SILVER PENNIES AND LINEN TOWELS

YEOMAN WITH MAUNDY GIFTS

SILVER PENNIES AND LINEN TOWELS

The Story of The Royal Maundy

BY
BRIAN ROBINSON
M.Sc., Ph.D., D.Sc., F.R.S.C.

SPINK
London

© 1992 Spink & Son Ltd., London

British Library Cataloguing in Publication Data
Robinson, Brian *1936–*
    Silver pennies and linen towels : the story of the royal maundy.
    1. Great Britain. Coins, history
    I. Title
    737.4941

ISBN 0–907605–35–4

Data input by Sandra Baldwin
Disk conversion and typesetting by Columns Design and Production Services Ltd, Reading
Printed in Great Britain by Grillford, Granby, Milton Keynes.

Dedicated to the Memory of
MR. LESLIE (Les) TAYLOR, D.F.M.,
a good friend with whom
I shared many an exciting
numismatic moment.

Contents

Foreword	ix
Preface and Acknowledgements	xi
List of Plates	xiv
List of Figures	xix
List of Tables	xx
List of Abbreviations	xxii

Chapter 1. Royal Charities other than the Royal Maundy — 1
  I. Daily Alms and Gate Alms — 2
  II. The King's Dole — 2
    i. The Common Bounty — 3
    ii. The Discretionary Bounty — 3
    iii. The Minor Bounty — 3
  III. Other Pensions — 3
  IV. Largesse — 4
  V. Educational Endowments — 5
  VI. Touching for the King's Evil — 5
  VII. Cramp Rings — 13

Chapter 2. The Royal Maundy — 18
  I. The Evolution of the Maundy Service — 19
  II. The Passing of the Loving Cup and the Drinking of the Monarch's Health at the End of the Maundy Service — 50
  III. The Liturgy of the Current Maundy Service — 51
  IV. The Etymology of Maundy Thursday — 55
  V. Venues for the Maundy Service — 58
  VI. The Maundy Recipients — 61
  VII. The Royal Almonry — 73

Chapter 3. The Maundy Money — 95
  I. The Evolution, Production and Specifications of Maundy Money — 95
  II. Mintages of the Maundy Coinage — 117
  III. The Issues, Types and Varieties of the Pre-1729 Post-Restoration Small Silver Coinage and of the Maundy Coinage — 136
    i. Charles II (29 May 1660–6 February 1685) — 141
    ii. James II (6 February 1685–11 December 1688 (declared to have abdicated)) — 149

iii.	William and Mary (13 February 1689–28 December 1694 (upon the death of Mary))	150
iv.	William III (28 December 1694–8 March 1702)	153
v.	Anne (8 March 1702–1 August 1714)	154
vi.	George I (1 August 1714–11 June 1727)	156
vii.	George II (11 June 1727–25 October 1760)	158
viii.	George III (25 October 1760–29 January 1820)	158
ix.	George IV (29 January 1820–26 June 1830)	165
x.	William IV (26 June 1830–20 June 1837)	167
xi.	Victoria (20 June 1837–22 January 1901)	168
xii.	Edward VII (22 January–6 May 1910)	178
xiii.	George V (6 May 1910–20 January 1936)	178
xiv.	Edward VIII (20 January 1936–10 December 1936 (abdicated))	183
xv.	George VI (10 December 1936–6 February 1952)	184
xvi.	Elizabeth II (6 February 1952 to date)	187

IV.	Die-axis Variations of the Pre-1729 Post-Restoration Small Silver Coinage and of the Maundy Coinage	191
V.	Maundy Money Proof Issues and Strikings in Metals other than Silver	194
VI.	The Groove on the Head of some Pre-1781 Silver Pennies	198
VII.	Brockages of the Post-Restoration Small Silver Coinage	200
VIII.	Economic Aspects of Collecting Maundy Money	201

Appendices

1.	Engravers and Designers of the Pre-1729 Post-Restoration Small Silver Coinage and of the Maundy Coinage	219
2.	The Banqueting House	231
3.	The Calendar	232
4.	Alms Dishes used in the Maundy Service	234
5.	Attendant Persons, excluding the Royal Almonry Officials, at the Royal Maundy Service	235
6.	Units of Weight	237
7.	The Trial of the Pyx	238
8.	Peter Blondeau and the Milled Coinage	241
9.	The Groat	244

Bibliography   248

Plates

Index   253

Foreword

SIR Arthur Bryant, in an oration in Westminster Abbey for The Queen's Silver Jubilee, said, 'One must first ask what Britain is. And I, who am no prophet, politician or social reformer, can only answer as a historian. Our past makes us . . . we must go back to the past to find an answer. . . .'

Dr. Brian Robinson has done just that in writing not only about the evolution of the Maundy Money but also of the history of the Royal Maundy Service as it has evolved through thirteen centuries. He goes back to the Gospel narrative when Jesus 'began to wash his disciples' feet and to wipe them with the towel'; and to the giving of the new commandment, 'love one another: as I have loved you, so you are to love one another'. He goes on to show how this simple and gracious act of humility is one which Christians in many lands have recalled regularly down the centuries as they have repeated the events of the first Maundy Thursday.

For nearly four hundred years, from the reign of Edward II to that of William and Mary, the Sovereign took an active part in the observance in England, including the washing of the feet of the poor. By contrast, from 1698 to 1931 no Sovereign attended the service and early in the 18th century the washing of feet was omitted from the ceremony. During this time the annual observance became less and less significant and questions began to be raised about its continuance. In 1837 a Report on the Civil List presented to the House of Commons stated:

> Considering that the sum distributed annually as alms and charity is applied in a manner suited rather to ancient than modern times, and is attended with some expense, it may not be inexpedient to consider whether the purposes of the Royal benevolence might not be more fully attained if some other and better mode of distribution were adopted.

150 years later the same question was raised more than once in Television interviews! Today the amount of money given is of small significance compared with the symbolic act of the Sovereign in recognising service to a local community, faithfully given by ordinary men and women pensioners in obedience to the commandment to love one another.

As recently as the 1930s, it was asserted that the service 'seemed to be in danger of becoming nothing but a picturesque, and perhaps, rather meaningless survival from the past'. The fact that this has not happened is due in no small measure to the skill and devotion of successive Secretaries of the Royal Almonry, but also to the decision of The Queen herself that the Service should normally be held in different parts of the country and only once every ten years in London. The Maundy pilgrimages made by The Queen around the country have been described by a former member of her Household as 'one of the most successful innovations of the reign'. There have been only four occasions since 1952 when Her Majesty has not attended the Maundy Service in person and she has been present at every Service since 1971.

The Office for the Royal Maundy was last revised in 1972 when the reading of the new commandment by the Lord High Almoner was introduced and provision made for greater participation by the congregation. The next revision, whenever it comes, will no doubt take account of the changes in liturgical language in recent years and also, perhaps, of the new provision made by the House of Bishops of the Church of England for the washing of the feet to be included in services on Maundy Thursday. The fact that the officers of the Royal Almonry, who are in attendance upon The Queen, are all girded with linen towels, dating from Queen Victoria's reign, might suggest that they could be required to wash the feet of some of the recipients before the arrival of the Sovereign, as frequently happened in earlier times. The Service would undoubtedly recover some of its lost symbolism if this were to happen.

'Silver Pennies and Linen Towels' takes us back to the past and many will be grateful to Dr. Robinson for the fruits of his historical scholarship and of his unrivalled knowledge of the Maundy coinage. But he is also at pains to write about the significance in the 1990s of an ancient ceremony which has taken on a quite new lease of life in the present reign. His book will be invaluable for those who will have a part in the continuing evolution of the ceremony in the 21st century. Meanwhile, we can all 'go back to the past' and take heart.

Right Rev. R. D. Say, K.C.V.O., D.D., D.C.L.
Lord High Almoner to H.M. The Queen, 1970–88

Preface and Acknowledgements

The Royal Maundy, a religious service full of beauty and colour, is held annually on Maundy Thursday, the day preceding Good Friday in the Christian Church. It is highly symbolic and of great antiquity, having its origins in the beginning of Christendom. One of the current service's characteristic features which has evolved over the centuries involves the distribution of various monetary gifts by the monarch, or an appointed deputy, to a selected group of elderly people. One of these gifts consists of a specially minted small silver coinage of pennies, twopences, threepences and fourpences, known as Maundy money and which is responsible for the numismatic interest in the ceremony. It is intended that the following study may appeal not only to those having either historical or liturgical interests in this ancient service but that it may also be accepted as a positive numismatic contribution to the study of the Maundy coinage and, hopefully, provide a reliable foundation upon which others may build.

Following the publication in 1977 of my previous work on the Royal Maundy,[1] much further related information, both published and, until now, unpublished, has come my way from various sources. This, together with the results from further research in this area pursued over the past twelve years, is incorporated into this present book. Consequently, compared with that of 1977, the present study is much modified and expanded. An entirely different and more comprehensive approach has been taken in the discussion of the historic evolution of the service and its various aspects, whilst the inclusion of much erstwhile unpublished material from the library archives and museum of the Royal Mint, together with a consideration of the various facets of diversification within the Maundy coinage, represent significant numismatic additions.

As with my previous study, earlier publications on the Royal Maundy have been important reference sources. Included in the more significant of these are the papers published between 1912 and 1930, inclusively, in the *BNJ* by Helen Farquhar on the Royal Maundy and other royal charities, although it is unfortunate that these studies are somewhat fragmentary and, more seriously, occasionally inaccurately quote data from original documentation. Other sources of information are the short monographs on the Royal Maundy by William Charlton, William John Hocking,[2] Cornelius Nicholls, E. E. Ratcliffe, E. E. Ratcliffe and P. A. Wright, Edgar Sheppard,[3] Lawrence E. Tanner and Peter A. Wright, the article concerning royal almsgiving by H. J. Bidwell, the book about the history of Whitehall by George S. Dugdale, the book on touching for the King's Evil and on cramp rings by Marc Bloch and the articles and book expounding the former subject by Noel Woolf.

Numismatically, *ESC* and the publications by George C. Brooke, Sir John Craig, H. A. Grueber, Edward Hawkins, Sir Charles Oman and Peter Seaby, have been invaluable.

It will become apparent later that the number of recipients for the Royal Maundy and the number of Maundy pence each of them receives is related to the sovereign's age in years at the time of the service. With regard to this, important works of reference are the publications which record the birthdays of our monarchs[4] and the compilations which quote, from A.D. 500 to 2000[5] and from A.D. 1066 to 2000,[6] the date of Easter Day[7], and thereby establish the date of the previous Thursday, namely Maundy Thursday, in each of these years.

Many individuals and institutions have made significant contributions to this study. Mr Graham P. Dyer, B.Sc., the Librarian and Curator at the Royal Mint, Llantrisant, gave me so generously of his time and expertise. Not only did he read and make many very useful detailed and general comments upon, and additions to, my manuscript in both its draft and second stages, but he also provided me with many significant pieces of numismatic data, many of these deriving from his own, as yet unpublished, research. Furthermore, during the several extremely warm welcomes which he extended to me at the Royal Mint, he made many stimulating and constructive suggestions, guided me through the relevant sections of the Mint's museum and subsequently provided me with photographs of many unique and previously unpublished numismatic items in the museum's collection for use in this present book, to which he has made such a significant contribution. Through the offices of Mr Dyer, I made contact with Dr C. E. Challis, Reader in Modern History at the University of Leeds, and Mr Harrington E. Manville of Washington, DC. Dr Challis put at my disposal his professional skill in the location and transcription of documents appertaining to Maundy distributions of the Tudor period. Mr Manville provided me with details, including photographs which were supplied by Mr Michael R. Dudley of the Ashmolean Museum, Oxford, of his collection of mis-strikes, including a significant number of brockages, of the post-1660 small silver coinage, together with the results of his survey of the *GM* for accounts relating to Maundy distributions. When I was effecting my initial research on the Royal Maundy, I had the opportunity of meeting the now late Dr Lawrence E. Tanner, C.V.O., M.A., F.S.A., F.R. Hist. Soc., who was the Secretary of the Royal Almonry from 1921 to 1964 and who had played a leading rôle in revitalizing the Maundy service in the 1930s.[8] During the very interesting and stimulating discussions which I had with him, Dr Tanner afforded me much help and valuable data which was not only employed in my then current undertaking but has been put to significant use in the present work. Dr Tanner's successor as Secretary of the Royal Almonry, Mr Peter A. Wright, C.V.O., has also provided me with much invaluable information which, in particular, relates to recent developments in connection with the Maundy service. Furthermore, he has loaned me a fine pictorial record of past Maundy ceremonies, made me a gift of a set of four Maundy purses and extended to me an invitation which made possible my membership of the congregation at the Maundy service held at Birmingham Cathedral in 1989. Miss M. M. Archibald, M.A., F.S.A. and her colleagues in the Department of Coins and Medals at the British Museum arranged for me to have access to the Museum's numismatic collection and the use of specimens therein for illustrative purposes. Several of my colleagues at the University of Manchester, namely Dr J. N. Adams, B.A., M.A. (Reader in Latin), Dr J. H. Denton, B.A. (Professor of Mediæval History), Dr H. D. Jocelyn, B.A., M.A., F.B.A. (Hulme Professor of Latin), Rev. Barnabas Lindars, S.S.F., M.A., D.D. (Rylands Professor of Biblical Criticism and Exegesis) and Dr Peter McNiven, M.A.

(Sub-librarian in the John Rylands University Library and Honorary Lecturer in Mediæval History), along with Mr Christopher Cove-Smith (Archivist to the National Westminster Bank plc), Mr A. V. Griffiths (Deputy Keeper of Paintings and Drawings at the British Museum) and Dr. M. M. N. Stansfield (Records and Public Sevices Manager of the Cathedral, City and Diocesan Record Office in Canterbury), all permitted me to take advantage of their professional fortes. The Very Rev. Peter Berry, M.A. (the Provost of Birmingham Cathedral), Mr Charles F. Green (the Lay Administrator to the Bishop of St Albans), Mrs Charlotte A. Hodgson (Assistant County Archivist (East Kent) and Archivist at the Cathedral, City and Diocesan Record Office in Canterbury) and Ms Diana Ward of Her Majesty's Stationery Office, Norwich, have provided me with very useful leads or artifacts in reply to my enquiries and Mr Bill Cotton, C.B.E., likewise supplied a somewhat amusing anecdote involving his father and the gift of Maundy coins that his paternal grandmother used to make to her children. The staff at the John Rylands University Library, Manchester, and at the Bodleian Library, Oxford, have put at my disposal their considerable facilities. The photographs of coins, other than those accredited elsewhere, are of specimens from the author's collection and are the work of Messrs Christopher Herbert and Andrew Jenkins, respectively the Principal and Senior Photographers at the Royal Mint. Mrs Sandra Baldwin undertook the daunting task of typing my manuscript and preparing it for submission to the printers. Last but, of course, not least I am mindful of the help given to me by my publishers, Spink and Son Ltd, and in particular that of Mr Douglas H. Saville who encouraged and guided my study toward its target, made many constructive comments upon my manuscript and played such a significant rôle in the process whereby it was transformed into this book.

To all these above persons, who were so generously liberal with their talents, expertise, time and help, I offer my most sincere gratitude, as I do to the many others who, through conversation over the past few years, have provided me with relevant leads and ideas.

December 1990

Brian Robinson
Eyam, Derbyshire

NOTES

1. Robinson (1977).
2. 1906, Appendix III, pp. 422–24.
3. 'The Royal Maundy' in Sheppard, Chapter 23, pp. 350–72.
4. *DNB*; Freeman-Grenville; *HBC*.
5. Cheney, pp. 83–161.
6. *OCEL*, pp. 935–53.
7. In the Latin Church, this is the Sunday following the first full moon on or after 21 March and hence it falls on any of the thirty-five days from 22 March to 25 April (Cheney, p. 7).
8. Tanner (1969).

List of Plates

(The Plates are located between pages 252 and 253)

The frontispiece, *Yeoman with Maundy Gifts*, is reproduced from an undated and unreferenced press cutting entitled *Links with the Past* and filed in the library at the Royal Mint.

Plate 10, Plates 14, 19, 28 and 32 to 37, Plates 46, 47, 71, 75, 79, 93 to 95, 98, 103 and 106, and Plates 48, 50 and 109 to 118 are reproduced by courtesy of Lord Beauchamp of Madresfield Court, Malvern, Worcestershire, the Royal Almonry Office, the Royal Mint and Mr Harrington E. Manville of Washington, DC, respectively. Plate 26 is reproduced from *BNJ*, 16 (1921–22), p. 214. Plates 3, 5, 6, 18, 20 and 31 are reproduced by arrangement with the British Library, the Trustees of the Tate Gallery, the Dean and Chapter of Canterbury, Thomson Regional Newspapers Ltd, Alan Lamb of Birmingham Cathedral and the London Evening News, respectively, and Plates 13 and 21, Plates 1, 2, 4, 7, 8, 16, 22, 23, 38 to 41, 51 to 54, 56 and 57, and Plates 29 and 30 are reproduced by arrangement with the Controller of Her Majesty's Stationery Office, the Trustees of the British Museum and Times Newspapers Ltd, respectively.

Unless otherwise indicated, coins, dies and punches are illustrated actual size. The obverses illustrated in Plates 55, 58, 60 to 64, 66, 68 to 70, 72, 74, 78, 87, 89 to 91, 96, 97, 101 and 102 are those of the corresponding fourpences. With the exceptions of Plates 68 and 101, or unless indicated to the contrary in the caption, the specific dates upon illustrated coins are purely exemplary, as are the legends on those coins so illustrated up to Plate 69, in which minor variations, which are described in the related Tables and text, often occur within the type.

1. The obverse and reverse of a gold angel of Edward IV
2. The obverse and reverse of a gold angel which has been pierced, possibly so that it could be threaded on a ribbon for use as a healing-piece
3. Robert White's etching showing Charles II touching for scrofula
4. The obverse and reverse of a touch-piece of Charles II
5. Ford Madox Brown's painting 'Jesus washing Peter's feet'
6. The part of the register in which is described the Maundy ceremonial as carried out by the monks of Canterbury in the fourteenth century
7. The obverse and reverse of a silver penny of John from the Rochester mint, moneyer Alisandre, ALISANDRE.ON.R
8. The obverse and reverse of a silver penny of John from the Rochester mint, moneyer Hunfrei, HUNFREI.ON.RO
9. The transcript of that section of the *Rotulus Misæ* for the eleventh year of the reign of John relating to Maundy Thursday and the Easter period

List of Plates xv

10. The miniature (actual size approximately 2¾ in × 2¼ in) showing Elizabeth I at one of her Maundies, probably that held on 11 April 1560
11. A red leather purse (actual size 7 cm × 10 cm) with long white leather strings of the type in which the Maundy allowances are presented
12. A white leather purse (actual size 7 cm × 10 cm) with long red leather strings of the type in which the Maundy money is presented
13. The Maundy Dish
14. Members of the Yeomen of the Guard, one of whom is carrying in the traditional manner the Maundy Dish bearing the charged white and red purses with long strings, on the Dean's Steps at Westminster Abbey immediately prior to a Maundy service
15. A white leather purse (actual size 7 cm × 10 cm) with short vivid Tudor green leather strings and a vivid Tudor green leather purse (actual size 7 cm × 10 cm) with short white leather strings, the types in which, from 1936 to 1979, was presented the clothing allowance, as the First Distribution in the Maundy service, to male and female recipients, respectively
16. S. H. Grimm's water-colour of the 1773 Maundy service in progress
17. The distribution of the Royal Maundy in 1842
18. On the Dean's Steps at Westminster Abbey following the Maundy service on 6 April 1950
19. At the entrance to St Albans Cathedral following the Maundy service on 18 April 1957
20. The Maundy distribution by Queen Elizabeth II, with the attendant distribution party, in Birmingham Cathedral on 23 March 1989
21. The Fish Dishes
22. S. H. Grimm's drawing of the Royal Almonry procession before the 1773 Maundy service
23. S. H. Grimm's water-colour showing the distribution of the provisions in the Ante-chapel of the Chapel Royal, Whitehall, during the 1773 Maundy ceremony
24. The obverse and reverse of a proof 1953 Coronation crown
25. The obverse and reverse of a proof 1977 Silver Jubilee crown
26. A water-colour sketch of the Maundy distribution on 25 March 1875
27. The distribution of the Royal Maundy by the Lord High Almoner (Lord Alwyne Compton, Bishop of Ely) in Westminster Abbey on 4 April 1901
28. On the Dean's Steps at Westminster Abbey following the Maundy service on 18 April 1935
29. George V making the Second Distribution during the Maundy service held in Westminster Abbey on 24 March 1932
30. George V and Queen Mary leaving Westminster Abbey following the Maundy service on 24 March 1932
31. Edward VIII with, on his left, the Lord High Almoner (the Archbishop of Canterbury) and, on his right, the Dean of Westminster, following the distribution of the Royal Maundy on 9 April 1936
32. Some of the recipients displaying their Maundy gifts after the Maundy service at St George's Chapel, Windsor Castle, on 26 March 1959
33. The purse of Bishop William Lloyd, Lord High Almoner from 1689 to 1702
34. The seal of Henry de Bluntesdon, Lord High Almoner from *c.* 1284 to *c.* 1305

xvi *Silver Pennies and Linen Towels*

35. The seal of Stephen Payne, Lord High Almoner from 1414 to 1419
36. The seal of the Royal Almonry Office during the reign of George VI
37. The present badge of office of the Lord High Almoner
38. Obverse and reverse of a third issue (1619–1625) silver penny of James I
39. Obverse and reverse of a third issue (1619- .625) silver twopence of James I
40. Obverse and reverse of an Oxford Declaration penny
41. Obverse and reverse of a silver Spanish dollar, countermarked on the bust with the effigy from the then current Maundy penny die and in 1804 in England issued for currency at five shillings each
42. The top and inside of an official Maundy case of 1907, containing the appropriate coins
43. The top and inside of an official Maundy case used during the reign of George V, containing appropriate coins
44. The top and inside of an official Maundy case of 1985, containing the appropriate coins
45. The top and inside of an official Maundy case of 1990, containing the appropriate coins
46. The obverse punches for the type 2 silver penny, twopence, threepence and fourpence of Charles II
47. The reverse punches for the small silver coinage of William III
48. The obverse and reverse of a 1674 silver penny with legend errors ($\times 3.3$)
49. The obverse and reverse of a 1679 silver twopence on an enlarged flan and the obverse and reverse of a normal 1679 silver twopence (all $\times 2$)
50. The obverse and reverse of a 1683 silver threepence struck on a flan of the fourpence diameter ($\times 2$)
51. The obverses and reverses of the types 1A to 1F silver pennies of Charles II
52. The obverses and reverses of the types 1A to 1F silver twopences of Charles II
53. The obverses and reverses of the types 1A and 1B silver threepences of Charles II
54. The obverses and reverses of the types 1A and 1B silver fourpences of Charles II
55. The obverse and four reverses of the type 2 small silver coinage of Charles II
56. The obverse and reverse of Nicholas Briot's pattern silver penny of Charles I
57. The obverses and reverses of Nicholas Briot's pattern silver twopences of Charles I
58. The obverse and four reverses of the small silver coinage of James II
59. The reverse of a silver threepence of James II dated 1685, showing a partially-struck central I ($\times 2$)
60. The obverse sub-types A and B, respectively, and the four reverses of the small silver coinage of William and Mary
61. The obverse and four reverses of the small silver coinage of William III
62. The obverse and four reverses of the small silver coinage of Anne
63. The obverse and four reverses of the small silver coinage of George I
64. The obverse and four reverses of the pre-1732 Maundy coinage of George II
65. The reverses of the post-1731 Maundy twopence and fourpence of George II
66. The obverse and four reverses of the type 1A Maundy coinage of George III
67. The reverses of the type 1B Maundy penny and fourpence of George III
68. The obverse and four reverses of the type 2 Maundy coinage of George III
69. The obverse and four reverses of the type 3 Maundy coinage of George III

List of Plates xvii

70. The obverse and four reverses of the type 4 Maundy coinage of George III
71. Top and side views of the obverse and the reverse dies for the type 4 Maundy fourpence of George III
72. The obverse and four reverses of the Maundy coinage of George IV
73. The Maundy threepence obverse of 1822 and that used from 1823 to 1830
74. The obverse and four reverses of the Maundy coinage of William IV
75. The obverse and reverse of a proof half-sovereign of 1831
76. The obverse and reverse of a silver Britannia groat of William IV
77. The obverse and reverse of a silver three-halfpence of William IV
78. The obverse and four reverses of the type 1 Maundy coinage of Victoria
79. The obverse and two reverses of the gold pattern quarter-sovereigns of 1853
80. The obverse and reverse of a copper quarter-farthing of Victoria
81. The obverse and reverse of a silver Britannia groat of Victoria (young head)
82. The obverse and reverses of copper half-farthings of 1839 and 1844
83. The obverse and reverse of a silver three-halfpence of Victoria
84. The obverse of a Maundy twopence of 1857 showing the legend error BRITANNIAE EEGINA (×3)
85. The obverse of a Maundy twopence of 1859 without the legend error BEITANNIAR (×3)
86. The reverses of Maundy twopences of 1861 with and without the 6 over 1 overstrike in the date (×3)
87. The obverse and reverses of the penny, twopence and fourpence and the obverse and reverse of the threepence of the type 2 Maundy coinage of Victoria
88. The obverse and reverse of a silver Britannia groat of 1888
89. The obverse and four reverses of the type 3 Maundy coinage of Victoria
90. The obverse and four reverses of the Maundy coinage of Edward VII
91. The obverse and four reverses of the type 1 Maundy coinage of George V
92. The obverse and reverse of a proof 500 millesimal fine silver threepence of 1927
93. The obverse and reverse of a uniface Maundy penny of 1931
94. The blank reverse die for the uniface Maundy penny of 1931
95. The soft reduction obverse punches for the proposed Maundy penny and twopence of Edward VIII
96. The obverse and four reverses of the type 1 Maundy coinage of George VI
97. The obverse of the type 3 Maundy coinage of George VI
98. The punch produced by the Royal Mint for the new reverse proposed in 1950 for the Maundy twopence
99. The obverse and reverse of a 500 millesimal fine proof silver threepence of 1937
100. The obverse and reverse of a proof copper-zinc-nickel threepence of 1937
101. The obverse and four reverses of the type 1 Maundy coinage of Elizabeth II
102. The obverse of the type 2 Maundy coinage of Elizabeth II
103. The memorandum from James William Morrison, the Deputy Master of the Mint, which authorised William Wyon to use the dies, sunk for the production of the 1831 Maundy coinage, for the striking of Maundy sets in fine gold
104. The Maundy set dated 1953 and struck in gold
105. The Maundy set dated 1952 and struck in copper
106. The obverses and reverses of the officially defaced Maundy penny, twopence and fourpence of 1936 and general currency 500 millesimal fine silver threepence of

1937 which were used as templates by the maker of the Maundy cases in 1937
107. The obverse of a Maundy penny of 1780 exhibiting a vertical groove on the bust (×3)
108. The obverse and reverse of an obverse brockage of the Maundy penny of George I which has been assigned to the year 1727 (×3)
109. The obverse and reverse of an obverse brockage of the type 1D silver twopence Charles II (×2)
110. The obverse and reverse of an obverse brockage of the type 2 silver penny of Charles II (×2)
111. The obverse and reverse of an obverse brockage of the type 2 silver fourpence of Charles II (×2)
112. The obverse and reverse of a reverse brockage of the 1683 silver penny (×2)
113. The obverse and reverse of a reverse brockage of the 1679 silver twopence (×2)
114. The obverse and reverse of an obverse brockage of the silver penny of James II (×2)
115. The obverse and reverse of an obverse brockage of the silver twopence of James II (×2)
116. The obverse and reverse of an obverse brockage of the silver threepence of James II (×2)
117. The obverse and reverse of an obverse brockage of the silver fourpence of James II (×2)
118. The obverse and reverse of an obverse brockage of the silver twopence of William and Mary (×2)

List of Figures

1. The two circlet designs, with and without pearls, as variously used on the crown on the reverse of the type 1 Maundy coinage of George III — 162
2. Uniface cross-sections of the proof and the ordinary Maundy fourpences of 1911 — 194

List of Tables

1. Expenses associated with the Maundy distributions of Henry VIII, from 1509 to 1517 and from 1538 to 1542 — 28
2. The distributors, other than the monarch, of the Maundy gifts since 1932 — 51
3. The venues, other than Westminster Abbey, of the Maundy service since 1953 and the associated anniversary or linked activity of the Queen in the locality — 62
4. Examples of the relationships between the monarch's age, the number of Maundy recipients and the number of pence in the Gift of Pennies — 65
5. The ages of the Maundy recipients in 1969 and the varying reasons given for their being chosen as such — 70
6. High Almoners as known to date — 75
7. Sub-almoners as known to date — 80
8. The small silver denominations and Maundy coins minted from 1668 to 1822 — 104
9. The respective proportions of the silver denominations which were struck from 1696 to 1698, from 1699 to 1756 and from 1757 to 1804 — 107
10. The annual production of Maundy money, in troy pounds, and the mintages derived thereof, from 1727 to 1816 — 108
11. Comparison between the annual Maundy money mintages and the requirements of the Maundy recipients for most years from 1727 to 1816 — 114
12. The annual mintages of Maundy coins from 1816 to 1988 — 121
13. Comparison between the annual Maundy money mintages and the requirements of the Maundy recipients for the years from 1816 to 1988 — 126
14. The fees paid in Maundy coins in connection with the Maundy service of 1909 — 131
15. The denominational compositions of the Gift of Pennies from 1946 to 1978 — 134
16. The total annual face value of each of the four Maundy denominations of 925 millesimal fine silver, issued under the operation of the Decimal Currency Acts 1967 and 1969 and the Coinage Act 1971, from 1971 to 1975 — 135
17. The annual mintages of the Maundy money from 1971 to 1975 — 135
18. The total annual face value of each of the four Maundy denominations of 925 millesimal fine silver, issued under the operation of the Coinage Act 1946, from 1965 to 1970 — 136
19. The frequency of die-sinking for the Maundy money from June 1741 to April 1812 — 138
20. The frequency of matrix and punch production for the Maundy money from June 1741 to April 1812 — 140

21.	The type 1 small silver coinage of Charles II	143
22.	The type 2 small silver coinage of Charles II	147
23.	The small silver coinage of James II	150
24.	The small silver coinage of William and Mary	151
25.	The small silver coinage of William III	153
26.	The small silver coinage of Anne	155
27.	The small silver coinage of George I	157
28.	The Maundy coinage of George II	159
29.	The types 1A and 1B Maundy coinage of George III	160
30.	The type 2 Maundy coinage (wire money) of George III	162
31.	The type 3 Maundy coinage of George III	163
32.	The type 4 (bull head) Maundy coinage of George III	164
33.	The Maundy coinage of George IV	166
34.	The Maundy coinage of William IV	167
35.	The type 1 (young head) Maundy coinage of Victoria	169
36.	The type 2 (jubilee head) Maundy coinage of Victoria	176
37.	The type 3 (old head) Maundy coinage of Victoria	177
38.	The Maundy coinage of Edward VII	179
39.	The Maundy coinage of George V	180
40.	The Maundy coinage of George VI	184
41.	The Maundy coinage of Elizabeth II	187
42.	The die-axis variations of the pre-1729 small silver coinage from 1668 and of the Maundy coinage	192
43.	Examples of market value comparisons between some twentieth-century Maundy sets and contemporary coins or proof sets of similar mintages	202
44.	Variations between 1953 and 1989, inclusively, of the sterling pound market values of the post-William IV Maundy sets	203

List of Abbreviations

BMJ	*British Medical Journal*
BNJ	*British Numismatic Journal*
CNJ	*Canadian Numismatic Journal*
CM	*Coin Monthly*
cm	centimetre or centimetres
d	penny or pence (pre-decimal)
d.	died
DNB	*Dictionary of National Biography*
dwt	pennyweight or pennyweights (troy) (see Appendix 6)
ESC	*The English Silver Coinage from 1649*, by Herbert Allen Seaby and P. Alan Rayner, fourth edition (London, 1974).
FDC	Fleur-de-coin
GM	*Gentleman's Magazine*
g	gram (gramme) or grams (grammes)
gr	grain or grains (troy) (see Appendix 6)
HBC	*Handbook of British Chronology*, edited by E. B. Fryde, D. E. Greenway, S. Porter and I. Roy (London, 1986)
HCM	*Home Counties Magazine*
in	inch or inches
£	pound or pounds (currency)
lb	pound or pounds (weight) (troy) (see Appendix 6)
mm	millimetre or millimetres
MS	Manuscript
MSCE	*The Milled Silver Coinage of England from Charles II to the Present Day, including Patterns and Proofs, with a Chapter on Maundy Money* (London, 1925)
NC	*Numismatic Chronicle*
NCirc	*Spink's Numismatic Circular*
NL	*Numismatic Literature*
NS	New Style (see Appendix 3)
OCEL	*The Oxford Companion to English Literature* (compiled and edited by Sir Paul Harvey (Oxford, 1967), Appendix III, *The Calendar*
OED	*Oxford English Dictionary*, second edition, 1989, prepared by J. A. Simpson and E. S. C. Weiner
ORM	*Office for the Royal Maundy*
OS	Old Style (see Appendix 3)

oz	ounce or ounces (troy) (see Appendix 6)
p	penny or pence (decimal)
PSAS	*Proceedings of the Society of Antiquaries of Scotland*
PRO	Public Record Office, London
s	shilling or shillings
SCMB	*Seaby's Coin and Medal Bulletin*

CHAPTER 1

Royal Charities other than the Royal Maundy

The organization of charity is currently a world-wide phenomenon. Indeed, it has become a significant business in itself and this has led to much adverse criticism in that it is alleged that the related administrative costs often swallow far too much of the received donations. Furthermore, the opportune establishment of political platforms upon some charitable organizations is far from desirable. Although in earlier times the benefits arising from charities were not so widely available, most possibly because of the lack of facile, or even any, means of communication, charitable organizations at a more localized level have been active in several parts of the world for centuries. In the United Kingdom alone, thousands of charities are registered and the benefits accruing from many of these, administrative costs apart, not only make a marked impact in this country but also afford a significant contribution to the well-being of the populations of the materialistically-poorer nations of our world. The literature upon charity and its management is extensive and many authors have made significant contributions in this area.[1] Although some of these studies include sections upon philanthropy in England, specific studies on the earlier aspects of this have also appeared.[2]

For many centuries, charity in the form of alms-giving was practised by the monarchs of several countries and, in this practice, the English kings and queens have been no exception, being involved not only with the Royal Maundy but also with many other charities. These have often been collectively termed maundy and have provided sometimes food, but usually money, for the needy. Such gifts were and, indeed, still are generally of a philanthropic nature and a practical illustration of the old motto *noblesse oblige*. Nevertheless, they have occasionally been employed by monarchs as public relations' exercises, either in attempts to enhance their popularity with their subjects or to acquaint the latter with their sovereign whose effigy, in recognizable form, appears for the first time from part-way through the reign of Henry VII on the obverse of some of the coinage, namely the profile issues of the testoon, groat and half-groat.[3] Other royal benevolences in earlier times were based upon the then accepted belief in the sacred and miraculous properties of royalty, one facet of which led to the acceptance that the royal touch, under prescribed conditions, could effect cures of specific diseases. This was perhaps the most striking manifestation of their claimed sacerdotal or even divine powers. Such exercises, however, also involved the monarch in material expense since one of them was accompanied by the gift of a gold coin as a healing-piece, to be used as an amulet (later this gift consisted of a touch-piece which, although initially of gold and later of silver, was not intended as coin of the realm), and the other was effected through the intercession of rings made of gold or silver. In order to place the Royal Maundy into perspective, these other royal charities are now briefly discussed.

I. DAILY ALMS AND GATE ALMS[4]

In times past it was usual for food distributions to be made to the poor from royal palaces, castles, inns of court, monasteries and universities. Although in some cases these gifts would consist of the scraps of food left after meals in these establishments, it was more common for specific quantities of food to be set aside for such purposes. Such gifts were sometimes made by the monarch as a means of seeking favour with the population or as a form of compensation for the occasional necessary requisitioning of labour or goods from his or her subjects.

In the Tudor period these offerings were called Daily Alms, signifying their distribution on a daily basis, although special distributions of such alms were sometimes also made around Easter and Christmas. Also during this period they were modified by the addition of a monetary distribution of 37s 11d per week divided between thirteen persons, equivalent to 2s 11d per week, or five pence per day per person. By the time of the reign of William and Mary, the monetary gift, which over a period of years utilized all four small denomination silver coins, namely the penny, twopence (half-groat), threepence (quarter-shilling) and fourpence (groat), had completely supplanted the food gift. Notwithstanding this, at the beginning of the nineteenth century both food and money were once again being used in the distribution of these alms. Thus, at the gatehouse at Lambeth during this period, thirty poor parishioners received food gifts together with, in halfpennies, twopence per week.

By 1843, the gift had become known as Gate Alms, in view of the venue of its distribution,[5] rather than Daily Alms, and it had been commuted entirely to a monetary distribution at Easter and Christmas of twenty-six shillings (representing a sum of six pence per week throughout the year) to each of 150 persons. This charitable distribution is still in effect and the Royal Gate Alms are still payable at Easter and Christmas.[6]

II. THE KING'S DOLE[7]

During the Tudor and Stuart periods, the distribution associated with this charity was usually made on Good Friday, the day following the distribution of the Royal Maundy on Maundy Thursday. Yet this was not invariably so since the distribution day for both these charities, on the occasions when the monarch was personally involved with the ceremonies, could be changed to suit his or her convenience. Thus, in some years we find the distribution of the King's Dole being made on Maundy Thursday, following the distribution of the Royal Maundy, and in other years we find a similar arrangement but with both ceremonies being held on Good Friday instead of Maundy Thursday. When the sovereign did not personally distribute this dole, his or her almoner was deputized, a practice that was also followed in connection with the distribution of the Royal Maundy.

Prior to the reign of Henry VIII, the sum distributed annually in this charity was variable but during this reign it was settled at £133 6s 8d, an amount equivalent to 200 marks, the mark having a value of two-thirds of a pound sterling. This remained the sum until Charles II increased it to £200. The main coinage denominations used in either of these distributions were the twopence and fourpence, with the occasional use of the penny.

By the end of the eighteenth century, the payment of the Dole had undergone modification in that it was by then paid at both Christmas and Easter, the majority of recipients receiving either five shillings or a half-guinea (10s 6d), with a few of them receiving a guinea (£1 1s). A century later the Dole had undergone further major modification by being divided into the following separate allowances known as Bounties.

i. The Common Bounty

In 1893, for example, this was distributed in two parts, one at Christmas and the other at Easter, to 1,300 persons who each received a total of ten shillings. Prior to 1848, the recipients of this bounty attended personally at the Royal Almonry for their gift. However, such practice then ceased because of the dangers and risks to the aged and infirm recipients incurred from the travelling thus involved and their associated exposure to the elements, together with the contemporary objection to the congregating of such a large number of people, the cleanliness of many which left much to be desired. At the suggestion of the Lord High Almoner, and with the sanction of Victoria, a new method of distribution was thus introduced whereby the clergy of the various dioceses throughout England and Wales petitioned on behalf of a certain number of candidates for this relief, themselves or their nominees receiving the total amount due which was then distributed by them to the recipients. This bounty, which can be regarded as the direct survivor of the King's Dole, is still in existence and is now payable in a single sum at Christmas.[8]

ii. The Discretionary Bounty

This has now ceased[9] but used to consist of an annual payment of £3 to each of certain people, approximately fifty in all, who were held in reserve as recipients of the Royal Maundy. Thus, in common with the latter recipients, they were selected from a class of the population who were contemporarily regarded as being of a status somewhat superior to that of those who received one of the other bounties.

iii. The Minor Bounty

This supplied various pensions and would appear, along with the now disbanded Discretionary Bounty described above, to have still been in effect in 1920 when a contemporary report reads:[10]

> The Minor Bounty, the Discretionary and Royal Gate Alms, were in accordance with ancient usage, distributed at the Royal Almonry Office last Monday and Tuesday[11] to some 700 aged, disabled, and meritorious persons. The recipients were selected by the Lord High Almoner assisted by the Sub-Almoner, and the payments were made and the arrangements conducted by Mr. Norgate[12].

III. OTHER PENSIONS

Old servants and others have also been in receipt of pensions paid from the royal purse. In the earliest extant accounts where such payments are mentioned, namely those for the year 1723–24, there appear the names of about one hundred and fifty individuals receiving pensions ranging from £1 to £16 per annum. In 1811 or 1812 the list was revised and the amounts reduced and, in 1838, the number of such recipients diminished to forty, half of whom received £5 and the other half of whom received £10, annually, a balance thus being liberated which the Lord High Almoner was able to apply generally in the interests of the poor and needy.[13] Current details regarding such pensions and payments are not publicly available.

IV. LARGESSE[14]

At times of certain royal pageantry, such as a coronation or a royal wedding, or during a royal progress, money was given to the poor. During the early Norman period these gifts, called largesse, were given in the form of silver pennies, the only coins minted at this time. However, by the Tudor period, when other denominations had also become available, usually twopences and occasionally fourpences were employed for this purpose.

These gifts, as with other royal benefactions, were not necessarily philanthropic in nature. Thus, the largesse presented at the coronation of William II in 1087 may have been an attempt to purchase the goodwill of those of his subjects that were reluctant to accept him as king. Mary Tudor's accession to the throne in 1553 was, likewise, not easily accepted by many of her subjects and, in this connection, it is significant that the money laid aside for largesse in her first regnal year exceeded that dispensed in any year during the reign of her late brother, Edward VI. One of the consequences of the spread of the Renaissance to Britain was the appearance on the coinage of a life-like effigy of the monarch whose stern, wise or benevolent face thus appears the way that he or she wished to be seen and remembered, subject, of course, to the skill of the engraver. Such a recognizable effigy appears, as mentioned earlier, for the first time from part-way through the reign of Henry VII (1485–1509) on the obverses of the profile issues of the testoon, groat and half-groat.[15] Consequently, the distribution of largesse from the beginning of this period onward may also have been used in some instances to help acquaint the populace with the sovereign by presenting it in this way with his or her portrait. This is evident from the distribution of silver medalets, especially struck by Nicholas Briot,[16] at the coronation of Charles I and at other royal functions of this king. These medalets bore a fine effigy of Charles but had little intrinsic value and, in fact, actual coin was still used as largesse on royal progresses.

Distributions of largesse appear to have continued into the reign of George II but the practice then fell into disuse and has not since been revived. They were usually carried out by the Almoner or the Court Heralds and, in connection with these latter officials, is found another royal gift that is also classed as largesse.

When in attendance at a royal function, the Heralds would claim their largesse in lieu of a fee as also, for example, did the King's Champion after he had delivered his challenge at a coronation when he thus claimed the gold cup from which the Monarch had drunk his health. Specific sums are, indeed, set aside in the royal accounts for payment of such largesse to the Heralds.

Often nobles and high-ranking ecclesiastics would distribute their own largesse to the poor. Likewise, the knights themselves would provide the largesse for the Heralds attending their investitures to the Orders of the Garter or Bath, as would the surviving family of a deceased noble whose funeral the Heralds attended.

V. EDUCATIONAL ENDOWMENTS

Royal patronage of education is long established and has been wide-spread. Foundations include that of Christ's Hospital by Edward VI, with further endowment by Charles II, and of Eton College by Henry VI. Although she was not actually the foundress of Westminster School, Elizabeth I made a new foundation whereby each of forty scholars received the yearly sum of £3 0s 10d for commons and two marks for a gown. A visit by her to this latter school is said to have occasioned a distribution of prizes consisting of Maundy coins, then simply newly struck normal coins of the realm, a custom that survives to the present day: in the seventeenth century 'the coins seem to have fallen to the composers of extemporary verses in Latin or Greek' and by 1898 'an annual grant of £2 in Maundy money was given for exercises in prose or verse'.[17] In 1337 an endowment was provided by Edward III of twopence per day for each of thirty-six poor scholars at King's Hall, Cambridge.[18]

Possibly as a relic of the royal foundations at several of the colleges has been the sum of £50 which was granted to two professors or readers in Arabic, one at the University of Cambridge and the other at the University of Oxford.[19] This first appears as an item in the accounts for 1724 and seems to have been of a recurrent nature but when and how it became almonry expenditure cannot be traced. The first known appointment is the nomination in 1748 of one Mr Richard Brown by the then Bishop of Salisbury acting in his capacity as Lord High Almoner. It has been suggested that at one time the Crown itself made the appointments to these two posts but later delegated the power to the Lord High Almoner. Up to 1812 these payments were made in full but were then subjected to certain tax deductions that amounted to as much as £15 in the course of a year, a large deduction from a salary of £50.[20]

VI. TOUCHING FOR THE KING'S EVIL[21]

The custom of healing by the royal touch was of great antiquity and was practised by the monarchs of many European countries. In England, the power of healing scrofulous sores by the touch was believed for centuries to be inherent in the sovereign, the virtue being imparted through the royal hand after it had been anointed with holy oil. Such healing ceremonies, which were performed with much solemnity, were usually held on Sundays but special powers were associated with those held on Good Friday.

The first king to touch for scrofula was Robert II of the Franks (996–1017), a man of great piety whose subjects credited him with the gift of healing not as a king but as a priest. In England, the belief in the curative power of a prayer and the royal touch grew up around Edward the Confessor (1042–1066). However, although he was revered as a man of God, Edward was only credited with one healing. It was not until nearly one hundred years later that Henry I (1100–1135), seeking substantiation of his own royalty, and not wishing to admit that he was imitating the French kings, remembered Edward's one reported cure and claimed the power of healing had descended to himself. In the process, a whole history of healings was posthumously fabricated for the Confessor who, it was claimed, after touching the diseased patients, ordered that they were to be maintained at the royal expense until they were cured or died.

However, irrespective of who was the first English monarch to practise the royal touch, during the thirteenth century the subsequent upkeep of the patients at royal expense until recovery or death was replaced by a monetary gift. This amounted to a labourer's wage for a day, or one penny, and was given by the king to each of the patients who had received his touch. Furthermore, the disease specifically treated by the touch had by then become known in England as the King's Evil, or Morbus Regius, and in France as Mal de Roi: it was later known by the all-embracing Latin name of Scrofula.

The disease, in fact, covered several pathological conditions which all gave rise to similar or related symptoms. True Scrofula was, and indeed still is, a tubercular infection of the lymph nodes which, if permitted to remain untreated, can result in the formation of suppurating sores. It is estimated that in London it used to affect about one per cent of the population, a figure that compares with some three per cent of the city's dwellers who annually became victims of smallpox. Furthermore, that the disease was not confined to the impoverished is evident from the fact that, in 1686, six pupils from Eton College were in receipt of the royal touch. Scrofula was not usually a fatal disease but it could be disfiguring and cause great distress. Being a condition in which natural remissions of the symptoms, or sometimes spontaneous cures, were known, it was inevitable that mystical and magical explanations should be sought. Thus, passing naked children, who were so infected, three times through a hole in a tree or stone was considered to be a cure for Scrofula: this act, symbolic of rebirth, supposedly freed them of their affliction. The hanging of a healing-piece, threaded on a white silk ribbon and put around the patient's neck during prayers after the sores had been touched by the sovereign, may well have echoed the same symbolism.

The gold angel was first introduced into the English coinage about 1465.[22] It took its name from its obverse design which depicts St Michael slaying the dragon of evil,[23] along with the legend carrying the royal name and titles (Plate 1). It has been suggested[24] that this design symbolizes the defeat of the Lancastrians by the House of York although, clearly, it could alternatively be associated with the healing of disease. Indeed, in this latter respect, it may be significant that the value of the coin, namely 6s 8d, (one third of a pound) was the contemporary professional fee for a physician or lawyer. The reverse of the coin carries a ship, in common with so many other coins, and, in abbreviated form, the legend PER CRUCEM TUAM SALVA NOS CHRISTE REDEMPTOR (By means of your Cross, save us Christ redeemer) (Plate 1) which suggests that it may well have been intended from its onset as a healing-piece.

Since only a rightful king was believed to possess the curative touch, it has been suggested that it may have been in an attempt to encourage the sick to come to him for healing that Edward IV (1461–1470 and 1471–1483), during the first part of his troubled reign, when he certainly aimed at fortifying himself upon the throne by the somewhat liberal use of the royal gift of healing, introduced the angel and thereby at once raised the value of the alms given to those who were touched from a silver penny to a gold coin worth 6s 8d.[25] However, it is generally believed that the angel was not regularly used in connection with royal healing ceremonies until the reign of Henry VII (1485–1509), other gold pieces probably having been donated in earlier ceremonies to replace the royal upkeep of the patients. It was certainly this latter monarch who codified the practices of the past into a divine service, thereby creating a ceremony for touching, and the alms, in the form of a gold coin that had previously been given, became a healing-piece. After receiving the royal touch, the patient would have the angel, which had been pierced (Plate 2), used for crossing their sores, threaded on a white silk ribbon and hung by the King's own hand around his or her neck. It was important that it should continue to be worn by the sufferer, thus establishing its rôle as an amulet, rather than a talisman, that also became a permanent memento of the King, an example of good sound public relations.

Henry VII thus established a pattern that was to survive for 160 years. Although his son, Henry VIII, does not appear to have been a very prolific toucher, it is noticeable that when he debased the coinage, including reducing the weight of the sovereign from 240gr to 200gr, the angel was kept at the same eighty grains which it had always been, thus raising its relative value to eight shillings, even though the fineness of the gold had been reduced. Edward VI restored its fineness, increasing its value still further, to ten shillings, a state of affairs that was maintained by Mary Tudor and Elizabeth I (except between 1562 and 1572). James I and Charles I both kept its value at ten shillings, but only by reducing its weight. This apparent reluctance by successive sovereigns to debase the angel implies that the coin was held in unusual regard and supports a case being made for some mystic association between angel-gold and the healing power.

It would appear that touching was not practised by the young and sickly Edward VI but his elder sister, Mary Tudor, took it on board very seriously as, indeed, she did the service of the Royal Maundy. The reverse legend on her angels was altered to read, in suitably abbreviated form, A DOMINO FACTUM EST ISTVD ET EST MIRABILE (It is the Lord's doing and it is marvellous) but too much should not be read into this since a similar legend, although now also including, in suitably abbreviated form, IN OCULIS NOSTIS (in our eyes), also appears on her sovereigns and ryals. During the service for touching, Mary pressed the sores of each patient with her hands. Later in the ceremony, for each patient she touched these infected areas with an angel, with which she made the sign of the cross, and subsequently threaded a white silk ribbon through a hole which had been made in the coin which she then hung around the sufferer's neck.

Elizabeth I made no changes to the angel, other than her titles in the coin's obverse legend. Bearing in mind that the whole concept of the miraculous nature of the royal touch began to be questioned upon the advent of the Reformation and, as a result, cramp rings[26] were discredited once and forever during the reign of Elizabeth I, it is somewhat surprising that this queen continued to touch for the King's Evil in virtually the same manner as had her elder sister. However, she removed from the associated liturgy a prayer that mentioned the Virgin and the saints and probably translated into English the Latin ritual of the previous ages[27] although, rather unexpectedly, she continued the practice of making the sign of the cross when presenting the healing-piece. One reason why Elizabeth had, in fact, initially laid her maiden hands upon the scrofulous was to establish that her possession of the related curative powers was the verification of her rightful sovereignty[28] as well as of theological truth,[29] and thus monarchial survival instincts clearly played a rôle in her adoption of the ritual.

James I was initially loath to touch at all because of his upbringing as a Calvinist and of his dislike of being in close contact with a large number of diseased and sick people. He was torn between, on the one hand, his regard for the ceremony as a superstitious rite and, on the other, the need to maintain what had become the Royal Health Service, the abandonment of which would have been a most unpopular act, and thereby to continue an ancient custom which enhanced public belief in the supernatural character of monarchial power. Not surprisingly, his royal survivalistic instincts predominated, as had those of Elizabeth I, and he practised the custom. However, to ease his conscience, on his angels he omitted the cross that had previously topped the ship's mast and also removed the words, or their abbreviation, ET EST MIRABILE from the reverse legends introduced by Mary Tudor, possibly sometimes used gold coins other than the angel as healing-pieces, refused to make the sign of the cross, amended the rubric to eliminate everything of a papist nature and treated the ritual as a prayer in which God was invoked to perform the healing. This handing it back whence it came marked the beginning of the end for the supposedly curative royal touch.

However, contrary to his father, Charles I was an ardent and prolific practitioner of touching. He was, indeed, the first monarch to effect it in Scotland, namely when, a few days after his Scottish coronation in 1633, he touched about one hundred sufferers inflicted with the Evil, a ceremony for which special angels were struck by Nicholas Briot.[30] Nevertheless, in London, Charles I, like his father, only touched around Easter and Michaelmas since in the summer months it was not only too hot but there was a risk of the King contacting disease, although both also touched on progresses. However, even during these periods all touching was either postponed or cancelled when plague was rife, for fear of the King's health. During the first phases of the Civil War, Charles I continued the practice but, after 1643, there were no further strikings of the angel and thus those coins as were in circulation had to suffice for the occasion. Furthermore, when during this period gold coins were unavailable, it is likely that Charles I used silver coins as healing-pieces although there is no evidence to suggest that he ever so used base-metal coins, of which, in fact, only farthings were available. When the supply of both gold and silver coins became exhausted, the patients had to supply their own, in doing so it being clear that they were genuinely seeking a cure and not the bounty. The eventual capture of the King put an end to his touching, a deciding factor to this effect possibly being the legend upon the gold angels of his reign that were supplied by the patients and read AMOR POPULI PRAESIDIUM REGIS (The love of the people is the King's defence) (Plate 2).

During Cromwell's period as Lord Protector, curative touching understandably fell into abeyance in England. Nevertheless, patients travelled to the Low Countries, often under the auspices of tours by sea that were organized by enterprising merchants of the time, to receive the touch from the exiled son (later to become Charles II) of the executed Charles I. For such ceremonies, ten shilling pieces (angels) and possibly other small gold coins, perhaps including some of those of James I, were used as healing-pieces. Alternatively, angels from earlier ceremonies or artifacts soaked in the executed King's blood allegedly taken from the scaffold were used during this period in England in attempts to treat the Evil. Indeed, many stories abound connecting relics of the executed King with miraculous cures and, well into the nineteenth century, his crowns and half-crowns, handed down through the generations, were still being used in the Shetland Islands to effect healings.

Following the Restoration in 1660, Charles II quickly re-established curative touching in England. He so first touched in the Banqueting House at Whitehall[31] on 23 June 1660, less than four weeks after his return and ten months before his coronation as King of England: 600 sufferers presented themselves. A month later, it was decided to limit the number of patients to 200 per ceremony. Furthermore, a pattern was soon established in that touchings took place on Fridays from 1 November to 18 December, then during the months of January and February and for a month at Easter, they being suspended during the summer months for fear that the hot weather and the associated disease amongst the public would present a threat to the King's health. Excluding those on royal progress, the number touched during a twelve month period was about four thousand and in the first four years following the Restoration some twenty-three thousand sufferers received the touch. An illustration of Charles II touching for scrofula (Plate 3) forms the frontispiece of John Browne's *Charisma Basilikon* (part 3 of *Adenochiradelogia*) published in 1684 and an example of such a ceremony, possibly the first effected after the Restoration, is described by Evelyn, as an entry in his diary under 6 July 1660:[32]

> His Majesty began first to touch for ye evil, according to custome thus: Sitting under his state in the Banqueting House, the chirugeons cause the sick to be brought or led up to the throne, where they kneeling, ye King strokes their faces and cheeks with both his hands at once, at which instant a chaplaine in his formalities says: 'He put his hands upon them and healed them.' This he said to everyone in particular. When they have been all totched, they come up again in the same order; and the other chaplaine kneeling, and having an angel of gold strung on white ribbon on his arme, delivers them one by one to His Majestie, who puts them about the necks of the touched as they passe, while the first chaplaine repeats: 'That is ye true light which came into ye world.' Then follows an epistle (as at first a gospel), with the liturgy, prayers for the sick, with some alteration, and then the Lord Chamberlain and the Comptroller of the Household brings a basin, ewer, and towel for his Majesty to wash.

From 1660 to 1664, in the absence of a suitable coin of his own issue, Charles II used foreign gold coins and those of Charles I, James I and Elizabeth I as healing-pieces. That there had been an initial intention to bring back the angel, if only for touching needs, is evident from the fact that in September 1660 Thomas Simon[33] was ordered to prepare sketches and dies for such a coin. Nevertheless, this idea was soon abandoned and only one trial-piece of the reverse is known. Subsequently, by a warrant dated 25 February 1664/5,[34] special healing-pieces were ordered of twenty-two carat fine gold (angel gold had been of a standard of 23 carats 3½ gr) with one troy pound to make 106 pieces, thus giving them a weight of 54.3 gr each. The dies were almost certainly the work of John Roettiers[35] and the first striking was about six thousand seven hundred pieces, namely enough to last about a year and a half.

These new healing-pieces, called touch-pieces, had no mark of value and were not intended to be coin of the realm but they had a bullion value of approximately ten shillings. Although the same emblems were still employed on these touch-pieces as had been traditional on the angel, the design was very different, with a further move, the first having occurred in the third coinage of James I, toward a representational ship (Plate 4). This ship can be identified with *The Sovereign of the Seas*, originally named *The Royal Sovereign*, which at that time was by far the largest ship afloat. However, the most manifest change in design lay in the whole piece being turned over, with what had been the reverse now becoming the obverse. Thus, the royal name and titles were now placed around the ship (Plate 4; compare with Plates 1 and 2) and a simpler, more direct, legend on the reverse, namely around St Michael, reads SOLI DEO GLORIA (Glory to God alone) (Plate 4), an inscription that no doubt reflects the influence of James I. In August 1684, the size of the touch-piece was reduced from 54.3 gr to 30.0 gr, a move that might be assumed to have been an economic measure, although it may have been influenced by the necessity for new dies. The results of a numismatic investigation of the touch-pieces of Charles II, and of those James II and Anne, which are of the same basic design, have been published.[36]

During the years from 1664 to 1684 the first, larger, touch-pieces were received by approximately seventy-nine thousand two hundred people. These, together with those who received the second, smaller, type and some further twenty-three thousand who received either foreign coins or coins from earlier reigns, afford a total of about one-hundred-and-five thousand people who were touched during the twenty-five years of the reign. Charles II clearly was, unlike his father, an ardent and prolific toucher.

James II first touched for the Evil on 4 March 1685, just four weeks after his brother's death, probably using some of the 1,905 touch-pieces left over from the previous reign. He was far more prolific a toucher than even his late brother had been and as many as 14,364 sufferers were presented to him in one year. As had been the practice in his late brother's reign, the ceremony was carried out weekly on Fridays in London, except during hot weather, but unlike his late brother, James put no limit upon the numbers he was prepared to touch at any one session, a figure which reached as high as 800 on a single day when he touched in the choir of Chester Cathedral. On average it would appear that he touched not less than 12,000 sufferers annually. By the middle of 1686, James, who had been converted to Catholicism in 1669, had begun replacing the Anglican clergy, who had previously officiated in the ceremony, with his own Romish priests, was introducing a Latin liturgy and was generally reverting to the original popish ritual of Henry VII. Whilst these moves served to discredit the practice of touching amongst Protestants and undoubtedly contributed to the increasing unpopularity of James that finally overtook him some few months after the birth of his son by his second wife, Mary of Modena, on 10 June 1688, since this birth would have ensured a Catholic succession to the throne, they do not appear to have affected the numbers coming to be touched. Apparently, considerable numbers still had sufficient faith in James, or at least in his gold, to lead them to seek his favour.

Obviously, the gold in the angel or, later, in the touch-piece, represented a substantial gift to the recipient patients. Indeed, in view of the large numbers of sufferers who were touched, it must have been a heavy charge upon the Exchequer, one estimate being in the region of £10,000 per annum. Those who were to receive this royal favour were chosen by the sovereign's surgeons who, in view of the considerable expense involved, were very careful in their examination of petitioners and in the keeping of registers, those successful being given an admission token or ticket[37] for the ceremony on the following day. To many sufferers, the gold was an essential part of the treatment and many such convinced believers in this form of metallotherapy were anxious to have the process repeated. In fact, the power of the royal pseudo physicians appeared to leave much to be desired, since so many patients returned time and again to be touched!

This potential form of abuse was checked by John Browne, a Chirugion in Ordinary to Charles II, James II and William III, who proposed that if such further visits to be touched were considered as being necessary, the patients should supply their own gold. However, as evidence that such abuse of this form of royal patronage actually occurred, we have Browne's account that 'there are another set of People who make it their study to cheat the King of his gold, who having been touched and received their gold are ready to sell and part with it; and were not this true and very commonly put in practice, without all question, His Majestie's touching Medals would not be so frequently seen and found in the Gold Smiths Shops'. In a further attempt to prevent such abuse, patients were required to bring with them certification from their parish where the minister was supposed to keep the appropriate register to ensure that they had not previously received the gold.

Although it was still practised after 1688 by James II in exile in France he was compelled, because of his reduced circumstances, to use silver rather than gold touch-pieces.[38] These were almost certainly made in England by the brothers Norbert and James Roettiers, an activity that helps to substantiate the contemporary accusations that they had been working surreptitiously for the exiled king and which were responsible for Norbert's hasty departure from England in 1695.[39]

In England, the newly enthroned William and Mary refused to touch. Like James I, William had been raised as a Calvinist and, as such, dismissed touching as 'silly superstition' which was anathema to him. However, unlike James I, he was not prepared to concede to any popular demand although this was likely to have been less than it was in earlier reigns since the Divine Right, which had helped to sustain the monarchy for so long, was by then becoming increasingly fragile as the Crown became more accountable to Parliament. Mary, his wife and the daughter of James II, may have been encouraged to refuse to touch out of respect for her husband's wishes although she may also have had some misgivings about practising the ritual whilst her father was still alive. It is reported that only once was William induced to touch, on which occasion he supposedly said to the patient 'God give you better health, and more sense!' Unfortunately, the enlightened spirit of these two monarchs was not appreciated by all, as is evident from one report which reads:[40]

> The parents of scrofulous children cried out against his cruelty; bigots lifted up their hands and eyes in horror at his impiety; Jacobites sarcastically praised him for not presuming to arrogate to himself a power which belonged only to legitimate sovereigns: and even some Whigs thought that he acted unwisely in treating with such marked contempt a superstition which had a strong hold on the vulgar mind: but William was not to be moved, and was accordingly set down by many High Churchmen as either an infidel or a Puritan.

With the dawn of the eighteenth century, medical science was beginning to revolt against the myths of the curative royal touch. Furthermore, when Anne succeeded to the throne in 1702, she had no desire to touch and, indeed, she claimed no divine right to do so. Nevertheless, her ministers advised compliance with a tradition that offered the only hope to sufferers from Scrofula and that, to remove this, would have been politically unwise. It should not go unnoticed that Anne was also probably induced to resume touching by way of asserting her hereditary right to the Crown (as, indeed, had been a motive of Elizabeth I) and flouting the Parliamentary right of William III and the House of Hanover. In addition, the popular clamour which led to Anne unpremeditatedly touching thirty patients at Bath on 6 October 1702, her first participation in the ritual, probably decided her to subscribe formally to the practice. However, the first announcement that she would touch for the Evil did not appear in the *London Gazette* until 15 March 1702/3,[41] almost eleven months after her coronation, and the related ceremony took place on 3 April 1703. Anne touched on Saturdays at 11 o'clock at St James's, sometimes in the courtyard, the number of patients, when mentioned, being either one hundred or two hundred. Admission tickets were issued every Friday at 3 o'clock in the afternoon at the New Guard Chamber in Whitehall. It would appear that a total of approximately nineteen thousand four hundred gold touch-pieces were issued during her reign.

Amongst those upon whom Anne laid her hands was one Samuel Johnson when he was two-and-a-half years old. Indeed, Dr Johnson was for all his life a Jacobite. Coming from Lichfield, as his family did, this meant a journey of three days and a stay of several nights in London for the young Johnson. The most likely date for his touching is 30 March 1712. He bequeathed the touch-piece that Anne had hung around his neck to Dr Taylor, the Prebendary of Westminster, who in turn left it to the Duke of Devonshire in whose possession it was in 1798. It is now in the British Museum and shows little wear although, according to his biographers, Johnson wore it all his life,[42] an act which, along with the royal touch, would appear to have been in vain for apparently he was never cured.[43]

Anne, who died on 1 August 1714,[44] last touched for Scrofula on 27 April 1714, a date which marked the final discontinuance of this ceremony in England and brought an end to the history of the gold touch-piece which had existed for just fifty years. The Hanoverians would have none of it. In fact, it is related that, soon after his accession, George I declined to touch the child of an English gentleman, referring him to the Pretender as possessing the hereditary power of the Stuarts. However, the service remained in the Book of Common Prayer until 1719 and, in view of their supposed curative powers, touch-pieces from earlier periods continued to circulate for many years amongst the sick. Furthermore, the Stuart Pretenders to the British throne continued curative touching in their various countries of residence, namely France, Italy and Scotland, but using silver touch-pieces. These were of the same basic design as the gold piece illustrated in Plate 4 and a numismatic investigation of them has been published.[45] The last Stuart to touch was Henry, Cardinal Duke of York, who died at Frascati on 13 July 1807 and was laid to rest in the crypt of St Peter's beside his mother, father (James Francis Edward Stuart, The Old Pretender and son of James II) and brother (Charles Edward Louis Philip Casimir Stuart, The Young Pretender, Bonnie Prince Charlie). Henry's death brought to an end the House of Stuart and the practice of touching for the King's Evil.[46]

It may be thought that the royal touch, representing as it did royal competition, would have been resented by the surgeons of the day but this was not the case. Indeed, this body gave its unqualified and ardent support to the practice. However, was touching genuine? In true cases of Scrofula, the psychological element can be eliminated although, in cases where a misdiagnosis had occurred, such factors may have played a part. Contemporary misdiagnosis may in other cases also have been responsible for the apparent royal miracle since the name Scrofula was often used to cover a large number of lesions of various kinds, some of which were benign and would by themselves disappear, often in a very short time. Certainly some, but far from all, of those touched recovered, but often only slowly, a recovery that is not surprising since it is known that tuberculous adenitis is in some cases a disease of temporary remission. In connection with these above clinical factors, it has been admitted that the royal surgeons made a very careful selection of patients for the royal healer, choosing those who experience told them showed a tendency to recovery. It may be claimed, with obvious justification, that the popularity of this treatment was connected with the gold coin or touch-piece received by each of the patients during the ceremony. Furthermore, relating to this it has been stated that 'some were cured of the King's Evil who never had any other evils than that of poverty, which brought more patients and more fame to those royal practitioners than they deserved'.[47] The early kings had no doubt conceived the royal touch in order to strengthen their fragile prestige and it was then easy for those later physician-sovereigns, who were not impostors in their beliefs, to proceed in terms of cause and effect, even if the latter was only partial. The sought after miracle could occur. Certainly, the royal touch was harmless which is more than can be said for many of the contemporary surgical procedures employed in the treatment of Scrofula or many of the claimed cures for it contained in the pharmacopoeia of olden times. From this purely negative viewpoint it is probably justifiable to claim that more than one poor sufferer may have owed a debt to his sovereign for the relief of his ills. Indeed, even quite late into the nineteenth century, the following incredible recipes for treating the condition were still being published:

(i) Take as much cream of tartar as lies on a shilling.
(ii) Drink for 6 weeks half a pint of strong decoction of devil's bit (a herb of the Scabious species).
(iii) Make a leaf of dried burdock into a pint of tea; take half a pint twice a day for 4 months, I have known this cure hundreds.
(iv) Mix a scruple of burnt sponge with four grains of rhubarb for a dose; take it night and morning in a cup of whey.

Only in recent times, in fact, have therapeutic agents been developed for the effective treatment of this disease.

VII. CRAMP RINGS[48]

As with touching for the King's Evil, cramp rings represented yet another of several sacred and miraculous aspects of royalty, the credibility of which was accepted in earlier times and which the monarchy thus sometimes attempted to exploit to its own advantage in order to gain popularity or, indeed, to establish its rightful claim to the throne.

During the Middle Ages, in common with the customs universally observed by the Catholic Church, the kings of England used to practise the Adoration of the Cross on Good Friday. Thus, by the early years of the fourteenth century, in the chapel where they happened to be at this time, the Cross of Gwyneth, a miraculous relic which, according to tradition, was made of wood from the true Cross presented by a pilgrim to Richard Cœur de Lion, and apparently taken from the Welsh by Edward I, was set up and the sovereign would prostrate himself before it in a prescribed fashion. However, by the reign of Edward II (1307–1327) and up to and including that of Henry V (1413–1422), an additional related act was concurrently practised specifically in England. After the prostrations, the king would proceed to the altar and offer a certain quantity of gold and silver in good new coins, namely florins, nobles and sterlings. He would then take these coins, redeeming them by an equivalent sum in ordinary coins, and from the redeemed coins would have made a number of rings which were considered to be capable of curing those who wore them of certain diseases.

In earlier documents it is not specified what these diseases were but by the fifteenth century it is clear that these talismans were reckoned to relieve muscular pains and spasms and, more especially, epilepsy for which they were supposedly particularly effective as a cure. Hence from this time onwards they became known as cramp rings, the cramp somewhat sacrilegiously being compared to the agony suffered by Christ on the Cross.

When such faith in these rings had reached its peak in England, it was natural to seek the support of legendary patrons. Thus grew the mediæval legend that Joseph of Arimathea, the disciple who is recorded as having buried Christ's body after its removal from the Cross, brought to England the act of healing epileptics by means of rings. Later, the patronage was placed under Edward the Confessor as, indeed, was that of touching for the King's Evil.

From the earliest of times, rings have been amongst the favourite instruments of magic, and epilepsy, with its attendant violent fits, was thus considered to have a diabolical origin and therefore to be more amenable than other diseases to such supernatural means of healing. In England, the ring of Edward the Confessor was one of the sacred relics in his shrine in Westminster Abbey and many miraculous cures are associated with it, the sick and infirm who sought help kneeling at the shrine. However, the earliest such cure for epilepsy, so-called cramp, only dates from the reign of Edward II. In the fifteenth century in Germany, rings made from begged deniers were employed as a treatment for gout. A silver ring made of five sixpences contributed by five different bachelors and conveyed by a bachelor to a smith who was also a bachelor was a reputed remedy for epilepsy, the numbers five being symbolic of the five wounds of the crucified Jesus. In other cases, rings made from the nails or screws taken from old coffins that had been dug out of a churchyard, or from nails from which a man had hanged himself, were supposed to have supernatural powers, with many other sources and related cures being on record. Thus, cramp rings were only one of a very general class of remedies of which the current wearing of copper bracelets by some sufferers from rheumatism and related disorders may be regarded as a modern manifestation.

In France, the coins redeemed as described above were themselves pierced and used as amulets (as were the healing-pieces in touching for the King's Evil), in the German-speaking St Gall region this ritual taking place on Christmas Eve, rather than on Good Friday as was the situation with the cramp rings. However, in both cases the principle was the same, namely the sanctification of metals from which healing talismans were made. Clearly, in this scenario the English monarchs of the fourteenth century only played a minor and passive rôle. Nonetheless, during these earlier times, the English and French monarchs were held by the populace to be wonderworkers endowed with sacred powers. Because of this, and since they had long been attributed with the power to cure scrofula by touching, it is not surprising that it eventually became believed that monarchs played an active rôle in the transmission of the curative powers to the cramp rings. Eventually, the English monarchs began to consider the production of cramp rings on Good Friday as they did their touching for the King's Evil, namely one of their supernatural functions. This assumption was easily accepted by the general credulity that was then prevalent in mediæval England and, indeed, in Europe generally. In fact, it was only one example of a magical procedure during this period being eventually taken over and monopolized by hereditary healers.

By the early part of the reign of Henry VI (1422–1461 and 1470–1471), it had become more convenient for basins full of the rings themselves to be placed for a moment at the foot of the cross during the Good Friday ceremony prior to their redemption with coin of the realm. Later, even the offering of the rings to the altar had ceased to be the central act in the rite and, by the time of Mary Tudor's reign, the then supposed divine force emanating from the touch of the royal hands which had been sanctified by unction, widely employed in the contemporary treatment of scrofula, had obliterated everything else in the production of cramp rings on Good Friday. Indeed, as early as 1462 it was written that:[49]

> The Kings of England at their very anointing receive such an infusion of grace from heaven, that by touch of their anointed hands they cleanse and cure those infected with a certain disease, that is commonly called the King's Evil, though they be pronounced otherwise incurable. Epileptics too, and persons subject to the falling sickness, are cured by means of gold and silver devoutly touched and offered by the sacred anointed hands of the kings of England upon Good Friday, during divine service (according to the ancient custom of the Kings of England); . . . The gift is not bestowed on Queens, as they are not anointed on the hands[50].

No mention is made in the contemporary Tudor missal[51] of the making of any offering although this probably took place after the prayers but was no longer considered to be of importance. Thus, the healing power that had hitherto been ascribed to the influence of the cross and the altar had been completely usurped by the ancient conception of sacred royalty.

However, with the coming of the Reformation the days of the cramp ring and, in the longer term, of royal healing in general, were numbered. Although records bear testimony to the popularity of the rings during the reign of Henry VIII, show that Edward VI continued to bless them and record that the Roman Catholic Mary Tudor conducted these rites with much vigour, the Court reverted to the Protestant faith in 1558 upon the accession of Elizabeth I and it was during her reign, probably toward its beginning, that the ceremonial finally fell into disuse and the cramp ring disappeared quite unobtrusively. For some time, rings blessed by former monarchs continued to be treasured and hoarded by the general public, then people gradually ceased to value these unpretentious artifacts which were not distinguishable by any external signs from those that were generally worn. Not a single cramp ring has come down to us or, if any have, we handle them without being aware of the fact. Elizabeth I had effectively killed this ancient rite.[52]

Neither epilepsy nor muscular spasm are amenable to psychiatric therapy so how did the cramp ring effect its cure? To account for this, it must be remembered that medical diagnosis was very unreliable in earlier times when it was without much precision and clinical definition. Thus, during this period it was certainly easy to diagnose, along with true cases of epilepsy and its attendant symptoms, many other kinds of nervous disorders, and pains, of a purely emotional origin that would be curable by the persuasion inherent in a talisman.

NOTES

1. F. E. Andrews, *Philanthropic Functions* (New York, 1956); R. H. Bremmer, *American Philanthropy* (Chicago, 1960); James Douglas, *Why Charity? The Case for a Third Section* (Beverly Hill, London and New Delhi, 1983): J. P. Gallagher, *The Price of Charity* (London, 1975); B. K. Gray, *Philanthropy and the State, or Social Politics* (London, 1908); Jørgen Lissner, *The Politics of Altruism. A Study of the Political Behaviour of Voluntary Development Agencies* (Geneva, 1977); C. S. Loch, *Charity and Social Life. A Short Study of Religious and Social Thought in Relation to Charitable Methods and Institutions* (London, 1910); W. A. Nielsen, *The Big Foundations* (New York and London, 1972); Nightingale.
2. David Gerard, *Charities in Britain, Conservation or Change?* (London, 1983); B. K. Gray, *A History of English Philanthropy, from the Dissolution of the the Monasteries to the Taking of the First Census* (London, 1905); W. K. Jordan, *The Charities of London, 1480–1660. The Aspirations and the*

Achievements of the Urban Society (London, 1960); W. K. Jordan, *The Charities of Rural England, 1480–1660. The Aspirations and the Achievements of the Rural Society* (London, 1961).
3. Challis (1989); McAlpine and Robinson (1981).
4. Bidwell, p. 545; Farquhar (1923–24).
5. In olden times, this bounty was paid at the gate of the Palace of Whitehall. The position of this gate is not quite clear but it may be inferred that it must have been somewhere in Whitehall since it is supposed that one of the gates of the palace stood on or about the same spot as did the former Almonry Office in Middle Scotland Yard where, until 1884, the distributions took place (Bidwell, p. 545).
6. Wright.
7. Bidwell, p. 545; Farquhar (1925–26).
8. See note 6 above.
9. See note 6 above.
10. *The Times* (3 April 1920), p. 13.
11. During the week preceding Easter in that year.
12. The Secretary of the Royal Almonry.
13. Bidwell, p. 545.
14. Farquhar (1925–26).
15. See note 3 above.
16. See Appendix 1.
17. Farquhar (1923–24), pp. 159-60.
18. Farquhar (1923–24), p. 158.
19. See notes 13 and 18 above.
20. See note 13 above. In fact, the Bishop of Salisbury was the Lord High Almoner from 1743 to 1747 only, in 1748 the position being held by the Archbishop of York (Table 6).
21. Bloch; Crawfurd (1911); Farquhar (1916, 1917, 1918, 1919–20); Gomme, pp. 165–75; E. L. Hussey, 'On the Cure of Scrofulous Diseases Attributed to the Royal Touch', *Archæol. J.*, 10 (1855), pp. 187–211 (see also p. 337); Miles; Cornelius Nicholls, 'On the Obsolete Custom of Touching for the King's Evil', *HCM*, 14 (1912), pp. 112–22; Woolf (1979, 1980, 1985); 'John Browne and the Royal Gift of Healing', *BMJ* (31 August 1895), pp. 555–56; 'The Royal Cure for the King's Evil'.
22. C. E. Blunt, 'Some Notes on the Coinage of Edward IV between 1461 and 1470 with Particular Reference to the Nobles and Angels', *BNJ*, 22 (1937), pp. 193–99; H. Schneider, 'An Unpublished Angel of Edward IV', *BNJ*, 26 (1950), p. 221; T. G. Webb Ware, 'Dies and Designs: the English Gold Coinage 1465–1485' *BNJ*, 55 (1985), pp. 95–133.
23. In heraldic terms the beast is not a dragon but a wyvern, having as it does only two legs (Woolf (1979), footnote 4 on p. 101).
24. Seaby, p. 76.
25. Bloch (quoted in Woolf (1979), p. 101).
26. See Section VII of Chapter 1.
27. Bloch, p. 190.
28. Likewise, the common opinion that only the lawful monarch could heal was the reason why the Lancastrians had earlier refused to admit that the House of York could possess the miraculous gift of healing, and no doubt vice versa. With each side trying to discredit the other, it is only too likely that some of this discredit overflowed onto the rite in general (Bloch, p. 65). Conversely when, from 1320 onward, the popularity of Edward II began to wane before the ever-increasing popularity of his rival, Edward III, the number of the sick seeking the former's touch fell: clearly, concomitant with his lack of prestige was a decline in his subjects' belief in his miraculous powers (Bloch, p. 59).
29. Crawfurd (1911), p. 76; 'The Royal Cure for the King's Evil', p. 1182.
30. See note 16 above.
31. See Appendix 2.
32. Quoted in 'The Royal Cure for the King's Evil', p. 1183. Illustrations showing the French kings Henry II and Henry IV, and Edward the Confessor and Mary Tudor, touching for Scrofula are also known (Crawfurd (1911), Plates facing pp. 58, 78, 18 and 68, respectively).
33. See note 16 above.
34. See Appendix 3.
35. See note 16 above.
36. Woolf (1979, 1990).

37. Woolf (1979), pp. 104, 108, 109, (1990), pp. 9, 10, 13, 14, 57, 58.
38. Woolf (1980, 1990).
39. See note 16 above; Woolf (1985) (In this article, Norbert's brother is initially incorrectly referred to as Philip (which was, in fact, the name of his uncle). However, it is evident from the remainder of the article that this was clearly a slip of the pen).
40. Quoted in 'The Royal Cure for the King's Evil', p. 1184.
41. See note 34 above.
42. The almost unworn appearance of the piece would appear to be incompatible with this biographical claim and has consequently led some to question its pedigree. In this connection it may also be significant that the Devonshire collection was essentially a seventeenth-century collection.
43. Woolf (1979), p. 113
44. *DNB*, Freeman-Grenville, *HBC*.
45. See note 38 above.
46. In France, the practice continued until the death of Louis XVI during the French Revolution. Afterward there was one brief and rather half-hearted unsuccessful attempt to effect its revival, namely on 3 May 1825 at the hands of Charles X when he touched 121 people following his coronation. In fact, Charles X was the last king of France whose sovereignty rested, even in semblance, on the antiquated principle of the divine right of kings.
47. Miles.
48. Bloch, pp. 92–107; Crawfurd (1955).
49. Crawfurd (1955), p. 171.
50. This did not deter our two Tudor queens or the last of the Stuarts from occupying the throne of England or from touching for scrofula. The reasoning may have been intended to apply to queens consort and not to queens regnant (Woolf (1979), p. 101 and note 5).
51. Crawfurd (1955), pp. 182–87.
52. Bloch, pp. 189–90.

CHAPTER 2

The Royal Maundy

Many previous authors have devoted their attention to the Royal Maundy. One of the earliest such studies appeared as long as 150 years ago.[1] It briefly covers the origin of the ceremony, Maundy Thursday's etymology and the Maundy money, and quotes details of the Maundy distributions as they were effected in 1572, 1731, 1814 and 1838, although this last described distribution was actually that to those Maundy men and women who were on the supernumeracy list, namely reservists[2]. Furthermore, it makes reference to the Maundy distribution by the Earl of Northumberland in the early part of the sixteenth century and describes the corresponding ceremonies as then practised by the Churches in Moscow, Rome and Seville, and by the Austrian monarchy in Vienna. During the 1920s, three thoroughly researched and extremely well-referenced articles appeared in the numismatic literature[3] although, unfortunately, these are somewhat fragmentary in composition and, more seriously, occasionally quote inaccurately from original documentary sources. Earlier in the century, four other studies, primarily historic rather than numismatic, of the subject appeared, two of which are published in the periodical literature[4] and the others constituting an appendix to a book[5] and a chapter in a book[6]. The secretariat of the Royal Almonry Office, the body responsible for the administration of the Royal Maundy, have described the evolution of the latter and of various related facets in a booklet that has appeared in two distinct formats, each of which has run into several editions. The first of these formats was published by the Royal Almonry Office at Buckingham Palace and its first edition, printed in 1936, was the work of the then Assistant Secretary of the Office:[7] by the time of the seventh edition[8], published in 1960, he had been joined by Mr P. A. Wright, the Office's present Secretary, as co-author. The completely revised format of the booklet, under the latter's sole authorship, was subsequently published by Pitkin Pictorials and has appeared in three editions.[9] Although they do not quote original reference sources, all the editions of both formats contain much interesting historic, together with some numismatic, information. Furthermore, they are very well illustrated, particularly the later format, of which the most recent edition has many of its illustrations in colour. Another discussion of the Royal Maundy,[10] interestingly highly personalized, was written by Dr L. E. Tanner who was the Secretary of the Royal Almonry from 1921 until 1964. This account deals with the revival of the ceremony during the 1930s, before which it 'seemed to be in danger of becoming nothing but a picturesque and, perhaps, rather meaningless survival from the past',[11] and its subsequent development up to the late 1960s. In more recent years another booklet, which ran into a third edition,[12] has appeared. However, apart from giving a very brief account of the Royal Maundy's evolution and descriptions of the main types of Maundy coins, this publication consists for the larger part of a contemporary price catalogue of this coinage as appertaining to North American valuations. Much of the information in the above publications that were then extant was utilized in a book[13] on the Royal Maundy published in 1977. Other publications have also made brief, but significant, contributions in this area.[14]

I. THE EVOLUTION OF THE MAUNDY SERVICE

The custom of providing guests upon their arrival with water, in order that they might wash their feet and thereby cleanse themselves of the dirt gathered from the road, is of great antiquity. Indeed, the practice is referred to several times in the Old Testament of the Holy Bible[15] and, in the Middle and Far East, it is still traditional to wash one's feet, in the fountain provided, prior to entering a mosque. As a further act of hospitality, the host, or one of the host's servants, would also sometimes personally carry out the washing of their guests' feet.

It can be seen from the Holy Bible that, toward the end of the Last Supper,[16] Jesus washed the feet of the twelve Apostles (Plate 5),[17] an act that could well be related to His earlier directive for them to choose the room for this feast in the house to which they would be led by following a man bearing a pitcher of water.[18] After performing this humble act, Jesus told the Apostles (gave them a *mandatum*) 'If I then, *your* Lord and Master, have washed your feet, ye also ought to wash one another's feet. For I have given you an example, that ye should do as I have done unto you'.[19]

Thus was the Maundy service conceived.

The Church's obedience to Christ's *mandatum* can be traced back to the fourth century, when in Northern Italy and Spain the feet of converts were washed at the end of Lent prior to their baptism,[20] and to the *pedilavium*, referred to by one writer[21] as the *mandatum* or *lavipedium* (*lavanda*[22]), which followed Holy Communion on Maundy Thursday. In fact, by the Middle Ages, Maundy Thursday had become one of the most complex days in the ecclesiastical year, being marked not only by the *pedilavium* but by six other special features. These were Tenebrae (a combined service of Mattins or Nocturns and Lauds, the principal ceremonial of which involved the gradual extinction of twenty-four candles which had been lit at the onset), the Reconciliation of Penitents, the Mass, the Consecration of the Oils, the Altars' Stripping and Washing, and the Loving Cup.[23]

The *pedilavium* is the ceremony whereby the feet of the poor or lower clergy are washed by the senior clergy, an act which in the Early Church was regarded as being symbolic of ecclesiastical humility and the removal of worldly spiritual pollution. However, by the Middle Ages it was directed mainly towards humility alone and was regarded as an act of self-abnegation and penance following the example of Jesus at the Last Supper.[24] The ceremony is also credited in the Early English Text Society's transcription of the *Early South English Legendary* as being held by St Brendan and his monks in the sixth century on Shire[25] Thursday. It was on the second occasion, during their famous voyage, when they arrived at the Isle of Sheep on Maundy Thursday that the ceremony took place and of which the literal translation from the old rhymed version of the event reads:[26]

So that their ship at the last to that isle drew–
On Shire Thursday they came thither: in great travail enough [after a difficult journey]
The Procurator came to them again and welcomed them anon,

> And kissed St Brendan's feet: and the monks, each one;
> And set them afterwards to supper, for the day it willed so [the time of day required it],
> And afterwards he washed their feet all: the Maundy for to do.
> They held there their Maundy–: and there they gan [did] stay
> On Good Friday all the long day: until Easter Eve.

Another reference to this event states that:

> In the miraculous legend of St. Brandon [sic], it is related that he sailed with his monks to the Island of Sheep, about the year 565 A.D.. This island, which abounded in sheep, was set down, in the ancient maps, in the middle of the Atlantic Ocean, near the Equator. Here on '*shere thursdaye*, after souper, he wesshe theyr feet, and kyssed them lyke as our lorde dyd to his dyscyples'.[27]

Other references are also known[28] appertaining to similar celebrations on Maundy Thursdays during the eighth and tenth centuries. Indeed, as early as the year 694, the seventeenth Synod of Toledo commanded all bishops and priests in positions of superiority, on pain of excommunication, to wash the feet of those subject to them.[29]

The practice of the *pedilavium* was not, however, confined to Maundy Thursday. Thus, in some monasteries it took place every Saturday, the feet of as many people being washed in the eastern side of the cloisters as there were monks in the house,[30] and in some abbeys linen was given to the poor after the ceremony.[31] Indeed, before the Norman Conquest, there was a daily Maundy for washing the feet of three of the poor attached to a monastery and for giving them food. Similarly, St Oswald, Archbishop of York, washed the feet of twelve poor men (no doubt symbolic of the number of Apostles) and fed them every day.[32] The physical strain of carrying out this office was great, especially to the aged and infirm and to those who effected the act by traversing the ceremonial hall kneeling. Indeed, it is recorded that in 992 St Oswald, who had been Bishop of Worcester before succeeding Oshitell as Archbishop of York in 972, 'passed to the Lord, on the day before the kalends of March [29th Feb] while (according to the usual custom) he was observing the Maundy before the feet of the poor'.[33]

At Lichfield Cathedral, and probably in other cathedrals destitute of cloisters, these early Maundy services took place in quires: for example, at York Minster the Maundy seats are probably those in the north quire aisle.[34] In the east alley of the cloisters of Worcester Cathedral is a bench table anciently used at the Maundy,[35] while in the south transept of Winchester Cathedral is a great oak settle which may have been the abbot's Maundy bench.[36] At Westminster Abbey, on a stone bench in the east cloister (the east cloister was the usual place for effecting the *pedilavium* in many churches[37]), sat the twelve beggars whose feet the abbot washed, with sundry solemn rites and signs of great humility, and under the nosing of the bench still remain the copper eyes from which hung the carpet upon which he knelt during the performance of this ceremony.[38] Indeed, this broad stone seat, which is in the northern-most bay on the west side of the east cloister, is known as the Maundy bench.[39]

The ceremony at Westminster Abbey, which goes back at least to the sixth century, has been described in the *Rites of Durham*,[40] which also describes the ceremony at Durham Cathedral, and reads:

> There was a goodly ceremony which the Prior [the Abbot, at Westminster] and the monks did use every Thursday before Easter, called Maundy Thursday. The custom was this. There were thirteen poor aged men [representing Christ and the twelve Apostles] appointed to come to the cloister at that day, having their feet clean washed, there to

remain till such time as the Prior and the whole convent did come thither at 9 o'clock or thereabouts; the aged men sitting between the parlour door [At Durham, this was north of the chapter house] and the church door, upon a fair long broad thick form . . . where the Abbot after certain prayers said, one of this servants did bring a fair bason with clean water, and the Abbot did wash the poor men's feet, all of them, one after another, with his own hand, and dried them with a towel, and kissed their feet himself. Which being done, he did very liberally bestow 30*d.* in money on every one of them, with seven red herring apiece, and did serve them himself with drink and three loaves of bread.

This account differs significantly from that briefly referred to elsewhere in which only twelve poor people underwent the *pedilavium* and no mention is made of gifts of food or money.[41] The monks at Westminster Abbey and Durham Cathedral also had Maundies in which they washed the feet of certain children.[42] The ritual followed in effecting the *pedilavium* varied among the different religious orders. For example, the Clugniacs merely touched with wetted fingers the feet of three poor men whereas the Benedictines and the Cistercians scrupulously washed the feet of the brethren, the abbot himself not being excused.[43]

Two accounts exist of the Maundy ceremony as carried out by the monks of Canterbury Cathedral in the Middle Ages. The first such description is based upon a translation of the text of the monastic ordinances which had primary reference to Canterbury and which were drawn up by Lanfranc of Bec who became Archbishop in 1070. From Lanfranc's Constitutions it has been deduced that in the years after the Norman Conquest the Maundy ceremony was practised as follows:[44]

The priest for the week at Low Mass celebrated Mass for the poor men who were to be at the Maundy. The Almoner and others charged for the duty then led them in. When Mass was done the priest gave them of the wafers which were offered but not consecrated, over which the sign of the Cross had been made in the name of the Lord. After this they were led away and given refreshment. After High Mass (for the Monks) the Body of Our Lord was laid up in the Easter Sepulchre (which in the later Middle Ages probably occupied the niche where now lies the so-called Chained Bible in the North Choir Aisle. This part of the structure, it should be remarked, was not in existence in the days of Lanfranc).

Meanwhile the Cellarer and Almoner and others concerned led the poor into the Cloister and caused them to sit side by side. Before entering the Cloister they evidently had a preliminary washing of feet in warm water, conducted by themselves. All things necessary for the Maundy stood prepared in suitable places, the Chamberlains had warm water ready in ewers, together with other vessels, and cloths with towels for feet and hands. The Cellarer provided jugs and drinks and all else of that kind. The servants of the Chamberlains were at hand, together with servants brought in for the occasion from other departments, all having been well-instructed with their duties. Mention is made of the boys of the monastery who will one day be monks. They and their master took part in the Maundy ceremonies, and had poor allocated to them. The rest of the brethren come and take up station before the poor assigned to them. The Abbot (at Canterbury the Archbishop) had two poor men. He now gave order to the Prior for striking the board thrice. This species of wooden gong was used since the bells were out of commission at this climax of Lent. Now the whole monastery adored Christ in the presence of His poor, genuflecting and bowing down. The Abbot or Cantor then intoned the antiphon *Dominus Jesus*.

Each brother now washed the feet of his poor man, wiping and kissing them, and touching them with his forehead. When the feet of all the poor were washed the Abbot took water and towel from two monks, while the monks themselves took like equipment from the servants. (The sequence of events here is not quite clear). Meanwhile the servants brought stoups and liquor to the Abbot and monks. The Prior struck the board thrice and all said in a low voice *Benedicite* (presumably going through the Canticle). When blessing was given the drink was given to the poor, and their hands were kissed. As the stoups were received back, two pence (or whatever the Abbot ordered) were given to each of the poor, with further kissing of hands. Those brethren who had died during the year had their poor, like the other monks, the Abbot allocating them to living brothers. Similarly those associates of the house for whom the Abbot decided in their life time that there should be a poor man.

So long as they are singing at this Maundy (say the Constitutions), that is while the feet and hands of the poor are being washed, those who wish may sit down, keeping to the custom in choir, that is, one shall sit between two who stand. While the drink is being served however, all who wish may sit side by side, not observing the order of alternate standing. The rites concluded with prayers.

We have received Thy mercy, O God, in the midst of Thy Temple; thou hast commanded Thy precepts, O Lord to be exactly observed. . . Assist, we beseech Thee O Lord this work of our service, and since Thou didst vouchsafe to wash the feet of Thy disciples, despise not the work of Thy hands, which Thou hast commanded us to imitate; that as the outward stains are washed away by them, so all our inward sins may be washed away by Thee.

So the monks proceed back to the Church, singing the Psalm *Miserere Have mercy on me, O Lord*, the great penitential Psalm.

The second version of mediæval Maundy at Canterbury, albeit as conducted sometime during the third century after the Conquest, is entered into the Dean and Chapter Register J among the Cathedral archives. The volume, compiled by John of Gore (a monk of Christ Church Priory), probably dates from 1315 to 1316 and contains a great amount of administrative memoranda, especially as relating to agricultural treaties and manorial matters. The pages of this register, namely 420 and 421 (Plate 6), which relate to the Maundy Thursday celebrations have been transcribed and translated to read, along with associated comments:[45]

Procedure to be followed by the Sub-Almoner on Maundy Thursday

Memorandum, that on the Wednesday after Palm Sunday, the Subalmoner should receive from the Cellarer certain tokens (signa), that is to say, for the Archbishop, if present, three tokens. And for the Prior, two tokens. And for each monk present, one token, and for each monk being away on journey, or having died during the previous year, one token. And for guests being 'religious' (i.e. visiting monks, and, probably clergy), one token for each of them.

He shall then deliver all the tokens to the Almoner who delivers them as is customary (by the hands of the Subalmoner), to the Subprior, three tokens; to the 'Third Prior,' and to the 'Fourth Prior' (the under-Subprior and his deputy), to each two tokens. To the Cellarer three tokens; to the Subcellarer, two. To the Precentor, two tokens; to the Sacrist, two tokens; to the Master Subsacrist, one. To the Chamberlain two tokens; to the Subchamberlain, one. To the Masters of the infirmary, four tokens. To the Penitenciaries, four. To the Granger, two. To the Refectorian, two; to his assistant (socio), one. To the *Hospitalarius*, one token. To the Cook, one. Item to each of the sick going about with a stick, one. The other tokens shall remain for distribution at the disposal of the Almoner, except that he shall deliver four to the Subalmoner, and to his servant in the Refectory, one. And to the Panterer's assistant, (garcio – 'garcon'), one.

On Maundy Thursday, after the Chapter Meeting, the Subalmoner shall go out into the 'Curia' and call in individual poor folk. He shall now lead them in through the Cloister to the Altar of St. John beside the Choir, and there shall celebrate Mass of the Holy Ghost. Mass being over, he is to lead back the Poor again through the Cloister into the Hall.

There each of them shall receive a loaf which is called 'smalpeys,' with peas, salt and three herrings, with as much drink as they like. What is left of the drink shall remain to the Almoner. The servants of the Almoner (*make ready? – text evidently incomplete here*) the bread, drink, peas and salt. And the 'Salter' must receive the herrings from the Cellarer and have them ready in the Hall, before the poor come back from the Cathedral. Afterwards the poor are to wash their feet, or before, if they so chose. After Mass for the Monks, while they are having their bread and drink, the poor, under the supervision of the Cellarer and the Granger, shall enter into the Cloister awaiting their Maundy. (*Details are not given, but this stage in the ceremonies probably correspond more or less with those related in the Lanfrancian version, above*). After the Mid-day meal, the Maundy being over, in the Convent (*i.e. the Maundy ceremony held among the monks themselves, when they washed each other's feet*), and the whole Church, the ale is carried into the Almonry and the Sub-Almoner shall deliver to each servant taking part in the Maundy, one gallon of ale *ex gratia*.

The topography of the latter ceremony has been found 'slightly puzzling' and has elicited the comments that 'the "Curia" where the Subalmoner goes to seek the poor might be the "Curia Monachorum" i.e. the Green Court, on the north side of the Cathedral. In such case the Cloister through which they are led must be, not the Great Cloister, but the infirmary Cloister of which part survives as the Cathedral end of the Dark Entry. The hall would probably be the Hall of the Almonry, in the Mint Yard, once among the present buildings of The King's School. If, however, the Cloister in question is the Great Cloister, then the Subalmoner will go to find the poor in the Precincts on the south side of the Cathedral, while the Hall will probably become the Refectory of the Monks, flanking the north side of the Cloister (the site now occupied by the Archdeacon of Canterbury's garden). The Altar of St. John where the flock of poor (there must have been quite a hundred of them) crowd to hear Mass, is specified by the chronicler Gervase of Canterbury as being in the south-eastern transept, on the left, facing east. This is curious, it may be remarked, as there are the remains of a splendid eagle of St. John scratched on the wall of the right-hand apse'.[46]

In both these above descriptions, and apparently in those of the ceremony as effected at Durham Cathedral and Westminster Abbey (see earlier), the Maundy recipients were required to effect a preliminary washing of their own feet. It may nowadays be suggested that this may have lessened the act of humility of those others who subsequently washed them. However, in mitigation, it should not be forgotten that so many people passed their lives in unspeakable filth and squalor during the Middle Ages, when comparatively civilized members of society only bathed at infrequent intervals.[47]

In the second account, it would appear that the total number of tokens received by the Sub-almoner from the Cellarer represents the number of poor who are to participate in the Maundy ceremony. In these circumstances, the number of ecclesiastical personnel of the priory, including those who were temporarily absent or who had died during the previous year, determined, to varying individual degrees, the number of Maundy recipients, similar to the present day system whereby such numbers are related to the monarch's age at the time of the distribution. That such tokens should originate from the Cellarer is understandable since their numbers issued would ultimately determine the quantity of food and wine which he would have to provide for the Maundy distribution. The subsequent delivery of these tokens by the Almoner, via the Sub-almoner, in varying numbers to the various members of the priory, and to others chosen at the discretion of the almoner, represents an allocation of the poor for their receipt of the Maundy rituals.

The custom of providing, along with gifts of clothes, food and money, a post-*pedilavium* substantial meal may have been a recognition by the Church of the previous fasting undergone by the recipients during Lent, although such a feast would appear in such circumstances to have been some three days premature. That such a breaking of the Lenten fast was a concession enjoyed not only by the poor Maundy recipients would appear to be the case in view of the following sarcastic portrayal, in verse, of a monastic celebration. Translated from some old and apparently contemporaneous writer, possibly one of those members of the secular clergy who regarded the monks which such well-known jealously, and supplied by Barnaby Googe in *The Popish Kingdome*, the account reads:[48]

> And here the monkes their Maundie make, with sundrie solemne rights
> And signes of great humilitie, and wondrous pleasant sights
> Ech one the other's feete doth wash, and wipe them cleane and drie,
> With hatefull minde, and secret frawde, that in their heartes doth lye;
> As if that Christ, with His examples, did these things require,
> And not to helpe our brethren here, with zeale and free desire;
> Each one supplying other's want in all things that they may,
> And He Himselfe a servaunt made, to serve us every way.
> Them straight the loaves doe walke, and pottes in every place they skinke,[49]
> Wherewith the holy fathers oft to pleasant damsels drinke.

Although the *pedilavium* had not, until recently, been performed in the Anglican Church since the early years of the eighteenth century,[50] Churches in other countries have long continued to practise, or have until recently practised, the ritual. Thus, in the Church of the Holy Sepulchre in Jerusalem, the Patriarch of the Greek Orthodox Church washes the right foot of each of twelve senior clerics, the Armenians hold a similar ceremony in their Cathedral of St James, Pope John XXIII restored the ceremony, after a lapse of some ninety years, in the Vatican on Maundy Thursday (similar services being also held in all Roman Catholic cathedrals) and the Archbishop of Seville used to perform the act for twelve paupers, after he had entertained them to a splendid meal, as did the Emperor of Austria, assisted by the archdukes of the blood royal.[51] The Archbishop of Moscow, too, used to wash the feet of twelve monks in his practice of the ritual[52] and other examples can also be found.[53] In all of these ceremonies, the twelve people ministered to were symbolic of the twelve Apostles.

The earliest known Maundy distribution involving an English monarch was, until recently, accepted as being that held in Rochester in Kent where, in 1213, John gave thirteen pence to each of thirteen poor men. The contemporary record of this ceremony is to be found in the *Rotulus Misæ-Anni Regni Regis Johannis Quarti Decemi*, a document that contains an account of the daily expenses of the Court of John during the fourteenth year of his reign. The relevant section of the transcript of this document[54] reads 'D Jovis in Cena Dñi in elemoš xiii. paupum quoz quitz ħuit xiii.d. apud Roffam xiiij.š. i. đ.'[55] (on Thursday at the feast of the Lord[56] for the alms of 13 paupers, each of whom had 13 pennies at Rochester, 14s 1d). It has been suggested[57] that the pennies used in this ceremony might well have been from the Rochester Mint where two moneyers, Alisandre and Hunfrei, are known to have produced pennies in 1205 (Plates 7 and 8). Furthermore, in relation to this ceremony, the statement has been made[58] that 'when King John had reigned for 13 years, he gave 13d each to 13 men at Rochester' which appears to suggest that the number of recipients and the magnitude of their monetary gift were related to the regnal year of the monarch. This relationship is, however, purely coincidental in this instance for, as will be seen below, in 1210 John had also administered his Maundy to thirteen recipients. Indeed, it is almost certain that, in both cases, the thirteen is symbolic of the twelve Apostles together with either Jesus or the angel who, according to tradition, came to the table at which Pope Gregory the Great was serving.

The ceremony of 1213 retained its credibility, as representing the earliest known Maundy distribution implicating an English monarch, until 1985 when it was reported that an examination by Arnold Kellett, the then Mayor of Knaresborough, of the *Rotulus Misæ* for the eleventh year of John's reign indicated that the Maundy had been distributed by John at that Yorkshire town in 1210.[59] From the transcript of the sections of this document relating to Maundy Thursday and the Easter period (Plate 9),[60] it can be seen that on 'Maundy Thursday at Knaresborough[61], in ma. . . the King to ten (possibly thirteen)[62] paupers[63] . . . 3s 1d for the sewing of Clothes of these paupers, 2s 2d[64] for 13 girdles[65], and 13 small knives, and 13 belts[66] for the same paupers and for 13[67] . . .'. Clearly, this account relates to a Maundy distribution to thirteen recipients. It later tells us that there was expended 'on Good Friday at the same place, for one thousand poor people whom the Lord King fed on the same day £4 3s 9d'.[68] That the King was still in Knaresborough on the following day is apparent when the account reads 'Saturday before Easter at Knaresborough'[69] but, by the following Tuesday, he had moved to Wakefield ('Tuesday next after Easter at Wakefield'[70]) whence, some days later, he is found in Nottingham[71] where he was on Easter Saturday.[72]

It is unfortunate that the only rolls of the above-mentioned series of records denominated *misæ* (expenses) now extant are those of the eleventh and fourteenth years of John's reign,[73] for earlier such documents may well have included records of expenses and venues of pre-1210 Maundy distributions. Indeed, a similar point was made in 1921[74] with regard to the roll of the fourteenth regnal year.

Although it is clear that 1210 now becomes the earliest year for which there is extant documentary evidence for a Maundy distribution associated with an English monarch, the gifts referred to are of personal apparel and the reference to the ceremony in 1213 at Rochester would at first sight appear to be the earliest mention in the royal accounts relating to the distribution of a definite sum of money, although line 2 of Plate 9 is incomplete and may, in its entirety, have referred to x(iii) (13) paupers each receiving 13 pence, a total expense of (xi)iij.s. j.d (14s 1d).

The first English monarch recorded to have become associated with the *pedilavium* was Edward II (1307–1327) who, in his nineteenth year (presumably of his reign since he did not succeed to the throne until he was just past his twenty-third birthday[75]), washed the feet of fifty poor men on 21 March.[76,77]

During the reign of his successor, Edward III (1327–1377), it became customary for the monarch, in addition to performing the *pedilavium*, to provide a meal, together with gifts of clothing, food and money, for the poor people involved. Thus, on 20 March 1361, an order was given to John de Newbury to purchase and deliver to Thomas de Keynes, the King's Almoner, '200 ells of cloth of Candelwykstrete, 50 pairs of slippers, 2 short towels of Paris (cloth) and 4 ells of linen of Flanders, for the next

Cena Domini.[78,79] It is possible that the bestowment of gifts was initially included in Maundy services as effected by the monarchy as a form of compensation for the strain and fatigue experienced by the old people whose feet were sequentially washed by three or four persons before the royal hands came into play in the *pedilavium*.[80] Although it was apparently not a formal Maundy distribution, Edward III, at a jubilee held in 1363 when he was fifty years old (clearly some time after his half-century birthday since he was born on 13 November 1312[81]), gave presents of food and clothing to fifty poor men.[82]

Why did this early monarchy adopt for itself a central rôle in the Maundy Thursday celebrations of the *pedilavium* and giving? Was it a practical illustration of the old motto *noblesse oblige*? Was it altruism? Was it an act of humility? Was it an exercise in public relations? Were they reinforcing their claimed miraculous powers for healing in such an imitation, or possibly emulation, of Jesus? Was it a manifestation of the powerful instinct for survival which the monarchy, along with the Church, has possessed from times immemorial? Perhaps a combination of some or all of these reasons provides the answer. Nevertheless, whatever their motive or motives, the ceremonial of the Maundy service as practised by the monarchy gradually developed and many records are preserved in manuscripts, held at the PRO and at the British Museum, that illustrate the length and depth to which this development had occurred by the Tudor period. Indeed, in England subsequent to the Dissolution of the Monasteries, many charities in which ecclesiastics had taken the chief rôle scarcely survived outside the precincts of the Court and possibly the condescension was considered to be all the more impressive when centred solely in the sovereign.[83]

To illustrate the format of the Maundy ceremony at this juncture, there exists the following record, extracted by Miss Helen Farquhar in 1927[84] from a sixteenth-century manuscript:[85]

> Ordre of the King's going to the Chapell on Shere Thursday and from thens in to the hall to the Maundy' 'First at suyche oure as shall please His Grace to appoynt at afternone a bisshopp and the deane of the chapell to be their redy revested to wayte upon the Kynge w^t all. . .[86] of the Chapell in their surplusses wayting in Lyckewyse
>
> Then the Kynge at his pleasure to come to the Lords and Noble men wayting on Hym w^{tout} any Sworde to be borne afore his grace at the tyme going or coming and so to passe strayte to the hye Aulter the Chapell[ain] begyngyng sūyce [service] thereto belonging the Kynge the Bysshop and the Deane to washe the Aulter and that don the Chapell[ain] the Bysshop and the Deane to passe through the . . . into the body of the Chapell the Bysshop and these to the Aulters as before saide. And this don to passe forth to the Kyng's closset and to wash the Aūter there in lycke manner and from there to the Quenes Closset as before is said.
>
> Item from thens the Chappell[ain] w^t the Bysshop and the Deane to goe before the Kynge in to the Hal and then the Kyng shall pause a little there. Then his grace to goe in the Wardrop of his Robes there to put on the gowne which he shall geve to some one of the pore men as shall lycke his grace and then to retorne into the Hall ageyne and then the Chapell[ain] to begyn sūyce [service] accustomed And then the towell and the Apron to be brought to the Kyng by the Kyng's Almoner and the Chamberlyn if so be present or the vice Chamberlyn in his Absence to take the towell and put it on the Kyng's hed lying the one pt on the one shulder and the other on the other sholder and to put on the Apron about hym knottying the twoo corners behind hym and so stande till that be don And in the mean tyme the Lordes and gentlemen to fetch towels and aprons for their sellfes. And then incontinent the Lordes and Noblemen to go to the lower end of the Hall and there to

receue of the officers of the Eurey and of the Amōry [almonry] basons of Silver w^t water in them to bryng to the Kyng to wasshe the pore menes fete begynnyng at the uppermost man sitting upon the righthand of the kyng as he standeth the Kyng's Almoners to beginne first to washe and the Kyng to folloe until they have don And the Lords and the Noble Men to receūe for ev̄ry pore man a gowne and a hod the Kynge begynnyng at the uppermost man as is aforesaid and so forth till the last man.

    Item in lycke manner to receūe for every pore man a payre of shoes and they to be geven in manner afore said.

    Item in lycke manner a Case of brede and messe of fyshe to be received in Dishes of Tree [wood] and to be delyūed in lyke manner before rehersed.

    Item in lyke manner an ashen Cuppe of wyne to be fetched for ev̄ry pore man and to be delyv̄d as afore is said.

    Item this don the Kynge shall geve his Towel and his Apron to the fyrst man that he did washe and so eūy man a towell and an Apron Item that don the Treasrer of the Kyng's Chamber for the tyme beying shall bring to the Kyng for eūy pore men an halpenny purse and as many pens in hit as there be poore men in nombre and that be delyūd as is befor sed. And this don the Kyng shall go ageyne into the Wardrobe and put off his gowne and hit shall be delyūd to the Almoner and he shall bere hit before the Kynge in to the hall and these the Kynge shall geve to suyche one of the pore men as shall please his grace – this done the Chapell shall begyne ageyne sūyce accostom̄d and that don the Kyng shall go to his Closett the Bisshop the Deane w^t all them of the Chapell and begyn sūyce there. And that don the Kyng to retorne to his chamber.

The original manuscript is believed to be in the handwriting of Thomas Hawley, Clarenceux, who was Rouge Croix in 1509 and Clarenceux in 1537 and died in 1557.[87] Although the account is chiefly concerned with the attendant ceremonial, with regard to the monetary gift it makes an interesting reference to 'an halpenny purse' with 'as many pens in hit as there be poore men in nombre'.

Such a reference is typical of all the extant Tudor account books in which such meticulous disposition is given to financial detail that, for instance, charges are entered of sums varying from a penny to less than a halfpenny each for the little leather bags used to contain the monetary gift.[88] Thus, in those of Henry VII it is recorded, for example, that in his seventh regnal year (when he was thirty-five years old[89]), thirty-eight poor men received thirty-eight 'smale-purses' at the price twenty pence.[90] A few years later, the differential between the King's age and the number of recipients had fallen by two as is evident from entries which read 'xvj[91] April [1500]. Shirethursday. Item to xliiij poer men in almes viij^{li} xvj^d.[92] Item for xliiij smale purses xxij^d,'[93] 'Shirethursday[94] [1501]. Item geven in almes to xlv poer men for ev[er]y of theym iij^s v [sic, an error in the MS for ix[95]]^d in all viij^{li} viij^s ix^d. Item for xlv smale purses for their money ij^s,'[96] and 'xxiiij March [1502] Shirethursday. Item to xlvj poer men in almes ev[er]y man iij^s x^d this day viij^{li} xvj^s iiij^d. Item for xlviij [sic, 48 not 46[97]] smale purses ij^s'.[98] – on the Maundy Thursdays of these years, the King was forty-three, forty-four and forty-five years old, respectively.

Similar data are also available for the Maundies of Henry VIII. Thus, in the Household Book running from 1 May 1509 to 23 March 1518 can be found, for one year, 'ij dozen purses for the Maundie viij^d' and, for the following year, 'two Duzon of rede psses for the maundy viij^d'.[99] Not only do these two entries indicate that the purses cost less than a halfpenny each[100] but from the latter it is also evident that a red purse was used when the sole monetary gift was the silver pennies, it being only later that a white purse was so employed when the red purse was used to contain the payment for the robe redemption.[101] These account books give, year by year, the rise in the numbers of recipients and the Gift of Pennies according to the King's advancing years.[102] For example, in 'Anno Primo Hen. VIII' on Good Friday,[103] 29 March 1510, is the entry 'Item to XX almsmen at the Kyng's Mandye evry of them having xx^d the piece, xxxiij^s iiij^d'. This, together with the corresponding entries for the next seven years, are summarized in Table 1 which also includes four similar entries from a later account book for the thirtieth to the thirty-third regnal years. Henry VIII was born on 28 June 1491[104] and, with respect to this, it is interesting to note from Table 1 that in the early Maundy distributions of his reign the number of recipients and the Gift of Pennies exceeded by two his age in years at the time of the ceremony (clearly the Year of Grace, the further year which, by God's grace, it was hoped the monarch might live, was included) whereas, in the last four distributions referred to, this differential had been reduced by one.

Table 1. Expenses associated with the Maundy distributions of Henry VIII, from 1509 to 1517 and from 1538 to 1542

Accountable, presumed to be regnal, year	Number of recipients	Number of pence received by each recipient	Total expense quoted for the gift of pennies	Number and cost of the purses	Reference
				see note:	see note:
1509–10	20	20	33s 4d	1	2
1510–11	21	21	35s 1d^3	1	4
1511–12	22	22	37s^5	1	6
1512–13	23	23	44s 1d	7	8
1513–14	24	24	48s	1	9
1514–15	25	25	52s 1d	7	10
1515–16	26	26	56s 4d^{11}	7	12
1516–17	27	27	60s 9d	7	13
1538–39	48	48	£9 12s	14	15
1539–40	49	49	£10 0s 1d	14	16
1540–41	50	50	£10 8s 4d	14	17
1541–42	51	51	£10 16s 9d	14	18

Notes to Table 1: *1*, Two dozen at a total cost of eight pence; *2*, BL Addit. MS 24481, fo. 25v; *3*, Farquhar (1927–28) (p. 117) quotes the total as xxxv^s ij^d. Regardless of this, the total would be expected to have been 36s 9d, namely the product of the number of recipients multiplied by the same figure representing the number of pence they each received (see Section I of Chapter 3), in this instance this being 21 × 21d. It is tempting to assume that contemporaries in those days were not well schooled and consequently could not get their arithmetic correct. Nevertheless, this assumption should not be made since accounts were carefully kept and accurately audited and, if arithmetical problems arise by reason of the figures they contain, this is because the accounts, which are summaries of much fuller 'particulars of account', do not spell out precisely every single detail of every single transaction. In this particular instance, the figure of 35s 1d is accurate, as may be shown by the total given for transactions on that particular page of the accounts, namely £528 1s 8d, which can only be reached if the Maundy entry is, indeed, 35s 1d (Challis); *4*, BL Addit. MS 21481, fo. 57; *5*, Again, the arithmetic would appear to be erroneous since the total would be expected to have been 22 × 22d, namely 40s 4d. However, the entry of 37s is correct and enables the page total to reach £774 17s which is the figure given by the accountant at the foot of that page of these accounts (Challis) (see also note *3*). All the other nine subsequent accounts of Henry VIII's Maundies which are quoted in this Table are arithmetically correct with respect to the expected numerical pattern; *6*, BL Addit. MS 21481, fo. 88; *7*, Three dozen at a total cost of twelve pence; *8*, BL Addit. MS 21481, fo. 119v, *9*, BL Addit. MS 21481, fo. 151v; *10*, BL Addit. MS 21481, fo. 185; *11*, Corrected from 8d in the account; *12*, BL Addit. MS 21481, fo. 216v; *13*, BL Addit. MS 21481, fo. 255; *14*, Not given; *15*, BL Arundel MS 97, fo. 12v; *16*, BL Arundel MS 97, fo. 69; *17*, BL Arundel MS 97, fo. 119; *18*, BL Arundel MS 97, fo. 183v.

In his first Maundy ceremony after he succeeded his father on 28 January 1547, the infant Edward VI, then in the tenth year of his life,[105] presented his gift of ten pence to each of twelve men, it being evidently considered that twelve was the minimum number of recipients since the Apostles were the prototype. The account of this ceremony also includes the statement 'Item more to said xij pore men at the same Maundy. Any [of] them xx^s in a purse instede of the Maundy gown'.[106] Clearly, this redemption of Edward VI's gown was effected since, belonging to a child, it would have been of no practical use to an adult recipient to whom the King obviously wished to present it. In the following year the number of men remained the same but each received eleven pence and, in the third year, each of twelve men received twelve pence, in both of these ceremonies the robe redemption allowance of twenty shillings also being paid as before.[107] Presumably when, in 1550, Edward had reached the thirteenth year of his age, the number of recipient males would have risen accordingly although, unfortunately, documentary evidence for this is unavailable.[108]

The death of Edward VI on 6 July 1553[109] brought to the throne his eldest half-sister, Mary Tudor. The following description of her Maundy of 1556 is given in part of a letter dated 3 May 1556.[110] It was written by Marco Antonio Faitta, the Secretary to Cardinal Reginald Pole (then the Papal Legate in England and, what was to be, its last Roman Catholic Primate), to Dr Ippolito Chizzola, a Doctor of Divinity, in Venice. After writing on other matters, Faitta continues:

... and on Holy Thursday, at 3 o'clock in the afternoon, the most Serene Queen performed the ceremony of the feet-washing, thus:–

Her Majesty being accompanied by the right reverend Legate and by the Council, entered a large hall, at the head of which was my Lord Bishop of Ely, as Dean of the Queen's chaplains, with the choristers of her Majesty's chapel. Around this hall on either side there were seated on certain benches, with their feet on stools, many poor women, to the number of forty and one, such being the number of the years of the most Serene Queen. Then one of the menials of the Court having washed the right foot of each of these poor persons, and this function being also next performed by the Under Almoner and also by the Grand Almoner, who is the Bishop of Chichester, her Majesty next commenced the ceremony in the following manner:– At the entrance of the hall there was a great number of the chief dames and noble ladies of the court, and they prepared themselves by putting on a long linen apron which reached the ground, and round their necks they placed a towel, the two ends of which remained pendant at full length on either side, each of them carrying a silver ewer, and they had flowers in their hands, the Queen also being arrayed in like manner. Her Majesty knelt down on both her knees before the first of the poor women, and taking in the left hand the woman's right foot, she washed it with her own right hand, drying it very thoroughly with the towel which hung at her neck, and having signed it with the cross she kissed the foot so fervently that it seemed as if she were embracing something very precious. She did the like by all and each of the other poor women, one by one, each of the ladies her attendants giving her in turn their basin and ewer and towel; and I vow to you that in all her movements and gestures, and by her manner, she seemed to act thus not merely out of ceremony, but from great feeling and devotion. Amongst these demonstrations there was this one remarkable, that in washing the feet, she went the whole length of that long hall, from one end to the other, ever on her knees. Having finished and risen on her feet, she went back to the head of the hall and commenced giving in turn to each of the poor women a large wooden platter with enough food for four persons, filled with great pieces of salted fish, and two large loaves, and thus she went a second time distributing these alms. She next returned a third time, to begin again, giving to each of the women a wooden bowl filled with wine, or rather, I think, hippocras; after which, for the fourth time, she returned and gave to each of those poor people a piece of cloth of royal mixture for clothing. Then returning for the fifth time she gave to each a pair of shoes and stockings; for the sixth time she gave to each a leathern purse, containing forty-one pennies, according to the number of her own years, and which in value may amount to rather more than half an Italian golden crown; finally, going back for the seventh time, she distributed all the aprons and towels which had been carried by those dames and noble ladies, in number forty-one, giving each with her own hand.

Her Majesty then quitted the hall to take off the gown which she had worn, and half an hour afterwards she returned, being preceded by an attendant carrying the said gown, and thus she went twice round the hall, examining very closely all the poor women one by one, and then returning for the third time, she gave the said gown to the one who was in fact the poorest and most aged of them all; and this gown was of the finest purple cloth, lined with martens' fur, and with sleeves so long and wide that they reached the ground. During this ceremony the choristers chaunted the miserere, with certain other psalms, reciting at each verse the words –

'In diebus illis mulier quæ erat in civitate peccatrix.'

Later in the letter Faitta writes 'I will not omit telling you that on Holy Thursday alms were distributed here in the Court to a great amount, to upwards of 3000 persons' and also describes how, on the following day, Good Friday, the Queen blessed cramp rings[111] and then touched the scrofulous.[112]

That such a letter, written within the Roman Catholic Church, should stress as it does the arduous rôle played by the Queen in the ceremony, and her fervour in carrying out this fatiguing ritual, is understandable since at that time she was the key figure in attempts to re-establish that faith in England after the Reformation effected by her father. Furthermore, an incidental testimony to the importance known to be attached by Mary Tudor to this Lenten observance occurs in a list of the presents she received on New Year's Day. These were given, for the most part, by high dignitaries of Church and State, nobles and titled ladies, and were both numerous and costly. However, amongst gifts, presumably from the more humble members of the Court, such as flowers, sweetmeats, trinkets and needlework, it is especially interesting to notice 'a table painted with the Maundy' and 'a table of needleworke of the Maundy'.[113]

In her Maundies, Elizabeth I appears to have followed closely the example set by her half-sister in most particulars, save perhaps as to the extent of her personal humiliation, and to have made elaborate preparation for them by royal warrant. For example, that for 'her Majesties Mawndye' in 1579, following the precedent of her father, is addressed to the Keeper of the Great Wardrobe in the following terms:[114]

> Wee woll and comaund you, that, immediatelye upon the sight hereof, ye delyver, or cause to be delyvered, to our welbeloved servaunt Rauf Hope, Yeoman of our Wardrobe of Robes, for those of our Mawndye, and our said Warderobe, theyse parcelles of stuff followinge; that is to say, first, one hundreth thirtye and fyve yerdes of russet cloth, to make fourety and fyve gownes for fourtye and fyve poore women; and fouretye and fyve piere of single soled showes for them. Item, two hundrethe fyvetye and eight elles of lynen cloth, aswell to make smockes for the said poore women, as also to be employed in the service of our said Mawndye. Item, twentie and six peire of bearinge and trussinge sheetes of two bredthes and a half of Hollande cloth, and two elles thre quarters longe the pere. Item, thirtye elles of diaper of elle quarter brode; and eighteene napkyns, cont' one elle longe the pere, for thuse of our said Warderobe. Item, one peire of presse sheetes, of

fower bredthes of Hollande cloth, and nyne elles longe the pere. Item, one curten for a presse, of lynen cloth, cont' seven bredthes and two elles longe. Item, thirtye elles of canvas, and the boultes of stronge rope to trusse the said stuff in. And that ye content and paye for making the premisses; and for cariadge of the same from our greate warderobe to the place wheare, God willing, we shall make our Maundye. And these our lres, signed with our owne hande, shall be your sufficient warraunte and dischardge in this behalf annempst us, our heires and successors. Geoven under our signett, at our Pallaise at Westm', the 12th daye of Marche, the 21st yeare of our reigne.   JO. SARUM.
To our trustie and welbeloved servaunte John Forteskewe, Esquier, Maister of our Great Wardrobe.
    Ex'p N. Pigeon.

In connection with Elizabeth I, a remarkable miniature depicting one of her Maundies exists (Plate 10), being in the possession of Lord Beauchamp of Madresfield Court, Malvern, Worcestershire. Until the true significance of this miniature was pointed out,[115] it was believed to represent the execution of Mary, Queen of Scots, with the throne in the back-ground, guarded by a soldier with a halberd, being taken for the block and the executioner, respectively. Although only measuring some 2¾" × 2¼", this miniature clearly shows one hundred or more figures, including the Maundy recipients, the Almonry Children, the officiating clergy, various members of the Court and Elizabeth I herself, wearing a white apron over a blue gown. She is followed by her principal Lady-in-Waiting, Blanche Parry who, because of the excellent portraiture of this miniature, is recognizable by comparison with her picture at Hampton Court and her monument in St Margaret's, Westminster.[116] When, in 1912, Lord Beauchamp lent this painting to the *Brussels Exposition de la Miniature*, where it was exhibited as no. 181,[117] it was attributed to Nicholas Hilliard (1547–1619), the well-known Elizabethan miniature painter. However, in 1961 it was stated to look 'more like an illumination which has been cut to fit a frame' and to be 'an excellent example of the Anglo-Flemish manuscript style' and was reattributed, from 'the draping of the costumes, the attitudes of the onlooking crowd and the conception of space' to 'a versatile limner of the Ghent-Bruges school who resided in this country'.[118] This reattribution was made more specific by the statement that 'its manner would better agree with the name of Levina Teerline than with that of Hilliard, according to what we know of the origin of that woman artist'. Furthermore, in the 1912 exhibition, the painting was provisionally dated 'vers 1563' but it was later thought that this date was probably a misprint and the illustrated Maundy distribution is that of 1560.[119] It has been claimed[120] that the style of dress corresponds with this assumption. The year 1563 is also eliminated since in that year and, indeed, in the following year, the Queen herself did not distribute the Maundy because plague was rife,[121] the distributions therefore being made on her behalf by her almoner.[122]

Two accounts of the Maundy ceremony in 1560 are, in fact, recorded, one of which reads:[123]

> Maundy Thursday, the Queen kept her Maundy in her Hall at the Court in the afternoon; and then gave unto twenty women so many gowns, and one woman had her best gown; and her Grace washed their feet; and in a new white cup she drank unto every woman, and then they had the cup. The same afternoon she gave unto poor men, women, and children, whole and lame, in St. James's Park, being two thousand people, and upwards, 2d. apiece.

The other report, which is essentially similar except that it also alludes to a monetary gift, has been quoted from *Mackyn's Diary*, the text of which somewhat corruptly reads:[124]

> The 11 day of April [1560] the Queen's grace kept her monde [Maundy] in her hall at the court at afternoon, and her grace gave unto 20 women so many gowns, and one woman had her best gown, and there her grace did wash their feet, and with a new white cup her grace drank unto every woman, and they had the cup and so her grace did likewise unto all, and every woman had in money [blank]. The same afternoon she gave unto poor men, women, and children, both whole and lame in Saint James' park 2d. apiece, a thousand people and upwards.

The reference to St James's Park at the end of both these accounts leaves no doubt as to Whitehall having been the venue for the ceremony.[125] In addition, it is clear that in both these reports the year referred to is definitely 1560. Why, then, do they only refer to twenty women recipients when the Queen, who was born on 7 September 1533,[126] was at the time of the Maundy ceremony twenty-six years old and therefore twenty-six, twenty-seven or twenty-eight female recipients would have been expected?[127] Possibly only twenty women were present and the gifts for the others were sent to them, as is sometimes the case at the present time when the Maundy recipients are too infirm to attend the service. Possibly it is a printer's error, a slip of the pen or the misreading in the original authority of a 0 for a 6, a not infrequent error, yet the figure of twenty recipients as alluded to in the two accounts would appear to be supported by a count of the tiny figures of the bedeswomen shown in the two front ranks of the miniature (Plate 10).[128]

Another record of one of Elizabeth I's Maundy services, namely that of 1572/3, is one which is presented in far greater detail[129] than was that of 1560. Preceded by the observation that 'At four of the clock on the Wednesday afternoon, the Queen and her Court removed to her Palace of Greenwich; where on the 19th of March the Order of the *Maundy* was thus observed', it continues:

> First, the Hall was prepared with a long table on each side, and forms set by them; on the edges of which tables, and under those forms, were layed carpets, and cushions for her Majesty to kneel, when she would wash them (*the poor*). There was also another table laid across the upper end of the Hall, somewhat above the foot pace for the Chappelan to stand at. A little beneath the midst whereof, and beneath the foot pace, a stool and cushion of estate was pitched, for her Majesty to kneel at during service time. This done, the holy-water basons, alms, and other things, being brought into the Hall; and the Chappelan and poor folks having taken their said places, the Yeomen of the Laundry, armed with a fair towell, and taking a silver bason filled with warm water and flowers, washed their feet, all, one after another, wiped the same with his towel, and so, making a cross a little above the toes, kissed them. After him, within a while followed the Sub-Almoner, doing likewise, and after him the Almoner himself also; then, lastly, her Majesty came into the Hall, and, after some singing and prayers made, and the Gospel of Christ's washing his disciples feet read, thirty-nine ladies and gentlewomen (for so many were the poor folks, according to the number of the years complete of her Majesty's age) addressed themselves with aprons and towels to wait upon her Majesty; and she, kneeling down upon the cushions and carpets under the feet of the poor women, first washed one foot of every of them in so many several basons of warm water and sweet flowers, brought to her severally by the said ladies and gentlewomen, then wiped, crossed, and kissed them, as the Almoner and others had done before. When her Majesty had thus gone through the whole number of thirty-nine (of which twentie sat on the one side of the Hall, and nineteen on the other), she resorted to the first again, and gave to each one certain yards of broad-cloth to make a

gown. Thirdly, she began at the first, and gave to each of them a pair of shoes. Fourthly, to each of them a wooden platter, wherein was half a side of salmon, as much lyng, six red herrings, and two cheat[130] loafs of bread. Fifthly, she began with the first again, and gave to each of them a white wooden dish with claret wine. Sixthly, she received of each Waiting Lady and Gentlewoman their towel and apron, and gave to each poor woman one of the same. And after this the Ladies and Gentlewomen waited no longer, nor served as they had done throughout the courses before; but then the Treasurer of the Chamber (Mr. Henneage) came to her Majesty with thirty-nine small white purses wherein were also thirty-nine pence (as they say) after the number of the years of her Majesty's age; and of him she received and distributed them severally; which done, she received of him several red leather purses, each containing twenty shillings, for the redemption of her Majesty's gown, which (as men say) by ancient order she ought to give to some one of them at her pleasure; but she, to avoid the trouble of suit, which accustomably was made for that preferment, had changed that reward into money, to be equally divided amongst them all, namely, twenty shillings apiece; and those she also delivered particularly to each one of the whole company; and so taking her ease upon the cushion of state, and hearing the choir a little while, her Majesty withdrew herself, and the company departed; for it was by that time the sun-setting.

W. L.[131]

There is one poignant similarity between this Maundy of Elizabeth I, an independent corroborating brief report of which has appeared,[132] and that of her half-sister in 1556.[133] In both, the Queen only washed the recipients' feet after they had been washed by others, namely a court menial, the Sub-almoner and the High Almoner, sequentially: apparently, too, the almoners, like the monarchs, were unwilling to handle the feet of the poor unless they had been prewashed, a reluctance which they shared with the clerics in much earlier ceremonies which were purely ecclesiastical and in which the Maundy recipients themselves were expected to carry out an initial washing of their own feet.[134]

Conversely, one significant difference is apparent between Elizabeth I's 1572/3 Maundy on the one hand and, on the other hand, her 1560 ceremony[135] and that of her half-sister's of 1556. In the last two, in accordance with the custom established in the Maundy services by the Tudor period, the Queen donated her Maundy robe to one of the Maundy recipients. However, in that of 1572/3, probably either because she recognized that all the recipients had a partial entitlement to it or in order to satisfy her vanity in not wishing to part with it,[136] Elizabeth I substituted a gift of twenty shillings in lieu for each recipient. Alternatively, it may be argued that Elizabeth was but reverting to the custom established by her late younger brother, Edward VI, who had also given each recipient a sum of twenty shillings in lieu of his gown, although the reason for this in his case was that such a gown, belonging to a child, would have been of no practical use to an adult recipient.[137] Indeed, although it is not referred to in the account of her Maundy in 1556, it is possible, in view of the monies set aside for the ceremony, that Mary Tudor also made a similar gift of twenty shillings to each recipient as well as donating her Maundy robe to one of them.[138] Furthermore, when Elizabeth I did not distribute her Maundy personally, the robe redemption allowance of twenty shillings still remained as part of the gift. For example, her almonry accounts relating to her Maundy in 1582 read:[139]

> Delivered to John Piers, Bishop of Sarum,[140] Her Majesty's High Almoner, as money wont to be delivered to Her Highnesses' own hands, which she distributed to divers poor

women, and now by him distributed for this year, to 48 of the said poor women, viz. to every poor woman in a white purse 48d. in memory of Her Majesty's age, £9. 12s.;[141] and to every of the said women in a red purse, 20s., in lieu of Her Majesty's own gown, £48; and for 12 dozen of purses, 13s. 4d. In all £58 5s. 4d..[142]

Likewise, we have an eye-witness account[143] of 17 April 1595, the date of Maundy Thursday in that year,[144] which tells us that the office 'of the Queenes Maundaye was performed' by 'Dr. Mathewes, Bisshop of Durham', the prelate 'washing the right foot of 57 severell women' and giving to each a 'redd purse and a whyt, as they say 40^s therein'.[145]

The introduction of this second monetary gift had necessitated the introduction of a second purse. The red purse used in earlier years to contain the Gift of Pennies[146] was now used to contain this robe redemption allowance and a white purse was consequently introduced to contain the pennies.

Although the robe redemption allowance was abandoned in 1731, it was restored in 1759,[147] since when it has survived through to the present day. Up to and including 1979, it was contained, along with the allowance in lieu of the food gift,[148] in a red leather purse with long white leather strings (Plate 11) which, loosely tied to the white leather purse with long red leather strings (Plate 12) containing the Gift of Pennies (the Maundy money[149]), was presented as the Second Distribution during the Maundy service. These gifts, in their purses, used to be carried to and during the service, prior to their distribution, on the Maundy Dish (Plate 13)[150] with the long strings of some of the purses hanging over the side of the dish. This was carried, on his head, by one of the Yeomen of the Guard (frontispiece and Plate 14), a body who are always in attendance at the Maundy service.[151] After 1979, the red purse with long white strings was also used to contain the allowance in lieu of the clothing gift[152] which, contained in other separate leather purses (Plate 15), had previously formed the basis of the First Distribution of the Maundy service. Thus, after 1979, the white purse with long red strings contained, as before, the Maundy money and the red purse with long white strings contained all the other allowances in normal currency. These purses, appropriately charged and loosely tied together, now constitute during the Maundy service the only distribution although this is apportioned through the service.

The question of the type of coin used for the robe redemption gift of twenty shillings since its introduction has been the subject of interesting numismatic speculation. In 1556, if she paid this allowance, Mary Tudor cannot have used the beautiful new sovereign which had been introduced during her reign since it was valued at thirty shillings. However, her late brother's sovereigns of twenty shillings were available, as were two of his half-sovereigns and two of his angels, and Elizabeth I most likely paid this sum as two angels in her earlier distributions since her sovereign of twenty shillings was of later date.[153] The question of the type of coin used for the allowance by Charles II and James II has also been considered, it being likely that in 1661 and 1662 it was of silver coin and in 1663 it was of gold coin whereas later, when the value of the gold coinage rose above its nominal value, James II and his immediate successors reverted to the use of silver coin.[154] Subsequently, however, a sovereign was used, a practice that continued until 1916 when this coin was substituted by a treasury note for £1[155] although it would appear that in 1932 a sovereign was again so used.[156] The allowance is currently presented as ordinary coin of the realm to the value of £1.[157]

Although by the Tudor period the monarch had become firmly and actively associated with the Maundy service, which consequently gave rise to the term Royal Maundy, it was by no means their sole prerogative at this period to effect such a ceremonial. Thus, the queen consorts also gave their Maundy as, for example, did Elizabeth of York, the wife of Henry VII, in 1502 when she gave 3s 1d to each of thirty-seven poor women (Elizabeth was then in her thirty-seventh year of age[158]) on Skere[159] Thursday[160] in a ceremony which also involved the *pedilavium*, although it is not known if Elizabeth actually carried out the preliminary cleansing.[161] Connected with this Maundy service of Elizabeth of York are statements in her privy purse accounts. In March, 1502 is entered 'Furst the same xxiiij[ti] day of Marche delivered to Maister Richard Pagn Aulmoigner to the Quene for xxxvij[ti] pore women every woman iij s̄. jd. for hir maunday upon Shire Thursday Cxiiij s̄. j d.'[162] and 'Item to John Walker yeoman aulmoigner for money by him paid for a cowle for Water xij d. for iij newe bolles xij d. for a basket iiij d. for flowres iiij d. for heting of watier at the kechin xij d. and for cariage of the same stuff from London to Richemount iiij d. for the Quenes Maundy upon Shirthursday. iiij s̄.',[163] the flowers referred to in this latter item being used in an attempt to render the *pedilavium* as pleasant as it might be. The following month we read 'Itm̄ for money be theim payed for the cariage of certain stuf[164] of the Quenes x d. and for the dyner and botehire of the said Maistres Alianor upon Shire-thursday ij s̄. viij d.'[165] and in December 1502 appears 'Itm̄ to the same Richard Smyth for Cxj yerdes of cloth for xxxvij poure women for the Quenes Maundye in the yere last passed every woman iij yerdes at ij s̄. viij d. the yerd xiiij li. xvj s̄. . . .'[166] Finally, in January 1503 is entered 'Itm for xxxvij payre shoes for xxxvij[ti] poure women at the Quenes Maundy at v d. the payre xv s. v d.'.[167]

One of the tyrannical acts of Henry VIII was to forbid Catherine of Aragon, after his marriage to her had been declared to be invalid by Archbishop Cranmer on 23 May 1533, to 'keep her Maundy', as had been her custom whilst she was queen. On 'the Princess Dowager', as she was then styled, declaring in 1535 her intention of doing so 'in spite of the King's order last year to the contrary', Henry gave his qualified consent that 'the King is content if she does not keep it as Queen; if so, she and others would be guilty of High Treason'.[168]

In addition, during the Tudor period it is also known that non-royal personages of either temporal or spiritual high rank gave their Maundy. Thus, for example, Henry, Lord Berkeley yearly clothed many poor people.[169] However, in such Maundies, the number of recipients was usually limited to the twelve symbolic of the Apostles.[170] Yet this was not the case in at least one of the annually-celebrated Maundies of Henry Algernon Percy, the fifth Earl of Northumberland (1477–1527) and then the most influential of all the nobles, a report of which reads:[171]

> Al Manner of Things Yerly Geven by my Lorde for his Maundy ande my Laidis and his Lordshippis Children As the Consideracion Why more playnly hereafter folowyth
>
> *Furst* My Lorde useth and accustomyth yerely uppon Maundy Thursday when his Lordship is at home to gyf yerly as menny Gownes to as manny Poor Men as my Lorde is Yeres of Aige with Hoodes to them and one for the Yere of my Lordes Aige to Come Of Russet cloth after iij yerddes of Brode Cloth in every Gowne and Hoode Ande after xij*d* the brode Yerde of Clothe
>
> *Item* My Lorde useth ande accustomyth yerly uppon Maundy Thursday when his Lordship is at Home to gyf yerly as manny Sherts of Lynnon Cloth to as manny Poure Men as his Lordshipe is Yers of Aige ande one for the Yere of my Lords Aige to come After ij yerdes dim. [*dimidius* = half] in every shert and after . . . the yerde

Item My Lorde useth and accustomyth yerly uppon the said Maundy Thursday when his Lordshipe is at Home to gyf yerly as manny Tren Platers [wooden trenchers] after ob. [*obolus*, a halfpenny] the pece with a Cast of Brede and a Certen Meat in it to as manny Poure Men as his Lordship is Yeres of Aige and one for the Yere of my Lordis Aige to come

Item My Lorde useth and accustomyth yerly uppon the said Maundy Thursday when his Lordship is at home to gyf yerely as many Eshen [ashen] Cuppis after ob. the pece with Wyne in them to as many Poure Men as his Lordship is Yeres of Aige and one for the Yere of my Lordis Aige to come

Item My Lorde useth and accustomyth yerly uppon the said Maundy Thursday when his Lordshipe is at home to gyf yerly as manny Purssses of Lether after ob. the pece with as manny Penys in every purse to as many poore men as his Lordshipe is Yeres of Aige and one for the Yere of my Lords Aige to come

Item My Lorde useth and accustomyth yerely uppon Maundy Thursday to cause to be bought iij Yerdis and iij Quarters of Brode Violett Cloth for a Gowne for his Lordshipe to doo service in Or for them that schall doo service in his Lordshypes Absence After iiij*s* viij*d* the Yerde And to be furrede with Blake Lamb Contenynge ij Keippe and a half after xxx skynnes in a kepe and vj*s* iij*d* the kepe and after ij ob. the skynne and after LXXV skynns for Furringe of the said Gowne Which Gowne my Lorde werith all the tyme his Lordship doith service And after his Lordship hath don his service at his said Maundy doith gyf to the pourest man that he fyndeth as he thynkyth emongs them all the said Gowne

Item My Lorde useth and accustomyth yerly uppon the said Maundy Thursday to caus to be delyvered to one of my Lordis Chaplayns[172] for my Lady If she be at my Lordis fyndynge and not at her owen To comaunde hym to gyf for her as manny Groits to as manny Poure Men as her Ladyshipe is Yeres of Aige and one for the Yere of hir Aige to come Owte of my Lordis Coffueres if sche be not at hir owen fyndynge

Item My Lorde useth and accustomyth yerly uppon the said Maundy Thursday to caus to be delyvered to one of my Lordis Chaplayns for my Lordis Eldest Sone the Lord Percy For hym to comaunde to gyf for hym as manny Pens of ij Pens to as manny Poure Men as his Lordshipe is Yeres of Aige and one for the Yere of his Lordshipes aige to come

Item My Lorde useth and accustomyth yerly uppon Maundy Thursday to cause to be delyverit to one of my Lordis Chaplayns for every of my Yonge Maisters My Lordis Yonger Sones To gyf for every of them as manny Pens to as manny Poore Men as every of my said Maisters is yeeres of Aige and for the Yere to come

By the antiquary Grose, this account is extracted from the voluminous details of the expenditure of this House contained in the *Northumberland Household Book* which was written, according to the custom of the time, with an entire absence of punctuation. It represents a practical illustration of the old motto *noblesse oblige* and shows that, not only like his sovereign did this very powerful nobleman, when he was at home on Maundy Thursday, bestow gifts of food, clothing (including his Maundy gown) and, in leather purses, pennies in number that he was years of age plus one penny for his year of life to come (the Year of Grace) to that same number of poor men, but he also ordered similar distributions to be made on behalf of his wife (substituting groats for pennies), his eldest son (substituting the equivalent value in half-groats for pennies), and his other children. Interestingly, in as much as it may shed light upon Northumberland's attitude to those members of society that were materialistically less fortunate than himself, no mention is made of his performing the *pedilavium*.

The manner in which a prince of the Church distributed his Maundy during the

Tudor period can be exemplified by reference to Cardinal Wolsey. Although he was Henry VIII's right hand, Wolsey, being a cardinal and the Papal Legate in England, was primarily a papal creature. Thus, his casting out by Henry was symbolic of the casting out of papal authority. On 17 October 1529 Wolsey was forced to surrender the Great Seal, forfeit most of his lands, possessions and offices, and retire from York Place, the archiepiscopal residence in Westminster, to his seat at Esher. However, some months later his enemies became fearful of the possibility that should he return to live in the proximity of the King, the latter might visit or recall him. Accordingly, they recommended that, since he was not now detained by the duties of the chancery, Wolsey should be sent to govern his diocese and he was thus banished to York. He subsequently lived happily at Carwood Castle, one of his residences as the Archbishop of York, some twelve miles distant from the city, but only a few months later he was arrested for high treason and during his consequent conveyance to London he was taken ill and reached only as far as Leicester Abbey where he died on 29 November 1530.

Wolsey commenced his journey northwards into exile[173] just prior to the end of Lent in 1530 and, by Easter, had reached Peterborough where he kept the Maundy Thursday celebrations, a chronicle of these events reading:[174]

> Then prepared the cardinall for his iournie into the north, and sent to London for liuerie clothes for his seruants, and so rode from Richmond to Hendon, from thence to a place called Rie, the next daie to Raistone where he lodged in the priorie; the next daie to Huntingdon, and there lodged in the abbeie; the next daie to Peterborow, and there lodged in the abbeie, where he abode all the next wéeke, & there he kept his Easter, his traine was in number an hundred and thréescore persons. Upon Maundie thursdaie he made his maundie, there hauing nine and fiftie poore men, whose feet he washed, and gaue euerie one twelve pence in monie, three els of good canuas, a paire of shoes, a cast of red herrings, and three white herrings, and one of them had two shillings.

It is apparent from this account that whereas the number of recipients was related to the Cardinal's age, the religious significance of the event was manifest by relating the number of pence in the Gift of Pennies to the number of Apostles. However, the significance of the lone gift of two shillings is not immediately obvious: could it be a robe redemption allowance and possibly, in such case, a reporting error for twenty shillings? From the account it is also evidential that Wolsey, unlike the fifth Earl of Northumberland, carried out the *pedilavium*. Indeed, Thomas Cranmer, the Tudor period's other famous cleric,[175] wrote of the Maundy ceremony 'we, in like manner, as Christ washed His desciples' feet at His Maundy, should be ready at all times to do good unto our Christian brothers, yea, even to wash their feet, which seemeth to be the most humble and lowly act that we can do unto them'.[176]

In some of the years when plague was rife, the monarch neither performed the *pedilavium* nor even distributed the Maundy gifts personally but deputized an official, usually the Royal Almoner, for these purposes. For example, plague was prevalent from January 1562/3[177] to December 1563 and, although it had almost ceased by the Easter of 1564,[178] a proclamation on 23 March 1563/4[179] announced that the Queen would not distribute her Maundy alms herself but that they would be given by her almoner to the poor in Windsor and Eton.[180] It was probably as a precaution against the possibility of his contacting plague, or simply because of his vanity, that the Bishop Almoner, deputizing for Charles I, kissed his own thumb whilst holding the washed feet of the Maundy recipients in his hand rather than kissing the feet themselves, although his chaplain appeared to exhibit more faith or courage, or both, in the following account of the Maundy service in 1633:[181]

> Relation of the Ceremony upon Maundy Thursday at Whitehall as I saw the 18 of April 1633.
>
> First there were placed along the right side of the Hall, 33 poore old men, the number of men answering to the age of the King. One of these men, viz.: Goodman Board of Kingston told me that he was aged 104 yeers, and that his father and grandfather lived to the age of 120 yeers; this man had all his teeth and his senses and understanding and memory very pfect.
>
> 2. Then came the Amners men and washed their feet wth water, wherein was boyled bayes and rosemary, which made it sweete and a redd colour like claret wine.
>
> 3. Then the Bp Almoner's Chaplain washed their feete, wiped them with a fine towell and kissed them on the instep and said the words mentioned underneath.
>
> 4. The Bp Almoner came psently after and satt downe in a chaire wth cushions before it and then the Quire sang after wch was read a Gospell.
>
> 5. Then the Bp Almoner washed their feete and taking their foote in his hand kissed his thumb on their foote and sayd Pray for the King and Queene and their royall issue and the Lord blesse you. Then the Bp gave euery one them I. a fine shirt. 2. three yards of broad cloth. 3. a pr of shoes. 4. a wodden platter wth green fish salmon, readherring and 2 loafs of bread. 5. A wodden dish with clarret wine. 6. Two purses one containing 20 shillings in newe silver, the other 33 new single pence.
>
> *Nota.* – Between every one of these p̃ticulars the Quire sang and the Bp rested hymselfe in his chaire till the Gard fetched the other.

In other Maundies during the reign of Charles I, the King was represented by his Almoner. Thus, on his way to Scotland from London on an expedition against Scots who had thought fit to rebel, Charles I came to York on 30 March 1639 where he broke his journey until the following 29 April. For 11 April 1639, when the King was thus certainly still present in the city and apparently in the Minster, it is recorded that 'on *Maunday Thursday* Doctor *Curle*, Bishop of *Winchester*, the King's Almoner kept the *Maunday* in the *Minster*, giving as the King's Gift to nine and thirty Poor Men, each of them four yards of Holland, three yards of Broad-Cloth, a pair of Shoes, a Wooden Platter, with a Jowle of Ling and another of Salmon, six Red Herrings, two Loaves of Bread, a Scale of Wine, twenty shillings in Money, nine and thirty single Pence, and Washed all their Feet'.[183] Other longer and slightly differing accounts of this ceremony read:[184]

> Upon *Thursday* before *Easter* the king kept his *Maunday* in the cathedral; where the bishop of *Ely* washed the feet of thirty nine poor aged men, in warm water, and dried them with a linnen cloth. Afterwards the bishop of *Winchester* washed them over again in white wine, wiped and kissed them. The king gave to every one of the poor men, a gown, of very good cloth, a holland shirt, new stockings and shoes. Also in one leathern purse every one had twenty pence [clearly a reporter's error for twenty shillings, which would have been the robe redemption allowance] in money given him, and in another purse thirty nine single pennies being the just age of the king.[185] Lastly each man had a wooden scale full of wine given him, scale and all, a joule of salt fish and a joule of salmon, with a six-penny loaf of bread. This ceremony, says my authority, was performed in the south isle of the minster. Near where the bells hang.

and:

> *Thursday* before *Easter* 1639
>
> The *Maundy* given in *York-minster* for the king, by the bishop of *Winchester* in manner as followeth, to thirty nine poor men sitting along one by another.
>
> *First*, the right foot of every of them washed in cold water by the bishop's pantler, and

six pence a piece given them in money: *Secondly*, washed again in claret wyne lukewarme by the bishop's chaplain: *Lastly*, washt againe and dryed by the bishop himselfe and kist every tyme.
2. To each of them three ells of course holland for a shirt.
3. To each of them a cloth gown of gray sreese.
4. To each of them one pair of shoes.
5. To each of them a wooden dubler whereon was a joule of *old ling*, a joule of *salmond*, six *red herrings* and two loaves of *bread*.
6. To each of them a little purse wherein was xx *s*. in money; and so many single pennies as the king was years of age, being thirty nine.
7. To every of them a little scale of *claret* wyne which they drak off, and so after a few prayers read the ceremony ended, and the poor men carried away all that was given them.

The same account also tells us that:

Upon *Good-Friday* the king touched for the king's-evil in the minster two hundred persons. Upon *Easter-Sunday* the king received the sacrament at the cathedral. On *Monday* he ordered seventy pound to be given to each of the four wards of the city; to be distributed amongst poor widows. On *Tuesday* and *Wednesday* he touched each day an hundred persons for the evil. At his leisure hours, his usual diversion, during his stay in *York*, was to play at a game called the *Balloon*.

Clearly the King's philanthropy and supernatural powers were very much in evidence at this period although, alas, at least as a public relations exercise it was to no avail for some ten years later he was to be executed. At Easter in 1642, Charles I was again in York, where he had been since the previous 18 March (having thought fit to so remove himself and the Court from London as the relationship between himself and his parliament grew worse) establishing his head-quarters in preparation for the Civil War which was imminent and where he once again kept his Maundy. However, once more his Almoner may have deputized for him, for although it is recorded with relation to this service that 'this Year also His Majesty kept His *Maunday* in the Minster upon the seventh of *April*',[186] an alternative source notes that '*April* 7. the king kept his maunday in the cathedral, where the bishop of *Winchester*, lord almoner, performed the usual ceremonies'.[187] However, the Bishop's 'usual' participation would not necessarily have precluded the King having carried out the *pedilavium*.

The course of the Civil War found Charles I at Easter during both 1643 and 1644 in Oxford where the Maundy service for each of these two years was thus held. Indeed, it has been suggested that the Oxford Declaration Penny, struck in 1644, was minted especially for use in the latter Maundy distribution.[188] It is known that plague forbade entry into Oxford by members of the public during the former Easter period but, since the Maundy recipients were within the city walls, this did not hinder the distribution[189] although whether it, and that in 1644, was made by the King in person remains unknown. Nevertheless, it is unlikely that he would have so exposed himself to the risk of contacting such infection and it is thought that the distribution, and the *pedilavium* if it was performed, would have been carried out under proxyship by the King's Almoner.[190] After 1644 the records are silent until the Restoration in 1660, it being probable during the remaining years of Charles I's reign, and certain during the Commonwealth period, that the ceremony remained in abeyance.

It was perhaps because of the frequent absences of his father from the Maundy service, or a desire to gain popularity with his subjects, that Charles II, not, one would have thought, the most devout of rulers, revived it with such fervour, as he did touching for the King's Evil. Thus, although plague made its appearance to a small extent in 1661, Charles was undeterred from personally carrying out the *pedilavium* in that year during the Maundy service, a report of which reads:[191]

> Whitehall on Thursday last (April 11th) His sacred Majesty according to the example of the King of Kings, as well as his Predecessors (the Kings and Queens of England) washed and kissed the feet of 31 poor men in the Great Hall at Whitehall this being the 31st year of his Majesty's age to whom God in Mercy to these late distracted Kingdoms grant a long and happy reign.

In this narrative, the political overtures relating to the Restoration are very obvious and, unfortunately, appear to have been made at the expense of recording details of any distribution of food, clothing or money. In fact, it had been anticipated in 1661 by William Sancroft, chaplain to Charles II, that the monetary gift would consist of 'first white purses in every purse 31 single pence, then red purses in every one of them 20s'[192] but it was not foreseen that Charles II would revert to personally effecting the *pedilavium*, probably since Sancroft's predictions used the 1633 distribution, as recorded above, as their model.[193] However, the deficiencies in these two accounts are rectified in a further report of the Maundy service of 1661:[194]

> April 11, 1661. Called Maunday Thursday: His Maj^y was pleased to wash 31 poor men's feet in the great hall in Whitehall, and gave every man a purse of white leather, in it 31 pence, and a red purse, in it a piece of gold, and a shirt, a suit of cloathes, shoes and stockings, a wooden dish, and a basket wherein was four loaves, half a salmon, a whole ling, and herrings red and white. Every man drank claret wine in the Hall, and after the service was done by the usual Vicar that belonged to the King's Chapel, also the sound of the organs, they all departed and said – God save the King.

Plague was again rife in London in 1663 but once again Charles II was undeterred from his personal adherence to the Royal Maundy. Following the statement that 'after part of Devine Service, his Majesty being girt with a towel first washed their feate and then wiped them', the narrative for the service in that year continues:[195]

> Then the Lord Almoner (that most prudent and reverend Prelate the Lord Bishop of Sarum[196]) delivered in his Majestys name to each of those poore men a purse wherein was a piece of Gold and 33 pence in silver, with allusion to so many yeares as his Majesty by God's blessing hath already lived.[197] After which his Lordship delivered to them one by one as before, cloth to make each of them a gown or coat and linen for shirts, then shoes and stockings, then loaves of bread, then salmon, herrings and other fish in so many several Dishes and all Beare and Wine at the delivery of each of these his Lordship minded them by some text of Scripture suitable to the occasion to be thankfull and pray for his Majesty. And then his Lordship came back to attend his Majesty, who, after the rest of Devine Service and an anthem sung, left those poore creatures praying and glorifying God for his Majesty.

Nonetheless, it would appear that with the passage of time Charles II's interest in personally administering the *pedilavium* tended to wane. This is evident from the renowned diary of Samuel Pepys. Part of the entry for 4 April 1667 reads 'and so home by coach, and there took up my wife and Mercer, who had been to-day at White Hall to the Maundy, it being Maundy Thursday; but the King did not wash the poor people's feet himself, but the Bishop of London did it for him, but I did not see it, . . .'[198] However, it is apparent from its final six words that this account by Pepys is second-hand and, furthermore, another contemporary account notes the King performing the rites in person during the 1667 Maundy service.[199]

Whether or not Charles II effected the *pedilavium* in 1667 is thus open to doubt but it does appear that, in his easy-going way, he might well have preferred during the later years of his reign to be deputized for in the Maundy service by his Almoner. Notwithstanding this, the monarch still took an active rôle in the service according to the prayers and ceremonies used by the House of Stuart which are preserved in the *Royal Cheque Book*. This contains an order of service in which, after certain prayers and lessons, the monarch, attended by the Lord Almoner and the White Staves, went to the poor men in order and, with a sprig of hyssop dipped in water, sprinkled their feet which he then wiped and kissed before returning to his chair of state. Then followed certain anthems, during the singing of which the Lord Almoner distributed shoes and stockings, clothes, woollen and linen, purses, bread and fish, the whole being concluded with special reference to the act of washing and kissing the feet and the Benediction. After the blessing, the Lord Almoner called for wine and drank to all the poor the King's health, bidding them to be thankful to God and pray for the King.[200] Following his accession to the throne, Charles II's more serious-minded younger brother, James II, was determined to revive the full Maundy ceremony and, within three months, it is apparent that he so succeeded:

> On Maundy Thursday, April 16, 1685, our gracious King James ye 2nd wash'd wip'd and kiss'd the feet of 52 poor men with wonderfull humility, and all the service of the Church of England usuall on that occasion was perform'd, his Majesty being present all the time.[201]

It was perhaps for politico-religious reasons, as is manifest, for example, from the specific reference to the Church of England in this narrative, that the participation of the pro-Roman Catholic James II in the Maundy service was considered of sufficient importance to be recorded with such emotion.

It has been generally accepted that the Maundy ceremony of 1685 was the last occasion when the *pedilavium* was carried out by an English monarch.[202] Nevertheless, considerable evidence is now available to show that this is not the case and that William III and his wife Mary, a partnership which succeeded after James II's ill-fated short reign, actively participated in the *pedilavium* during some of their Maundies. Thus, in his observance of the ceremony as practised in the English Court, Delaune reported in 1690:[203]

> On the Thursday before Easter, called Maundy Thursday, the King or his Lord High Almoner, assisted by the Sub-Almoner, was wont to wash the feet of as many poor men as his Majesty had reigned years, and then to wipe them with a towel (according to the pattern of our Saviour). After this he gave every one of them two and a half yards of woollen cloth with which to make a suit of clothes; also linen cloth for two shirts, as well as a pair of stockings and a pair of shoes; three dishes of fish in wooden platters, one of salt salmon, a second of green fish or cod, a third of pickle-herrings – red herrings or red sprats – a gallon of beer, a quart bottle of wine, and four sixpenny loaves of bread, also a red leather purse with as many single pence as the King is years old, and in such another purse as many shillings as the King has reigned years. The Queen doth the like to diverse poor persons.

Furthermore, a contemporary obverser, F. Colsoni, wrote in 1693 'le Jeudy Saint, le Roy, selon une fort ancienne coutume, lave les pieds à tout autant de vieillards, qu'il a d'années; et la Reine de même à autant de vieilles femmes, qu'elle a d'années'.[204] However, in the third edition of this work, probably published in 1710,[205] by which time, in fact, William III had been dead and Anne had reigned for some eight years, we read 'mais le Roy G.III. (Guillaume III) a laissé l'intendance de cette ceremonie à son grand Aumonier ou un Evêque du Royaume'.²⁰⁶ A statement by Meige in 1693 regarding the ceremony of 'Washing the Feet' that, during the reign of William III, it 'is done sometimes by the King himself and in his absence by the Lord Almoner'²⁰⁷ is clearly in accord with Delaune's account and Colsoni's earlier statement but has been dismissed as a diplomatic ploy.²⁰⁸ Certainly, in 1693 Mary alone distributed the Maundy, a contemporary account stating:²⁰⁹

> The queen this day, according to custom, distributed in the banqueting house, money to a great many poor persons, 43 men and 31 women [the numbers corresponding to the ages of King William and Queen Mary]; the crowd was so great, a woman and a boy were pressed to death.

Nonetheless, an indication of William III's involvement with a subsequent Maundy service and its *pedilavium*, namely that which took place in 1698, is apparent from the entry in the *Protestant Mercury* of 20–22 April 1698:²¹⁰

> Yesterday being *Maundy-Thursday*, His Majesty came to the *Banqueting-house* from *Kensington*, and Washed the Feet of 12 Poor Men; and gave them Money, and Cloth to make them Garments.

It is interesting that, according to this account, the custom of relating the number of recipients to the monarch's age, which by then had become well established, was not adhered to in the 1698 service. Rather, the twelve Apostles appear to have been the prototype, as they had been in some of the pre-Tudor Maundy ceremonies and many of those of a purely ecclesiastical nature. The favourable politico-religious ramifications of this move and, indeed, of this whole narrative are obvious, concerning as it does the divine activities of this ultra-Protestant monarch. Furthermore, its publication in the *Protestant Mercury* is clearly not coincidental. Apparently contrary to this account is another source which notes that the Maundy distribution in 1698 was made by the Sub-almoner²¹¹ although this does not preclude the possibility that the King effected the *pedilavium* since such apportionment of duties within the Maundy service had been the general practice over the previous two centuries. Nevertheless, in the subsequent year the King was certainly deputized for by his High Almoner in the Maundy distribution which, according to the following report, was not accompanied by the *pedilavium*:

> The 6th instant being Maundy Thursday, 49 old men met in the Guard Room at Whitehall (it being the same number as the King is yeares of Age)²¹³ when they dined on Beef according to Custom after which the Right Reverend Father in God, the Lord Bishop of Litchfield [sic] and Coventry, Lord Almoner to the King, gave to each of them 2 Purses in one of which were as many silver Pence as His Majestie's Years of Age, and in the other 20s in money, then each of them had given him 2 yards of Broadcloth for a Coat, 4 yards of Linnen Cloth for a shirt, with New Shoes and Stockings and also a Salt Cod with Salmon 2 dozen Herrings on a Platter with a Bowl of Wine, etc. This has been Customary and practised time out of mind in all Reigns whatsoever.²¹²

Not only is the above report of the 1698 Maundy service the last currently known record of a British monarch effecting the *pedilavium* but no documentary evidence is known to suggest that the sovereign took any active rôle in the service for the next 233 years: Anne was too infirm to attend and the Hanoverian Georges and their successors were content to act by proxy. In as much as it continued to be the responsibility of the Royal Almonry, the service retained its royal connection but successive sovereigns took little or no interest either in it or the Almonry beyond appointing a new High Almoner as vacancies occurred²¹⁴ and occasionally attending the distribution as spectators. For example, George III and eight other members of the royal party have been shown in the royal pew (Plate 16) observing the Maundy distribution of 1773 in the Chapel Royal, Whitehall, and another illustration (Plate 17) shows, on its far right side, a young Victoria similarly engaged in 1842.

Notwithstanding the lack of active royal involvement, the Maundy service continued to be held annually, with the High Almoner or the Sub-almoner deputizing for the monarch. Although between 1688 and 1724 the reports of the contemporary Maundy services are 'somewhat vague',[215] the following reasonably detailed account of the ceremony in 1731 has appeared:[216]

> *Thursday, April 15.* Being Maundy-thursday, there was distributed at the Banquetting house, *Whitehall*, to 48 poor Men, and 48 poor Women (the King's Age 48) boiled Beef and Shoulders of Mutton, and small Bowls of Ale, which is called Dinner; after that, large wooden Platers of Fish and Loaves, *viz.* undress'ed, 1 large old Ling, and 1 large dryed Cod; 12 red Herrings, and 12 white Herrings, and 4 half quarter Loaves; each Person had one Platter of this Provision; after which was distributed to them Shoes, Stockings, Linen and Woollen Cloth, and leathern Bags with 1 Penny, 2 Penny, 3 Penny, and 4 Penny Pieces of Silver, and Shillings; to each about 4l. in Value.[217] His Grace the Ld Archbishop of *York*, Ld High Almoner, performed the annual Ceremony of washing the Feet of a certain Number of Poor in the Royal Chappel, *Whitehall*, which was formerly done by the Kings themselves, in imitation of our Saviour's Pattern of Humility, etc. *James II. was the last King, who perform'ed this in Person*[218]'.

Another closely related account of the 1731 Maundy service provides essentially identical information but incorrectly gives its date as 5 April[219] (Easter Sunday fell on 18 April in 1731[220]) and an alternative contemporary narrative[221] of it appears to be at serious variance[222] with the then long-established relationship between the monarch's age and the magnitude of the Gift of Pennies[223] when it allots the 'silver pence, twopences, threepences and groats' according to the 'years his Majesty had reigned and the number of shillings to the King's age': clearly these aspects of this latter report are erroneous.

One of the significant points of the first two closely-related accounts is their indication that, although the King was not personally involved in any manner with the ceremony, the *pedilavium* was still carried out by his deputizing official, namely the Lord High Almoner. Similarly, a brief account of the Maundy service for 1732 reads:[224]

> Being *Maunday Thursday*, Dr. Gilbert, sub-almoner, wash'd the feet, and distributed alms to 49 (the king's years) poor people of both sexes.

In the ceremony of 1736, the officiating deputizing clergy once again administered the *pedilavium*. Thus:

> On Thursday, April 23rd, 1736, the Rev. Dr. Gilbert, Sub-Almoner, in the absence of the Archbishop of York,[225] distributed at Whitehall, to 53 poor men and women, his Majesty's alms, viz.: to each, three ells of Holland, a piece of cloth for a coat, a pair of shoes and stockings, a purse with 20 shillings, and 53 silver pence, a loaf of bread, and a wooden platter of fish. In Duke Street Chapel, his grace the Archbishop of York, assisted by Drs. Gilbert and Hatter, washed the feet of so many poor persons.[226]

However, in the following year the distribution of the King's alms on Maundy Thursday to fifty-four poor men and fifty-four poor women was not accompanied by the *pedilavium*, a situation which has prevailed to the present day.[227]

Nevertheless, the connection of the *pedilavium* with the Royal Maundy has remained manifest in the service in two symbolic forms. It had become the general practice during Tudor times to sweeten the water, which was to be used for the washing of the recipients' feet, with wine and appropriate herbs and flowers. Such additions were made in attempts to minimize the degree of unpleasantness and the inherent danger in the rite by disguising the recipients' bodily odours, in particular those of their feet, and by guarding against possible infection, respectively. In later Maundy services, as in some of those in Tudor times, sweet-scented nosegays were also employed for the former effect[228] and the traditional nosegays carried by some of the officials in the modern service (Plates 18[229] and 19[230]) are symbolic of this practice. In the same way, a bunch of herbs is provided for judges at assizes.[231] Those nosegays currently used in the Royal Maundy are assembled during the night prior to Maundy Thursday, from cheerfulness (a small double narcissus), cupressus, daffodils, rosemary, thyme, violets and white stocks, by Mrs Bennett-Levy who receives a Maundy set as a fee for this service.[232] The second symbolism in the current Maundy service relating to the *pedilavium* of old is the towels which are worn over the right shoulder and tied around the waist as part of the traditional attire of the Lord High Almoner, the Sub-almoner and the Secretary and the Assistant Secretary of the Royal Almonry for the service (see Plates 18 to 20). Until 1936, the Children of the Royal Almonry[233] also wore similar towels.[234] It has already been related[235] how, in the 1556 Maundy service, Mary Tudor gave to the Maundy recipients the towels and aprons which had been used in the *pedilavium*. The linen towels later symbolically worn by the officials were, until about 1880, retained after the service by their wearers. However, this privilege was then withdrawn, since when the linen has been returned to the Royal Almonry after use to be laundered for the next ceremony. The pieces of linen currently used in the service have been so used since 1883.[236]

The suggestion has been made that the symbolism of the nosegays and the towels in the current Maundy service is lost on the majority of people and, for the few who are aware of its significance, it 'is a striking reminder that the sovereign today does not undertake this act of humility', namely the *pedilavium*. Further criticism, apparently of liturgical symbolism in general, proceeds 'The symbolism is exceedingly unhelpful. Those who order the worship of a church need to ask sometimes, "Why do we do this? Is this symbolism saying what we want said?" Ritual becomes dangerous, and a religion of its own, when the meaning is lost, and it becomes an end in itself'.[237]

It would appear that there may be many who regret the abandonment of the *pedilavium*, after so many centuries, by the Anglican branch of the Catholic Church.[238] However, although it has not, as yet, been reintroduced into the Maundy service, it has been resurrected by this branch of the Church in recent years. Thus, during the Eucharist of Maundy Thursday, it has been interspaced between the end of the Sermon and the beginning of the Prayers of Intercession and the subsequent Communion. Those who are to have their feet washed by the priest are usually chosen to be representative of the church community and, because of spacial restrictions, are usually limited to six in number rather than the traditional twelve symbolic of the Apostles. Yet the restoration of this ceremony has not been as widespread as that of other traditional Holy Week practices. Possibly, it may not have the same meaning and significance in our modern culture as it did in earlier days and its performance may not be genuinely helpful to worship and could so easily degenerate into a farce. Indeed, unlike most Holy Week rituals, its real benefit is not to onlookers, for it is not visually impressive, but to participants. Therefore, the majority of a congregation may probably be largely unmoved or, even worse, faintly amused or a little embarrassed.[239]

Although by 1737 it had become stripped of both the monarch's direct involvement and the *pedilavium*, the Maundy distribution continued to be made on a regular annual basis. This is exemplified by the following brief accounts of some of those distributions made during the second half of the eighteenth century:

Being *Maundy Thursday* [1754], the sub-almoner distributed his majesty's alms to 54 poor men and women in the manner following. To each three ells of holland, a piece of woollen-cloth, a pair of shoes and stockings, 20s. in a purse, 54 silver-pence, two-pences and three-pences, a loaf and a platter of fish.[240]

His majesty's alms was distributed [in 1755] to 54 poor men and women; to each 3 ells of Holland, a piece of woollen cloth, a pair of shoes and stockings, 20s. in a purse, 54 silver pence, two-pences and three-pences, a loaf, and platter.[241]

Being *Maunday Thursday* [1765], his majesty's bounty to 27 poor men and women was distributed at *Whitehall* as usual.[242]

Being *Maunday Thursday* [1766], his majesty's alms were distributed in *White-hall* chapel, to 28 poor men and women; to each three ells of holland, a piece of woollen cloth, a pair of shoes and stockings, 20 shillings in a purse, 27 [*sic*, 28?] silver pence, two-pences, and three-pences, a loaf of bread, and a platter of fish. One of the women who received the alms was 105 years of age.[243]

Being *Maunday Thursday* [1767], his Majesty's alms were distributed as usual to 29 poor men and women; to each three ells of holland and a piece of woollen cloth, a pair of shoes and stockings, 20 shillings in a purse, 29 silver two-pences and three-pences, a loaf, and a platter of fish.[244]

Being Maunday Thursday [1772], his Majesty's alms were distributed to twenty nine poor men and women, in the usual manner.[245]

Being Maunday-Thursday [1774], his Majesty's alms were distributed to thirty-five poor men and women, three ells of holland, a piece of woolen cloth, a pair of shoes and stockings, 20 shillings in a purse, 35 silver pence, a loaf of bread, and a platter of fish, to each.[246]

Presumably, in the above eleven post-1730 Maundy distributions, only the male recipients received the gift of clothes since, for female recipients from 1724 onward, it was commuted for an allowance of thirty-five shillings.[247] This change was a welcome one in every respect and was made in order to circumvent during the service the unseemly trial fitting and exchanging by some of the female recipients of their clothing gift, which was not made to measure.[248]

The male recipients' gift of clothing, at the time consisting of three ells of fine linen, three yards of woollen cloth of a russet colour, a pair of shoes and a pair of stockings, remained until 1882. It, too, was then replaced, with the permission of Queen Victoria, by an allowance of forty-five shillings, the price formerly paid by the Lord Chamberlain for each such individual gift. This change was introduced because some of the male recipients were too poor to meet the expense of having the cloth component of their gift made up into clothing.[249] In 1973, the clothing allowance for both males and females was increased to £3 in normal currency and has since remained unchanged.[250]

Until 1936, the clothing allowances were distributed in paper packets[251] which were carried in a brocaded silk bag by the Secretary of the Royal Almonry prior to their distribution by the Lord High Almoner.[252] This practice was then modified, a further two leather purses, one white with short vivid Tudor green leather strings and the other a vivid Tudor green with short white leather strings (Plate 15), being introduced to carry the gift for the male and female recipients, respectively.[253] When the Maundy Dish (Plate 13) was used to carry the other gifts, in white and red leather purses with long strings of red and white leather, respectively, for what was then called in the Maundy service the Second Distribution,[254] the purses containing the clothing allowance, with their short strings tied in bows, were carried on a second alms dish, smaller than the Maundy Dish,[255] and were presented to the recipients during what was termed the First Distribution.[256] From 1971, the two so called Fish Dishes (Plate 21) were used to carry the charged purses for the Second Distribution and the Maundy Dish was used to carry the clothing allowance in its purses prior to their presentation in the First Distribution.[257] After 1979, the use of these short-stringed purses ceased and the clothing allowance was then, as now, included along with the other allowances in the red purses with long white strings. The reason for this withdrawal of the short-stringed purses was to reduce the number of distributions and thereby the physical strain on the Queen, in view of her advancing years and the related increase in the number of recipients.[258]

An interesting pictorial record of the Maundy ceremony of 1773 exists in the form of an indian-ink sketch and two water-colours. All three pieces are the work of Samuel Hieronymus Grimm.[259] They were commissioned by the Rev. Dr Richard Kaye, F.R.S.,[260] the then Sub-almoner to George III, who in that year distributed the Maundy, probably the first occasion on which he did so.[261] For over twenty years Grimm was closely associated with Kaye and the former's earliest known commission from the latter was this ceremony of 1773.[262]

The sketch (Plate 22) depicts the Royal Almonry procession en route from the Almonry Office, then in Scotland Yard, to the Chapel Royal. It is led by two members of the Yeomen of the Guard with halberds who precede the Sergeant of the Guard upon whose head is being carried, in the traditional manner, the Maundy Dish containing the charged Maundy purses, some of which have their strings hanging over the edge of the dish. Following the Sergeant of the Guard are, in order, two Gentlemen of the Almonry, a chaplain in robes, the Sub-almoner (Dr Kaye), an official who is possibly the Treasurer of the Chamber (analogous to the current Secretary of the Royal Almonry) and, finally, a further four Gentlemen of the Almonry.[263] Of further interest are the towels, worn around the waists of the six Gentlemen, symbolic of the *pedilavium*, as are the nosegays carried by the two ecclesiastics.[264] An interesting account relating to the conveyance of the Maundy alms in the manner illustrated in this sketch appeared in 1893,[265] and again in 1902 in a slightly modified form which reads:[266]

> Till the construction of the new street into Whitehall, a few years ago, a very curious little ceremony used to take place, viz. the conveyance of the alms from the Almonry office and residence of the Lord High Almoner in Scotland Yard to the Chapel at Whitehall. Suddenly confronted by this procession, a wanderer who chanced to be straying in the byways of the neighbourhood of the Chapel Royal would have been struck with surprise and wonder at the attire of the figures who took part in it, for some of them were in mediæval, and some in modern, dress, some in clerical vestments, others in lay garments. He would, perhaps, have been startled if, unawares, he had met the detachment of stalwart beef-eaters, with their halberds over their shoulders, escorting one of their number, who bore on his head a large gilt salver, filled with the curious old-fashioned red and white purses with their strings hanging round like a fringe. And he might have marvelled at the Sub-Almoner, at his bevy of lay officials, and his company of children, who, representing the children of the Almonry (one of the divisions of the Alms) carried bright bunches of flowers and wore white linen scarves that were emblematic of the sweet flowers and towels

used at the obsolete ceremony of the feet washing. The little band would glide slowly by, and, before the uninitiated spectator could recover his astonishment, pass through the door of the Chapel Royal at Whitehall and join the Lord High Almoner, the Sub-Almoner and the staff of the Chapel, and then take part in the service of prayer and thanksgiving, and in the ceremony of the distribution of the royal gifts.

The water-colours (Plates 16 and 23) are regarded as Grimm's most important historical work. Done from nature for Dr Kaye in 1773, they were exhibited the following year.[268] The distribution of the provisions, namely the Maundy dinner, in the Ante-chapel of the Chapel Royal is represented in Plate 23. The platters carrying loaves and fishes are clearly visible in front of each recipient, as are capacious baskets under the tables.[269] In all, 147 carefully drawn figures are shown. Plate 16 shows the distribution of the Maundy money, in the Chapel Royal itself, by Dr Kaye whose august figure, gird with a towel symbolic of the *pedilavium*, is seen handing a purse to one of the thirty-five male recipients (George III then being in his thirty-fifth year[270]). The white and red purses, lying on the silver-gilt Maundy Dish, are passed along by a chain of Gentlemen of the Royal Almonry to Dr Kaye, in front of whom is an official, perhaps the Treasurer. The male recipients are already holding their clothing gift of broad cloth, linen and shoes and the female recipients await their turn. The King himself, in scarlet, together with Queen Charlotte and other members of the royal party, is watching the distribution from the royal pew, the choir is in attendance and visitors of all ranks are present.[271] Altogether there are 186 carefully drawn figures in the piece.

James Basire engraved plates from both water-colours in 1789 and 1777, respectively, and from them were produced prints that are marked in the lower right and left corners, respectively, of their borders 'Publish'd as the Act directs' on '23.ᵈ April 1789' and '27.ᵗʰ March 1777', respectively.[272] Some of these prints were coloured after the original paintings, the latter being ultimately presented by Dr Kaye to George III and eventually passed, as part of the King's Library, into the custody of the British Museum.[273]

Complementing the fine pictorial record afforded by Plates 16, 22 and 23 of the celebration of a Maundy distribution during the earlier years of the reign of George III is the following narrative of the ceremony as it was held toward the end of his reign, namely on 7 April[274] 1814:[275]

> According to annual custom, on Maundy Thursday, 1814, the royal donations were distributed at the Chapel Royal, Whitehall.
>
> In the morning the sub-almoner, the secretary to the lord high almoner, and others belonging to the lord chamberlain's office, attended by a party of the yeomen of the guard, distributed to seventy-five poor women, and seventy-five poor men, being as many as the king was years old, a quantity of salt fish, consisting of salmon, cod, and herrings, pieces of very fine beef, five loaves of bread, and some ale to drink the king's health. . . . A procession entered, of those engaged in the ceremony, consisting of a party of the yeomen of the guard, one of them carrying on his head a large gold dish, containing one hundred and fifty bags, with seventy-five silver pennies in each, for the poor people, which was placed in the royal closet. They were followed by the sub-almoner in his robes, with a sash of fine linen over his shoulder, and crossing his waist. He was followed by two boys, two girls, the secretary, and another gentlemen, all carrying nosegays. The Church evening service was then performed, at the conclusion of which the silver pennies were distributed, and woollen cloth, linen, shoes, and stockings to the men and women,[276] and a cup of wine to drink the king's health.

This report makes clear that the celebration began in the morning, implies that it did not end until later afternoon or early evening since the 'Church evening service' was performed during its final stages and, from the break in the middle, suggests that it was divided into a morning and an afternoon component. Such a division of the Royal Maundy between the morning and the afternoon is known to have occurred in 1826.[277]

Some of the Maundy recipients would sell their gifts of food for much less than their full value, in some cases receiving no more than five shillings for a gift that had a contract price of thirty shillings. In view of this, William IV endorsed in 1837 an arrangement, affirmed by Victoria in the following year, whereby an allowance of thirty shillings per recipient in lieu of this gift was introduced.[278] This was presented, along with the robe redemption allowance of twenty shillings,[279] in the red leather purse.[280] Apart from its decimalization, the magnitude of the food allowance has remained unchanged and is still presented, as £1.50 in normal currency, as one of the monetary gifts in the red purse. For some years, a 1953 coronation crown (Plate 24) formed part of this allowance. However, this practice had no historical significance, it merely being thought that the recipients would appreciate a specimen of this coin as part of their Maundy gifts, and it ceased after 1976 when stocks of the crown became exhausted. The recipients in 1977 received a silver jubilee crown of that year (Plate 25) as part of the allowance but since then the gift has been composed totally of normal currency.[281]

The first Maundy ceremony at which the monetary allowance in lieu of the food gift was presented was the first of Victoria's long reign, namely that held on 12 April 1838:[282]

> Upon this occasion (the first of the Royal charity in the new reign) the distribution took place with the usual forms, which, in consequence of the repairs of Whitehall Chapel, have not been observed since the year 1829.[283] At 3 o'clock the procession, consisting of the Yeomen of Her Majesty's Body Guard, under the command of Mr. Ellerthrope, Clerk of the Check, the children of the Chapel Royal, the gentlemen of the Chapel Royal, the priests of the Chapel Royal, the Sub-Almoner (the Dean of Carlisle), the Sub-Dean (Rev. Dr. Sleath), the Secretary and Yeoman of the Almonry (Mr. J. Hanby), the Groom of the Almonry (Mr. J. Jones), four children from the National School, Westminster, two children from the National School of St. George, Hanover-square, then entered the chapel, and took their respective stations.
>
> The Yeoman, who carried the gold dish which contained the alms, deposited it upon a table prepared for that purpose.
>
> Divine service then commenced, and after the first anthem ('Blessed is he who considereth the poor and needy'), the Sub-Almoner and officers of the almonry distributed to each woman 1l. 15s. and to each man shoes and stockings.[284] After the second anthem ('Hide not thou thy face from me, etc.') the Sub-Almoner distributed to each man woollen and linen cloth. After the third anthem ('O Lord, grant the Queen a long life'), the Sub-Almoner, etc., distributed to both men and women purses of money. Each white purse contained 19 silver pennies (being the age of Her Majesty) and each red purse 2l. 10s.
>
> The Maundy men and women received upon this occasion for the first time 1l. 10s. each, as a commutation in lieu of all provisions with which they had heretofore been supplied. This arrangement was sanctioned by his late Majesty William IV, and confirmed by the Queen.

A pictorial record (Plate 17) of the distribution in 1842 not only shows the young Victoria observing from the royal pew on the far right side but also partially visible are three of the nine ceiling panels that were painted by Rubens for the Chapel Royal.[285] Another pictorial record of a Victorian Maundy distribution is in the form of a very rapid and clever sketch in water-colour (Plate 26), signed by W. J. Colville, and given to the late Sir Spencer Ponsonby-Fane by an artist friend in 1875. It is claimed that in this latter illustration the distribution is being made by one Dean Stanley.[286] However, this is surprising since neither then nor at any other period did a person by this name hold either the position of High Almoner or Sub-almoner.[287] The first Maundy distribution of the reign of Edward VII has also been illustrated in an artist's impression (Plate 27). This shows the Lord High Almoner, then Lord Alwyne Compton, Bishop of Ely, distributing the Maundy gifts in 1901, on 4 April,[288] in Westminster Abbey[289] which by then had become the regular venue for the service.[290]

From illustrations (Plates 16 and 17) and surviving narratives it is apparent that, although the monarch played no active rôle in the Maundy service during the 233 years following 1698, they or other members of the royal family sometimes attended as spectators. Thus, for example, Queen Alexandra, the wife of Edward VII, and her sister, the Empress of Russia, attended the service on two occasions, namely those held in 1907 and 1909, being accompanied at the former celebration by the four children of the Prince of Wales.[291] Similarly, in 1920 the royal party consisted of Princess Christina, Princess Louise (Duchess of Argyll), Princess Beatrice, Princess Marie-Louise, Princess Alice (Countess of Athlone), the Earl of Athlone, Lady May Cambridge, the Grand Duke Michael and the Countess de Torby, the distribution being made by Dr Armitage Robinson (the Dean of Wells and Lord High Almoner to the King), Canon Edgar Sheppard (the Sub-dean of his Majesty's Chapels Royal and Sub-almoner), Mr T. T. Norgate, (the Secretary of the Royal Almonry) and Mr W. Folland, his assistant.[292]

However, during the early parts of the twentieth century, the royal connection remaining with the Maundy service resulted almost entirely from the presence of the Princesses Helena Victoria and Marie-Louise (Plate 28[293]). 'The hardy annuals', as they so described themselves, worked untiringly for charity and one or the other, usually both, made a point of attending the Maundy distribution unless they were unavoidably prevented from doing so.[294] Thus, from 1926 to 1943 and from 1926 to 1956, respectively, they attended the service on twelve and twenty-eight occasions, respectively.[295] However, this attendance notwithstanding, by the third decade of this century the service 'seemed to be in danger of becoming nothing but a picturesque and, perhaps, rather meaningless survival from the past.'[296] Indeed, as early as 1841 it was written that 'the changes which have gradually been introduced into the distribution of the "Maundy" lead to the conclusion that the ceremony will gradually sink into disuse'[297], some thirty-five years later it was stated that 'although the mandate, or Maunday, is now little more than an empty ceremony . . .'[298] and, when referring to the Maundy service it was more recently recorded that 'in England (except among Roman Catholics), the distribution of "maundy money" is all that remains of this ceremony'.[299]

The Maundy service's revitalization, which was not without its difficulties, owes much to the late Dr Lawrence E. Tanner, C.V.O. who, in 1921, was appointed as Secretary of the Royal Almonry, a position which he held until 1964. The problems associated with bringing about the service's revival have been discussed. As a first step it was essential to strengthen the royal connection with the ceremony. This was achieved very satisfactorily, to a large measure because of the whole hearted co-operation of Rev. Lancelot Jefferson Percival (Plate 28) who was not only the Sub-almoner but also the Sub-dean of the Chapels Royal, the latter position keeping him in touch with the Royal Court. Ultimately, and following the suggestion to Dr Tanner from Princess Marie-Louise (Plate 28), as they were leaving Westminster Abbey following the Maundy service in 1931, that the sovereign should once again attend the service and make the distribution in person, George V was approached to this effect and consequently made the Second Distribution during the service in 1932.[300] After describing the First Distribution, namely that of packets containing the allowances in lieu of clothing, by the Lord High Almoner (Dr Armitage Robinson, the Ven. Dean of Wells and formerly Dean of Westminster), the report of this service continues:[301]

> Thus the service came to an event the like of which (so our readers are aware) has not taken place since the reign of King James II. – the distribution of the Royal Maundy by the Sovereign's own hand. The ceremony followed the same lines as the first distribution. In this case, the Secretary,[302] carrying his white bouquet, went before the King. The great gold dish was borne along by a Yeoman of the Guard. From it the Assistant Secretary[303] took by the long strings one red and one white purse, which he gave to the Sub-Almoner, from whom the King took them, to present them to each bowing, or curtsying, and evidently deeply affected recipient of this bounty. In each red purse was £1 in gold,[304] representing part of the Maundy, and 30s in lieu of provisions, formerly given in kind; and in each white purse were as many pence as the King is years of age, given in newly coined pieces of one, two, three, and four pennies, being the balance of the Maundy.
>
> Two anthems were sung while the congregation was privileged to watch this historic scene [Plate 29], one being Tallis's "If ye love Me, keep My Commandments" and the other that triumphant "Zadok the Priest" by Handel' . . . 'and to the sound of bells and organ the great procession attended their Majesties down the choir and the nave and so to the West Door and the sunny spring morning [Plate 30].

The precedent for the re-establishment of the monarch's active participation in the Maundy service was thus set, through the inspiration of Princess Marie-Louise, by George V. However, he was subsequently unable to attend other services during his lifetime and for the next three years the royal rôle was once again reduced to that of spectator, it being interesting to note that in 1935 the Queen, then Princess Elizabeth, attended for the first time.[305] Nevertheless, since 1932, successive monarchs have taken an active interest in the service and, apart from the exceptions listed in Table 2, they have personally distributed the gifts.[306] The distribution in 1936 was made on 9 April by the uncrowned king, Edward VIII,[307] the late Duke of Windsor[308] who abdicated on 10 December 1936 before his coronation. This Maundy service was, in fact, almost the first public ceremonial of his short reign[309] (Plate 31). Similarly, the distributions in 1952 and 1953 were made, on 10 and 2 April, respectively, by Elizabeth II[310] prior to her coronation on 2 June 1953.

II. THE PASSING OF THE LOVING CUP AND THE DRINKING OF THE MONARCH'S HEALTH AT THE END OF THE MAUNDY SERVICE

It has been stated that the loving cup, the *caritatis potum*,[311] passed round at the end of the early Maundy services as, for example, at the end of that of Elizabeth I in 1560,[312] was an adaptation by the Christian Church of the wassail-bowl of Saxon times. This, instead of being abolished upon the introduction of Christianity, was adopted under the above name for use in religious ceremonies.[313] Alternatively, the cup circulated by Jesus during the Last Supper could have been the prototype.[314]

Table 2. The distributors, other than the monarch, of the Maundy gifts since 1932[1]

Year	Distributor of the Maundy gifts
1933	The Sub-almoner, Rev. L. J. Percival
1934	The High Almoner, Archbishop C. G. Lang
1935	———
1937	———
1938	———
1939	The Sub-almoner, Rev. L. J. Percival
1941	The High Almoner, Archbishop C. G. Lang
1942	———
1943	———
1947	The High Almoner, The Bishop of Lichfield (Rt Rev. E. S. Woods)
1949	———
1954	The High Almoner, The Bishop of St Albans (Rt Rev. E. M. Gresford-Jones)
1960	H.M. Queen Elizabeth, The Queen Mother
1964	H.R.H. The Princess Royal (Countess of Harewood)
1970	H.M. Queen Elizabeth, The Queen Mother

Note to Table 2: *1*, Wright.

Whatever the origin, drinking the monarch's health became a fairly regular practice at the completion of the Maundy services during the seventeenth and eighteenth centuries. A general example is present in the Order of Service for the Maundy used by the House of Stuart,[315] a specific application of this being found in a contemporary report of the service for 1664, concluding 'after the blessing the Lord Almoner calls for wine and drinks to all the pore the King's health'.[316] Furthermore, under the date 1709 it was still written that 'after the Blessing The Lord Almoner calls for Wine and drinks to all ye poore the King's health and bids them be thankfull to God and Pray for the King'.[317] This statement appears strange since the monarch at that time was a woman, namely Anne, who had by then been on the throne for seven years: clearly the account is simply a repetition from an earlier period.[318] Nevertheless, it would appear to indicate that, even after the monarch had ceased by the end of the seventeenth century to take an active rôle in the Maundy service, their health was still drunk at its termination. Such a custom was extended into the nineteenth century, as is evident from the account of the Maundy service of 1814.[319] However, it has now been abandoned for many decades, probably since the gift of provisions was commuted for a monetary allowance after 1837.

III. THE LITURGY OF THE CURRENT MAUNDY SERVICE

The order for the modern Maundy service can be illustrated by reference to that held in Birmingham Cathedral on 23 March 1989 and which the author had the privilege of attending.

Some two hours before the service was to begin, the recipients began to gather in a nearby hotel whence, about one-and-a-half hours later, they were led in procession, under the guidance of the six wandsmen,[320] into the cathedral. Here they took their assigned seats on either side of the nave and on the inside edges of the two aisles. About fifteen minutes later, when the congregation were seated, there entered the cathedral an attachment of the Yeomen of the Guard,[321] eight of whom took up regular positions down either side of the nave, with others, about half-dozen, being stationed at its west end.

The cathedral and the Royal Almonry processions then began to form in the nave and the south aisle, respectively. With the arrival of the Queen and the Duke of Edinburgh, the congregation stood and, during the singing of the hymn 'Praise to the Holiest in the height', the processions passed into the choir in the following order:

THE CATHEDRAL PROCESSION
THE CRUCIFER AND TAPERERS
THE CHILDREN OF HER MAJESTY'S CHAPEL ROYAL, ST JAMES'S PALACE[322]
THE CHORISTERS OF BIRMINGHAM CATHEDRAL
THE GENTLEMEN OF HER MAJESTY'S CHAPEL ROYAL, ST JAMES'S PALACE[323]
THE LAY CLERKS AND CHORAL SCHOLARS OF BIRMINGHAM CATHEDRAL
THE ORGANIST AND MASTER OF THE CHORISTERS OF BIRMINGHAM CATHEDRAL
THE ORGANIST, CHOIRMASTER AND COMPOSER OF HER MAJESTY'S CHAPEL ROYAL
THE SUCCENTOR AND CHAPLAIN

A VERGER
THE DIVISIONAL COMMANDER, THE SALVATION ARMY
THE MODERATOR OF THE UNITED REFORMED CHURCH, WEST MIDLANDS PROVINCE
THE SUPERINTENDENT OF THE WEST MIDLAND BAPTIST ASSOCIATION
THE CHAIRMAN OF THE BIRMINGHAM DISTRICT OF THE METHODIST CHURCH

A VERGER
THE GREATER CHAPTER

A VERGER
THE ARCHDEACON OF BIRMINGHAM
THE ASSISTANT BISHOP
THE SUFFRAGAN BISHOP OF ASTON
THE DIOCESAN REGISTRAR
THE CHANCELLOR OF THE DIOCESE
THE CATHEDRAL CHURCHWARDENS
THE LORD BISHOP OF BIRMINGHAM
THE BISHOP'S CHAPLAIN

A VERGER
THE RESIDENTIARY CHAPTER OF BIRMINGHAM CATHEDRAL
THE HEAD VERGER
THE PROVOST
HER MAJESTY THE QUEEN[324]
HIS ROYAL HIGHNESS THE DUKE OF EDINBURGH
HER MAJESTY'S SUITE
HER MAJESTY'S LORD-LIEUTENANT FOR THE WEST MIDLANDS

THE ROYAL ALMONRY PROCESSION

A VERGER
THE CLERK OF THE CHEQUE AND ADJUTANT

THE SERGEANT-MAJOR OF THE YEOMEN OF THE GUARD
THREE MEMBERS OF THE YEOMEN, CARRYING ON THEIR HEADS THE MAUNDY
DISH AND THE TWO FISH DISHES, CONTAINING THE ALMS
THE YEOMEN IN ATTENDANCE
THE CHILDREN OF THE ROYAL ALMONRY[325]
THE WANDSMEN
THE ASSISTANT SECRETARY OF THE ROYAL ALMONRY
THE SECRETARY OF THE ROYAL ALMONRY
THE SERJEANT OF THE VESTRY OF HER MAJESTY'S CHAPEL ROYAL
THE SUB-ALMONER
(The Reverend Canon A. D. Cæsar)
THE CLERK OF THE CHAPEL, BUCKINGHAM PALACE
THE LORD HIGH ALMONER
(The Lord Bishop of St Albans)

The Queen, the Duke of Edinburgh, the Lord High Almoner, the Sub-Almoner and the Secretary and Assistant Secretary of the Royal Almonry, along with the cathedral's clergy, passed through the choir and took up their positions in the sanctuary. The alms dishes bearing the purses were placed on a table centrally positioned in the choir and stood guard over by a Yeoman. After the passing of the processions, the eight Yeomen in the nave's passage moved outwards and took up positions by the columns, where they remained throughout the service, and the congregation became seated.

The service opened with the Lord High Almoner reading the Exhortation 'I give you a new commandment; Love one another; as I have loved you, so you are to love one another' (St John 13. 34). The Succentor (Rev. Philip Wells) then began the prayers with the Kyres, the Lord's Prayer and versicles and responses, sequentially. This was followed by the choir singing Psalm 138, after which the Archdeacon of Aston (Ven. John Cooper) said a prayer for humility,[326] preceded by versicles and responses. The senior canon (Rev. Douglas McLean) then said a prayer for the Queen, also preceded by versicles and responses. Following a further contribution from the choir, namely the singing of the anthem 'Lord, for thy tender mercy's sake', by an unknown composer of the sixteenth century, the Duke of Edinburgh read the First Lesson (St John 13. 1–16).

The Maundy gifts, a white leather purse with long red leather strings containing the Maundy money and a red leather purse with long white leather strings containing the other monetary gifts in ordinary currency, tied together by their strings, were then distributed to the recipients on the southside of the Cathedral. The congregation stood throughout the distribution, during which the choir sang the anthem '*Ubi caritas et amor*', to music by Maurice Duruﬂe, and Psalm 51, 2–3, to music by Samuel Sebastian Wesley, but the recipients and those behind them were allowed to sit when the wandsmen so indicated.

The distribution party (Plate 20) was led by the Secretary of the Royal Almonry, Mr Peter A. Wright,[327] walking backwards and indicating each of the recipients in turn to the Queen who was immediately following him. The gifts were taken, one at a time, off the Maundy Dish by the Assistant Secretary of the Royal Almonry, Mr Derek Waters,[328] and were passed in turn to the Sub-almoner, Rev. Anthony Douglass Cæsar,[329] and the Lord High Almoner, Rt Rev. John Bernard Taylor,[330] who gave them to the Queen as they were required by her for presentation to the recipients. The Maundy Dish was carried by a member of the Yeomen of the Guard who was followed by the Clerk of the Cheque and Adjutant, the party being completed by the Sergeant-Major of the Yeomen of the Guard followed by the four Children of the Royal Almonry. The members of the procession returned to their places at the end of this distribution.

The provost (Very Rev. Peter Berry) then read the Second Lesson (St Matthew 25. 31–45) which was followed by the distribution of the Maundy gifts, now taken from the two Fish Dishes,[331] to the recipients on the north side of the Cathedral, in the same manner as before. This distribution was accompanied by the choir singing a further two anthems, firstly the Gradual for Maundy Thursday (Philippians 2. 8–9), to music by Anton Bruckner, and then 'Zadok the priest' (I Kings 1. 39–40), to music by George Frideric Handel.

After the return of the distribution party to their places, and following further versicles and responses by the canon, two prayers of thanksgiving, one for the Queen and one for the suffering and needy, were said by the precentor (Rev. Canon Lorys M. Davies) and a general thanksgiving was said by all, successively. After the singing by all of the hymn 'O Thou who comest from above', to the tune Hereford, and a final prayer for the people of the Diocese and the whole Church by the Lord Bishop of Birmingham, the service ended with the singing of the National Anthem by the whole congregation followed by the Blessing pronounced by the Bishop. The recession then took the following order:

THE CRUCIFER AND TAPERERS
A VERGER
THE RESIDENTIARY CHAPTER OF BIRMINGHAM CATHEDRAL
THE HEAD VERGER
THE PROVOST
HER MAJESTY THE QUEEN
HIS ROYAL HIGHNESS THE DUKE OF EDINBURGH
HER MAJESTY'S SUITE
HER MAJESTY'S LORD-LIEUTENANT FOR THE WEST MIDLANDS
THE CLERK OF THE CHAPEL, BUCKINGHAM PALACE
THE LORD HIGH ALMONER
THE SERJEANT OF THE VESTRY OF HER MAJESTY'S CHAPEL ROYAL
THE SUB-ALMONER
THE SECRETARY OF THE ROYAL ALMONRY
THE ASSISTANT SECRETARY OF THE ROYAL ALMONRY
THE CHILDREN OF THE ROYAL ALMONRY

A VERGER
THE CLERK OF THE CHEQUE AND ADJUTANT
THE SERGEANT-MAJOR OF THE YEOMEN OF THE GUARD
THE YEOMEN CARRYING THE DISHES
THE YEOMEN IN ATTENDANCE

A VERGER
THE DIOCESAN REGISTRAR
THE CHANCELLOR OF THE DIOCESE
THE LORD BISHOP OF BIRMINGHAM
THE BISHOP'S CHAPLAIN

A VERGER
THE DIVISIONAL COMMANDER, THE SALVATION ARMY
THE MODERATOR OF THE UNITED REFORMED CHURCH, WEST MIDLANDS PROVINCE
THE SUPERINTENDENT OF THE WEST MIDLAND BAPTIST ASSOCIATION
THE CHAIRMAN OF THE BIRMINGHAM DISTRICT OF THE METHODIST CHURCH

A VERGER
THE SUFFRAGAN BISHOP OF ASTON
THE ASSISTANT BISHOP
THE ARCHDEACON OF BIRMINGHAM
THE GREATER CHAPTER
THE SUCCENTOR AND CHAPLAIN
THE ORGANIST, CHOIRMASTER AND COMPOSER OF HER MAJESTY'S CHAPELS ROYAL
THE ORGANIST AND MASTER OF THE CHORISTERS OF BIRMINGHAM CATHEDRAL
THE LAY CLERKS AND CHORAL SCHOLARS OF BIRMINGHAM CATHEDRAL
THE GENTLEMEN OF HER MAJESTY'S CHAPEL ROYAL, ST JAMES'S PALACE
THE CHORISTERS OF BIRMINGHAM CATHEDRAL
THE CHILDREN OF HER MAJESTY'S CHAPEL ROYAL, ST JAMES'S PALACE

This royal event, splendid in its colour and pageantry, nevertheless had a moving simplicity as Queen and subject drew together during the traditional giving and receiving.

IV. THE ETYMOLOGY OF MAUNDY THURSDAY

The various names and their derivations for the Thursday of Holy Week, the day preceding Good Friday in the Christian calendar, have been the subject of wide discussion.

In parts of the north of England, the name Kiss Thursday, alluding to the kiss of Judas, has been used.[332] During mediæval times it was called the Birthday of the Chalice, or the Eucharist, in memory of the institution of the Holy Eucharist.[333] In European Roman Catholic countries, the day is called Holy Thursday,[334] a name which, along with the more generally accepted Great Thursday, has also been used in the Russo-Greek churches.[335] In Austria it was known as Antlatz-Tag (Remission Day), from the reconciliation and readmission into the Church of penitents prior to their restoration to communion at Easter.[336] Likewise, in Germany it was the day when penitents, in these cases wearing sprigs of green leaves or herbs, were customarily readmitted to the Church and hence it became popularly designated as Green Thursday.[337] This name also relates to the eating, in some areas, of green herbs to prevent diseases and to the wearing of green vestments by the priests of certain denominations on this day.[338] The name White Thursday has also been used since in some churches it is the time when the colour of the Lenten vestments is changed from violet to white in memory of the institution of the Blessed Sacrament.[339]

Manuscripts from the twelfth to the sixteenth centuries may be searched in vain for the name Maundy Thursday as relating to this day since, in such documents, its name can appear as Sheer(e), Sher(e), Shier, Shir(e), Shyre, Shear, Shor(e), Shorp, Shrift, Scer(e), Scher(e), Schir(e), Schyr(e), Schor, Skere, Skeyre, Skire, Char(e) and *Sc.* chyris Thursday, as it is variously spelt.[340] Furthermore, in many instances such a description is written as one word, examples being Sheerthursday, Shorthursday, Shorpthursday and Scherethursday, or is hyphenated as, for example, in Shore-thursday.[341]

It has been postulated that these names for the Thursday of Holy Week arise from the old root name Skier, signifying pain and affliction,[342] presumably an allusion to the suffering of Jesus on the Cross. Others thought them to relate to the custom of men polling their heads and beards as a token of grief for Jesus' betrayal[343] or, as postulated by John Myre in the fourteenth century, as a preparation for Easter. This latter suggestion was reiterated two centuries later when it was recorded that 'it is also in England called Sher-Thursdaye, for in old fader's dayes the people wolde that daye *shere* theyr heedes, and clyppe theyr berdes, and poll theyr heedes, and so make them honest ayenst Eester Day':[344] alternative accounts of this custom have also been given.[345] Although it has been suggested that 'this seems a questionable "popular" derivation', it has been given wider significance in that the trimming of their hair and beards was included in the ritual whereby penitents sought readmission to the Church on the Thursday of Holy Week and it thus relates to the cleansing of the soul.[346] In a related explanation, it has been stated that Shere Thursday was the occasion when 'a priest should shave his crown, so that there be nothing between God and him, and men should make them clean within their souls and without'.[347] However, contrary to the above, it has been affirmed, but arbitrarily so, that with regard to such head shearings 'whatever the custom may have been in that respect, it has nothing to do with the name'.[348]

Nevertheless, the above ritualistic shearings were associated with spiritual cleansing and it has been widely accepted that the meaning underlying the words sheer, etc. is cleansing and, incidentally, although it is not mentioned as a possibility in the *OED*,[349] the present-day words char or charwoman (cleaning lady) and chore (cleaning task) may also be so derived. In connection with the Thursday of Holy Week, sheer, etc. appear to have been applied as an allusion to the purification of the soul by confession[350] or to the practice of washing the altar[351] on that day,[352] acts in preparation for the imminent festival of Easter.[353] Alternatively, the prototype for this concept of cleanliness could be the act of Jesus at the Last Supper whereby he washed the Apostles' feet.[354] Cleansing is certainly the underlying theme of all the above acts and reference has, in fact, been made to the meaning of sheer as *mundus*, Latin for clean.[355] The possible extrapolation of *mundus* to maundy (or one of its forms[356]) is obvious although, irrespective of the validity of this derivation, by the seventeenth century the term Maundy Thursday had superseded Sheer Thursday and its many forms which have, indeed, been completely set aside in modern parlance. Other possible derivations of the word maundy and its various forms have, however, been suggested.

Bishop Kingdon postulated that the name may originate from the now obsolete word maundye or maundaye meaning a feast (thus, to make one's maundy: to feast[357]).[358] Indeed, the naming of the day as Feast Thursday, from the feast in honour of the Lord's Last Supper, was long retained in the early Church.[359] A feast is also inferred from the passage 'the Maundye of Chryste with hys Apostles upon Shere Thursday'.[360] It is interesting here that Shere is used to qualify the Thursday and that Maundye relates to the Last Supper itself. This quoted passage is from a mediæval manuscript[361] and in many other such documents Maundy, or one of its forms, similarly relate to this feast (for example, 'this day is called Schir Thursday or ellis the day of Cristes Maundy, that is Maundy Thursday'[362]). Only later did Maundy displace Sheer, or one of its variants, in the qualification of this Thursday. Furthermore, reference to the Last Supper is also made in the Latin-derived name for the day, namely *Cena Domini*,[363] *Cœna Domini*[364] or *Cœnæ Domini*,[365] as it is variously spelt, and we have 'The daye of Cene that we calle Sherethursdaye' as used in the late fourteenth century.[366] Kingdon further remarks, in connection with this possible derivation, that 'there is a French word, *mandè*, which seems to have been used for a feast, and then for the feast for the poor; and there is an English word, maundy, which means a feast or meal given to the poor. This really seems the best derivation for this name, whether these words have any connection or not with the French *mandè* and the English maund, both of which mean "basket"'.[367] This statement clearly implies that Maundy alludes to the meal which used to be given to the recipents as part of the ceremonial distributions on the day preceding Good Friday.

A maund, which according to Dr Samuel Johnson originates from the Saxon (mand) or French (mande),[368] is an early English word, for a type of wicker or other woven basket, which is now only in use in specific localities.[369,370] The word Maundy has been related to it and has been stated by Johnson to be 'derived by Spelman[371] from mande, a hand-basket in which the king was accustomed to give alms to the poor'.[372] Such an appellation, which seems to confine the term to that part of the Maundy ceremony which consists of the giving of alms,[373] was also favoured by later authors[374] and mentioned by others.[375] However, it was arbitrarily and somewhat abruptly dismissed by Skeat who, with regard to Maundy Thursday, states that 'Spelman's trumpery guess, that the word is derived from *maund*, a basket, is one of the fables which are so greedily swallowed by the credulous',[376] it is 'not connected with maund, a basket',[377] 'the derivation from *maund*, a basket, is wrong'[378] and 'the popular derivation from *maund*, a basket, is utterly wrong'.[379]

To maund, meaning to beg, whose possible sources are the French mendier and quémander, to beg, is a verb used from the sixteenth to the eighteenth century. Relating to it are a maunder, to maunder, a maunderer, maundering, maunding and to maund it, which mean a beggar, to beg, a professional beggar, begging, the act of begging and to go a begging, respectively.[380] In connection with these definitions, the claim was made in 1779 that '*Maundy Thursday* is the *poor people's* Thursday, from the Fr. *maundier*, to beg. The King's liberality to the poor on that Thursday in Lent; a season when they are supposed to have lived very low. *Maundiant* at this day in French is a beggar'.[381] This possible derivation of Maundy, implying begging, has been mentioned, but without any criticism or comment, by several authors.[382]

Notwithstanding all the above, it has been most generally accepted[383] that Maundy is derived from the command, at one time written as commaund,[384] of Jesus at the Last Supper: 'A new commandment have I given under you' *Mandatum novum do vobis* 'that ye love one another; as I have loved you, that ye also love one another'.[385] In fact, these words, spoken by the Lord High Almoner, begin the Maundy service following the processional hymn[386] although this is only of relatively recent innovation for in the Order of Service as given in 1902 no such words are used.[387] However, from records going back to the thirteenth century and beyond, it is clear that the service was always known as the *Mandatum* (mandate) and that the gifts used were supplied *pro mandeto regis*.[388] The same derivation has also led to the day being referred to as *dies mandati* (day of the mandate).[389]

V. VENUES FOR THE MAUNDY SERVICE

The annual Maundy distribution of early times was made at a variety of locations which, being mainly to suit the monarch's own convenience, were often wherever the Court happened to be in residence at Easter. Such venues included Eton, Greenwich (being part of her palace at Greenwich and where Elizabeth I presented many of her Maundies[390]), Richmond, Westminster (Whitehall), and Windsor (where from the twelfth century there was a definite almonry with a tower now known as the Garter Tower[391]). For example, Elizabeth I distributed her Maundies of 1560 and 1572 in the Great Hall at Whitehall[392] and in the Great Hall at the Palace of Greenwich[393], respectively. A proclamation on 23 March 1563/4 announced that her almoner, on her behalf, would distribute the Queen's alms to the poor at Windsor and Eton.[394]

The early Maundies of Charles I were held at Whitehall as, for example, was that in 1633, when the Bishop Almoner deputized for him.[395] However, during the Civil War this became impossible and the distributions were made in whatever city he happened to be occupying at the time. Thus, in 1639[396] and 1642[397], just prior to the War, they were held in York, in both cases his almoner being deputed for the King, and in 1643 and 1644 they were held in Oxford.[398]

Following the Restoration on 9 May 1660, the Maundy service returned to Whitehall and the Banqueting House[399] became the venue for most of these services (for example, that of 1661[400]), an organ being lent for those held there on thirteen occasions between 1662 and 1683.[401] In 1698 the Banqueting House became used as the Chapel Royal.[402] From then until 1813 it also became the regular annual venue for the Maundy ceremony, with the service and the distribution of the Maundy money taking place in the Chapel proper and the clothes and food parcels being distributed in the Ante-chapel.[403] A fine pictorial record of one of these ceremonies, namely that of 1773, exists (Plates 16, 22 and 23).

In 1814, as a consequence of internal building alterations in preparation for musical festivals which were to be held, under the patronage of Queen Charlotte, in aid of Germans who had suffered during the Napoleonic Wars, the Ante-chapel became unavailable for use in the Maundy ceremony. A lean-to building was therefore erected against the Chapel's wall that faced Whitehall Gardens, and extending the whole length of the building. This temporary structure was duly equipped with forms, tables and other necessaries and every effort was made to ensure the comfort of the Maundy recipients. In the event, the clothes and provisions continued to be distributed annually within this temporary building until the distribution of provisions and the dinner were replaced by a monetary allowance after 1837.[404] Indeed, in 1829 the Chapel itself was closed for eight years whilst its roof was reconstructed[405] and during this period the whole of the Maundy service was conducted in the lean-to accommodation. Two contemporary accounts illustrate how the celebration was effected under these transient arrangements. That for 1826 reads:[406]

> MAUNDY THURSDAY:– At his Majesty's Chapel, Whitehall, the usual annual Royal donations were distributed to as many poor men and women as the King is years old, viz. 64 of each. A temporary building had been constructed at the back of Whitehall Chapel for the occasion, which was divided into two compartments, the larger for the reception of the Maundy men and women.
>
> At the ends, seats were prepared for the accommodation of the visitors, who were

admitted by tickets; the smaller room was fitted up with shelves, as a store larder, on which were arranged the salt fish, loaves of bread, etc. to be distributed.

About eleven o'clock the Maundy people arrived, and were arranged by the attendants, the men at one table, and the women at the other.

Morning Service:– The Maundy people being seated, Mr. Hanby, secretary to the lord high almoner, and Mr. James, groom of the almonry, attended by the Yeoman guards, with an usher, ordered the tables to be covered with damask cloths, and supplied every man and woman with a loaf weighing one pound and a half. The attendants then placed on both tables a number of wooden dishes, on which were pieces of fine beef, weighing three and three quarter pounds a-piece. At twelve o'clock, the sub-almoner, the Rev. Dr. Goodenough, entered the room in his robes, attended by the secretary, and having inspected the tickets of admittance of the Maundy people, pronounced the following Grace before Meat:– 'Bless, O Lord, this Royal Maundy to the use of these thy servants, and dispose their hearts to the praise of the Holy Name, with gratitude to their Royal benefactor, through Jesus Christ, our Lord. Amen.'

The Doctor then inspected the quality of the meat, and having seen that all were supplied with a piece of beef, said the Grace after Meat:– 'Grant O Lord, in the hearts of these people grateful obedience to the Royal dispenser of these thy blessings, and cause them to look up to thee as the Supreme Author of every good, through Jesus Christ our Lord.'

The cloths were then removed, and a wooden platter, on which were four loaves, two salt salmon, two salt cod, eighteen salt herrings, and eighteen red ditto, was placed before each person, which the sub-almoner inspected. The distributors then produced several leather flagons filled with ale, and a quantity of wooden ale-cups, out of which the sub-almoner drank to the health of King George 4th, which was also drank [sic] by the recipients, who shortly afterwards departed with their load of provisions.

At two o'clock the recipients re-assembled in the interior of the Chapel, to receive the remainder of the King's Maundy.

Afternoon Service:– At three o'clock the Yeoman usher, followed by eleven Yeoman [sic] in their state dresses, and one bearing a large gold dish, on which were one hundred and twenty eight purses, each purse containing a sovereign, and small silver pennies, as many as the King is years old; Mr. House, the King's serjeant of the vestries; the sub-almoner, followed by two girls and two boys from the Westminster National School, selected for their good conduct; the secretary, and the groom of the almonry, etc. etc., formed in procession, all wearing white scarfs [sic], and carrying nosegays.

Mr. Cooper played a solemn piece, on the procession entering the Chapel.

The procession advanced up the aisle; the sub-almoner and two Yeomen took their station within the altar, the officers and children on seats in front of the organ, and others along the aisle, and etc.

The appropriate Church-service for the day was then read by the Rev. Dr. Vivian, the Rev. Messrs. Knapp, Barham, and Pack.

The gentlemen of the Chapel Royal were Messrs. Gore, Goulden, Molyneux, and the young gentlemen of the Chapel Royal.

The other account refers to the ceremony of 1833,[407] by which time it was being conducted in its entirety in the lean-to building:

His MAJESTY's Royal Maundy was distributed on Thursday to 68 aged and infirm men and 68 women, as many as the KING is years old, all of whom were aged above 60 years, and some of them exceeded the age of 80 years. At twelve o'clock, the officers of the Almonry entered the temporary building at the back of Whitehall Chapel, where the distribution took place. The Maundy people were arranged round tables. The Sub-Almoner having repeated a prayer, shoes and stockings and woollen clothes were distributed. A Yeoman of the guard then advanced, having a large gold dish covered with purses, each purse containing a sovereign and 68 silver penny pieces. A purse was given to each person, commencing with the women. The Officers of the Wine-cellar then presented the Sub-Almoner and attendants with a cup of wine to drink the KING's health. The Maundy men and women were afterwards served, and were permitted to retain the cup. A loaf of bread was then supplied to each person.

The reopening of the Chapel Royal in Whitehall resulted in the return to it, in 1838, of the Maundy ceremony, a report of the service in that year having already been given.[408] A pictorial representation of the distribution being made four years later (Plate 17) clearly shows the interior of the building.

The annual venue for the Maundy service continued to be the Chapel Royal from 1838 until 1890 when the building's use as a chapel ceased and it was lent to the Royal United Service Institute as a home for its museum. Consequent upon this change, which took effect from 1 January 1891[409] and came to an end in 1963 when the building was restored as the Banqueting House, the venue of the Maundy service was moved, by command of Queen Victoria, to Westminster Abbey.[410] It was subsequently held there annually until 1953, with the exceptions of 1902, 1911 and 1937 when it was held in St Paul's Cathedral because the Abbey was being prepared at these times for the coronations of Edward VII, George V and George VI. A report of the service, and related events, as held on 25 March 1937 reads:[411]

> The stately and symbolic ceremony of the Royal Maundy lost nothing of its beauty this year in being transferred from Westminster Abbey, closed in preparation for the Coronation, to St. Paul's Cathedral. It had not been held in the Cathedral since 1911. Although the distribution was not made by the King in person, as was the case last year when King Edward VIII attended the Abbey to bestow alms on the aged poor, there was a large congregation to see the ancient rite performed.
>
> Two members of the Royal Family were present at the service – Princess Helena Victoria and Princess Marie Louise. Both carried nosegays, the modern equivalent of the sweet herbs used in days gone by as a supposed protection against the plague.
>
> A year ago the coins used as Maundy gifts bore the head of King George V. On Thursday some had been specially struck with the image of King George VI. The King is in his forty-second year – as was his brother 12 months ago – so that for two successive years there were 84 recipients of the Maundy – one of each sex for each year of the King's age. Some of the old people on Thursday were so frail that they had to be assisted to and from their seats in the chancel.
>
> As 12 o'clock struck, the procession came up the central aisle to the chancel – a long line of figures whose offices lined up the ceremony with that fuller commemoration centuries ago, when monarchs washed the feet of their humble subjects, as did Christ those of His disciples. Queen Elizabeth herself performed this task at Greenwich Palace, but James I [sic] and subsequent sovereigns deputed the duty to archbishop or bishop, until the custom was abolished.[412]
>
> At the head of the procession was the cross bearer, followed by the choirs of the Chapel Royal and of St. Paul's, the children of the Chapel Royal being in scarlet and gold. Minor canons and prebendaries preceded the Bishop of London, who was supported by the Dean and Chapter of St. Paul's. Then came the sergeant-major of the Yeomen of the Guard, and the yeomen, carrying high above their heads the round dish of silver gilt on which rested the purses containing the Royal alms.
>
> Next followed the children of the Royal Almonry. They were dressed in white and, symbolical of the washing of the disciples feet, were girt with white towels, as were the Gentlemen of the Royal Almonry and, under his cope, the Lord High Almoner, the

Archbishop of Canterbury, before whom walked the Sub-Almoner, Prebendary L. J. Percival. Then came the clergymen in academical robes, representing the recipients of the Royal alms, and, finally, the King's Bodyguard of the Yeomen of the Guard, who marched with stately tread and shouldered blades into the chancel. Here two of the bodyguard detached themselves and took up their positions, like guards, at the head of the choir stalls.

During the procession the hymn 'Praise my soul, the King of Heaven' was sung. The service followed the established form. There were four anthems. While the first distribution of the Maundy purses was taking place – the green, containing £1 15s., to each woman, and the white, with £2 5s., to each man, these amounts being allowances in lieu of clothing – there was sung Wesley's 'Wash me thoroughly from my wickedness.'

In the second distribution the red purses contained 'each £1, representing part of the Maundy: and £1 10s., an allowance in lieu of provisions, formerly given in kind': and the white purses 'as many pence as the King is years of age, and given in Silver Pennies, Twopences, Threepences and Fourpences, being the balance of the Maundy.' The choir, whilst this was in progress, sang Tallis's 'If ye love Me, keep My commandments' and Handel's triumphant 'Zadok, the priest.'

A prayer for the King and the general thanksgiving, followed by the Old Hundredth and the Blessing, brought the service to a close. The National Anthem was sung and the procession passed out of the chancel in the order in which it entered.

The High Commissioner for New Zealand (Mr. W. J. Jordan) and Mr. Walter Nash (Finance Minister) attended the Maundy service and afterwards had luncheon with the Archdeacon of London.

The Abbey was undergoing similar preparation in 1953 for the coronation of Elizabeth II, again necessitating a change of venue for the Maundy service to St Paul's Cathedral.

From 1954 to 1970 the service was held only in alternate years at Westminster Abbey and then again held there in 1973, 1977 and 1981. In the intervening years it took place, by command of the Queen,[413] at the venues listed in Table 3. In connection with the post-1954 services which have been held at locations other than Westminster Abbey, the choice of venue has often been linked either with a visit by the Queen elsewhere in the locality or with an anniversary (Table 3).

The 1957 ceremony at St Albans Cathedral (Plate 19) was the first time in over two hundred years that it had been held outside of London, and its celebration in 1982 in Wales, namely at St Davids Cathedral, was the first outside of England. As yet, its visit to Carlisle in 1978 represents the furthest journey northward for the Royal Maundy. Although a few of the recipients at this service were members of the Church of Scotland in that city, the service itself has not yet crossed the border into Scotland even though, from the time the crowns were united in 1603, this has been theoretically possible.[414] Perhaps one day it might and, indeed, the Queen has recently made a suggestion to this effect.[415] However, such a service would, of necessity, be of an œcumenical nature.[416]

VI. THE MAUNDY RECIPIENTS

In and prior to the early mediæval period, the number of people to whom the Maundy rites were administered on the day preceding Good Friday was usually twelve, symbolic of the number of the Apostles, or thirteen, symbolic of the Apostles together with either Jesus or the angel who, according to tradition, came to the table at which Pope Gregory the Great was serving. Thus, in the ceremonies held at Knaresborough in

Table 3. The venues, other than Westminster Abbey, of the Maundy service since 1953 and the associated anniversary or linked activity of the Queen in the locality

Year	Maundy ceremony venue	Anniversary or linked activity of the Queen in the locality
1955	Southwark Cathedral	Golden jubilee of the Diocese[1] (see also note 2)
1957	St Albans Cathedral	Compliment to its Bishop who had been appointed Lord High Almoner[3]
1959	St George's Chapel, Windsor	Court customarily in residence at Windsor Castle during Easter[4] (see also note 5)
1961	Rochester Cathedral	Five-hundredth anniversary of the granting of the city's charter. Visit also came a few weeks after the enthronement of its new bishop who, some nine years later, was to be appointed as Lord High Almoner[6], (see also note 7)
1963	Chelmsford Cathedral	(see notes 8, 9)
1965	Canterbury Cathedral	The mother-church of the kingdom. Later in the day, the Queen visited Christ Church College[10]
1967	Durham Cathedral	First time in a Northern Province for several centuries, thereby allowing a northern congregation to witness the service[10] (see also note 11)
1969	Selby Abbey	Year in which a special festival was held marking the 900th anniversary of the founding of the abbey[10]
1971	Tewkesbury Abbey	The 500th anniversary of the battle of Tewkesbury and the 850th anniversary of the consecration of the abbey[10]
1972	York Minster	The 500th anniversary of the consecration of the present building[10]
1974	Salisbury Cathedral	Commencement of the commemoration of the founding of the diocese 900 years earlier[12]
1975	Peterborough Cathedral	Where Cardinal Wolsey distributed his Maundy in 1530[13]
1976	Hereford Cathedral	In commemoration of the foundation of the see in the seventh century[13]
1978	Carlisle Cathedral	Founded as an Augustian priory in 1123[13]
1979	Winchester Cathedral	The 900th anniversary of its cathedral[13]
1980	Worcester Cathedral	The 1,300th anniversary of the diocese[13]
1982	St Davids Cathedral	Year after the cathedral building had celebrated its 800th anniversary[14]
1983	Exeter Cathedral	The 850th anniversary of the consecration of the high altar. Also recalled the fact that Stephen Payne, who was High Almoner from 1414 to 1419, was also Dean of Exeter from 1415 to 1419 and it is from his seal that that of the Royal Almonry is probably derived[15]
1984	Southwell Minster	The centenary of its becoming the cathedral of the then new diocese of Southwell[16]
1985	Ripon Cathedral	The 150th anniversary of the then minster becoming the cathedral church of the newly-formed diocese of Ripon and the 1,100th anniversary of the granting of the city's first royal charter, both being celebrated in 1986[17]
1986	Chichester Cathedral	see note 8
1987	Ely Cathedral	Christianity there goes back to 673, it had been a cathedral city since 1109 and four of its bishops had held the office of Lord High Almoner[18]
1988	Lichfield Cathedral	The first cathedral had been consecrated there in 700 and the construction of the present building, the third on the site, was begun in 1195. The Rt Rev. Edward Sydney Woods, the Bishop of Lichfield, was Lord High Almoner from 1946 to 1953[19]

Table 3. *(continued)*

Year	Maundy ceremony venue	Anniversary or linked activity of the Queen in the locality
1989	Birmingham Cathedral	The building had been consecrated in 1715. The centenary of the granting of the city's charter. Afterwards, the Queen formally opened the cathedral's song school and meeting rooms[20] and in the afternoon she opened the New Halls development of the National Exhibition Centre in the city[21] (see also note 22)
1990	Newcastle Cathedral	see note 8

Notes to Table 3: *1*, Tanner (1969), p. 127; *2*, The fact that this service proved to be so successful led to the Queen deciding that, from time to time, it should continue to be held at places other than Westminster Abbey (Tanner (1969), pp. 127–28); *3*, Tanner, p. 128; *4*, Wright (1981), p. 21; *5*, On this occasion the Queen occupied her special stall in the choir as Sovereign of the Order of the Garter (Wright, (1971), p. 18; *6*, Wright (1981), pp. 21, 22; *7*, This was one of the few occasions when all the Maundy recipients were able to be present, a remarkable achievement considering that their average age is around eighty years, and it was the first time that the traditional lessons were read from the New English Bible which had been published earlier that year (Wright (1981), pp. 21, 22); *8*, There was no linked activity or celebration on this occasion (Wright); *9*, An unusual form for the distribution of the gifts occurred on this occasion when, because of the smallness of its Cathedral Church of St Mary the Virgin, St Peter and St Chad, the recipients had to sit on the end seat of each pew in the three aisles and the nave and the distribution followed a figure of eight pattern around the cathedral (Wright (1981), p. 22); *10*, Wright (1981), p. 22; *11*, This was the first time the service was televised (Wright (1981), p. 22); *12*, Wright (1981), pp. 22, 23; *13*, Wright (1981), p. 23; (see also page 37); *14*, ORM, St Davids Cathedral, 8 April 1982, p. 11; *15*, ORM, Exeter Cathedral, 31 March 1983, p. 11 (see also page 79 and Plate 35); *16*, ORM, Southwell Minster, 19 April 1984, p. 11; *17*, ORM, Ripon Cathedral, 4 April 1985, p. 11; *18*, ORM, Ely Cathedral, 16 April 1987, p. 11; *19*, ORM, Lichfield Cathedral, 31 March 1988, p. 11; *20*, ORM, Birmingham Cathedral, 23 March 1989, p. 11; *21*, Wright; *22*, Following this Maundy service, the recipients, together with their companions, were entertained to a buffet-style lunch in the Council House Extension at the invitation of the Lord Mayor and City Council of Birmingham. This was a generous and thoughtful act which, it was hoped, may have created a precedent for the future (Wright). Certainly, such a meal is reminiscent of the Maundy feast of earlier times.

Yorkshire in 1210 and at Rochester in Kent in 1213, John administered his Maundy to thirteen poor men in each case. The fact that, at the time of the latter ceremony, John had reigned for thirteen years, which appears to have been suggested, albeit prior to the documentation relating to the former ceremony had been discovered, as being significant with relation to the number of recipients, would appear to be purely coincidental.[417]

It has been stated that the custom of relating the monarch's age at the time of the ceremony to the number of recipients dates at least as far back as 1363, the year in which the then fifty-year-old Edward III presented gifts to fifty poor men.[418] However, this was not a formal Maundy distribution but was made at a jubilee celebrating the King's fiftieth birthday. Notwithstanding this, an order had in fact been given some two years previously, namely on 20 March 1361, for cloth, footwear and towels for the next *Cena Domini* (Maundy Thursday), the magnitude of this order clearly suggesting that fifty recipients were administered to in the 1361 Maundy ceremony during which the *pedilavium* was also effected. Furthermore, his predecessor, Edward II had, thirty-five years earlier, administered the *pedilavium* to fifty poor men, at a time when he was forty-one years old.[419] Clearly, it would seem that, around this period, fifty was regarded as being the most desirable number of recipients.

It would appear that Henry IV (1399–1413) was the first monarch to decree that the number of Maundy recipients should be related to the sovereign's age.[420] Certainly, by the beginning of the Tudor era and up to the present time, the number of recipients, with the exception of the Maundies of Edward VI, and the number of pence each received in the Gift of Pennies have been related to the monarch's age at the time of the service. This relationship, which has undergone minor variations during this period, can be discussed with reference to the information presented in Tables 1 and 4. This indicates that, for the Maundies of Henry VII and the early Maundies of Henry VIII, the number of recipients was determined by the King's age on his next birthday following the service, plus one more to represent the Year of Grace, the further year which, by God's grace, it was hoped that the monarch might live. Nevertheless, in the majority of the other examples listed in Table 4, the relationship omitted the consideration of the Year of Grace. However, in the 1582 and 1814 Maundies of Elizabeth I and George III, respectively, the number of recipients (in the latter case, both that number of males and females) is the same as the monarch's years of age at the time of the ceremony.[421] Furthermore, although at the time of his first two Maundy distributions, Edward VI was only in the tenth and eleventh year, sequentially, of his life, on each occasion there were twelve recipients, no doubt because twelve was regarded as a minimum since the Apostles were the prototype.[422] Whether that same number of recipients in 1549 represented a continuation of this principle or an attempt to relate to the King's age is unknown: it is unfortunate that no records have as yet been found concerning the number of recipients in 1550, by which time the young King was in the thirteenth year of his age.[423] Accounts of Elizabeth I's Maundies of 11 April 1560,[424] and 17 April 1595,[425] when the Queen was in her twenty-seventh and sixty-second year of age,[426] state that the recipients were twenty and fifty-seven women, respectively. Possibly the Maundy gifts were sent to some recipients who were too infirm to attend the ceremony,[427] a practice also often followed in such situations in more recent Maundy services.[428]

The statement has been made that 'Henry IV (1399–1413) seems to have been the first sovereign who decreed that the recipients should number as many old men and as many old women as he was years of age'.[429] However, prior to the reign of William and Mary, it would appear that only either male or female recipients were chosen, according to the sex of the monarch (Table 4). Then, during the joint reign, William III also made his presentations to men only, in numbers according to his age, although it has been noted that concomitantly 'The Queen doth the like to diverse poor persons', presumably women whose number related to her years of age since it was reported elsewhere 'et la Reine de même à autant de vieilles femmes, qu'elle a d'années'.[430] Furthermore, when Mary, presumably in her husband's absence, distributed the Maundy in 1693, she did so to both men and women in numbers relating to William's and her age, respectively (Table 4).[431]

Clearly, by the time of the joint reign the relationship between the number of Maundy recipients and the age of the sovereign at the time of the ceremony had become well established. Yet, contrary to this, is the narrative by Thomas Delaune in 1690, relating to the Royal Maundy as conducted in that year, in which he states that the recipients were 'as many poor men as his Majesty had reigned years'.[432] However, it is highly likely that Delaune was misinformed upon this point. Interestingly, his account is also unique with respect to the reference to a monetary gift of shillings which, furthermore, he again relates in magnitude to the number of years of the King's

Table 4. Examples of the relationships between the monarch's age, the number of Maundy recipients and the number of pence in the Gift of Pennies

Monarch	Monarch's birthday[1]	Date of the Maundy ceremony[2]	Monarch's age[3]	Number of recipients	Number of pence per recipient	Reference
Henry VII	28 July 1457	8 April 1501	43	45 men	45	4
Henry VIII	28 June 1491	29 March 1510[5]	18	20 men	20	6
Henry VIII	—	3 April 1539	47	48 men	48	7
Edward VI	12 October 1537	7 April 1547	9	12 men	10	8
Edward VI	—	29 March 1548	10	12 men	11	9
Edward VI	—	18 April 1549	11	12 men	12	9
Mary Tudor	18 February 1515/6[10]	2 April 1556	40	41 women	41	11
Elizabeth I	7 September 1533	12 April 1582	48	48 women	48	12
Charles I	19 November 1600	11 April 1639	38	39 men	39	13
Charles II	29 May 1630	11 April 1661	30	31 men	31	14
Charles II	—	16 April 1663	32	33 men	33	15
William and Mary	30 April 1662[16]	13 April 1693	42[17] and 30[18]	43 men and 31 women	see note 19	20
William III	14 November 1650	6 April 1699	48	49 men	48[21]	22
George II	30 October 1683	15 April 1731	47	48 men and 48 women	see note 23	24
George III	4 June 1738	7 April 1814	75	75 men and 75 women	75	25
Victoria	24 May 1819	12 April 1900	80	81 men and 81 women	81	26
George V	3 June 1865	1 April 1915	49	50 men and 50 women[27]	50[28]	29
Elizabeth II	21 April 1926	11 April 1974	47	48 men and 48 women	48	30

Notes to Table 4: *1, DNB;* Freeman-Grenville; *HBC; 2,* Confirmed from the dates given for Easter Days in Cheney, pp. 83–161; *OCEL,* pp. 935–53; *3,* In years, on the occasion of the Maundy service; *4,* PRO, E101/415/3, fo. 49v (see also page 27 and note 95); *5,* Easter Day in 1510 fell on 31 March (Cheney, pp. 83–161; *OCEL,* pp. 935–53) and the Maundy service in that year was held on Good Friday (see page 28); *6,* BL Addit. MS 21481, fo. 25v; *7,* BL Arundel MS 97, fo. 12v; *8,* PRO, Accounts of Sir William Cavendish, vol. 5; *9,* PRO, Accounts of Sir William Cavendish, vol. 6; *10,* See Appendix 3; *11, Calendar of State Papers and Manuscripts; 12,* BL Harl. MS 1644; *13,* Torr, p. 100; Drake, i, p. 137 and footnote *t; 14,* BL Harl. MS 3795; *Mercurius Politicus* (1661); *15,* BL Harl. MS 829; *16,* The birthday of Mary, that of William being given immediately underneath: *17,* The age of William; *18,* The age of Mary; *19,* Not quoted; *20,* Dugdale, p. 71; *21,* See note 213 to Chapter 2; *22, Dawks' Newsletter,* no. 439; *23,* The total gifts cost approximately £4 (see note 217 on page 88); *24, GM,* 1 (1731), p. 172; *25, London Interiors,* pp. 47, 48; Ratcliffe and Wright, p. 14; *26,* Charlton, pp. 213–14; *27,* Some of the recipients could not attend the service and the gifts were therefore sent to them (Farquhar (1929–30), p. 218); *28,* When George V was fifty years old, namely in his fifty-first year, the recipients were fifty-one men and fifty-one women who each received fifty-one Maundy pence (Charlton, p. 215), not fifty men and fifty women who each received fifty Maundy pence as was later stated (*ESC,* pp. 210–11); *29,* Farquhar (1929–30), p. 218; *30,* Wright.

reign. In 1698, the Apostles as a prototype appear to have been reverted to when, in his Maundy of that year, William III administered the *pedilavium* and gave gifts to twelve poor men.[433] Nevertheless, in the following year the number of recipients was related to the King's age in years[434] and from the reign of George I onward they have been an equal number of men and women, the number of each being related to the sovereign's age as shown in Table 4.

Who are the Maundy recipients and how and why are they chosen?

Amongst the Rawlinson manuscripts[435] are several petitions to be placed upon the Maundy list of Charles II, many of them from men who had been wounded in either the Dutch War of 1666 or in the service, presumably during the Civil War, of the King's late father, Charles I. For example, the petition of one Thomas Philip in 1682 reads:

> To the King's most Excell^t Ma^{ty}
> The humble Petition of Thomas philip
> That yor Pet^r lost his left Arme in yor Ma^{ts} Ship the portsmouth upon the 25th of July 1666 in fighting The Dutch, By which he is disabled from Working for his lyvelyhood as formerly.
> May it therefore please yor sacred Ma^{ty} to Signify yor Royall pleasure That yor Pet^r shall be one of yor Ma^{ts} Maundy men to receive yor Ma^{ts} Royall Bounty upon Maundy Thursday next
> And yor Pet^r shall (as in Duty bound) ever pray etc.

That this petition was successful is confirmed by the immediately subsequent entry in the manuscript:

> At the Court at Whitehall Octob^r 29 1682 His Ma^{ty} being sensible of the pet^r's losing of his left Arme in his Ma^{ts} Service and of his poverty, Is etc.[436]

Similarly, the acceptance of several petitions submitted four years earlier for inclusion in the 1678 Maundy list is exemplified by that of one Thomas Collyer, the success of which is indicated by the entry:

> At the Court at Whitehall
> The Pet^r having been Maymed in the service of His Ma^{tys} Royall Father is hereby commended by His Ma^{ty} to the Right Reverend ffather in God John Ld Bp of Rochester Ld Almoner to His Ma^{ty} to admit the Pet^r into the number of such poor men that are to partake of His Ma^{ts} Bounty on Maundy Thursday next.

These manuscripts also include petitions for inclusion in the list of Maundy recipients from men other than those wounded whilst engaged in military service. For example, that of one Robert Ward reads:

> To the King's most Excellent Ma:^{ty}
> The humble Petition of Robert Ward late a Labourer in Scotland Yard.
> That yor Pet^r having served yor Ma^{ty} as a Labourer ever since your happy Restauration, first in yor Ma^{ts} privy Garden and afterwards at yor Ma^{ts} works in Scotland Yard, till such tyme as hee was Maymed there by a fall with a Burthen [burden] upon him, and being seventy three years of age and upwards, very weake, and Infirm, and disabled to do further service by reason thereof, is like to be endured to great poverty unless received by yor Ma^{tys} accustomed Clemonsy and Goodness.
> And therefore most humbly Prayers That yor Ma^{ty} will be gratiously pleased to grant that yor Pet^r may be admitted into the number of such poor old men as are to partake of yor Ma^{ts} Bounty on Maundy Thursday next
> And yor Pet^r shall ever prayer

and its immediately subsequent acceptance reads:

At the Court at Whitehall October 29. 1682 His Ma:^ty in consideration of the Pet^rs long services as a Labourer in his Ma^ts Pryvy Garden, and being maymed by a fall in His Ma^ts Service, and of his now great Age and poverty Is gratiously pleased to Recomend the Pet^r to the Right Revered ffather in God John Ld Bp of Rochester Ld Almoner to His Ma^ty to admit the Pet^r into the number of those poor men who are to partake of His Ma^ts Bounty on Maundy Thursday next.   W. Glascock.

It is interesting that a similar petition had also been successfully submitted by Ward in 1678: clearly then, as until 1957,[437] it was possible for Maundy recipients to receive such a gift on more than one occasion.

Although the above and others of the petitioners referred to in these manuscripts were ultimately placed on the Maundy list, there were far too many in total for all so to succeed. It was probably partly to reduce this pressure on the funds available for the Royal Maundy that Charles II founded the Royal Hospital at Chelsea for the treatment and care of those disabled by wounds or old age.[438]

An interesting recipient of the Royal Maundy around the turn of the eighteenth century was Mrs Frances Ochs, the widow of John Ralph Ochs junior who, prior to his death in July 1788, had been an engraver at the Tower Mint until 1787 and a Mint employee for some fifty years.[439] Some few weeks following her husband's death, Mrs Ochs was appointed, on 20 August 1788, as office sweeper at the Mint at an annual salary of £10.[440] This appointment was used, basically, as a means of providing the late former Second Engraver's widow with a source of income since the work involved could be delegated for a much lower sum. Further evidence for this policy is apparent in a letter dated 10 October 1806, subsequent to Mrs Ochs' death earlier in the year, from the Deputy Master to the Master of the Mint. This letter indicated not only that by her death had the office sweeper's post become vacant, but that for a long time before her death Mrs Ochs had been infirm and quite helpless from age, and consequently the sweeping had been carried out for upwards of sixteen years by one of the Deputy Master's servants who was then residing at the office.[441] Another manifestation of the Mint's caring for Mrs Ochs is apparent in the Master's annual successful recommendation that she become a recipient of the King's Maundy. Thus, on 1 March 1797 the Deputy Master sent to the Master the usual petition of Mrs Ochs to become a partaker of His Majesty's Maundy, annexing along with this the Master's recommendation which he had had the goodness to sign in former years.[442] Similarly, in 1803 we find the Deputy Master sending to the Master for Mrs Och's petition with which he had called the day before.[443] Some two years later, on 20 March 1805, the Deputy Master is once again recorded as forwarding to the Master the yearly petition from Mrs Ochs to partake in the King's bounty at Easter on the recommendation of the Master and requesting the signing of a letter to the Archbishop of York[444] which would make sure of her so partaking.[445]

Generally speaking, in earlier times when the Maundy service was confined to London,[446] the recipients were recommended by that city's clergy from those applying to the Royal Almonry for assistance, preference being given to those who had formerly been householders and had paid rent and taxes, and to those who had been employers but had fallen on hard times.[447] Indeed, regarding the qualities of the recipients at the turn of the nineteenth century, it was stated in 1902 that 'the people who are selected for this class of charity [the Royal Maundy] are of a somewhat superior position to those receiving gifts from other classes',[448] a similar sentiment having also been expressed in 1893.[449]

Furthermore, when the service was confined to the Capital, a situation which prevailed for over two hundred years until 1956, it had been possible for the recipients, having once been admitted to the Maundy list, to remain on it for the rest of their lives.[450] In effect, they regarded the gift as a small pension and an honoured privilege.[451] In these circumstances, a royal succession would usually result in there being too many potential recipients for the first Maundy service of the new reign. According to tradition, the Maundy list was immediately reduced to a number corresponding to those required, those being selected who had been longest on the list. The remainder were placed in a supernumerary position and were provided for out of surplus funds[452] until they may have been elected to fill vacancies, caused by death or otherwise, in the list or to meet the requirement of the further male and female recipients as each year passed: in the meanwhile, no new appointments were made.[453] Thus, for example, the first Maundy distribution that took place during the reign of Victoria, namely that on 12 April 1838, required only nineteen males and nineteen females as recipients since the new Queen was then in the nineteenth year of her age. However, her late uncle, William IV, had been born on 21 August 1765 and had died on 20 June 1837[454] and for the next distribution of his reign, had he lived, seventy-three male and seventy-three female recipients would have thus been required. Clearly, the requirement for the first distribution of Victoria's reign could not accommodate all the potential recipients on the late King's accumulated list. Consequently, Victoria ordered that these potential recipients of her late uncle's who would not therefore attend the distribution should still receive their payments at the Royal Almonry. That this was effected is confirmed by a contemporary report of the 1838 Maundy service which begins:[455]

> The Queen's Royal alms were distributed yesterday at Whitehall Chapel. According to ancient usage, the number of men and women who partook of the Royal Maundy upon this occasion was reduced to the age of the Sovereign. The poor and aged persons exceeding that number, who were upon the Royal Maundy lists of his late Majesty William IV, have been placed on supernumerary lists, to fall into vacancies as they occur, and will continue to receive the Royal charity during their lives.

and by another report which appeared three days later:[456]

> The Queen's Royal alms were distributed on Saturday by Mr. Hanby, at the Almonry-office, to the Maunday men and women placed on the supernumerary lists, owing to the difference of the ages between the late King and her present Majesty. Both men and women received 2*l*. 10s. and 19 silver pennies (being the age of the Queen). To the men woollen and linen clothing, shoes and stockings were given, and to the women in lieu of clothing 1*l*. 15s. each. The Maunday men and women also received 1*l*. 10s., a commutation instead of the provisions heretofore distributed.

Similarly, in February 1901, after the death of Victoria, at the age of eighty-one years, on 22 January 1901,[457] the Lord High Almoner petitioned Edward VII, who had been born on 9 November 1841,[458] to follow the precedent adopted on the demise of William IV. The new King consented to this proposal. As a result, the numbers of men and women on the late Queen's list of Maundy recipients were reduced to the numbers required according to Edward VII's age and the other surviving recipients of the last Maundy of the previous reign were placed on a supplementary list, to be absorbed as vacancies occurred. It was further ordered that in the meantime no fresh appointments were to be made.[459]

In 1957, after over two hundred years, the Maundy service was held for the first time outside London, namely at St Albans. This necessitated a revision of the rules relating to the selection of recipients who in that year were chosen from within the boundaries of the St Albans diocese. Consequently, it was decided that in future years a successful applicant should receive the gift on the one occasion only. However, in order to honour the earlier promise, recipients selected prior to 1956 received an equivalent sum by post and were given the opportunity still to attend the service whenever it was held in London.[460]

The Maundy recipients are chosen from the elderly (Plate 32), namely those who are over sixty[461] or sixty-five[462] years old. For example, in the 1965, 1969 and 1971 Maundy services the average ages of the male and female recipients were eighty-one and eighty, seventy-six and seventy-six, and seventy-five and seventy-seven, respectively.[463] Furthermore, one of the female recipients in 1965 was the first known Maundy centenarian of recent time although one of those in the 1633 ceremony and one in receipt of the 1766 distribution claimed to be 104 and 105 years old, respectively.[464] Some 200 years later, in 1838, it was reported that 'Elizabeth Love, a Maundy woman, aged 110, died on Saturday last'.[465] Maundy recipients can be selected from anywhere in the United Kingdom. For convenience this is in practice usually limited to the area where the ceremony is being held and they are chosen, upon the recommendation of the local clergymen, for the service they have given to the Church or community,[466] a principle that is attested to by the information presented in Table 5.

It is apparent that well over a hundred years ago the concept of royal charity was subject to adverse criticism since, in 1875, it was thought necessary to write 'so far from censuring or despising such acts of condescension on the part of the royal and noble towards their poorer brethren and sisters, we ought rather to regret that so few opportunities occur in a year for bringing into contact and contrast the squalid poverty of "St. Giles" with the wealth and luxury of "St. James" '.[467] This statement, made at a time by which the Maundy distribution had become firmly established as being confined to London, appears to accept the then contemporary status quo with regard to the heinous social injustices appertaining throughout society, the 'good olde days', by unquestionably highlighting such gross dissimilarities in living standards. Even worse, it accepts such deprivation within the Capital in that it provided the platform for *noblesse oblige*.

The current method by which the Maundy recipients are selected and, moreover, of the Maundy distribution in general, has also been subject to modern censure.[468] Following the statement that for the Royal Maundy 'the old people are carefully selected from the area's respectable poor', the censurer continues that 'it takes a short walk, down the Embankment to Waterloo Bridge and across to Waterloo Station, to see that, at any rate in Westminster, more needy people may be found on every park bench late at night'. Furthermore, whilst subsequently acknowledging that 'the ceremony is, of course, symbolic', which presumably thereby justifies the current method and criteria employed in choosing the recipients, the critic proceeds 'though it is perhaps unfortunate that it symbolizes a kind of charity that is outdated: doles from on high to those who will surely be receiving such attention from the state as they require. The conception of the "deserving poor" dies hard, and goes some way towards explaining why charity is so often so disliked by the working class. In the past it has seemed to demand of its recipient, not just gratitude, nor even just exemplary conduct,

Table 5. The ages of the Maundy recipients in 1969[1] and the varying reasons given for their being chosen as such

Age in years	Reason for their being chosen as a Maundy recipient
	MALE RECIPIENTS
86	A conscientious worker all his life in the Congregational and Anglican churches; lay preacher for 65 years
——	A willing helper in his local village to every community organisation, namely the British legion, cricket club, W.I., etc.
85	Long service as verger, bellringer and sidesman. Active member of christian study group
——	Has served twenty-three years on Road Safety committee, school governor and considerable public relations work in industry
83	Service in both wars, fifteen years voluntary service to the National Savings movement and a churchwarden for twenty-eight years
81	During fifty years service to his Parish Church he has held virtually every office at some time or another in which it is possible to serve
——	Billeting officer in the last war; regarded in his neighbourhood as the most kindly man in the Parish
80	Local historian, life chairman of Ottley Cottage Homes Trust, youth management work, billeting officer and food and shelter adviser in the last war
——	Three times Mayor of Goole, diocesan reader for 40 years and at present Chairman of the Goole Darby and Joan Club
79	Highly respected citizen, well known for his charitable works for the poor and needy in the St Vincent Society
78	Has been blind for twenty-five years but in that time has influenced many young lives by his christian standards and teaching
——	Retired Methodist minister and former chaplain to R.A.F., to several hospitals and to the National Children's Home
77	Forty-seven years service as a doorman and collector at Boston Spa
——	Baptised, confirmed and married in Selby Abbey. For thirty-five years headmaster of Church School, Clerk to the Parish Council
76	Active Sunday School worker, secretary of the Children's Society, has served the British Legion since 1920. During the war he and his wife cared for fourteen evacuees
——	Considerable public service as a magistrate, councillor, school governor and trade union official
——	Trained the Selby Abbey choirboys for forty years and has raised over £1000 himself for local charities
——	Served with the RAMC for sixteen years, has served the aged and poor, he is a 'great and kindly character and his religion is deep and sincere'
——	While organist of his local church, he maintained and repaired the church bells and the turret clock and raised £300 himself to have the organ repaired
75	An active Salvation Army worker for fifty-eight years
——	He has devoted the whole of his active life to the voluntary service of the church and community. For forty-three years he looked after the Church garden and the boiler!
——	Regular communicant and church worker, caring in a voluntary capacity for the churchyard and the war memorial
——	Holds the B.E.M. for long service to the agricultural community; keen churchman and an outstanding character in Malton
74	A man who associates himself with all church and good cause efforts in the village in which he lives
——	Clerk to the Parish Council, churchwarden for half a century and local councillor
73	Has been a blood donor since 1927, life governor of York hospital and a Methodist local

Table 5. *(continued)*

Age in years	Reason for their being chosen as a Maundy recipient
——	preacher for twenty-one years
——	Started the West Riding library service, secretary of the National Savings movement, special constable, village school teacher and member of the Parochial Council for thirty years
——	Active member of the British Legion, Parochial Church councillor, and forty years service to the local church
——	Clerk to parochial charities, service with the British Legion, Northern Dairies' welfare, R.A.O.B. and childrens' sports
72	Has helped to run a Darby and Joan Club for many years. A voluntary verger and a chorister for fifty years
——	In addition to Sunday School and Youth training, he has served TocH and Lifeboat Institution and helped to start a local swimming club and blood donor panel
71	Has specialised in helping the old and infirm. Former youth worker, special constable and twenty years service to the Parish Council
——	Despite the fact that he lost two sons in action in the War, he has continued to give much service to Church work
——	Active service in both wars, forty-three years service to the Parish Council and a chorister for over half a century
70	Hospital visitor for thirty years; considerable service to orphans and the blind; has helped to promote good music in Selby
69	Former youth worker and steward in Selby Congregational Church
——	Apart from nursing an ailing wife for many years, he has devoted most of his spare time to visiting and helping the sick in local hospitals
——	Thirty years service in the Royal Observer Corps, an extremely generous man and church organist for forty years
68	Youth leader, sports organiser, ran a Forces Canteen in the War, fifteen years work for 'Save the Children Fund'
67	Special constable, a verger for thirty years, a loyal Church worker in every way
66	Red Cross worker, twenty years as secretary of Agricultural Workers Union, considerable work in Church and Sunday School affairs
——	Over fifty years service to his Church as sexton, gardener, verger, bellringer; also a chorister when he was not acting as organ blower!
65	A lifetime of service to the Scout movement and various young people's organisations. A Methodist local preacher for forty-three years

FEMALE RECIPIENTS

100[2]	Sunday school teaching and Youth work. Now almost blind
91	Has actively supported several charitable organisations, enrolling member of the Mother's Union
——	Sick visitor and baby sitter. Has cared for altar linen for thirty years. Known and loved in the village of Terrington
86	Oldest inhabitant at South Milford. Service to church and community in many ways. Always raising money for good causes
——	Regular attender at Parish Church. Sunday School teacher. Has known real poverty but never complains
85	National Savings group collector, Women's Institute member and secretary for fifteen years. Twenty-three years service as a Methodist steward
——	Her vicar writes an essay of 350 words concerning her many good works and activities, mainly to the sick and elderly, and the church as a whole, never accepting a penny for expenses

(continued)

Table 5. *(continued)*

Age in years	Reason for their being chosen as a Maundy recipient
84	Secretary of a Baptist Sisterhood for forty years and active choir member. Bible class leader
——	A soldier's widow and has served and made things for the church for over fifty years. Has also helped the British Legion
82	By personal effort she has raised several hundred pounds for the Church. Ready to help anyone at anytime
——	Widow of Salvation Army Officer, and continues to serve the Selby Corps in a most active way
80	Service to Mothers' Union and Women's Institute. Has shown great courage in adversity and overcome physical disabilities
79	Widow of Borough Surveyor. W.V.S. work in War. Service to Church choir and York Musical Society
——	Life long church worker in Sunday School and Mothers' Union. Member of Parish Council and Women's Institute.
——	Voluntary sacristan for twenty years and, as member of Catholic Women's Needlework Guild, helped to provide for the children of unmarried mothers
——	Ardent Church missionary worker. Y.W.C.A. service and inaugurated the Yorkshire services of Women's World day of Prayer
78	Y.M.C.A. canteen worker and British Red Cross duties. Hospital visitor and Sunday School worker for twenty-five years
——	Founder member of local Townswomen's Guild. Considerable service to R.S.P.C.A., W.R.V.S., R.N.L.I. and Dr Barnado's
——	Often deputizes for the vicar to preach in an Old People's Home. Retired schoolteacher. Sunday School superintendent, organist, helper at Darby and Joan Club
77	W.R.V.S. duties for twenty-six years. Church magazine distributor and Clothing Officer for Selby U.D.C.
——	Home-help, active sick visitor; has looked after and cleaned the Village Hall and distributed magazines for the Church
——	Cared for evacuees during the War. Housekeeper at the vicarage. Regular church worshipper and helper
——	Health visitor, care of school clinics, district nurse and midwife, loyal church worker
76	Founder Women's Institute committee member, thirty years on Parish Council, choirmistress at church, Mothers' Union secretary, etc.
——	Health visitor, St. John's Ambulance work, started and now runs an Over-sixty Club. The 'mother of the village' at Church Fenton
75	Fifty years service to the Catholic Women's League; keen worker for Oxfam and Church missions
74	Being the widow of a verger, she has spent many years looking after the church linen, sick visiting, etc.
——	W.V.S. war duties, 'meals on wheels' service, and a leading light in promoting Save the Children Fund and a local Darby and Joan Club
73	Service to Darby and Joan Club and Women's Institute, Methodist Church organist for fifty-six years and still going strong!
——	W.R.V.S. and Civil Defence service for fifteen years. Has continued active social work despite acute arthritis
——	Her family have a tradition of service to the Church and community covering three centuries. She has organised National Savings and Mothers' Union and been President of the Women's Institute for twenty-one years
72	Many years service to the Parish Council, Women's Institute and Church of England Children's Home
——	In her village she is loved by all; cares for the sick and dying; she started an Over-sixty Club and a foot clinic for the elderly

Table 5. *(continued)*

Age in years	Reason for their being chosen as a Maundy recipient
——	Forty years service to Women's Institute and thirteen years to Darby and Joan Club. Local treasurer of Church of England Children's Society, vice-chairman of Old People's Centre
71	Many years service in helping the blind, 'meals on wheels' and National Children's Home. Methodist class leader
70	Sick visitor to Homes and Hospitals and local Church magazine distributor, a woman of fine christian character
69	Service in World War I, and in the W.L.A. in World War II. On Parish Council for fifteen years and School Management Board
——	Has served on several Scout and Guide committees, Mothers' Union and Church Council
——	Active church worker and secretary of the Union of Catholic Mothers for several years
——	Has helped in Brownies, Y.M.C.A., W.R.V.S., Guides, Missions to Seaman, British Red Cross – to name but a few!
67	During the war her home was an emergency 'Rest Home' for Officers and evacuees. Leader in W.R.V.S. and Darby and Joan Club
65	Town missioner and Sunday School worker; an active, wise and charitable soul
——	A great comforter to the lonely and the sick. Has cared for scores of bedridden people

Notes to Table 5: *1*, This Maundy service was held in Selby Abbey on 3 April 1969. The recipients, forty-three men and forty-three women, had average ages of seventy-five and seventy-seven years, respectively. They were chosen from churches of various denominations from an area corresponding roughly with the Archdeaconry of York, and a few places to the south of Selby which have a special historical link with Selby Abbey; *2*, There was a centenarian on the list of Maundy recipients when the service was held in Canterbury Cathedral in 1965 but the lady in question was unable to attend on the day. However, another centenarian, Ada Daniel, both had all her faculties and was in attendance to receive her Maundy gifts at the service held in York Minster in 1972 (Wright).

but submission to an economic and social *status quo*'. Perhaps the reintroduction of the *pedilavium* into the service for the Royal Maundy would obviate at least some of this condemnation!

VII. THE ROYAL ALMONRY

In former times, all great men, learned institutions, such as the Colleges and the Inns of Court, and, before the Reformation, every monastery in England had, as an important officer of their households, an almoner whose business it was to distribute alms to the poor. In this practice, the monarch was no exception.

Many examples have already been quoted whereby, during the Maundy service, either the High Almoner or the Sub-almoner deputized totally for the monarch in the latter's absence or distributed the Maundy gifts on behalf of his sovereign when the latter performed the associated *pedilavium*. Even when not so deputizing at the service, it was, and still is, the High Almoner's duty to be in attendance upon his king or queen at this time.

The office of High Almoner, or Lord High Almoner as it is also styled, is one of great antiquity and dignity. Appointment to it is made by the sovereign by Letters Patent under the Great Seal. Whilst during early times, the position was almost always bestowed on one of the monarch's chaplains, who was known as the King's Almoner or as Our Almoner, lately the office has been usually held by a bishop or by a distinguished ecclesiastic. The first half of the thirteenth century witnessed sometimes two or three almoners in office at the same time but John Leukenor, the holder of the position from 1228 to 1245, is the one who is the most frequently mentioned (Table 6), the others being what we would now call Sub-almoners.[469]

By the fifteenth century, the office had increased in prestige. For example, in 1440 John de la Bere was granted the position of Great Almoner for life and in 1476 John Gunthorpe is described as the King's High Almoner. Although High Almoner remains the official title, the holder of the office is usually referred to as the Lord High Almoner and was formerly recognized as one of the Great Officers of State, sharing the title of High only with the Lord High Chancellor, the Lord High Treasurer, the Lord High Constable and the Lord High Admiral.[470]

The High Almoner should not be confused with the Hereditary Grand Almoner, this being an ancient title which is held, by hereditary descent, by the Marquess of Exeter. Described by Burke as 'joint Hereditary Grand Almoner in fee', his only duty was to take part in the procession at the coronation of the sovereign and to distribute the coronation medals amongst those assembled. Nevertheless, although the Hereditary Grand Almoner was present at Queen Victoria's coronation, the throwing of the medals was not done by his Lordship but by the Treasurer of the Household.[471]

Today, the duties of the Lord High Almoner are far less onerous than they were previously. For example, in the reign of Edward I, the unknown author of *Fleta* (II., c.23) tells us:[472]

> The High Almoner has to collect the fragments from the Royal table, and distribute them daily to the poor, to visit the Sick, poor widows, prisoners, and other persons in distress; he reminded the King about the bestowal of his alms, especially on Saints' Days, and was careful that the cast-off robes, which were often of high price, should not be bestowed on players, minstrels or flatterers, but their value given to increase the King's Charity.

and in 1755 it was recorded:[473]

> The Lord High Almoner disposes of the King's Alms, and for that use receives (besides other moneys allowed by the King) all deodands[474] and *bona felonum de se* to be that way disposed. Moreover, the Lord High Almoner hath the privilege to give the King's dish to whatsoever poor men he pleases; that is, the first dish at dinner which is set upon the King's table, or instead thereof *4d. per diem*. Next he distributes to twenty-four poor men, nominated by the parishioners of the parish adjacent to the King's Palace of residence, to each of them 4d. in money, a twopenny loaf, and a gallon of beer, or instead thereof 3d. in money, to be equally divided among them every morning at seven of the clock at the court-gate; and every poor man, before he receives the Alms, is to repeat the Creed and the Lord's Prayer in the presence of one of the King's Chaplains, deputed by the Lord Almoner to be his Sub-Almoner; who is also to scatter new-coined twopences in the towns and places where the King passeth through in his progress, to a certain sum by the year. Besides there are many poor pensioners to the King and Queen below stairs, that is, such as are put to pension, either because they are so old that they are unfit for service, or else the widows of such of His Majesty's Household servants that died poor, and were not able to provide for their wives and children in their life-times; everyone of these hath a competency duly paid them.

Apart from a small fee, currently paid in Maundy coins, for attendance at the Maundy service,[475] the only emolument known to have been attached to the office of Lord High Almoner was the right in earlier times to occupy an official residence in

Table 6. High Almoners as known to date[1]

Dates	Name and notes
c. 1103–c. 1130	WILLIAM THE ALMONER
1159–77(?)	FROGER
	Archdeacon of Derby c. 1155; Bishop of Seez c. 1160
1177 (June)–1189 (Feb.)[2]	ROGER THE TEMPLAR
1210[2]–11	THOMAS THE ALMONER
–1228	JOHN BRAZ d. 1228
1228 ⎱ –36	JOHN LEUKENOR (or LE ARKER)
1229 ⎰	The Templar; Warden of Ospringe Hospital
	GEOFFREY (DE SUTTON)
	The Templar
1236 ⎫	JOHN LEUKENOR (as above)
1236 ⎬ –40	GEOFFREY (as above)
1236[2] ⎭	W(ALTER LE BUTILER) 'the Almoner'
1240 ⎫	JOHN LEUKENOR (as above)
1240 ⎬ –42	WALTER LE BUTILER 'our Almoner' (as above)
1241[2] ⎭	BRO. RICHARD 'the King's Almoner'
1242 ⎫	JOHN LEUKENOR (as above)
1242[2] ⎬ –45	ROGER DE CRAMFELD 'the King's Almoner'
1243[2] ⎭	WALTER (LE BUTILER) (as above)
1245–53	ROGER DE CRAMFELD (as above)
	The Templar
1253(?)–1256	SIMON THE CHAPLAIN
	'Sometime the King's Almoner'
1257(?)–1280(?)	JOHN DE COLCHESTER
	Chaplain to the King
1284[2]–1305[2]	HENRY DE BLUNTESDON
	Archdeacon of Dorset 1297–1316
1306–12[2]	JOHN DE LECK
	Bishop of Dunkeld 1309–12; Archbishop of Dublin 1311–13
1312–16[2]	BERNARD DE KIRKEBY
	Vicar of Collegiate Ch. of Norton 1311–15
1316(?)–27[2]	ADAM DE BROME
	Founder and Provost of Oriel Coll., Oxon., 1326–32; Archdeacon of Stowe 1320; d. 12 June 1332
1327[2]	WALTER DE LONDON
	Prebendary of London c. 1331–36; Dean of Wells 1335–50; d. 1350
c. 1340–?	PHILIP WESTON
	Prebendary of London 1338
1348–49	JOHN DE LA CHAMBRE
	Dean of Windsor 1348–49; d. June 1349
1355[2]–67[2]	THOMAS DE KEYNES
	Dean of St Stephen's, Westminster; 1355–67; d. 1367
1371[2]–73[2]	ROBERT DE WHITBERGH
1377[2]–84[2]	WILLIAM WALSHAM
1392[2]–98[2]	RICHARD FELDE or DE LA FELD (ATFELD)
	Canon of Windsor 1390–1401; d. 1401
1400 (March)[2]–?	ROBERT ESLAKBY
1402–13	ROBERT GOWE (or GOUGH)
	Canon of Windsor 1400–32
1414–19	STEPHEN PAYNE
	Dean of Exeter 1415–19; d. May 1419
1422–31	JOHN SNELL
	Archdeacon of London 1422–31; Canon of Windsor 1425–31; (resigned 1431)

(continued)

Table 6. *(continued)*

1431–32	JOHN DE LA BERE (*see below*)
	King's Clerk
1432–38	ROBERT FELTON
	Canon of Windsor 1428–32; Prebendary of London 1433–38; d. 1438
1439/40–47	JOHN DE LA BERE
	Prebendary of Exeter 1434; Dean of Wells 1446; Bishop of St Davids 1447
1448–67[2]	HENRY SEVER
	1st Provost of Eton College 1440–42; Prebendary and Chancellor of St Paul's Cathedral 1449–71; Warden of Merton Coll., Oxon., 1455–71
1468–76	JOHN GUNTHORPE
	Warden of King's Hall, Cambridge, 1467; Archdeacon of Essex 1472–78; Dean of Wells 1472–98
1476 (February–November)	ALEXANDER DE LYE (LEE)
	Canon of Windsor 1469–80
1476 (November)–1483[2]	THOMAS DANETT
	Principal of St Alban Hall, Oxon., 1468–83; Dean of Windsor 1481–83; d. 19 September 1483
1483 (May–December)	WALTER FELDE (or FIELD)
	Provost of King's Coll., Cambridge, 1479–99
1483 (December)–1485	JOHN TAILLOUR
	(Probably the John Taylor who was Provost of Oriel Coll., Oxon., 1478–92, and Chancellor of Exeter Cathedral *c.* 1486)
1485–95	CHRISTOPHER URSWICK
	Prebendary of St Stephen's, Westminster, 1485; Dean of York 1488–94; of Windsor 1496–1505
1495–97	RICHARD FITZJAMES
	Warden of Merton College, Oxon., 1483–1507; Bishop of Rochester 1497; of Chichester 1504; of London 1506–22
1497–(?)1504	RICHARD MAYHEW
	President of Magdalen College, Oxon., 1480–1505; Bishop of Hereford 1504–16
(?)1504–07	CHRISTOPHER BAINBRIDGE
	Dean of York 1503; of Windsor 1505; Bishop of Durham 1507–08; Archbishop of York 1508–14; Cardinal 1512
1507–09	JOHN EDNAM (or EDENHAM)
	Archdeacon of Taunton 1505; of Norwich 1508; Prebendary and Treasurer of St Paul's, London, 1509
1509–14	THOMAS WOLSEY
	Dean of Lincoln 1509; Bishop of Lincoln 1514; Archbishop of York 1514; Cardinal 1515
1514–21	RICHARD RAWLINS
	Canon of Windsor 1508, Warden of Merton College, Oxon., 1508–21; Bishop of St David's 1523–26
1521–23	JOHN LONGLAND
	Dean of Salisbury 1514–21; Bishop of Lincoln 1521–47
1523–31	EDWARD LEE
	Archdeacon of Colchester 1523; Canon of St Stephen's, Westminster, 1530; Archbishop of York 1531–45
1532–38	EDWARD FOX
	Provost of King's Coll., Camb., 1528–38; Bishop of Hereford 1535; d. 1538

Table 6. *(continued)*

1539–(?)1547	NICHOLAS HEATH Archdeacon of Stafford 1534; Bishop of Rochester 1540; of Worcester 1543; Archbishop of York 1555–60
1547–53	RICHARD COX Dean of Ch. Ch., Oxon., 1546–53; of Westminster 1549; Bishop of Ely 1559–81
1553–56	GEORGE DAY Bishop of Chichester 1543–51 and 1554–56; d. 1556
1556–58	FRANCIS MALLET Canon of Windsor 1543–70; Prebendary of Westminster 1553–58; Dean of Lincoln 1554–70
1558–61	WILLIAM BILL Master of Trin. Coll., Camb., 1558; Dean of Westminster 1560–61; d. 15 July 1561
1561–72	EDMUND GHEAST (or GUEST) Bishop of Rochester 1560–71; of Salisbury 1571–77
1572–76	EDMUND FREAKE Bishop of Rochester 1572; of Norwich 1575; of Worcester 1584–93
1576–90	JOHN PIERS (or PEIRSE) Bishop of Rochester 1576; of Salisbury 1577; Archbishop of York 1589–95
1590–96	RICHARD FLETCHER Bishop of Bristol 1589; of Worcester 1593; of London 1594–96; d. 15 June 1596 (1595 TOBIE MATTHEW, Bishop of Durham, acted as Deputy Lord High Almoner. The reason was that Bishop Fletcher had offended Queen Elizabeth I by his second marriage (February 1595), was forbidden the Court and suspended from exercising episcopal functions)
1597–1605	ANTHONY WATSON Bishop of Chichester 1596; d. 10 September 1605
1605–19	LANCELOT ANDREWES Dean of Westminster 1601–05; Bishop of Chichester 1605; of Winchester 1619–26
1619–28	GEORGE MONTAIGNE Bishop of Lincoln 1617; of London 1621; of Durham 1627; Archbishop of York 1628; d. 24 October 1628
1628 (July)	BARNABY POTTER Provost of Queen's Coll., Oxon., 1615–26; Bishop of Carlisle 1628/9–41
1629–(?)1638	FRANCIS WHITE Bishop of Norwich 1629; of Ely 1631–38; d. February 1638
1639[2]–45	WALTER CURLL Bishop of Winchester 1632; deprived 1645
1660–62	BRIAN DUPPA Bishop of Winchester 1660–62; d. March 1662
1662–75	HUMPHREY HENCHMAN Bishop of Salisbury 1660; of London 1663–75; d. October 1675
1675–83 (November)	JOHN DOLBEN Dean of Westminster 1662–83; Bishop of Rochester 1666–83; Archbishop of York 1683–86
1684 (March)–1689	FRANCIS TURNER Dean of Windsor 1683–84; Bishop of Rochester 1683–84; of Ely 1684–90

(continued)

Table 6. *(continued)*

1689–1702	WILLIAM LLOYD
	Bishop of St Asaph 1680; of Lichfield and Coventry 1692; of Worcester 1700–17
1703 (February)–1714	JOHN SHARP
	Archbishop of York 1691–1714; d. February 1714
1714 (March)–1715	GEORGE SMALRIDGE
	Dean of Ch. Ch., Oxon., 1713–19; Bishop of Bristol 1714–19
1715^2–18	WILLIAM NICOLSON
	Bishop of Carlisle 1702–18; of Derry 1718; Archbishop of Cashel 1727
1718–23^2	RICHARD WILLIS
	Bishop of Gloucester 1714; of Salisbury 1721; of Winchester 1723–34
1723^2–43	LANCELOT BLACKBURNE
	Bishop of Exeter 1717; Archbishop of York 1724–32; d. April 1743
1743–47^2	THOMAS SHERLOCK
	Bishop of Salisbury 1734; of London 1748–61
1747^2–58	MATTHEW HUTTON
	Archbishop of York 1747–57; of Canterbury 1757–58; d. March 1758
1758–61	JOHN GILBERT
	Archbishop of York 1757–61; d. 9 August 1761
1761–76	HONBLE. ROBERT HAY-DRUMMOND
	Archbishop of York 1761–76; d. December 1776
1777 (January)–1807	WILLIAM MARKHAM
	Archbishop of York 1777–1807; d. November 1807
1808–47	HONBLE. EDWARD HARCOURT
	Archbishop of York 1807–47; d. November 1847
1847–69	SAMUEL WILBERFORCE
	Bishop of Oxford 1846; of Winchester 1869–73
1870–82	HONBLE. GERALD WELLESLEY
	Dean of Windsor 1854–82; d. September 1882
1882–1906	LORD ALWYNE COMPTON
	Dean of Worcester 1879–86; Bishop of Ely 1886–1905; d. April 1906
1906–33	JOSEPH ARMITAGE ROBINSON
	Dean of Westminster 1902–11; of Wells 1911–33; d. May 1933
1933–45	COSMO GORDON LANG
	Archbishop of Canterbury 1928–42; d. December 1945
1946–53	EDWARD SYDNEY WOODS
	Bishop of Lichfield 1937–53; d. January 1953
1953–70 (resigned)[3]	EDWARD MICHAEL GRESFORD JONES
	Bishop of St Albans 1950–69[4]; d. October 1983
1970–88 (resigned)[3]	RICHARD DAVID SAY
	Bishop of Rochester 1961–88
1988 to date[3]	JOHN BERNARD TAYLOR
	Bishop of St Albans 1980 to date

Notes to Table 6: *1*, Tanner (1957–58); *2*, There is doubt as to the exact date of the appointment, resignation, or death of the person named but there is a definite reference to him as the King's Almoner in that particular year; *3*, Wright; *4*; *Who's Who*, 1981, p. 1056.

Scotland Yard.[476,477] However, the following extract from Bishop Samuel Wilberforce's letter to Mr Gladstone of 21 September 1869, announcing his resignation of the office, shows that it had advantages other than emoluments:[478]

> I will not disguise from you that it is a great surrender: 1st, from its connection with the Queen; and 2nd, from its large opportunity of charity. . . . The personal advantages of the entree and the right of passing through the Park, which I have enjoyed for twenty-two years, I understand you that I retain as Prelate of the Garter.

Three of the early High Almoners have each endowed us with an interesting personal artifact.

The first of these is kept at Hardwicke Court, near Gloucester. It is a Lord High Almoner's purse made of green satin and gold lace (Plate 33) which belonged to Bishop William Lloyd, the Lord High Almoner to William and Mary and to William III alone after Mary's death. It is believed the purse was given to Lloyd by Queen Anne.[479]

Among the muniments of Westminster Abbey are six documents connected with Henry de Bluntesdon, Almoner to Edward I and Edward II from about 1284 to about 1305.[480] It would appear from these documents that shortly after the disastrous fire in 1298 which destroyed so many of the conventual buildings at Westminster, de Bluntesdon loaned to the monastery the sum of one hundred pounds. This sum was gradually, year by year, being repaid to him by the monks but in 1311 he decided to release them from the remaining balance of their debt, namely fifty pounds, on the condition that they donated this sum toward the rebuilding of the chapel in the monastic infirmary which had been destroyed by the fire.[481] The present interest in these documents, however, lies not so much in their contents as in the fact that to four of them de Bluntesdon appended his seal.[482] This seal (Plate 34) is the second part of the tripartite legacy from the early High Almoners, delineating as it does the earliest known representation of a king's almoner distributing alms to the poor It is circular, of red wax, bears the inscription SIGILLUM SERVI DEI (Seal of God's Servant) and depicts the Almoner holding in his right hand a basket whilst with his left hand he is distributing the alms that he has taken from the basket to an eager crowd awaiting his donations with outstretched hands.[483]

The third and final part of the legacy from the early almoners is to be found in another seal (Plate 35), that of Stephen Payne,[484] the King's Almoner from 1414 to 1419, in the May of which year he died. The seal bears the inscription SIGILLUM OFFICII ELEMOSINARII REGIS HENRICI QUINTI ANGLIE (Seal of the Almoner's Office of King Henry the Fifth of England) and shows the Almoner under a canopy holding in his arms a ship on wheels. An alms box in the form of a silver ship on wheels, which could be passed around a table, was frequently used in the fifteenth and sixteenth centuries.[485] It is possible that during the course of time the original significance was forgotten, the wheels were lost and there emerged a ship, launched on a Tudor sea, which came to be accepted as the official seal of the Royal Almonry (see Plate 36),[486] a seal which is, however, of uncertain date.[487]

Alternatively, the Royal Almonry could owe the representation of the three-masted ship in full sail on its seal to the benefaction of Cardinal Wolsey. In 1512, Thomas Wolsey[488] began to build a ship, the famous *Henry Grace de Dieu*, *The Royal Harry*, which he presented to Henry VIII and which was launched in 1515. Wolsey was King's Almoner from 1509 to 1514 and, in this capacity, he had *The Royal Harry* represented upon the seal which he used in connection with this office, a seal which could have acted as the prototype for the current seal of the Royal Almonry.[489] Another possible origin for the ship on the latter seal may lie in the ship which appears upon the reverse of the angel (Plate 1) or the later touch-piece (Plate 4), artifacts which were used in connection with another royal charity, touching for the King's Evil.[490]

During 1976, a badge of office for the Lord High Almoner was produced in gold (Plate 37). This bears, essentially, the seal of the Royal Almonry and is worn, around his neck, by the Lord High Almoner during the Maundy service.[491] The Almonry seal is also now embroidered at the top of the arms of the black gowns which are worn by its Secretary and Assistant Secretary during the Maundy service.[492]

A list has been published[493] (Table 6) of the High Almoners who are known to have held office since the beginning of the twelfth century. It is probably complete from about 1400, although there are gaps in the earlier period which have yet to be filled.[494] In this compilation, the position held at the date, or the approximate date, of appointment as High Almoner has been noted along with subsequent preferments. The starting point for this list is not intended to suggest that the office of Almoner did not exist before the twelfth century. Indeed, it is likely to have existed from a much earlier period but records of its incumbents are not available.[495] A similar list (Table 7) has also been compiled of the Sub-almoners as known from 1382 to date.[496] Although from about the middle of the eighteenth century the succession is continuous, for the period prior to this the list is far from complete. The reason lies in the common failure to record officially this appointment in both earlier and later times and it was, indeed, only possible to recover the names of many of those listed from their accidental documentary description as the King's Under (or Sub) Almoner.[497] Since the beginning of this century, the Sub-almoner has also undertaken the duties of Sub-dean of Chapels Royal, Deputy Clerk of the Closet and Domestic Chaplain, thereby affording between the Royal Almonry and the Chapel Royal a useful link since the Maundy service is still regarded as a Chapel Royal service.[498]

Table 7. Sub-almoners as known to date[1]

1382 (January)[2]	JOHN DE STONE
1444 (April)[2]	JOHN KETTE
	Canon of Windsor 1437–55
1449 (December)[2]–1454[2]	THOMAS PASSHE
	Canon of Windsor 1449–89
1471[2]–72[2]	JOHN BLAKEWYN
	Dean of St Mary, Shrewsbury, 1471; d. 1485
1486[2]	RICHARD BROMFELD
	Rector of Fordham
1507[2]–11[2]	JOHN HAWKESFORD
	Vicar of Brystall, Yorkshire
1529[2]	DR CLYFTON
	(Probably Gamaliel Clifton: Canon of Windsor 1522–41; Dean of Hereford 1530–41; d. 1541
1540[2]	HUGH CURWEN
	Dean of Hereford 1541; Archbishop of Dublin 1555–67; Bishop of Oxford 1567–68
1548[2]–50[2]	WILLIAM TODDE
	Rector of Northehill 1550
1561 (December)[2]	THOMAS NORLEY

Table 7. *(continued)*

	Prebendary of Worcester 1560–70; of Westminster 1563–70; d. 1570
1574 (October)[2]	WILLIAM ABSOLON
	Prebendary of Rochester c. 1576–86
1578[2]	WILLIAM SONCHE
	Rector of Spetisbury, Dorset; ? Canon of Salisbury 1586
1595[2]	JOHN DIX
	Prebendary of St Paul's, London, 1599
1608[2]	ROBERT SCOTT
	Master of Clare College, Camb., 1612–20; Dean of Rochester 1615–20
1619[2]–c. 1630	JEROME BEALE
	Master of Pembroke College, Camb., 1619–30
1661 (May)[2]–1667[2]	THOMAS GORGES
	Prebendary of Westminster 1661–67; d. 1667
?–1667	WILLIAM JOHNSON
	Prebendary of St Paul's, London, 1666–67, Archdeacon of Huntingdon 1666–67
1671[2]–73	RICHARD PERRINCHIEF
	Prebendary of Westminster 1664–73; d. 1673
1674–89	WILLIAM HOLDER
	Sub-dean of Chapels Royal
1689[2]–1713[2]	RALPH BATTELL
	Sub-dean of Chapels Royal
1716–22	ROBERT CANNON
	Prebendary of Westminster 1715–22; Dean of Lincoln 1721–22
1726[2]–40	JOHN GILBERT
	Dean of Exeter 1726–40; Archbishop of York 1757–61; Bishop of Llandaff 1740; of Salisbury 1748
1752[2]–57	RICHARD TERRICK
	Master of the Temple 1748–53; Bishop of Peterborough 1757; of London 1764–77
1757–61 (resigned)	THOMAS NEWTON
	Prebendary of Westminster 1757–61; Bishop of Bristol 1761–82
1762–(?)1773	JOHN THOMAS
	Prebendary (1754) and Dean of Westminster 1768–93; Bishop of Rochester 1774–93
1773(?)–1784	SIR RICHARD KAYE, BT.
	Prebendary of Durham 1777–84; Dean of Lincoln 1783–1809
1784–1809	WILLIAM VINCENT
	Head Master of Westminster 1788–1802; Dean of Westminster 1802–15
1810–16	WILLIAM CAREY
	Head Master of Westminster 1803–14; Bishop of Exeter 1820; of St Asaph 1830–46
1816–19	WILLIAM PAGE
	Head Master of Westminster 1815–19; d. September 1819
1819–31	EDMUND GOODENOUGH
	Head Master of Westminster 1819–28; Dean of Wells 1831–45
1831–43	ROBERT HODGSON
	Dean of Carlisle 1820–44
1843 (October)–1846	SAMUEL WILBERFORCE
	Dean of Westminster 1845; Bishop of Oxford 1845–69; of Winchester 1869–73; Lord High Almoner 1847–69

(continued)

Table 7. *(continued)*

1846 (February)–1871	RICHARD WILLIAM JELF Canon of Ch. Ch., Oxon., 1830–71; Principal of King's College, London, 1844–68
1871–82	ERNEST ROLAND WILBERFORCE Canon of Winchester 1878–82; Bishop of Newcastle 1882; of Chichester 1895–1907
1882–83	RANDALL THOMAS DAVIDSON Dean of Windsor 1883–91; Bishop of Rochester 1891; of Winchester 1895; Archbishop of Canterbury 1903–28
1883–99 (resigned)	ROBERT EYTON Prebendary of St Paul's, London, 1885; Canon of Westminster 1895–99
1899–1921	EDGAR SHEPPARD Sub-dean of Chapels Royal 1884–1921
1922–41	LANCELOT JEFFERSON PERCIVAL Sub-dean of Chapels Royal 1922–42
1942–48 (resigned)	WALLACE HAROLD ELLIOTT Sub-dean of Chapels Royal 1942–48
1948–65 (resigned)[3]	MAURICE FREDERIC FOXELL Sub-dean of Chapels Royal 1948–65[3]
1965–79 (resigned)[3]	JOHN SEYMOUR DENNIS MANSEL Sub-dean of Chapels Royal 1965–79[3]
1979 to date[3]	ANTHONY DOUGLASS CÆSAR Sub-dean of Chapels Royal 1979–91[3]

Notes to Table 7: *1*, Tanner (1957–58); *2*, There is doubt as to the exact date of the appointment, resignation or death of the person named but there is a definite reference to him as the Sub-almoner in that particular year; *3*, Wright.

NOTES

1. 'On the Custom of the Maundy', pp. 133–35.
2. See page 68.
3. Farquhar (1921–22, 1927–28, 1929–30).
4. Charlton; Nicholls.
5. Hocking (1906), Appendix III, pp. 422–24.
6. Sheppard, Chapter 23, pp. 350–72.
7. Ratcliffe.
8. Ratcliffe and Wright.
9. Wright (1966, 1971, 1981).
10. Tanner (1969).
11. Tanner (1969), p. 122.
12. Trowbridge.
13. Robinson (1977).
14. J. Pearson Andrew, 'Distribution of Maundy Money by the Monarch', *World Coin News*, no. 14 (4 April 1978), p. 23, illus. (quoted in *NL*, 104 (1980), p. 119); F. E. Ballin, 'Maundy Money Celebrations in England', *Coins, incorporating Coins and Medals*, 10, no. 7 (July 1973), pp. 9–11, illus. (quoted in *NL*, 95 (1976), p. 57); Brand, pp. 83–86; Brown; P. H. Ditchfield, *Old English Customs* (London, 1901), pp. 72, 257–61; Feasey, pp. 95–113; Gomme, pp. 35, 36, 147, 312–13; Hole, pp. 38, 39, 146; J. P. Jones, 'The Royal Maundy', *Texas Numismatic Association News*, 17, no. 4 (April 1976), p. 9 (quoted in *NL*, 97 (1977), p. 86); Brenda R. Lewis, 'Special Coins of Maundy Thursday', *Coins*, 30,

no. 4 (April 1983), pp. 64–70, illus. (quoted in *NL*, 110 (1983), p. 57); Nightingale, pp. 298–99; John Ryton, 'Changing Face of the Royal Maundy', *Coin and Medal News* (April 1985), p. 23; Richard J. Trowbridge, 'The Story of Maundy Money', *CNJ*, 21 (1976), pp. 148–54.
15. Genesis 18. 4; 19. 2; 24. 32; 43. 24.
16. St John 13. 1–16 (see also St Matthew 26. 20–29; St Mark 14. 17–26; St Luke 22. 14–38).
17. St John 13. 4,5.
18. St Mark 14. 13, 14; St Luke 22. 10–12.
19. St John 13. 14, 15.
20. Nicholls, p. 8; Urry, p. 12.
21. Skeat (1910), p. 367.
22. Feasey, p. 96.
23. Davies, J. G., pp. 46–50.
24. Farquhar (1921–22), p. 202.
25. Maundy – see Section IV of Chapter 2.
26. 'The Early South-English Legendary' or 'Lives of Saints', edited by Carl Hortstmann, *Early English Text Society*, 87 (original series) (1887), p. 229, lines 23–30 (partially quoted in Nicholls, p. 8).
27. 'On the Custom of the Maundy', pp. 133–34. St Brendan (*c.* 486–*c.* 575) was born probably near Tralee and died at Annadown. He became a monk and a priest and founded several monasteries in western Ireland, of which that at Clonfert in Galway was the most famous. In common with many other Irish monks, he was a great traveller. Although very few details regarding his life can be asserted with certainty, his cult was certainly very strong in Ireland (from the ninth-century martyrologies onwards), Wales, Scotland and Brittany. This cult owed much to the famous *Navigation of St Brendan*, an account of his sea voyage with a band of monks to a promised island of a paradise on earth in the Atlantic Ocean, which became one of the most famous and enduring stories of Western Christendom. Its immense popularity is evident from the survival of 116 mediæval Latin manuscripts of the text, and of versions in Middle English, French, German, Flemish, Italian, Provençal and Norse. However, most translations of the voyage are souped up and are utterly unreliable and none of them should be regarded as representing an authentic biography. The story only appeared some three hundred years after Brendan's historical death, probably as the work of an unknown expatriate Irish monk of the late ninth or early tenth century. It is a mixture of fact, fantasy and literary borrowing, and has been authoritatively described as a 'visionary fairy tale', 'a delightful fiction', and 'a romance of the 10th – 11th centuries' which 'transformed the historical, seafaring abbot into a mythical adventurer'. However, the voyage has attracted recurring speculation as being one of the various candiates for a pre-Columbus discovery of America and the recent journeys of Dr Timothy Severin have established the possibility of the Hebrides, the Faroes, Iceland and Newfoundland being reached by a type of craft which would have been available to Brendan (D. H. Farmer, *The Oxford Dictionary of Saints* (Oxford, 1978), pp. 54, 55; 'The Voyage of St Brendan' in *The Age of Bede*, translated by J. F. Webb and edited with an introduction by D. H. Farmer (Auckland, Harmondsworth, Markham, New York and Ringwood, 1983); *The Voyage of Saint Brendan: Journey to the Promised Land*, translated with an introduction by John J. O'Meara (Dublin and Atlantic Highlands, 1978)).
28. Nicholls, p. 9.
29. Thurston, p. 306 (quoted in Farquhar (1921–22), p. 204).
30. Feasey, p. 108.
31. See note 30 above.
32. See note 30 above.
33. 'The Chronicle of Melrose', in *The Church Historians of England*, translated from the original texts, with preface and notes, by Joseph Stevenson, vol. 1, part 2–vol. 5, part 1 (London, 1853–58), iv, part 1 (1856), pp. 100, 104.
34. Feasey, pp. 107, 109; Nicholls, p. 10.
35. Feasey, p. 107; Nicholls, p. 10.
36. Tanner (1956).
37. See note 36 above.
38. See notes 35, 36 above.
39. See note 36 above (see also Bond, p. 69).
40. Quoted in Bond, p. 69 (see also pp. 78–80).
41. Feasey, p. 107.

42. Bond, pp. 70, 78–80.
43. Feasey, p. 109.
44. Urry, pp. 12–14.
45. Urry, pp. 13, 15.
46. Urry, p. 14.
47. Urry, p. 13.
48. Brand, p. 83; Gomme, p. 313; Nicholls, p. 9.
49. Skinke, Anglo-Saxon scenc, meaning 'to draw liquor' (Nicholls, p. 9).
50. See page 44.
51. Wright (1981), p. 2.
52. Charlton, p. 207; Wright (1981), p. 2.
53. Charlton, pp. 206–8.
54. 'Rotulus Misæ Anni Regni Regis Johannis Quarti Decimi'; transcript published in *Documents Illustrative of English History in the Thirteenth and Fourteenth Centuries Selected from the Records of the Department of the Queen's Remembrancer of the Exchequer*, edited by H. Cole (London, 1844), p. 258.
55. See also Farquhar (1921–22), pp. 209–10.
56. Maundy Thursday.
57. Farquhar (1921–22), p. 210.
58. Hole, p. 38.
59. *Guardian* (2 April 1985), p. 1. The Knaresborough Mayor's interest was connected with the fact that in 1975 the Maundy service took place in nearby Ripon.
60. Hardy, pp. 161–62.
61. Line 1 of Plate 9.
62. Line 2 of Plate 9; x possibly xiij.
63. Inferred by analogy with lines 3 and 5 of Plate 9.
64. Line 3 and ii. d on line 4 of Plate 9.
65. For the clothes?
66. For the knives?
67. Lines 4 and 5 of Plate 9.
68. Lines 11–13 of Plate 9.
69. Line 24 of Plate 9.
70. Line 27 and the beginning of line 28 of Plate 9.
71. Line 33 of Plate 9.
72. Line 39 of Plate 9.
73. Hardy, pp. xvi, xvii.
74. Farquhar (1921–22), p. 209.
75. *DNB*; Freeman-Grenville; *HBC*.
76. This date is possibly in error, since Maundy Thursday fell on 20 March in 1326 (Cheney, p. 158; *OCEL*, p. 940). However, it could be correct since the celebration of the Maundy was sometimes effected on Good Friday as, for example, was that of Henry VIII in 1510 (BL Addit. MS 21481). Only in later years was the ceremony invariably fixed to be on Maundy Thursday, before this it being possible to postpone it until the following day by order of the monarch (Farquhar (1927–28), p. 117).
77. Wardrobe Roll, 19, Ed. II., 25, I Q.R. (quoted in Feasey, p. 110).
78. Maundy Thursday (see Section IV of Chapter 2), which in 1361 fell on 25 March (Cheney, p. 158; *OCEL*, p. 940).
79. Close Roll, 34, Ed. III (quoted in Feasey, p. 110).
80. Farquhar (1921–22), p. 207.
81. See note 75 above.
82. Charlton, p. 208.
83. Farquhar (1921–22), p. 204.
84. Farquhar (1927–28), pp. 114-16.
85. College of Arms MS M7, fo. 26 (quoted in Farquhar (1927–28), p. 114).
86. This gap should be filled with two short words, such as 'the clergy' or 'the choir' (Farquhar (1927–28), p. 114).
87. Farquhar (1927–28), p. 114.
88. Farquhar (1927–28), p. 116.

89. Henry VII was born on 28 January 1456/7 (see Appendix 3), not on 28 July as stated by Freeman-Grenville (p. 20). Whilst Henry VII's regnal years from his second year onwards did run from 22 August to 21 August, and within this framework his seventh regnal year ran from 22 August 1491 to 21 August 1492 (Cheney, p. 23), when he acceded to the throne on 22 August 1485 he deliberately claimed that his reign had begun the day before. This was simply a device by him to ensure that all those who fought against him on Bosworth Field were, indeed, traitors to his rule and therefore had forfeited all their lands and possessions to him by that act of treachery (Challis).
90. BL Addit. MS 7099.
91. Not 18 April as stated by Farquhar (1927–28), p. 118.
92. Not viij^{li} x^s 1^d as quoted by Farquhar (1927–28), p. 118.
93. PRO, E101/415/3, fo. 19r.
94. Not Sheirs Daye as quoted by Farquhar (1927–28), p. 118.
95. This is simply a scribal error because if each of the men had received forty-five pence, namely 3s 9d, then the total sum would indeed have amounted to £8 8s 9d as the manuscript indicates.
96. PRO, E101/415/3, fo. 49v.
97. This may be a scribal error, although it is conceivable that forty-eight were actually purchased and two were kept over for subsequent use.
98. PRO, E101/415/3, fo. 89v.
99. BL Addit. MS 21481.
100. When three dozen purses became required for later Maundies, their cost still remained at four pence per dozen (Farquhar (1927–28), p. 117 and Table 1.
101. See pages 33 and 34. In earlier times, the purses used in the Maundy service were of tawed (alum-dressed) sheep or goat skin and hand sewn. In the nineteenth century they were often made by poor children in the industrial schools. The modern purses are machine sewn and the alumed leather has been replaced by leather which, produced by newer methods, is superior in many respects to the ancient type. However, in size and style the modern purses closely resemble their predecessors (Wright (1981), p. 24).
102. See Section VI of Chapter 2.
103. It was not until later that the ceremony was invariably fixed to be on Maundy Thursday. If, to suit the monarch's convenience for instance, it was omitted on that day, it was performed on the next day, namely Good Friday (Farquhar (1927–28), p. 117).
104. See note 75 above.
105. Edward VI was born on 12 October 1537 (*DNB*; Freeman-Grenville, *HBC*).
106. PRO, Accounts of Sir William Cavendish, vol. 5.
107. PRO, Accounts of Sir William Cavendish, vol. 6.
108. Farquhar (1927–28), p. 118.
109. See note 75 above.
110. *Calendar of State Papers and Manuscripts.*
111. See Section VII of Chapter 1.
112. See Section VI of Chapter 1.
113. John Nichols, *Illustrations of the Manners and Expenses of Antient Times in England* (1797) (quoted in Nicholls, pp. 18, 19).
114. Nichols, ii, p. 297.
115. Sir Lionel Henry Cust, *King Edward VII and his Court. Some Reminiscences* (London, 1930), pp. xiii, xiv.
116. Farquhar (1927–28), p. 110; Ratcliffe and Wright, pp. 4–6.
117. Farquhar (1927–28), p. 111.
118. E. Auerbach, *Nicholas Hilliard* (London, 1961), pp. 53, 54, 287–88.
119. See note 117 above.
120. Ratcliffe and Wright, p. 6.
121. Nichols, i, pp. 147–49.
122. Crawford.
123. Nichols, i, pp. 83–85.
124. Dugdale, p. 18.
125. See note 124 above.
126. See note 75 above.

127. See Section VI of Chapter 2.
128. Farquhar (1927–28), pp. 111–12.
129. Nicholls, pp. 20–22; Nichols, i, pp. 325–27; (see also Appendix 3).
130. Cheat bread was good wheaten bread, though inferior to manchet which was the finest made (Nicholls, p. 21).
131. W. L. are the initials of William Lambarde, the learned topographical antiquary (Nichols, i, p. 327).
132. Nichols, i, p. 325 (footnote 4).
133. See page 29.
134. See pages 20, 21 and 23.
135. See page 31.
136. Farquhar (1927–28), p. 114; Wright (1981), p. 4.
137. See note 133 above.
138. Farquhar (1925–26), p. 83.
139. BL Harl. MS 1644, fo. 5.
140. Salisbury.
141. Erroneously quoted as £11 12s by Farquhar (1925–26), p. 83.
142. Farquhar ((1925–26), pp. 83, 84; (1927–28), p. 112) appears to have mistakenly believed that the Queen herself delivered her Maundy in 1582.
143. BL Addit. MS 5832, fo. 219 (quoted in Farquhar (1927–28), p. 112).
144. Cheney, p. 159; *OCEL*, p. 945.
145. If the date is correct, the number of female recipients should have been sixty-two (Elizabeth I was born on 7 September 1533 (*DNB*, Freeman-Grenville, *HBC*) and so she was in her sixty-second year of age on 17 April 1595) and the two gifts of money should therefore have totalled £1 5s 2d (£1 + 62d) (Farquhar (1927–28), p. 113).
146. See, for example, page 27.
147. Bidwell, p. 545; Farquhar (1929–30), p. 225; Sheppard, p. 356.
148. See page 48.
149. See Section I of Chapter 3.
150. See Appendix 4.
151. See Appendix 5.
152. See page 45.
153. Farquhar (1925–26), pp. 83, 84.
154. Farquhar (1929–30), pp. 223–25.
155. Charlton, p. 215; Farquhar (1929–30), p. 217.
156. See page 50.
157. Wright.
158. See note 75 above.
159. See Section IV of Chapter 2.
160. Nicholls, p. 12.
161. Farquhar (1921–22), p. 206.
162. Nicholas, p. 1.
163. Nicholas, p. 4.
164. Probably clothing or provisions for the Maundy recipients.
165. Nicholas, p. 5.
166. Nicholas, p. 74.
167. Nicholas, p. 85.
168. *Letters and Papers of Henry VIII*, 22 and 23 March 1535 (quoted in Farquhar (1927–28), p. 123).
169. See note 114 above.
170. Farquhar (1927–28), p. 124.
171. *Northumberland Household Book*, edited by Thomas Percy, late Bishop of Dromore, from the manuscript then in the possession of the Duke of Northumberland (1727) (quoted in Charlton, pp. 208–9; Farquhar (1927–28), p. 124; Nicholls, pp. 12–15).
172. There were eleven priests in the Earl's household (Nicholls, p. 14).
173. Not, as stated by Nicholls (p. 15) 'in the hey-day of his prosperity', although his train did consist of 160 horse, and seventy-two wagons, loaded with the relics of his furniture: if this was poverty, how great must have been his wealth (John Galt, *Life of Cardinal Wolsey*, third edition (London, 1846), p. 193).

174. *Holinshed's Chronicles of England, Scotland and Ireland*, 6 vols (London, 1807–8), iii (1808), p. 570. When Raphaell Holinshed first compiled these chronicles (2 vols (London, 1577)), he included data to the year 1577. Subsequently (3 vols (London, 1586–87)) he extended them to the year 1586 and also added 'occurrences and accidents of fresh memorie' which included the account of Wolsey's Maundy celebration of 1530.
175. Cranmer was the first protestant Archbishop of Canterbury who, as a victim of the cold and calculating power politics of Mary Tudor and the Papal Legate, Reginald Pole, was falsely convicted of heresy and burnt at the stake in Oxford on 21 March 1556. Throughout history, countless thousands have suffered cruel and agonizing deaths in the cause of religion or politics: Cranmer so died for both such reasons.
176. Farquhar (1921–22), pp. 202–3; Feasey, p. 112; Jaspar Ridley, *Thomas Cranmer* (Oxford, 1962).
177. See Appendix 3.
178. Nichols, i, pp. 147–48.
179. See note 177 above.
180. Crawford; Nicholls, pp. 22, 23.
181. BL Harl. MS 1026.
182. Farquhar (1921–22), p. 205.
183. Torr, p. 100.
184. Drake, i, p. 137 and footnote *t*, respectively.
185. Charles I was born on 19 November 1600 (*DNB*, Freeman-Grenville, *HBC*) and so on 11 April 1639 he would have been only thirty-eight years old although he would have been in his thirty-ninth year.
186. Torr, p. 103.
187. Drake, i, p. 144.
188. Farquhar (1927–28), pp. 122–23, 129; (see also page 101).
189. Farquhar (1927–28), p. 122.
190. Farquhar (1929–30), p. 216.
191. *Mercurius Politicus* (1661).
192. BL Harl. MS 3795.
193. Farquhar (1929–30), p. 223.
194. *Topographical History of London* (The Gentleman's Magazine Library), edited by G. L. Gomme (London, 1904), pp. 173–74.
195. BL Harl. MS 829 (see also *Mercurius Politicus* (1663)).
196. See note 140 above.
197. Charles II was born on 29 May 1630 (*DNB*, Freeman-Grenville, *HBC*); the Year of Grace was therefore included, in spite of the phrase 'hath already lived'.
198. *The Diary of Samuel Pepys*, p. 257 (see also *The Diary of Samuel Pepys, a New and Complete Transcription*, edited by Robert Latham and William Matthews (London, 1974), vol. 8, p. 150).
199. *Mercurius Politicus* (1667).
200. Feasey, pp. 110–11.
201. *Chapels Royal Register of Births, Deaths and Marriages* (quoted in Charlton, p. 211; Farquhar (1929–30), p. 219; Sheppard, pp. 352–53).
202. See, for example, Bidwell, p. 545; Charlton, p. 211; Farquhar (1925–26), p. 88; Feasey, p. 110; *GM*, 1 (1931), p. 172; Hocking (1906), Appendix III, p. 423; Nicholls, pp. 23, 24; Walford, p. 368.
203. Thomas Delaune, *Angliæ Metropolis, or the Present State of London* (1690), p. 114 (quoted in Farquhar (1929–30), p. 219; Hocking (1906), Appendix III, p. 423; Ratcliffe and Wright, pp. 10, 13; Sheppard, p. 353; Wright (1981), pp. 9, 10). This account would appear to be at serious variance with the then long-established custom, in that it claims that the Gift of Pennies was presented in red (rather than the customary white) leather purses and that a gift of shillings, related in magnitude to the King's regnal year as was the number of recipients, was also presented. Clearly the report is erroneous and, amongst other matters, almost certainly the latter gift was, in fact, the robe redemption allowance of twenty shillings.
204. *Le Guide de Londres pour les Etrangers* (London, 1693) (quoted in Brand, p. 84).
205. *The BL General Catalogue of Printed Books in 1975*, vols 1–360 (Munich, New York and Paris, 1979–87), lxvi, p. 494.
206. See note 204 above.
207. *New State of England* (1693), p. 196 (quoted in Farquhar (1929–30), p. 219).
208. Farquhar (1929–30), p. 219.

209. Quoted in Dugdale, p. 71.
210. *Protestant Mercury* (London), no. 258 (Wednesday, 20 April to Friday, 22 April, 1698), 403 verso (in the Bodliean Library, Oxford).
211. *Dawks' Newsletter*, no. 289 (quoted in Farquhar (1929–30), p. 220).
212. *Dawks' Newsletter* (1699).
213. William III was born on 14 November 1650 (*DNB*, Freeman-Grenville, *HBC*) and so on 6 April 1699 he would have been only forty-eight years old although he would have been in his forty-ninth year.
214. Tanner (1969), p. 122.
215. Bidwell, p. 545; Sheppard, p. 355.
216. *GM*, 1 (1731), p. 172.
217. This presumably refers to the *total* value of each gift since, in 1731 when George II was in his forty-eighth year of age, each recipient would have received forty-eight pence, namely four shillings. This, along with the robe redemption allowance of £1, would have been the total monetary gift received by each male: each female would have received a further £1 15s which had, from 1724 onward, replaced their gift of clothing (see note 152 above).
218. This final sentence is surprising in view of the then available literature which has been quoted above and which clearly establishes that William III was the last British monarch to effect the *pedilavium*.
219. Walford, p. 368. The error was also quoted, without comment, in Ratcliffe and Wright, p. 13.
220. Cheney, p. 160; *OCEL*, p. 948.
221. *London Journal* (17 April 1731) (quoted in Farquhar (1929–30), p. 226).
222. Farquhar (1929–30), p. 226.
223. See Section I of Chapter 3.
224. Gomme, p. 35.
225. The Lord High Almoner (Table 6).
226. Feasey, p. 111.
227. Feasey, pp. 111–12.
228. Farquhar (1921–22), p. 213; Wright (1981), p. 23.
229. Standing in front of George VI and Queen Elizabeth are the Children of the Royal Almonry (see Appendix 5) and to the right of the Queen is the Lord High Almoner (Rt Rev. Edward Sydney Woods, Bishop of Lichfield). To his left stands Mr Lawrence E. Tanner, the Secretary of the Royal Almonry, and Mr Egbert E. Ratcliffe, the Assistant Secretary of the Royal Almonry, is standing directly behind the King.
230. Standing to the centre rear of the Queen and the Duke of Edinburgh is Mr Peter A. Wright, the Assistant Secretary of the Royal Almonry, and standing to the Queen's rear left. and partially obscured by a cleric, is Dr Lawrence E. Tanner, the Secretary of the Royal Almonry. Two of the Children of the Royal Almonry (see Appendix 5) are standing at the extremities of the front row.
231. Wright (1981), p. 23.
232. Mrs Bennett-Levy, personal communication; Wright (1981), p. 9.
233. See note 151 above.
234. See note 231 above.
235. See page 30.
236. See note 231 above.
237. Perham, p. 26.
238. Nicholls, pp. 28, 29.
239. Perham, p. 181–83.
240. *GM*, 24 (1754), p. 188. This account refers to the distribution made on 11 April 1754, at which time George II was in his seventy-first year of age. Thus, it would be expected that seventy-one men and seventy-one women would each have received seventy-one pence in small silver coin.
241. *GM*, 25 (1755), p. 183. This account refers to the distribution made on 27 March 1755, at which time George II was in his seventy-second year of age. Thus, it would be expected that seventy-two men and seventy-two women would each have received seventy-two pence in small silver coin. It would appear that the author merely repeated the previous year's figure, a figure which is itself questionable.
242. *GM*, 35 (1765), p. 195. This account refers to the distribution made on 4 April 1765, at which time George III was in his twenty-seventh year of age: the number of recipients is therefore correctly quoted.
243. *GM*, 36 (1766), p. 149. This account refers to the distribution made on 27 March 1766, at which time George III was in the twenty-eighth year of his life.

244. *GM*, 37 (1767), p. 190. This account refers to the distribution made on 16 April 1767, at which time George III was in the twenty-ninth year of his life, in accordance with which are both the number of recipients and the magnitude of their Gift of Pennies.
245. *GM*, 42 (1772), p. 198. This account refers to the distribution made on 16 April 1772, at which time George III was in the thirty-fourth year of his life. Therefore, thirty-four men and thirty-four women should each have received the gifts. It would appear that the writer of this report was unaware of the relationship between the monarch's age and the number of recipients and, not having the details of the 1772 distribution, merely repeated the figure from five years earlier.
246. *GM*, 44 (1774), p. 185. This account refers to the distribution made on 31 March 1774, at which time George III was in the thirty-sixth year of his life, namely he was thirty-five years old. It would appear that in this instance it was the latter factor which determined the number of recipients and the magnitude of their Gift of Pennies.
247. Bidwell, p. 545; Charlton, p. 212; Nicholls, p. 25: incorrectly quoted as thirty-four shillings in Farquhar (1929–30), p. 217; Sheppard, p. 355.
248. Bidwell, p. 545; Charlton, pp. 212–13; Sheppard, pp. 355–56.
249. Bidwell, p. 545; Charlton, p. 213; Farquhar (1929–30), p. 217; Nicholls, p. 25; Sheppard, pp. 357–58.
250. See note 157 above.
251. Charlton, p. 214; Nicholls, p. 25; Sheppard, pp. 358–59; Tanner (1969), p. 126.
252. Tanner (1969), p. 126.
253. See note 252 above.
254. See page 34.
255. See note 252 above.
256. See note 157 above.
257. Wright (1981), p. 24.
258. See note 157 above.
259. Clay.
260. (1736–1809), D.C.L., F.S.A., Sub-almoner, Prebendary of Southwell and Durham, Archdeacon of Nottingham, Dean of Lincoln (1783–1809), Baronet (December 1787).
261. See Table 7.
262. Clay, p. 90.
263. Clay, p. 58.
264. See note 50 above.
265. Bidwell, p. 546.
266. Sheppard, pp. 360–61.
267. By 1893 the old Almonry Office in Scotland Yard had been demolished, to make way for a new street into Whitehall, and the Chapel had been closed (Bidwell, p. 546; Dugdale, pp. 117–18).
268. Clay, p. 56.
269. Clay, pp. 56, 57.
270. See note 75 above.
271. Clay, p. 57.
272. The Act in these cases refers to the Engravers' Act 1735, the so-called Hogarth Act, which first established the possibility of creating a copyright on a print (Ronald Paulson, *Hogarth: His Life, Art and Times*, vols 1 and 2 (New Haven and London, 1971), pp. 359–75, 379, 391 and 128–29, 132, 219, 435–36, 489–90, respectively). Since this Act administered itself, there was never any registry of works published or information about how may impressions were printed. It is therefore purely conjecture but it is usually assumed that an engraved plate of the eighteenth century would normally have from five hundred to a thousand impressions taken from it (personal communication from Mr A. V. Griffiths, Deputy Keeper of Paintings and Drawings at the British Museum).
273. See note 263 above.
274. Cheney, p. 160; *OCEL*, p. 950.
275. *London Interiors*, pp. 47, 48; Ratcliffe and Wright, p. 14; Walford, p. 368.
276. Surely an error by the reporter, since the female recipients' clothing allowance was replaced by an allowance of thirty-five shillings from 1724 onwards (see note 152 above).
277. Squibb; (see also page 58).
278. Bidwell, p. 545; Charlton, p. 212; Farquhar (1929–30), p. 217; Nicholls, p. 25; Sheppard, pp. 256–57.
279. See pages 33 and 34.

280. Charlton, p. 213–14; Farquhar (1929–30), p. 217; Nicholls, p. 25; Sheppard, pp. 358–59.
281. See note 157 above.
282. *The Times* (13 April 1838), p. 5.
283. See Section V of Chapter 2.
284. The clothing gift for men was not commuted for money until 1882 (see note 152 above).
285. See Appendix 2.
286. Farquhar (1921–22), pp. 213–14.
287. See Tables 6 and 7.
288. Cheney, p. 160; *OCEL*, p. 951.
289. Wright, p. 7.
290. See note 283 above.
291. See note 36 above.
292. *The Times* (3 April 1920), p. 13.
293. On the front row, viewed from left to right, is seen Rev. Lancelot J. Percival (Sub-almoner), Princess Marie-Louise, Rt Rev. Cosmo Lang, (Archbishop of Canterbury and Lord High Almoner), Princess Helena Victoria and Canon Percy Dearmer. Standing immediately behind these is a group of five clerics and between the immediate rear of the third and fourth of these from the left is standing Mr Lawrence E. Tanner, the Secretary of the Royal Almonry.
294. Tanner (1956); (1969), p. 122; *The Times* (27 December 1956), p. 10.
295. Tanner.
296. See note 214 above.
297. *London Interiors*, p. 48.
298. Walford, p. 369.
299. *OED*, ix, p. 492.
300. See note 10 above. The monarch's active participation in the service also resulted in an increased interest in, and consequent demand for, the Maundy money in 1932 (*NCirc*, 40 (June 1932), final page).
301. *The Times* (26 March 1932), pp. 10, 12.
302. Of the Royal Almonry (Mr Lawrence E. Tanner).
303. Of the Royal Almonry (Mr Egbert E. Ratcliffe).
304. The robe redemption allowance was commuted from a gold sovereign to a treasury note for £1 in 1916 (see note 254 above). This apparent reversion to the use of a sovereign in 1932 may have been made as a recognition of this particular service's rather special nature, involving as it did the return of the monarch's active participation in the ceremony after 233 years.
305. Wright (1966), p. 8.
306. Ratcliffe and Wright, pp. 24, 27; Wright.
307. His father, George V, had died on 20 January 1936 (Freeman-Grenville).
308. It is interesting that a Maundy set dated 1936, presumably one that had been retained by the King as a momento on the occasion of his distribution, was sold in the auction of the jewellery and related precious artifacts which had belonged to the late Duchess of Windsor (*Sacra Moneta*).
309. Ratcliffe (1936), p. 11.
310. Her father, George VI, had died on 6 February 1952 (Freeman-Grenville).
311. Davies, J. G., p. 50; Feasey, p. 113; Nicholls, p. 10.
312. See pages 31 and 32.
313. Nicholls, p. 10.
314. Farquhar (1921–22), p. 201.
315. See page 41.
316. Manuscript in the Cathedral Library at Salisbury (quoted in Charlton, p. 211).
317. Charlton, p. 212; Farquhar (1929–30), pp. 218–19.
318. Farquhar (1929–30), p. 219.
319. See page 47.
320. See note 151 above.
321. See note 151 above.
322. See note 151 above.
323. See note 151 above.
324. Carrying a traditional nosegay, as were the Duke of Edinburgh, each of the Children of the Royal Almonry, the Secretary and the Assistant Secretary of the Royal Almonry, the Sub-almoner and the Lord High Almoner (see note 50 above).

325. See note 151 above.
326. This is known as the Maundy Prayer (Wright (1981), p. 24) and proceeds 'Lord Jesus Christ, who before instituting the Holy Sacrament at thy Last Supper, washed the feet of thine Apostles; teach us, by thine example, the grace of humility; and so cleanse us from all stain of sin that we may worthily partake of thy holy mysteries; who with the Father and the Holy Spirit art one God, world without end. *Amen*'.
327. Gird with a traditional towel (see note 50 above).
328. See note 327 above.
329. See note 327 above.
330. See note 327 above.
331. See note 150 above.
332. Feasey, p. 95 (footnote).
333. See note 22 above.
334. Charlton, p. 204; Nicholls, p. 5.
335. Charlton, p. 204.
336. See note 22 above.
337. See note 335 above.
338. See note 335 above.
339. Nicholls, p. 5; *OED*, xv, p. 223.
340. Farquhar (1921–22), p. 199; Feasey, p. 95; *OED*, xv, p. 223.
341. *OED*, xv, p. 223.
342. See note 332 above.
343. Quoted in Feasey, p. 95.
344. *Festival*, fo. xxx, p. 2 and fo. xxxi, printed by Wynkyn de Worde (quoted in Charlton, p. 204; Farquhar (1921–22), p. 211; *GM*, 49 (1779), pp. 290–91; Nicholls, p. 5).
345. BL Harl. MS 2247, p. 85 (quoted in Farquhar (1921–22), pp. 199, 211); *OED*, xv, p. 223.
346. Nicholls, pp. 5, 6.
347. Thurston, p. 88 (quoted in Farquhar (1921–22), p. 211).
348. William Langland, *The Vision of William Concerning Piers the Plowman*, edited by W. W. Skeat (London, 1867), notes, pp. 379–80, B. Pass. XVI, p. 140.
349. iii, pp. 30, 51, 169, respectively.
350. Feasey, p. 95; *OED*, xv, p. 223.
351. Feasey, pp. 105–7.
352. Jeremy Collier, *Ecclesiastical History*, 2 (1714), p. 197 (quoted in Brand, p. 85; Charlton, pp. 202–3; *GM*, 49 (1779), p. 349; Sheppard, p. 351); Feasey, pp. 105–7.
353. Farquhar (1921–22), p. 199.
354. Brand, p. 85; Charlton, p. 202; *GM*, 49 (1779), p. 349.
355. Brand, p. 85; *GM*, 49 (1779), p. 349; Sheppard, p. 351.
356. Usually spelt maundye and maunday in documents of the sixteenth or seventeenth, and eighteenth centuries, respectively (Farquhar (1921–22), pp. 211–12), and having many other forms, namely maunde(e,y), mande(e), monde(e), mawnde(e), maundie, mandy, manday, mawndy(e), mawndaye and mawneday (*OED*, ix, p. 492).
357. *OED*, ix, p. 492.
358. Quoted in Charlton, p. 203.
359. Charlton, p. 203.
360. Quoted in Brand, p. 85.
361. Quoted in Charlton, p. 204; *OED*, ix, p. 492.
362. See note 358 above.
363. Quoted in Cheney, p. 46; Feasey, p. 110; *GM*, 49 (1779), pp. 290–91.
364. Feasey, p. 95.
365. Nicholls, p. 5.
366. *OED*, xv, p. 223.
367. See note 358 above.
368. Johnson.
369. See note 368 above.
370. Charlton, pp. 201–2; *OED*, ix, pp. 490–91; Sheppard, p. 350–51.
371. Sir Henry Spelman (1562–1641) was one of the most distinguished of English antiquaries (Charlton, p. 201).

372. See note 368 above.
373. Nicholls, p. 4.
374. Brand, p. 84; Feasey, p. 96; Nichols, i, p. 325 (footnote 3).
375. Charlton, pp. 201–2; Farquhar (1921–22), p. 212; Nicholls, p. 4; Sheppard, pp. 350–51.
376. Skeat (1882), p. 359.
377. Skeat (1910), p. 367.
378. See note 348 above.
379. William Langland, *The Vision of William Concerning Piers the Plowman*, edited from numerous manuscripts with preface, notes and a glossary by W. W. Skeat (Oxford, 1886), ii, preface, notes and glossary, p. 239, B. Pass. XVI, p. 140.
380. *OED*, ix, p. 491.
381. *GM*, 49 (1779), p. 354.
382. Brand, p. 85; Charlton, p. 202; Sheppard, p. 351.
383. Nicholls, p. 4; *OED*, ix, p. 492; Onions; Skeat (1882), p. 359; (1910), p. 367; Stephen Skinner, *Etymologicon Linguæ Anglicanæ* (Londoni, 1669) (quoted in Nichols, i, p. 325 (footnote 3); *The Diary of Samuel Pepys*, p. 257 (footnote).
384. Farquhar (1921–22), p. 212; Sheppard, p. 350.
385. See note 324 above.
386. See Section III of Chapter 2.
387. Sheppard, pp. 362–68.
388. See note 36 above.
389. Cheney, p. 48; Johnson; Nicholls, p. 4; *OED*, ix, p. 492; xv, p. 223; Onions; Skeat (1882), p. 359; (1910), p. 367.
390. Dugdale, p. 17.
391. See note 36 above.
392. See note 312 above.
393. See pages 32 and 33.
394. See page 37.
395. See page 38.
396. See pages 38 and 39.
397. See page 39.
398. See note 397 above.
399. See Appendix 2.
400. See page 40.
401. Dugdale, p. 71
402. See note 399 above.
403. Dugdale, pp. 108–9.
404. Bidwell, p. 545; Dugdale, pp. 108–9; Sheppard, p. 357.
405. Dugdale, p. 108.
406. Squibb.
407. *John Bull*. Presumably only the male recipients received the clothing gift since for female recipients it was commuted for a monetary allowance of thirty-five shillings from 1724 onward. However, the account makes no reference to this extra monetary gift for the ladies.
408. See note 148 above.
409. Dugdale, p. 109; Sheppard, pp. 50–52.
410. Tanner (1969), p. 128.
411. *The Times* (27 March 1937), p. 9.
412. The latter statement is obviously erroneous (see pages 41 and 42).
413. Tanner (1969), pp. 127–28.
414. However, for several centuries before the crowns were united in 1603, the Scottish monarchs had been active in presenting their alms. Thus, mention has been made (*Accounts of the Lord High Treasurer*, vol. i, p. 71 (quoted in Farquhar (1921–22), p. 208)) of the items which composed the gifts of James III and an account exists (quoted in Farquhar (1921–22), p. 210) of the *pedilavium* as performed by Margaret, the wife of Malcolm III, and of this king's offerings on Maundy Thursday. Furthermore, the earliest known coins especially struck as Maundy money in the British Isles were 2,550 twelvepenny groats of James IV, produced for the Maundy service held in Scotland in 1512 and using the 11lb 1½oz

of bullion from one of the great silver wine jugs which the King gave to David Scott, Master of the Scottish Mint for this purpose (Seaby and Purvey; Farquhar (1921–22), p. 200; Stewart, Ian H., pp. 265–66 and Plate XXXVI; (see also page 112)).

415. See note 157 above
416. See note 157 above.
417. See pages 24 and 25.
418. Robinson (1977), p. 45.
419. See pages 25 and 26.
420. Tanner (1969), p. 120; Wright (1981), pp. 2, 4.
421. A correlation which has also operated in some of the more recent distributions (Wright).
422. See note 108 above.
423. See note 108 above.
424. See note 392 above.
425. See note 254 above.
426. *DNB*; Freeman-Grenville; *HBC*.
427. Farquhar (1927–28), p. 111.
428. See, for example, note 27 to Table 4.
429. Tanner (1969), p. 120.
430. See note 315 above.
431. See page 42.
432. See note 430 above.
433. See note 431 above.
434. See note 431 above.
435. MS Rawlinson D. 18 fo. 75–77 (in the Bodleian Library, Oxford).
436. The etc. refers to that part of the consent accompanying an earlier petition, namely that of one Robert Ward, which is presented in full on the next page of the present text.
437. See page 69.
438. See note 36 above.
439. See Appendix 1.
440. PRO, Mint 4/21.
441. PRO, Mint 4/24.
442. See note 440 above.
443. PRO, Mint 4/23.
444. The Lord High Almoner at that time (see Table 6).
445. See note 441 above.
446. See Section V of Chapter 2.
447. Bidwell, p. 545; Charlton, p. 215; Sheppard, p. 359.
448. Sheppard, pp. 359–60.
449. Bidwell, p. 545.
450. The previously-described cases of Robert Ward and Mrs Ochs are specific cases whereby recipients appeared in the Maundy list in more than one year.
451. Wright (1966), p. 18.
452. The Discretionary Bounty (see Section II, Sub-section ii, of Chapter 1).
453. See note 449 above.
454. See note 426 above.
455. See note 282 above.
456. *The Times* (16 April 1838), p. 5. The gift of 2*l*. 10s. was clearly composed of the robe redemption allowance of £1 and the 1*l*. 10s. commutation in lieu of provisions mentioned in the account.
457. See note 426 above.
458. See note 426 above.
459. Sheppard, pp. 359–60.
460. See note 451 above.
461. *OED*, ix, p. 492; *The Times* (13 April 1838), p. 5.
462. See note 36 above.
463. See note 295 above.
464. See pages 38 and 45, respectively.

465. See note 282 above.
466. Tanner (1969), p. 121; Wright.
467. See note 298 above.
468. Nightingale, pp. 298–99.
469. Ratcliffe and Wright, pp. 20, 23, 24; Tanner (1957–58); Wright (1981), pp. 16, 17.
470. See note 469 above.
471. Ratcliffe and Wright, p. 24; Tanner (1957–58).
472. Quoted in Ratcliffe and Wright, p. 23.
473. John Chamberlayne, *Present State of Great Britain*, thirty-eighth edition, 2 parts (London, 1755) (quoted in Ratcliffe and Wright, pp. 23, 24; Wright (1981), p. 17).
474. Objects which had been the immediate cause of the death of a human being, such as a carriage that had run over and fatally injured somebody. They were given to the monarch, as the Lord's anointed, in expiation, they or the money raised from their sale being then used for pious purposes (Bidwell, p. 545; Tanner (1957–58)).
475. Wright (1981), p. 18.
476. Ratcliffe and Wright, p. 24; Wright (1981), p. 18.
477. The Almonry Office used to occupy premises in Scotland Yard but in 1884 these were demolished to permit the construction of a new street into Whitehall (Bidwell, p. 546; Dugdale, pp. 117–18). It is now housed in Buckingham Palace.
478. Ratcliffe and Wright, p. 24.
479. Wright (1981), pp. 3, 17.
480. He was also Archdeacon of Dorset from 1297 until his death in 1316.
481. See note 36 above.
482. Tanner (1956); *The Times* (24 March 1937), p. 19.
483. *The Times* (24 March 1937), p. 19; Wright (1981), pp. 2, 3.
484. Stephen Payne was also Dean of Exeter from 1415 to 1419. He came from Durham and it is interesting that, for some yet unknown reason, his seal (without alteration) was later adopted by Greatham Hospital in West Hartlepool near Durham, where it is still so used (Tanner (1956); *The Times* (24 March 1937), p. 19; Wright (1981), p. 18).
485. For instance, William de Wykeham refers to such an alms box in his will (*The Times* (24 March 1937), p. 19).
486. The present seal is similar except that its legend reads SIGILL : ELEEMOSYN : ELIZABETHAE : II : D : G : BRITT : OMNIUM REGINAE : F : D :.
487. Tanner (1956); *The Times* (24 March 1937), p. 19; Wright (1981), pp. 2, 18.
488. Thomas Wolsey was created a cardinal in 1515 and, as such, but after his fall from political power in October 1529, he presented his Maundy in 1530 at Peterborough (see note 394 above).
489. Ratcliffe and Wright, p. 23.
490. See note 112 above.
491. Wright; Wright (1981), p. 24.
492. Wright (1981), pp. 4, 5.
493. Tanner (1957–58).
494. The results of an earlier attempt (Sheppard, pp. 369–72) to compile such a list left much to be desired. Relative to Table 6, it omits nearly as many names as it quotes and, also, it makes no attempt to trace the names of almoners before Thomas Wolsey was appointed to such office in 1509.
495. See note 493 above.
496. See note 493 above.
497. See note 493 above.
498. Wright (1981), p. 18.

CHAPTER 3

The Maundy Money

I. THE EVOLUTION, PRODUCTION AND SPECIFICATIONS OF MAUNDY MONEY

The Maundy ceremony of 1213, in which John gave thirteen pence[1] to each of thirteen poor men, has been stated as being the earliest record in which a definite monetary sum is mentioned in connection with the Maundy distribution although it was cautiously added that 'this is no proof that no earlier exists'.[2] As mentioned earlier in connection with the discussion relating to the number of recipients in the Maundy service,[3] the thirteen pence given to each of them in the distribution of 1213 was also probably symbolic of the twelve Apostles together with either Jesus or the angel who, according to tradition, came to the table at which Pope Gregory the Great was serving. That, at the time of the ceremony in 1213, John had reigned for thirteen years, which appears to have been suggested as being of significance with relation to the number of recipients and the magnitude of their monetary gifts,[4] would seem to be purely coincidental.

In the Maundy distributions from the beginning of the Tudor period up to the present, the number of pence each recipient received in their Gift of Pennies (Maundy money) has been related to the monarch's age in years at the time of the ceremony. This relationship has, however, undergone some minor variations during this period, as is evident from the examples presented in Tables 1 and 4 and the related text. These indicate that, for the maundies of Henry VII and the early such ceremonies of Henry VIII, the number of pence received by each of the recipients was determined by the age of these kings on their next birthday following the distribution plus one more to represent the Year of Grace, the further year which, by the grace of God, the monarch might live. In the majority of the other examples listed, including the later distributions of Henry VIII, the number of pence in the Gift has been the same as the number of years of age of the monarch on their next birthday following the ceremony. Exceptions to this in Table 4 are the Maundies of Elizabeth I and George III of 1582 and 1814, respectively, in which each recipient received the same number of pence as the monarch was years of age at the time of the ceremony, a relationship which is not uncommon for some of the more recent distributions.[5] The report[6] that in the Maundy ceremony of 1731[7] the number of pence received by each recipient was allotted according to the number of years for which George II had then reigned is probably incorrect.[8]

Relating to the majority of the examples quoted in Table 4 is the current method, which has been practised for many decades, of determining both the number of Maundy recipients and the magnitude of their Gift of Pennies. Thus, when the monarch is x years old on his or her next birthday following the Maundy service, x pence in the form of Maundy coins are given to each of x male and x female recipients.

The Maundy coinage consists of silver pennies, twopences, threepences and fourpences. A complete sequence of these four coins of uniform dates is known as a Maundy set and, having a total face value of ten pence, it therefore represents in the Gift of Pennies ten years of the sovereign's age. Thus, for each multiple of ten years, each recipient receives one set of Maundy coins, with the remaining years being represented in the Gift by the appropriate single coins. For example, in the Maundy distribution of 1914, when George V was in his forty-ninth year, forty-nine men and forty-nine women each received, in a white leather purse with long red leather strings,[9] forty-nine pence consisting of five silver fourpences, four silver threepences, five silver twopences and seven silver pennies, namely four complete sets plus one fourpence, one twopence, and three pennies.[10] In the following year, each recipient received five sets of coins, namely fifty pence, and in the next year each were given an additional silver penny.[11] Similarly, in 1948, when George VI was in his fifty-third year of age, fifty-three men and fifty-three women each received five sets of the coins plus a Maundy threepence.[12]

The weight, fineness and values of the coinage of the realm has been legally established in the past as part of the succession of Mint Indentures (see, for example, notes 13 and 14) which have been made between the Crown and the various Masters of the Mint, and, in more recent times, have been statutorily determined by several Coinage Acts (see, for example, notes 15 and 16). As regards the silver penny, twopence, threepence and fourpence, these properties remained constant from 1601[17] until 1817.[18] For this period, the weights have been variously imprecisely, and sometimes incorrectly, stated[19] but they can be precisely calculated, from the data presented in the Mint Indenture of 1770, as 7.7419, 15.4839, 23.2258 and 30.9677 gr, respectively. The finenesses of all the four denominations was 11oz 2dwt of fine silver and eighteen pennyweights of alloy, namely the 92.5% silver plus 7.5% alloy mixture known as sterling silver, and 744, 372, 248 and 186 such coins, respectively, were contained in one troy pound.[20] By the Mint Indenture of 1817, the millesimal fineness 925 of the Maundy coinage remained unchanged but, as a consequence of the reduction of silver to a token coinage with the introduction of the gold standard,[21] the weights of the coins were reduced so that one troy pound would contain 792, 396, 264 and 198, respectively; namely they would weigh 7.27272, 14.54545, 21.81818 and 29.09090 gr, respectively.[22] Since then, the weights of the Maundy coinage have remained unchanged although the Coinage Act 1870 notes, along with the millesimal fineness 925, not only these imperial weights but also their metric equivalents, namely 0.47126, 0.94253, 1.41379 and 1.88506 g, together with imperial remedy allowances of 0.03030, 0.06060, 0.09090 and 0.12121 gr per piece and metric remedy allowances of 0.00196, 0.00392, 0.00589 and 0.00785 g per piece, respectively.[23] In the Coinage Act 1971 the millesimal fineness is again 925 but only the metric weights are quoted: these are as in the Coinage Act 1870 although in the later Act the remedy allowances are increased to 0.0056, 0.0093, 0.0138 and 0.0170 g, respectively.[24]

Unlike their weights, fineness and values, the physical dimensions of the Maundy coinage, like the gold coinage and all the rest of the pre-decimal coinage, are not controlled by law. However, such measurements are regulated by the Royal Mint. Thus, for many years now, Maundy coins, which have always had plain edges, have had, in ascending denominational order, diameters of 0.439, 0.529, 0.640 and 0.694 in

(11.15, 13.44, 16.26 and 17.63 mm) and edge thicknesses of 0.026, 0.035, 0.035 and 0.038 in (0.66, 0.89, 0.89 and 0.96 mm).[25]

The Maundy coinage retained the millesimal fineness 925 until it was debased, following the issue dated 1920, to an alloy containing only 50% of silver, a fate it shared with the other silver coinage of the realm at this time. From January to March 1920, minting in 925 sterling silver continued but only sixpences, threepences and Maundy money were struck during this period.[26] From then until October 1946, the production of the 500 millesimal fine silver coinage at particular periods utilised four specific alloys, referred to as 500A, 500B, 500C (all three of which were introduced from 1920) and 500Z, which was introduced from 1927. They were composed of 50% silver along with 50% of copper, 40% of copper plus 10% of nickel, 45% of copper plus 5% of manganese and 40% of copper plus 5% of each of nickel and zinc, respectively.[27] Of the Maundy coins struck over this period, those dated from 1921 to 1937 are made of alloy 500A which gave the coins a better appearance than did alloys 500B, 500C and, at first, 500Z. However, a method was then found of treating the blanks, after which those composed of alloy 500Z gave the best results on coining. Consequently, Maundy coins struck from 1938 to 1946 are composed of alloy 500Z.[28] Contrary to the statement relating to the Maundy sets which were included in the 1937 proof sets that 'these cannot be distinguished from the ordinary Maundy coins which are of proof quality',[29] it is now interesting to note that the Maundy coins struck for the Maundy service and related uses in 1937 are of composition 500A whereas alloy 500Z was used for the striking of those Maundy sets which were to be included in the proof sets issued in that year.[30]

After World War II, Britain had to repay the United States of America the eighty-eight million ounces of silver which it had received from that country under the Lend-Lease agreement during the war period (1939–1945). It was decided that the most satisfactory manner by which this debt could be met was to withdraw all the silver coin then in circulation and replace it with a base metal coinage of relatively little intrinsic value.[31] Thus, from October 1946 onwards[32] the coinage of Britain that had previously contained silver was 100% debased to an alloy of 75% copper and 25% nickel,[33] the cupro-nickel coins struck in 1946 all bearing the date 1947.[34]

However, it was decided at this juncture that, unlike the rest of the 500 millesimal fine silver coinage, the Maundy money should, in fact, revert to the millesimal fineness 925, namely sterling silver, from the 500 millesimal fine silver to which it, along with the rest of the 925 millesimal fine silver coinage, had been debased from 1921 onward. Thus, by virtue of the Coinage Act 1946, the Maundy coins issued from 1947 onward have been of such 925 millesimal fineness. Not only did this reversion involve only a very small amount of silver but it led to an easement of working and was also of great sentimental value.[35] This latter aspect is illustrated by the following extract from the seventy-seventh Annual Report of the Deputy Master and Comptroller of the Royal Mint for the year 1946.[36] After referring to the cessation of the manufacture of silver coins as being the outstanding event of that year, the Report continues:

> The use of silver in English coinage, which has been continuous since the seventh century, is not, however, to disappear entirely, the decision, welcome to scholars and aesthetes, having been taken to resume the use of the sterling standard in Maundy Money, the silver penny, twopence, threepence and fourpence. Of these coins, the English silver penny was instituted about 700 A.D. and gave its later name of the sterling to our whole currency

system. The fourpence was added in 1279, the twopence in 1351 and the threepence in 1551. All were struck in sterling silver (silver of 925 millesimal fineness), with one brief interruption on Henry VIII's debasement of all coinage, until the general change in 1920, in which these small coins were included with the rest.

The Act of 1946 thus restores to their ancient standard all those silver coins which antedate the discovery of argentiferous America, with the addition of the threepence when struck for use in the Maundy service, while all those introduced after that date, including the threepence if required for circulation, are converted to cupro-nickel.

Sir John Craig, the author of that report, expresses similar sentiments when he states, in connection with the total debasement effected by the Coinage Act 1946, that 'the four Maundy coins were excepted and were restored to 925 fineness; they remain the memorial of a coinage standard which had endured with one short break from the Saxon kings'.[37] Indeed, the present-day striking of the silver penny as part of the Maundy money keeps intact a link which goes back approximately one thousand three hundred and fifty years to the introduction of the silver sceattas,[38] the first English pennies.[39]

The procedure for the production of the Maundy money begins with a letter to the Deputy Master of the Royal Mint from the Secretary of the Royal Almonry, setting out the quantity of each denomination required for the coming year,[40] a quantity restricted to the amount which the sovereign has authorized.[41] For example, such a letter relating to the Maundy distribution of 1989 was received in August 1988 and asked for the delivery of the said coin to the Royal Almonry Office by 10 February 1989[42] (in 1989, Maundy Thursday fell on 23 March). All the subsequent manufacturing processes, including the provision of the necessary silver bullion, are handled by the Royal Mint[43] but the Royal Almonry pays for the Maundy coins required for use in connection with the Maundy service.[44]

The Maundy money has always been legal tender. However, since they were not meant to be obtainable by the public, it has been stated[45] that for many years, although these are not stipulated, they were not included in the Trial of the Pyx.[46] Regardless of whether or not this is true,[47] the Maundy coinage has for a long time now been subject to the Trial. In over seven hundred years up to 1974, only five adverse verdicts had been delivered by the juries of these Trials.[48] Therefore, the failure of the Maundy coinage with relation to the Trial of the Pyx Order 1975, which came into operation on 20 December in that year, is worthy of note since it constitutes only the sixth such adverse verdict in over seven centuries. Following the deliverance of its verdict, the jury was addressed by the Queen's Remembrancer, J. H. Jacob, at Goldsmiths' Hall on Friday, 21 May 1976, the relevant part of his speech reading:[49]

> Today, Gentlemen of the Juries, your verdict on the silver Maundy coins has brought to light a slight discrepancy but a discrepancy nevertheless. In order to appraise the significance of this error, it might be helpful if I were to make a few passing observations on this noteworthy occasion.
>
> Your verdict on the Maundy coins, which is, of course, of special significance to Her Majesty the Queen herself, has reversed the famous Biblical verdict on King Balshazzar. For him, the writing on the wall was that he was weighed in the balances and found wanting, whereas for the Maundy coins the writing on the scroll is that they were weighed in the balances and found abounding. For the coins themselves were found to be fulsome and goodly [when assayed by comparison with the standard trial plate, they were on the whole found to be within the permitted variation from finenes, the amount of the variation

being 1.5 parts per thousand above standard fineness]. Indeed, I should emphasise that your verdict on the Maundy silver shows that the coins were not underweight but that they were slightly overweight – as [sic] which of us is not? The amount of this variation for all the 31 Maundy coins weighed in bulk was .77 grams above the standard weight compared with the permitted variation of .36 grams, a difference of .41 grams in respect of the coins that were tested, which according to my poor mathematics is at least much below the much discussed 4½% prospective increase.

The Royal Mint, I am sure, would be the first to recognise and regret this discrepancy. It should be noted that this is the first time since 1926 that the verdicts at this Trial relating to United Kingdom coinage have shown a discrepancy from the permitted tolerances. In spite of the most advanced technology used in the processes of the production of coins, the human element must surely enter at some stage, and if this is so, one can say that to err is human and one can add that to err once in 50 years is surely remarkable and surely forgivable. Moreover, it may be of interest to the Master of the Mint to know that the error this year puts him in excellent though unexpected company, for in 1926 when the discrepancy in the United Kingdom coinage occurred, the then Master of the Mint was none other than Winston Spencer Churchill, and that fact should be put in the scales in Mr Healey's[50] favour.

The Royal Mint, I have no doubt, is always aiming at perfection but the pursuit of perfection is perhaps an unattainable ideal though a famous judge is reported to have remarked about one of his brother judges – I hasten to add that this was in the last century – that he was a great and wise and learned judge and had all the virtues without one redeeming vice. On the other hand, I am sure there is a moral in the biblical story about the handsome Absalom of whom it is recorded that from the sole of his foot to the crown of his head there was no blemish in him, but he turned out nevertheless to be a rebellious son.

The discrepancy in the silver Maundy coins will of course be brought to the attention of the proper authorities to deal with as they think fit. I doubt, however, the extra silver used in minting these coins would cause the Chancellor of the Exchequer a sleepless night or even the raising of the famous eyebrows, still less will he need to rush back to prepare an emergency budget. Both in volume and in value, the error relating to the silver Maundy coins borders on the negligible, if not infinitesimal. So far as volume is concerned, the number of Pyx pieces of United Kingdom coinage which were submitted to Trial amounted to nearly 100,000 consisting of 2,000 gold sovereigns and a vast quantity of cupro-nickel coinage, whereas the number of silver Maundy coins was only 31; and so far as the total value of the U.K. coinage is concerned, this amounted to over £45 millions, whereas the total value of the Maundy silver was £113.82. In these circumstances, the proper authorities may well feel that they could follow the example of the fair and firm football referee who when he spots that a member of one team is guilty of an infringement which leaves the advantage to the other team, he would play the advantage rule and waive the game to go on. I think this may be a proper case for playing the advantage rule and everyone would be happy if the worthy recipients who have received these Maundy coins should not be disturbed, even though the 1976 silver Maundy coins, perhaps because they are errant coins, may acquire a greater collectors' value.

In the light of all the above circumstances, I venture to think that the discrepancy relating to the silver Maundy coins revealed by your verdicts should not detract from the high reputation and esteem in which the Royal Mint has always been held. As you know, the Royal Mint is a large exporter and has received the Queen's Award to Industry and it enjoys a notable and pre-eminent record in the production of millions of coins of all denominations, shapes, and sizes and metals. Despite this unhappy lapse, your verdicts will, I am sure, give great comfort and satisfaction to Mr Christie, the Deputy Master and

Comptroller of the Royal Mint and his staff, since on the whole they constitute a well-deserved tribute to the admirable way in which they carry out their responsibilities and highly skilled duties.

I hope, nevertheless, it will not be taken amiss, if I were to remind you of the helpful remark which a wise judge is reported to have addressed to the prisoner in the dock who after a long and gruelling trial was acquitted by the jury. The report quotes the judge as saying, 'As you have been acquitted by the jury, it is my duty to discharge you. You are free to go, but don't do it again!'.

When, during the early Middle Ages, a monetary gift was first included in the Maundy ceremony,[51] the silver penny was the only coin in use. Even though the groat (fourpence), quarter-shilling (threepence) and half-groat (twopence) were introduced into general currency in 1351,[52] 1551[53] and 1351,[54] respectively, with the groat having been first introduced experimentally, with a low mintage, in 1279,[55] it still remained, until long after the most recent of these dates, the exclusive rôle of the silver penny to be used as Maundy money. Thus, during the reign of Elizabeth I, various orders were made pertinent to the minting of pennies for the Royal Maundy. For example, on 2 April 1574,[56] John Lonison, the then master worker at the Royal Mint,[57] was ordered to coin into the 'single penny', for the Queen's private use, 10lb of 11oz 2dwt fine silver, enough to produce approximately £30 worth of coin,[58] at the rate of 720 to the troy pound.[59] Similarly, in the *Acts of the Council* for 1576 is the entry '18th April, Mr. Martin officer of the Mint[60] to deliver £12 in pence for H.M.'s service on Maunday Thursday',[61] an order which must have been designed to meet the requirements of the following day[62] and shows that the money must have been in some already preserved stock.[63] Nearly two years later, on 18 March 1577/8,[64] there exists a 'Warrant to the Warden of the Mint for delivery of £13 in new pence for Maundy',[65] Maundy Thursday falling on 27 March in 1578.[66] From these orders it is apparent that about ten shillings in pence was added year by year to meet the increasing age of Elizabeth who would, in 1578, have required £8 8s 9d, namely 2,025 (45 × 45) pennies, as against £7 14s 1d, namely 1,849 (43 × 43) pennies, in 1576.[67]

Elizabeth I's death on 24 March 1603[68] witnessed the end of the House of Tudor and brought to the throne of England its first monarch of the House of Stuart, James VI of Scotland, then also becoming James I of England. This new king, who immediately took a keen interest in the Mint and its coinage, arranged for a regular supply of small moneys by means of a clause in the Indenture of 1604, which ordered that in every 100lb of coined silver there should be 2lb in half-groats, 1½lb in pence and ½lb in halfpence, the moneyers receiving an additional 1d per lb for the more exact sizing of these coins. However, it was not until the Indenture of 31 March 1619 that the Mint accounts during this reign make reference to 'the maundye'[69] when 61lb of sterling are recorded as being coined into small moneys for charity but the denominations were not stated. In the next year, 50lb of sterling silver was again used for the same purpose and in 1624-25 there was a third 'extraordinary' purchase of 75lb of the metal at eighteen pence per pound troy over price,[70] which was likewise converted into small pieces for distribution.[71] The above-mentioned clause in the Indenture of 1604 indicates the intention to strike silver twopences and halfpennies, as well as pennies. Some twenty years later the silver twopence had joined the silver penny in the moneys presented to the Maundy recipients. This is evident from a letter from the Bishop of London, endorsed 'March 16, 1625[72] – Bishop of London for his Mat Warrant for Maundaie money' and directed 'to the Right Honorable Sir Edward Conway, Kt. Principal Secretary to his Maties at Court or elsewhere':[73]

> My Lord, ye Maundy Thursday draws on and ther wilbe I suppose some difficulty to gett ye Kings Hand whilst his Ague holds him w^h I hope in God shall not be long. I am bold therefore to goe ye ferst way beseeching y^r Ldp to gett his hand as soone as it shall please yr Ldp for ye money gotten by warrant must be coyned into pence [Plate 38] and twopences [Plate 39] for ye Maundy distribution to ye por w^h will require some tyme, it is a thing of course and done every yeare, but ye indisposition of ye King requires such a Mediator as yr Lordship. So wth my harty prayer for yr Ldp's health and happinesse I remayne ready for your Comandements.
>
> GEO LONDON.

Mr. Subalmoner will wayte uppon youe wth ye bill, London House, March 16, 1624.[74]

This incursion of the silver twopence into the seventeenth-century Maundy money would, however, appear to have been short-lived. Thus, in the accounts of the Maundy ceremonies of Charles I in 1633 and 1639, of Charles II in 1661 and 1663 and of William III in 1699, it is reported that the monetary gift was made in 'new single pence',[75] 'single Pence'[76] or 'single pennies',[77] 'single pence',[78] 'pence in silver'[79] and 'silver pence',[80] respectively.[81] Furthermore, there is no reason why any of these coins should have been struck using special dies, so long as the coins were bright, new and bore the monarch's effigy, since at these times the main criterion was that the gift should ultimately be spendable. The coins were therefore probably struck using dies from ordinary currency production.[82] It has been arbitrarily suggested[83] that the now unique penny dated 1558 may have been struck in numbers sufficient for the Maundy distribution of 23 March 1558/9[84] and again, without any positive evidence,[85] that the Oxford Declaration Penny (Plate 40), struck in 1644, was issued solely for use in the Maundy ceremony which took place in Oxford in that year.[86] In 1644, Charles I was in his forty-fourth year of age at the time of the Maundy ceremony and it seems amazing to suggest that 1,936, namely 44 × 44, Oxford Declaration pennies ever existed. If they did so, it has been suggested that the current rarity of such pieces could be the result of many of them, over a period of some three hundred and fifty years, becoming lost because of their diminutive size, whilst support for such a mintage was claimed because of the existence of three varieties of this penny.[87] Nevertheless, the validity of such support is questionable since it is often the case that more than one pair of dies exist from which rare coins have been struck, strikings on different occasions using dies at random, thus leading to variations within the coinage. For example, one of the rarest of English coins is the VIGO five-guineas of 1703, of which about twenty pieces were struck: amongst the surviving specimens of these, there is evidence for the use of no fewer than three obverse dies.[88]

Over a period of some two to three years following the Restoration on 9 May 1660, several issues of what have been termed hammered silver coins were struck but the quality of striking of some is commensurate with certain of them having been machine made and struck in a collar. These issues contain variously the penny, twopence, threepence and fourpence.[89] One of them, which is complete in that it contains all four denominations, became known as the Undated Maundy money or Simon's Maundy money. This has been stated as probably[90] or definitely[91] having been struck for exclusive use as Maundy money, a claim which has also been extended[92] to all these issues. However, although not excluding the use of some of these coins in the Maundy distribution, it has been suggested that all these small silver coins were produced for general circulation, since there are examples of the Simon's Maundy threepence bearing a harp with either four, five or six strings, indicating the use of several dies in the striking of that particular denomination and thus implying a substantial mintage,[93] and worn specimens of these early small silver coins of Charles II in general often appear.[94]

Such an interpretation of the latter observation is, however, open to question since worn specimens of the four small silver denominations issued up to the latter part of the eighteenth century also often appear. Although this could suggest that these coins were likewise issued for general circulation, their very low mintages from 1727 onward, as discussed later, renders this very unlikely. It is far more feasible that the occurrence of such worn specimens could simply be the result of the Maundy recipients in these earlier times spending this monetary gift. Even during the nineteenth century some of the Maundy threepences found their way into general circulation.[95] In fact, in design those issued from 1845 to 1926 are indistinguishable from the silver threepence struck during this period for general circulation whereas the other three denominations, having no such comparable coins in general circulation, were not readily acceptable by traders, although they were, of course, legal tender. However, worn specimens sometimes appear of the Maundy pennies, twopences and fourpences issued during the first half of the nineteenth century, suggesting their limited circulation around this period.[96] Indeed, as recently as 1926 a letter to the Royal Mint reported that a Maundy fourpence dated 1925 had been found in circulation in Ireland.[97] Furthermore, the silver threepence of the Maundy design was also struck as a non-Maundy coin from 1834 to 1844, with the exception of 1842,[98] as was the silver twopence in 1838, 1843 and 1848,[99] but only for use in certain of the Colonies. Nevertheless, because of this, worn specimens of these issues frequently appear.

The first strikings, as a milled coinage,[100] of the silver twopence and the silver penny, threepence and fourpence, occurred in 1668[101] and 1670, respectively (Table 8) and it has been claimed[102] that from this latter date the production of these four small silver denominations was confined exclusively to the supplying of Maundy money. On the other hand it has been more cautiously stated that 'the money was first struck under Charles II for this purpose,[103] and the practise still continues',[104] such a claim, and a similar one by another authority,[105] not thereby excluding the use of the money for other purposes, including that of general circulation. Indeed, the exclusive use of these coins from 1668 onward for Maundy purposes has been refuted by many authorities. Three of these place between 1729 and 1731, inclusively, the issue of these four denominations solely for use as Maundy money,[106] an observation in 1730 recording that 'the greatest part of silver now remaining in the nation, and most likely to remain, is in sixpences and shillings'[107]. Other sources place the date of the beginning of such exclusive use for these coins at sometime during the reign of George III.[108] It may be thought contrary to both these conclusions that neither Snelling nor Ruding in their classic and then definitive works upon the English coinage, published in 1762 and 1817,[109] respectively, refer to Maundy sets, or even Maundy coins, whilst they both clearly describe the types of silver pennies, twopences, threepences and fourpences issued up to the periods of their publication. However, around this period the Maundy ceremony generally had assumed a very low profile[110] and such an omission by these two authorities may thus be understandable.

Clearly, the evolution of the four small silver denominations into the Maundy coinage is enigmatic, and opinions have varied widely. When the coins became used for Maundy purposes is not necessarily synchronous with their removal from general circulation and may be denominationally dependent. Obviously, the solution may be far from simple or clear cut, although the following considerations do permit conclusions to be reached.

That there was a need from 1660 onward, as there had been previously, for a small-denomination currency cannot be doubted. On 5 June 1661, Henry Slingsby, 'Officer of the Mint' suggested the introduction of 1¾d, 1½d and ⁵/₄d pieces in silver, besides being anxious to retain the silver penny in currency.[111] In the event, new silver threepences and fourpences were introduced into the public currency in January 1662/3.[112]

In the accounts of the Trial of the Pyx for 9 July 1663, 4 July 1664 and 4 August 1669, all the silver coins are classed together, namely as '2s 6d., 1s., 6d., 4d., 3d., 2d., 1d., and ½d.', '5s., 2s. 6d., 1s., 2d., and 1d.' and '5s., 2s. 6d., 1s., 4d., 3d., 2d., and 1d.', respectively. However, contrary to this, in the account for 16 January 1671, the small denominations are placed apart from the others, namely '5s., 2s. 6d., and 1s.' by the statement ' "and other silver taken from the same pyx", 4d., 3d., 2d., and 1d.'. It was recognized that 'this is the only occasion on which the distinction occurs' and subsequently noted that the accounts for 21 January 1672 and 14 February 1673 read as that for 4 August 1669 and that those for 20 February 1674, 14 June 1677 and 1679, 5 August 1681 and 7 November 1684 all read '5s., 2s. 6d., 1s., 6d., 4d., 3d., 2d., and 1d.'. However, the one exception led to the conclusion that 'the fact that the four lowest denominations of silver were noted separately in the record of this trial seems to place them in a class apart from the ordinary currency and to confirm the belief that the type with interlinked C's was used for Maundy purposes.'[113] Although this statement might be interpreted as disregarding their use as normal currency, the very inclusion of the four small silver denominations in the Trials of the Pyx is suggestive of their use as general purpose currency. This supposition is confirmed by the Indenture of 8 October 1670 which had ordered these coins with the general currency, namely 186 fourpences, 248 threepences, 372 twopences and 700 pennies, each to the troy pound.[114]

To prevent the abuses and frauds associated with the privately issued base-metal token coinage of pennies, halfpennies and farthings, a copper coinage of the halfpenny and farthing, of which both contained as much copper in weight as was their true intrinsic value less the charges for coining and uttering, was announced by proclamation on 16 August 1672. Concurrently, it was also declared that heretofore for the same reasons the officers of the Mint had been commanded 'to cause many thousands of pounds of good sterling silver to be coined into single pence and twopences, that so there might be good money currant [sic] among the poorest of our subjects, and fitted for their smaller traffic and commerce' but that this remedial measure had failed, partially because of the hoarding of these silver coins.[115] Nevertheless, it is clear that these official copper coins were not intended to displace the small silver from general circulation. In fact, although by 1674 or 1675 the production of the latter was falling,[116] the relief afforded by the copper coinage introduced in 1672 was only partial and confined to the silver penny and twopence, it having no effect upon the threepence and fourpence.[117] Nearly twenty years later, in February 1691/2,[118] a letter from the Duchess of Grafton, who desired Letters Patent to make pennies and twopences of coarse alloy, whilst being adversely critical of the

104 *Silver Pennies and Linen Towels*

Table 8. The small silver denominations and Maundy coins minted from 1668 to 1822

Date	1d	2d	3d	4d	Date	1d	2d	3d	4d	Date	1d	2d	3d	4d
1668		✓			1707	✓	✓	✓	✓	1746				
1669	✓	✓	✓	✓	1708	✓	✓	✓	✓	1747[7]				
1670	✓	✓	✓	✓	1709					1748[7]				
1671	✓	✓	✓	✓	1710	✓				1749	4	4	4	4
1672	✓	✓	✓	✓	1711					1750				
1673	✓	✓	✓	✓	1712					1751[9]				
1674	✓	✓	✓	✓	1713					1752				
1675	✓	✓	✓	✓	1714					1753	✓	4	4	4
1676	✓	✓	✓	✓	1715					1754				
1677	✓	✓	✓	✓	1716					1755				
1678					1717	3				1756				
1679	✓	✓	✓	✓	1718	✓				1757				
1680	✓	✓	✓	✓	1719					1758				
1681	✓	✓	✓	✓	1720	✓	✓	✓	✓	1759	✓	✓	✓	✓
1682	✓	✓	✓	✓	1721	✓				1760				
1683	✓	✓	✓	✓	1722	4	4	4	4	1761[5]				
1684	✓	✓	✓	✓	1723					1762[7]	✓	✓	✓	✓
1685	✓	✓	✓	✓	1724					1763				
1686	✓	✓	✓	✓	1725					1764[5]				
1687	✓	✓	✓	✓	1726					1765	10			
1688	✓	✓	✓	✓	1727					1766	✓	✓	✓	✓
1689					1728[5]					1767[7]	✓	✓	✓	✓
1690	1				1729					1768[7]				
1691	✓	✓	✓	✓	1730[6]					1769[7]				
1692	✓	✓	✓	✓	1731	✓				1770	✓	✓	✓	✓
1693	✓	✓	✓	✓	1732					1771[7]				
1694	✓	✓	✓	✓	1733	4	4	4	4	1772				
1695					1734[6]					1773[7]				
1696					1735					1774[7]				
1697				2	1736[7]					1775[7]				11
1698					1737					1776	✓	✓	✓	✓
1699	✓	✓	✓	✓	1738[7]	✓				1777[7]				
1700	✓	✓	✓	✓	1739	✓				1778[7]	✓	✓	✓	✓
1701					1740					1779				
1702	✓	✓	✓	✓	1741[8]					1780				
1703					1742[7]					1781				
1704	✓	✓	✓	✓	1743					1782[7]				12
1705					1744	4	4	4	4	1783[7]				
1706					1745[7]					1784				✓

Date	1d	2d	3d	4d
1785[7]				
1786				
1787[7]				
1788[7]				
1789[7]				
1790[7]				
1791				
1792				
1793[7]				
1794[7]				
1795				
1796[7]				
1797				
1798[7]				
1799[7]				
1800[13]				
1801[13]				
1802[13]				
1803[13]				
1804[13]				
1805[13]				
1806[13]				
1807[13]				
1808[13]				
1809[13]				
1810[13]				
1811[13]				
1812[13]				
1813[13]				
1814[13]				
1815[13]				
1816[13]	14	14	14	14
1817	✓	✓	✓	✓
1818	14	14	14	14
1819	✓	✓	✓	✓
1820	14	14	14	14
1821	✓	✓	✓	✓
1822		15		

Notes to Table 8: √, Denominations exist according to Hawkins and *ESC* and are present in the British Museum Collection. Complete uniformly-dated sequences marked √√√√ are also confirmed by Grueber; *1*, Exists according to Grueber (p. 136) but not according to Hawkins (p. 390) or to *ESC* (p. 200). A specimen is not in the British Museum Collection which makes Grueber's claim doubtful; *2*, Exists according to *ESC* (p. 186) (only one of two examples known) but not according to Hawkins (p. 397). The specimen exhibited at the Ordinary Meeting of the British Numismatic Society on 31 March 1948 was thought to be unique (see note 2 to Table 25); *3*, Exists according to Grueber (p. 144) but not according to Hawkins (p. 406). A specimen is not in the British Museum Collection which makes Grueber's claim doubtful; *4*, The absence of all the denominations with these dates might be explained by the fact that, for Royal Maundy purposes, such coins would not be required since, in 1722, 1733 (see also note 5 to Table 10), 1744 (see also note 7 to Table 10) and 1749, Maundy Thursday fell before 25 March, namely on 22, 22 and 23 March, respectively (*OCEL*, pp. 935–53), and the OS calendar (see Appendix 3) was still in use in England. However, these were the only post-1706 years in which this combination of OS calendar with a pre-25 March Maundy Thursday occurred (*OCEL*). The absence of all four denominations in some of the other years between 1706 and 1752 (the NS calendar (see Appendix 3) was adopted in England on 1 January 1752) was obviously therefore caused by other factors, such as that referred to in note 7 or the use of coins struck in even earlier years for the Maundy distribution in these years; *5*, See note 3 to Table 10; *6*, See note 4, and then note 3, to Table 10; *7*, The absence of Maundy coins bearing some of these dates was probably caused by the contemporary practice of the Master of the Mint to purchase, at the most financially expedient intervals, some one hundredweight or so of silver, even though the purchase price, that of bullion, would still have been above the coinage price of sixty-two shillings per troy pound which thereby prevented the Mint striking silver for general currency (see Section II of Chapter 3). This silver was then struck, using the most recently available dies, into enough Maundy coins to satisfy the requirements for several years, in order to save starting men and machines more often to produce the very low mintages required for individual years (Craig (1953), p. 247); *8*, See note 6 to Table 10; *9*, See note 8 to Table 10; *10*, The penny dated 1765 exists according to the Dean of Bocking (quoted by Farquhar (1929–30), p. 249), *ESC* (pp. 32, 208) (only one or two examples known) and Trowbridge (p. 24) (twenty to fifty examples known) but not according to Hawkins (p. 417). No penny dated 1765 is in the British Museum Collection, nor was one in an otherwise complete collection of normal Maundy money, namely excluding proof and other than silver issues, offered for sale in 1977 (*NCirc*, 85 (1977), pp. 556–57). Linecar (*An Advanced Guide to Coin Collecting* (London, 1970), p. 198) doubts its existence, as does the present author since no silver was coined into pennies in 1765, although small quantities were coined into the other three small denominations (Table 10); *11*, According to Hawkins (p. 417), a fourpence dated 1765 does not exist. However, this is clearly erroneous since not only does the Dean of Bocking claim its existence (quoted by Farquhar (1929–30), p. 249) but *ESC* (pp. 32, 187) estimates five to ten examples exist, a specimen is in the British Museum Collection and specimens have been offered for sale on several occasions during the past quarter-century (see, for example, *NCirc*, 85 (1977), p. 557; *SCMB*, (July 1976), p. 270; Spink Coin Auction, 1980; 1987, p. 19 (see also note 5 to Table 29); *12*, Dr G. H. Bullmore is quoted (*ESC*, p. 187) as pointing out that the 1776 fourpence appears with a defective 6 which appears much like a 5. No fourpence dated 1775 is as yet known (*ESC*, p. 187) nor, indeed, is one likely to be found since there was no mintage of silver into Maundy money in that year (Table 10), and that so minted in 1776 (Table 10) produced coins bearing the latter date; *13*, The Maundy coins dated 1800 represent those of a frozen date, in that not only were they struck in 1800 but also in some of the subsequent years up to, and including, 1816. Furthermore, during this period of sixteen years several new dies were sunk but these were all dated 1800. Further elaboration upon this situation, with its possible raison d'être, is presented in Section III, Sub-section viii, of Chapter 3; *14*, According to Hawkins (p. 418) and Grueber (p. 151), the type 4 (bull head) Maundy coinage of George III exists bearing these dates but such coins do not exist according to *ESC* (p. 215): specimens are not in the British Museum Collection which casts doubt upon Grueber's claim. It is fairly certain that Maundy coins bearing these dates were not struck. However, such coins were minted in these years but they did not bear these dates but those on the most recently prepared obverse dies (Dyer) (see also note 13); *15*, Complete sets have been issued annually from 1822 to date.

problems associated with the small size of the silver pennies and twopences then in circulation, also indicated that the former, although becoming rarer, was still a circulating coin.[119] Furthermore, specimens of the milled small silver coinage of Charles II and of Simon's Maundy Money are still quite common, in spite of their smallness, with the related predisposition to having become misplaced over the past three hundred or so years, and their having to survive the Great Recoinage of 1696 to 1698. Clearly, large quantities, far in excess of the Maundy requirements, must have been struck.[120]

Considerable diversification within the small silver denominations of William and Mary is known.[121] This not only indicates, from the legend variations, that several dies were used but also, because of the bust variations, that more than one punch was sometimes also used in the production of individual denominations of these coins of particular dates. This, in turn, suggests a considerable production of such coins, namely one significantly above that only necessary for the requirements of the Royal Maundy.

From the foregoing considerations it may be concluded that, up to the end of the reign of William and Mary, the small silver coinage was struck for general circulation and found only incidental utility in the Maundy service, this latter use being often probably restricted to the silver penny.[122]

Mary died on 28 December 1694[123] and so the Maundies of 1695, 1696 and 1697 would have been made either by, or on behalf of, William III alone. If the production of a special coinage for Maundy distribution had become established by this time, then surely small silver bearing William III's bust would have been produced in one or more of these years, especially since the Great Recoinage of 1696 to 1698 was then being undertaken. In fact, with the exception of the probably unique fourpence dated 1697,[124] the earliest date which appears on these coins is 1698 (Table 8). However, it is possible that stocks of the small silver of William and Mary were high enough for Maundy purposes during these first three years of William III's reign. Alternatively, it has been suggested that the hiatus in 1696 and 1697 was probably the result of the objection raised by the workmen to the carrying out of the Indenture[125] ordering that eighteen ounces in every hundredweight (100lb) of silver should 'be in groats, threepences, twopences and pence', whilst the small total of silver coined in 1695 could answer for the lack of such pieces in that year.[126] However, such an objection could not have prevented the carrying out of the terms of the Indenture, since this was a formal binding agreement between the Crown and the Master of the Mint.[127] Indeed, not only would it appear to be likely that the small total of silver, variously quoted as twenty pounds troy to the value of £62,[128] or £160,[129] coined in 1695 would have been struck as the small silver denominations, but for the following year it is significant that a striking of £60 in silver is quoted separately from that of £2,511,853.[130] This latter large sum reflects the beginning of the Great Recoinage of 1696 to 1698 involving the production of sixpences, shillings, half-crowns and crowns.[131] Perhaps, in 1695 and 1696, the dies which had been used to produce the small silver dated 1694 (this being the last bearing the conjoint busts of William and Mary) were used to strike the Maundy requirements of William III alone.

The proportion of the various silver denominations which were struck from 1696 to 1698, 1699 to 1756 and 1757 to 1804 are presented in Table 9. It is apparent that the average annual rate of minting of the four small silver denominations from 1696 to 1698, namely 11,004 troy pounds (£34,111), is far greater than that of these denominations which were produced from 1699 to 1756, during which period the average annual rate was some eighty-four troy pounds (£274). From a consideration of the information presented in Table 10, the majority of the total minted during the latter period must have been struck in its earlier years. Thus, because of its not inconsiderable mintage, it would appear that the small silver of William III was, like that of earlier reigns, struck for general circulation with an only incidental utility as Maundy money. That this use may have been limited to the silver penny is suggested by the account of the distribution in 1699, when all four small silver denominations were actually issued (Table 8), which reports that one purse contained 'as many silver Pence as His Majesties' Years of Age'.[132] Indeed, it has been stated that 'only the penny was used during Newton's lifetime [25 December 1642–20 March 1727] for the Maundy ceremonial'.[133] Nevertheless, the £34,111 of small silver struck during the former

Table 9. The respective proportions of the silver denominations which were struck from 1696 to 1698, from 1699 to 1756 and from 1757 to 1804[1]

Date	Proportion[2]	Denomination	Weight (troy lb)	Value (£)
1696 to 1698	2/10	Crown	433,557	1,344,027
	3/10	Half-crown	650,335	2,016,039
	4/10	Shilling	867,114	2,688,053
	1/10	Sixpence	216,778	672,012
	18oz per 100lb	Small money[3]	33,011	102,334
1699 to 1756	2/10	Crown	67,426	209,020
	3/10	Half-crown	101,139	313,531
	4/10	Shilling	134,852	418,041
	1/10	Sixpence	33,713	104,511
	18oz per 100lb	Small money[3]	5,133	15,912
1757 to 1804	2/3	Shilling	40,834	126,586
	1/3	Sixpence	20,416	63,289
	Approximately £60 per annum	Small money[3]	883[4]	2,737[4]
Totals coined from 1696 to 1804		Crown	500,983	1,553,047
		Half-crown	751,474	2,329,570
		Shilling	1,042,800	3,232,680
		Sixpence	270,907	839,812
		Small money[3]	39,027	120,983

Notes to Table 9: *1*, From the account made out by James William Morrison, the Deputy Master of the Mint, on 1 November 1804 and transmitted to the Earl of Liverpool (PRO, Mint 1/16); *2*, In relation to these proportions, Morrison writes 'From the time of the Recoinage in the Reign of King William III (in conformity with the Acts of Parliament and the Indentures of that time) a Regulation was established at the Mint to coin the several species of Silver Monies in the following proportions, viz. 2/10 into Crowns 3/10 into Half crowns 4/10 into Shillings and 1/10 into Sixpences, reserving out of every 100 lbs Troy 18oz to be coined into small Maundy Monies. This regulation continued until the year 1757, when the Master of the Mint was directed by Warrant of Treasury dated July 1757, to coin the Bullion imported into the Mint in that year into Shillings and Sixpences only. After this period, no distinct rule appears to have been adhered to in coining the different Silver Monies. Excepting the Small Monies, no Coinage of Silver seems to have taken [place] till the year 1787, and this consisted solely of Shillings and Sixpences. The proportion has been taken at 2/3 of Shillings and 1/3 Sixpences, which it is conceived will be found nearly correct. But as the Comptrollment roll does not distinguish the respective species of Monies, it is very difficult from the other Books to obtain a perfectly accurate Account'; *3*, Pennies, twopences, threepences and fourpences; *4*, Clearly, this total ignores the £5,791 which was struck as silver threepences in 1762 and 1763.

108 *Silver Pennies and Linen Towels*

Table 10. The annual production of Maundy money, in troy pounds, and the mintages derived thereof, from 1727 to 1816[1]

Date of delivery from the moneyers to the Mint office	Weight of silver (in troy pounds) used to produce denomination (mintage figure, calculated from the weight[2], is given in the associated parentheses)				Annual total of of Maundy money in sterling currency
	1d	2d	3d	4d	
25 February 1727	16(11,904)	17(6,324)	17(4,216)	16(2,976)	£204 12s
13 April 1728[3]	17(12,648)[3]	15(5,580)[3]	15(3,720)[3]	—[3]	£195 16s
26 March 1729	15(11,160)				£186
26 March 1730[4]				15(2,790)	
22 April 1731	21(15,624)	14(5,208)	13(3,224)		£190 16s
17 March 1733[5]	33(24,552)[5]	31(11,532)[5]	11(2,728)[5]	12(2,232)[5]	£269 14s
24 April 1734[4]					
2 April 1735	28(20,832)	29(10,788)	13(3,224)	16(2,976)	£266 12s
31 March 1737	36(26,784)	34(12,648)	16(3,968)	17(3,162)	£319 6s
14 April 1739	42(31,248)	22(8,184)		16(2,976)	£297 12s
18 March 1741[6]	47(34,968)[6]	13(4,836)[6]	30(7,440)[6]	30(5,580)[6]	£372
2 March 1744[7]	37(27,528)[7]	15(5,580)[7]	8(1,984)[7]	8(1,488)[7]	£210 16s
19 March 1746	17(12,648)	13(4,836)	4(992)		£105 8s
22 August 1746	65 + 2oz (48,484)	65 + 6oz (24,366)	69(17,112)	70 + 4oz (13,082)	£837
27 March 1751[8]	30[9](22,320)[8]				£93
4 March 1752	18 + 9oz + 6 dwt (13,969)				£58 4s ½d (58)[10]
28 March 1753	19(14,136)				£58 18s (59)[10]
1 April 1754					
20 February 1755					
25 February 1756	20(14,880)	19(7,068)			£120 18s (121)[10]
2 March 1757	19(14,136)				£58 18s
8 March 1758	29(21,576)				£89 18s
21 March 1759	24(17,856)	10(3,720)			£105 8s (105)[10]
12 March 1760	16(11,904)	9(3,348)	9(2,232)	9(1,674)	£133 6s (133)[10]
11 March 1761[3]	10(7,440)[3]				£31 (31)[10]
9 March 1763	18(13,392)	23(8,556)	uncertain[11]	54(10,044)	see note 12
11 April 1764[3]			5(1,240)[3]		£15 10s (15)[10]
27 March 1765		2 + 2oz (808)	2 + 2oz (537)	1 + 8oz (310)	£18 12s (19)[10]
12 March 1766	23 + 6oz (17,484)	30 + 7oz (11,377)	21 + 4oz (5,291)	20 + 7oz (3,829)	£297 12s (298)[10]

30 March 1770	13(9,672)		6(1,488)	3(558)	£68 4s (68)[10]
7 April 1772	31(23,064)	32(11,904)	22(5,456)	23(4,278)	£334 16s (335)[10]
6 March 1776	29 + 9oz(22,134)	30(11,160)	21(5,208)[13]	21(3,906)	£315 8s 6d
31 December 1779	32(23,808)	17(6,324)[14]	17(4,216)[14]	16(2,976)[14]	£254 4s (254)[10]
28 November 1781	20(14,880)				£62 (62)[10]
31 December 1784	23 + 8oz (17,608)	17 + 10oz (6,634)	12 + 10oz + 12gr (3,183)	11 + 18gr (2,047)	£202 11s (203)[10]
24 October 1787[15]	40(29,760)[15]	25(9,300)[15]	20(4,960)[15]	20(3,720)[15]	£325 10s
21 March 1792	40 + 7oz (30,194)	8 + 8oz (3,224)	14(3,472)	18(3,348)	£251 17s 6d (252)[10]
16 December 1795	42 + 10oz + 14 dwt (31,911)	17 + 5oz + 1 dwt (6,481)	17 + 7oz (4,361)	16 + 9oz +15 dwt (3,127)	£293 11s 11d (295)[16]
25 March 1800[17]	13 + 9oz(10,230)	6(2,232)	5(1,240)	4(744)	£89 2s 6d (91)[10]
March 1801[17,18]	13 + 2oz + 1 dwt + 8gr (9,828)[18]			——[18]	£53 7s (33)[19]
April 1802[17,18]	6(4,464)[18]	5(1,860)[18]	5(1,240)[18]	——	£62 (62)[10]
March 1803[17,18]	13 + 6oz (10,044)[18]	3 + 4oz (1,240)[18]	3 + 3oz (806)[18]	3 + 3oz (605)[18]	£72 6s 8d (72)[10]
21 March 1804[17,18]	13 + 4oz (9,920)[18]	4 + 3oz (1,581)[18]	3 + 8oz (909)[18]	3 + 9oz (698)[18]	£77 10s (78)[10]
22 January 1805[17,18]	31 + 3oz (23,250)[18]	9 + 1oz (3,379)[18]	8 + 5oz (2,087)[18]	10 + 3oz (1,907)[18]	£182 18s (183)[10]
12 February 1807[17,18]	20(14,880)[18]	5(1,860)[18]	5(1,240)[18]	5(930)[18]	£108 10s (108)[10]
21 February 1809[17,18]	19(14,136)[18]	6(2,232)[18]	6(1,488)[18]	6(1,116)[18]	£114 14s (115)[10]
7 April 1810[17,18]	20(14,880)[18]	——	——	7(1,302)[18]	£120 18s (121)[10]
24 March 1812[18]	13(9,672)[18]	1 + 6oz (558)[18]	2 + 6oz (620)[18]	uncertain	£52 14s (53)[10]
24 March 1813[18]	11(8,184)[18]	6(2,232)[18]	7(1,736)[18]	5(930)[18]	£89 18s (90)[10]
23 March 1814[18]	31(23,064)[18]	7(2,604)[18]	——	7(1,302)[18]	£161 4s (161)[10]
15 April 1816[18]	6(4,464)[18]	6(2,232)[18]	6(1,488)[18]	8(1,488)[18]	£80 12s

(*continued*)

Notes to Table 10: *1*, These data were drawn from accounts in the PRO by Mr G. P. Dyer, the Librarian and Curator at the Royal Mint; *2*, These totals are calculated on the basis of sixty-two shillings to one troy pound (see Appendix 6); *3*, Maundy coins bearing the date corresponding to this year are not known (Table 8). This silver was therefore most probably minted using the most recently available dies at the time; *4*, There were deliveries of coin on 26 March 1730 and 24 April 1734 but the denominations are not specified and so far it has not been possible to establish whether or not Maundy coins were included; *5*, The date given is NS and is thus 17 March 1732 OS (see Appendix 3), the year in which this delivery was therefore made and which thereby accounts for the fact that Maundy coins dated 1733 are unknown whereas all four denominations dated 1732 are known to have been minted (Table 8); *6*, The date given is NS and is thus 18 March 1740 OS (see Appendix 3), the year in which this delivery was therefore made and which thereby accounts for the fact that Maundy coins dated 1741 are unknown whereas all four denominations dated 1740 are known to have been minted (Table 8); *7*, The date given is NS and is thus 2 March 1743 OS (see Appendix 3), the year in which this delivery was therefore made and which thereby accounts for the fact that Maundy coins dated 1744 are unknown whereas all four denominations dated 1743 are known to have been minted (Table 8); *8*, No Maundy coins dated 1751 were struck but the penny dated 1750 was issued (Table 8) and most likely forms the basis of this delivery; *9*, For 27 March 1751, one account gives 60lb but this seems to be an error made some years later; *10*, The figures in parentheses for these totals were published some thirty-eight years ago (Craig (1953), pp. 418–19) and clearly in most instances represent the result of rounding either up or down; *11*, The delivery of 9 March 1763 included £1,185 of silver in threepences (Dyer) but it is not clear how many of these were set aside for the Maundy. Likewise, in 1762, Officially £100, but possibly significantly more (Mays, James O'Donald; p. 139), of the £4,117 (Dyer) (quoted elsewhere Craig (1953), p. 418) as £3,162), was coined into threepences; *12*, Officially £100, but possibly significantly more (Mays, James O'Donald; p. 139), of the £4,117 (Dyer) (quoted elsewhere Craig (1953), p. 418) as £2,629) in silver minted in Dublin as Lord Lieutenant (Craig (1953), pp. 246–47; Mays, James; Mays, James O'Donald). *13*, No threepences dated 1776 are known (Table 8). This silver was therefore minted into threepences using the then most recently available dies; *14*, No twopences, threepences and fourpences were struck bearing the date 1779 (Table 8). Since the delivery was made on the last day of 1779, it is surely possible that this silver, and, indeed, some of that used in striking pennies, was used to produce coins dated 1780; all four denominations bearing this date exist (Table 8); *15*, No Maundy coins dated 1787 were struck but all four denominations dated 1786 were minted (Table 8) and most likely form the basis of this delivery; *16*, The rounding up or down (see note 10) would appear to have gone a little astray; *17*, Some of the figures for the first decade of the nineteenth century are a little problematical. The most reliable source is the Mint Master's annual account and this has been followed in the present instance; *18*, Maundy coins bearing the date corresponding to these years are unknown (Table 8). This silver was therefore most probably minted using the most recently available dies at the time, those dated 1800. This would explain the very frequent occurrence of Maundy coins so dated (see Table 8 and the related note *13*); *19*, The figure 33 (Craig (1953), p. 419) is probably a misprint for 53 since the rounded down total has been quoted elsewhere (Dyer).

period still represents only 1½ per cent of the total silver coined (Table 9), in accord with the above-mentioned Indenture, and such a small proportion may be considered as being too small to have been of much use in ordinary transactions. Furthermore, if the small silver denominations of William III were struck for general circulation, it might be expected some would have been coined in one or more of the various provincial mints operating during the Great Recoinage of 1696 to 1698, namely at Bristol, Chester, Exeter, Norwich and York. However, there is no evidence that this occurred, in so far as none of the small silver denominations are known which carry any of the distinguishing letters associated with these mints.

In 1702, an abortive attempt was made to reduce the standard of the smaller coins.[134] Whilst opposing any idea of changing the alloy for the then current larger pieces, the Mint authorities suggested 'that if small money which by continual use weares away fast and is apt to be lost were coined of coarse alloy as is done in several countries provided it were well coyned to prevent counterfeiting such money would weare longer and be less apt to be lost than that now in use'. They qualified this statement 'by small money we understand Groats, Threepences, Twopences and Pence, unless the penny by reason of its smallness be made of copper'. This suggests that all four of the small silver coins were then in general circulation. However, it would appear that they were primarily of the two larger denominations since the statement has been made that by 1701 'the silver penny and twopenny were in any case out of date for trade; they were "curios and toys for children" ' and furthermore, following 1701 'virtually no new coins below the sixpence were produced for sixteen years; although the small silver coins from penny to fourpence, stopped during the Great Recoinage [but see above], were resumed at the previous ratio of 1½ per cent of silver coined, the quantity was too trifling to matter'.[135]

All four of the small silver denominations dated 1706 are fairly common. Nevertheless, strictly speaking, they ought not to have been required for Maundy use in that year since, according to the Julian OS calendar then in operation,[136] Maundy Thursday did not occur in 1706 but occurred twice in 1705 (on 5 April and 21 March) and then next in 1707 (on 10 April).[137] It would therefore appear that the coins dated 1706 may have been required as general currency, not forgetting their possible use, particularly that of the two smaller denominations, in other royal charities.[138]

In 1711, James Clerk and Joseph Cave, conjoint engravers at the Scottish Mint, sought payments for making 'puncheons and Letters for Small Coynes, viz. Fouer Pence, Three Pence, Two Pence and One Penny, the sum of £70'.[139] In fact, an obverse and reverse die pair for a twopence of the same date and with the Edinburgh mintmark[140] is known,[141] as are two pattern groats dated 1711 and with the Edinburgh mintmark, one in copper[142] and one in silver[143] and both, no doubt, from the same die.[144] Nonetheless, apart from the two patterns, the worn appearance of which suggests that they were not of the period but of later strikings,[145] it would appear that small silver coins dated 1711 and bearing the Edinburgh mintmark were not struck. This was understandable since the Edinburgh Mint, reopened in 1707 following the Act of Union of Scotland with England, was closed forever on 4 August 1710.[146] It is suggested that the worn appearance of the above-mentioned dies is caused through age, not by use.[147]

It has been stated that 'it is obvious that Maundy was not in question and the bare suggestion of making these little pieces for Anne's new Scottish coinage shows that in her effort to establish parity between the sister countries, the small silver currency was given consideration'.[148] In other words, the four small silver denominations must at that time have been in use in England as general currency. Alternatively, these dies could reflect a regional variation in demand, namely a preference for low value denominations north of the Border, as was apparent much later with respect to the Britannia groats and silver threepences.[149] On the other hand, the post-Union striking of Anne's coinage at the Edinburgh Mint only involved the production of crowns (in 1707 and 1708), half-crowns (from 1707 to 1709), shillings (from 1707 to 1709) and sixpences (in 1708 and 1709) in silver, the four small silver denominations being conspicuous by their absence. This, together with the late date, namely 1711, on the above-mentioned artifacts, might indicate that, whatever the latter's real significance, small silver denominations were not in demand in Scotland, a situation which may, or may not, have also prevailed south of the Border, and which could suggest a connection of the above-mentioned dies for small silver denominations with potential Maundy uses in Scotland.

Notwithstanding the raison d'être of the intended small silver coinage for Scotland, for several centuries before the Crowns were united, the Scottish monarchs had been active in presenting their alms.[150] Indeed, the earliest known coin especially struck as Maundy money in the British Isles is the twelvepenny groat of James IV, of which 2,550 were struck for distribution during the Maundy service held in Scotland in 1512, the source of the bullion for these coins being one of the King's great silver wine jugs which he gave to David Scott, Master of the Scottish Mint, to be so used.[151] Thus it might be argued that the above-mentioned artifacts with the Edinburgh mintmark could have been indicative of an intended Maundy ceremony in Scotland. This supposition is further supported not only by the fact that the Act of Union of Scotland with England, passed on 6 March 1707, became law from the following 1 May but also because the crowns of the two countries had been united since 1603 when James VI of Scotland succeeded to the throne of England as James I. Actually, the report announcing the Edinburgh-mintmarked pattern groat of 1711 in copper incorporated the statement that 'it seems, however, from this discovery that a series of the Maunday money was intended to be struck in 1711'.[152] Nevertheless, although Anne was more popular with the Scots than had been William III, who had snubbed them and virtually begun the process, which had forced the Act of Union on them, through the offices of a number of London-based and influential Scotsmen, it is still doubtful whether such a royal visitation would have been considered prudent since it would almost certainly have received an extremely hostile reception and was difficult to imagine.[153] On the other hand, by this time the monarch appears to have lost all direct involvement with the Maundy service in England, being deputized for by the High Almoner or the Sub-almoner.[154] Thus, a similar Scottish proxy in a Maundy service north of the Border could well have obviated the necessity of an associated royal visit.

The introduction into general circulation of the regal copper farthing and halfpenny in 1672 could well have begun the displacement of the impractically-small silver penny and twopence from general circulation[155] and thereby their exclusive use as Maundy coins and largesse, respectively.[156] Although it has been considered that this process was probably not completed until the introduction of the impractically large copper penny and twopence in 1797,[157] it would appear that these two silver denominations had, for all practical purposes, disappeared from general circulation at a much earlier date. By the beginning of Sir Isaac Newton's time as Master of the Mint, from 25 December 1699 until his death at the age of eighty-four years on 20 March 1727,[158] the silver penny and twopence, as has already been stated, were, 'in any case out of date for trade; they were "curios and toys for children" ',[159] although there may have been a regional variation in demand for them. Clearly, the penny and twopence were too small for easy handling whereas the silver threepence and fourpence[160] certainly remained in general use, being not only of a reasonable size but also useful at a time when there would otherwise have been considerable inconvenience in making transactions because of the large gap between the values of the halfpenny and sixpence prior to the introduction of the cartwheel penny and twopence in 1797. In point of fact, John Arbuthnot in his *History of John Bull* relates the manner by which John's friend, Sir Roger, discouraged creditors by setting them 'a telling a thousand Pounds in Sixpences, Groats, and Three-penny Pieces'.[161] This suggests that such coins were then to be found in circulation and, significantly, does not mention the penny or twopence which must have been too rare for Sir Roger to acquire.[162] It is of related interest that when a small silver coinage was struck for general circulation in 1762 and 1763, it was as threepences and not as any of the other three small denominations.[163]

From 1727 to 1816, during which period the striking of the other silver coinage in Great Britain was so sporadic because of the effects of the Mint's shortage of silver,[164] small quantities of silver were set aside, on an almost annual basis, for the production of Maundy money (Table 10). Clearly, the number of coins struck from this operation are far too small (Table 10) to have been of any practical use in general circulation and yet their mintages are in significant excess of those required for the Royal Maundy (Table 11). This indicates that, as well as being used in the Gift of Pennies in the Royal Maundy, this small silver coinage also adopted a corresponding rôle in other royal charities, such as the Daily and Gate Alms, the King's Dole and largesse. Furthermore, when, after 1783, the coins became regularly available as uniformly-dated sets (Table 8), some probably found their way into souvenir-type gifts.

During the eighteenth-century silver shortage at the Mint, the London Lead Company were its occasional suppliers of this bullion as necessary. Thus was read, at a meeting of the Company's Court of Assistants held on 30 January 1766, the following letter dated 19 December 1765:[165]

> Gentlemen, I waited on you today by Direction of the Mint to acquaint you that they have not at present any Silver in the Office and as the Coinage of the small Money for the Maunday approaches, the Office is under the necessity of reminding you of the terms of your Charter and to desire you would forthwith order some Silver to be sent in as the same is always appropriated for the Service of the Maunday.
>
> Wm. Chamberlayne
> Sollicitor to the Mint.

The Company, however, were of the opinion that they were under no obligation to supply silver to the Mint at a financial loss to themselves, but were prepared to do so at the then current full market value, views which were transmitted to Mr Chamberlayne when he visited the Court on 27 February 1766.[166] The current significance of this letter is its illustration of the fact that, despite it being completely without silver, the Mint was still obliged to produce Maundy money and therefore had to procure the necessary small quantities of the metal. With regard to this obligation in this particular year, it is evident that Maundy coins of all four denominations (Tables 8 and 10) and to a total

Table 11. Comparison between the annual Maundy money mintages and the requirements of the Maundy recipients for most years[1] from 1727 to 1816

Year of the Maundy ceremony[2]	Monarch's age in years at the time of the ceremony[3]	Total number of pence required for the recipients[4]	Number of Maundy pence minted[5]	Excess Maundy pence not required for the recipients	Percentage excess[6]
1727	66	8,978	49,104	40,126	447
1728[7]	44	4,050	46,872	42,822	1,057
1729	45	4,232	44,640	40,408	955
1731	47	4,608 }[9]	46,872	37,462	398
1732	48	4,802			
1733[7,8]	49	5,000	64,728	59,728	1,195
1735	51	5,408 }[9]	63,984	52,958	480
1736[7]	52	5,618			
1737	53	5,832 }[9]	76,632	64,750	545
1738[7]	54	6,050			
1739	55	6,272 }[9]	71,424	58,654	459
1740	56	6,498			
1741[7]	57	6,728 ⎫			
1742[7]	58	6,962 ⎬[9]	89,280	68,390	327
1743	59	7,200 ⎭			
1744[7,8]	60	7,442 }[9]	50,592	35,462	234
1745[7]	61	7,688			
1746	62	7,938 ⎫			
1747[7]	63	8,192 ⎪			
1748[7]	64	8,450 ⎬[9]	226,176	183,906	435
1749[7,8]	65	8,712 ⎪			
1750[7]	66	8,978 ⎭			
1751[7]	67	9,248	22,320	13,072	141
1752	68	9,522	13,969	4,447	47
1753	69	9,800	14,136	4,336	44
1754	70	10,082	—	4,054	40
1755	71	10,368	—	3,768	36
1756	72	10,658	29,016	18,358	172
1757	73	10,952	14,136	3,184	29
1758	74	11,250	21,576	10,326	92
1759	75	11,552	25,296	13,744	119
1760	76	11,858	31,992	20,134	170
1761[7]	22	1,058 }[9]	7,440[10]	5,230	237
1762	23	1,152			
1764[7]	25	1,352	3,720	2,368	175
1765	26	1,458	4,464	3,006	206
1766	27	1,568 ⎫			
1767[7]	28	1,682 ⎪			
1768[7]	29	1,800 ⎬[9]	71,424	64,452	924
1769[7]	30	1,922 ⎭			
1770	31	2,048 }[9]	16,368	12,142	287
1771[7]	32	2,178			
1772	33	2,312 ⎫			
1773[7]	34	2,450 ⎪			
1774[7]	35	2,592 ⎬[9]	80,352	70,266	697
1775[7]	36	2,732 ⎭			
1776	37	2,888 ⎫			
1777[7]	38	3,042 ⎬[9]	75,702	66,572	729
1778[7]	39	3,200 ⎭			

Table 11. *(continued)*

Year of the Maundy ceremony[2]	Monarch's age in years at the time of the ceremony[3]	Total number of pence required for the recipients[4]	Number of Maundy pence minted[5]	Excess Maundy pence not required for the recipients	Percentage excess[6]
1779	40	3,362	}[9] 61,008	54,118	785
1780	41	3,528			
1781	42	3,698	}[9] 14,880	3,260	28
1782[7]	43	3,872			
1783[7]	44	4,050			
1784	45	4,232	}[9] 48,613	35,355	267
1785[7]	46	4,418			
1786	47	4,608			
1787[7]	48	4,802	}[9] 78,120	52,090	200
1788[7]	49	5,000			
1789[7]	50	5,202			
1790[7]	51	5,408			
1791[7]	52	5,618	}[9] 60,450	48,128	391
1792	53	5,832			
1793[7]	54	6,050			
1794[7]	55	6,272			
1795	56	6,498	}[9] 70,464	35,634	102
1796[7]	57	6,728			
1797[7]	58	6,962			
1798[7]	59	7,200			
1799[7]	60	7,442			
1800	61	7,688	21,390	13,702	178
1801[7,11]	62	7,938	12,804	4,866	61
1802[7,11]	63	8,192	14,880	6,688	82
1803[7,11]	64	8,450	17,360	8,910	105
1804[7,11]	65	8,712	18,600	9,880	113
1805[7,11]	66	8,978	}[9] 43,896	25,670	141
1806[7,11]	67	9,248			
1807[7,11]	68	9,520	}[9] 26,040	6,718	35
1808[7,11]	69	9,800			
1809[7,11]	70	10,082	27,528	17,446	173
1810[7,11]	71	10,368	}[9] 29,016	7,990	38
1811[7,11]	72	10,658			
1812[7,11]	73	10,952	12,648	1,696	15
1813[7,11]	74	11,250	21,576	10,326	92
1814[7,11]	75	11,552	}[9] 38,688	15,278	65
1815[7,11]	76	11,858			
1816[7,11]	77	12,168	17,856	5,688	47

Notes to Table 11: *1*, Excluding 1730 and 1734 (see note *4* to Table 10) and 1763 (see note *11* to Table 10); *2*, The year refers to NS (see note *8* and Appendix 3); *3*, DNB, Freeman-Grenville, *HBC*; *4*, Calculated from the relationship that when the monarch was x years old on their next birthday following the Maundy service, x pence in the form of Maundy coins were given to each of x male and x female recipients, although some of the Maundy services of George III, at least as exemplified by that in 1814 (Table 4), may have used the monarch's age in years *at the time* the service; *5*, Calculated from the data presented in Table 10; *6*, Calculated from: (excess Maundy pence not required for the recipients/total number of pence required for the recipients) × 100; *7*, Maundy coins bearing these dates are not recorded (Table 8) (see note *7* to Table 8); *8*, See note *4* to Table 8; *9*, It is assumed that in the years when no silver was set aside to produce Maundy coinage (Table 10), that required was produced from the most immediate previously allocated silver, usually in the form of already-struck coin using the dies of the most immediately available year (see also note *7* to

(continued)

face value of £297 12s (Table 10) were minted in 1766 but that no further silver was then coined until 1770 (Tables 8 and 10).

It was the practice around this period for the Master of the Mint to purchase at intervals some hundredweight or so of silver, however high the price, from which were then produced at one minting enough Maundy coins to suffice for several years and which thus explains the absence of certain dates on these coins (Table 8). For years in which silver allocations were made (Table 10) but for which Maundy coins bearing the related dates are unknown (Table 8), it is likely that the most recently-used dies were employed for minting. Such operations were effected in order to save starting men and machines on an annual basis for so small a mintage[167] and to maximize the use of dies.[168] However, notwithstanding such measures, the coins were still produced at a loss which meant that they were not issued for general use.[169]

From the above it may be concluded that, although for the preceding three decades the situation is far from clear cut, from 1727 onward the small silver coinage has been produced solely for Maundy purposes. Nevertheless, some of it was spent by the Maundy recipients and thereby found its way into general circulation, where the earlier small silver coinage was still in use. It would appear, however, that from the beginning of the eighteenth century, such use of the small silver coinage in general circulation was largely confined to the threepence and fourpence.

Although further evidence would appear to be unnecessary in order to establish that the small silver denominations, with the exception of the threepences dated 1762 and 1763,[170] issued from the beginning of the reign of George II were struck only for Maundy purposes, it may be significant that these denominations of George II's coinage are different from all the other denominations of this reign in that around 1740 the bust on the latter was changed from a young to an old type. This difference may be extrapolated into their being used for different purposes, namely as Maundy money and as general currency, respectively. However, such an interpretation may be unnecessary and may simply underestimate, and therefore ignore, the hard-headed engravers at the Mint during the eighteenth century whose working philosophy was that if good tools were available they need not be replaced. Thus, whereas the punches for the rest of the coinage were probably becoming worn and required replacing, thereby giving the opportunity to introduce a bust more commensurate with the King's advancing years, it would appear that the punches for the small silver were still in satisfactory condition. Since a new punch would take three weeks or so of an engraver's time to produce, it would appear that bust uniformity within the post-1740 coinage was sacrificed for some twelve weeks of an engraver's time.[171]

The earliest ceremony in which the use of the penny to fourpence sequence as Maundy money is reported is that of 1731,[172] in which year all four coins were issued. Nonetheless, it does not necessarily follow that similar complete denominational sequences were used in all subsequent Maundy ceremonies. After 1731, complete uniformly-dated sequences were actually only issued in sixteen of the years before 1799

Notes to Table 11. *(continued)*
Table 8); *10*, This figure takes no account of a possible contribution from the considerable quantity of silver, namely £1,674 (Dyer) (the total silver, namely that of the small coinage, struck in 1762 has been quoted elsewhere (Craig (1953), p. 418) as £3,162), which was coined into threepenny pieces dated 1762; *11*, All the Maundy coins struck from 1801 to 1816 were struck using dies dated 1800: hence the very frequent occurrence of the 1800 Maundy coinage (see also Section III, Sub-section viii, of Chapter 3).

(Table 8). Although it is possible that sequences struck in one year could also have been used in the distributions of subsequent years, or that mixed-date complete sequences may have been used in some years, it is clear that during this period the silver penny was issued more frequently (Tables 8 and 10) and in significantly larger numbers (Table 10) than any of the other three denominations. Thus, it would appear that, even after 1731, the silver penny might have been the only coin used in the Gift of Pennies in some years until toward the end of the eighteenth century. However, although only the penny was issued dated 1754 and 1755 (Table 8), contemporary reports[173] indicate that the Gift in these two years consisted of 'silver pence, two-pences and three-pences'.[174] Likewise, only these three smaller denominations are described as being used in the distribution of 1766,[175] although complete penny-fourpence sequences were struck with this date (Table 8), and in the following year only the twopence and threepence (no Maundy money dated 1767 was struck (Table 8) and it is likely that these coins were dated 1766) were reportedly so used.[176] Table 8 suggests that it was probably only from 1784 onward that the complete penny to fourpence sequence, now also uniformly dated, of Maundy money became annually utilized in the Maundy service. The accounts of the Maundy distributions for 1814, 1826 and 1833 in which the gift is stated to consist of 'seventy-five silver pennies', 'small silver pennies' and '68 silver penny pieces', respectively,[177] would, however, appear to contradict this generalization but, possibly, these statements should not be taken too literally.

II. MINTAGES OF THE MAUNDY COINAGE

During the course of the eighteenth century, the mintage of silver sank lower and lower, slowing from a trickle in the first half of the century to a virtual standstill in the second, as the so-called silver famine took effect. This famine, however, was confined to the coinage, for there was no shortage of silver bullion in the country. Nevertheless, so long as its price stayed above the coinage price of sixty-two shillings per troy pound there was no reason why it should be brought voluntarily to the Mint for coinage and, indeed, even if it were, there would have been the obvious temptation for the new full-weight coinage either to be hoarded or melted down for its bullion value.[178]

Although during this period the Mint was apparently not very active and senior officers seemed to be content to leave their work to deputies, this inactivity was the fault of Government in not providing the circumstances in which silver bullion could be presented for coinage. The Mint was ready to do what was asked of it. For example, it coped very well with the Great Gold Recoinage of the 1770s. Furthermore, it was careful to maintain the professional skills associated with coining, particularly amongst the assay masters and engravers, these being key areas which if not protected could have led to a proliferation in counterfeiting with an associated loss of confidence by the public in their coins.[179] Thus, the Mint produced the Maundy coinage when asked to do so (Tables 8 and 10).

From 1731 to 1751, although not in every year, crowns and half-crowns were issued, as were shillings from 1727 to 1752 and sixpences from 1728 to 1751. However, the total of this mintage was only £226,697 and, of this, £136,431 was produced in a single year, namely 1745.[180] This coin, along with some dated 1746, bears the name LIMA under the bust since the bullion for it was seized in the North Atlantic by two British privateers, the 'Duke' and the 'Prince Frederick', from two French treasureships which were en route from Peru carrying booty consisting principally of pieces of eight (eight reales) bearing the Lima mintmark.[181]

Silver had also been obtained from another fortuitous haul of foreign booty in 1702. Following the outbreak of the war of the Spanish Succession in that year, an Anglo-Dutch naval expedition sacked the town of Vigo in Galicia and either destroyed or captured the Spanish treasure fleet and their French escorts which had arrived there from Vera Cruz, via Havana, on 23 September 1702. However, the Anglo-Dutch attack did not occur until the following 23 October and in the interim the Spanish authorities had removed virtually all the bullion from the fleet, firstly to the security of Lugo and then across country to their fortress of Segovia.[182] Consequently, the widely-held claim, both contemporary and modern, that subsequent to the battle a great quantity of treasure was carried to England, quantified by at least one source as eleven million pieces of eight,[183] is erroneous. Indeed, another source, mindful of the fact that a great deal of the bullion had already been landed prior to the attack, limited the booty to 'a respectable amount'.[184] Furthermore, an indication of the actual dimension of this plunder is available from the statement on 16 June 1703 by the Keeper of the Mint, Isaac Newton, to the effect that till that date the total metal handed in to him was 4,504lb 2oz of silver and 7lb 8oz 16dwt of gold and less than a tenth of this, or 321lb 2oz 13dwt, had been used to coin £1,000. Thus, the total worth of the silver was approximately £14,000, far removed from 'a great quantity of treasure'.[185] Nonetheless, in commemoration of this military exploit, which was publicized throughout Britain by the propaganda machine of the Government as a famous victory, with the attendant distribution of knighthoods, etc., the name VIGO was placed below Anne's bust on some of the shillings dated 1702 and on all the crowns, shilling and sixpences, and most of the half-crowns, dated 1703.[186]

Returning to the reign of George II, it can be seen that, excluding 1745, the average annual production of silver over the remaining twenty-four years from 1727 to 1751 was only £3,761. Furthermore, the surrender of bullion under their licences by the native mining companies ceased about 1750 and dried up entirely when it was discovered that their obligatory offer of silver to the Mint did not have to be made at below the market price. As a result, and until 1816, the minting of silver coinage was even more severely limited. From 1752 to 1801, £143,313 was so minted and, of this, a total of £79,198 was struck as shillings in 1758 and as sixpences in 1757 and 1758 and £55,459 was struck as shillings and sixpences in 1787. These issues were special commissions for the Bank of England who, wishing to oblige their customers at Christmas time in these years with new shillings and sixpences, sent in bullion to the Mint at a loss: that the Bank issued these coins with care is evident from the fact that it still had £22,800 of them in stock in 1798.[187] A further £5,791, struck as silver threepences in 1762 and 1763, resulted from a Treasury Order to coin £10,000 of such coins after yet another treasure, of nearly £1,000,000, was taken at sea.[188] Officially £100, but possibly significantly more,[189] of the silver minted in 1763 was also used to produce shillings for use as largesse[190] on the occasion of the Duke of Northumberland's arrival in Dublin as Lord Lieutenant.[191]

In 1797 the Bank of England issued as currency, for 4s 9d each, Spanish and Mexican dollars (pieces of eight)[192] which had been marked on their bust with the little oval stamp bearing the head of George III, used at Goldsmith's Hall for distinguishing the Plate of the Kingdom and being the duty mark which had been stamped on the

Plate since 1784.[193] The Bank of England sent to the Mint a total of 2,325,099¾[194] (or 2,323,288[195]) of these dollars to be so countermarked. However, only £354,000[196] in such marked coins were issued to the Bank which soon, on 28 September 1797, recalled even these because of problems associated with counterfeiting.[197]

When, at the beginning of 1798, the price of silver at long last fell below sixty-two shillings per troy pound, a group of ten London bankers, including its most vociferous member, Magens Dorrien Magens, notified the Mint that they would send in silver bullion to be minted into shillings and sixpences. In all, some 9,895lb, equivalent to some £30,000, was so delivered and more was apparently on the way to give a final total which might well have reached some 100,000lb. Meanwhile, in February 1798 the problems associated with the British currency had been taken on board by a reconstituted Privy Council Committee on Coin actively led by Lord Liverpool, a committee which was cognisant of the renewed activity at the Mint which by the beginning of May 1798 was close to releasing the coins minted from the London bankers' silver. However, on 9 May 1798 the Committee ruled that this work of the Mint was lawless, a ruling regularized on 21 June 1798 by statute, and all the related bars, scissel and coin were melted into ingots and sold and the original owners repaid. A few of the shillings went astray and eventually found their way, under the name of Dorrien and Magens shillings, into various cabinets.[198]

The Bank of England then reverted to the expedient of producing a substitute silver coinage. From 21 September to 6 November 1799, further dollars to the weight of 409,992oz were marked with the small oval counterstamp used two years earlier but these were never issued to the public[199] and, indeed, why they were ever so stamped is not clear. In 1804 a third attempt was made to issue such dollars, at a currency value of five shillings each, a Treasury Warrant to the Royal Mint dated 2 January 1804 authorizing the officers 'to prepare the necessary means of stamping in an octagon form, the head now used for impressing the Silver penny, omitting the Inscription, on such silver Spanish Dollars'[200] as were sent by the Bank.[201] It was idly hoped that this changed countermark (Plate 41) would offer a greater degree of protection against counterfeiting than had the duty stamp used in the 1797 issue, since the larger head was capable of more rapid identification and the Maundy penny could be used as a touchstone in cases of questionable stamps.[202] From January to May, 415,080 dollars were so countermarked but the counterfeiting problem was not finally overcome until later in 1804 when Matthew Boulton, F.R.S., at his Soho works in Birmingham, overstruck completely the dollars with the effigy and titles of the King of England on one side and the figure of Britannia with the inscriptions Five Shillings Dollar and Bank of England, together with the date, 1804, on the other. The striking of these coins continued until 1815,[203] with their nominal value being raised to 5s 6d on 18 March 1811. They were supplemented in June 1811 by silver bank tokens for three shillings and 1s 6d, both of which were struck by the Royal Mint rather than by Boulton and issued until 1816.[204] In total, £4,457,649 of Bank of England tokens were made by Matthew Boulton and the Mint between 1804 and 1815[205] and this, together with the counterstamped dollars issued in 1797 and 1804, gave a total issue of £5,009,860 4s 9d.[206]

Throughout the whole of the above period from 1727 to 1816, when the striking of silver coinage in Britain for general currency use was so infrequent and even then mainly so very restricted quantitatively, the production of the small silver denominations, namely the penny, twopence, threepence and fourpence, continued on a fairly regular, albeit limited, basis (Tables 8 and 10). Furthermore, apart from the trifle expended in the later eighteenth century to provide small silver coin for the Royal Maundy, the Mint never used any of its surplus funds to purchase bullion for coinage.[207] Clearly, the requirements of coin for the Royal Maundy had to be met.

Nevertheless, from the data presented in Table 10, simple calculation shows that these coins were produced in considerable excess of what was required for presentation to the recipients of the Royal Maundy during this period (Table 11). Analogous treatment of the mintage figures for the Maundy coinage from 1816 to 1988 (Table 12) likewise indicates that, during this later period, coins in significant excess of the requirements of the Royal Maundy recipients were also produced (Table 13).

During the eighteenth century it is possible that these excess mintages may have been employed for presentation in other royal charities[208] which, along with the Royal Maundy, were often collectively referred to as Maundy. The possibility that they were used for general circulation, where there was certainly a deficit of coinage for use as small change during this period, appears to be unlikely in view of the overall small quantities of these coins that were issued. It has been suggested that in some years, when all four denominations were issued, some of the coins may have been used as presentation sets.[209] This practice was certainly very common with sets issued during the reign of Victoria and the first seven years of the reign of Edward VII, when they were available through the banks for purchase by the general public. When, as part of efforts begun in 1851 to effect a Mint rationalization, the company of Hunt and Roskell, London jewellers and goldsmiths, were in 1852 appointed to act as the Royal Mint's agents for the sale of its proof issues, these also included the Maundy coinage. Thus, the retail trade in its proof and Maundy coin issues was removed from the Royal Mint by this arrangement which appears to have continued until the early 1870s.[210] It is interesting that a proof Maundy set dated 1871 in an original Hunt and Roskell presentation box was recently reported.[211]

There is no doubt that the retail trade in Maundy sets prior to 1909 was a significant factor responsible for the excess of these coins minted although other secondary causes also operated. Thus, in the 1790s various Masters of the Mint[212] appear to have given Maundy pennies to the Queen, a spontaneous act and a little piece of gallantry by the Masters who no doubt thought the delicate tiny silver coins to be an ideal gift for a lady.[213] Indeed, from early in her reign, Victoria began to ask annually for Maundy coins for her own private use, the first such payment being one of £10 in Maundy money made on 31 March 1846.[214] Other Maundy sets were given to those officiating at, and helping with, the Maundy service and to officials at the Mint. That the Mint's officers may sometimes have been a source of these coins in the dealers' trays is evident from a note, written in 1824 by William Wyon[215] to Matthew Young, one of Britain's most sought-after numismatic traders of the early nineteenth century, that begins 'Dr Sir, I have been able to procure you a supply of Maundy monies between 20 & 30 setts'.[216] There is some evidence that, in the 1840s, the sets in excess of those given to the official recipients and the various helpers at the Maundy service were retained by the Mint until the following Christmas when they could be purchased by Mint officers, no doubt for use as presents.[217] Sets were also given, as they still are, as prizes to the pupils at Westminster School[218] and small quantities of Maundy twopences and fourpences, (half-groats and groats, respectively) were supplied to various of the colleges at the Universities of Cambridge (for example, Gonville and Caius) and

Table 12. The annual mintages of Maundy coins from 1816 to 1988[1]

Date	Denomination			
	1d	2d	3d	4d
1816[2]	4,752	2,376	1,584	1,584
1817	10,296	—	—	1,386
1818	9,504	—	—	1,188
1819[2]	6,336	1,980	1,320	792
1820	7,920	1,584	—	990
1821[2]	3,960	1,980	—	—
1822	11,880	5,940	3,960	2,970
1823	12,672	3,960	2,640	1,980
1824	9,504	3,168	2,112	1,584
1825	8,712	3,960	3,432	2,376
1826	—	—	—	—
1827	7,920	—	3,168	2,772
1828	—	—	—	—
1829	—	—	—	—
1830	—	—	—	—
1831[3]	10,296	4,752	3,960	3,564
1832	8,712	3,564	2,904	2,574
1833	—	—	—	—
1834	—	—	—	—
1835	—	—	—	—
1836	—	—	—	—
1837	—	—	—	—
1838	8,976	4,488	4,312	4,158
1839[4]	—	—	4,356	4,125
1840	—	—	—	—
1841	7,920	3,960	2,904	2,574
1842	8,976	4,488	4,356	4,125
1843	7,920	4,752	4,488	4,158
1844	—	—	—	—
1845	—	—	—[5]	—
1846	—	—	—[5]	—
1847	—	—	—	—
1848	—	—[6]	—	—[7]
1849	—	—	—[8]	—[7]
1850	—	—	—[8]	—[7]
1851	7,128	—	—[8]	—[7]
1852	7,920	—	—	—
1853[9]	—	—	—[8]	—[7]
1854	—	—	—[10]	—
1855	—	—	—[10]	—
1856	—	—	—[10]	—
1857	—	—	—[10]	—
1858	—	—	—[10]	—
1859	—	—	—[10]	—
1860	—	—	—[10]	—
1861	—	—	—[10]	—
1862	—	—	—[10]	—
1863	—	—	—[10]	—
1864	—	—	—[11]	—
1865	—	—	—[11]	—
1866	—	—	—[11]	—

(continued)

Table 12. *(continued)*

Date	1d	2d	3d	4d
1867	—	—	—[11]	—
1868	—	—	—[11]	—
1869	—	—	—	—
1870	9,002	5,347	—[12]	4,569
1871	9,286	4,753	—	4,627
1872	8,956	4,719	—	4,328
1873	7,932	4,756	—	4,162
1874	8,741	5,578	—	5,937
1875	8,459	5,745	—	4,154
1876	10,426	6,655	—	4,862
1877	8,936	7,189	—	4,850
1878	9,903	6,709	—	5,735
1879	10,626	6,925	—	5,202
1880	11,088	6,247	—	5,199
1881	9,017	6,001	—	6,203
1882	10,607	7,264	—	4,146
1883	11,673	7,232	—	5,096
1884	14,109	6,042	—	5,353
1885	12,302	5,958	—	5,791
1886	15,952	9,167	—	6,785
1887	17,506	8,296	—	5,292
1888	14,480	9,528	—	9,583
1889	14,028	6,727	—	6,088
1890	13,115	8,613	—	9,087
1891	21,743	10,000	—	11,303
1892	15,525	11,583	—	8,524
1893	21,593	14,182	8,976	10,832
1894	18,391	12,099	—	9,385
1895	17,408	10,766	—	8,877
1896	17,380	10,795	—	8,476
1897	16,477	11,000	—[12]	9,388
1898	16,634	11,945	—[12]	9,147
1899	17,402	14,514	—	13,561
1900	17,299	10,987	—	9,571
1901	17,644	13,539	—	11,928
1902[13]	21,278	14,079	—	10,117
1903	17,209	13,386	—	9,729
1904	18,524	13,827	—	11,568
1905	17,504	11,139	—	10,998
1906	17,850	11,325	8,800	11,065
1907	18,388	13,238	8,760	11,132
1908	18,150	14,815	—	9,929
1909	2,948	2,695	1,983	2,428
1910	3,392	2,998	1,440	2,755
1911[14]	1,913	1,635[15]	1,991	1,768
1912	1,616	1,678	1,246	1,700
1913	1,590	1,880	1,228	1,798
1914	1,818	1,659	982	1,651
1915	2,072	1,465	1,293	1,441
1916	1,647	1,509	1,128	1,499
1917	1,820	1,506	1,237	1,478

Table 12. *(continued)*

Date	Denomination			
	1d	2d	3d	4d
1918	1,911	1,547	1,375	1,479
1919	1,699	1,567	1,258	1,524
1920	1,715	1,630	1,399	1,460
1921	1,847	1,794	1,386	1,542
1922	1,758	3,074	1,373	1,609
1923	1,840	1,527	1,430	1,635
1924	1,619	1,602	1,515	1,665
1925	1,890	1,670	1,438	1,786
1926	2,180	1,902	1,504	1,762
1927	1,647	1,766	1,690	1,681
1928	1,846	1,706	1,835	1,642
1929	1,837	1,862	1,761	1,969
1930	1,724	1,901	1,948	1,744
1931	1,759	1,897	1,818	1,915
1932	1,835	1,960	2,042	1,937
1933	1,872	2,066	1,920	1,931
1934	1,919	1,927	1,887	1,893
1935	1,975	1,928	2,007	1,995
1936	1,329	1,365	1,307[15]	1,323
1937[16]	——	1,472	1,351	1,325
1938	1,275	1,374	1,350	1,424
1939	1,253	1,436	1,234	1,332
1940	1,375	1,277	1,290	1,367
1941	1,255	1,345	1,253	1,345
1942	1,243	1,231	1,325	1,325
1943	1,347	1,239	1,335	1,335
1944	1,259	1,345	1,345	1,345
1945	1,367	1,355	1,355	1,355
1946	1,479	1,365	1,365	1,365
1947	1,387	1,479	1,375	1,375
1948	1,397	1,385	1,491	1,385
1949	1,407	1,395	1,395	1,503
1950	1,527	1,405	1,405	1,515
1951	1,480	1,580	1,468	1,580
1952	1,024	1,064	1,012	1,064
1953	1,050	1,025	1,078	1,078
1954	1,088	1,020	1,076	1,076
1955	1,036	1,082	1,082	1,082
1956	1,100	1,088	1,088	1,088
1957	1,168	1,094	1,094	1,094
1958	1,112	1,164	1,100	1,100
1959	1,118	1,106	1,172	1,106
1960	1,124	1,112	1,112	1,180
1961	1,200	1,118	1,118	1,188
1962	1,127	1,197	1,125	1,197
1963	1,133	1,131	1,205	1,205
1964	1,215	1,137	1,213	1,213
1965	1,143	1,221	1,221	1,221
1966	1,206	1,206	1,206	1,206
1967	1,068	986	986	986
1968	964	1,048	964	964

(continued)

Table 12. *(continued)*

Date	Denomination			
	1d	2d	3d	4d
1969	1,002	1,002	1,088	1,002
1970	980	980	980	1,068
	1p	2p	3p	4p
1971[17]	1,018	1,018	1,018	1,108
1972	1,026	1,118	1,026	1,118
1973	1,004	1,004	1,098	1,098
1974	1,138	1,042	1,138	1,138
1975	1,050	1,148	1,148	1,148
1976	1,158	1,158	1,158	1,158
1977	1,240	1,138	1,138	1,138
1978	1,178	1,282	1,178	1,178
1979	1,188	1,188	1,294	1,188
1980	1,198	1,198	1,198	1,306
1981	1,288	1,178	1,178	1,288
1982	1,218	1,330	1,218	1,330
1983	1,228	1,228	1,342	1,342
1984	1,354	1,238	1,354	1,354
1985	1,248	1,366	1,366	1,366
1986	1,378	1,378	1,378	1,378
1987	1,512	1,390	1,390	1,390
1988	1,402	1,526	1,402	1,402

Notes to Table 12: *1*, Mintages for the years from 1816 to 1870 are taken from Parliamentary Returns (see notes *5, 6, 7, 11*), for the years from 1871 to 1976 they are taken from the Royal Mint annual reports of the Deputy Master and Comptroller, 1870 to 1975–76, and from 1977 to 1988 they were supplied by Mr G. P. Dyer, the Librarian and Curator at the Royal Mint. All the figures up to 1869, inclusively, and those for the threepence up to 1908, inclusively, were calculated from the weight of coin pyxed (see Appendix 7) and issued. Consequently, since individual coins vary in standard weight, the figures cannot be regarded as being precise (Dyer). The mintages from 1816 to 1972 are also quoted in *ESC*, pp. 235–37. Up until World War II, these figures relate to the number of coins *issued* by the Mint during the years in question, *not* the number of coins bearing these dates (Dyer; *ESC*, p. 231); *2*, No Maundy coins were issued dated 1816, 1819 or 1821 (see Table 8 and the related note *14*); *3*, A proof Maundy set was part of the 1831 proof set (see Section V of Chapter 3); *4*, A proof Maundy set was part of the 1839 proof set (see Section V of Chapter 3); *5*, The mintages of the silver threepences for 1845 and 1846 are quoted ('Accounts of all gold, silver, and copper monies of the Realm, coined at the Royal Mint, from the 1st day of January 1816 to the 31st day of December 1847', in *Return to an Address of the Honourable The House of Commons*, 13 December 1847) as 1,319,208 and 52,008, respectively, figures which clearly include those pieces struck for general circulation. The mintages of the Maundy threepences for these years have been confirmed by the Royal Mint (Dyer); *6*, The mintage of the silver twopence for 1848 is quoted ('Account "of all gold, silver, and copper monies of the Realm, coined at the Mint, from the 1st day of January 1848 to the 31st day of December 1853." ' in *Return to an Order of the Honourable the House of Commons*, 31 January 1854) as 266,112, a figure which clearly includes the 261,360 silver twopences dated 1848 which were issued for use in British Guiana (Pridmore, p. 275). The mintage of the Maundy twopence for 1848 has been confirmed by the Royal Mint (Dyer); *7*, The mintages of the silver fourpences from 1848 to 1851 and of 1853 are quoted (source as given in note *6*) as 716,958, 384,318, 598,158, 35,458 and 16,038, respectively, figures which obviously include the Britannia groats issued in these years. Nevertheless, the mintage of 4,158 quoted in this source for the silver fourpence of 1852 clearly reflects only the Maundy fourpence, notwithstanding that Britannia groats were also issued in that year. The mintages of the Maundy fourpences for these years have been confirmed by the Royal Mint (Dyer). In the next return ('Account "of all gold, silver, and copper monies of the Realm coined at the Mint, for each year from the 1st day of January 1854 to the 31st day of December 1863 (in continuation of Parliamentary Paper, No. 447, of Session 1863)" ' in *Return to an Order of the Honourable The House of Commons*, 12 July 1864), the groats and fourpences are listed separately; *8*, The mintages of the silver threepences from 1849 to 1851 and of 1853 are quoted (source as given in note *6*) as 131,208, 954,888,

Oxford (for example, Brasnose, Magdalen,[219] and Oriel) for use in customary distributions. Thus, Gonville and Caius received sixty fourpences in 1935, Brasnose took delivery of an undisclosed number of fourpences in 1929, and again in 1937, and of twelve in 1935, and Oriel in both 1937 and 1938 got seventeen fourpences and thirty-five twopences, although the later delivery was an error. However, it would appear that this use of the Maundy coinage was discontinued soon after this period, for in 1953 Brasnose asked for some more fourpences but, after an unenthusiastic reply from the Mint, the matter was dropped, and in the same year Oriel asked for fourpences and twopences but were refused.[220] At Gonville and Caius it would appear that any practice involving Maundy coins may have ceased some decades ago and is unlikely to be revived now.[221] It is interesting that in the Royal Mint's Ninety-Sixth Annual Report of the Deputy Master and Comptroller for 1965, Mr John Hasting (later Sir Jack) James writes, on page 2, 'and some time ago when I delved in our silver recovery operations with the faint hope that I might find a hardy remaining groat to help an Oxford College to pay its annual toll, I was rewarded by finding dozens, largely from north of the Border'.

As early as 1841, the number of Maundy coins struck was insufficient to meet the total demands of those, including the Bank of England, who had become accustomed to making applications to the Mint for them. That the Mint resisted attempts to increased their mintage, and thereby reduce their rarity, to meet this increased demand is apparent in a letter of 1 April 1874, from C. W. Fremantle (later Hon. Sir Charles Fremantle, K.C.B.), the Deputy Master and Comptroller of the Mint, to one F. May Esq. at the Bank of England, which reads:[222]

My dear Mr. May,
    I am very sorry to say that it is impossible to let the Bank have any more Maundy Monies.

483,553 and 36,168, respectively, figures which clearly include those pieces struck for general circulation. The mintages of the Maundy threepences for these dates have been confirmed by the Royal Mint (Dyer); *9*, A proof Maundy set was part of the 1853 proof set (see Section V of Chapter 3); *10*, The mintages of the silver threepences from 1854 to 1863 are quoted (source as given in note 7) as 1,471,734, 387,838, 1,018,248 1,762,728, 1,445,928, 3,584,328, 3,410,088, 3,299,208, 1,160,808 and 954,888, respectively, figures which clearly include the pieces struck for general circulation. The mintages of the Maundy threepences for these years have been confirmed by the Royal Mint (Dyer); *11*, The mintages of the silver threepences from 1864 to 1868 are quoted ('Account "of all gold, silver, and copper moneys of the Realm coined at the Mint, for each year from the 1st day of January 1860 to the 31st day of December 1869, etc. (in continuation of Parliamentary Paper No. 157, of Session 1868–9)." ' in *Return to an Order of the Honourable The House of Commons* 30 May 1870) as 1,335,048, 1,746,888, 1,905,288, 717,288 and 1,461,768, respectively, figures which clearly include the pieces struck for general circulation. The mintages of the Maundy threepences for these years have been confirmed by the Royal Mint (Dyer); *12*, The mintages of the 1870, 1897 and 1898 Maundy sets have apparently been incorrectly quoted as 4,458, 9,388 and 9,147, respectively (*Coin Year Book 1975*, p. 189). However, see note *1*; *13*, A matt proof Maundy set was part of both the long and short proof sets of 1902 (see Section V of Chapter 3); *14*, A proof Maundy set was part of the long and short proof sets with gold, and the proof set without gold, of 1911 (see Section V of Chapter 3); *15*, The mintage of the 1911 and 1936 Maundy sets have apparently been incorrectly quoted as 1,786 and 1,323, respectively (*Coin Year Book 1975*, p. 190). However, see note *1*; *16*, A Maundy set was part of the silver and bronze proof sets of 1937 (see Section V of Chapter 3); *17*, The British currency was decimalized on 15 February 1971 (*ESC*, p. 225), resulting in the Maundy coins being declared legal tender for one, two, three and four new pence (p) (*ESC*, p. 210), namely with a face value multiplied by a factor of 2.4. Since it is not possible to distinguish between some of the issues of Maundy threepences and some of those issued for normal currency, such threepences issued from 1870 onwards thus became worth 3p, more than the old sixpence which became legal tender for 2½p until 30th June 1980 when it was demonetized. Thus, these threepences were demonetized and then remonetized with an increase in value, surely a unique occurrence in the case of a British coin (*ESC*, p. 210).

126 Silver Pennies and Linen Towels

Table 13. Comparison between the annual Maundy money mintages and the requirements of the Maundy recipients for the years from 1816 to 1988

Year of the Maundy ceremony	Monarch's age in years at the time of the ceremony[1]	Total number of pence required for the recipients[2]	Number of Maundy pence minted[3]	Excess Maundy pence not required for the recipients	Percentage excess[4]
George III (born 4 June 1738[1])					
1816	77	12,168	20,592	8,424	69
1817	78	12,482	25,344	12,862	103
1818	79	12,800	23,760	10,960	86
1819	80	13,122	17,424	4,302	33
1820	81	13,448	19,008	5,560	41
George IV (born 12 August 1762[1])					
1820	57	6,728	19,008	12,280	183
1821	58	6,962	15,840	8,878	128
1822	59	7,200	47,520	40,320	560
1823	60	7,442	36,432	28,990	390
1824	61	7,688	28,512	20,824	271
1825	62	7,938	36,432	28,494	359
1826	63	8,192	—	28,240	345
1827	64	8,450	—	27,982	331
1828	65	8,712	—	27,720	318
1829	66	8,978	—	27,454	308
1830	67	9,248	—	27,184	294
William IV (born 21 August 1765[1])					
1831	65	8,712	45,936	37,224	427
1832	66	8,978	34,848	25,870	288
1833	67	9,248	—	25,600	277
1834	68	9,522	—	25,326	266
1835	69	9,800	—	25,048	256
1836	70	10,082	—	24,766	246
1837	71	10,368	—	24,480	236
Victoria (born 24 May 1819[1])					
1838	18	722	47,520	46,798	6,482
1839	19	800	—	46,720	5,840
1840	20	882	—	46,638	5,288
1841	21	968	34,848	33,880	3,500
1842	22	1,058	47,520	46,462	4,391
1843	23	1,152	—	46,368	4,025
1844	24	1,250	—	46,270	3,702
1845	25	1,352	—	46,168	3,415
1846	26	1,458	—	46,062	3,159
1847	27	1,568	—	45,952	2,931
1848	28	1,682	—	45,838	2,725
1849	29	1,800	—	45,720	2,540
1850	30	1,922	—	45,598	2,372
1851	31	2,048	46,728	44,680	2,182
1852	32	2,178	47,520	45,342	2,082
1853	33	2,312	—	45,218	1,956
1854	34	2,450	—	45,070	1,840
1855	35	2,592	—	44,928	1,733
1856	36	2,732	—	44,788	1,639

Table 13. *(continued)*

Year of the Maundy ceremony	Monarch's age in years at the time of the ceremony[1]	Total number of pence required for the recipients[2]	Number of Maundy pence minted[3]	Excess Maundy pence not required for the recipients	Percentage excess[4]
1857	37	2,888	——	44,632	1,545
1858	38	3,042	——	44,478	1,462
1859	39	3,200	——	44,320	1,385
1860	40	3,362	——	44,158	1,313
1861	41	3,528	——	43,992	1,247
1862	42	3,698	——	43,822	1,185
1863	43	3,872	——	43,648	1,127
1864	44	4,050	——	43,470	1,073
1865	45	4,232	——	43,288	1,023
1866	46	4,418	——	43,102	976
1867	47	4,608	——	42,912	931
1868	48	4,802	——	42,718	890
1869	49	5,000	——	42,520	850
1870	50	5,202	51,436	46,234	889
1871	51	5,408	50,764	45,356	839
1872	52	5,618	49,170	43,552	775
1873	53	5,832	47,556	41,724	715
1874	54	6,050	57,109	51,059	844
1875	55	6,272	50,029	43,757	698
1876	56	6,498	56,648	50,150	772
1877	57	6,728	56,178	49,450	735
1878	58	6,962	59,725	52,763	758
1879	59	7,200	58,748	51,548	716
1880	60	7,442	57,842	50,400	677
1881	61	7,688	59,295	51,607	671
1882	62	7,938	55,183	47,245	595
1883	63	8,192	59,985	51,793	632
1884	64	8,450	61,069	52,619	623
1885	65	8,712	60,846	52,134	598
1886	66	8,978	74,890	65,912	734
1887	67	9,248	68,730	59,482	643
1888	68	9,522	85,332	75,810	796
1889	69	9,800	65,298	55,498	566
1890	70	10,082	80,153	70,071	695
1891	71	10,368	100,419	90,051	869
1892	72	10,658	86,251	75,593	709
1893	73	10,952	120,213	109,261	998
1894	74	11,250	107,057	95,807	846
1895	75	11,552	101,376	89,824	778
1896	76	11,858	99,802	87,944	742
1897	77	12,168	102,957	90,789	746
1898	78	12,482	104,040	91,558	734
1899	79	12,800	127,602	114,802	897
1900	80	13,122	104,485	91,363	696
		Edward VII (born 9 November 1841[1])			
1901	59	7,200	119,362	112,162	1,558
1902	60	7,442	116,832	109,390	1,470
1903	61	7,688	109,825	102,137	1,329
1904	62	7,938	119,378	111,440	1,404

(continued)

Table 13. *(continued)*

Year of the Maundy ceremony	Monarch's age in years at the time of the ceremony[1]	Total number of pence required for the recipients[2]	Number of Maundy pence minted[3]	Excess Maundy pence not required for the recipients	Percentage excess[4]
1905	63	8,192	110,702	102,510	1,251
1906	64	8,450	111,160	102,710	1,216
1907	65	8,712	115,672	106,960	1,228
1908	66	8,978	113,776	104,798	1,167
1909	67	9,248	23,999	14,751	160
1910	68	9,522	24,728	15,206	160
		George V (born 3 June 1865[1])			
1911	45	4,232	12,924	8,710	206
1912	46	4,418	15,510	11,092	251
1913	47	4,608	16,226	11,618	252
1914	48	4,802	14,686	9,884	206
1915	49	5,000	14,645	9,645	193
1916	50	5,202	14,045	8,843	170
1917	51	5,408	14,455	9,047	167
1918	52	5,618	15,046	9,428	168
1919	53	5,832	14,703	8,871	152
1920	54	6,050	15,012	8,962	148
1921	55	6,272	15,761	9,489	151
1922	56	6,498	18,461	11,963	184
1923	57	6,728	15,724	8,996	134
1924	58	6,962	16,028	9,066	130
1925	59	7,200	16,688	9,488	132
1926	60	7,442	17,544	10,102	136
1927	61	7,688	16,973	9,285	121
1928	62	7,938	17,331	9,393	118
1929	63	8,192	18,720	10,528	129
1930	64	8,450	18,346	9,896	117
1931	65	8,712	18,667	9,955	114
1932	66	8,978	19,629	10,651	119
1933	67	9,248	19,488	10,240	111
1934	68	9,522	19,006	9,484	100
1935	69	9,800	19,832	10,032	102
		Edward VIII (born 23 June 1894[1])			
1936	41	3,528	13,272	9,744	276
		George VI (born 14 December 1895[1])			
1937	41	3,528	13,626	10,098	286
1938	42	3,698	13,769	10,071	272
1939	43	3,872	13,155	9,283	240
1940	44	4,050	13,267	9,217	228
1941	45	4,232	13,084	8,852	209
1942	46	4,418	12,980	8,562	194
1943	47	4,608	13,170	—	186
1944	48	4,802	13,364	—	178
1945	49	5,000	13,562	—	171
1946	50	5,202	13,764	—	165
1947	51	5,408	13,970	—	158
1948	52	5,618	14,180	—	152
1949	53	5,832	14,394	—	147

Table 13. *(continued)*

Year of the Maundy ceremony	Monarch's age in years at the time of the ceremony[1]	Total number of pence required for the recipients[2]	Number of Maundy pence minted[3]	Excess Maundy pence not required for the recipients	Percentage excess[4]
1950	54	6,050	14,612	—	142
1951	55	6,272	15,364	9,092	145
Elizabeth II (born 21 April 1926[1])					
1952	25	1,352	10,444	9,092	672
1953	26	1,458	10,646	9,188	630
1954	27	1,568	10,660	9,092	580
1955	28	1,682	10,774	—	541
1956	29	1,800	10,892	—	505
1957	30	1,922	11,014	—	473
1958	31	2,048	11,140	—	444
1959	32	2,178	11,270	—	417
1960	33	2,312	11,404	—	393
1961	34	2,450	11,542	—	371
1962	35	2,592	11,684	—	351
1963	36	2,738	11,830	—	332
1964	37	2,888	11,980	—	315
1965	38	3,042	12,132	9,090 ≡ 909 sets	299
1966	39	3,200	12,060	8,860 ≡ 886 sets	277
1967	40	3,362	9,942	6,580 ≡ 658 sets	196
1968	41	3,528	9,808	6,280 ≡ 628 sets	178
1969	42	3,698	10,278	6,580 ≡ 658 sets	—
1970	43	3,872	10,152	6,280 ≡ 628 sets	162
1971	44	4,050	10,630	6,580 ≡ 658 sets	—
1972	45	4,232	10,812	—	155
1973	46	4,418	10,698	6,280 ≡ 628 sets	142
1974	47	4,608	11,188	6,580 ≡ 658 sets	143
1975	48	4,802	11,382	—	137
1976	49	5,000	11,580	—	132
1977	50	5,202	11,482	6,280 ≡ 628 sets	121
1978	51	5,408	12,988	6,580 ≡ 658 sets	122
1979	52	5,618	12,198	—	117
1980	53	5,832	12,412	—	113
1981	54	6,050	12,330	6,280 ≡ 628 sets	104
1982	55	6,272	12,852	6,580 ≡ 658 sets	105
1983	56	6,498	13,078	—	101
1984	57	6,728	13,308	—	98
1985	58	6,962	13,542	—	95
1986	59	7,200	13,780	—	91
1987	60	7,442	14,022	—	88
1988	61	7,688	14,268	—	86

Notes to Table 13: *1*, Freeman-Grenville; *2*, See note *4* to Table 11; *3*, Calculated from the data presented in Table 12; *4*, See note *6* to Table 11.

The rule is to strike one Journey weight[223] each year, £146, and of this the Bank have just over half, viz, £75.

I do not think we are justified in striking more, as we ought not to make the Maundy Money too common – and perhaps I may add that the more we strike the more numerous the applications will be both to the Bank and the Mint, and 'our last state will be worse than the first'!

Yours very sincerely
C. W. Fremantle

On the other hand, it is stated in the Twenty-Fourth Annual Report of the Deputy Master of the Mint, 1893,[224] that 'there was an increase in the amount of Royal Maundy Money issued, mainly attributable to the adoption of new designs[225] for the coinage early in the year': clearly the mintage was related to collector demand.

In 1903 a small reform was effected by the then Deputy Master of the Mint[226] when the Maundy list was reduced by some 200 names, mostly those of charwomen and labourers,[227] although this action is not overtly apparent from the mintage figures given in Table 12. In fact, by 1908 the supply of Maundy coins was to some extent out of control. For example, it had then for some time apparently been the prerogative of the Chief Clerk 'to gratify people whom he desired to oblige' and some of these had received as many as forty-eight sets.

In order to instill greater control into the production and supply of the Maundy coinage such that the value of the coins to the recipients would be enhanced, a very significant reduction in their mintages came into effect in 1909 (Table 12). From then on, as well as those given to the recipients of the Royal Maundy, sets were only made available to those who had some genuine claim, such as the Banks of England, Scotland and Ireland,[228] to those officiating at, and helping with, the Maundy service (as fees) (Table 14), to the Mint's Deputy Master for his personal allocation and for distribution amongst the Mint's senior and long-standing employees, to the Mint for distribution to its visiting dignitaries and to the sovereign as a personal allowance.[229] There are in existence printed handouts which give a brief historical account of the Maundy service and Maundy money. These are almost certainly the work of William John Hocking who, as Assistant Superintendent of the Operative Department of the Royal Mint, was the author of a catalogue, in two volumes, of the coins, tokens, medals, dies and seals in the Royal Mint's museum at the beginning of this century[230] and the handouts' format closely resembles the account of the Royal Maundy given in the first volume of this catalogue.[231] The purpose of these handouts is not recorded but they were no doubt supplied to some of those who were fortunate enough to be given or sold Maundy sets by the Royal Mint.

The Maundy coins given to each of the recipients at the Maundy service are contained in a white leather purse with long red strings. However, from toward the end of the nineteenth century, those sets presented to others have been contained in official Maundy presentation cases.[232] These cases, which are not available to the Maundy recipients,[233] are manufactured for the Mint and used to be sold for the benefit of the Royal Mint Self Help Society (later the Royal Mint Provident Society), an organisation of the Mint's manual employees.[234] That the Society was grateful for this additional income which, for example, amounted to £5 0s 7d[235] and £2 2s 0d[236] for the years from 1903 to 1904 and from 1926 to 1927, respectively, is evident from an entry in its report and statement of accounts for the year 1901–1902 which reads 'we desire to record the thanks of the Society to the Deputy Master for his kindness in presenting

Table 14. The fees paid in Maundy coins in connection with the Maundy service of 1909[1]

Recipients of the fee	Monetary value of the fee £	s	d	Number of Maundy sets in the fee[2]
The King's Scholars, Westminster[3]	2	0	0	48
The King's Almshouses, Westminster[4]	6	0		
Four children of the National Schools of St John and St Margaret's Westminster, for attendance at the Abbey to represent the Children of the Almonry, five shillings each[5]	1	0	0	24
The Sub-almoner[6,7]	3	0	0	72
The Secretary[6]	2	0	0	48
The Assistant to the Secretary[6]	1	0	0	24
The Dean of Westminster		3	4	4
The Canons of Westminster, five at 2s 6d		12	6	15
The Minor Canons of Westminster, six at 2s 6d		15	0	18
The Organist		2	6	3
The Schoolmaster of the Choristers		—		—
The Vergers, ten at ten pence		8	4	10
The Lay Vicars, twelve at 2s 6d	1	10	0	36
The Choristers, twenty-four at ten pence	1	0	0	24
The Clerk of the Works		2	6	3
The Portress		—		—
The Organ Blower			10	1

Notes to Table 14: *1*, Data supplied by Mr G. P. Dyer, the Librarian and Curator at the Royal Mint; *2*, Calculated using the fact that one Maundy set is equivalent to ten pence, namely a penny, a twopence, a threepence and a fourpence; *3*, This was really a prize that had been sanctioned by Elizabeth I; *4*, This was a dole of ancient date; *5*, These were given as good conduct prizes; *6*, These were personal gifts to the present holders of these positions and were to cease when they retired; *7*, The Lord High Almoner's old fee of £4 had already lapsed.

the Society with the profits from the sale of Maundy Cases'.[237] Other Maundy sets have been contained in cases that have originated from diverse private sources (for example, Spink and Son Ltd and various jewellers) and many of which are marked accordingly.

By the mid-1960s, a considerable degree of commercialism had become associated with the Maundy coinage, apparent from the substantial increases in its market values about this time.[238] This situation had two somewhat unsavoury consequences. Firstly, it led to the harassment of the recipients of the Royal Maundy by unscrupulous coin dealers, often outside the very place of worship where they had but a short time ago received their gift from the royal hands. Such despicable activity would appear to have been of long standing for in 1902 or thereabout it was reported, with regard to the situation appertaining around the turn of the nineteenth century, that 'as soon as the service is over, crowds of buyers eagerly throng around the old people, who take a price for their coins. The rate they usually charge is four or five times the face value of the coins. The purses are sometimes disposed of at from one to two shillings each, according to the state of the market. In 1897, owing to the Diamond Jubilee, it is said there was a great demand for Maundy money, and that fabulous prices were offered by the American visitors in London desirous of taking back with them sets of these interesting curiosities'.[239] However, a significant difference exists between these early ceremonies and those of more recent times. In the former, up to that of 1956, when they were apparently acquiescent with regard to the subsequent sale of their Maundy coins, the recipients of the Royal Maundy usually remained on the Maundy list for the rest of their lives and regarded the gift as a small pension. On the other hand, for the recipients of the post-1956 distributions it was a unique occasion and the gift of Maundy coins consequently would have a sentimental value which it did not possess for the recipients in earlier times. The second undesirable consequence of the association of commercialism with the Maundy coinage was that it resulted in profiteering by some of those who received sets as fees[240] or as extraneous gifts which they were intended to accept as a privilege rather than for their ultimate financial gain.

The unwelcome pressure upon the old recipients, manifest from the former eventuality in more recent years, has caused much concern. In fact, a few weeks following the Maundy service in 1965, it was raised in the House of Lords[241] by Lord Wade whose question on the Order Paper asked of Her Majesty's Government:

> what steps, if any, have been taken to safeguard recipients of Maundy Money from persistent pestering by persons wishing to purchase such Maundy Money; and whether any offences have been committed against such recipients.

Lord Beswick, in reply, stated that:

> My Lords, I understand that this year the Royal Almonry Office arranged for the recipients of Maundy Money to be warned to expect approaches from coin dealers. I am aware that certain approaches made to recipients after the Maundy Service were reported in the Press; but so far as we know none of the incidents reported constituted a criminal offence, . . .

to which Lord Wade rejoined:

> My Lord, while I recognise that the recipients of Maundy Money are free to sell if they so wish, although I believe the great majority do not wish to do so, may I ask the noble Lord whether he would agree that to harass old people in an endeavour to get them to sell, sometimes at less than the true value, is to be deplored? Can any practical steps be taken to discourage this type of exploitation?

Lord Beswick's answer, which brought this item to a close, reads:

> My Lords, it is conceivable that the Newspaper Proprietors' Association could recommend their members not to accept from coin dealers the sort of advertisement which appeared in the Press at the time of the Canterbury Service at Easter. I understand it is also being considered whether the prior publication of the list of recipients could be withheld. As for the rest, this of course, as the noble Lord says, is not a criminal offence, but there is a matter of good taste involved, and I should like to think the noble Lord's Question underlines that fact.

In an attempt to obviate the other above-mentioned eventuality resulting from the associated commercialism, and as a result of moves initiated by Mr John Hastings (later Sir Jack) James, the Deputy Master of the Mint,[242] the mintage of the Maundy coinage was, from 1967, further reduced,[243] an action which is apparent from the figures presented in Table 12.[244] Thus, whilst the spectrum of the extraneous recipients[245] remained unchanged, the number of Maundy sets which some of them received was reduced and the sets so given to Mint officials were sometimes those of earlier years.[246]

In 1970[247] it was anticipated that a further reduction in the mintages of the Maundy coinage might have been imminent when it was stated that 'there is a prospect that Maundy sets will become considerably rarer during the early 1970s' since 'the Treasury is anxious to reduce perks – as opposed to wages – received by special branches of the Civil Service. And the 300 or so Maundy sets distributed to long-serving Royal Mint employees each year certainly come into this category' and 'if they ceased to be issued the total annual mintage of Maundy sets would drop sharply to something in the region of 600'. With respect to this possibility, it was reported that the Mint's spokesman 'refused to confirm that there was any immediate prospect of cutting off Maundy awards to Mint workers, many of whom are uneasy at the switch of work from Tower Hill to Llantrisant, South Wales' and that he said 'there are no official plans to change the system by which our employees are given Maundy sets'. Presently, the Royal Mint's employees of five years standing are given the opportunity, shortly after Maundy Thursday, to purchase from the Mint a set of the current Maundy coins. Subsequently, at intervals of approximately seven years, they are likewise offered a further set, but then not necessarily of the most recent minting. Bearing in mind that such employees also have to provide a written undertaking that they will not resell these sets, this arrangement is obviously more of a sentimental rather than financial nature and, as such, it should not be condemned.

Nevertheless, however desirable the mintage reduction of the Maundy coinage in 1967 may have been, it may be considered[248] that the excess Maundy coins annually minted is still disproportionately large relative to that required for distribution to the Maundy recipients. In every year until 1984, the former exceeded the latter (Table 13) even though, theoretically, the sole purpose for producing the coins is for the latter use. It may be argued that were it not for these excess mintings, numismatists might be largely deprived of their source of these coins. However, under these circumstances, could not the Maundy recipients then be more actively encouraged to sell some of their Maundy coins, perhaps retaining one representative set for themselves for sentimental reasons? As is evident from the fact that the 1989 Maundy set was retailing at £75 during its year of issue, a price which would no doubt have also been much greater if the mintages of these coins had been restricted to the numbers required by the Maundy recipients, such a sale would provide them with considerable extra money. This was, indeed, the original concept underlying the Gift of Pennies, it not being intended for the ultimate benefit of others as is manifest when Maundy sets, which have either been given as fees, etc. or have belonged to a Maundy recipient who has died, enter the retail market.[249]

From Table 13 it can be seen that from 1942 to 1950 and from 1951 to 1964, with the exception of 1953, Maundy pence in annual excesses of 8,562 and 9,092, respectively, were produced in addition to the requirements of the Maundy recipients. Furthermore, it is possible to calculate the denominational compositions of these excess mintages from the compositions of the individual Gifts of Pennies for these years (Table 15), the figures presented in Table 12 and the fact that the number of Maundy recipients is twice that of the number of pence in the Gift of Pennies.[250] Such numeration shows that from 1946 to 1950 the excess mintage consisted of 855 sets plus twelve pennies, in 1951 and 1952 and from 1954 to 1961 it consisted of 908 sets plus twelve pennies, in 1953 it was 916 sets together with twenty-six pennies and a twopence and from 1962 to 1964 it included 909 sets with two pennies. Clearly there is a pattern within these results but the significance of the annual oddment excesses, which exhibit an amazing degree of denominational regularity, together with the interesting digression from this in 1953, involving as it does one twopence, is far from obvious. Similar calculation using the corresponding data in Tables 12 and 15, from 1965 to 1978, establish that the excess mintings are, indeed, the actual number of sets indicated by equivalence in Table 13. It is also interesting to note from Table 13 that, from 1967 and onward, an excess of 628

Table 15. The denominational compositions of the Gift of Pennies from 1946 to 1978[1]

Year	Sets	1d	2d	3d	4d
1946	5	1			
1947	—		1		
1948	—			1	
1949	—				1
1950	—	1			—
1951	—		1		—
1952	2		—		—
1953	—			1	—
1954	—	1		—	—
1955	—		1	—	—
1956	3				
1957	—	1			
1958	—		1		
1959	—			1	
1960	—				1
1961	—	1			—
1962	—		1		—
1963	—			1	—
1964	—	1		—	—
1965	—		1	—	—
1966	4				
1967	—	1			
1968	—		1		
1969	—			1	
1970	—				1
1971	—	1			—
1972	—		1		—
1973	—			1	—
1974	—	1		—	—
1975	—		1	—	—
1976	5				
1977	—	1			
1978	—		1		

Note to Table 15: *1*, Information from *Catalogue of Ancient, English, and Foreign Coins*, Glendining and Co., London, 6 and 7 December 1978, pp. 44–46.

Maundy sets was produced in the years when the Maundy service was held in Westminster Abbey (Table 3) whereas in the other years, when it visited the provinces (Table 3), 658 such sets were produced.

The *Royal Mint: Hundred and Fifth Annual Report of the Deputy Master and Comptroller for the Year 1st April 1974 to 31st March 1975* quotes returns relating to the United Kingdom silver and cupro-nickel currency. In relation to the Maundy money, these returns, which are in pounds sterling, cover the period from 1971 to 1975[251] and are reproduced in Table 16. By dividing these sums by the respective denomination to which they refer, the mintage figures given in Table 17 are derived. As can be seen, apart from those coins dated 1975, differences exist between these derived mintages and those given in Table 12, which are also re-quoted, in parentheses, in

Table 16. The total annual face value of each of the four Maundy denominations of 925 millesimal fine silver, issued under the operation of the Decimal Currency Acts 1967 and 1969 and the Coinage Act 1971, from 1971 to 1975[1]

Year	Face value, in pounds sterling, of the denomination			
	1p	2p	3p	4p
1971	7.50	13.20	19.80	30.00
1972	9.88	21.60	29.64	43.20
1973	10.06	20.12	33.00	44.00
1974	11.81	21.70	35.43	47.24
1975	10.50	22.96	34.44	45.92

Note to Table 16: *1*, The source of this information is *Royal Mint: Hundred and Fifth Annual Report of the Deputy Master and Comptroller for the Year 1st April 1974 to 31st March 1975* (London), Appendix VII, p. 64.

Table 17. The annual mintages of the Maundy money from 1971 to 1975

Year	Mintage derived from the data in Table 16 and, in parentheses, given in Table 12, for the denomination			
	1p	2p	3p	4p
1971	750(1,108)	660(1,018)	660(1,018)	750(1,108)
1972	988(1,026)	1,080(1,118)	988(1,026)	1,080(1,118)
1973	1,006(1,004)	1,006(1,004)	1,100(1,098)	1,100(1,098)
1974	1,181(1,138)	1,085(1,042)	1,181(1,138)	1,181(1,138)
1975	1,050(1,050)	1,148(1,148)	1,148(1,148)	1,148(1,148)
Total	5,259(5,610)	5,077(5,428)	4,979(5,330)	4,975(5,326)

Table 17.[252] In reply to enquiry, it has been stated by the Royal Mint that the reason for these differences is that the coins struck in a financial year are not necessarily all issued in that year, and thus the data presented in the Annual Report are merely statements of the face values of coins issued in each of the five financial years and do not mean that all the coins were accordingly dated.[253] However, the very small differences between the 1973 derived figures and those obtained from Table 12, namely two sets, is particularly hard to rationalize on the above basis. Furthermore, it might be expected, in the light of the Royal Mint's comments, that over the five-year period quoted the total for the derived and quoted mintage figures would approach equality in the case of each denomination. In fact, in each case the latter exceeds the former and, even more surprising, it is in each instance of the same magnitude, namely 351 coins (Table 17).

An equally surprising and analogous difference, but this time of an excess of seventy coins for each denomination, becomes apparent if similar calculations and comparisons are effected upon the equivalent information (Table 18) contained in the *Royal Mint: Hundred and First Annual Report of the Deputy Master and Comptroller for the Period 1st January 1970 to 31st March 1971*,[254] namely that for the years from 1965 to 1970, the last six pre-decimal years, and the corresponding figures presented in Table 12.

Table 18. The total annual face value of each of the four Maundy denominations of 925 millesimal fine silver, issued under the operation of the Coinage Act 1946, from 1965 to 1970[1]

Date	Face value of the denomination											
	1d			2d			3d			4d		
	£	s	d	£	s	d	£	s	d	£	s	d
1965	4	15	4	10	3	8	15	5	6	20	7	4
1966	4	19	3	9	18	6	14	17	9	19	17	0
1967	4	11	1	8	8	6	12	12	9	16	17	0
1968	4	1	8	8	17	4	12	5	0	16	6	8
1969	4	2	8	8	5	4	13	9	6	16	10	8
1970	4	6	1	8	12	2	12	18	3	18	13	8

Note to Table 18: *1*, The source of this information is *Royal Mint: One Hundred and First Report of the Deputy Master and Comptroller for the Period 1st January 1970 to 31st March 1971* (London), Appendix VII, p. 86.

III. THE ISSUES, TYPES AND VARIETIES OF THE PRE-1729 POST-RESTORATION SMALL SILVER COINAGE AND OF THE MAUNDY COINAGE

Prior to a chronological discussion of this subject, the diversification which is widespread throughout the post-Restoration small silver and the early Maundy coinage must be placed into perspective by considering the process by which such coinage was manufactured.

Up to the issues dated 1800, the striking of the coins from blanks was accomplished using hardened dies which themselves were sunk in part using hardened punches as templates. These punches were either carved in relief directly onto soft steel, which was subsequently hardened, or were raised from a hardened matrix which had been cut, namely engraved in intaglio, onto soft steel. Whatever their origin, an observe punch simply bore the monarch's effigy (Plate 46) and one for the reverse was unlikely to carry more than the denominational numeral surmounted by the crown (Plate 47). Consequently, on each die sunk on soft steel from a master punch, all the other details, such as letters, digits and rim denticles, had to be filled in using small hand punches, as had been the practice since the Middle Ages, after which the die was hardened before being used for the striking of coin.[255]

Because of this hand finishing, differences arise between each individual die prepared for the production of one particular type and denomination of coin. Such differences may be of a minor nature involving, for example, the precise spacing and positioning of letters and numbers, or may be of a more noticeable character involving, for example, variations in punctuation, the inversion of letters, the use of incorrect (for instance, an inverted V for an A) or damaged[256] letters or those of the font for a different size of coin, or the overstriking of an erstwhile inserted incorrect letter or number. Such varieties,[257] where known, are referred to in the appropriate Tables of this section although there is no doubt that further examples within this coinage remain to be discovered by the discerning numismatist. Nevertheless, such multiformity is simply an unavoidable consequence of the method of die manufacture and therefore has no design significance. It does, however, enable coins struck from individual dies to be fairly readily identified and this, in turn, makes it possible to estimate the number of dies used for a particular coinage.

Many errors may be manifest on just one coin, as is illustrated by the 1674 penny shown in Plate 48. This belongs to the type 2 small silver coinage of Charles II, the normal legends for which read CAROLVS·II·DEI·GRATIA (Charles II, by the Grace of God) on the obverse and ·MAG·BR·FRA·ET·HIB·REX· (King of Great Britain, France and Ireland) on the reverse. Apart from the mark (a post-striking nick) on the reverse central C and the obvious two curved clips, an examination of the legends of this particular coin reveals several interesting errors.[258] The King's name would seem to have been correctly sunk in the die with all the letters from the same font, although the top of the R is not struck up, giving it an appearance of a letter K. However, this is not unusual and, indeed, similar weaknesses are apparent in the tops of the C and O of the same word and on several of the reverse letters, including the R in REX. However, the die-sinker became too enthusiastic when punching the regnal number but probably thought that a stop punched over the extra I would patch up the error and avoid starting afresh. Nevertheless, it would appear that he then went from bad to worse. His next letter should have been a D, but either it is over another letter, possibly a V, or from a very damaged punch. Progressing to the first letter of the next word we have what might be taken to be mis-shapen G but is unlikely to be so since it would surely not have been made in that form on the small hand punch. It would seem that the die-sinker had a damaged C-punch and punched it in the wrong way round, namely forwards, on the die: perhaps he had missed or lost the original G-punch and thereby attempted to fashion an impromptu substitute. Indeed, following his error with the regnal number, the die-sinker of this particular obverse appears to have become extremely careless, not only in his choice of hand punches but also in his spacing and positioning of them on the die, this being manifest in the grossly off-kilter alignment noticeable in GRATIA. On the reverse of this coin there is only one error but it is a major one. As it had possibly been when the obverse die was prepared, the G-punch was apparently also missing when the reverse die was being completed.[259] In this instance yet another method for rectifying this deficiency was apparently attempted, namely the use of an incorrect letter from the font for a slightly larger coin, the silver twopence being the obvious choice. The result of this substitution is the appearance of MAC instead of MAG in the reverse legend.

Brockages of the small silver denominations of the seventeenth and eighteenth century are also known,[260] as are examples of these denominations which exhibit evidence of off-centre and double striking and of striking using cracked dies. Of particular interest, too, are such coins which are obviously struck on the wrong size of flan, probably usually one of abnormal thickness which expands during striking to give a resulting coin of abnormal diameter. Known examples are a twopence dated 1679 with a diameter of 1.5cm,[261] another twopence dated 1679 with a diameter of 1.6cm (Plate 49) and weighing 1.1783g, namely 22% heavier than the average weight for a normal twopence[262] of diameter 1.4cm and 16% lighter than the average weight for a normal threepence[263] of diameter 1.75 cm, some five to ten examples of pennies dated 1680 on twopence-size flans but thinner,[264] a threepence dated 1683 with a diameter of a corresponding fourpence (Plate 50) and weighing 26.25g, namely 13% heavy for the threepence and 15.3% light for the fourpence,[265] some five to ten examples of threepences dated 1685 struck on fourpence-size flans[266] and a threepence dated 1687/6 of diameter 2.4cm[267] which is exceptionally large, the normal fourpence being only 1.9cm in diameter.

Notwithstanding all of the above, the really significant feature of the multiformity within this coinage of the pre-1800 period is not the die varieties or the mis-strikes but the master punch varieties. Fortunately, for the period from 1741 until 1812, records exist of the actual number of dies which were sunk (Table 19) and punches (Table 20) and matrices (Table 20) which were produced for the Maundy coinage. Understandably, the number of dies sunk greatly exceeds the number of punches and matrices which were prepared. Furthermore, the production of a new punch was usually effected only to introduce the coinage of a new reign or of a new design within a reign[268] but was sometimes also necessary, where possible using an available matrix, to replace a punch that had either become too worn[269] or had sustained unacceptable damage.[270] A catalogue of those existing matrices, punches and dies in the Royal Mint Museum that have been used in the production of the small silver and Maundy coinage up to that of Edward VII, inclusively, has been published[271] although in this compilation those early matrices which are described with legends are almost certainly, in fact, dies.[272] The museum also houses the similar artifacts used in the production of the subsequent Maundy issues.

By the end of the eighteenth century, techniques had improved and the Mint engravers had found it possible to produce more or less fully-lettered punches lacking, at most, only the last digit or two of the date. These punches, used to sink the dies, were raised from fully-inscribed matrices that were carefully checked for errors.

Table 19. The frequency of die-sinking for the Maundy money from June 1741 to April 1812[1]

Period	1d Obverse	1d Reverse	2d Obverse	2d Reverse	3d Obverse	3d Reverse	4d Obverse	4d Reverse
1741–43								
1744	3	14	6	5		6	6	6
1745								
1746	4	4		4	2	2	2	2
1747–49								
1750		1		1		1		1
1751	2	10	2	6	3	6	3	6
1752								
1753		2						
1754	3	5						
1755	2	4						
1756								
1757		4						
1758		6						
1759	4	—		4				
1760								
1761		3						
1762					26	22		
1763	5	2	3	1	6	9	3	
1764								
1765			2		2		3	
1766	4	6	2	3	1	3	2	2
1767–69								
1770	2	3			2	1	2	4

Table 19. *(continued)*

Period	1d Obverse	1d Reverse	2d Obverse	2d Reverse	3d Obverse	3d Reverse	4d Obverse	4d Reverse
1771								
1772	3	7	6	5		3	1	2
1773–12 Dec.1777	6	10		5	3	2	4	4
12 Dec. 1777–26 Jan. 1780	—	—	2	2	2	4		3
26 Jan. 1780–13 Nov. 1782	3	8						
13 Nov. 1782–25 Feb.1784								
25 Feb.1784–19 Jan. 1785	2	4	4	4		4	4	4
19 Jan. 1785–29 Mar. 1786								
29 Mar. 1786–25 Apr. 1788	4	6	4	5	2	6	6	6
25 Apr. 1788–29 Jan. 1791								
29 Jan. 1791–14 June 1792	6	6	8	8	6	6	6	5
14 June 1792–28 Mar. 1794								
28 Mar. 1794–23 Mar. 1796	4	4	4	4	7	3	7	3
23 Mar. 1796–25 Sept. 1799								
25 Sept. 1799–14 May 1802	4	4	4	4		4	6	4
14 May 1802–12 Oct. 1803	4	4	3	3	3	2	3	2
12 Oct. 1803–7 Dec. 1805								
7 Dec. 1805–3 June 1807	2	2	3	3	5	3	3	3
3 June 1807–30 Dec. 1809	4							
30 Dec. 1809–4 Apr. 1812								
Total	77	135	53	67	70	87	61	57

Note to Table 19: *1*, This information was abstracted from the library archives of the Royal Mint by its librarian and curator, Mr G. P. Dyer. They are present in two accounts, one of which runs from 1741 to 1773, (PRO, Mint 14/10) and the other which runs from 1773 to 1812 (PRO, Mint 14/11, 14/12 and 14/13). Unlike the former, the latter account does not directly quote the numbers of dies sunk but these can be readily inferred by comparison of the appropriate figures given for numbers in the pool with those left good in the immediately previous inventory. The figures relate to the number of dies sunk and not necessarily to the number of dies finished. The practice was undoubtedly to leave new dies soft and unfinished, completing the missing details and then submitting those particular dies to the hardening process only when they were actually required for the coining press. Thus, some dies might remain in stock for years before being finished. This is the reason that, for instance, no die-sinking is recorded in 1760, a year in which we know that Maundy coins were struck (Table 8). Other such examples can be found by appropriately comparing the data in Table 8 with that in this present Table.

Table 20. The frequency of matrix and punch production for the Maundy money from June 1741 to April 1812[1]

Period	1d Matrices[2]	1d Punches[3]	2d Matrices[2]	2d Punches[3]	3d Matrices[2]	3d Punches[3]	4d Matrices[2]	4d Punches[3]
9 June 1741–22 Dec. 1744		0 + 1						
22 Dec. 1744–8 Feb. 1760								
8 Feb. 1760–18 Nov. 1766	$1^4 + 0$	$1^5 + 0$	$1^4 + 0$	$1^5 + 0$	$1^4 + 0$	$1^6 + 1^6$		$1^5 + 0$
18 Nov. 1766–26 Jan. 1780								
26 Jan. 1780–13 Nov. 1782		$0 + 1^7$						
13 Nov. 1782–25 Feb. 1784								
25 Feb. 1784–19 Jan. 1785								$0 + 1^8$
19 Jan. 1785–29 Mar. 1786								
29 Mar. 1786–25 Apr. 1788							$1 + 0$	
25 Apr. 1788–29 Jan. 1791								
29 Jan. 1791–14 June 1792	$1^9 + 1^9$	$2^9 + 1^9$	$1^9 + 1^9$	$2^9 + 1^9$	$0 + 1^9$	$1^9 + 1^9$	$1^9 + 1^9$	$4^{9,10} + 1^9$
14 June 1792–28 Mar. 1794								
28 Mar. 1794–23 Mar. 1796		$0 + 1^{11}$		$0 + 1^{11}$		$0 + 1^{11}$		$0 + 1^{11}$
23 Mar. 1796–30 Dec. 1809								
30 Dec. 1809–4 Apr. 1812[12]								
Total	2 + 1	3 + 4	2 + 1	3 + 2	1 + 1	2 + 3	2 + 1	5 + 3

Notes to Table 20: *1*, See note *1* to Table 19. The numbers of matrices and punches prepared were established from the account running from 1773 to 1812 in a manner analogous to that employed to establish the number of dies sunk; *2*, The figures on the left and right sides of the addition signs refer to the number of obverse and reverse matrices, respectively; *3*, The figures on the left and right sides of the addition signs refer to the number of obverse and reverse punches, respectively; *4*, The account of 18 November 1766 shows that this obverse matrix was prepared since 8 February 1760 but it does not indicate the date of production; *5*, This new obverse punch, presumably that of the new king, George III, was reported on 8 February 1763 as having been prepared; *6*, The preparation of a new obverse punch, presumably bearing the bust of the new king, George III, and of a new reverse punch, reported on 25/29 June 1762 and 30 September 1762, respectively, were obviously required in relation to the large issue of silver threepences for that year (see page 118); *7*, Examination of the appropriate coins leaves little doubt that by 1780 the reverse punch for the penny had deteriorated badly, it presumably being this factor which brought about the preparation of this new reverse punch. Concurrently with its introduction, the groove on the effigy (see Section VI of Chapter 3) was eliminated but since this defect had been tolerated for so long it is unlikely that its removal was of paramount consideration; *8*, This additional reverse punch indicates that produced for the new reverse designs for the wire money of 1792; *9*, Indicative of the new obverse and reverse designs for the wire money of 1792; *10*, This suggests that some of the punches raised for the wire money fourpence were faulty. Indeed, from a pool of five obverse punches, three were set aside to be defaced on 14 June 1792; *11*, The new reverse punch for the issues dated 1795 and 1800; *12*, Other drafts of these accounts between 1809 and 1812 give slightly different figures but those presented here seem to be the most reliable.

Consequently, this change in die-making technique abruptly eliminated the previous common cause of blundered inscriptions but provided a new opportunity for errors to be made. Thus, although varieties now become less likely to occur and are sometimes much more difficult to identify, those that do arise often do so as a consequence of either defective repair work on a partially damaged die, often evident as mis-spelling, or the careless punching of a date digit.[273]

Unless otherwise or more specifically referenced, information for the remainder of this section has been obtained from standard sources.[274] Furthermore, those coins illustrated in the Plates that are referred to in this section, with the exceptions of Plates 68 and 101, are, with respect to their dates, and unless otherwise stated, purely exemplary of their particular type or sub-type. Also of a similar nature are the legends on those coins that are referred to in this section and illustrated up to Plate 69, in which minor variations, which are described in the related Tables and text, often occur within the type. Unless otherwise specified, the illustrated obverses are those of the fourpences.

i. Charles II (29 May 1660–6 February 1685)[275]

Following his restoration on 9 May 1660, Charles II made his state entry into London and ascended to the throne twenty days later, on his birthday, although his regnal years are reckoned from the death of his father on 30 January 1648/9.[276] On 27 June 1660, a general order was made directing the preparation of dies, puncheons, etc. for the making of gold and silver coins and in the same month a warrant was issued ordering the Wardens of the Mint to furnish irons for coining money, and to cause their chief engraver, Thomas Simon,[277] to grave the King's effigies thereon. On 20 July following, an indenture was entered into with Sir Ralph Freeman, the Master of the Mint, which provided for the coinage of the same pieces and of the same value as those which had been coined in the time of Charles I. Understandably, the King was in a hurry to have money issued bearing his effigy but Simon, a careful workman, was not to be rushed and the Mint's authorities were slow in getting to work. Reminders were sent to the Wardens on 18 August and 21 September and, on the latter date, the King also sent under his own hand to Thomas 'Simons', as one of the chief gravers, 'to lay aside all occasions, and forthwith to prepare the original or master puncheons and charges, and also some dies or stamps for the gold and silver coins, according to the said order of the 27 June without fail'. The resultant minting certainly commenced before the end of the year, because the Mint returns between 20 July and 31 December show that 543lb of silver (£1,683 6s in value) was coined. However, this did not alleviate the demand for coinage and, on 29 January 1661, French, Portuguese and Spanish coins were ordered to be 'current of and in England, as if they had been sterling money'. Furthermore, a proclamation of 7 September 1661, ordering that the money of the Commonwealth was not to be current after the following 30 November, was extended by several subsequent proclamations until May of the next year.

In spite of the availability of newer techniques and the invention of more advanced machinery, it was initially decided that the coinage of the new monarch would be produced using the then well-established method known as hammering.[278] There is no doubt that Simon, who may to a certain extent have had the co-operation of Thomas Rawlins[279] in some of this work, would have produced a milled[280] currency but his aspirations in this direction were thwarted by the persistent jealousy of the moneyers and he was thereby compelled to follow the old-fashioned methods of the previous reign.

The pre-1668 small silver coinage of this reign (Table 21) has been arranged in various ways. Hawkins[281] arranges it in four issues, Webb[282] extends this to six (a division accepted, albeit with a slight alteration in order, by Morrieson[283]) and Graham[284] returns to a quadripartition. In the current study, the small silver coinage of the whole reign (29 May 1660–6 February 1685) has been divided into two types, the undated (type 1), which consists of the pre-1668 issues, and the dated (type 2). The coins of type 1 (Table 21) were initially struck from 1660 to 1663, during which period six sub-types, A–F, of each of the penny (Plate 51) and twopence (Plate 52) and two sub-types, A and B, of each of the threepence (Plate 53) and fourpence (Plate 54) were minted. All the coins of type 1 carry on their obverse the King's bust represented in profile and facing to the left, are with or without a mintmark[285] and have a variously-abbreviated Latin legend (Table 21) which translates as 'Charles II, by the Grace of God, King of Great Britain, France and Ireland'. All their reverses are similar, excepting either the presence or absence of the mintmark: the arms of England are quartered with those of France in the first and fourth quarters and those of Scotland and Ireland are in the second and third quarters, respectively, and all are enclosed together in a plain square-topped shield.[286] The ends of a cross fleury project slightly beyond the edges of this shield and the whole is surrounded by the variously punctuated (Table 21) legend CHRISTO AVSPICE [one type 1C penny (Table 21) reads AVSPCE] REGNO (I Reign under the Auspice of Christ).

It is the type 1 small silver coins (less the penny and twopence of type 1F and the threepence and fourpence of type 1B), which can be divided into three issues (each consisting of one of more of the above sub-types), that formed what has been referred to as Charles II's hammered small silver coinage produced using Simon's various dies. These first, second and third issues, the bust on all of which includes a single-arched crown, are distinguished by being without inner circles or a mark of value, without inner circles but with a mark of value (the appropriate Roman numeral behind the bust)[287] and with dotted inner circles and a mark of value, respectively, and the component small silver denominations have been well documented.[288]

For the first issue, only the penny (type 1A, with the mintmark on the obverse only, and type 1B, without a mintmark) and the twopence (type 1A, with the mintmark on the obverse only) are known.[289] Ruding's Plate XXXIII, no. 4, illustrates what is apparently a first issue twopence with the mintmark on both its obverse and reverse although the related text relates it to what is clearly a type 1A twopence. As mentioned by Graham[290] in connection with another of Ruding's plates, these were reproduced from Folkes[291] and 'to rely upon a plate executed without the aid of photography is to lean upon a bruised reed'. It is presumably the type 1A penny and twopence which have been referred to as patterns.[292]

As with the first issue, only the penny and twopence are present in the second issue which contains these denominations both as type 1C, with the mintmark on both its obverse and reverse, and as the physically smaller type 1D, with the mintmark confined to the reverse and with the bust extending to the bottom of the coin.[293] Although they are not quite so well made as are the corresponding denominations of the coins known as the Undated or Simon's Maundy money, the type 1F penny and twopence (see

Table 21. The type 1 small silver coinage of Charles II

No.	Sub-type	Denomination		Varieties, remarks, etc.
1	A	1d	(i)	Obverse: CAROLVS. II. D.G. MAG. BRIT. FR. ET. HIB. REX[1,2]
				Reverse: with stops; harp,? strings[2]
			(ii)	Obverse: CAROLVS II D G MAG BRIT FR ET H REX[2]
				Reverse: no stops; harp,? strings[2]
			(iii)	Obverse: CROLVS. II. D. G. MA. B. F. ET. HI. REX.[3]
2	—	2d	(i)	Obverse: as 1(i)[4,5]
				Reverse: with stops; harp, 5 strings[2]
			(ii)	Obverse: as 2(i) but no stops and minute pellet on either side of the mintmark[2]
				Reverse: harp, 5 strings[2]
			(iii)	Obverse: CAROLVS II D G MAG BRIT FR FT H RFX[2,4]
				Reverse: no stop after REGNO; harp, 5 strings[2]
			(iv)	Obverse: CAROLVS. II. D: G: MAG: B: FR: ET. H. REX[2,4]
				Reverse: with stops; harp, 5 strings[2]
3	B	1d	(i)	Obverse: CPOLVS II D. G. M. BP. F. HI. PFX.[1,6], legend clearly unfinished[6]; pellet over the King's bust in place of the usual mintmark[6]
				Reverse: with stops; harp,? and 5 strings[6]
			(ii)	Obverse: CAROLVS II D G M BR F ET H REX[1,6]
				Reverse: no stops; harp,? strings[6]
4	—	2d		Obverse: CAROLVS. II. D: G·MAG·B·FR·ET. H. REX[4,7]
				Reverse: CHRISTO · AVSPICE · REGNO ·; harp,? 4 strings[7]
5	C	1d	(i)	Obverse: · CAROLVS · II: D: G: M: B: F: ET · H: REX ·.[1,7]
				Reverse: · CHRISTO · AVSPICE · REGNO ·; harp, 5 strings[7]
			(ii)	Obverse: as 5(i)[8]
				Reverse: · CHRISTO · AVSPCE · REGNO ·.[8]
6	—	2d	(i)	Obverse: as 5(i) but without stop before CAROLVS[4,7]
				Reverse: as 5(i) but harp, ? 4 strings[7]
			(ii)	Obverse: reads M., F. and HI. and II. for value[3]
7	D	1d		Obverse: CAROLVS. II. D. G. M. B. F. &. H. REX.[1,9]
				Reverse: with stops; harp, 4 strings[9]
8	—	2d		Obverse: as 7 but with G ·, B · and & ·.[4,7]
				Reverse: with stops[7]
9	E	1d	(i)	Obverse: CAROLVS II D G MAG: BR: FR: ET. HIB REX[10]
				Reverse: as 5(i)[10]
			(ii)	Obverse: CAROLVS. II. D. G. M. BR. FR. ET. HIB. REX[1,10]
				Reverse: as 5(i)[10]
			(iii)	Obverse: CAROLVS. II. D: G: M B F ET HIB REX[1,10]
				Reverse: as 5(i)[10]
			(iv)	Obverse: CAROLVS. II. D G M. B. F. ET. HIB REX[10]

(continued)

Table 21. *(continued)*

No.	Sub-type	Denomination		Varieties, remarks, etc.
				Reverse: as 5(i)[10]
			(v)	Obverse: CAROLVS. II. D. G: M: B: F: ET. HIB: REX.[10]
				Reverse: as 5(i)[10]
			(vi)	Obverse: MAG BR FR RT HIB[1]
			(vii)	Obverse: MAG B F ET HIB[1]
10	—	2d	(i)	Obverse: CAROLVS. II. D: G: MAG: BRI: FRA: ET. HIB. REX[4,11]
				Reverse: as 5(i) but harp,? strings[11]
			(ii)	Obverse: as 10(i) but with stop before CAROLVS and after REX[11]
				Reverse: as 10(i)[11]
			(iii)	Obverse: CAROLVS. II. D. G. MAG: BRI: FRA: ET. HIB: REX[4,11]
				Reverse: CHRISTO – AVSPICE ᛫ REGNO; harp? strings[11]
			(iv)	Obverse: CAROLVS. II. D: G: MAG: BRI: FR: ET. HIB: REX[10]
				Reverse: no stops; harp,? strings[10]
			(v)	Obverse: CAROLVS. II. D: G: MAG: BR: FR: ET. HIB: REX[4,10]
				Reverse: as 5(i) but harp, ?5 strings[10]
			(vi)	Obverse: King's name is mis-spelt CAROLLVS[3]
			(vii)	The British Museum's collection contains a forgery of this coin
11	A	3d		Obverse: .CAROLVS. II. D. G. M. BR. FR. ET. HI. REX.[11]
				Reverse: as 5(i) but harp, 4 strings[11]
12	—	4d	(i)	Obverse: .CAROLVS. II. D. G. MAG. BR. FR. ET. HIB. REX.[11]
				Reverse: as 5(i)[11]
			(ii)	Obverse: as 12(i)[11]
				Reverse: as 12(i) but omits stops before CHRISTO and after REGNO[11]
			(iii)	Obverse: as 12(i) but omits stops before CAROLVS and after REX[11]
				Reverse: as 12(i)[11]
13	F	1d		Obverse: CAROLVS. II D. G. M. B. F &. H. REX[1,12]
				Reverse: no stop after REGNO and harp, 6 strings[12]
14	—	2d		Obverse: as 13 but with stops after II and F[1,12]
				Reverse: as 5(i) but no stop after REGNO and harp, 7 strings[12]
15	B	3d	(i)	Obverse: as 13 but with stop after II[12]
				Reverse: no stop after REGNO; harp, 5 strings[12]
			(ii)	Obverse: as 15(i)[12]
				Reverse: as 15(i) but harp, 4 strings[12]
			(iii)	Obverse: as 15(i)[12]
				Reverse: as 15(i) but harp, 6 strings[12]
16	—	4d		Obverse: CAROLVS. II D G. M B F & H REX[12]
				Reverse: as 13[12,13]

Notes to Table 21: *1*, ESC, p. 205; *2*, Graham, p. 70; *3*, Hocking (1906), p. 118; *4*, ESC, p. 199; *5*, Graham, p. 69; *6*, Graham, p. 71; *7*, Graham, p. 73; *8*, Robinson; *9*, Graham, p. 74; *10*, Graham, p. 78; *11*, Graham, p. 77; *12*, Graham, p. 79; *13*, A harp with 7 strings has also been observed on a type 1B fourpence (Robinson).

below), the pennies and twopences of type 1C and 1D show a quality of striking commensurate with their having being machine made[294] and being, when struck, confined in a collar. However, they are still classed as part of the second hammered issue and it is highly probable that Simon made the punches[295] for such a coinage. Furthermore, it has been suggested that the coins themselves of types 1C and 1D, and all four of the small silver denominations known as the Undated or Simon's Maundy money, which were also machine made (see below), were actually struck by Simon outside the precincts of the Mint on a machine, the modus operandi of which he kept a secret.[296] Alternatively, it has been suggested that the location for this work may, in fact, have been the Tower after the order was issued to Simon 'to bring in and deliver to the officers of His Majesty's Mynt all such counter puncheons, charges, letters and dyes and all other tools and engines for coining by way of the press and hammer as he hath in his custody' since this order, on 24 January 1661/2,[297] did not depose him from office but was simply made to restrict the manufacture of the coins of the realm to the confines of the Tower Mint.[298] It is interesting that not only do the type 1D penny and twopence differ from those of type 1C by virtue of their obverse effigies extending to the bottom of the coin and the replacement of ET by the ampersand in their obverse legend (Table 21), but these features are also present of the coins known as the Undated or Simon's Maundy money (see below and Table 21). Clearly they can be regarded as a connecting link between this latter coinage and the type 1C of the second issue. In addition to the types 1C and 1D twopences, a further twopence within the second issue has been recorded. In the absence of the naturally-sequential type 1B twopence,[299] this further twopence is now so type-designated. It is of type 1A but with the mark of value, namely a II, added behind the bust and, accordingly, it may be regarded as a connecting link between the first and second issues. Very few specimens of this coin exist and those which do are all apparently from the same die. They were probably struck immediately upon the issue of the value mark warrant using the reverse die from the last coining of the first issue. It is doubtful whether they were accompanied by a corresponding penny.[300]

A warrant dated 19 January 1662/3[301] was issued for the striking of threepences and groats which had not been ordered by the earlier indenture.[302] Consequently were struck the third issue of the small denominational silver coins, namely the type 1E penny and twopence and the type 1A threepence and fourpence. Although these coins are usually placed together and all have a mintmark on both their obverse and reverse, dissimilarities, involving the legend, quality of work, arches of the crown and locks of hair on the bust, between the penny and twopence on the one hand and the threepence and fourpence on the other have led to a tendency to separate the two smaller denominations from the two larger ones.[303] These coins have been placed before those of types 1C and 1D by one authority and before those of type 1D by another:[304] the latter relative positions are certainly supported by the Trials of the Pyx[305] held on 9 July 1663 and 4 July 1664 when the third issue hammered coins are included only in the former and what would appear to be coins of the second issue, types 1C or 1D, in the latter.[306] Furthermore, it is almost certain that the Trial of the Pyx of 4 August 1669 contained, along with the Simon's Maundy money (see below), examples of this third issue coinage,[307] which are today by far the most common of the small silver denominations of the hammered coinage of Charles II.

As mentioned above, types 1C and 1D of the penny and twopence show properties commensurate with their having been machine made and therefore both might be regarded as a milled coinage. Nevertheless, the first small silver denominations which are usually so designated are the type 1F penny and twopence and the type 1B threepence and fourpence. All these four coins are similar in design. They carry a bust of the King which now includes a double-arched crown, are somewhat better struck than the pennies and twopences of types 1C and 1D, and collectively they have become known as the Undated Maundy money or Simon's Maundy money. It is likely, however, that they were not reserved exclusively for Maundy purposes because worn specimens sometimes occur and there are examples of the threepence which bear a harp with four, five and six strings, respectively (Table 21), thus indicating the use of several reverse dies for that particular coin, suggesting a substantial mintage.[308] Reverse-die variation in the fourpence of this sub-type has also been observed, involving the use of either large or small capital letters and variations in the punctuation (the presence or absence of a stop after REGNO) in the legend and the use of a six-stringed harp and an apparently two-stringed, albeit badly damaged, harp in the coat of arms.[309] Furthermore, die-axis variation within the twopence and fourpence of this sub-type has been observed, in spite of it being a milled coinage.[310] A thorough investigation of multiformity within this so-called Simon's Maundy money and, indeed, further such research into the earlier small silver denominations of Charles II, would be of interest.

In 1662, the Mint entered into an agreement with Peter Blondeau[311] to erect and superintend the working of his new machinery for coining in the Tower. Machinery was also introduced for rolling the metal into sheets and for cutting out from these blank discs of the requisite size, instead of producing the sheets by hand hammering and shaping the blanks by hand shearing as formerly practised. Thus, in England in 1663, milled coinage production almost completely superseded that of hammered coinage production and, included in the new issue of the coinage which subsequently appeared, was a small silver coinage of all four denominations (type 2) (Plate 55 and Table 22).[312] The possible exception was the striking of the third issue hammered pieces which may have continued for some further five or six years (see above).

The obverse and reverse tools for all this new coinage were produced by John Roettiers.[313] On all the denominations, both silver and gold, it is interesting, and probably significant, that Roettiers' design shows the bust of the King in profile facing to the right whereas that on Simon's earlier hammered coinage of the reign was likewise represented but facing to the left.[314] Furthermore, one of the characteristic features of both the large and the small silver denominations of the new milled coinage is the use of the King's monogram, a C, in the reverse design. On the four larger silver pieces, the crown, half-crown, shilling and sixpence, the four shields in the quarters, which between them carry the royal coat of arms,[315] are separated by four linked double Cs in the field.[316] Such a linked double C also occurs on the obverses of some of Charles II's official pattern farthings[317] and four large interlinked Cs form part of the reverse design of private pattern farthings in pewter and in copper.[318] However, the shields used on the larger silver denominations were found to be too intricate for reproduction in the space available on the four smaller denominations[319] which thus have on their reverses four, three and two interlinked Cs and a single C, according to their value. In addition, the fourpence is also decorated on the four quarters of the field between the interlinked Cs with a rose, thistle, fleur-de-lis and harp, the national

Table 22. The type 2 small silver coinage of Charles II

No.	Date	Denomination		Varieties, remarks, etc.
17	1668	2d		probably a pattern[1]
18	1670	1d	(i)	with blundered date[2]
19	——	2d		
20	——	3d		
21	——	4d		
22	1671	1d		
23	——	2d		
24	——	3d	(i)	reads GRΛTIΛ[3]
			(ii)	reads GRVTIA[4,5]
			(iii)	reads GRΛTIA[4]
25	——	4d		
26	1672[6]	1d	(i)	2 over 1[6]
27	——	2d	(i)	2 over 1[6]
			(ii)	with a clear-cut date (?)[7]
28	——	3d	(i)	2 over 1[6]
29	——	4d	(i)	2 over 1[6]
30	1673	1d		
31	——	2d		
32	——	3d		
33	——	4d		
34	1674	1d	(i)	reads ƆRACIA[3,10]
			(ii)	reads ƆRATIA[8,9,10,11]
35	——	2d		
36	——	3d		
37	——	4d	(i)	4 over 6[5]
38	1675	1d	(i)	see note 11
39	——	2d		
40	——	3d		
41	——	4d		
42	1676	1d	(i)	reads ƆRATIA[8,10,11]
43	——	2d		
44	——	3d	(i)	6 of date over 5[4,5]
			(ii)	reads ERA instead of FRA[4,5]
45	——	4d	(i)	7 of date over 6[3,5,12]
			(ii)	second 6 of date over 5[5,12]
			(iii)	large lettering and figures[3]
46	1677	1d	(i)	reads ƆRATIA[8,9,10,11]
			(ii)	reads GRATIA.RE.X[3]
			(iii)	reads ƆRATIA.REX[3,10,11] (i.e. as (i))
47	——	2d	(i)	reads CAROLVS II.[3]
48	——	3d		
49	——	4d	(i)	reads CAROLVS:I.I[3]
			(ii)	A partly over R in CAROLVS[13]
50	1678	1d	(i)	reads ƆRATIA[3,8,9,10,11]
51	——	2d	(i)	8 of date over 6[3,9,14] and CAROLVS II.[3]
			(ii)	8 of date over 6[3,14] and CAROLVS.II.[3]
52		3d	(i)	large lettering[3]
53		4d	(i)	8 of date over 7[5,12]
			(ii)	8 of date over 6[3,5,12]
54	1679	1d[15]	(i)	no stop after DEI or CAROLVS[3]
55	——	2d	(i)	blundered HIB[3]
			(ii)	HIB over FRA[14]

(continued)

Table 22. (continued)

No.	Date	Denomination		Varieties, remarks, etc.
			(iii)	blundered DEI[3]
			(iv)	two specimens known on large flans[16]
56	——	3d[17]	(i)	O of CAROLVS over A[3,4,5]
			(ii)	broken die[3,18]
57	——	4d[17]	(i)	fine lettering[3]
			(ii)	heavy lettering[3]
			(iii)	no stop after CAROLVS or DEI[3]
58	1680	1d	(i)	on flan of 2d size and thinner. Five to ten examples are known[8]
59	——	2d	(i)	80 of date over 79[9,14,19]
60	——	3d	(i)	double cut 6 in date[19]
			(ii)	very badly cracked die[18,19]
61	——	4d		
62	1681	1d		
63	——	2d		
64	——	3d	(i)	1 of date over 0[4,5,19]
65	——	4d	(i)	1 of date over 0[5,12,19]
66	1682	1d	(i)	2 of date over 1[8,9,19]
			(ii)	large lettering on obverse[19]
			(iii)	ERA for FRA[8,9]
67	——	2d	(i)	2 of date over 1[9,14,19]
			(ii)	2 of date over 1, reads ERA for FRA[14,18]
68	——	3d	(i)	2 of date over 1[4,5,19]
69	——	4d	(i)	2 of date over 1[5,12,19]
			(ii)	2 of date over 1 and no stop after CAROLVS[19]
70	1683	1d	(i)	no stop after CAROLVS[19]
			(ii)	3 of date over 2[9]
71	——	2d	(i)	3 of date over 1[13]
			(ii)	3 of date over 2[9,14,19]
72	——	3d	(i)	large 3 in date[19]
			(ii)	large flan of 4d diameter[20]
73	——	4d		
74	1684	1d	(i)	4 of date over 3[8]
			(ii)	no stop after CAROLVS[19]
75	——	2d	(i)	no stops after CAROLVS or DEI[18]
76	——	3d	(i)	4 of date over 3[4,5,19]
77	——	4d	(i)	4 of date over 3[5,12,19]

Notes to Table 22: *1*, Farquhar (1929–30), pp. 231–32; Ratcliffe and Wright, p. 19; (see also Section IV of Chapter 3); *2*, Linecar (1978); *MSCE*, p. 74 (the blunder shows the 0 looking like a 9 (Harding (1982))); *3*, Linecar (1978); *MSCE*, p. 74; *4*, *ESC*, p. 190; *5*, Trowbridge, p. 14; *6*, All the usual small silver pieces of 1672 have this overdate (*ESC*, pp. 184, 190, 199, 205; Linecar (1978); *MSCE*, p. 74); *7*, Linecar (1978); *MSCE*, p. 74 (see also *ESC*, p. 199); *8*, *ESC*, p. 205; *9*, Trowbridge, p. 15; *10*, see page 137; *11*, Since pennies reading ɔRATIA exist for 1674, 1676, 1677 and 1678, it has been suggested (*ESC*, p. 205) that 'one might logically expect a specimen dated 1675 to appear one day'. However, bearing in mind the nature of die sinking during this period (see page 136), this suggestion does not follow. The 1674 and 1677 obverses with this error are certainly struck from the same die (Manville) and it is therefore likely that the 1676 and 1678 obverses with this error also originated from this die. However, in 1675, the moneyer may have simply chosen an alternative obverse die, namely without this error, since it is possible that more than one were sunk, finished and concurrently available; *12*, *ESC*, p. 184; *13*, Manville; *14*, *ESC*, p. 199; *15*, The 9 in the date on some of these coins resembles a damaged 0 with a short tail added to its right lower extremity, namely to give ϑ (see also note 2), on others the tail is added to an undamaged 0 to give ϙ and on yet others, the rarest, an inverted 6 is used; *16*, See page 137 and Plate 49; *17*, Of all the type 2 small silver coinage of Charles II, the threepence and fourpence dated 1679 are by far the most common; *18*, See Plate 46; *19*, Linecar (1978); *MSCE*, p. 75; *20*, See page 137 and Plate 50.

emblems of England, Scotland, France and Ireland, respectively, which thus represent Charles II's continuing claim to the thrones of these countries. Of all this new coinage, only the four small denominations carry, in the form of the interlinked Cs, a mark of their value.[320]

The type 2 small silver coinage of Charles II, which probably owes its origin to patterns, one for a penny (Plate 56) and two for a twopence (Plate 57), of Charles I by Nicholas Briot,[321] has obverse and reverse legends which read, respectively, with minor variations (Table 22), CAROLVS·II·DEI·GRATIA (Charles II, by the Grace of God) and, along with the varying dates, ·MAG·BR·FRA·ET·HIB·REX·, an abbreviation of MAGNÆ BRITANNIÆ FRANCISE ET HIBERNIÆ REX (King of Great Britain, France and Ireland).

The type 2 twopence was initially minted in 1668 but it was not until 1670 that the other three denominations first made their appearance (Table 8). It has been proposed[322] that this lone issue of the twopence in 1668 was produced because the King was at that time 'about to goe a progress', thus presumably requiring these coins for largesse.[323] Alternatively, it has been suggested[324] that it was a pattern by Roettiers although this claim had neither appeared previously nor has subsequently in any of the well-established numismatic literature, or elsewhere. Nevertheless, credence is lent to this suggestion by the observation that the twopence of 1668 has a die-axis opposite to that of all the other twopences, and, indeed, pennies, threepences and fourpences which were issued annually from 1670 to 1684.[325]

ii. James II (6 February 1685–11 December 1688 (declared to have abdicated))[326]

All the tools for the coinage of this reign were designed and engraved by John Roettiers.[327] The larger silver denominations, the crown, half-crown, shilling and sixpence, of James II differ little from those of his elder brother except that the obverse bust and name are changed accordingly and the spaces between the shields on the reverse remains blank, since the initial I of IACOBVS (James) could not be used in a manner analogous that of the corresponding C of his late brother.

However, on the small silver denominations (Table 23), the monogram I is used and appears on the reverses as I, II, III and IIII, according to the denomination (Plate 58).

The central I of the III on the reverses of the threepences is often only weakly or partially struck (Plate 59) as a consequence of the mismatching of the obverse and reverse dies, with a resultant metal theft from the central I by the effigy.[328] The obverse and reverse legends of this issue read IACOBVS·II·DEI·GRATIA (James II, by the Grace of God) and, together with the varying dates, ·MAG·BR·FRA·ET·HIB·REX· (King of Great Britain, France and Ireland), respectively. A new obverse die was obviously prepared for the striking of the 1688 fourpence since the legend on these coins finishes at the immediate rear of the bust's neck whereas for the corresponding denomination dated 1686 or 1687/6, the A of GRATIA is beneath the truncation of the rear of the neck. In fact, the fourpence of 1688 is the only coin in this whole issue of small silver in which none of the obverse legend is underneath the neck's truncation.[329]

Table 23. The small silver coinage of James II

No.	Date	Denomination		Varieties, remarks, etc.
78	1685	1d		
79	——	3d	(i)	on flan for the groat. Five to ten examples known[1]
			(ii)	reversing sideways[2]
80	1686	1d		
81	——	2d	(i)	small o in IACoBVS[2]
			(ii)	—— and reads IΛCoBVS[2,3]
82	——	3d	(i)	small o in IACoBVS[2]
			(ii)	die flaw on some specimens[4]
83	——	4d	(i)	date over crown[2,5,6]
84	1687	1d	(i)	7 of date over 8[2]
			(ii)	7 of date over 6[7]
85	——	2d	(i)	ERA for FRA[3]
86	——	3d	(i)	7 of date over 6[1,2]
			(ii)	—— on flan 2.4 cm diameter[8]
87	——	4d	(i)	7 of date over 6[5,6] (on all coins?)
88	1688	1d	(i)	last 8 of date over 7[2,5,7]
89	——	2d	(i)	——[2,3,5]
90	——	3d	(i)	——[1,2,5]
91	——	4d	(i)	——[5,6]
			(ii)	no stop after FRA[2]

Notes to Table 23: *1*, *ESC*, p. 191; *2*, Linecar (1978); *MSCE*, p. 75; *3*, *ESC*, p. 200; *4*, Harding (1980); *5*, Trowbridge, p. 16; *6*, *ESC*, p. 185; *7*, *ESC*, p. 206; *8*, Harding (1982).

iii. William and Mary (13 February 1689–28 December 1694 (upon the death of Mary))[330]

The obverse design of the small silver coinage of this reign (Table 24) includes the jugate busts of the King and Queen with that of the former at the front (Plate 60). Of this design on the two larger denominations, two distinct sub-types, A and B, exist. These can be readily distinguished by the absence or the presence, respectively, on the threepence and fourpence of a tie to the wreath which is around the King's head (Plate 60).[331] Furthermore, on the threepence and fourpence of 1689 and, indeed, also on the two smaller denominations of this date, the legend is continuous over the busts. Only the bust of sub-type A occurs on coins dated 1689 and 1690, whilst the bust of sub-type B occurs on coins dated 1692 and 1693 (and the threepences dated 1694) and both sub-types of bust are found on coins dated 1691 (and the fourpences dated 1694).[332] The conjoint busts on all the pennies and twopences are of sub-type A.[333]

The use of a cypher, in this case W and M intertwined, returned in the reverse designs of some of the larger silver denominations, whence it had been lost when the coinage of Charles II was replaced by that of his younger brother. However, the King's monogram which had been evident, in appropriate numbers, on the reverses of the small silver coinage of the two immediately preceding reigns was now replaced by a large Arabic numeral, showing the value of the piece, surmounted by a crown[334] (Plate 60). No doubt space limitations were to a large extent responsible for this change on the small silver coinage which gave four reverse designs which have remained essentially unchanged through to the current Maundy coinage. Although James and

Table 24. The small silver coinage of William and Mary

No.	Date	Denomination		Varieties, remarks, etc.[1]
92	1689	1d[2]	(i)	reads ETREGINA6[3]
			(ii)	reads GVIELM∧S[3]
			(iii)	reads GVLIEMAS[1,4]
			(iv)	reads GVIELMVS[5]
93	—	2d	(i)	legend continuous above the bust[6]
			(ii)	no stop after D G or REGINA 1629[7]
94	—	3d	(i)	no stop after date[7]
			(ii)	no stop after or before date[7]
			(iii)	no stops on the reverse[7,8]
			(iv)	hyphen stops on the reverse[8]
			(v)	LMV in GVLIELMVS over MVS[8]
95	—	4d	(i)	.GVL...G., A.1689M[7]
			(ii)	GVL...G., A.1689M[7]
			(iii)	similar but GV below bust[7]
			(iv)	similar but A.1689.M[7]
			(v)	GVL...G, A.1689M[7]
			(vi)	similar but berries in hair[7]
			(vii)	similar without berries, A.1689.M[7]
			(viii)	similar but A1689.M[7]
			(ix)	similar but berries in hair[7]
			(x)	G below bust[7]
			(xi)	GV below bust[9]
			(xii)	G below bust, stop before G[9]
			(xiii)	G below bust, with berries in wreath[9]
96	1690	1d[10]	(i)	D G., no stop after date[3]
97	—	3d	(i)	D G., no stop after date[3]
			(ii)	D G., stop after date[3]
			(iii)	GVLIELMVS·, D G, no stop after date
			(iv)	GVLIELMVS, D· G., no stop after date, 9 over 6
98	—	4d	(i)	D. G., no stop after date[3]
			(ii)	D. G, no stop after date[3]
99	1691	1d	(i)	1 of date over O[4,5] (all pennies have this overdate[3])
			(ii)	stop above head, D. G., .1691[3]
			(iii)	stop above head, D G., .1691[3]
			(iv)	stop after ET., —— 1691[3]
			(v)	stop after ET., —— .1691[3]
100	—	2d	(i)	.1691
101	—	3d	(i)	long space between REGINA and date[3]
			(ii)	reads ETREGINA[3]
			(iii)	sub-type A[8]
			(iv)	sub-type B[8]
102	—	4d	(i)	sub-type A[9]
			(ii)	sub-type A, 1 of date over 0[3,9]
			(iii)	sub-type B[9]
103	1692	1d	(i)	2 of date over 1[5]
			(ii)	no stop after G, 2 of date over 1[3]
104	—	2d	(i)	no stop after G, small date[3]
105	—	3d	(i)	G below bust[8]
			(ii)	GV below bust[3,8] .1692[3]
			(iii)	GVL below bust[3,8] .1692[3]
			(iv)	.GV below bust ——[3]
106	—	4d	(i)	small letters on obverse and reverse[3,9] and all stops[3]

(continued)

Table 24. *(continued)*

No.	Date	Denomination		Varieties, remarks, etc.[1]
			(ii)	small letters on obverse and reverse, no stops after date and 2 of date over 1[3]
			(iii)	small letters on obverse, large letters on reverse,[3,9] all stops, MARIA[3]
			(iv)	large letters on both sides,[3,9] all stops[3]
107	1693	1d	(i)	stop after ET[3]
			(ii)	stop above head[3]
108	——	2d	(i)	3 of date over 2[3,4,6]
			(ii)	——, no stop after G[3]
			(iii)	GV under bust[6]
109	——	3d	(i)	3 of date over 2, G under bust[3]
			(ii)	3 of date over 2, GV under bust[3]
			(iii)	G below bust[8]
			(iv)	GV below bust[8]
110	——	4d	(i)	3 of date over 2[3,9]
111	1694	1d	(i)	stop above head[3]
			(ii)	stop after ET[3]
			(iii)	no stops on obverse[3,5]
			(iv)	HI for HIB[5]
112	——	2d	(i)	4 of date over 3[6]
			(ii)	GVLI, D.G, HIBREXET[3]
			(iii)	——, D.G., ——[3]
			(iv)	——, ——, HI.REX.ET[3]
			(v)	ditto MARIA[3]
			(vi)	—— but GVL[3]
			(vii)	—— but MARLA[3]
			(viii)	GVLI under bust[6]
			(ix)	HI for HIB,[3,11] GVL under bust[6]
113	——	3d	(i)	G below bust[8]
			(ii)	——, reads MARIA[3,8]
			(iii)	GV below bust[3,8]
			(iv)	GVL below bust[3,8]
114	——	4d	(i)	sub-type A[9]
			(ii)	sub-type B[9]

Notes to Table 24: *1*, On the small silver denominations of William and Mary and of William III there are a large number of small inscription errors, particularly where the use of V or A is concerned (*ESC*, p. 185); *2*, The date is difficult to read, it having been very badly punched into the die, but all pieces with the legend continuous over the busts on the obverse are of this date (*ESC*, p. 206; Linecar (1978); *MSCE*, pp. 75, 76); *3*, Linecar (1978); *MSCE*, p. 76; *4*, Trowbridge, p. 18; *5*, *ESC*, p. 206; *6*, *ESC*, p. 200; *7*, Linecar (1978); *MSCE*, p. 75; *8*, *ESC*, p. 191; *9*, *ESC*, p. 185; *10*, All the pennies from 1690 to 1694 have the obverse legend broken by the jugate busts (*ESC*, p. 206); *11*, Hocking (1906), p. 131.

Norbert Roettiers[335] and, to a small extent, George Bower[336] were responsible for the obverses and reverses of the large majority of the coinage of this joint reign, the artists responsible for the small silver obverses and reverses are unknown although it has been suggested that the type A busts are possibly the work of Bower.

The obverse and reverse legends read, respectively, GVLIELMVS·ET·MARIA·D·G· (William and Mary, by the Grace of God) and, along with the date, ·MAG·BR·FR·ET·HIB·REX·ET·REGINA· (King and Queen of Great Britain, France and Ireland), although many minor variations within both of these, involving the absence of stops, spelling errors and changes in letter spacing, are known (Table 24). No reference on the small silver coinage is made to the House of Orange whereas on the larger denominations, where space permits the use of a coat of arms on the reverse, the arms of Orange (azure, billetty and a lion rampant Or) are superimposed, initially as an escutcheon and, from 1691, as a centrepiece.[337]

iv. William III (28 December 1694–8 March 1702)[338]

The obverse dies for the small silver coinage of William III (Plate 61 and Table 25) were the work of John Croker[339] and carry the legend GVLIELMVS·III·DEI·GRA· (William III, by the Grace of God). The reverse design remains essentially the same as

Table 25. The small silver coinage of William III

No.	Date	Denomination		Varieties, remarks, etc.[1]
115	1697	4d		probably unique[2]
116	1698	1d	(i)	6 of date above the crown[3]
			(ii)	9 of date above the crown[3]
			(iii)	reads IRA for FRA[3,4,5]
			(iv)	reads HI. BREX[3,4]
			(v)	reads HI BREX[5]
117	——	2d	(i)	date partly above the crown[3]
118	——	3d		
119	——	4d		
120	1699	1d		
121	——	2d		
122	——	3d		
123	——	4d		
124	1700	1d	(i)	one 0 partly over the crown[3]
125	——	2d		
126	——	3d		
127	——	4d	(i)	no stop after date[3]
128	1701	1d	(i)	no stop after III[3]
			(ii)	no stop after MAG or ET[3]
129	——	2d		
130	——	3d	(i)	1's of date like Z⁶ (ς70ς[3]), small lettering[3,6]
			(ii)	1's of date like J⁶ (]70][3]), large lettering[3,6]
			(iii)	GBA for GRA[6]
131	——	4d		
132	1702	4d[7]		

Notes to Table 25: *1*, See note *1* to Table 24; *2*, This was exhibited by Mr Albert Baldwin at the Ordinary Meeting of the British Numismatic Society on 31 March 1948, as reported in *BNJ*, 25 (5, third series, parts 1–3) (1945–48), p. 352; *3*, Linecar (1978); *MSCE*, p. 77; *4*, *ESC*, p. 206; *5*, Trowbridge, p. 19; *6*, *ESC*, p. 192; *7*, This is the only coinage of William III that is dated 1702. It was certainly either issued prematurely in anticipation of the King continuing to live or was a case of incorrect dating since William III died on 8 March 1701/2 and so did not see the beginning of the year 1702 which began on 25 March according to the OS calendar then in use in Britain (see Appendix 3). Since the dates in use upon the coinage at this period adhered to the OS calendar, all thoughts of this fourpence's appearance before William's death can therefore be dismissed (Farquhar (1912), p. 264). That these coins were struck in considerable number is evident from the delivery, on 25 March 1702, of 114lb 6oz of silver (Dyer; Snelling, p. 54) which, at sixty-two shillings per troy pound, would be equivalent to a face value of £354 19s (Craig (1953), p. 417, quotes a corresponding figure of £359), namely 21,297 fourpences.

that introduced on the small silver coinage of William and his late queen, namely large crowned and value-denoting Arabic numerals. These, for William alone, are surrounded by the legend ·MAG·BR·FRA·ET·HIB·REX· (King of Great Britain, France and Ireland) along with the varying dates (Plate 61) (the penny of 1699 has no stop after ET and the 1701 twopence appears not to have a stop after BR). The tools were engraved by Croker or an Assistant Engraver. As in the case of the joint reigns, no reference to the House of Orange is made on the small silver denominations whereas the four larger silver denominations, carrying as they do the appropriate royal coats of arms on their reverses, include in these the Lion of Orange as a centrepiece.[340]

The Maundy distribution was, by William III's reign, long-established at its London venue and was no doubt regarded as a London ceremony. It may therefore not be surprising that the small silver denominations were not struck at the provincial mints, at Bristol, Chester, Exeter, Norwich and York, in so far as none are known which carry any of the distinguising letters associated with these mints, during the Great Recoinage of 1696 to 1698. However, it must be borne in mind that these coins, with the possible exception of the silver penny, were being struck for general circulation around this period[341] and the London connection would therefore have been irrelevant. The hiatus, with the exception of the unique fourpence dated 1697, in the small silver coinage from 1695 to 1697 has already been discussed.[342]

v. Anne (8 March 1702–1 August 1714)[343]

The small silver coinage of Anne (Plate 62 and Table 26) was the work of John Croker[344] or his assistant, Samuel Bull.[345]

It has been noted that, specifically in connection with the Maundy coinage, 'there is a slight change in portraiture in 1705–6'[346] although this is neither qualified nor is it immediately obvious upon comparative examination of the appropriate coinage. However, two distinct busts, with the associated punches, exist for both the threepences and fourpences within this issue.[347] In addition, although they would appear no longer to exist, it seems that several different reverse punches were cut and used to sink the dies employed in the striking of the specific denominations within this issue. For example, microscopic examination of the twopences of 1703, 1705, 1706 and 1707 readily show differences in the crown and in its position relative to the denominational 2. Similar differences, now obvious to the naked eye, are encountered on the twopence of 1708, although it would appear that the same punch was subsequently used in the production of the dies for the twopences of 1709, 1710 and 1713. The larger crowns and the larger and more open 4s on the fourpences of 1710 and 1713, relative to those struck in earlier years, are also readily apparent.[348]

The obverse legends read ANNA·DEI·GRATIA· (Anne, by the Grace of God), although on the twopences dated 1706, 1709 and 1710 the stop after DEI is omitted, apparently because the die-sinker ran out of space: for presumably the same reason, it appears in the fourpence dated 1710 as DEI·. The reverse design is based upon the by then well-established large crowned Arabic numerals 1, 2, 3 and 4. However, the reverse legends, as published[349] and as observed from examination of the author's and the British Museum's collections, are worthy of comment since not only do they herald the use of the colon in the legendary punctuation of the small silver denominations but, in certain cases, they are also at variance with the reverse legends associated with the

Table 26. The small silver coinage of Anne[1]

No.	Date	Denomination		Varieties, remarks, etc.
133	1703	1d		
134	——	2d		
135	——	3d	(i)	7 of date above the crown[2,3]
			(ii)	7 of date not above the crown[2,4]
136	——	4d		
137	1704	2d	(i)	all date well above the crown[3,5]
			(ii)	no stops on obverse[3,5,6]
138	——	3d		
139	——	4d	(i)	no stop on obverse[4]
140	1705	1d		
141	——	2d		
142	——	3d		
143	——	4d		
144	1706	1d	(i)	0 of date over the crown[3,7]
145	——	2d	(i)	no stop after DEI[3]
146	——	3d		
147	——	4d		
148	1707	2d		
149	——	3d		
150	1708	1d		
151	——	2d	(i)	with a large crown, as the half-groats of 1709, 1710 and 1713[5]
152	——	3d		
153	——	4d		
154	1709	1d	(i)	reads M A G.[1]
			(ii)	reads M AG.[1]
155	——	2d	(i)	see 2d of 1708
			(ii)	no stop after DEI[3]
156	——	3d	(i)	no stop after date[8] (see also note 1)
157	——	4d		
158	1710	1d		
159	——	2d	(i)	see 2d of 1708
160	——	3d		
161	——	4d	(i)	larger crown, as the groat of 1713[9]
			(ii)	unusual lock of hair above the head and heavier tie[3,10]
162	1711	4d		Unique patterns in copper and silver, both with the Edinburgh mintmark, are known (see page 000)
163	1713	1d	(i)	3 of date over 0[3,6,7]
			(ii)	——, no stop after DEI[3]
164	——	2d	(i)	see 2d of 1708
165	——	3d	(i)	much larger bust[2]
			(ii)	two distinct curls over head[3]
166	——	4d	(i)	see 4d of 1710
			(ii)	very close date[3]

Notes to Table 26: *1*, The reverse legend variation of this coinage is discussed in the text (see pages 154 and 156); *2*, *ESC*, p. 192; *3*, Linecar (1978); *MSCE*, p. 77; *4*, Trowbridge, p. 19; *5*, *ESC*, p. 201; *6*, Trowbridge, p. 20; *7*, *ESC*, p. 207; *8*, Robinson, B., previously unpublished observation. Seven specimens were examined. All other Maundy coins of Anne have a stop after the date and it would therefore be of interest if a similar threepence of 1709 could be found; *9*, *ESC*, p. 186; *10*, The fourpences of 1703 to 1706, 1708 and 1709 have two curls above the head band and an ornamented brooch, namely ☉, those of 1713 have only one curl above the head band and a plain brooch, namely ●, and both busts appear on the fourpences dated 1710.

(*continued*)

pre-Union and post-Union issues of the other silver denominations, namely the crown, half-crown, shilling and sixpence. On these four larger denominations, the reverse legend, which translates into English as 'Queen of Great Britain, France and Ireland', reads ·MAG·BR·FRA·ET·HIB·REG· on the former issues and on the latter issues ·MAG·BRI·FR·ET·HIB·REG·, with minor modifications involving the absence of stops or their replacement by colons, and with the one exception of a very rare variety of the sixpence of 1707, the reverse legend of which reads . . .BR·FRA. . ., namely pre-Union.[350] However, the reverse legends of the threepences and fourpences dated 1703, 1704 and 1705 and the threepence dated 1707 exhibit a different abbreviation, ·MAG·BR·FR·ET·HIB·REG·, whereas the threepence and fourpence dated 1706 bear the reverse legend ·MAG·BR·FRA·ET·HIB·REG·, the expected pre-Union abbreviation. Those dated 1708, 1709, 1710 and 1713 read ·MAG·BRI·FR·ET·HIB·REG·, the expected post-Union abbreviation. The reverse legends of all the twopences conform with those of the four larger silver denominations, with the exception of the twopence dated 1707 which reads ·MAG:BR:FRA:ET:HIB:REG:, namely a pre-Union legend which also largely exhibits colons in place of stops. Colons also partially replace the stops in the reverse legends of the twopences dated 1703 and 1704 and 1709 which, conforming with the pre-Union and post-Union reverse legends associated with the larger silver denominations, read ·MAG:BR:FRA:ET·HIB·REG·, ·MAG:BR:FRA:ET·HIB:REG: and ·MAG:BRI:FR:ET·HIB:REG:, respectively, only the colons of the 1709 piece having being noted previously. The reverse legends of the pennies are those associated with the pre-Union and post-Union larger silver denominations with the exception of that dated 1706 which reads ·MAG·BR·FR·ET·HIB·REG·: a specimen of each of those dated 1708 and 1703 have no trace of a stop after HIB and REG, respectively, and of two further specimens dated 1703, one has stops only before and after MAG and the other has no stop after REG and only traces of stops after FRA, ET and HIB – clearly partial die-blocking had occurred.

vi. George I (1 August 1714–11 June 1727)[351]

By the reign of George I it had become the duty of the Assistant Engraver to engrave the reverse master tools for the coinage. Accordingly, whereas the obverse master tools for the small silver coinage of this king (Plate 63) were engraved by John Croker, the Chief Engraver, those of the reverse (Plate 63) are said to be the work of Johann Rudolph Ochs senior.[352]

The gold and large silver coinages of not only George I, but also of George II and the pre-1816 such coinages of George III, with the exception of some of the small-denominational gold, are characterized by very detailed legends. These refer to both the British and German titles of these kings, 'Georgius Dei Gratia Magnæ Britanniæ, Franciæ, et Hiberniæ Rex, Fidei Defensor, Brunsviciensis et Luneburgensis Dux, Sacri

---

Notes to Table 26. *(continued)*
The punches exist for both these obverses, which have been associated with pre- and post-Union issues, respectively (Hocking (1910), p. 20), although with respect to this it would appear that the change-over in 1710. The punches exist for both these obverses, which have been associated with pre- and post-Union issues, along with a third obverse punch related to that of the post-Union period but with two curls above the head-band (Hocking (1910), p. 20). None of the twopences and pennies of this reign have curls above the head bands and all have a plain brooch: only one obverse punch for each of these two denominations is known (Hocking (1910), p. 20).

Romani Imperii Archi-Thesaurarius et Elector' (George, by the Grace of God, King of Great Britain, France and Ireland, Defender of the Faith[353], Duke of Brunswick and Luneburg, Arch-Treasurer and Elector of the Holy Roman Empire). On the coinage of George I these titles are suitably abbreviated to, for example, GEORGIVS [whereas on the coins of George I, no regnal number appears, a II or III is added on the coinage of his son and great-grandson, respectively] D·G·M·BR·FR·ET·HIB·REX·F·D· (on the obverse) and BRVN·ET·L·DVX·S·R·I·A·TH·ET·EL·, together with the date (on the reverse), variously punctuated by omission of stops. On the corresponding coinage of the second and third Hanoverian monarchs, the titles are retained but rearranged, the obverse legends thus reading GEORGIVS II [or III] DEI·GRATIA· and that on the reverse reading, along with the date, M·B·F·ET·H·REX·F·D·B·ET·L·D·S·R·I·A· T·ET·E·, variously punctuated by omission of stops. However, the impracticality of using such legends on the small silver coinage was recognized. Consequently, these coins bear only the British titles of these monarchs. In the case of both the small (Table 27) and larger silver coinage of George I, no regnal number appears. For the obverses, the legends read GEORGIVS·DEI·GRA· (George, by the Grace of God), with the first stop missing on the 1726 penny and the third stop missing on the 1718 and 1727 pennies, and ·MAG·BRI·FR·ET·HIB·REX·, along with the date, for the reverse, excepting the pennies of 1716, 1718, 1720 and 1723 which read BR· instead of BRI·,

Table 27. The small silver coinage of George I

No.	Date	Denomination		Varieties, remarks, etc.
167	1716	1d	(i)	reads ·1716· (var.A)[1]
			(ii)	reads ·1716 (var.B)[1]
168	1717	2d	(i)	no stop after GRA[2]
169	——	3d		
170	——	4d		
171	1718	1d	(i)	no stop after GRA[2]
			(ii)	no stops after GRA or GEORGIVS[2]
172	1720	1d	(i)	reads HIPEX[2,3,4]
173	1721	2d	(i)	no stop[4]
174	——	3d		
175	——	4d		
176	1723	1d	(i)	reads GEORGIVS.[2]
			(ii)	reads GEORGIVS[2]
177	——	2d		
178	——	3d	(i)	reads F.R[5]
179	——	4d		
180	1725	1d	(i)	reads FR.ET.[2]
			(ii)	reads FR.ET.[2]
181	1726	1d		
182	——	2d		
183	1727	1d	(i)	no stop after GRA[2]
184	——	2d	(i)	reads GEOrgIVS[2]
			(ii)	reads GEORGIVS[2]
185	——	3d	(i)	obverse legend finishes nearer the bust[2]
186	——	4d	(i)	wide space in the legend below 4[2]

Notes to Table 27: *1*, Robinson, B. 'Two Varieties of the 1716 Maundy Penny', *NCirc*, 89 (1981), pp. 275–76 (the two obverses as illustrated in this article are in the wrong order); *2*, Linecar (1978); *MSCE*, p. 77; *3*, *ESC*, p. 207; *4*, Trowbridge, p. 21; *5*, Robinson.

the penny of 1725 which correspondingly reads RR.[354] and the penny of 1716, on some of which the first stop is missing.[355]

vii. George II (11 June 1727–25 October 1760)[356]

The obverse master tools for the Maundy coinage of George II (Plate 64 and Table 28) were the work of John Croker,[357] the Chief Engraver and, in common with the practice at the time, those for the reverse (Plate 64) were engraved by the Assistant Engraver, John Sigismund Tanner.[358] The 2 and 4 on the reverses of the twopence and fourpence, respectively, are larger on those coins dated 1732 and onward (Plate 65). Clearly, the production of the new punches was effected so that the size of the resulting 2 and 4 would be better matches for the 1 and 3 on the other two denominations.

The obverse legends read GEORGIVS·II·DEI·GRATIA· (George II, by the Grace of God) and that on the reverse is the same as that on the similar coins of the previous reign, with the possible exception of the threepence of 1739 which appears to have all the stops missing except for those after BRI and FR.[359]

Apart from the restriction in their legends to the King's British titles alone, a further difference between the Maundy coinage of George II and the other coinage of this reign relates to the change in the portrait, namely to an older bust, which was effected in 1739 on the gold and in 1740 on the copper coins, and in 1743 on the silver coinage with the notable exception of the Maundy coinage. Throughout the whole of the reign this latter coinage retains on its obverse the young bust portrait. Whether this difference sets these coins apart, namely for specialized use in the Maundy distribution, or whether it is simply the result of the hard-headed economic philosophy of the then engravers at the Mint, is debatable.[360]

viii. George III (25 October 1760–29 January 1820)[361]

This long reign witnessed the minting of four types of Maundy money.

The designer and engraver of the obverses of the coins of type 1 (Table 29) was John Ralph Ochs junior[362] and the reverse master tools, the design of which had remained essentially unchanged since the small silver coinage of 1689, were probably engraved by a junior engraver whose name is not recorded. The obverses carry a young head effigy of the King and the legend GEORGIVS·III·DEI·GRATIA· (George III, by the Grace of God). The reverse legend is the same as that on the similar coins of the previous reign.

This type 1 coinage is divided into two sub-types, A and B. The former (Plate 66) was issued intermittently dated from 1763 to 1786, with the exclusion of the pennies dated 1781, 1784 and 1786 and the fourpences dated 1784 and 1786 (Tables 8 and 29). Until now, the penny dated 1781 and all the four denominations dated 1784 and 1786 have been assigned to a sub-type B. However, cognisant of the data which are currently presented in Table 20, it is clear that the twopence and threepence dated 1784 and 1786 belong to type 1A since for neither of these denominations were new obverse or reverse punches produced. On the other hand, a new reverse punch was made for the penny which was first struck dated 1781, and then again dated 1784 and 1786, in which the crown and figure 1 have a flatter design than beforehand (Table 20 and Plate 67). Likewise, a new reverse punch with similar characteristics was produced for the fourpences which were struck dated 1784 and 1786 (Table 20 and Plate 67). It would

Table 28. The Maundy coinage of George II

No.	Date	Denomination		Varieties, remarks, etc.
187	1729	1d	(i)	no stop after GRATIA[1]
			(ii)	struck on thick flan, perhaps a proof[2]
188	——	2d	(i)	smaller obverse letter 9[1]
189	——	3d	(i)	slightly differing in lettering and crown[3]
190	——	4d	(i)	stop above head[1]
191	1731	1d		
192	——	2d		
193	——	3d	(i)	small letters on obverse[1,4,5]
194	——	4d		
195	1732	1d	(ii)	slight variety of the bust[1,4,6]
196	——	2d	(i)	small o in GEoRGIVS[1]
197	——	3d	(i)	stop over head[1,4,5]
198	——	4d		
199	1735	1d		
200	——	2d		
201	——	3d		
202	——	4d		
203	1737	1d		
204	——	2d		
205	——	3d		
206	——	4d		
207	1739	1d		
208	——	2d	(i)	cracked die[1]
209	——	3d		
210	——	4d		
211	1740	1d		
212	——	2d		
213	——	3d		
214	——	4d		
215	1743	1d		
216	——	2d	(i)	3 of date over 0[2,4,7]
217	——	3d	(i)	large lettering[1] on both sides[4,5]
			(ii)	stop above head, small lettering[1,4,5]
218	——	4d	(i)	3 of date over 0[4]
219	1746	1d	(i)	6 of date over 3 or 5[6,8]
			(ii)	over 3?[6]
220	——	2d		
221	——	3d	(i)	6 of date over 3[5] (on all coins?[9])
			(ii)	6 of date over 5[4]
222	——	4d		
223	1750	1d		
224	1752	1d	(i)	2 of date over 0[1,6,8]
225	1753	1d	(i)	3 of date over 2[6]
226	1654	1d		
227	1755	1d	(i)	colon after GRATIA[1]
228	1756	1d		
229	——	2d		
230	1757	1d	(i)	——[6]
231	1758	1d		
232	1759	1d	(i)	——[1]
233	——	2d		
234	1760	1d	(i)	GEORGIVS[1]
235	——	2d		
236	——	3d		
237	——	4d		

Notes to Table 28: *1*, Linecar (1978); *MSCE*, p. 78; *2*, Montagu, p. 17; *3*, Montagu, p. 16; *4*, Trowbridge, p. 22; *5*, *ESC*, p. 193, *6*, *ESC*, p. 208; *7*, *ESC*, p. 202; *8*, Trowbridge, p. 23; *9*, Harding (1980).

Table 29. The types 1A and 1B Maundy coinage of George III

No.	Date	Denomination		Varieties, remarks, etc.
238	1762[1]	3d[1]		
239	1763	1d	(i)	proof condition[2]
240	——	2d		
241	——[3]	3d[3]		
242	——	4d		
243	——	1d		proof[2,4]
244	——	2d		proof[4]
245	——	3d		——
246	——	4d		——
247	1765	2d[5]		
248	——	3d[5]		
249	——	4d[5]		
250	1766	1d		
251	——	2d	(i)	● on nose of bust (5 specimens examined)[6]. Do specimens without ● exist?
252	——	3d	(i)	1766[7]?
			(ii)	REX[7]?
253	——	4d		
254	1770	1d		
255	——	3d		
256	——	4d		
257	1772	1d	(i)	D of DEI touches hair[7]
258	——	2d	(i)	second 7 of date over 6[7,8]
			(ii)	1772/6[2]
259	——	3d	(i)	small letters on obverse[2,7,9]
			(ii)	large letters on obverse, with very large III[2,7,9]
			(iii)	large letters on obverse, with small III[2,7,9]
260	——	4d	(i)	2 of date over 0[2,7,10]
261	1775	4d		see no. 264
262	1776	1d	(i)	double cut
263	——	2d	(i)	reads MA G[6]
264	——	4d	(i)	defective 6 appears very much like 5. A genuine groat of 1775 is not known[10,11]
265	1779	1d		
266	1780	1d		
267	——	2d	(i)	BR-1[7]
268	——	3d		
269	——	4d		
270	1781	1d[12]		
271	1784	1d[12]		
272	——	2d		
273	——	3d		
274	——	4d[12]		
275	1786	1d[12]		
276	——	2d		
277	——	3d		
278	——	4d[12]	(i)	large lettering on obverse[2,8]

Notes to Table 29: *1*, This is the commonest of all the Maundy(?) coins, with specimens having been seen from over thirty dies (*ESC*, p. 193; Trowbridge, p. 24). The £3,162 minted in 1762 (Craig (1953), p. 418) were, without doubt, all produced as these threepences since no other silver coins bearing this date were issued. They were issued as general currency (*ESC*, p. 193); *2*, Trowbridge, p. 24; *3*, This is the second most also appear, from the quality of the coins, that concomitantly with the introduction these new reverse punches, the opportunity was also taken to sink new obverse dies, at least for the threepence and fourpence.

Since the issue of the jubilee head obverse of Victoria, the design of the crown on the reverse of the Maundy coinage and, indeed, of the whole reverse, has, disregarding very slight modifications resulting from die re-engraving, remained unchanged. However, on the earlier Maundy issues considerable multiformity is evident between the crown designs on the coins of different reigns or of different types or sub-types within a reign. Nevertheless, within such groups, major dissimilarities between the crowns are rare but one such difference, involving an interesting variation in the circlet of the crown on the reverses of the type 1A Maundy coinage of George III is apparent.[363] Thus, the twopence, threepence and fourpence proof issues of 1763, of which very few specimens are known, and the threepence and fourpence of 1765 which, along with the corresponding twopence, and excluding the unique fourpence dated 1697,[364] are the rarest of the non-proof Maundy coins known, have a circlet design with pearls (Figure 1). This feature is not confined to these extremely rare coins, for it is also present on other threepences of this sub-type, namely those of 1763 (non-proof), 1766, 1770, 1772, 1780, 1784 and 1786. On the other hand, the pellets (pearls) are

---

common of all the Maundy(?) coins, with specimens having been seen from over thirty dies (Trowbridge, p. 24). Much of the £2,629 minted in 1763 (Craig (1953), p. 418) was produced as these threepences, which were issued for general currency (*ESC*, p. 193), since apart from the £100 (*ESC*, p. 143), but possibly significantly more (Mays, James O'Donald; Seaby, p. 139), produced as Northumberland shillings (Mays, James; Mays, James O'Donald) and the eighteen, twenty-three and fifty-four troy pounds used to produce Maundy pennies, twopences and fourpences, respectively, (Table 10), no other silver coins bearing this date were struck. Within a few years of their striking, some of the threepences dated 1763 were destined to find their way to the other side of the world. On 16 January 1770, during his first journey of exploration around the world, Captain James Cook anchored his ship, 'Endeavour', in an inlet on what was, in fact, the northern coast of the South Island of New Zealand. During his three week stay he soon established from the indigenous population, cannibalistic maoris, that his was the first such ship to visit the area. Consequently, in accord with colonial tradition, Cook, on 31 January 1770, named the inlet Queen Charlotte Sound, after the wife of the then King of England, George III, and formally claimed it and the adjacent lands for his king. As a physical manifestation of this action, he had erected by his crew a post, setting forth his ship's name and the date, and flying the Union flag. The native population not only gave their consent to the construction of this erection but promised never to pull it down and, in return, Cook gave every one of them a present 'of one thing or another' and to one in particular, an old man who had paid several visits to the crew during the previous fortnight, he gave 'silver, three penny pieces dated 1763; and Spike Nails with the King's Broad Arrow cut deep in them'. In Cook's words, all these gifts were 'things', that he 'thought were most likely to remain long among them' and within these the old man's gift of coins was no doubt of further significance in that through it was left a durable portrait of the King in his new colony. Such an interpretation may also be placed upon the fact that among the artifacts left in 'a Tower or Pile of Stones' which Cook's party had erected on the top of a nearby hill two days previous was 'a Piece of Silver Coin', but this coin was not further defined (*Captain Cook's Journal during his First Voyage round the World made in H.M. Bark 'Endeavour' 1768–71. A Literal Transcription of the Original MSS*, edited by W. J. L. Wharton (London, 1893), pp. 182–92); *4*, See Section V of Chapter 3; *5*, These are the rarest of the non-proof or non-pattern Maundy coins known. Nevertheless, the claim that only five to ten (*ESC*, pp. 10, 187, 193, 202), or even twenty to fifty (Trowbridge, pp. 23, 24), examples of each are known is most likely to be an underestimate, since specimens have been offered for sale on several occasions during the past quarter-century (see, for example, *NCirc*, 85 (1977), p. 557; *SCMB*, 1976, p. 270; Spink Sale no. 9 (1980), p. 52, lot 356; no. 62 (1987), p. 19, lot 491). On 27 March 1765, 808 twopences, 537 threepences and 310 fourpences, presumably dated accordingly, were delivered to the Mint Office (Table 10), figures which also support the current observation that the fourpence of these three coins is the rarest; *6*, Robinson; *7*, Linecar (1978); *MSCE*, p. 78; *8*, *ESC*, p. 202; *9*, *ESC*, p. 193; *10*, *ESC*, p. 187; *11*, No silver deliveries were made to the Mint Office during 1775 (Table 10), supporting the absence of the 1775 groat; *12*, These coins are of type 1B, all the other coins listed in the Table being of type 1A.

absent in the circlets of the crowns on the reverses of the proof penny of 1763, of which very few specimens are known, and the extremely rare twopence of 1765, both of which have this feature (Figure 1) in common with the crowns on all the remaining coins of the type 1A. The exception is the threepence dated 1762, for which more than thirty dies exist[365] and in which the use of either circlet designs has been noted.[366] Clearly, the presence of such pellets can be used to confirm, along with die-axis[367] and other[368] evidence, whether or not a twopence or fourpence dated 1763 is a proof and also to check the authenticity of a fourpence dated 1765 where date-tampering may be suspected.

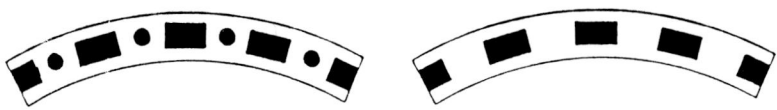

Figure 1

The type 2 Maundy coinage of George III was issued as a complete four-denominational sequence dated 1792 (Plate 68 and Table 30). Lewis Pingo[369] was the designer of the obverses (which now carry as effigy an armoured bust) and the reverses of this coinage and also the engraver of the tools via which it was produced. Because of the thin script of the denominational numerals on these coins, which is particularly apparent on the twopence, threepence and fourpence, this type 2 coinage is referred to as wire money. Whether there is a historical reason for the introduction of this thin script or whether it was merely an artistic experiment by Pingo is not known. In any case, it was not repeated.

The obverse and reverse legends read the same as those on the type 1 issues. However, on the wire money no stops are used in the obverse legend whilst on the reverse the date is now placed below the denominational numeral. The reverse legend now starts at the 7 o'clock position, rather than at the 1–2 o'clock position as on the previous type and earlier issues.

The type 3 Maundy coinage of George III (Plate 69 and Table 31) was struck as two complete four-denominational sequences, dated 1795 and 1800. The obverse was again of the armoured bust design, as used on the type 2 Maundy coinage, by Lewis Pingo[370] who engraved the corresponding tools. Pingo was also probably the designer of the

Table 30. The type 2 Maundy coinage (wire money) of George III

No.	Date	Denomination		Varieties, remarks, etc.
279	1792	1d		
280	——	2d		
281	——	3d	(i)	a variety is known with large letters on the reverse[1]
282	——	4d		

Note to Table 30: *1*, Linecar (1978); *MSCE*, p. 78.

reverse, the punches for which are said to have been prepared by a junior engraver, as was the contemporary practice.[371] The obverse and reverse legends read as for those on the type 2 coinage. However, no stop is present after FR and there is a varying presence or absence of stops in the obverse legend.

Table 31. The type 3 Maundy coinage of George III

No.	Date	Denomination		Varieties, remarks, etc.
283	1795	1d	(i)	no stop on obverse[1]
			(ii)	large letters no (stops?)[1]
284	——	2d		
285	——	3d		
286	——	4d		
287	1800	1d[2]		
288	——	2d[2]		
289	——	3d[2]		
290	——	4d[2]		

Notes to Table 31: *1*, Linecar (1978); *MSCE*, p. 79; *2*, Three or four varieties exist (see note *13* to Table 8).

From the obverse punch of the penny for this type 3 coinage were sunk dies which were hardened in immediate form, namely bearing only an effigy, and used in 1804 by the Bank of England to counterstamp Spanish dollars (Plate 41) which subsequently circulated in Britain for five shillings each.[372]

It is evident that the dies for the type 2 Maundy coinage of George III, those dated 1792, were used in that year to produce coins sufficient for the requirements of not only that year but also for the two subsequent years since no silver was struck into Maundy coin in 1793 and 1794 (Table 10). Likewise, the type 3 dies with the reverse dated 1795 were employed to strike in that year sufficient coins for that and the subsequent four years (Table 10). However, type 3 dies with the reverse dated 1800 were used on an almost annual basis up to 1816 (Table 10) to produce the Maundy coinage as it was required. Furthermore, during this total period, other dies for all the denominations of this coinage type were sunk (Table 19), clearly for use as wear took its toll, but the reverse date, 1800, remained unchanged,[373] since Maundy coins dated from 1801 to 1816[374] are unknown (Table 8). The freezing of the date in this manner over such a long period, namely sixteen years, is remarkable and was clearly a conscious decision on the behalf of the Mint. Although no official explanation for this has so far been uncovered, it probably arises from the fact that, as a result of the minting of silver by it in the April and May of 1798 having taken place without the knowledge of the Privy Council Committee on Coin which had been set up on the previous 7 February to deliberate upon its runnings, the Mint had been forbidden by statute on 21 June 1798 to strike silver coinage, a prohibition which was not abrogated until midway through 1816.[375] On the other hand, it was still obliged during this period to produce the small silver coinage required for the Royal Maundy. In attempting to resolve the paradoxical situation with which it was thus confronted, one wonders if the Mint attempted to meet its obligation to produce Maundy money in a manner, namely by using a frozen date, that would not draw attention to the fact that it was minting silver contrary to the 1798 legislation, albeit only in small amounts.

The type 4 Maundy coinage of George III (Plate 70 and Table 32) is part of what is known as the bull head or laureate head coinage because of the bust on the obverse, the designer of which was Benedetto Pistrucci.[376] Both Thomas Wyon junior and William Wyon[377] were responsible for the engraving of the obverse master tools and for the design and production of the reverse dies.[378]

Table 32. The type 4 (bull head) Maundy coinage of George III[1]

No.	Date	Denomination		Varieties, remarks, etc.
291	1817	1d		
292	——	2d	(i)	BRITANNIARUM[2]
293	——	3d		
294	——	4d		
295	1818	1d		
296	——	2d	(i)	BRITANNIARUM[2]
297	——	3d		
298	——	4d		
299	1820	1d		
300	——	2d		
301	——	3d		
302	——	4d		

Notes to Table 32: *1*, See note *14* to Table 8; *2*, Robinson.

The legend on the obverses of the type 4 coinage reads the same as that on the earlier types, except that a U replaces the V in the King's name, it includes the date[379] and no stops are present. The reverse legend, however, is significantly different from that of the earlier types and issues and reads BRITANNIARUM[380] REX FID: DEF:[381] (King of Britains, Defender of the Faith). This change was a consequence of two political events, the Act of Union with Ireland in 1800, which removed the need specifically to refer to Ireland in the legend, and the signing of the Treaty of Amiens on 27 March 1802 by which George III surrendered his title of King of France. Underneath the denominational number of the penny there also appears a stop which in the similar position on the three larger denominations is replaced by a cinquefoil (rose or rosette).

The dies for the type 4 Maundy coinage of George III have no necks (see, for example, Plate 71) and therefore could not be used with a collar, unlike the situation with all the other bull head coinage which was struck in collars. However, the type 4 Maundy coinage is noticeably different from the earlier types of Maundy coins which had all been struck in the by then vacated Tower Mint. Although the former exhibit fishtailing and sheared edges, features characteristic of coins struck without the use of a collar, in quality they lie between the earlier issues and the subsequent more uniform and exactly-struck issues of George IV and onward which were all struck in collars, as is not only evident from the superior quality of the coins but also because the dies employed in their striking, which are in the museum of the Royal Mint, have necks.[382] The bull head Maundy coinage was the first such coinage struck in the then only recently-opened and newly-erected mint building, the Royal Mint, on Tower Hill[383] and as such a newly installed Boulton screw-press may have been employed in its production. However this may be, in 1822 'a new coining press for striking His Majesty's Maundy monies' was purchased on behalf of the Company of Moneyers and installed in the new Mint,[384] concurrent with the introduction of the use of a collar in the striking of Maundy coins. It was presumably this press that, along with the eight screw-presses that were in use on almost every working day of the year, was accommodated in the coining-press-room at the Royal Mint in 1859 when it was described as 'a small hand-press, which does only two days' work in the year' and as 'the French toy-press' that 'produces only the silver Maunday pennies given by Her Majesty or her agents to poor pensioners on Maunday Thursday, according to ancient custom'.[385] Currently, the Maundy coinage is produced in the Proof Coin Unit at the Royal Mint but a special press is no longer used for its striking.

At the Great Recoinage of 1816, a weight reduction in the silver coinage, including the Maundy coins, was effected from sixty-two shillings to sixty-six shillings per troy pound, although the millesimal fineness of 925 was retained. Consequently, at this juncture the weights of the Maundy penny, twopence, threepence and fourpence were reduced from 7.7419, 15.4839, 23.2258 and 30.9677 gr to 7.27272, 14.54545, 21.81818 and 29.09090 gr, respectively.[386]

ix. George IV (29 January 1820–26 June 1830)[387]

All the Maundy coins of this reign (Plate 72 and Table 33) carry on their obverses the bust of the King, designed and engraved by Benedetto Pistrucci.[388] However, whereas the earlier issues of the other denominations struck also use this bust, the King's almost immediate dislike of it led, after some time, to the adoption for these denominations of a bust of George IV by Sir Francis Chantrey:[389] Pistrucci, having apparently refused to copy Chantrey's bust for a medal was therefore excluded as the engraver for this later coinage, the tools being accordingly prepared by William Wyon.

With the Maundy coins of this reign were introduced some major modifications in the design which, to date, has remained fundamentally unchanged. By comparison with the pattern which had been followed since the small silver coinage of William and Mary, all but the date in the reverse legend was removed into the obverse legend, which now reads GEORGIUS IIII D.G. BRITANNIAR. REX F. D. (George IV, by the Grace of God, King of Britains, Defender of the Faith) and begins at the 7 o'clock position. The date, in turn, was moved into a more central position on the reverse and divided by the value-denoting Arabic numeral which, whilst still remaining crowned, was now placed within an oak-wreath. The tools for these reverses were designed and engraved by Jean Baptiste Merlen.[390]

The bust on the 1822 Maundy threepence is of the same size as that on the twopence and thus smaller than that on the other threepences of this reign (Plate 73). According to Hawkins,[391] the first punch for the dies for the 1822 threepence broke and, since there was not enough time to raise another one with a proper-sized head, a die was made using the punch for the twopence. Alternatively, the economical use of time and a maximization of its resources may have been deciding factors when this decision was taken by the Mint.

Table 33. The Maundy coinage of George IV

No.	Date	Denomination		Varieties, remarks, etc.
303	1822	1d		
304	——	2d		
305	——	3d		2d-size bust[1]
306	——	4d		
307	——	1d		proof[2,3]
308	——	2d		——
309	——	3d		——
310	——	4d		——
311	1823	1d		
312	——	2d		
313	——	3d		
314	——	4d		
315	1824	1d		
316	——	2d		
317	——	3d		
318	——	4d		
319	1825	1d		
320	——	2d	(i)	T over B of BRITANNIAR[4]
321	——	3d		
322	——	4d		
323	1826	1d		
324	——	2d	(i)	T over B of BRITANNIAR[4]
325	——	3d		
326	——	4d		
327	1827	1d		
328	——	2d		
329	——	3d		
330	——	4d		
331	1828	1d		
332	——	2d		
333	——	3d		
334	——	4d		
335	——	1d		proof[2]
336	——	2d		——
337	——	3d		——
338	——	4d		——
339	1829	1d		
340	——	2d		
341	——	3d		
342	——	4d		
343	1830	1d		
344	——	2d		
345	——	3d		
346	——	4d		

Notes to Table 33: *1*, See page 165; *2*, Davies, Peter J., p. 40; *ESC*, p. 216; *3*, Montagu, p. 102; *4*, Salzman, pp. 44, 98. Other sources (Davies, Peter J. p. 40; Gaspar, p. 360) have quoted this error as B over T. However, microscopic examination by the present author clearly indicates a T over a B, namely a Mint error, and further shows that the twopences of both 1825 and 1826 were struck using the same obverse die.

x. William IV (26 June 1830–20 June 1837)[392]

The obverses for the Maundy coinage of this reign (Plate 74 and Table 34) were engraved by William Wyon.[393] The bust was based on a model by Sir Francis Chantrey[394] and the legend reads GULIELMUS IIII D: G: BRITANNIAR: REX F: D: (William IV, by the Grace of God, King of Britains, Defender of the Faith). The reverses (Plate 74) were designed and cut by Merlen.[395]

Table 34. The Maundy coinage of William IV

No.	Date	Denomination	Varieties, remarks, etc.
347	1831	1d	
348	——	2d	
349	——	3d[1]	
350	——	4d	
351	——	1d	proof[2]
352	——	2d	——
353	——	3d[1]	——
354	——	4d	——
355	——	1d	proof in gold[3]
356	——	2d	——
357	——	3d[1]	——
358	——	4d	——
359	1832	1d	
360	——	2d	
361	——	3d[1]	
362	——	4d	
363	1833	1d	
364	——	2d	
365	——	3d[1]	
366	——	4d	
367	1834	1d	(i) see note 4
368	——	2d	——
369	——	3d[1,5]	——
370	——	4d	——
371	1835	1d	
372	——	2d	
373	——	3d[1,5]	
374	——	4d	
375	1836	1d	
376	——	2d	
377	——	3d[1,5]	
378	——	4d	
379	1837	1d	
380	——	2d	
381	——	3d[1,5]	
382	——	4d	

Notes to Table 34: *1*, Two slightly different obverses for the threepences have been recorded. Obverse 1 has low hair (Davies, Peter J., p. 43), a small head and the right legs of both Ns in BRITANNIAR pointing toward beads (Davies, Peter J., p. 43; Salzman, p. 47) and obverse 2 has high hair (Davies, Peter J., p. 43), a larger head and the right legs of both Ns in BRITANNIAR pointing towards spaces (Davies, Peter J., p. 43; Salzman, p. 47). Only obverse 1 appears on threepences dated from 1831 to 1833, both obverses are variously used on those coins dated from 1834 to 1836 and either obverse 1 (Davies, Peter J., p. 43; Salzman, p. 47) or obverse 2 (Robinson) appear on the threepences dated 1837; *2*, Davies, Peter J., p. 44; *ESC*,

(*continued*)

At the beginning of the reign of William IV, the decision was taken that, in order that it could be easily distinguished from the sixpence, the half-sovereign, whilst retaining the usual weight and fineness, should be reduced in diameter from about 19.4mm to 17.9mm. This resolution also allowed the necessary obverse dies to be made from the same master tools as used in the production of the Maundy fourpence (in the event, such small half-sovereigns were not well received and were only struck in 1831 (as proofs) (Plate 75) and 1834).[396] It is also likely that the dies for the Maundy threepence and the Britannia groats of 1836 and 1837[397] (Plate 76) came from the same master tools, although officially-documented evidence for this is lacking.[398] By analogy with the issues of Victoria, it would appear that the silver three-halfpence of 1834–1837 (Plate 77) had its own master tools.[399]

xi. Victoria (20 June 1837–22 January 1901)[400]

Three types of Maundy coins were issued during this long reign.

Type 1 (Plate 78) was minted from 1838 to 1887 (Table 35). The young head bust on the obverse was designed and engraved by William Wyon[401] while the reverse was, like the previous issue, the work of Merlen,[402] although it has also been suggested that it was of Merlen's design but engraved by William Wyon.[403]

The obverse legend reads VICTORIA D: G: BRITANNIAR: REGINA F: D: (Victoria, by the Grace of God, Queen of Britains, Defender of the Faith).

The master tools used to produce the obverse dies for the type 1 Maundy twopence were also used to produce the dies for the obverses of the pattern quarter-sovereigns in gold (Plate 79) which were struck in 1853,[404] and the quarter-farthing (Plate 80) which was struck in 1839 and from 1851 to 1853 (all for use solely in Ceylon) and as proofs in 1852 (bronzed), 1853 (both bronzed and in copper) and 1868 (in bronze and in cupro-nickel).[405] Likewise, the master-tools for the Maundy threepence and the Britannia groat (Plate 81)[406] were interchangeable,[407] as were those for the Maundy fourpence and the two types[408] of the half-farthing[409] (Plate 82): the first of these was struck in 1839 and the second from 1842 to 1844, in 1847, from 1851 to 1854, in 1856 and, as bronze and cupro-nickel proofs, in 1868.[410] The Victoria three-halfpence (Plate 83) had its own master tools.[411]

By a proclamation dated 19 May 1845, the threepence, which was similar in design to the Maundy threepence, was given general currency use in Britain[412] whereas such use in selected of the colonies had begun with the threepences struck from 1834 and onwards.[413] Furthermore, although no threepences dated 1847, 1848 and 1852 were minted for general currency in Britain, it has been claimed that it is possible that during this time this denomination was again produced for colonial use.[414] However, it was later stated that 'threepences of 1847, 1848, 1852 and maybe 1869' and 'threepences of 1923 and 1924' 'were issued only in the Maundy sets'.[415] In the evaluation of these opposing claims, mintage figures must be believed although it must be borne in mind

---

Notes to Table 34. *(continued)*
p. 215; Montagu, pp. 108–9, 114; *3*, Davies, Peter J., p. 44; *ESC*, p. 216; Montagu, p. 111; *4*, An alleged proof Maundy set dated 1834 may merely be a proof-like early strike of the normal Maundy issue (see page 194); *5*, The threepence was also struck for various colonial general currency uses in 1834 (mintage 401,016), 1835 (mintage 491,040), 1836 (mintage 411,840), and 1837 (mintage 42,768: the order was for £3,500 (280,000), a large portion of which bore the date 1838) (Pridmore, p. 273).

Table 35. **The type 1 (young head) Maundy coinage of Victoria**[1]

No.	Date	Denomination	Varieties, remarks, etc.
383	1838	1d	
384	——	2d[2]	
385	——	3d	see note 3
386	——	4d	
387	——	1d	proof[4]
388	——	2d	——
389	——	3d	——
390	——	4d	proof[4,5]
391	——	1d	proof in gold[6]
392	——	2d	——
393	——	3d	——
394	——	4d	——
395	1839	1d	
396	——	2d	
397	——	3d	
398	——	4d	
399	——	1d	proof[7]
400	——	2d	——
401	——	3d	——
402	——	4d	——
403	1840	1d	
404	——	2d	
405	——	3d	
406	——	4d	
407	1841	1d	
408	——	2d	
409	——	3d	
410	——	4d	
411	1842	1d	
412	——	2d	
413	——	3d	
414	——	4d	
415	1843	1d	
416	——	2d[2]	
417	——	3d	
418	——	4d	
419	1844	1d	
420	——	2d	
421	——	3d	
422	——	4d	
423	1845	1d	
424	——	2d	
425	——	3d	
426	——	4d	
427	1846	1d	
428	——	2d	
429	——	3d	
430	——	4d	
431	1847	1d	
432	——	2d	
433	——	3d	
434	——	4d	

(*continued*)

Table 35. (continued)

No.	Date	Denomination	Varieties, remarks, etc.
435	1848	1d	
436	——	2d[2]	
437	——	3d	
438	——	4d	
439	1849	1d	
440	——	2d	
441	——	3d	
442	——	4d	
443	1850	1d	
444	——	2d	
445	——	3d	
446	——	4d	
447	1851	1d	
448	——	2d	
449	——	3d	
450	——	4d	
451	1852	1d	
452	——	2d	
453	——	3d	
454	——	4d	
455	1853	1d	
456	——	2d	
457	——	3d	
458	——	4d	
459	——	1d	proof[7]
460	——	2d	——
461	——	3d	——
462	——	4d	——
463	1854	1d	
464	——	2d	
465	——	3d	
466	——	4d	
467	1855	1d	
468	——	2d	
469	——	3d	
470	——	4d	
471	1856	1d	
472	——	2d	
473	——	3d	
474	——	4d	
475	1857	1d	
476	——	2d	(i) BRITANNIAE EEGINA[8]
477	——	3d	
478	——	4d	
479	1858	1d	
480	——	2d	
481	——	3d	
482	——	4d	
483	1859	1d	
484	——	2d	(i) BEITANNIAR[9]
485	——	3d	
486	——	4d	

Table 35. *(continued)*

No.	Date	Denomination		Varieties, remarks, etc.
487	1860	1d		
488	——	2d		
489	——	3d		
490	——	4d		
491	1861	1d		
492	——	2d	(i)	6 of date over 1[10]
493	——	3d		
494	——	4d		
495	1862	1d		
496	——	2d	(i)	No colons behind D and G[11]
497	——	3d		
498	——	4d		
499	1863	1d		
500	——	2d		
501	——	3d		
502	——	4d	(i)	Flaw over 63. On all?[12]
503	1864	1d		
504	——	2d		
505	——	3d		
506	——	4d		
507	1865	1d		
508	——	2d		
509	——	3d		
510	——	4d		
511	1866	1d		
512	——	2d		
513	——	3d		
514	——	4d		
515	——	2d		proof[13]
516	1867	1d		
517	——	2d		
518	——	3d		
519	——	4d		
520	——	1d		proof[14]
521	——	2d		——
522	——	3d		——
523	——	4d		——
524	1868	1d		
525	——	2d		
526	——	3d		see note *15*
527	——	4d		
528	——	1d		proof[13]
529	——	2d		——
530	——	3d		——
531	——	4d		——
532	1869	1d		
533	——	2d		
534	——	3d		
535	——	4d		
536	1870	1d		
537	——	2d		
538	——	3d		

(continued)

Table 35. *(continued)*

No.	Date	Denomination	Varieties, remarks, etc.
539	——	4d	
540	1871	1d	
541	——	2d	
542	——	3d	
543	——	4d	
544	——	1d	proof[16]
545	——	2d	——
546	——	3d	——
547	——	4d	——
548	1872	1d	
549	——	2d	
550	——	3d	
551	——	4d	
552	1873	1d	
553	——	2d	
554	——	3d	
555	——	4d	
556	1874	1d	
557	——	2d	
558	——	3d	
559	——	4d	
560	1875	1d	
561	——	2d	
562	——	3d	
563	——	4d	
564	1876	1d	
565	——	2d	
566	——	3d	
567	——	4d	
568	1877	1d	
569	——	2d	
570	——	3d	
571	——	4d	
572	1878	1d	
573	——	2d	
574	——	3d	
575	——	4d	
576	——	1d	proof[17]
577	——	2d	——
578	——	3d	——
579	——	4d	——
580	1879	1d	
581	——	2d	
582	——	3d	
583	——	4d	
584	1880	1d	
585	——	2d	
586	——	3d	
587	——	4d	
588	1881	1d	
589	——	2d	
590	——	3d	

Table 35. *(continued)*

No.	Date	Denomination	Varieties, remarks, etc.
591	——	4d	
592	——	1d	proof[17]
593	——	2d	——
594	——	3d	——
595	——	4d	——
596	1882	1d	
597	——	2d	
598	——	3d	
599	——	4d	
600	1883	1d	
601	——	2d	
602	——	3d	
603	——	4d	
604	1884	1d	
605	——	2d	
606	——	3d	
607	——	4d	
608	1885	1d	
609	——	2d	
610	——	3d	
611	——	4d	
612	1886	1d	
613	——	2d	
614	——	3d	
615	——	4d	
616	1887	1d	
617	——	2d	
618	——	3d	
619	——	4d	

Notes to Table 35: *1*, Intra-denominational minor multiformities within this type have been observed. The obverses of the pennies dated from 1880 to 1887 have more and smaller beads than those of the pennies dated from 1838 to 1879 (Salzman, p. 40), although a parallel variation claimed for the reverses (Salzman, p. 40) would appear to be too general since the reverses of the pennies dated from 1881 to 1883 revert to large beads (Robinson). Whereas no varieties were observed for the reverses of the twopences, apart from the overstrike referred to in the Table (see note *10*), two variations of the obverse are apparent, those from 1880 to 1887 having much longer beads than those from 1838 to 1879 (Salzman, p. 44). Two authorities have noted multiformities within the threepences, which from 1845 were also struck for general circulation in Britain and had, since 1834, with the exception of 1842, also been struck for such use in certain of the colonies (Pridmore, pp. 273–74). These authorities, although differing qualitatively, are quantitatively largely complementary with respect to their date spectra. According to one, obverses from 1867 to 1879 have more rounded truncation fronts and more, longer beads than noted on coins from 1838 to 1868, with an overlap in 1867 and 1868, and those from 1880 to 1887 have, relative to those earlier, a thinner pony tail which ends in a hook shape: two reverses are also noted, that from 1867 to 1887 having more, and smaller, beads than that from 1838 to 1868, again with an overlap in 1867 and 1868 (Salzman, p. 47). The other authority notes four obverse varieties, namely 1 'right leg of 1st. 'N' in 'Brit' to bead. 'G' has right serif', 2 'lowest hair wave covers top of ear. 'G' has left and right serif', 3 'right leg of 1st. 'N' in 'Brit' to space. 'Victoria' close 'DG'' and 4 'right leg of 1st. 'N' in 'Brit' to bead. Gap after 'Victoria'', and two reverse varieties, namely A 'large border beads. Cross away from beads' and B 'small border beads. Cross nearer beads', with a die combination through this type of threepence as used for Maundy money of 1A (1838–1861), 2A (1859, 1862–1867), 3B (1868–1879) and 4B (1880–1887) (Davies, Peter J., pp. 69, 73, 74). Other combinations also exist for some of this denominational type which was used as general currency (Davies, Peter J., pp. 69–71). No multiformity within the fourpence of this type has been detected. As well as these more general multiformities, microscopic examination reveals that, throughout all the four denominations of this type, examples of die damage, usually evident from the presence of damaged letters in the legends, and die repair,

(continued)

that before 1864, when Thomas Graham, F.R.S., the Warden and Master Worker of the Mint from 1855 to 1869, introduced a rigid dating system,[416] the year of striking is not necessarily the same as the date on the coin. Up to, and including, 1926, the threepences issued for general currency purposes retained the same design as those produced for Maundy purposes. However, they can be readily distinguished since the former have a somewhat dull surface whereas the latter have a proof-like quality with polished fields and, furthermore, they tone much more easily than the former, being often bluish or quite dark.[417]

After forty years of usage, a design change was sought for the young head bust on the silver and gold coinage of Victoria. This resulted, after some nine years of deliberation and experimentation,[418] in the introduction of such a coinage bearing a new effigy. This became known as the jubilee head coinage since its eventual introduction purposely coincided with the Queen's Golden Jubilee which fell in June 1887. Consequently, the threepences issued for normal currency purposes in 1887 were of both the young head and the jubilee head types and the Maundy coinage for 1887

Notes to Table 35. *(continued)*
often resulting in obvious overstriking, abound. However, such faults are of little, if any, numismatic significance although their detection within a particular denomination could provide an estimation of the number of dies used for its striking. Only those instances where incorrect letter punches have been used to effect die repairs, together with one instance in which it appears that punctuation has been omitted, are specifically referred to in the Table and its accompanying notes; *2*, Twopences were struck in 1838 (mintage 1,045,440), 1843 (mintage 902,880) and 1848 (mintage 261,360) for use as general currency in some of the colonies, primarily in British Guiana (Pridmore, pp. 274–75); *3*, A few examples of the 1838 threepences which were struck for general currency uses in the colonies read BRITANNIAB (*ESC*, p. 194; Gaspar, pp. 359–60): the legend of the Maundy threepence for 1838 is without error. Other varieties of the threepences which were issued for general circulation from 1845 to 1887 have been documented (Davies, Peter J., pp. 69–71; Salzman, pp. 47, 48); *4*, Davies, Peter J., p. 73; *ESC*, p. 218); *5*, Montagu, p. 156; *6*, Davies, Peter J., p. 73; *ESC*, p. 218; Montagu, pp. 141–42; *7*, Davies, Peter J., p. 73; *ESC*, p. 218; Montagu, p. 157; *8*, This legend error (Plate 84) has hitherto been unrecorded. Microscopic examination clearly shows that in both places it results from the sinking of an E over a damaged or worn R on the die. Examination of the legend on the 1856 Maundy twopence shows that it was struck from a considerably worn die and the sharp and error-free legend on the 1858 Maundy twopence indicates the use of a new obverse die in its striking; *9*, This error has been reported as an E over the first R of BRITANNIAR (Davies, Peter J., p. 74; Salzman, pp. 44, 98) and, more cautiously, as 'reads BEITANNIAR' (Gaspar, p. 360). However, it does not appear on three specimens of the Maundy twopence of 1859 (see, for example, Plate 85) examined by the present author although on all these three coins the legend was in poor condition, obviously the result of using a worn obverse die. This was clearly renewed in the following year as it is evident from the condition of the 1860 Maundy twopence. The existence of this reported blundered die variety clearly indicates the use of at least two obverse dies during the striking of the 1859 Maundy twopence (Davies, Peter J., p. 74; *ESC*, p. 218; Salzman, pp. 44, 98); *10*, This overdate (Plate 86) has also been suggested (Salzman, p. 98) as being, maybe, 1 over 6, namely a Mint error. However, it was confirmed, by the Chief Engraver at the Mint in September 1970, as being 6 over 1 (Dyer). Although it has by some sources (Trowbridge, p. 29; *ESC*, p. 218) been associated with the Maundy set of that year without any further qualification, it is by others (Davies, Peter J., p. 29; Salzman, p. 98) correctly confined to the twopence. Nevertheless, a specimen of this denomination is known (Plate 86), and another was offered for sale some eleven years ago (Harding, 1980), in which the overdate is absent. Clearly more than one reverse die was sunk for the striking of the Maundy twopence of 1861; *11*, During microscopic examination by the present author, no traces whatsoever of colons, or any other punctuation, could be detected, whereas traces of colons following F and D, namely as F· and D·, in which both letters were also double struck, were noticeable. The Maundy twopence dated 1863 has very distinct colons following D, G, F and D, all four of which were also sharply struck; *12*, Harding (1980); *13*, In the Royal Mint Collection (see Section V of Chapter 3); *14*, Davies, Peter J., p. 74; *ESC*, p. 218; Montagu, p. 157; *15*, An extremely rare variety *struck for general circulation* reads RRITANNIAR (*ESC*, p. 194; Gaspar, pp. 359–60); *16*, Davies, Peter J., p. 74; *ESC*, p. 218; *NCirc*, 97 (1989), p. 235, item 4826; *17*, Davies, Peter J., p. 74; *ESC*, p. 218.

was of the former type since Maundy Thursday in that year was on 7 April,[419] namely a few weeks before the Golden Jubilee and the issue of the associated currency. It was not until 1888 that the type 2 Maundy coinage, namely that bearing the jubilee head, first appeared.

The jubilee head bust was designed by Sir Joseph Edgar Boehm[420] and the tools for the obverses of the Maundy coinage, in common with the rest of the associated silver coinage, were engraved by Leonard Charles Wyon.[421] On the penny, twopence and fourpence the obverse legend is continuous over the bust, as it is on the type 1 Maundy coinage (Plate 78), and reads the same as that on this earlier type (Plate 87). However, the obverse legend on the type 2 threepence reads VICTORIA DEI GRATIA BRITT: REGINA F: D: (Victoria, by the Grace of God, Queen of Britains, Defender of the Faith) with its continuity broken by the protrusion of the top of the Queen's crown between GRATIA and BRITT: (Plate 87). This brings the threepence into line with the jubilee head sixpence and shilling upon which the same obverse legend, likewise divided, also appears. This move might perhaps be seen as a belated recognition of the threepence's status as a normal circulating coin since 1845:[422] since its introduction, the young head general currency threepence had been indistinguishable in design from the corresponding Maundy threepence, the legend of which was of a different form to those on the larger young head silver denominations. On the other hand, the obverse legend on the 1888 Britannia groat (Plate 88)[423] is the same as those on the type 2 penny, twopence and fourpence and, like these, it is continuous over the bust. Such a similarity might suggest that this groat has a rather special nature. Yet there is also an argument that the retention of the legend then existing on the Maundy coinage for the Britannia groat of 1888 resulted from it having an administrative advantage in that it meant that the unexpected issue of this groat in that year did not require a new Royal Proclamation, the coins still falling within the terms of the description contained in the Proclamation of 5 July 1838.[424]

The reverses of the type 2 Maundy coinage were based upon Merlen's design introduced in 1822 but incorporated a slightly modified crown on all four denominations and a bolder and squarer-looking denominational 2 on the twopence. This reverse was designed and engraved by Leonard Charles Wyon and has since been used continuously up to the present day.

The type 2 Maundy coinage was only issued for five years (Table 36). In effect, the jubilee head coinage never really gained favour with the public. Furthermore, from all informed sources it met with a storm of disapproval which was directed particularly at the lack of artistic merit in the effigy of the Queen and even more specifically against the ridiculously small crown which is on her head. Clearly, she was wearing a hat which did not suit her. This hat actually exists and is kept amongst the Crown Jewels, apparently having been made upon orders from Victoria who wore it on suitable occasions because she found the full-size crown too heavy.[425] It is unfortunate that an artist of the very high calibre of Sir Joseph Edgar Boehm[426] designed such an ill-liked obverse, the replacement of which was never in doubt. The new design, common to the gold, silver and copper coinage, was introduced in 1893[427] and gave rise to what is known as the old head coinage. The new effigy was designed by Sir Thomas Brock,[428] whose initials, T. B., appear just below the bust's truncation,[429] and was engraved by George William De Saulles.[430]

Concomitantly with the change on the coinage from the jubilee head to the old

Table 36. The type 2 (jubilee head) Maundy coinage of Victoria

No.	Date	Denomination	Varieties, remarks, etc.
620	1888	1d	
621	——	2d	
622	——	3d[1,2]	
623	——	4d	
624	——	1d	proof[3]
625	——	2d	——
626	——	3d[1]	proof[3,4]
627	——	4d	proof[3]
628	1889	1d	
629	——	2d	
630	——	3d[1]	
631	——	4d	
632	1890	1d	
633	——	2d	
634	——	3d[1]	
635	——	4d	
636	1891	1d	
637	——	2d	
638	——	3d[1]	
639	——	4d	
640	1892	1d	
641	——	2d	
642	——	3d[1,2]	
643	——	4d	

Notes to Table 36: *1*, Slight multiformity on both the obverse and reverse of the threepences of this type have been observed by two authorities. One of these (Salzman, p. 48) notes three obverses, namely 1 '(1887–1889) Crowned "Jubilee" bust faces left. 7 jewels on left side of dome of crown. Dot on either side of cross on top of crown. 121 bts. A of REGINA points to space', 2 '(1887–1889) 6 jewels. Dots replaced by line projecting from beneath either side of cross on top of crown', and 3 '(1889–1893) Dots restored in place of lines on either side of cross. 126 bts. A of REGINA points to bt.', and two reverses, namely A '(1887–1893) Crowned figure 3 divides date. A single row of pearls constitutes the upper horizontal line of horizontal band on crown' and B '(1890) Pearls replaced by two parallel lines' with a die combination through the type of 1887 (1A, 2A) (see note 2) 1888 (2A), 1889 (1A, 2A, 3A), 1890 (3A, 3B), 1891 (3A), 1892 (3A) and 1893 (3A) (see note 2). The above obverse varieties correspond well with those of the other authority (Davies, Peter J., p. 71), namely 1 '7 pearls left side of crown. 2 dots each side of crown', 2 '1st. 'I' of 'Victoria' to bead. 2 lines each side of cross' and 3 '1st. 'I' of 'Victoria' to space. 2 dots each side of cross', which are also accompanied by three variations in the reverse, namely A 'Cross patée plain. Thin low outline under *fleur de lis*', B 'Cross patée has border. High outline under *fleur de lis*' and C 'Thick cross patée border. Double line across crown', with a die combination through the type of 1887 (1A, 2A) (see note 2), 1888 (1A, 2A), 1889 (1A, 1B, 2A, 2B, 3A, 3B), 1890 (3A, 3C), 1891 (3A), 1892 (3A) and 1893 (3A) (see note 2). Whereas these two authorities coalesce to a large degree with regard to obverse multiformity, little or no semblance is apparent with regard to that of their reverses. The present author has observed that Maundy threepences of this type show, on their obverses, two dots on each side of the cross on the top of the crown for those dated 1888 (proof) and from 1890 to 1892, which have been replaced by two lines on those dated 1888 (non-proof) and 1889, observations which concur with those quoted above, whilst on their reverses all six coins show a single row of pearls across the top of the crowns' circlet, namely as reverse A of Salzman (p. 48), with none showing its replacement by the two parallel lines; *2*, The type 2 (jubilee head) threepence was also struck dated 1887 and 1893 but in both cases this was for general currency, not Maundy, purposes; *3*, Davies, Peter J., p. 75; *ESC*, p. 218; *4*, A method for distinguishing between the proof and the non-proof Maundy threepence dated 1888 is presented in note *1*.

head, the obverse legend was modified, some say at the request of the Queen herself,[431] by the addition of IND·IMP·. An abbreviation of INDIAE IMPERATRIX, this addition was made to the Queen's titles to draw attention to the fact that she was by then Empress of India. Indeed, she had been proclaimed as such in 1876 and the title had, in fact, appeared in the legends of the coins of British India since 1877. The obverse legend of the type 3 Maundy coinage (Plate 89 and Table 37) thus reads VICTORIA·DEI·GRA·BRITT·REGINA·FID·DEF·IND·IMP· (Victoria, by the Grace of God, Queen of Britains, Defender of the Faith, Empress of India).

As were their obverses, the reverses of the type 3 Maundy coinage were engraved by De Saulles and utilized, as had those of type 2, the modification of Merlen's design.

Table 37. The type 3 (old head) Maundy coinage of Victoria

No.	Date	Denomination	Varieties, remarks, etc.
644	1893	1d	
645	——	2d	
646	——	3d[1]	
647	——	4d	
648	1894	1d	
649	——	2d	
650	——	3d[1]	
651	——	4d	
652	1895	1d	
653	——	2d	
654	——	3d[1]	
655	——	4d	
656	1896	1d	
657	——	2d	
658	——	3d[1]	
659	——	4d	
660	1897	1d	
661	——	2d	
662	——	3d[1]	
663	——	4d	
664	1898	1d	
665	——	2d	
666	——	3d[1]	
667	——	4d	
668	1899	1d	
669	——	2d	
670	——	3d[1]	
671	——	4d	
672	1900	1d	
673	——	2d	
674	——	3d[1]	
675	——	4d	
676	1901	1d	
677	——	2d	
678	——	3d[1]	
679	——	4d	

(continued)

xii. Edward VII (22 January 1901–6 May 1910)[432]

The only type of Maundy coinage issued during this reign (Plate 90 and Table 38) was similar in design to the type 2 and 3 of Victoria except for two changes. The first of these is the replacement of the bust of Victoria by one of Edward, designed by George William De Saulles[433] whose initial, DeS., appears just below the bust's truncation. The other involves the legend, which was not only modified to accommodate the change in name and sex occasioned by the accession of Edward VII (although the change from IMPERATRIX to IMPERATOR is not obvious in the common abbreviation to IMP) but was also enlarged by the addition of OMN (an abbreviation of OMNIUM), indicative of the then nature of the British Empire. The legend thus reads EDWARDVS VII D: G: BRITT: OMN: REX F: D: IND: IMP: (Edward VII, by the Grace of God, King of all Britains, Defender of the Faith, Emperor of India): the V has now replaced U in the King's name (and was to remain on the coinages of George V and George VI), thus reversing a change which had been effected in the obverse legend with the introduction of the type 4 coinage of George III.

xiii. George V (6 May 1910–20 January 1936)[434]

The Maundy coinage of this reign (Table 39) can be divided into four different types. These, however, unlike the very distinct types of Maundy coinage issued during the reigns of George III and Victoria, differ only by virtue of either slight design changes resulting from either minor modifications in the effigy or from re-engraving, or from changes in the composition of the alloy from which the coins were struck.

The type 1 Maundy coins (Plate 91) are dated from 1911 to 1920 and are similar in design to those of the previous reign except that they carry a bust of George V, prepared from plaster casts made by Sir Bertram Mackennal[435] whose initials, B. M., appear on the bust's truncation, and bear the obverse legend GEORGIVS V D . G. BRITT : OMN : REX F . D . IND : IMP : (George V, by the Grace of God, King of all Britains, Defender of the Faith, Emperor of India). As with the issues of the earlier reigns, the coins are of 925 millesimal fineness.

In April 1920, the silver coinage of Britain suffered a debasement to a millesimal fineness of 500, the Maundy coinage being no exception. Of the four different alloys thus used to produce the so-called silver coinage, the Maundy coins struck from 1921 to 1937 were composed of that consisting of 50% silver and 50% copper.[436] Since the Maundy coinage dated 1920 which was required for distribution on the Maundy

---

Note to Table 37: *1*, Two slightly different obverses and three slightly different reverses for the threepence have been recorded. On obverses 1 and 2, respectively, there are 129 and 122 beads, the Is of REGINA and FID point to the left of and to a bead (Salzman, p. 48) and the second I of VICTORIA points to a space and a bead (Davies, Peter J., p. 72). On the reverses A, B and C, respectively, there is a plain cross patée with a thin low outline under the fleur de lis, the pearls on the circlet are more distinct and in a different position to the jewels below, and the ribbon is unbalanced, with its right end thicker than the left (Davies, Peter J., p. 72). Both die combinations 1A and 2A exist on threepences dated 1893 and 1894 (Davies, Peter J., p. 72; Salzman, p. 48) (the Maundy threepences so dated which were examined by the present author are of combinations 1A and 2A, respectively), threepences dated from 1895 to 1898 are all of combination 2A and those dated 1899, 1900 and 1901 are of combinations 2B, 2A and 2C, respectively (Davies, Peter J., p. 72).

Table 38. The Maundy coinage of Edward VII

No.	Date	Denomination	Varieties, remarks, etc.
680	1902	1d	
681	——	2d	
682	——	3d[1]	
683	——	4d	
684	——	1d	matt proof[2]
685	——	2d	——
686	——	3d[1]	——
687	——	4d	——
688	1903	1d	
689	——	2d	
690	——	3d[1]	
691	——	4d	
692	1904	1d	
693	——	2d	
694	——	3d[1]	
695	——	4d	
696	1905	1d	
697	——	2d	
698	——	3d[1]	
699	——	4d	
700	1906	1d	
701	——	2d	
702	——	3d[1]	
703	——	4d	
704	1907	1d	
705	——	2d	
706	——	3d[1]	
707	——	4d	
708	1908	1d	
709	——	2d	
710	——	3d[1]	
711	——	4d	
712	1909	1d	
713	——	2d	
714	——	3d[1]	
715	——	4d	
716	1910	1d	
717	——	2d	
718	——	3d[1]	
719	——	4d	

Notes to Table 38: *1*, Two slightly different obverses and two slightly different reverses for the threepence have been observed. On obverses 1 and 2, respectively, there are 129 and 122 beads, the colon after IND points to a bead and a space, the right upright of the N of OMN points to a space and a bead (Salzman, p. 48), the IND: IMP are spaced and close and the I of BRITT points to a space and a bead (Davies, Peter J., p. 79). On the denominational 3 of reverses A and B, the former's diagonal stroke is longer, its base is further from the bow of the ribbon (Salzman, p. 48), and its base curve has a longer neck and ends in a smaller ball (Davies, Peter J., p. 79). Threepences dated 1902 and 1903 are all of die combination 1A, those dated 1904 are of combinations 1A, 1B, 2A and 2B (Davies, Peter J., p. 79; Salzman, p. 48), those dated 1905 are of combinations 1B (Davies, Peter J., p. 79) and 2B, those dated 1906 are of combinations 1B and 2B and those dated 1907 to 1910 are all of 1B (Davies, Peter J., p. 79 and Salzman, p. 48). The Maundy threepences dated from 1904 to 1906 which were examined by the present author are all of combination 1B; *2*, These matt proof Maundy coins (*ESC*, p. 219) were included in the long and short matt proof specimen sets of 1902 of which 8,066 and 7,057, respectively, were issued (see Section V of Chapter 3).

Table 39. The Maundy coinage of George V

No.	Date	Denomination	Varieties, remarks, etc.
720	1911[1]	1d[2]	
721	——	2d[2]	
722	——	3d[2]	
723	——	4d[2]	
724	——	1d	proof[3]
725	——	2d	——
726	——	3d	——
727	——	4d	——
728	1912[1]	1d	
729	——	2d	
730	——	3d	
731	——	4d	
732	1913[1]	1d	
733	——	2d	
734	——	3d	
735	——	4d	
736	1914[1]	1d	
737	——	2d	
738	——	3d	
739	——	4d	
740	1915[1]	1d	
741	——	2d	
742	——	3d	
743	——	4d	
744	1916[1]	1d	
745	——	2d	
746	——	3d	
747	——	4d	
748	1917[1]	1d	
749	——	2d	
750	——	3d	
751	——	4d	
752	1918[1]	1d	
753	——	2d	
754	——	3d	
755	——	4d	
756	1919[1]	1d	
757	——	2d	
758	——	3d	
759	——	4d	
760	1920[1]	1d	
761	——	2d	
762	——	3d	
763	——	4d	
764	1921[4]	1d	
765	——	2d	
766	——	3d	
767	——	4d	
768	1922[4]	1d	
769	——	2d	
770	——	3d	
771	——	4d	

Table 39. *(continued)*

No.	Date	Denomination	Varieties, remarks, etc.
772	1923[4]	1d	
773	——	2d	
774	——	3d	
775	——	4d	
776	1924[4]	1d	
777	——	2d	
778	——	3d	
779	——	4d	
780	1925[4]	1d	
781	——	2d	
782	——	3d	
783	——	4d	
784	1926[4]	1d	
785	——	2d	
786	——	3d	
787	——	4d	
788	1927[4]	1d	
789	——	2d	
790	——	3d	
791	——	4d	
792	1928[5]	1d	
793	——	2d	
794	——	3d	
795	——	4d	
796	1929[5]	1d	
797	——	2d	
798	——	3d	
799	——	4d	
800	1930[6]	1d	
801	——	2d	
802	——	3d	
803	——	4d	
804	1931[6]	1d	(i) obverse uniface exists[7]
805	——	2d	
806	——	3d	
807	——	4d	
808	1932[6]	1d	
809	——	2d	
810	——	3d	
811	——	4d	
812	1933[6]	1d	
813	——	2d	
814	——	3d	
815	——	4d	
816	1934[6]	1d	
817	——	2d	
818	——	3d	
819	——	4d	
820	1935[6]	1d	
821	——	2d	
822	——	3d	
823	——	4d	

(continued)

Table 39. *(continued)*

No.	Date	Denomination	Varieties, remarks, etc.
824	1936[6]	1d	
825	——	2d	
826	——	3d	
827	——	4d	

Notes to Table 39: *1*, Type 1; *2*, The Maundy penny and fourpence (Salzman, pp. 41, 53), threepence (Davies, Peter J., pp. 90, 91; Salzman, p. 49) and twopence (Robinson) dated 1911 have, at the back of the neck above the B.M. on the truncation, a hollow which on the first three denominations is absent on the coins for the following year and onward; *3*, Davies, Peter J., p. 92; *ESC*, p. 219. These proof Maundy sets were included in the long, medium and short proof sets of that year, of which 2,812, 952 and 2,243, respectively, were issued (see Section V of Chapter 3); *4*, Type 2; *5*, Type 3; *6*, Type 4; *7*, The Royal Mint Collection contains twelve uniface Maundy pennies of George V (Plate 93). These were clearly struck in 1931 since the corresponding blank reverse die (Plate 94) is, on its body, dated 1 6 31, namely 1 June 1931. Unfortunately, the raison d'être of these pieces is, as yet, unknown (Dyer).

Thursday of that year had been struck before April, the debasement only became manifest in the Maundy money in 1921 whereas the currency threepences[437] of 1920 are equally common in 925 and 500 millesimal fine silver.[438] Thus, the type 2 Maundy coinage of George V differs from that of type 1 only by its metallic composition and is dated from 1921 to 1927.

During the 1920s, George F. Hill, then Keeper of Coins and Medals at the British Museum (ultimately becoming the Museum's director) and a member of the Royal Mint Advisory Committee which deliberated upon the design of coinage, condemned the numerals on the Maundy coinage as being in the worst commercial style, making the further point that their hatching was quite unnecessary.[439] However, Hill's criticism fell on stony ground for action was neither then taken, nor has been since, which has resulted in any modification whatsoever to the basic design of the Maundy coinage.

During 1926, the effigy by Mackennal on the British coinage was modified, with the result that the head was reduced in size, its details were made in lower relief and more sharply defined, and the stops on the B. M. were removed and the resulting BM was placed nearer to the rear of the neck's truncation.[440] This modified effigy was introduced into the coinage used for general circulation in either 1926 or 1927, depending upon the denomination, but did not make its appearance on the Maundy coinage until 1928 whence it gave rise to the reign's type 3 such coinage which is dated 1928 and 1929.[441]

Unlike the type 2 and type 3 Maundy coins of this reign which result from changes which are also manifest upon the appropriate coinage in general circulation, the type 4 Maundy coinage, which carries the bust of George V and is dated from 1930 to 1936, arose from changes limited to the Maundy coinage and results from the production of sharpened up re-engraved reverse tools. This provided for longer beads and wider edges[442] and also rectified the previous situation whereby the wreath on the threepence had been out of centre and the orb was detached from the crown on the twopence.[443] Further changes resulting from this re-engraving of the reverse tools include the introduction of smaller date numerals on the twopence and fourpence,[444] the replacement of a thick irregular foliage by one thin and symmetrical[445] and other modifications to the crown. These include the replacement of the three large centre pearls by three smaller ones,[446] the replacement of bordered by plain crosses pateé on the penny, twopence and fourpence (the pre-1930 threepence already had the plain cross pateé) and changes to the upper and lower borders in the circlets. A smaller, thicker and squarer denominational 2 with bolder hatching was also introduced.[447]

As mentioned earlier, the silver threepence which was introduced into general currency in Britain from 1845 onwards was, in design, indistinguishable from its Maundy contemporary, a situation which prevailed until 1926. However, beginning in 1927, with a total mintage of only 15,000 which was confined to the proof sets of that year, and continuing, with the exception of 1929, until the end of the reign of George V in 1936, a threepence of millesimal fineness 500 was issued for general currency which had a reverse design different from that of the Maundy threepence. This design, by Kruger Gray,[448] consists of three interlaced oak sprigs, each bearing an acorn and a leaf (in the centre of which is the artist's monogram, G) and a legend THREE PENCE together with the date (Plate 92).

xiv. Edward VIII (20 January 1936–10 December 1936 (abdicated))[449]

Patterns were produced for the proposed coinage of this monarch.[450] The effigy for this coinage was designed by Thomas Humphrey Paget[451] whose initials, HP, appear just below the bust's truncation. However, these patterns did not include the Maundy coinage since work on the master tools required for its production was incomplete by the time of the Abdication[452] and had only reached the stage of having produced two soft reduction obverse punches, one for the penny and one for the twopence (Plate 95). The effigies on these two punches are, not surprisingly, the same as those on the pattern coins of the other denominations which were struck. However, the legends of both punches read EDWARDVS VIII D : G : BR : OMN : REX F : D : IND : IMP. (Edward VIII, by the Grace of God, King of all Britains, Defender of the Faith, Emperor of India), namely the same as those on the pattern bronze farthing, halfpenny and penny and nickel-brass threepence,[453] but different from those on the pattern 500 millesimal fine silver threepence, sixpence, shilling, florin, half-crown and crown,[454] not only by virtue of the nature of the abbreviation but also because on these latter denominations the royal titles are divided between both obverse and reverse legends. Such a restriction of the royal name and titles to an obverse legend on the Maundy coinage had been in effect since 1822, and had also applied to the silver threepences (up to 1926 these were, in fact, of the same design as the Maundy threepence) issued as general currency until 1936. By analogy, there is no doubt that, unlike the 500 millesimal fine silver pattern threepence, a Maundy threepence of Edward VIII would have carried the royal name and titles totally as an obverse legend, as on the punches for the penny and twopence. Indeed, apart from a new effigy and the associated change of name in the obverse legend, there is no reason why the designs of Edward VIII's Maundy coinage should have been different from those of his father's and, in fact, there is no evidence to suggest that they would have been.[455]

The death of George V occurred on 20 January 1936 and the Royal Maundy for that year was distributed by Edward VIII.[456] Thus, the Maundy coinage of 1936, although bearing the effigy of George V, might be regarded as being that of Edward VIII.[457]

xv. George VI (10 December 1936–6 February 1952)[458]

The Maundy coinage issued during this reign (Table 40) is of three different types. These are differentiated either by the composition of the alloy from which they were struck or by their obverse legend.

The type 1 Maundy coinage (Plate 96), issued from 1937 to 1946, is similar to that of the type 4 of George V except that the bust of George VI by Thomas Humphrey Paget,[459] whose initials, HP, appear just below the truncation, replaces that of George V and the obverse legend, to take account of the new king, reads GEORGIVS VI D : G : BR : OMN : REX F : D : IND : IMP., the royal titles being the same, and likewise abbreviated, as those on the proposed Maundy coinage of Edward VIII.

In 1946, as for the preceding twenty-five years, the British silver coinage, including the Maundy coinage, was of 500 millesimal fineness. Mention has already been made of the total debasement in that year of this coinage which was to be used for general

Table 40. The Maundy coinage of George VI

No.	Date	Denomination	Varieties, remarks, etc.
828	1937[1]	1d	
829	——	2d	
830	——	3d	
831	——	4d	
832	——	1d	proof[2]
833	——	2d	——
834	——	3d	——
835	——	4d	——
836	——	1d	matt proof[3]
837	——	2d	——
838	——	3d	——
839	——	4d	——
840	1938[1]	1d	
841	——	2d	
842	——	3d	
843	——	4d	
844	1939[1]	1d	
845	——	2d	
846	——	3d	
847	——	4d	
848	1940[1]	1d	
849	——	2d	
850	——	3d	
851	——	4d	
852	1941[1]	1d	
853	——	2d	
854	——	3d	
855	——	4d	
856	1942[1]	1d	
857	——	2d	
858	——	3d	
859	——	4d	
860	1943[1]	1d	
861	——	2d	
862	——	3d	

Table 40. *(continued)*

No.	Date	Denomination	Varieties, remarks, etc.
863	——	4d	
864	1944[1]	1d	
865	——	2d	
866	——	3d	
867	——	4d	
868	1945[1]	1d	
869	——	2d	
870	——	3d	
871	——	4d	
872	1946[1]	1d	
873	——	2d	
874	——	3d	
875	——	4d	
876	1947[4]	1d	
877	——	2d	
878	——	3d	
879	——	4d	
880	1948[4]	1d	
881	——	2d	
882	——	3d	
883	——	4d	
884	1949[5]	1d	
885	——	2d	
886	——	3d	
887	——	4d	
888	1950[5]	1d	
889	——	2d	
890	——	3d	
891	——	4d	
892	1951[5]	1d	
893	——	2d	
894	——	3d	
895	——	4d	
896	——	1d	matt proof[3]
897	——	2d	——
898	——	3d	——
899	——	4d	——
900	1952[5]	1d	
901	——	2d	
902	——	3d	
903	——	4d	
904	——	1d	struck in copper[3]
905	——	2d	——
906	——	3d	——
907	——	4d	——

Notes to Table 40: *1*, Type 1; *2*, Superficial examination cannot distinguish these proof coins from the ordinary Maundy coins which are also of proof quality (*ESC*, p. 220). However, those coins struck for the Maundy service and related uses in 1937 are of alloy composition 500A, namely 50% silver and 50% copper, whereas alloy 500Z, namely 50% silver, 40% copper, 5% nickel and 5% zinc, was used to produce those Maundy sets which were to be included in the proof sets issued in 1937 (Dyer) (see page 97); *3*, See Section V of Chapter 3; *4*, Type 2; *5*, Type 3.

circulation, whilst concomitantly the Maundy coinage was returned to its pre-1921 millesimal fineness of 925, namely sterling silver. This change gave rise to the reign's type 2 Maundy coinage, issued dated 1947 and 1948, which differs from that of type 1 only in as much as it is of millesimal fineness 925.

Relating to the granting of independence to India, it was ordered by proclamation on 22 December 1948 that the words INDIAE IMPERATOR should be omitted from the royal style and titles on the coinage from 1 January 1949 onwards. Thus, the type 3 Maundy coinage, issued dated from 1949 to 1952, is as that of type 2 except that IND : IMP. is omitted from the obverse legend (F:D: is also expanded to FIDEI DEF.). The obverse legend thus reads GEORGIVS VI D : G : BR : OMN : REX FIDEI DEF. (George VI, by the Grace of God, King of all Britains, Defender of the Faith) (Plate 97).

The number four in the date of the Maundy coinage of George VI varies according to denomination. Thus, on the penny and fourpence it appears as 4 whereas on the twopence and threepence it appears with an additional serif, namely as 4, a relationship which also applies to both fours in the date 1944. The significance, if any, of these differences is not apparent but its consistency within denominations certainly indicates it relates to the different sets of figure punches used. The same relationship also exists between the fours on the four denominations of the Maundy sets dated 1954, 1964, 1974 and 1984 whereas, in the reverse direction, the four appears as 4 on all four denominations dated 1934 and 1854 and as 4 on the penny, twopence and fourpence and as 4 on the threepence of the sets dated 1924, 1914, 1904, 1894 and 1884. A shorter serif is also sometimes used. Thus, on the coins dated 1874, the four appears as 4 on the fourpence and penny and as 4 on the threepence and twopence, on those dated 1864 we find 4 on the fourpence and 4 on the other three denominations, from 1849 to 1844 the penny, twopence and threepence again have 4 whereas the fourpence has 4 (namely only a very short serif), a relationship which also applies to both the fours in 1844, and the fours on all the denominations dated from 1843 to 1840, 1834 and 1824 are of the design 4.

In 1950, the Mint proposed to change the design of the denominational 2 on the reverse of the Maundy twopence to what it considered to be the more artistic and dignified shape that it possessed before 1888, and a punch (Plate 98) was produced accordingly. However, no such change was effected since the King, George VI, did not approve of this intention. He was of the opinion that the then, and indeed still, current design of the denominational 2 is more in keeping with the corresponding numerals on the other three denominations,[460] a view with which the present author concurs.

The commencement of the reign of George VI heralded a new design for the 500 millesimal fine silver threepence issued for general currency which, as with the design used on the corresponding denomination from 1927 to 1936 (with the exception of 1929 when no threepences were struck for general currency), is different from that used on the Maundy threepence. The new coin (Plate 99) has on its reverse St George's shield superimposed upon a full-blown Tudor rose which divides the date and below which are the designer's initials, K. G. (Kruger Gray[461]). Also different from the Maundy threepence is the legend in that not only is it differently abbreviated in part but it is divided between the obverse and reverse of the coin. That on the former reads GEORGIVS VI D : G : BR : OMN : REX and on the latter reads FID: DEF: IND: IMP together with THREE PENCE. This coin was struck dated from 1937 to 1945.

However, only those dated from 1937 to 1941 were issued for general currency in Britain, those dated from 1942 to 1944 being struck only in small quantities for use in the West Indian and other colonies.[462] All those struck and dated 1945 were supposedly melted down but at least one escaped the melting pot.[463] The proof set of 1937 is of interest in that it contains three different threepences. These are the Maundy threepence (but of a different alloy composition from those struck for Maundy purposes[464]), the 500 millesimal fine silver threepence struck for general circulation and the then conceptually-new copper-zinc-nickel (79:20:1 parts) dodecagonal threepence (Plate 100). This last was introduced for use as general currency to provide an acceptable coin, of value between a penny and a sixpence, in place of the silver threepence which, outside of Scotland and Wales, had become increasingly abhorred after the turn of the century.[465]

xvi. Elizabeth II (6 February 1952 to date)[466]

Two types of Maundy coinage (Table 41) have so far been minted during this present reign.

Table 41. The Maundy coinage of Elizabeth II

No.	Date	Denomination	Varieties, remarks, etc.
908	1953[1]	1d	
909	——	2d	
910	——	3d	
911	——	4d	
912	——	1d	matt proof[2]
913	——	2d	——
914	——	3d	——
915	——	4d	——
916	——	1d	in gold[2]
917	——	2d	——
918	——	3d	——
919	——	4d	——
920	1954[3]	1d	
921	——	2d	
922	——	3d	
923	——	4d	
924	1955[3]	1d	
925	——	2d	
926	——	3d	
927	——	4d	
928	1956[3]	1d	
929	——	2d	
930	——	3d	
931	——	4d	
932	1957[3]	1d	
933	——	2d	
934	——	3d	
935	——	4d	
936	1958[3]	1d	
937	——	2d	

(continued)

Table 41. *(continued)*

No.	Date	Denomination	Varieties, remarks, etc.
938	——	3d	
939	——	4d	
940	1959[3]	1d	
941	——	2d	
942	——	3d	
943	——	4d	
944	1960[3]	1d	
945	——	2d	
946	——	3d	
947	——	4d	
948	1961[3]	1d	
949	——	2d	
950	——	3d	
951	——	4d	
952	1962[3]	1d	
953	——	2d	
954	——	3d	
955	——	4d	
956	1963[3]	1d	
957	——	2d	
958	——	3d	
959	——	4d	
960	1964[3]	1d	
961	——	2d	
962	——	3d	
963	——	4d	
964	1965[3]	1d	
965	——	2d	
966	——	3d	
967	——	4d	
968	1966[3]	1d	
969	——	2d	
970	——	3d	
971	——	4d	
972	1967[3]	1d	
973	——	2d	
974	——	3d	
975	——	4d	
976	1968[3]	1d	
977	——	2d	
978	——	3d	
979	——	4d	
980	1969[3]	1d	
981	——	2d	
982	——	3d	
983	——	4d	
984	1970[3]	1d	
985	——	2d	
986	——	3d	
987	——	4d	
988	1971[3,4]	1p	
989	——	2p	

Table 41. (continued)

No.	Date	Denomination	Varieties, remarks, etc.
990	——	3p	
991	——	4p	
992	1972[3]	1p	
993	——	2p	
994	——	3p	
995	——	4p	
996	1973[3]	1p	
997	——	2p	
998	——	3p	
999	——	4p	
1000	1974[3]	1p	
1001	——	2p	
1002	——	3p	
1003	——	4p	
1004	1975[3]	1p	
1005	——	2p	
1006	——	3p	
1007	——	4p	
1008	1976[3]	1p	
1009	——	2p	
1010	——	3p	
1011	——	4p	
1012	1977[3]	1p	
1013	——	2p	
1014	——	3p	
1015	——	4p	
1016	1978[3]	1p	
1017	——	2p	
1018	——	3p	
1019	——	4p	
1020	1979[3]	1p	
1021	——	2p	
1022	——	3p	
1023	——	4p	
1024	1980[3]	1p	
1025	——	2p	
1026	——	3p	
1027	——	4p	
1028	1981[3]	1p	
1029	——	2p	
1030	——	3p	
1031	——	4p	
1032	1982[3]	1p	
1033	——	2p	
1034	——	3p	
1035	——	4p	
1036	1983[3]	1p	
1037	——	2p	
1038	——	3p	
1039	——	4p	
1040	1984[3]	1p	
1041	——	2p	

(continued)

Table 41. *(continued)*

No.	Date	Denomination	Varieties, remarks, etc.
1042	—	3p	
1043	—	4p	
1044	1985³	1p	
1045	—	2p	
1046	—	3p	
1047	—	4p	
1048	1986³	1p	
1049	—	2p	
1050	—	3p	
1051	—	4p	
1052	1987³	1p	
1053	—	2p	
1054	—	3p	
1055	—	4p	
1056	1988³	1p	
1057	—	2p	
1058	—	3p	
1059	—	4p	
1060	1989³	1p	
1061	—	2p	
1062	—	3p	
1063	—	4p	
1064	1990³	1p	
1065	—	2p	
1066	—	3p	
1067	—	4p	

Notes to Table 41: *1*, Type 1; *2*, See Section V of Chapter 3; *3*, Type 2; *4*, The British currency was decimalized on 15 February 1971, resulting in the Maundy coins being declared legal tender for one, two, three and four new pence (p). However, no modification to the reverse design was necessary since the denominational numbers are without qualification: the Maundy coinage is above denominations!

The type 1 coinage was only issued in 1953 (Plate 101). It is similar to that of the type 3 coinage of George VI except that the Queen's bust, by Mary Gillick,[467] has replaced that of her father and, to take account of the new monarch, the obverse legend, which now begins about the 1 o'clock position rather than the 7 o'clock position as in the previous six reigns, reads ELIZABETH II DEI GRA : BRITT : OMN : REGINA F : D : (Elizabeth II, by the Grace of God, Queen of all Britains, Defender of the Faith).

The bust on these coins has been the focus of much adverse criticism in that it is of low relief and lacks details. What might appear as wear is, in fact, the condition of this type 1 coinage as struck. However, this is not a defect as is widely believed and suggested by statements such as 'the low relief and lack of details was corrected by die retouching for subsequent years' and 'I have seen a sharper striking of the 1953 set, but this was an early striking. The die must have produced the low relief coins very quickly, resulting in the normal "weak" strikes'.[468] Rather, the soft effect was that actually desired by Mrs Gillick.[469] Nevertheless, for the following year and onward, the tools were retouched to afford coins with a sharper bust.

The year 1954 also witnessed the introduction of the type 2 Maundy coinage of the reign. In view of the situation that by then some of the Commonwealth's countries had adopted a republican constitution, the title of BRITT: OMN: was removed from the Queen's coinage titles by order of a proclamation on 4 October 1953. The type 2 coinage therefore differs from that of type 1 in that, as well as having a better-defined bust, its obverse legend reads ELIZABETH II DEI GRATIA REGINA F : D : (Elizabeth II, by the Grace of God, Queen, Defender of the Faith) (Plate 102).

With regard to the production of Maundy money over recent years, new reverse dies are produced each year, being sunk from a partially-dated punch and then completed by hand.[470] However, it is the general practice at the Royal Mint to make new obverse dies only as and when necessary. Thus, with so few Maundy coins being required annually, it is therefore possible that a current obverse die will be utilized in subsequent minting. Notwithstanding, this does not explain the continued use of the effigy designed by Mary Gillick on the Maundy coinage subsequent to the introduction into Britain on 15 February 1971 of decimal currency bearing a new bust of the Queen by Arnold Machin.[471] The retention was not an economic measure but an expression of affection for a charming portrait of the Queen. Although it had been widely expected and was, indeed, first thought that the Machin effigy would be adopted for the Maundy coinage at the time of decimalization, the Royal Mint Advisory Committee, on reflection, felt that it would be a pity to lose so admirable a portrait as the Gillick effigy and this recommendation was accepted by the Queen.[472] For the same reason, it also survived the general introduction into the British coinage in 1985[473] of a second new bust of the Queen, that by Raphael Maklouf.[474]

IV. DIE-AXIS VARIATIONS OF THE PRE-1729 POST-RESTORATION SMALL SILVER COINAGE AND OF THE MAUNDY COINAGE

The die-axis of a coin refers to the position of the design on its reverse relative to that on its obverse and it is indicated by an arrow, the positions of which in the two extreme cases are ↑ and ↓. Thus, if the coin with its obverse facing upward is turned over sideways and the reverse design then appears the right way up, the coin's die-axis is denoted as ↑ whereas, under such circumstances, if the reverse design is upside down the die-axis is shown as ↓.[475] In between these two extremes, the reverse design may be inclined to the left or to the right into one of an infinite number of positions which would be indicated accordingly. The results of so surveying all the silver penny, twopence, threepence and fourpence coins dated between 1668 and 1727, inclusively, and the post-1728 Maundy coinage to 1989 are presented in Table 42.[476]

As can be seen, no die-axis variation within the coins of a particular type occurs, with the exception of the dated milled coins (type 2) of Charles II. In these, the lone coinage of the twopence dated 1668, of which five specimens were examined, has a die-axis ↑, namely opposite to that of all the subsequent strikings of all the four denominations of this type. This observation, together with that that the die-axes of proof Maundy coins are often opposite to those of the corresponding non-proof strikings (see below), may lend credence to the suggestion that the twopence struck in 1668, the pioneer of John Roettiers' coinage of crowned Cs, is a pattern by this die-sinker[477] although, apparently contrary to this hypothesis, specimens of this coin are fairly common.

However, die-axis displacement in proof Maundy coins relative to the corresponding non-proof issues is observed elsewhere. For example, the four proof Maundy coins in each of the sets dated 1763, 1838 and 1839,[478] and 1871[479] have their die-axes 180° displaced relative to those of the non-proof, although sometimes apparently proof-like, issues. Thus, all sixteen of these proof Maundy coins have their die-axes ↑ [480] which thereby provides a clear differentiation between these coins and their non-proof, but probably proof-like, equivalents which have their die-axes ↓. There would appear to be little reason why the other Victoria (type 1) proof Maundy coins, namely those dated

Table 42. The die-axis variations of the pre-1729 small silver coinage from 1668 and of the Maundy coinage

Monarch	Inclusive dates on the coins. The coin type, where there is more than one (see Section III of Chapter 3), is in parentheses	Die-axis[1]
Charles II	1668[2](2)	↑ [3]
	1670–1684[4](2)	↓ [3]
James II	1685–1688	↓
William and Mary	1689–1694[5]	↓
William III	1698–1702[6]	↓
Anne	1703–1713[7]	↓
George I	1716–1727[7,8]	↓
George II	1729–1760[7,9]	↓
George III	1762–1780 (1A)[7,10]	↓
	1781–1786 (1B)[7,11]	↓
	1792 (2)[10]	↑
	1795 and 1800 (3)[10]	↑
	1817, 1818 and 1820 (4)[10]	↑
George IV	1822–1830	↑
William IV	1831–1837	↓
Victoria	1838–1887 (1)	↑
	1888–1892 (2)	↑
	1893–1901 (3)	↑
Edward VII	1902–1910	↑
George V	1911–1920 (1)	↑
	1921–1927 (2)	↑
	1928 and 1929 (3)	↑
	1930–1936 (4)	↑
George VI	1937–1946 (1)	↑
	1947 and 1948 (2)	↑
	1949–1952 (3)[12]	↑
Elizabeth II	1953 (1)	↑
	1954–1990 (2)	↑

Notes to Table 42: *1*, In each case, at least three specimens of each denomination were examined; *2*, Only the twopence was issued; *3*, Reverse die-axes are indicated by ↑ or ↓ when the date in the legend is at the top or bottom, respectively; *4*, None of the four denominations were issued dated 1669 (see Table 8); *5*, No twopence dated 1690 would appear to exist (see Table 8); *6*, Apart from an apparently unique fourpence dated 1697, which was not examined, and fourpence dated 1702, none of the four denominations were issued dated 1702 and from 1695 to 1697 (see Table 8); *7*, Of the four minor silver denominations, not all, or even none at all, exist bearing certain of the dates within these inclusive periods (see Table 8); *8*, None of the four denominations were issued bearing the dates 1714 and 1715 (see Table 8); *9*, None of the four denominations were issued bearing the date 1728 (see Table 8); *10*, None of the four denominations were issued bearing the dates 1761, 1787 to 1791, 1793, 1794, 1796 to 1799, 1801 to 1816, 1819 and 1821 (see Table 8); *11*, Only the pennies and fourpences dated 1784 and 1786 are of type 1B, the corresponding twopences and threepences being of type 1A (see Section III, Sub-section viii, of Chapter 3); *12*, The probably-unique Maundy set in copper dated 1952 (see page 197) also has the die-axis ↑.

1853, 1867, 1878 and 1881 (Table 35) should not have their die-axes similarly displaced. Indeed, this criterion has been employed to establish as proof issues two Maundy twopences dated 1866 and all four component coins of two Maundy sets dated 1868 which are part of the Royal Mint Collection.[481] Nevertheless, the coins of the Victoria (type 2) proof Maundy set dated 1888 have their die-axes ↑, namely the same as the corresponding non-proof issues. In this instance, a change in the die-axis was probably not effected in order to obviate the possible introduction of die mis-matching involving metal-flow problems consequent upon the incompatibility between the obverse and reverse dies.[482] The bottom of the bust on the jubilee head which was used on the obverse of the type 2 coinage is of a considerable area and also of high relief and should not, therefore, be opposite to the crown, the feature on the reverse that requires the most metal.[483]

Since the introduction of the jubilee head coinage, the die-axes of not only the Maundy coins but of all coins of the United Kingdom have remained upright, namely ↑.[484] Thus, the Maundy sets dated 1902, 1911 and 1937 which are included in the official proof specimen sets issued in these years have the same die-axes as the other Maundy sets and coins bearing these dates, and the threepences in the proof sets of 1893 (type 3) and 1887 (type 2)[485] both have their die-axes ↑, the same as the corresponding non-proof issues. Indeed, the 1831 Maundy sets included in the proof sets of that year have the same die-axis as the corresponding Maundy coins issued for other purposes.[486] It would be interesting to extrapolate these investigations to include the proof Maundy sets dated 1822 and 1828 (Table 33) and those in gold dated 1831, 1838 and 1953 (Tables 34, 35 and 41).

The uniformity in die-axes which, from Table 42, is apparent within the small silver and Maundy coins of a particular type or reign, with the exception of the 1668 twopence and some of the proof issues, is not shared by some of the pre-1668 small silver issues of Charles II (Plates 51–54 and Table 21). Thus, of the specimens examined, the die-axes of the pennies of types 1A and 1B are 1 × ↖ and 1 × ↓, and 1 × ↗, 1 × ↘ and 4 × ↖, respectively, and those of the corresponding twopences are 2 × ↑, 1 × ↗, 1 × →, 1 × ↘, 4 × ↙, 1 × ← and 1 × ↖, and 1 × ↗, respectively. Similarly, almost random die-axes are observed for the type 1E pennies and twopences, 1 × ↗, 2 × →, 2 × ↘, 1 × ↓, 2 × ↙, 1 × ← and 2 × ↖, and 1 × ↗, 1 × →, 3 × ↘, 2 × ↙, 2 × ← and 1 × ↖, respectively, and the corresponding type 1A threepences and fourpences, 1 × ↗, 2 × ↘, 1 × ↙ and 1 × ↖, and 1 × ↗, 2 × ↘, 1 × ↙, 1 × ←, 1 × ↖ and 1 × ↑, respectively, which were examined. Clearly, in these sub-types of the type 1 hammered issues, randomization of the die-axis is apparent. However, on the contrary, the die-axes of the types 1C and 1D pennies and twopences which have been examined were 2 × ↓, 2 × ↓, 2 × ↓ and 5 × ↓, respectively, this uniformity lending further credence to the suggestion that these coins, because of their quality of striking, were machine made.[487] A similar uniformity of die-axis is also shared by the type 1F penny and twopence and 1B threepence and fourpence, together known as the Undated Maundy money or Simon's Maundy money and usually designated as the first small silver milled coinage: all four denominations of five of the six such sets which have been examined have die-axes ↓. However, those of the sixth set were, in order of increasing denomination, ↓, ←, ↓ and →, and a type 1B threepence with a die-axis ← has also been noted: it may be significant with respect to their machine-made origin that the die-axis variations, where noted, within the Simon's Maundy money are related by right angles. Furthermore, accompanying these die-axis variations in the Simon's Maundy money, legend dissimilarities have also been observed and there is clearly a need for further research into this coinage.[488]

V. MAUNDY MONEY PROOF ISSUES AND STRIKINGS IN METALS OTHER THAN SILVER

Within the gold and larger silver denominations, plain edges are a likely characteristic of proof issues whose non-proof counterparts struck for general circulation are correspondingly grained or lettered.[489] However, all the Maundy coinage has plain edges and, consequently, other criteria must be sought for differentiating its proof issues. In doing so, care must be taken since many Maundy coins and sets issued after the beginning of the reign of William IV, especially early strikes, and occasionally some earlier issues have a proof-like appearance[490] and could well be mistaken for proofs. For example, the Maundy coins of the current reign are regarded by some as representing proof strikings of an extremely low mintage in the British series. Furthermore, many superb proof-like specimens of early strikes abound in the Maundy coins of William IV and only careful examination of the edge and field will distinguish them from a genuine proof, although even experts find such differentiation sometimes impossible. In their January 1974 Bulletin, Seaby listed for sale 'MS206. **William IV** Maundy set, 1834. F.D.C. *Toned.* (Although no record of any proof Maundy set exists for this date the striking is so sharp that we feel we must advertise the set "proof like"). **Plate 5**. £90'. The related illustration, of the obverse of the fourpence and the reverses of all the four coins, shows a frosted effigy on the fourpence. On Wednesday, 4 April 1979, Glendining and Co. sold for £210 'Lot 312. Proof Maundy Set, 1834 (ESC–). *Brilliant and exceedingly rare*': was this the same set as sold five years earlier by Seaby, resulting from the evolution of its description from proof-like into proof? The converse of this situation arises with the 1911 proof Maundy set on which, although the striking is crisp, the field is often quite ordinary, a problem which can be exaggerated if the coins are toned. In this particular situation, the proof set can be distinguished from the non-proof set by unifacial cross-section observation of the fourpence. On the proof the rim is flat and even, the result of turning to remove the burrs raised during the striking involving multiple blows, whereas on the ordinary issue it is tapered (Figure 2) and, under a magnification of ×20, shows minor nicks and is less neat and regular than the proof issue: the other three denominations do not exhibit such differences, presumably since the proof penny, twopence and threepence are too small to have been similarly de-burred.

Figure 2

From 1970 onward, proof sets of the British coinage have been issued annually and in large numbers (not surprisingly, these do not contain specimens of the contemporary Maundy issues). Prior to this, proof sets of the British coinage were issued only for the years of some particular historical significance, such as a coronation or a jubilee, or more specifically for the Festival of Britain in 1951, as the mid-century set of 1950, and concurrent with the introduction of new coinage-designs. Of these pre-1970 sets, those issued in 1953 (40,000 sets of ten coins, crown to farthing), 1951 (20,000 sets of ten coins, crown to farthing), 1937 (5,501 sets of four coins, five pounds to half sovereign), 1927 (15,000 sets of six coins, crown to threepence), 1893 (six sets of ten coins, five pounds to threepence and 556 sets of six coins, crown to threepence), 1887 (797 sets of eleven coins, five pounds to threepence and 287 sets of seven coins, crown to threepence) and 1826 (about 400 sets of eleven coins, five pounds to farthing) are devoid of a specimen of the contemporary Maundy set.[491] However, contemporary-dated Maundy sets are included in the other pre-1970 British proof set issues, namely those of 1937[492] (26,402[493] sets of fifteen coins, crown to farthing), 1911 (2,812 sets of twelve coins, five pounds to Maundy penny, 952 sets of ten coins, sovereign to Maundy penny and 2,243 sets of eight coins, halfcrown to Maundy penny), 1902 (matt finish) (8,066 sets of thirteen coins, five pounds to Maundy penny and 7,057 sets of eleven coins, sovereign to Maundy penny), 1853 (only a few sets of sixteen coins, sovereign to quarter farthing: the content of sets of this date may, however, vary[494]), 1839 (about three hundred sets of fifteen coins, five pounds and sovereign to farthing) and 1831 (220[495] sets of fourteen coins, two pounds to farthing).[496]

Along with those which were included in the above proof specimen collections, proof Maundy sets were issued dated 1888 (very rare), 1881, 1878 (both extremely rare), 1871 (eleven to twenty examples known), 1867, (extremely rare), 1853 (very rare), 1839 (rare), 1838 (extremely rare),[497] 1831 (rare), 1828 (five to ten examples known), 1822 (eleven to twenty examples known)[498] and 1763.[499]

Many of these proof Maundy coins can be distinguished from their non-proof counterparts because they exhibit some of the features which are normally employed generally to effect such differentiations. These include more sharply defined design details, a generally superior quality field, a sometimes wedge-shaped cross section which is often accentuated by the presence of vertical burrs thrown up in striking (the author has noted such features on proof Maundy fourpences of 1831 and 1838) and a firmness of beading around the rim. This last feature is particularly apparent on the 1763 proof Maundy coins, when compared with the corresponding non-proof issues and is a consequence of the use in the striking of the former of a collar to hold the dies and the blank together which coincidentally, by restricting the outward flow of metal during the striking process, prevents the distortion and loss of shape of the beads which is apparent on the non-proof issues.[500] However, the fish-tailing, or bifurcationing, on the uprights of legend lettering, another feature characteristic of the uncontrolled outward flow of metal during the striking of non-proof coins, namely without the use of a collar,[501] is not apparent on the 1763 non-proof Maundy coinage which has been examined by the author. Also absent on the edges of the proof 1763 Maundy coins is the single step or raised witness line normally associated with the use of a collar in the striking process.[502]

Late eighteenth-century proofs usually show a disregard for standard weight and fineness.[503] In accord with the former is the observation that the weights of the proof pennies, twopences, and threepences of 1763 in the Royal Mint and British Museum collections, 0.773 and 0.777, 1.193 and 1.197 (two other specimens weigh 1.161 and 1.172 g), and 1.957 and 1.957 g, respectively, are significantly greater than the weights of corresponding non-proof specimens, 0.508 and 0.458, 0.993 and 0.962, and 1.482 and

1.518 g, respectively. However, the corresponding proof fourpences only weigh 2.039 and 1.934 g, weights that not only exhibit considerable disparity, unlike those of the other corresponding proof pairs, but are not significantly different from those of corresponding non-proof specimens, namely 1.964 and 2.015 g. It has been suggested that a twopence of 1729 which is struck on a thick flan is perhaps a proof.[504]

Probably the most obvious difference between the proof and non-proof Maundy coins of 1763, and of the young head issues of Victoria, is that the die-axes of the proofs are upright, ↑,[505] whereas of the non-proofs they are inverted, ↓.[506] Indeed, such a difference permitted the following recent facile detection of further proof Maundy issues within the young head series of Victoria. In about 1866, Hunt and Roskell, the London jewellers and goldsmiths that, since 1852, had been appointed to act as the Mint's agents for the sale of its proof issues, put together two sets, from sovereign to farthing and of mixed dates, for a presentation. This never materialized and the sets were ultimately, in 1968, returned to the Royal Mint by the Foreign Office. Included in each of these two sets was a Maundy set dated 1866 and, whereas the die-axes of the component pennies, threepences and fourpences are all ↓, indicating they are ordinary Maundy issues, the die-axes of the two twopences are both ↑, in accord with their being classified as proof issues. The Royal Mint's collection also contains two Maundy sets dated 1868, all eight component coins of which have die-axes ↑. Again, this confirms their classification as proof issues, a designation which is further supported by their quality.

The die-axes of the proof Maundy set of 1888 and its non-proof analogue are both ↑, probably because in the jubilee head type 2 Maundy coinage an inverted axis would have resulted in die mis-matching,[507] and no die-axis differences exist between the Maundy sets included in the proof sets of 1831, 1902, 1911 and 1937 and those issued for Maundy and related purposes, although those coins struck for the Maundy service and related uses in 1937 are of a different alloy composition from those sets struck for inclusion in the 1937 proof sets (Table 40). Unfortunately, it has not been possible to effect a comparable die-axis study between the proof and non-proof Maundy coins dated 1828 and 1822. However, the observation that the die-axis of the twopence dated 1668 is ↑, namely opposite to that of all the subsequent issues of this denomination issued from 1670 to 1684, lends credence to the suggestion that this initial issue is a pattern.[508]

Apart from the matt proof Maundy sets of 1902, other more recent Maundy sets having a matt finish have been claimed as proofs. Thus, such a set dated 1937 is a component of a matt proof set of that year, comprising the sixteen pieces of crown to farthing which, it was claimed, were all struck from sand-blasted dies, it being understood that it was the practice around this time to make a small number of matt proofs, probably in order to facilitate photography.[509] Similar allegedly matt proof sets are also known dated 1951[510] and 1953,[511] both of which are again claimed to have been struck from sand-blasted dies. However, even bearing in mind that the Queen's effigy on the 1953 Maundy set is in very low relief and lacks detail,[512] the four coins in the 1953 matt set, which had been purchased from Seaby in July 1953, exhibit even significantly poorer detail. Furthermore, microscopic comparison of this set with that of a matt proof Maundy set of 1902 shows that on the former the matt finish is relatively very coarse and appears as if it might have been added, by either chemical or mechanical means, *after* the coins had been struck from normal dies. This is also a possibility in the case of the above two matt-finish sets of the previous reign.[513]

Sets of Maundy coins in metals other than 925 and 500 millesimal fine silver are known. Thus, proof sets in gold have been struck bearing three dates. The first of these was 1831, with respect to which a minute of 23 March 1831 (Plate 103) exists.[514] From James William Morrison, the Deputy Master of the Mint, it authorized the Moneyers and Clerk of the Irons to allow William Wyon to strike off a series of proof impressions in fine gold from the dies prepared for striking the 1831 Maundy coins. Although the reference to it is deleted, it would appear from this document that the initial intention had been to strike in gold twelve such sets, a minting which would certainly agree with the recent estimate that from five to ten examples are known.[515] A similar estimate has also been advanced for the number of those sets struck in gold and dated 1838 which are extant.[516] The third issue of a Maundy set struck in gold comprises the probably unique 1953 set (Plate 104) which recently came to light in the saleroom where it appeared with a 'copy letter relating' from Monnaies Numismatic Consultants Ltd and a statement to the effect that it had been purchased for the Norweb Collection in 1960 from Kreisberg. The sale catalogue contained a statement to the effect that the Royal Mint had no record of a reason, if indeed there was one, for the striking of this set but that it was possible that the metal came from the small quantity of gold traditionally and unofficially held by the Mint's Assay Office, thereby perhaps explaining the absence of a formal record. In ascending denominational order, the pieces weight 1.226, 1.843, 2.641 and 2.941g (18.9, 28.4, 40.8 and 45.4 gr).[517]

A very interesting, and probably unique, Maundy set struck in copper is dated 1952 (Plate 105). When this set was sold, as part of the Norweb Collection, in 1985 its source was not recorded, although it was known that it had been purchased for the Collection in 1963, and it was accompanied by a 'copy letter relating' from Monnaies Numismatic Consultants Ltd which confirmed the composition of the component coins as copper, with weights and specific gravities, in ascending denominational order, of 0.6335, 0.9235, 1.3520 and 1.5994 g and 8.94, 8.97, 8.90 and 8.91.[518] The raison d'être for these coins is far from clear. It is interesting to speculate whether, subsequent to the striking of the normal Maundy coins for 1952 and the death of George VI, the blanks for these copper coins were prepared and struck with a view to examining the feasibility, aesthetic and otherwise, of starting to produce the Maundy coinage in copper concomitantly with the introduction of a new obverse punch and the beginning of the new reign. On the other hand, an accompanying note in the sale catalogue states that, 'while there would appear to be no precedence for striking a set of Maundy money on specially-prepared copper blanks, one possible theory could be that the set was originally destined for a specialist manufacturer of cases for Maundy coins in order that the necessary recess measurements could be accurately gauged'. At first sight, this explanation may appear untenable since it would surely have been more obvious, more facile and much cheaper simply to have provided such a manufacturer with a specimen of one of the ordinary Maundy sets which were, and still are, readily available. If thought necessary, in order to eliminate any numismatic value such a set may have had, a simple defacing could have been effected. Indeed, the coins used as templates by the case maker in 1937 consisted of a Maundy penny, twopence and fourpence, all dated 1936, and a threepence, dated 1937, as issued for general currency, all four of which were defaced by having a hole of some three millimetres in diameter drilled through their centres (Plate 106). Perhaps it was thought that a set struck in copper would be similarly worthless, but why take the considerable trouble to make the special blanks in copper and subject them to individual striking rather than simply deface, if thought necessary, an ordinary Maundy set of, say 1952, for use as such templates in 1953? Sadly, no further light could be cast upon this question by the Royal Mint. In reply to an inquiry as to the raison d'être of this Maundy set in copper, and also of that in gold dated 1953, the Deputy Master and Comptroller, Dr D. J. Gerhard, replied 'unfortunately no record appears to have survived here of why these particular sets were made and I fear that in consequence it is not possible to add any information to that given in the catalogue entries. All I can perhaps say is that there have been occasions in the past when base metal strikes were made of gold or silver coins to serve as a pattern for the case maker, so that the suggestion in the catalogue with regard to the copper set may not be altogether naïve', the word naïve having been used in the original inquiry. Subsequently, the Librarian and Curator of the Royal Mint, Mr G. P. Dyer, in reply to a further inquiry commented 'I am sorry to say that there is nothing I can add to the Deputy Master's letter of 16 December 1985. It is, alas, all too often the case that no records were kept of the striking of unusual pieces of this nature'.

VI. THE GROOVE ON THE HEAD OF SOME PRE-1781 SILVER PENNIES

A groove appears on the head of the effigy of several of the pre-1781 George III Maundy pennies (see, for example, Plate 107), of some of the earlier silver pennies, notably those of Anne, William and Mary, and William III, and of a few of the fourpences of these earlier issues. Following an inquiry to him from Mr Harrington E. Manville as to the origin of this defect, and after a subsequent examination of several such impaired coins, Mr G. P. Dyer, the Librarian and Curator at the Royal Mint, arrived at the following conclusions.[519]

That this blemish might be caused through the development of a defect on the head punch from which the obverse dies were sunk is clearly not the case since, according to the die records, only one head punch was employed from 1763 to 1786 (Table 20). Further confirmation of this arises from the examination of pennies themselves which were issued over this period and which all appear to come from a single punch. It therefore follows from the absence of the groove on the pennies of 1781, 1784 and 1786 that there was no such defect on the punch. Furthermore, where the groove is present on the earlier coins it varies considerably in its position from die to die and thus cannot be a feature of the punch.

The fact that the defect manifests itself as a depression on the coins eliminates most of the explanations which assume the use of imperfect dies. A crack in the die or, more seriously, a fragment breaking away from the die would appear as a raised flaw on the coin, whilst rough filing of the surface of the die would similarly produce raised striations on the coin. A depression on the coin could only be caused by a raised flaw on the die and this would be unusual. A defective punch which could have this effect has already been excluded whilst the nature and frequency of the groove itself eliminates the occasional presence of foreign matter on the surface of the die.

It is conceivable that this defect might be the result of damage incurred during the removal of such troublesome little coins from the coining press which may have necessitated the use of some kind of mechanical device and, if used inexpertly, this may have effected some damage to the coin.[520] However, were this to be the case, the damage marks could be expected to vary in extent, and probably also in position, from coin to coin whereas, in fact, the contrary is the case. On those coins that come from the same pair of dies, the groove is remarkably consistent. This consistency also eliminates another possible explanation, namely that it is the result of filing the blank to adjust its weight. Any such filing marks are hardly likely to have been so uniform.

The real explanation for this defect appears to be that it is a consequence of metal-flow problems at the moment when the blank is struck by the obverse and reverse dies. Upon impact, the metal flows outward, upward and downward in order to fill the design on the dies. In these circumstances, for the metal to enter all the interstices of the designs there has to be compatibility between the obverse and the reverse. That is to say, those parts on the obverse which require most metal ought to be opposed on the reverse by areas that require relatively small amounts of metal to form the design, and vice versa. If areas of high relief oppose each other, there may not be enough metal available to fill both the obverse and the reverse designs and the problem is exacerbated if the blank is already too thin for good minting practice. The result of this situation can be ghosting of the kind which is seen on the large bronze pennies of George V struck during the early part of the reign when the combination of a thin blank with a head which required too much metal produced a situation in which the flow of metal into the head left a corresponding hollow, or ghost, on the reverse. Not until an effigy of smaller dimensions was introduced in 1928 was this ghost finally exorcized.[521]

Examination of the appropriately defective silver pennies establishes that the groove on the obverse is opposite the figure 1 on the reverse.[522] This means that the former is normally vertical. However, it would appear to be highly significant that on those specimens examined in which the dies were noticeably offset, the direction of the groove was similarly offset from the vertical and follows the slope of the figure 1. This strongly suggests that there was a basic incompatibility between the obverse and the reverse designs. That the effect is not consistent presents no problem to this above explanation since the extent of the depression is likely to be a function of the form of the dies and, given the somewhat crude nature of die-sinking as practised at that time and the degree of hand filing necessary to finish the dies, there were bound to be variations from die to die. Thus, for example, an obverse die in 1763 produced a defective coin when it was used with one reverse die but a perfect coin when it was used with another.

Examination of post-1780 silver pennies suggests that when a new reverse punch was introduced, apparently in 1781 (Table 20), this problem associated with metal flow disappeared and with it the groove. Certainly, the new punch appears to have a flatter crown and figure 1 than had the previous punch (Plates 66 and 67) and it is reasonable to suppose that this produced a greater degree of compatibility with the existing obverse punch. Nevertheless, it is likely that the elimination of the groove, however desirable in itself, was not the reason for the production of the new reverse punch since this defect had been tolerated for so long and, furthermore, there seems little doubt from the coins that by 1780 the first reverse punch had deteriorated badly and that its replacement was long overdue.

This above explanation for the groove was also accepted by Spink and Son Ltd in their Manville Auction when, appended to the description of lot 359, a Maundy set dated 1780, is the comment that 'the vertical line on the bust of many George III

Pennies (and sometimes other Maundy coins) results from a poorly-designed match between obverse and reverse dies. The thick I on the reverse requires too much metal on these thin coins and there is not enough to fill in the high parts of the obverse – leaving a depression exactly opposite the numeral'.[523]

Dyer's only doubt in relation to the above explanation concerned the sharpness of the groove and, in an attempt to resolve this, some of his colleagues at the Royal Mint agreed, in 1980, to attempt to reproduce it using a pair of modern Maundy penny dies. Unfortunately, in the event this experiment was not performed.

Another defect within the small silver coinage which is a consequence of the mis-matching of the obverse and reverse dies is apparent on some of the small silver denominations of James II, and in particular on some of the threepences. In these, metal theft by the effigy, which is in considerably high relief, results in the central I in the III on the reverse being only weakly or partially struck. The effect is particularly noticeable toward the bottom half of the I (Plate 59), as would be expected since this is opposite to the area of highest relief on the effigy, an area which itself, as a result of its high relief and metal theft by the central I, often lacks sharpness on its most raised details.

VII. BROCKAGES OF THE POST-RESTORATION SMALL SILVER COINAGE

Originally, the term brockage was applied to any mis-struck or broken coin but it is now restricted to a coin which has one side struck in relief, as normal, but with the same design incuse on the other side. They are produced when a coin becomes lodged in one of the dies and the next blank thereby receives impressions from the exposed face of this coin and the opposite die.[524] Obverse brockages are far more common than those of reverses, a simple reflection of the practice of engraving the obverse design on the lower die (the pile) and the reverse design on the upper die (the trussel)[525] and the fact that a coin lodged in the upper die would be more likely to go unnoticed than would one in the lower die.

The earliest reference to such mis-strikes of the post-Restoration small silver coinage relates to three obverse brockages, those of a penny of Charles II's 'fourth coinage, by Simon',[526] a twopence of James II and a penny of William and Mary.[527] Eighty-two years were to elapse before the next report of such a mis-strike appeared in the literature,[528] in this instance that of an obverse brockage of a penny of George I (Plate 108) which was assigned to the year 1727 by comparison of its obverse with those of the seven issues of George I silver pennies, including the two varieties of the 1716 silver penny (Table 27). Of prime significance in this investigation was the position of the stop between GEORGIVS and DEI in the obverse legends of these eight coins. On the pennies of 1716 (varieties A and B), 1718, 1720 and 1723, this stop is located well over to the left side, namely GEORGIVS· DEI,[529] whereas on the three later penny issues, those dated 1725, 1726 and 1727, this stop occupies a far more mid-way position which is only slightly toward the left. Nevertheless, a major difference between the obverse legends of the first two of these latter three pennies and that dated 1727 exists: whereas the former two bear a stop after GRA, this feature is absent on the later coin.[530] It was the almost equi-distance of the stop between GEORGIVS and DEI and the absence of a stop after GRA in the obverse legend of the brockage that initially allowed its assignment to the year 1727, this being further confirmed by a more detailed microscopic comparative examination of it and the obverse of three normal pennies dated 1727.

A current private cabinet[531] also contains several brockages of the small silver coinage, namely those of the obverse of a machine made (type 1D) (pierced) twopence (Plate 109) and a type 2 penny (Plate 110) and fourpence (Plate 111) of Charles II, of the reverse of a 1683 penny (Plate 112) and a 1679 twopence (Plate 113), of the obverse of a penny (pierced) (Plate 114), twopence[532] (Plate 115), threepence (Plate 116) and fourpence (Plate 117) of James II and of the obverse of a twopence of William and Mary (Plate 118). It certainly should be possible to date all but the first of the above obverse brockages using an approach similar to that taken with the obverse brockage of George I as described above.

It is interesting to speculate as to why this particular type of mis-strike occurs. Certainly, brockages of the seventeenth and eighteenth centuries are rare since during these periods coins were produced using hand-fed presses and so, even if the causative lodged coin went unnoticed, such irregularities, when produced, should have been readily observed and thereby picked out. Could it be that specimens were deliberately produced and allowed into circulation or a collector's cabinet as an act of devilment by various of the press operators?[533]

VIII. ECONOMIC ASPECTS OF COLLECTING MAUNDY MONEY

The mintages of the Maundy coinage (Tables 10 and 12) are very low by comparison with those of most other British coins, being similar to those of such coins which are regarded as having considerable rarity and a correspondingly high market value. On this basis, it has been recognized for several years[534] that, as a collector's item, Maundy coins are certainly very undervalued. In fact, they can be regarded as currently representing proof sets of modern British coinage with annual mintages of approximately a thousand and, in connection with the former property, it may be significant that Spink and Son Ltd recently offered, as available for sale from their Bullion Department, Royal Mint FDC British Proof Sets (1970–1982), Royal Mint FDC British Proof Sets (1983–1982 [sic]) and Maundy Sets 1990 FDC.[535] To exemplify the relatively low market value of the Maundy coinage, comparable valuations between various twentieth-century Maundy sets or complete Maundy set types and various of their contemporary coin and proof set issues of similar mintages are presented in Table 43. Similar comparisons are difficult to make between the earlier Maundy sets and selected of their contemporary coins but, considering likewise their low mintages, it is probable that these are also grossly undervalued. For example, the jubilee head sets issued between 1888 and 1892, inclusively, have a total mintage of only 22,440 (Table 12) and it is likely that only a minority of these still exist in FDC condition, yet such a set can be purchased for about £55. Similarly, £250 would purchase an FDC specimen of the 1792 wire money set, of which very few can be available, and a specimen of the 1763 proof Maundy twopence (EF-FDC), of which those extant can probably be counted on the fingers of one's hands,[536] was offered for sale in 1988 for only £375.[537]

The above discussions have been limited to considerations based upon relative availability, as suggested from relative mintages. That the demand for a commodity exerts a very important rôle with relation to its value is of paramount importance[538] and in 1977 it was formally recognized in connection with Maundy coinage.[539] It was

Table 43. Examples of market value[1] comparisons between some twentieth-century Maundy sets and contemporary coins or proof sets[2] of similar mintages

Maundy set (mintage[3])	Comparable coin or set, A (mintage, value)	Approximate rarity[4] of Maundy set relative to A	Calculated value[5] of Maundy set in terms of A	Current market value of the Maundy set
1954–1970 (18,348[6])	1972 proof 25p (100,000, 15)	5.5	82.5	45
1966 (1,206)	—	83	1,245	—
1953 (1,025)	—	98	1,470	230
—	1953 proof set (40,000, 30)	39	1,170	—
—	1934 crown (932, 850)	0.9	765	—
1914 (982)	—	0.95	808	45
1949–1952 (5,280[6])	1951 proof set (20,000, 50)	3.8	190	40[7]
1950 (1,405)	—	14	700	40
1927–1936 (17,362[6])	1927 proof set (15,000, 175)	0.85	149	40[8]
1927 (1,647)	1927 threepence (15,000, 30)	9	270	40
1932 (1,835)	1932 wreath crown (2,395, 180)	1.3	234	40
1934 (1,887)	1934 wreath crown (932, 800)	0.5	400	—
1936 (1,307)	1936 wreath crown (2,473, 250)	1.9	475	60
1910 (1,440)	—	1.7	425	—
1908 (8,760)	—	0.3	75	35

Notes to Table 43: *1*, All the values are quoted in pounds sterling; *2*, All the coins or proof sets were valued as in FDC condition; *3*, Abstracted from Table 12; *4*, Obtained by dividing the mintage figure in the second column by the corresponding figure in the first column; *5*, Calculated by multiplying the number of times the Maundy set is rarer than the comparable coin or proof set by the latter's market value; *6*, Total mintage of the sets between the indicated dates, inclusively (taken from Table 12); *7*, This is an average value and excludes the set dated 1952 which retails for about £60; *8*, This is an average value and excludes the set dated 1936 which retails for about £60.

subsequently reiterated when, with regard to Maundy sets, the statement that 'considering their low mintage, the prices at which they sell are relatively low' was followed by 'this demonstrates that rarity alone does not mean high values – there also has to be a demand. Although Maundy money is purchased by an ardent band of collectors worldwide, their number is small and their interest is mainly in earlier issues'.[540] This situation was illustrated by reference to one of the white leather Maundy purses containing twenty-one Maundy coins, namely five sets plus a penny, which had been presented at the Maundy service in 1977. Although such an item is rarely offered for sale, it failed to find a buyer at a Christie auction in 1988, being sold only later, privately, for £280. Perhaps the small size of the Maundy coinage is detrimental to its market value, public opinion often being so fickle. On the contrary, however, a Maundy set contains *four* coins.

Changes which have occurred from 1953 to date in the retail prices of post-William IV Maundy sets are exemplified in Table 44. As can be seen, these increased steadily during the ten years following 1953. Subsequently, in common with other British coins, they rose very rapidly during the following two years and then remained almost static during the next five years. From 1970, probably because of some recognition of the investment potential in these sets or an increasing numismatic increase in them, their market values, unlike those of other modern British coins, experienced a steady increase over the subsequent six years after which, until 1982, the market again became quiescent. At this latter juncture, a sharp increase in the market values of these sets occurred, caused apparently by overseas investment interests. However, this intense activity was short-lived and, over the past year or two, the prices commanded by such sets have decreased by some ten to twenty percent.

Table 44. Variations between 1953 and 1989, inclusively, of the sterling pound market values[1] of the post-William IV Maundy sets

Year of valuation	Victoria (type 1)	Victoria (type 2)	Maundy sets of: Victoria (type 3)	Edward VII	George V	George VI	Elizabeth II[2]
1953	0.9	1.75	1	1	1.4	1.75	13[3]
1961	1.4	2.25	1.5	1.5	2.25	2.4	4.5
1963	2.75	4.5	2.25	2.25	4	4.25	5.25
1965	12	17	11	11	15	15	20
1970	15	18	—	—	16	16.5	24
1976	25	30	22	22	28	27	35
1989	55[4]	55	40	35[5]	40	40	45

Notes to Table 44: *1*, Value of sets in UNC/FDC condition. The source of the data for the five years quoted from 1953 to 1970 is *Coins, Medals and Currency*, 28 March 1970, p. 6, in which are also quoted the corresponding data for the earlier types of Maundy and small silver coinage; *2*, Excluding the set dated 1953; *3*, This value refers to the 1953 set which is, in itself, a single type issue of 1,025 sets (Tables 12 and 41) currently retailing at about £230 each; *4*, The earlier sets of this type are some 30% more expensive; *5*, Excluding the sets dated 1909 and 1910 which retail at around £45 and £60 each, respectively.

Clearly, the investment potential of the modern Maundy sets has not yet been recognized by, amongst others, the collector of modern British proof sets. By comparison with these latter sets, the Maundy sets, which are also of proof quality, have extremely low mintages (Table 12) and yet they can be purchased for about £45 each.[541] Furthermore, unlike the other British proof coins issued by the Royal Mint, the Maundy coins do have an investment potential. Indeed, because of their very small mintages, even a slight increase in numismatic or investment interest in the Maundy coinage could soon lead to demand outstripping availability, with a resulting significant upward movement in its market value.

A few cautionary notes should be sounded for the purchasers of post-William IV Maundy oddments with the intention of making up Maundy sets. The first of these can be illustrated by reference to the 1953 Maundy distribution when the Queen, being in her twenty-seventh year, presented to each of twenty-seven male and twenty-seven female recipients twenty-seven Maundy pence,[542] namely two sets, each of ten pence face value, plus a threepence and a fourpence. These last two coins often come on the market at a cost of some £20 each and at such prices may appear to be bargains, bearing in mind that the complete 1953 Maundy set would cost about £250. However, the penny and twopence are not likewise available as single pieces. Thus, pre-purchase consideration must be given to the monarch's age in the year by which Maundy oddments are dated. However, such consideration need only be applied when contamplating the purchase of such coins dated after 1908.

Prior to 1909, Maundy sets in their year of issue were readily available through the banks to the general public,[543] a situation which is reflected in their significantly greater mintages (Table 12). In the likely event that some of these sets may ultimately have been split up, probably usually by the spending of the threepence which, apart from its proof-like quality, was indistinguishable from the threepence in general circulation after 1844,[544] this would have relieved, at least partially, the restrictions upon Maundy oddment availability related to the monarch's age. However, the fragmentation of Maundy sets in this way, by the passage of the component threepence into general circulation where, from 1845 to 1926, with the exception of those Maundy sets dated 1847, 1848, 1852, 1923 and 1924, it has a non-proof counterpart,[545] leads to a second caution for the oddment collector since the Maundy penny, twopence and fourpence, having no generally-circulating counterparts, remained unused and often appear for sale as part sets. However, to complete these properly is extremely difficult since the circulated Maundy threepences have usually become impaired and individual uncirculated specimens are very difficult to obtain. Quite frequently such completions are effected using uncirculated specimens of the threepences which were issued for general circulation and which, not being proof-like, are readily detectable in such made-up sets by the experienced eye.

NOTES

1. The fact that this ceremony was held at Rochester has led to the suggestion (Farquhar (1921–22), p. 210) that the pennies so used might well have been from the Rochester Mint where two moneyers, Alisandre and Hunefrei, are known to have produced pennies in 1205 (Plates 7 and 8).
2. See page 25 and Farquhar (1921–22), p. 209.
3. See Section VI of Chapter 2.
4. Hole, p. 38.
5. Wright.
6. *London Journal* (17 April 1731) (quoted in Farquhar (1929–30), p. 226).
7. *GM*, 1 (1731), p. 172.
8. Farquhar (1929–30), p. 226.
9. See page 34.
10. Farquhar (1929–30), p. 218.
11. Charlton, p. 215; (see also note 28 to Table 4).
12. E. E. Ratcliffe, *The Royal Maundy*, fourth edition (London, 1948), p. 25.
13. *Mint Indenture*, 28 November 1770 (filed in the Royal Mint Library, Llantrisant).
14. *Mint Indenture*, 6 February 1817 (filed in the Royal Mint Library, Llantrisant).
15. *The Coinage Act 1870* (filed in the Royal Mint Library, Llantrisant).
16. *The Coinage Act 1971* (filed in the Royal Mint Library, Llantrisant).
17. See note 13 above.
18. See note 14 above.

19. Charlton, pp. 218–19; Hawkins, p. 7; Henfrey, p. 281, Snelling, p. 51.
20. See note 13 above and Appendix 6.
21. Craig (1953), pp. 284–85; (see also Appendix 8).
22. See note 14 above and Appendix 6.
23. See note 15 above.
24. See note 16 above.
25. Unpublished official data from the Royal Mint, made available through the courtesy of its Librarian and Curator, Mr G. P. Dyer.
26. See note 25 above.
27. See note 25 above and Craig (1953), p. 355.
28. See note 25 above.
29. *ESC*, p. 220, footnote 1.
30. See note 25 above.
31. Kelly, p. 1; Seaby, p. 169.
32. See note 25 above.
33. See note 31 above.
34. See note 25 above.
35. Dyer.
36. *Annual Report of the Deputy Master and Comptroller of the Royal Mint for the Year 1946*, p. 1.
37. Craig (1953), p. 357.
38. Previous authors (see, for example, Brooke, pp. 13–15; Craig (1953), pp. 5–7; Oman, pp. 17–20) have made this link only as far back as the introduction of the silver penny by Offa, King of Mercia from 757 to 796.
39. G. P. Dyer, *The Royal Mint. An Illustrated History* (Llantrisant, 1986), p. 5.
40. See note 35 above.
41. See note 5 above.
42. See note 35 above.
43. See note 35 above.
44. See note 5 above.
45. Craig (1953), p. 285.
46. See Appendix 7.
47. See note 35 above.
48. See note 46 above.
49. Jacob, pp. 26, 27 (see also *Royal Mint. Hundred and Sixth Annual Report of the Deputy Master and Comptroller for the Year 1st April 1975 to 31 March 1976* (London, 1976), Appendix XI, pp. 73–76).
50. Denis Healey, M.P., Chancellor of the Exchequer, and thereby Master of the Royal Mint, whose bushy eyebrows (see later in the address) were well characterized.
51. See page 25.
52. Oman, p. 176; Seaby, pp. 66, 67.
53. Seaby, p. 92.
54. Oman, p. 177; Seaby, pp. 66, 67.
55. Oman, pp. 160–61; Seaby, p. 60.
56. Maundy Thursday fell on 8 April in that year (Cheney, p. 159; *OCEL*, p. 945).
57. Craig (1953), p. 124; Symonds (1916), p. 77.
58. Farquhar (1927–28), p. 119.
59. Symonds (1916), p. 78.
60. Richard (later Sir Richard) Martin was the Warden of the Mint (Craig (1953), pp. 123–24).
61. Symonds (1916), pp. 78, 79 (quoted in Farquhar (1927–28), p. 119).
62. Maundy Thursday fell on 19 April in 1576 (Cheney, p. 159; *OCEL*, p. 945).
63. See note 58 above.
64. See Appendix 3.
65. Symonds (1916), p. 79 (quoted in Farquhar (1927–28), p. 119).
66. Cheney, p. 159; *OCEL*, p. 945.
67. See note 58 above.
68. *DNB*; Freeman-Grenville; HBC.
69. Henry Symonds, 'The Mint-marks and Denominations of the Coinage of James I, as Disclosed by the

Trials of the Pyx, with Historical Comments on the Procedure and Notes on the Mint Accounts of the Period', *BNJ*, 9 (1912), p. 227.

70. During this period, the Mint operated on both a silver and a gold standard (bimetallism) which meant that the face value of coinage in either of these metals ought to be its intrinsic value, less only the cost of manufacture and distribution. Thus, a problem arose when the value of the bullion required to produce coins exceeded the face value of the coins which would be produced from it. Naturally, owners of silver, for example, would not sell it below the market value to the Mint which, in turn, would not purchase silver to produce coins at a loss. Only when cheap silver came on the market from military conquests as, for example, in 1702 and 1745 (see pages 117 and 118), did its economical coining take place. At other times, the Mint sometimes had to pay a premium when it purchased the silver necessary to meet its obligation to strike the Maundy coinage.

    Although from 1662 onwards coinage produced in Britain was exclusively of the milled type (see Appendix 8), even by 1696 most of the silver coin in circulation was still of the hammered type and included coins issued as far back as the reign of Elizabeth I. Any new and full-weight coins issued during this period had rapidly vanished from circulation when their bullion value exceeded their face value. The Great Recoinage of 1696 to 1698 proved to be an expensive failure as an attempt to rectify this situation. In fact, the problem was not finally settled until 1816 when Britain adopted gold as its sole standard and silver was reduced to a token coinage (Craig (1953), pp. 186, 256; Kelly, pp. 1–3).

71. Could this have been using the term 'maundye' in a more general sense (see page 1) to include, for example, the King's Dole which was also distributed at Easter (see Section II of Chapter 1)? Certainly, the sum required for the Gift of Pennies in the Maundy distributions of James I would only have utilized a few percent of the total production of small silver coinage indicated in these Mint accounts.

72. This is March 1624 OS and 1625 NS (see Appendix 3) (Farquhar (1925–26), p. 86).

73. PRO, State Papers Domestic, vol. 185, no. 63 (quoted in Farquhar (1927–28), p. 86; see also Farquhar (1927–28), p. 119).

74. James I died on 27 March 1625, eleven days after the Bishop had written this letter, and the coins must have therefore been distributed on the following 14 April (Maundy Thursday) by, or on behalf of, Charles I. Indeed, it is clear that they were charged to the latter's account, in so much as a Signet Office warrant under 'Maundye, 2nd April, 1625' was delivered to the Treasurer of the Chamber to pay £133 6s 8d to the Lord Almoner or his Sub-almoner to be distributed that Easter in Alms (Farquhar (1925–26), p. 87, (1927–28), p. 120).

75. BL Harl. MS 1026.

76. Torr, p. 100.

77. Drake, i, p. 137 and footnote *t*.

78. BL Harl. MS 3795.

79. BL Harl. MS 829 (see also *Mercurius Politicus* (1663)).

80. Dawks' Newsletter (1699).

81. However, these references should not, perhaps, be taken too literally (Wright) in view of the reports that in the 1814, 1826 and 1833 distributions, by which times it was well established that all four denominations of the Maundy coinage were used in the Gift of Pennies, the Gift was nevertheless described as 'seventy-five silver pennies' (*London Interiors*, pp. 47, 48; Ratcliffe and Wright, p. 14), 'small silver pennies' (Squibb) and '68 silver penny pieces' (*John Bull*), respectively.

82. Farquhar (1927–28), p. 125, (1929–30), pp. 235, 238.

83. Farquhar (1925–26), p. 124.

84. See note 64 above.

85. Steward, Ian H., p. 266.

86. Farquhar (1927–28), pp. 122–23, 129.

87. Farquhar (1927–28), p. 122.

88. See note 35 above.

89. See Section III, Sub-section i, of Chapter 3.

90. Hawkins, p. 378.

91. Grueber, p. 130.

92. Nicholls, pp. 26, 27.

93. Graham, pp. 67, 68.

94. Oman, p. 330.

95. *ESC*, p. 216.

96. Salzman, pp. 97, 98, 100.
97. See note 35 above.
98. Pridmore, pp. 273–74. The statement that 'the silver threepence was extended from the Maundy to the public service in August 1839 (Craig (1953), p. 312) would appear to be erroneous.
99. Pridmore, pp. 274–75.
100. See Appendix 8.
101. The twopence dated 1668 has been suggested as being a pattern produced by the die-sinker John Roettiers (see Appendix 1) (Farquhar (1929–30), pp. 231–32; Ratcliffe and Wright, p. 19), although, apparently contrary to this hypothesis, specimens of this coin are fairly common. Alternatively, it has been suggested that it might owe its origin to the fact that the King was 'now about to goe a progress' (PRO, MS T.29, vol. ii, p. 312, 1 September 1668. *Treasury Minute Book* (quoted in Farquhar (1929–30), p. 239)), namely to a requirement for largesse (see Section IV of Chapter 1).
102. Graham, p. 68; Grueber, p. 130; Hawkins, p. 385; Henfrey, p. 277; Oman, p. 333; W. S. Thorburn, *The Coins of Great Britain and Ireland*, third edition, revised and enlarged by H. A. Grueber (London, 1898), p. 76.
103. Namely, for distribution during the celebration of the Royal Maundy.
104. W. C. Hazlitt, *The Coin Collector* (Edinburgh, 1905), p. 252 (see also p. 185).
105. Hocking (1906), p. 116.
106. Brooke, p. 222; Farquhar (1927–28), p. 127; Sutherland, pp. 175, 181.
107. John Conduitt, *Observations upon the Present State of our Gold and Silver Coins, 1730* (London, 1774), pp. 219–20, quoted by Wm. A. Shaw, *Select Tracts and Documents Illustrative of English Monetary History 1626–1730* (London, 1896).
108. *ESC*, pp. 209–10.
109. The second and third edition of the latter work, published in 1819 and 1840, also fail to refer to Maundy sets or Maundy money.
110. See pages 45 and 49.
111. *Calendar of State Papers Domestic*, 5 June 1661, p. 3 (quoted in Farquhar (1929–30), p. 240; see also (1923–24), p. 164).
112. Farquhar (1929–30), p. 240 (see also Graham, pp. 66, 67).
113. Symonds (1915).
114. BL Addit. MS 18759, fo. 63B (quoted in Farquhar (1929–30), p. 232).
115. Peck, p. 605.
116. Farquhar (1921–22), p. 223.
117. Farquhar (1929–30), p. 241.
118. See note 64 above.
119. BL Addit. MS 18759, fo. 100 and 101 (quoted in Farquhar (1929–30), pp. 241, 246).
120. Farquhar (1929–30), p. 242.
121. See Table 24.
122. See page 101.
123. See note 68 above.
124. See note 2 to Table 25.
125. PRO, *Treasury Papers*, vol. xlii, no. 37 (quoted in Farquhar (1912), p. 265).
126. Farquhar (1912), p. 265.
127. See note 35 above.
128. Snelling, p. 54.
129. Craig (1953), p. 416.
130. See note 35 above.
131. Public demand does not seem to have played a decisive rôle in shaping Mint policy since, if they were being struck for general currency (see below in the text), it might be expected that the small coins would have been required in greater numbers than the larger denominations.
132. See notes 80 and 81 above.
133. Craig (1946), p. 31.
134. PRO, *Treasury Papers*, vol. lxxx, no. 105 (quoted in Farquhar (1929–30), p. 246).
135. Craig (1953), p. 219.
136. See note 64 above.
137. Cheney, p. 160; Farquhar (1929–30), p. 247; *OCEL*, p. 948.

138. See Sections I–V of Chapter 1.
139. Farquhar (1929–30), p. 247; Hocking (1914–15), p. 14; Rayner, p. 9; Stewart, Ian Halley. The petition was referred by Mr Lowndes, the Secretary to the Treasury, to Isaac Newton (the Master of the Mint) and other officers of the Mint who reported favourably upon the charges claimed for engraving but disallowed Clerk and Cave's further claim for £90 submitted on account of the 'extraordinary trouble during the coinage'. Clerk and Cave were paid in 1712 (Hocking (1914–15), pp. 14, 16).
140. A letter E under the effigy.
141. Hocking (1914–15), pp. 11, 12, 16; Wingate.
142. Wingate.
143. Burns, Hocking (1914–15), p. 16.
144. Burns.
145. Burns; Stewart, Ian Halley.
146. Craig (1953), p. 210; Sutherland, p. 181.
147. See note 144 above.
148. Farquhar (1929–30), p. 247. There was at the time a great need for small silver in Scotland (Burns).
149. See note 35 above.
150. Farquhar (1921–22), pp. 108, 110.
151. Seaby and Purvey; Farquhar (1921–22), p. 200; Stewart, Ian H., p. 265–66 and Plate XXXVI (see also note 414 to Chapter 2).
152. See note 142 above.
153. Christopher Cove-Smith, Archivist to the National Westminster Bank, personal communication, 1989; Hocking (1914–15), p. 16.
154. See page 42.
155. Farquhar (1929–30), p. 240; Oman, p. 333.
156. Farquhar (1929–30), p. 226.
157. Farquhar (1929–30), p. 240.
158. Craig (1953), p. 198.
159. See note 135 above.
160. See Appendix 9.
161. John Arbuthnot, *The History of John Bull*, edited by Alan W. Bower and Robert A. Erickson (Oxford, 1976), p. 62.
162. Brown.
163. See notes *1* and *3* to Table 29.
164. See Section II of Chapter 3 and note 70 above.
165. G. C. Brooke, 'The Coinage with Roses and Plumes', *NC*, 14, fifth series (1934), pp. 51–56.
166. See note 165 above.
167. See note *7* to Table 8.
168. See note *3* to Table 10.
169. Craig (1953), p. 247.
170. See note 163 above.
171. See note 35 above.
172. *GM*, 1 (1731), p. 172; (see also page 43).
173. *GM*, 24 (1754), p. 188; 25 (1755), p. 183.
174. The twopences and threepences which were used in these distributions were probably dated 1746, being those then most recently available (Table 8).
175. *GM*, 36 (1766), p. 149.
176. *GM*, 37 (1767), p. 190.
177. See pages 47, 58 and 59, respectively, and note 81 above.
178. Dyer and Gaspar (1982) (see also note 70 above).
179. See note 35 above.
180. Craig (1953), p. 246.
181. Seaby, pp. 136–37.
182. Kamen.
183. Seaby, p. 132.
184. Oman, p. 345.
185. See note 182 above.

186. See note 183 above.
187. See note 180 above.
188. Craig (1953), pp. 246–47 (see also notes *1* and *3* to Table 29).
189. Mays, James O'Donald; Seaby, p. 139.
190. See Section IV of Chapter 1.
191. Craig (1953), pp. 246–47; Mays, James; Mays, James O'Donald.
192. Other foreign silver, albeit in only small amounts but including the ecu of Louis XVI of France, the half-dollar of the USA and the half, one, two and four reale pieces, was similarly countermarked (Kelly, pp. 22–24 and Plates I and II).
193. Craig (1953), p. 261; Kelly, p. 22.
194. Kelly, p. 24.
195. Craig (1953), p. 261.
196. See note 194 above.
197. Craig (1953), p. 261; Kelly, pp. 31, 32.
198. Craig (1953), pp. 261–62; Dyer and Gaspar (1982); Seaby, p. 140.
199. Kelly, p. 42.
200. Small quantities of other pieces, such as dollars of the USA and two and four reale pieces, were likewise counterstamped (Kelly, p. 50 and Plate III).
201. PRO, Mint 1/15 (quoted in Kelly, p. 50). The necessary die was sunk from the corresponding punch used in the production of the Maundy penny. This die, bearing only the effigy, was then hardened for use in raising the bust on each dollar individually.
202. Kelly, p. 50.
203. Craig (1953), p. 262.
204. Craig (1953), pp. 262–63; Kelly, pp. 71–81 and Plates IV–VI.
205. Craig (1953), p. 263.
206. Kelly, p. 142.
207. Craig (1953), p. 170.
208. See Sections I–V of Chapter 1.
209. Craig (1953), p. 247; Farquhar (1929–30), p. 248.
210. See note 35 above.
211. *NCirc*, 97 (1989), p. 235, item 4826.
212. These were Philip Stanhope, fifth Earl of Chesterfield (1789–1790), George Townsend, Earl of Leicester (1790–1794) and Sir George Yonge, bart. (1794–1799).
213. See note 35 above.
214. PRO, Mint 6/66.
215. See Appendix 1.
216. Porritt, A., *Matthew Young and his Numismatic Correspondents a Century and a Half Ago* (Newcastle upon Tyne, 1967), p. 6.
217. See note 35 above.
218. Farquhar (1923–24), p. 160. The story goes that, when he was a boy, the late Mr Billy Cotton, the well-known band-leader, was to have been the recipient of such a prize but that it was withheld from him because of his naughtiness. Although this tale is not accurate there is, nonetheless, a ring of truth in it. His son, Mr Bill Cotton, C.B.E., affirmed that his father did not, in fact, go to Westminster School but to St Margarets in Dean Farrer St and he also recalled that his grandmother told him that whereas all her other nine children were given Maundy money [under what was presumably a purely domestic arrangement], because of his general tendency to get himself into hot water, though apparently not for any particular misdemeanour, his father did not receive any.
219. Farquhar (1923–24), p. 159.
220. See note 35 above.
221. John Porteous, Senior Bursar at Gonville and Caius College, Cambridge, personal communication.
222. Filed in the Royal Mint Library, Llantrisant.
223. One journey weight = sixty troy pounds which, at sixty-six shillings per pound = £198. Probably the requirements of the Royal Almonry had been subtracted in this particular instance (Dyer).
224. p. 14.
225. See Section III, Sub-section xi, of Chapter 3.
226. Sir William Grey Ellison-Macartney, formerly the Member of Parliament for South Antrim.
227. See note 35 above.

210 Silver Pennies and Linen Towels

228. These three banks were the bodies who, since they helped the Royal Mint by distributing the general silver coinage to the public, were therefore regarded as being legitimate recipients of the Maundy money.
229. Their distribution as prizes at Westminster School and the occasional supplying of a small number of twopences and fourpences to various colleges of Cambridge and Oxford Universities also continued.
230. Hocking (1906, 1910).
231. Hocking (1906), Appendix III, pp. 422–24.
232. The cases were, until 1910, rectangular (measuring approximately 10 × 3 × 1.5 cm), covered in black, or sometimes dull-red, leather (a red leather-covered case measuring some 10.5 × 4 × 1.7 cm was also occasionally used) and embossed, in gold, with either the royal coat of arms or a crown, accompanied by either MAUNDY MONEY or MAUNDY COIN, usually together with the corresponding year date (Plate 42). During the reign of George V, rectangular cases, but now measuring some 11.5 × 3.5 × 2.2 cm (Plate 43), remained in use although octagonal cases made a brief appearance during this period. All these cases were covered in bright-red leather and were embossed, in gold, with the royal coat of arms and MAUNDY MONEY, as were all subsequent Maundy cases and boxes. However, they were now only dated sporadically. In 1937, case-dating ceased altogether and, furthermore, a red square Maundy money container was introduced. Amongst the first of these were red cardboard boxes (6.8 cm square × 1.3 cm) containing the necessary four recesses. However, such boxes were only of transient issue and the exclusive use of the red leather covered case (some 6.2 cm square × 2.0 cm), all but the earliest of which now also had the Royal Mint Crest imprinted, in black, on the inside of their lids (Plate 44), was soon established. This design remained essentially unchanged until 1989, other than in 1952 and 1953 when sharper-cornered square cases covered in royal blue and maroon leather, respectively, were used. From 1989 onward, the four coins were housed in a hard plastic inset and, to accommodate this, the case was internally redesigned and increased in size (to 7.7 cm square × 2.2 cm) (Plate 45).
233. Wright.
234. This society also financially benefitted from the proceeds of the sale of postcards of, and by, the Royal Mint (Dyer).
235. Balance sheet, 1903–4, of the Royal Mint Self Help Society (filed in the Royal Mint Library, Llantrisant).
236. Balance Sheet 1926–27, of the Royal Mint Provident Society (filed in the Royal Mint Library, Llantrisant).
237. Report and Statement of Accounts of the Royal Mint Self Help Society for 1901–2, quoted in the meeting of its committee held on 25 February 1901 (filed in the Royal Mint Library, Llantrisant).
238. See Table 44 and Section VIII of Chapter 3.
239. Spink and Son, Ltd. Likewise, an increased interest in and consequent demand for the Maundy money occurred in 1932 (*NCirc*, 40 (June 1932), final page) when, after 233 years, the monarch once again became actively associated with the service, George V personally making the Second Distribution which included that of the Maundy money (see page 50).
240. For example, some of the choirboys (Dyer).
241. *Hansard*, 266, no. 77 (19 May 1965), House of Lords, 16/1965.
242. See note 35 above.
243. See notes 35 and 233 above.
244. Also at this time, the striking of VIP proofs was stopped since they had become too valuable to collectors, this action being an example of the manner by which the numismatic market can shape Mint policy (Dyer).
245. These were then, and still are, those who receive sets as fees for their help with, or participation in, the Maundy service (for example, the clergy, choir, Yeomen, maker of the nosegays) and those who receive them from the sets which are made available for distribution at the discretion of the sovereign (one hundred sets being currently struck annually for her household) and the Master of the Mint (Wright), together with those pupils at Westminster School who receive them as prizes in the years when the Maundy service is held in Westminster Abbey (Farquhar (1923–24), p. 160; Wright).
246. See note 35 above.
247. 'Maundy Sets go Scarce', *Coins, Medals and Currency Weekly*, 3 (21 March 1970), no. 48, p. 1.
248. Brian Robinson, 'Mintage Requirements of the Royal Maundy', *Coin Monthly*, (September 1978), pp. 69–71.
249. See note 248 above.

250. See note *4* to Table 11.
251. Appendix VII, p. 64.
252. Brian Robinson, 'A Look at Maundy Mintages', *Coin Monthly*, (April 1978), p. 77.
253. Personal communication to the author.
254. Appendix VII, p. 86.
255. Gaspar, p. 358. The engraving department at the Mint was reorganized in 1705, after the deaths of Roettiers and Harris (see Appendix 1), as a result of which an establishment of three salaried engravers was laid down for die work: a chief (at a salary of £200 per annum) usually carved the obverse matrix or punch, a second (at a salary of £80 per annum) traditionally had responsibility for the production of the reverse matrix or punch, and a probationer (also at a salary of £80 per annum which might during training have been paid to his teacher) did the letters. Although this was only a short career ladder, to scale it took a considerable time. However, all three rungs were endowed with considerable status, and private commissions were often forthcoming, as they were for the Mint's assayers. Thus, these positions were quite lucrative which ensured that the Mint's staff was amongst the best available.

 The policy underlying this establishment was that the Mint should attract young talent from which it should train its own artists and, to encourage this further, it was in 1715 further suggested that each apprentice should be given a few years in Paris. However, the policy failed, the multitudinous mints of the Continent of Europe being a better, and thereby more attractive, school for such craftsmen than the solitary mint in England. Consequently, about half the engravers employed by the Mint in the eighteenth and early nineteenth centuries were recruited from among the Dutch, French, German, Italian, Portuguese and Swiss.

 The heavy work of raising punches from matrices and sinking dies from punches was the business of the smith, or smith-assistant to the engravers, the former sinker of irons (Craig (1953), pp. 201–4).
256. The appearance in the legend of letters such as C, D, E, F, G, O, R and T, which are broken or very weakly struck about their upper part, is probably the result of die-pull resulting from the uncontrolled outward metal flow during the striking process in which collars were not used (see page 195) and not a reflection of a correspondingly damaged letter sunk into the die.
257. It would appear that some of these so-called varieties are incorrectly so referred to since, for example, where an error is the responsible feature, the error-free coin may not exist, or a particular form of punctuation may be the only one that does, or an overdate may be without its non-overdated counterpart.
258. H. E. Manville, 'British Variety Notebook I', *Error-Variety News*, no. 223, pp'. 40–42.
259. It must be borne in mind that the two dies which were employed in the production of the coin may have been produced considerable periods of time apart. Dies were valuable and were used as long as possible, if necessary after overpunching dates, sometimes more than once, on an otherwise functional die (Manville).
260. See Section VII of Chapter 3.
261. Harding (1982).
262. Around a mean of five coins, the percentage variation in the weights of these was from −3.6 to +5.7.
263. Around a mean of five coins, the percentage variation in the weights of these was from −4.5 to +3.5.
264. *ESC*, p. 205.
265. In the H. E. Manville Collection (winter 1989–90). Intradenominational weights of the type 2 small silver coinage of Charles II vary over a range of *c.* 9%. This is because the Trial of the Pyx at this time was based upon the average of *large* batch sampling: it was only later that Isaac Newton attempted to relate such an investigation to individual coins. Even so, the Maundy coinage by 1760 still shows considerable intradenominational weight variation, over some 9, 5, 8 and 4% for the penny, twopence, threepence and fourpence, respectively.
266. *ESC*, p. 191.
267. See note 261 above.
268. See notes *5, 6, 8, 9* and *11* to Table 20.
269. See note *7* to Table 20.
270. See, for example, the punch for the threepence in Plate 46.
271. Hocking (1910).
272. Dyer and Gaspar (1980), pp. 118–19.
273. Gaspar, p. 358.
274. *ESC*; Grueber; Hawkins; Linecar (1977); Rayner; Seaby.

275. See note 68 above.
276. See note 64 above.
277. See note 215 above.
278. See note 100 above.
279. See note 215 above.
280. See note 100 above.
281. pp. 375–78.
282. pp. 94–98 and Plate IV.
283. pp. 120–24.
284. pp. 58–62.
285. The mintmark on the coinage of Charles II is a crown. Those of his hammered issues which are so marked are the last of the British coinage to bear a mintmark since the realm's subsequent coinage includes the date of its year of issue in its designs.
286. These are the last small silver coins which carried the royal coat of arms.
287. A warrant issued on 28 November 1661 ordered that the value of the several pieces being coined under the Indenture of 20 July 1660 should be indicated upon them.
288. *ESC*, Farquhar (1929–30), pp. 226–39; Graham; Grueber; Hawkins; Morrieson; Webb.
289. It is unfortunate that Ruding, whilst illustrating in his Supplement Plate VI ((1840), iii) two Charles II pieces (nos 11 and 12 and both clearly of type 1B) and describing both of them as pennies in the related text ((1840), ii, p. 377), refers to them elsewhere as a twopence and a penny ((1840), ii, p. 336, footnote 2). On this latter authority, which would certainly appear to be erroneous, some early authors (for example, Morrieson, pp. 120–21; Webb, p. 95) have accepted the existence of a twopence of what would be of type 1B, namely without a mark of value or a mintmark, although Morrieson (p. 121) did express some doubt. However, Farquhar ((1929–30), p. 234) is of the opinion that since the type 1B penny exists then why should not a corresponding type 1B twopence?
290. p. 63.
291. Martin Folkes, *Tables of English Silver and Gold Coins* (London, 1763).
292. Webb, p. 95.
293. The bust extends to the bottom of the coin in both the penny and twopence of type 1D and in all four denominations of the Simon's Maundy money, namely the penny and twopence of type 1F and the threepence and fourpence of type 1B. On all these coins, the obverse legend begins from their bottom left (*c*. the 7 o'clock position) whereas on all the other coins of type 1, in which the obverse legend is unbroken in this manner by the bust, the former begins from the top right (*c*. the 1 o'clock position).
294. This is further supported by the uniformity of their die-axes (see Section IV of Chapter 3).
295. Not the dies, as stated elsewhere (*ESC*, p. 198), since hammered and milled dies are not interchangeable (Dyer).
296. Graham, pp. 65, 66.
297. See note 64 above.
298. Farquhar (1919–30), pp. 230–31.
299. See note 289 above.
300. Graham, pp. 59, 73 and Plate VI; Farquhar (1929–30), pp. 227–28, 237 (see also note 287 above).
301. See note 64 above.
302. Farquhar (1929–30), p. 228–29.
303. Morrieson, p. 122; Webb, p. 96.
304. Webb, pp. 95–97 and Morrieson, pp. 121–22, respectively.
305. See note 46 above.
306. Symonds (1915), pp. 346–47.
307. Farquhar (1929–30), p. 239; Symonds (1915), pp. 347–48.
308. Graham, pp. 67, 68.
309. Robinson.
310. See Section IV of Chapter 3.
311. See note 100 above.
312. See note 100 above.
313. See note 215 above.
314. It was in this reign that the practice was established whereby the sovereign's bust in profile is placed in a direction contrary to that of their predecessor. Clearly, in this case, the direction on the milled coinage

of Charles II, being opposite to that on the coinage of this father, was seeking to ignore the interposing Commonwealth pieces.
315. McAlpine and Robinson (1978, 1979).
316. *ESC*, pp. 36–41, 84–87, 129–32, 163–64.
317. Peck, pp. 119–20 and Plate 6.
318. Peck, pp. 126–27 and Plate 7.
319. Craig (1953), p. 166.
320. *ESC*, pp. 184–85, 190, 199, 204–5.
321. Farquhar (1929–30), p. 239.
322. See note 321 above.
323. See Section IV of Chapter 1.
324. Farquhar (1929–30), pp. 231–32; Ratcliffe and Wright, p. 19.
325. Robinson (1986); (see also Section IV of Chapter 3).
326. See note 68 above.
327. See note 215 above.
328. See Section VI of Chapter 3.
329. See note 309 above.
330. See note 68 above.
331. *ESC*, pp. 185, 191. For the fourpence, a specimen of each of the sub-type A and sub-type B obverse punches exist, as does another such sub-type B punch which is broken (Hocking (1910); p. 14): the presence of this broken punch suggests that, in the absence of a matrix, two varieties of the sub-type B bust may be detectable by examination of the appropriate fourpences. Neither punches for the sub-types A and B threepences have survived.
332. *ESC*, pp. 185, 191.
333. *ESC*, pp. 200, 206.
334. The fourpences dated from 1689 to 1691 have a small crown whereas on those dated from 1692 to 1694 the crown is much larger. Evidently, at least two different reverse punches were used during the striking of the fourpence of the joint reign.
335. See note 215 above.
336. See note 215 above.
337. See note 315 above.
338. See note 68 above.
339. See note 215 above.
340. See note 315 above.
341. See pages 106 and 107.
342. See page 106.
343. See note 68 above.
344. See note 215 above.
345. See note 215 above.
346. Rayner, p. 10.
347. See note *10* to Table 26.
348. See note 309 above.
349. *ESC*, pp. 186, 192, 201.
350. *ESC*, p. 168.
351. See note 68 above.
352. See note 215 above.
353. During the second decade of the sixteenth century, several approaches were made by Henry VIII, and by Cardinal Wolsey of the King's behalf, to the Vatican for honours to match the titles already bestowed on the kings of France and Spain. Since Henry had already fought for the Holy See against a schismatic Louis XII and was then very active in the struggle against the spread of Lutheranism, Pope Leo X drew up a short list of possible titles which, once they had been approved by the cardinals, were forwarded to Henry for him to make the most suitable choice. In the event, on 11 October 1521, Leo promulgated his bull conferring on Henry his coveted title Fidei Defensor (Defender of the Faith).

The King believed that the title was made to him and his heirs for ever. However, it had really been just intended for him personally and not the hereditary title which it became. It was an Act of Parliament in 1543, subsequently repealed by Mary Tudor but later restored by Elizabeth I, which joined the title in perpetuity to the English monarchy. To this latter Henry VIII thus gave one of the few additions to its style which have endured the test of time, even if, since 1534, and yet more so since 1559, it has been an incongruous one. Titles such as King (or Queen) of France and of Ireland, and of Emperor (or Empress) of India have all vanished (See Section III, Sub-sections viii and xv of Chapter 3) but Fidei Defensor lives on, regardless of the fact that the faith was that of the Vatican and that the supporting Act of Parliament must be suspect at least to the successors of the original donors, if not to others.

George I was, in fact, the first monarch to put Fidei Defensor among his titles, this being the one legacy which he has left to the succeeding English coinage to date. The fears that Anne might be succeeded by her brother, a Roman Catholic, were set at rest by the accession of this king. It was Sir Isaac Newton, the Master of the Mint, who consequently wanted to add to the King's title 'Defender of the Faith', brought up to date by adding 'of Protestants', an addition which would thus have read 'Fidei Protestantium Defensor'. In the event, the unamended title was put upon the coins for the first time, without change from the form adopted by Henry VIII (Craig (1946), pp. 55, 56, 102; Oman, p. 348). It is an irony that the title originally given the Henry VIII because of his defence of Roman Catholicism was eventually assumed by George I as a result of his defence against this faith.

354. See note 309 above.
355. See note *1* to Table 27.
356. See note 68 above.
357. See note 215 above.
358. See note 215 above.
359. See note 309 above.
360. See page 116.
361. See note 68 above.
362. See note 215 above.
363. See note 309 above.
364. See note *2* to Table 25.
365. See note *1* to Table 29.
366. See note 309 above.
367. See Section IV of Chapter 3.
368. See Section V of Chapter 3.
369. See note 215 above.
370. See note 215 above.
371. See note 255 above.
372. See notes 200 and 201 above and page 119.
373. This clearly accounts for the observation that, for each denomination dated 1800, three or four varieties exist, these being caused by dissimilarities resulting from the use of large and small letters on the obverse and reverse, the presence or absence of stops on the obverse, a variation in the distances between the figures of the date and being with or without hair curling over the left shoulder on the effigy (Hocking (1906), p. 159; Linecar (1978), p. 186; Montagu, pp. 28, 29; *MSCE*, p. 79.). The last variation probably indicates that another obverse punch was produced during the course of this sixteen-year period. However, if this was so, such an action must have been effected after 4 April 1812 (see Table 20).
374. In 1816, Maundy Thursday fell on 11 April (Cheney, p. 160; *OCEL*, p. 950) and thus the required Maundy coinage would have been struck from the type 3 dies dated 1800 since the striking of the bull head coinage, of which the type 4 Maundy coinage is a part, did not begin until the early summer of 1816 (Craig (1953), pp. 284–85).
375. Craig (1953), pp. 284–85. During the intervening years, the Bank of England struck a token silver coinage as an expedient (see page 119).
376. See note 215 above.
377. See note 215 above.
378. The Great Recoinage of 1816 witnessed the introduction of the standard practice whereby the designer or engraver (and, in the case of William Wellesley Pole, the Master of the Mint) would append their initials (on the crown of 1818–1820, Pistrucci appended his whole surname) to the design of a coin, usually on or below the truncation at the neck of the bust. However, in the case of the Maundy coinage, this did not become the practice until the introduction of the type 3 such coinage of Victoria in 1893 (see page 175).

379. This type 4 Maundy coinage is the only small silver coinage which carries the date on its obverse, namely underneath the effigy. All other issues from that of the type 2 of Charles II up to the present time are dated, albeit sometimes in differing places, on their reverses.
380. With the exception of the twopences of 1817 and 1818 (see Table 32).
381. The first standard use of the colon in legendary punctuation on the Maundy coinage: it had appeared, but only sporadically, on the reverse legends of the Maundy coins of Anne (see Section III, Sub-section v of Chapter 3).
382. Dyer and Gaspar (1980).
383. Craig (1953), pp. 270–71.
384. Parliamentary Return no. 322, 13 June 1836, p. 46 (filed in the Royal Mint Library, Llantrisant).
385. *The Mechanics' Magazine* (8 July 1859), p. 21.
386. See page 96.
387. See note 68 above.
388. See note 215 above.
389. See note 215 above.
390. See note 215 above.
391. p. 421.
392. See note 68 above.
393. See note 215 above.
394. See note 215 above.
395. See note 215 above.
396. G. P. Dyer, 'The Small Half-Sovereigns of William IV', NCirc, 86 (1978), pp. 470–71.
397. See note 160 above.
398. See note 35 above.
399. See Section III, Sub-section xi of Chapter 3 and note 89 to the Appendices.
400. See note 68 above.
401. See note 215 above.
402. See note 35 above.
403. Rayner, p. 19.
404. G. F. Crowther, *A Guide to English Pattern Coins in Gold, Silver, Copper, and Pewter from Edward I to Victoria, with their Value* (London, 1887), p. 51.
405. Peck, pp. 415–16 and Plate 33; PRO, Mint 14/14 and 14/15.
406. See note 160 above.
407. PRO, Mint 14/14 and 14/15; G. P. Dyer and P. P. Gaspar, 'A Victorian Groat of 1837', *SCMB* (December 1983), pp. 307–10.
408. These are distinguished by the fact that below the date on the type 1 issue, which was only struck for use in Ceylon, there is a rose with three leaves attached to each side of it whereas for the type 2 issue, which was also current in Britain, this single rose is replaced by a rose, thistle and shamrock joined, to make it uniform with the design on the three larger denominations, the farthing, halfpenny and penny, which too were current in Britain. (Peck, pp. 413–14 and Plate 33). The quarter-farthing (Plate 80), which was only ever issued for use in Ceylon, was consequently solely of the former design type (Peck, pp. 415–16 and Plate 33).
409. Although originally issued for use in Ceylon, the half-farthing was subsequently made current in Britain by a proclamation dated 13 June 1842 (Peck, p. 413).
410. Peck, p. 413; PRO, Mint 14/14 and 14/15.
411. PRO, Mint 14/14 and 14/15; (see also note 89 to the Appendices).
412. Hocking (1906), p. 180; (see also note 89 to the Appendices).
413. Pridmore, pp. 267, 273–74.
414. *ESC*, p. 194.
415. Salzman, pp. 98, 99.
416. Craig (1953), p. 323.
417. *ESC*, p. 194.
418. Dyer and Stocker.
419. Cheney, p. 160; *OCEL*, p. 951.
420. See note 215 above.
421. See note 215 above.

422. See note 35 above.
423. See note 160 above.
424. See note 35 above.
425. Dyer and Stocker; Forrer, 1 (1904), p. 204.
426. See note 215 above.
427. Both jubilee head and old head threepences dated 1893 were issued in that year as general currency.
428. See note 215 above.
429. See note 378 above.
430. See note 215 above.
431. See note 35 above.
432. See note 68 above.
433. See note 215 above.
434. See note 68 above.
435. See note 215 above.
436. See page 97.
437. The silver threepence had been proclaimed as general currency in Britain on 19 May 1845 and, until 1927 (see below in the text), those so struck were indistinguishable in design from those struck for Maundy purposes.
438. Salzman, p. 99 (note 129). It is claimed that 'these coins are distinguished by examining their "ring" – a low note indicates sterling silver whilst a higher note debased silver' (Davies, Peter J., p. 91).
439. See note 35 above.
440. Davies, Peter J., p. 92; *ESC*, p. 219; Salzman, p. 49.
441. The BM on the truncation of the post-1927 Maundy coins of George V is sometimes very poorly defined.
442. Salzman, pp. 41, 45, 49, 53.
443. See note 35 above.
444. Salzman, pp. 45, 53.
445. Davies, Peter J., p. 92.
446. See note 445 above.
447. See note 309 above.
448. See note 215 above.
449. Freeman-Grenville; HBC.
450. Dyer (1973); *ESC*, pp. 73, 110, 123, 157, 182, 196; Peck, pp. 510–12 and Plate 48.
451. See note 215 above.
452. Dyer (1973), p 14.
453. Dyer (1973); Peck, pp. 510–12 and Plate 48.
454. Dyer (1973); *ESC*, pp. 73, 110, 123, 157; 182, 196.
455. Dyer; Dyer (1973), p. 14.
456. See page 50 and Plate 31. In 1952, Elizabeth II similarly distributed her first Royal Maundy on 10 April (Cheney, p. 160; *OCEL*, p. 952) using that year's Maundy coinage which carried the effigy of her late father who had died on the previous 6 February (Freeman-Grenville; *HBC*).
457. See note 308 to Chapter 2.
458. See note 449 above.
459. See note 215 above.
460. See note 35 above.
461. See note 215 above.
462. Pridmore, pp. 268, 274.
463. *ESC*, p. 197.
464. See note 436 above.
465. Craig (1953), pp. 353–54.
466. Freeman-Grenville.
467. See note 215 above.
468. Harding (1979).
469. See note 35 above.
470. See note 35 above.
471. See note 35 above. At least one source ('Maundy Sets go Scarce', *Coins, Medals and Currency Weekly*,

3 (21 March 1970), p. 1) incorrectly assumed what was widely anticipated that the bust on the Maundy coinage would correspondingly change when it stated 'this year's [1970] Maundy coins are the last that will bear the "young" head of Queen Elizabeth II designed by Mary Gillick. Next year the Maundy obverse will be changed to Arnold Machin's "Commonwealth Queen" used on the British decimal coins and all modern Commonwealth issues bearing the Queen's effigy'.

472. See note 35 above.
473. See note 35 above.
474. See note 215 above.
475. Peck, p. xv.
476. Robinson (1986).
477. Farquhar (1929–30), pp. 231–32; Ratcliffe and Wright, p. 19; (see also Section V of Chapter 3).
478. See note 309 above.
479. *NCirc.*, 97 (1989), p. 235, item 4826.
480. An upright die-axis is, indeed, usual for eighteenth-century proofs (Dyer and Gaspar (1980), p. 118).
481. See Section V of Chapter 3.
482. See Section VI of Chapter 3.
483. Similar considerations may also have dictated some of the pre-1888 die-axis reversals noted in Table 42 both between issues and types.
484. See note 35 above.
485. Maundy sets dated 1887 are of type 1 (see Section III, Sub-section xi, of Chapter 3).
486. See note 309 above.
487. See Section III, Sub-section i, of Chapter 3.
488. See note 309 above.
489. Dyer and Gaspar (1980), p. 117.
490. This property was noted over one and a half centuries ago in a eulogy by the contemporary well-known numismatic trader, William Till, on 'the beauty and production of those small pieces termed Maundy money' which reads 'they are finely executed and well struck up. Indeed, in some instances they are like proofs' (*An Essay on the Roman Denarius and English Silver Penny; Shewing their Derivation from the Greek Drachma of Ægina. To which is Appended a List of English and Scotch* [sic] *Pennies from the Conquests, together with their Several Degrees of Rarity; an Account of the Farthings of Queen Anne; a List of Books necessary to the Collectors of Medals; Transactions of the Numismatic Society, with a List of its Members; as well as that of Collectors of Medals in England and the Continent; likewise of Medal Engravers, with an Addenda, etc.* (London, 1837), pp. 107–11.
491. *ESC*, p. 237; Peter Seaby and P. Frank Purvey (editors), *Standard Catalogue of British Coins*, Volume I. *Coins of England and the United Kingdom*, revised sixteenth edition (London, 1978), p. 303.
492. The Maundy sets struck in 1937 for the Maundy service and related uses are of a different alloy composition from those which were struck for inclusion in the proof sets of that year (see note 2 to Table 40).
493. See note 35 above.
494. See note 35 above.
495. See note 35 above.
496. See note 491 above.
497. *ESC*, pp. 10, 218.
498. *ESC*, pp. 10, 216.
499. It is recorded (*ESC*, pp. 10, 187, 193, 202, 208) that only one or two examples of each of the penny, threepence and fourpence and three or four examples of the twopence are known. However, this is clearly an underestimate since, to the author's knowledge alone, a complete set is in the British Museum's collection and another is in private ownership, the Royal Mint's collection contains the penny, twopence and threepence (curiously, the accompanying fourpence is of the non-proof issue) and two further twopences are in private cabinets.
500. Dyer and Gaspar (1980), pp. 117, 122, 124.
501. Dyer and Gaspar (1980), pp. 117, 121–22.
502. Dyer and Gaspar (1980), pp. 118, 124–26.
503. Dyer and Gaspar (1980), p. 118.
504. Montagu, p. 17.
505. With respect to the proofs of 1763, this observation concurs with the general observation that late

eighteenth-century proofs usually have an upright die-axis (Dyer and Gaspar (1980), p. 118).
506. See Section IV of Chapter 3.
507. See Section IV of Chapter 3.
508. See Section IV of Chapter 3 and note 477 above.
509. *Norweb*, p. 147, lot 729.
510. Spink Coin Auction no. 62 (1987), p. 18, lot 464.
511. *Norweb Collection Sale, English Coins – Part 3* (1986). Spink Coin Auction no. 56, p. 130, lot 1169.
512. See page 190.
513. See note 309 above.
514. PRO, Mint 9/114.
515. See note 498 above.
516. See note 497 above.
517. *Norweb*, p. 153, lot 747.
518. *Norweb*, p. 149, lot 733.
519. See note 35 above.
520. During the eighteenth century, the Maundy coinage was struck during the summer months when the handling of the small coins was at its easiest because of the better natural light and the absence of the finger-numbing cold weather of winter (Dyer).
521. Peck, pp. 501–2.
522. Microscopic examination of, for example, those pennies of Anne on which no groove appears nevertheless shows on the effigy a noticeable depression which is opposite to the figure 1 on the reverse (Robinson).
523. Spink Sale no. 9 (1980), p. 52, lot 359.
524. Seaby, pp. xix.
525. Such an arrangement was effected because the lower die lasted much longer than the upper one, which received the main shock of the hammer blow during the minting process, and the obverse design tended to require more skilled and careful engraving (Seaby, pp. xiii, xiv).
526. Type 1D or 1F?
527. *NCirc* (September 1904), column 7850, in which these three coins, as items 7860, 7863 and 7865, were being offered for sale at 1s 6d, 1s 6d and 3s 6d, respectively.
528. Brian Robinson, 'A Maundy Penny Brockage of George I', *NCirc*, 94 (1968), pp. 329–30.
529. A feature they also share with the twopences, threepences and fourpences dated 1717, 1721, 1723 and 1727 and the twopence dated 1726.
530. A similar stop appears on the pennies dated 1716 (varieties A and B), 1720 and 1723 but not on those dated 1718.
531. The H. E. Manville collection (winter, 1989–90).
532. Is this the specimen which was offered for sale in 1904 as item 7863 in note 527 above?
533. See note 35 above.
534. Robinson (1977), pp. 75–80.
535. *NCirc*, 98 (1990), p. 169, items 3565, 3566 and 3567 (at £5, £10 and £65, respectively, plus 15% VAT).
536. *ESC*, pp. 10, 202; Trowbridge, p. 23.
537. *NCirc*, 95 (1987), p. 305, item 6646.
538. Demand certainly surfaced at the sale of the jewellery and other precious artifacts which had belonged to the late Duchess of Windsor when a Maundy set dated 1936 (the year in which her late husband, as the then uncrowned Edward VIII, had distributed the Royal Maundy) was sold for 13,200 Swiss francs, some one hundred times the £55 or thereabouts which the coins are worth (Sacra Moneta).
539. Robinson (1977), p. 80.
540. Andrew Moore, 'Mint Attraction', *Weekend Telegraph* (18 March 1989), p. 3.
541. Purchasers of the Maundy sets in their year of issue have to pay a premium for the privilege of owning a set of the current Maundy money, since over the subsequent two years their market value depreciates to a stable figure some thirty-five percent below their original purchase price.
542. See pages 65 and 134.
543. See page 130.
544. See page 168.
545. See note 544 above.

APPENDICES

APPENDIX 1

Engravers and Designers of the Pre-1729 Post-Restoration Small Silver Coinage and of the Maundy Coinage

Boehm; Sir Joseph Edgar[1]

Sir Joseph Edgar Boehm was an artist of considerable reputation. Of Hungarian nationality, he was born on 4 July 1834 in Vienna where his father, Josef Daniel Böhm, a gem engraver and one of the foremost European medallists of his day, was director of the Imperial Mint. In 1848, Böhm junior came to England where he worked for three years, mainly at the British Museum. This was followed by periods of study – he originally trained as a medallist – in Italy, Paris and Vienna before he settled in London in 1862 and took out letters of naturalization three years later.

As a sculptor he was widely sought after and his works are many and widespread. In 1881 he was appointed by Queen Victoria as Sculptor in Ordinary, in 1882 he was made a Royal Academician and he was created a baronet in 1889.

A gentlemanly artist, his career enjoyed unbroken success until 1887 when his effigy of the Queen on the jubilee head coinage was the subject of widespread adverse criticism, although his medals commemorating the jubilee in gold, silver and bronze are of somewhat superior work. It has been suggested by one who knew him well that the widespread hostility to the effigy on the coinage proved fatal: he died very suddenly in his studio at 25 Wetherby Gardens, London, on 12 December 1890.

Bower; George[2]

George Bower (or Bowers) was a British medallist who worked in London from 1650 to 1689. In January 1664 he was appointed Engraver to the Royal Mint and Embosser in Ordinary, an office which he held until his death on 1 March 1689/90.[3]

He worked mainly on the production of medals and is not known to have engraved any dies for the coins of either Charles II or James II. It would appear, however, that he was responsible for both the obverse and reverse of the half-guinea and tin halfpenny and farthing of 1689 and the type A busts of William and Mary on the small silver coinage.

Briot; Nicholas[4]

Nicholas Briot, a Frenchman and celebrated coin-engraver and medallist, was born at Damblein in Lorraine in about 1579. He was Chief Engraver at the Paris Mint from 1606 to 1625. As early as 1615 he submitted to the authorities at this mint a new method which he had invented or improved for the striking of coins and medals 'which made them more perfectly round than they had ever been before'. However, he became disgusted with the treatment which he subsequently received, when his efforts to persuade the authorities to introduce this machinery were all in vain, and this, together with the fact that he was being hard-pressed by his creditors, caused him to flee to England at sometime between 16 September and 31 October 1625. He was subsequently employed at the Mint, at least from 1628, when he engraved coin dies for Charles I, and on 27 January 1633 he was appointed as Engraver General in England. Between 1635 and 1639 he also held the office of Master of the Mint in Scotland.

It has been said that during the Civil War he retired to Oxford where he died in about 1646. However, it would appear that he returned to France in 1642 or 1644, whence he returned to England very soon afterwards. It is suggested that from 1642 to 1646, in his capacity as Engraver, he followed Charles I to York and to Oxford during the Civil War. Indeed, at the Restoration, the name of his widow, Esther Briot, was one of those which were ordered to be placed on the list for relieving the servants of Charles I, the sum of £3,000 having been due to her husband at the time of his death.

Brock; Sir Thomas[5]

Sir Thomas Brock was a British sculptor. He was born in 1847 at Worcester, where his father was a decorator, and was educated at the Government School of Design in that city. He came to London and studied at the Royal Academy where he was awarded both silver and gold medals. He became a pupil, and later an assistant, of J. H. Foley, the sculptor and, after the latter's death, completed the numerous works unfinished by his predecessor.

Brock's career as a sculptor was long and distinguished. In the Royal Academy Exhibition of 1898 he had no less than five sculptures, on 16 January 1883 was elected an Associate of the Royal Academy and in 1891 was made a Royal Academician. He was the designer of the British coinage introduced in 1893 and of the head of Queen Victoria for the official Diamond Jubilee Medal of 1897 issued by the Royal Mint.

Bull; Samuel[6]

Samuel Bull was British and one of three engravers who were hired in 1695 by Henry Harris, the Chief Engraver at the Mint, to assist with the pressure of work brought about by the Great Recoinage of 1696 to 1698, although whether Harris paid his wages, unlike the case with John Croker[7], is not recorded. At Christmas 1698 he was appointed an Assistant Engraver (or Probationer Engraver) at the Mint. In this capacity, and before his death in 1726, he actively assisted John Croker in his work as Chief Engraver, cutting the reverse dies for a number of medals executed by the latter.

Chantrey; Sir Francis Legatt[8]

Chantrey was born near Norton, then in Derbyshire, on 7 April 1781. His father, who died in 1793, was a carpenter and small farmer who lived at Jordanthorpe, near Sheffield. The young Chantrey received his primary education at the village school and was first employed as a grocer in Sheffield. In 1797 he was attracted to the shop window of a carver, named Ramsay, in Sheffield and subsequently became apprenticed to him for seven years. Ramsay was also a dealer in prints and plaster models and Chantrey soon showed artistic tastes which were encouraged by J. Raphael Smith, the mezzotint engraver whom he met at Ramsay's.

Chantrey began his artistic work by drawing portraits and landscapes in pencil and was taught carving in stone by a statuary. For the latter part of his articles he made a composition with Ramsay, near whose shop he hired a room where he spent his leisure time studying alone. By 1802 he was executing portraits in crayons and miniatures in Sheffield at from two to three guineas each. Also in that year he moved to London and went to the Royal Academy where he was allowed to study for a limited time although he was not admitted as a student. Whilst in London he continued to make a living from the painting of portraits, for which he was now charging twenty guineas each.

In 1803 he was also employed in wood carving and, from the following year onward, he appears to have devoted himself almost exclusively to sculpture, his first commissions coming from friends in Sheffield. In 1807 he wrote 'orders increase and marble costs money' but then his financial struggles, if any, came to an end when in that year he married his cousin, a Miss Wale, who brought him considerable property. Consequently, he moved to a house of his own, built two more houses and a studio and laid in a stock of marble. His fame as a sculptor increased, as did his fees for commissions. He successfully competed for the statue of George III for the Guildhall and in 1822 he was paid, at the King's insistence, 300 guineas for his bust of George IV. His busts included those of most of the distinguished men of his time and it was to portrait sculpture that Chantrey owed his fortune and fame. The latter was augmented greatly by the grace and tender sentiment which he exhibited in his treatment of children, the most celebrated of all his works probably being the group of sleeping children in Lichfield Cathedral. He made graphic records in sketch-books of his travels in Britain and Europe, it probably being the contents of one of these books which furnished the contributions by Chantrey to Rhodes' *Peak Scenery*, published in 1818, with engravings by W. B. and G. Cook.

Chantrey received many honours. In 1815 he was elected an Associate, and in 1818 a full member, of the Royal Academy, to whose interests he was always devoted. He was an honorary D.C.L. of Oxford University and an honorary M.A. of Cambridge University and was elected to fellowship of both the Society of Antiquaries and the Royal Society. In 1835 he was knighted by William IV.

It was at the height of his fame and popularity that he died suddenly, of a heart attack, on 25 November 1842 and, in keeping with his life long affection for Sheffield, was buried in his native village in a tomb previously prepared by himself. He died childless and left the reversionary interest of the bulk of his considerable property, after the death of his widow, to the Royal Academy to make some provision for its president and to found the fund, known as the Chantrey Bequest, thereby establishing a national collection by the purchase of the most valuable works in sculpture and painting executed in Great Britain by artists of any nation.

Croker, John[9]

Henry Harris, who had been at the Mint in a junior capacity since the time of Charles II, was appointed as Engraver in April 1690 consequent upon the death of George

Bower[10] on 1 March in that year. He was appointed Die Engraver in February 1697 when, finding himself unable to carry out the associated work, he hired Johann Crocker, a German jeweller, though never paying him any wages.

Crocker had been born in Dresden on 21 October 1670. His father, a wood carver and cabinet maker to the Electoral Court of Saxony, had died when his son was very young but his mother ensured that the boy received a sound education. Ultimately, his godfather, a near relation, took him as an apprentice into his business of a goldsmith and jeweller in Dresden. In his leisure hours, the young Crocker worked at medal engraving and attempted to improve his knowledge of drawing and modelling. At the termination of his apprenticeship he practised as a jeweller in most of the large towns in Germany, then he came to England via Holland toward the end of 1691. In England he engaged himself to a jeweller, learnt die-sinking and eventually began to work exclusively as a medallist. Following the death of Harris, sometime before 12 October 1704, Johann Crocker, or John Croker as he was by then calling himself, was appointed on 7 April 1705, from a list of five candidates, as Chief Engraver at the Mint, a position that he was to hold until his death in London on 21 March 1740/1.

Johann Crocker's change of name to John Croker was related to his naturalization, by a special Act of Parliament. This latter was necessary since, as an alien, he would have been debarred from office at the Mint by a statute[11] passed earlier to keep foreigners in general, and William III's Dutchmen in particular, out of well-paid positions. As will be seen in later entries in this Appendix, other ploys were also used to overcome the effects of this Act and thereby permit the Mint to recruit from Europe many of its engravers, necessary since the art of coin die engraving was not then practised to any great extent in Great Britain.

De Saulles; George William[12]

George William De Saulles, whose paternal grandfather was a Frenchman, was born in Birmingham in 1862. He was trained at the Birmingham School of Art where he won several prizes and a scholarship. Nevertheless, he did not take up the latter but became apprenticed to Wilcox, a Birmingham die-sinker. Upon completion of his apprenticeship, De Saulles went to London in 1884 to work for John Pinches but four years later he returned to Birmingham to work for the medallist Joseph Moore. Learning that the post of Engraver at the Royal Mint had become vacant with the death of Leonard Charles Wyon,[13] De Saulles was recommended for the position by Thomas Brock.[14] He was ultimately appointed at the end of 1892 after a trial period and held this appointment until his sudden and unexpected death in 1903.

De Saulles' death coincided with the demise of the post of Engraver at the Royal Mint. This latter change resulted from the introduction, just before the commencement of the reign of Edward VII, of two modern Janvier reducing machines which were imported from Paris and which rendered unnecessary the practice of engraving any part of the steel dies by hand. Previous reducing machines in use at the Mint had been rather primitive and, until these new machines were acquired, it had not been practical to accept designs for coins from persons other than engravers employed at the Mint. However, from the beginning of the twentieth century, the title of Engraver became something of a misnomer and Designer is, strictly speaking, more correct.

Gillick; Mary[15]

Mary Gillick was the daughter of Thomas Tutin of Nottingham. In 1905 she married Ernest Gillick, A.R.A. She studied sculpture at the Royal College of Art and her works include several bronze bas-relief portraits and bronze portrait memorials and medals for the Royal Mint, the Royal Society, the Physical Society, and other institutions. She died on 27 January 1965.

Gray; George Edward Kruger[16]

Born on 25 December 1880 in Kensington, the son of Edwin Charles Kruger, a merchant of St Helier, Jersey, and his wife Frances Hester, the daughter of John Dafter Harris of Bath, he did not assume the surname Gray until his marriage in 1918 to Audrey Gordon, the daughter of the Rev. John Henry Gray. The young Kruger was educated at the Merchant Taylors' School, Great Crosby and, afterwards, at the Bath School of Art where he won a scholarship to the Royal College of Art. From 1905 he exhibited water-colours at the Royal Academy, his earlier such works being landscapes, flower studies and portraits.

However, it was not until after World War I, during which he served with the Artists' Rifles and the camouflage section of the Royal Engineers, that he gained positive success in the types of designing for which he became known. In 1923, a group exhibit of coinage at the Royal Academy included casts from original models of the half-crown, florin and farthing pieces which he had executed for the Union of South Africa. Thereafter, he was widely employed as a designer of coins and seals. As part of this, he was responsible for the reverse designs of the 500 millesimal fine silver coinage of George V introduced in 1927 and for the reverse designs of the 500 millesimal fine silver, introduced in 1937, and a large majority of the later cupro-nickel coins of George VI.

He also designed and executed a large number of stained-glass windows, was prominent in heraldic designs and effected various miscellaneous artistic commissions. His success as a designer was securely based on his knowledge of heraldry and of the materials in which he worked.

Kruger Gray died at Chichester on 2 May 1943 and was survived by his wife and the one son of his marriage.

Machin; Arnold[17]

Arnold Machin was born in 1911, the son of William James Machin of Stoke-on-Trent. He was educated at the Stoke School of Art, the Derby School of Art, and the Royal College of Art where he was awarded the silver medal and travelling scholarship for sculpture in 1940. Two of his works in terracotta, St John the Baptist and The Annunciation, were purchased by the Tate Gallery in 1943. From 1951 to 1958 he was a tutor at the Royal College of Art and from 1958 to 1967 he was a master of sculpture at the Royal Academy School. He was elected an Associate of the Royal Academy in 1947 and a Royal Academician in 1956 and was awarded the O.B.E. in 1965.

Mackennal; Sir Bertram[18]

Mackennal was born in 1863 in Melbourne, the son of John Simpson Mackennal, also a sculptor. After studying in Paris, he was to become one of the leading sculptors of his day. He was elected in 1909 an Associate of the Royal Academy, in 1912 a M.V.O. and in 1922 a Royal Academician. He was knighted in July 1921. He died on 10 October 1931.

Maklouf; Raphael[19]

Raphael Maklouf, a sculptor in bronze and a painter, was born in Jerusalem on 10 December 1937. From 1953 to 1958 he studied art at the Camberwell School of Art, under Dr Karel Vogel. Portraits by him have included those of the Queen and of the Duke of Edinburgh.

Merlen; Jean Baptiste[20]

Jean Baptiste (Johann Baptist) Merlen was a medallist and coin engraver of Flemish origin but apparently came over to England from France, where he had been engaged in medal work under the First Empire. He was appointed, at the request of Benedetto Pistrucci, as his assistant on 11 February 1820. The aliens' law (Statute of Limitations[21]) was in this instance evaded by calling his employment temporary and paying him £4 4s by the week instead of £200 by the year. He did not find his period of employment at the Mint an altogether happy one, partly because he considered that he was underpaid and partly because he became caught up in the feudings between Pistrucci and the Wyons,[22] he, too, occasionally having disagreements with both these parties. He retired in 1844 at the age of seventy-five years.

Ochs; John Ralph junior[23]

Johann Rudolf Ochs (or Ocks) senior was a Swiss gem, and coin, engraver. He was born in Berne in 1673 and became employed as an Assistant Engraver at the Tower Mint from 1727 until 1748 although he had worked for the Mint previous to this. His son, also Johann Rudolf, was born in 1704.

Ochs junior became an employee of the Mint and, indeed, whilst in the same official position that his father had held, he was to design and engrave the dies for both sub-types A and B of the type 1 Maundy money of George III. Hawkins states that Ochs junior held a position at the Mint for seventy-two years[24] which means that, since he died at the age of eighty-four years, he would have first been so employed when he was twelve years old: possibly some of the father's years at the Mint were credited to the son. However, the son certainly served the Mint for some fifty years, during the first twenty of which he was not on the establishment but after which he was appointed as Third Engraver, on 1 December 1757, and Second Engraver in about 1768. When, in 1779, he was at last offered the post of Chief Engraver he declined it, since he felt that at seventy-four years of age he was scarcely equal to it, and Lewis Pingo[25] was appointed to the position.

By 1786, Ochs was over eighty years old and totally unable to discharge the duties of an engraver. In the following year he was retired and granted a pension which was apportioned between that to which he was entitled as the former Second Engraver and that to which he would have been entitled as the former Chief Engraver. Ochs died at Battersea in 1788, presumably in early July because his pension was only paid until the fifteenth day of that month, and his Will was produced in the Mint Office on 5 August 1788.

Paget; Thomas Humphrey[26]

Thomas Humphrey Paget was born in 1893 at Croxley Heath, near London. It was small wonder that he soon became attracted to art, since his father was a well-known painter and illustrator and two uncles were also artists. Ultimately, he studied at the Central School of Arts and Crafts and at the Royal Academy Schools where he was awarded the Landseer Scholarship. This sound training was interrupted by naval service during World War I but, following demobilization, he found work as a sculptor and a short time later returned to the Central School as a visiting teacher.

In 1922, the newly-appointed Deputy Master of the Mint, Sir Robert Johnson, distressed at the poor state of numismatic art in Britain, secured the establishment of a standing advisory committee which, as part of its remit, was to assist him in locating and training young artists interested in this specialised and difficult art form. Among the most active members of this committee was Prof. Derwent Wood of the Royal College of Art and it was he who, in 1923, first introduced Paget to the Mint by including the latter's name in a list of artists to be asked to design a medal for the British Empire Exhibition at Wembley. The consequent invitation from the Mint was readily accepted by Paget but the subsequent competition was won by Percy Metcalfe, another of Derwent Wood's young artists. However, in December 1923, and again at Derwent Wood's suggestion, Paget was once more invited, along with other artists, to submit designs for a medal to be awarded to nurses at the Bristol Royal Infirmary. This time he was the successful candidate.

Following his success with the Bristol medal, Paget concentrated almost entirely on this type of work and produced, in the process, a long line of distinguished medallic portraits. Nevertheless, it was to be some years before he established himself as a senior member of the Royal Mint's panel of artists. In the meantime, his commissions were of a rather routine nature whereas the more important work, especially on new coinages, went to Kruger Gray[27] and Percy Metcalfe.

In fact, Paget secured his reputation as a result of one of his private commissions when, in 1935, he was asked to design a medal for the Honourable Company of Master Mariners and for the obverse of this he produced a fine portrait of the Prince of Wales who was Master of the Company. This portrait was widely admired and Paget was asked by the Deputy Master of the Mint to prepare a low-relief version as a possible effigy for coinage. His initial attempt was disappointing but in the late summer of 1936, by which time the Prince had become Edward VIII, a much improved model was approved for use on the coins and medals of the new reign. His design based on the Golden Hind was recommended for the reverse of the new halfpennies.

Following the Abdication on 10 December 1936, most of this work was scrapped and an urgent situation resulted which dictated that Paget alone should be commissioned to prepare the uncrowned effigy for the coins and medals of George VI. This he did brilliantly, in little more than a month producing what has been described as the classic coinage head of the twentieth century. His reputation was assured but the commissions which should have now come his way were frustrated by World War II.

At the onset of the War, he moved out of London and settled in Broom Cottage, Burwash Common, Sussex. In 1942 he married Winifred Turner, a well-known sculptor, colleague at the Central School and the daughter of Alfred Turner, R.A., a former member of the above-mentioned Royal Mint Advisory Committee.

At the end of the war came a highly productive period for Paget in the production of designs for a wide range of seals, medals and coins. However, not all was success. The portrait of the Queen by Mary Gillick[28] was preferred for the coins of the new reign and the obverse by Arnold Machin[29] and Christopher Ironside's reverses were chosen for the decimal coinage. Nevertheless, his last major commission, a medallic portrait of the Duke of Edinburgh, ranks as his best.

Paget died in April 1974. He had been a large, shy and kindly man with a natural reserve, not least apparent in his lack of active involvement, at least in his later years, in any of the artists' societies. He felt keenly the lack of official recognition which he thought his work had deserved and insisted that had he been a Royal Academician he would have received a knighthood for producing the two effigies for the United Kingdom coinage in the space of only a few months. However, at the time he was told that he was too young and he found small consolation in the award, some years later, of an O.B.E.. The idea that he signed his work HP, although he was Tom to his family and friends, because Sir Humphrey Paget would sound better when the expected honour came, appears to derive from a family joke in his youth.

Pingo; Lewis[30]

Thomas Pingo came to England sometime between 1742 and 1745. He was appointed as Assistant Engraver at the Mint in 1771. Of his several sons, Lewis, who had been born in 1743, was ultimately apprenticed to his father at the Mint and, after only a few further years, he was appointed to succeed his father upon the latter's death in 1776. Then, on 30 December 1779, he was appointed as Chief Engraver to succeed Richard Yeo who had held the position for eleven years before his death earlier in that year: John Ralph Ochs junior[31] was initially offered the post but at the age of seventy-four years he felt that he was scarcely up to it.

Other relatives of Ochs and Pingo were, indeed, employed at the Mint in subordinate posts. This, together with the numerous occasions that sons followed their fathers into engravers' positions at the Mint, examples of which can be found in the Roettiers, Ochs, Pingo and Wyon families,[32] suggest a degree of nepotism.

Lewis Pingo died at Camberwell on 26 August 1830.

Pistrucci; Benedetto[33]

Benedetto Pistrucci, an Italian gem and cameo carver, was born in Rome on 29 May 1784. He left that city in 1814 to seek his fortune in Paris whence he fled to England prior to the approach of the allied armies. By 1817 he was settled in the village of Brompton. When Thomas Wyon junior, the Chief Engraver, died on 22 September 1817, William Wellesley Pole, the Master of the Mint, blind to the home talents inherent in the Wyons,[34] wished to appoint Pistrucci to the post. However, he was unable to do so since the position was effectively banned to aliens by statute.[35] Consequently, the post was nominally left vacant but Pistrucci was paid and given an official residence.

Even though he received a handsome income from the Mint and private commissions, the situation regarding his terms of employment soon became a source of contention for Pistrucci, who claimed that he had been led to believe that he would be ultimately formally appointed as Chief Engraver, and caused him largely to disregard the duties for which he was paid over the next thirty years. His appointment as Chief Medallist, on 15 January 1828, failed to defuse the situation, no doubt because William Wyon was concomitantly appointed as Chief Engraver. In October 1839, Pistrucci left for Rome at whose mint he had been appointed Chief Engraver. However, since the salary he received was too low for him, after eighteen months he returned to England in 1841 and to the Mint where he continued to engrave dies for medals.

In this work, however, as in all his work on both medals and coins, some would claim that he ignored the technical aspects of coin and medal making whilst others would agree that he was technically brilliant and innovative. In practice, much of his work was of no use although it received international recognition for its artistic quality. Around this time, the Mint had become concerned about the expense of employing him and he had ceased to live in his Mint house by 1849 when he had moved to Fine Arts Cottage, Old Windsor. He subsequently moved to Flora Lodge, Englefield Green, near Windsor, where he died on 16 September 1855.

Rawlins; Thomas[36]

Thomas Rawlins, medallist and playwright, was born about 1620. He appears to have received training as a goldsmith and gem-engraver and to have worked under Nicholas Briot[37] at the Mint. An ardent royalist, he served both Charles I and Charles II. His first dated medal is of 1641 and throughout the Civil War he worked on the production of the King's coins and medals, having followed Charles I to Oxford at the War's outbreak. He was formally appointed Chief Engraver of the Mint in March 1647/8,[38] evidently after the death of Briot, but in 1649, following the death of Charles I, he appears, understandably, to have fled to France. However, 1652 saw his return to England where, until the Restoration, he earned a precarious livelihood and had a somewhat fraught time during the Commonwealth. Nevertheless, at the Restoration he was reinstated as Chief Engraver at the Mint, the pro-Commonwealth Thomas Simon[39] being thereby demoted to one of the Engravers of the King's arms, shields and stamps. Rawlins died in 1670.

Roettiers; James, John and Norbert[40]

Jan (John) Roettiers, Roettier or Rotier, as his surname has been variously spelt, was born on 4 July 1631. He was the eldest son of Philip, a medallist and goldsmith in Antwerp, although it is doubtful if Jan was born in that city. He became a medallist and stonecutter and his earliest known medals are of 1660, or possibly 1656.

In 1661, he and his brother Joseph, and later his other brother Philip, were invited to England to work at the Mint as engravers by Charles II who had become acquainted with them during his exile. John Roettiers' competition with Thomas Simon in early

1662, referred to in the next entry of this Appendix, resulted in the former being made one of the Chief Engravers at the Mint with the responsibility for the preparation of the new milled coinage.[41] From then on for nearly half a century the Roettiers family was to dominate English coin design.

John Roettiers was undoubtedly one of the best engravers ever employed at the Mint. Two of his sons, James and Norbert (altogether he had three sons, his eldest, John, not appearing to have been a medallist, and five daughters) followed in their father's profession and both became Assistant Engravers at the Mint. Indeed, when their father, whilst still Chief Engraver, became ill with a muscular disease, possibly *paralysis agitans*, which affected him in both hands in 1688–1689, he was compelled to delegate most of his work to his two sons. Possibly, too, he made the most of this affliction to avoid working for William and Mary, regarded as usurpers by the Roettiers family who had a particular loyalty to the Stuarts. Indeed, their Jacobite sympathies led to Norbert fleeing to France in 1695, where he went to work with his uncle Joseph at the Paris Mint, and to James being dismissed in 1697: he died the following year. John Roettiers continued to occupy the Graver's House at the Tower at least until after he was removed from office about 1697. He then moved to Red Lion Square. Toward the end of his life he became very ill, among his ailments being a lameness in his right hand. He died in 1703 and was buried in the Tower of London.

The relevant portions of the genealogy of the Roettiers family have been conveniently summarized in diagrammatic form.[42]

Simon; Thomas[43]

Probably the most celebrated English medallist of the seventeenth century and generally recognized as the greatest artist among all those who have engraved dies for the British coinage, Thomas Simon, or Symon, Symons or Symonds, as his name is variously spelt on documents of that century (his surname has also appeared as Simons, Symond or Simonds in the numismatic literature), but Simon as he himself spelt his name on his famous Petition Crown of 1663, is of uncertain date of birth. There is no confirmation of the tradition that he was a Yorkshireman. However, it is known that he was baptized on 26 April 1618 at the French Protestant Church in Threadneedle Street and that, like his father, he sought a wife in the Channel Islands, marrying Elizabeth, daughter and sole heiress of Cardin Fautrant of Guernsey.

When he was aged about fifteen and a half, he was apprenticed to George Crompton, a London goldsmith, for an eight-year term beginning on 30 August 1633. However, some two years later he transferred to the service of, and commenced a new seven-year apprenticeship with, Edward Greene, also a member of the London Goldsmiths' Company but, more significantly, the Chief Engraver at the Mint. This introduced Simon into service at the Mint where he received instruction from Nicholas Briot.[44]

On Greene's death at the end of 1644, the post of Chief Engraver was granted by Parliament jointly to Edward Wade and Thomas Simon, by letters patent dated 4 April 1645. Wade died shortly before the end of 1648 and it was thus that when new appointments were made to all the Mint's posts after Charles I's execution, Thomas Simon became the new Commonwealth government's sole Chief Engraver, his patent being dated 25 April 1649. He received a fresh grant of the position of sole Chief

Engraver for the Mint and Seals from Oliver Cromwell on 15 February 1655, held jointly with that of Medal Maker for the State, his tenure for the posts being confirmed by letters patent issued on 9 July 1656.

His work during the Commonwealth period was extensive and so, not surprisingly, at the Restoration Thomas Rawlins,[45] the royalist medallist, was reinstated as the sole Chief Engraver in recognition of his services to the late King during the Civil War. Nevertheless, Simon successfully petitioned for employment at the Mint, becoming actively occupied in making the dies for the hammered English coinage of 1660 (Rawlins clearly not being thought capable of the task) and on 2 June 1661 being granted the office of 'one of the Engravers of the King's arms, shields and stamps'.

However, in the January of the following year he was in disagreement with the Roettiers brothers,[46] the contemporary rival engravers, with regard to producing dies for the proposed new milled coinage. In the following month, after a competition between them which should have involved their each engraving a trial-piece for a silver crown and producing a pattern crown in silver, although it is not clear whether any such patterns were produced, the King decided in favour of the Roettiers brothers and Simon's employment at the Mint then practically ceased. It would appear that the former owed their victory over Simon neither because they possessed greater skill as engravers nor because they enjoyed greater favour at the Court, in view of Simon's earlier connections with the Commonwealth government, but to their ability to produce dies that would not crack, as Simon's had, under the pressure of the then recently introduced machinery employed to strike the milled coinage.

Simon's famous Petition Crown, a belated attempt to combat the Roettiers brothers, was produced in 1663 and in April and September of 1664 he was engaged in engraving seals for the King's service. Records show that in April 1665, Simon made a claim for £35 in payment for 'altering the stamps of the fourpenny, threepenny, twopenny and penny by way of the mill'. Since this claim is of later date than that in which he was displaced by the Roettiers brothers, it indicates that he worked on the production of dies for the minor coinage almost until his death during the Great Plague in 1665, although whether he actually died of the plague is far from certain.

Tanner; John Sigismund[47]

Johann Sigismund Tanner was a native of Saxe-Gotha and practised in his early life the carving and engraving of snuff-boxes, gun-locks, etc.. He came to England in 1728 and worked at the Mint as an apprentice to John Croker[48] from January 1728/9.[49] When Croker died in March 1740/1,[50] Tanner succeeded him as Chief Engraver, a position which he held until 1768 when he was retired on full pay. He died in David Street, London, on 14 March 1775.

Wyon; Leonard Charles[51]

Leonard Charles Wyon, the eldest son of William Wyon,[52] was born in one of the houses in the Royal Mint in 1826. As well as being educated at Merchant Taylors School in London, he was taught art by his father and also inherited considerable skill in engraving. By the age of sixteen years he had already made several medals and in 1844 he was appointed as Second Engraver, when the position became vacant upon the retirement of Merlen.[53] At the age of twenty-four years, in 1851, he followed in his father's footsteps at the Mint, but with the title of Modeller and Engraver. He held this position until his death on 20 August 1891.

Wyon; Thomas junior[54]

Thomas Wyon senior was born in 1767 and thirty years later was to be found with one of his three younger brothers, Peter, established in business at Lionel Street in Birmingham where Thomas engraved dies for a large number of the token issues of the late eighteenth century. However, because there was not enough work for both of them in Birmingham, Thomas moved to London and settled in a street on the west side of Blackfriars' Bridge Road. Eleven years later, on 30 September 1816, after he had already been working at the Mint for some time, he was appointed as Chief Engraver of His Majesty's Seals but this position was not part of the Royal Mint establishment. He died in London on 18 October 1830.

Thomas Wyon senior's contributions to the Mint were not great, unlike those of his eldest son, Thomas junior, and in spite of the latter's very short life. Thomas Wyon junior was born in Birmingham in 1792 and, after a few years, moved with his father to London. At the age of fourteen years he was apprenticed to his father and soon showed great promise and received many awards as a medallic engraver. At the Mint he was appointed, on 20 November 1811, as Probationary Engraver and, on 13 October 1815, as Chief Engraver, he being then only twenty-three years old. However, his very promising career was cut short by his death, from pulmonary tuberculosis, at the Priory Farmhouse in Hastings on 22 September 1817.

Wyon; William[55]

William Wyon, the son of Peter Wyon,[56] was born in Birmingham in 1795 and was apprenticed to his father in 1809. He was the finest artist of all the Wyons and received many associated honours. At the invitation of his uncle, Thomas Wyon senior,[57] he visited London in 1812 and again in 1815, on the latter occasion helping his uncle. Shortly after Thomas Wyon junior[58] was appointed Chief Engraver to the Mint, William was appointed, on 25 May 1816, as Assistant Engraver, although objections were raised on the grounds of kinship, even though William had been so chosen after open competition. When Thomas junior died in 1817, the position of Chief Engraver was left vacant because of Pole's inability to appoint Pistrucci[59] to the post. Nevertheless, William Wyon did the work without receiving the salary associated with the office. This inequitable situation was relieved on 15 January 1828 when he was appointed as Chief Engraver and received some financial recompense for his work during the previous few years. William Wyon remained actively engaged in his work at the Mint until, toward the end of his life, his left side was paralysed as the result of a stroke. He died at Brighton on 29 October 1851.

The relevant portions of the genealogy of the Wyon family have been conveniently summarized in diagrammatic form.[60]

APPENDIX 2
The Banqueting House[61]

Several Banqueting Houses have, in fact, occupied the same site in Whitehall as part of Whitehall Palace. This was itself created from York Place, the official London residence of the Archbishops of York, in 1529 when Henry VIII took possession of the latter following Cardinal Wolsey's fall from favour.

The first Banqueting House was a temporary structure erected in 1572, the second was built in 1581 to be followed by the construction of a third in 1607. Following the destruction of this building by fire on 12 January 1618/9,[62] the building which was ultimately to become the main host to the Maundy service after the Restoration was constructed by Inigo Jones between 1619 and 1622.

In fact, after the Restoration, the Maundy Service was only one of the many functions for which this historic building was used, others including the reception of ambassadors, the ceremony of touching for the King's Evil and the holding of lotteries and auctions. It was in the Banqueting House on 13 February 1688/9[63] that the Crown was offered to William and Mary and it was from this building that Charles I was led, by means of a passage broken through the wall, onto the scaffold where he was beheaded on 30 January 1648/9.[64]

The building still stands in Whitehall and is well worth a visit. Of particular interest is the ceiling, covered as it is by nine canvas panels that were painted by Peter Paul Rubens and set in a richly decorated wooden framework comprising nine spaces, five oval and four rectangles in three rows of three. These paintings symbolize, with particular reference to James I, the benefits and glories of Stuart monarchical rule. Ironically, Charles I who commissioned them ultimately passed beneath them on his way to the scaffold. The canvases were first planned in 1621, sketched by Rubens during his stay in London, painted by him in Antwerp, completed in 1634 and installed in the following year. As his reward, Rubens received a payment of £3,000 and a knighthood.

On 4 January 1697/8,[65] most of the Whitehall Palace, including the Chapel Royal, was destroyed by fire. However, the Banqueting House survived and four days later, on 8 January, it was selected to take the place of the ruined chapel. In view of the overwhelming evidence that the Banqueting House had been so adopted by William III, it is surprising that so many writers on Whitehall claim that its formal conversion into the Chapel Royal did not occur until the accession of the House of Hanover in 1714. This common error probably arises from the fact that George I appointed a panel of preachers, at a fixed stipend, to officiate regularly in the Chapel.

APPENDIX 3

The Calendar[66]

English historical documents and literary remains are dated in various ways. Throughout the Middle Ages in England, and in some countries for much longer, the calendar in use was that known as the Julian calendar and reckoning by this was known as the Old Style (OS), as distinct from the New Style (NS), namely reckoning by the Gregorian calendar introduced by Pope Gregory XIII in 1582 (see below).

The Julian calendar was named after Julius Cæsar who, in 45 B.C., set it up to consist of a common year of 365 days with every fourth year to consist of an extra day to account for the discrepancy between the calendar of 365 days and the solar year which was calculated by astronomers as 365¼ days. However, the current year was counted when deciding every fourth year which therefore gave a leap year every three years. This error rapidly accumulated until the emperor Augustus removed it by ordaining that twelve successive years should consist of 365 days only. The next leap year was then A.D. 4 and thereafter, as long as the OS calendar continued, every fourth year in the modern sense.

The year in this Roman calendar began on 1 January. However, in the Middle Ages, in attempts to break with pagan antecedents, the Christian Church preferred one of its own major festivals to mark the beginning of the year. Thus, early English chronicles usually preferred a year beginning on Christmas Day and from the latter part of the twelfth century, according to a mode of reckoning which began on the Continent of Europe, the Feast of the Annunciation (Lady Day) on 25 March became the first day of the year for most purposes in England and remained the legal and official mode of reckoning in England until the reform of the calendar in 1751 (see below).

The reckoning of the solar year as 365¼ days was a slight overestimate and by the sixteenth century this annual error had caused, cumulatively, an error of ten days. However, this was overcome by the bull of Pope Gregory XIII on 24 February 1582 which ordered the introduction and use of a reformed calendar. This arranged for the elimination of these accumulated ten days by decreeing that 15 October followed immediately upon 4 October in 1582 and that future difficulties were to be avoided by making only the fourth of the end-years of successive centuries a leap year, with occasional exceptions, at A.D. 2000, 4000, etc. to rectify the slight over-correction thus made. The bull also decreed that the year was to begin on 1 January.

The application of this very desirable reform, which introduced dating by the Gregorian calendar, was, unfortunately, subjected at the time to the very pronounced religious and political hostilities which were then manifest. Broadly speaking, Roman Catholic countries and states adopted the NS calendar either immediately or before the end of the sixteenth century, whilst Protestant states did likewise either early or late in the eighteenth century and Russia, the Balkan States and Greece followed suit in the twentieth century.

Thus, after 1582 Englishmen had to reckon with the fact that some continental countries, namely those of the Roman Catholic persuasion (and Scotland from 1600), had agreed to adopt the Gregorian (NS) calendar and so, from then until 1752 (see below), English writers sometimes give a double year-date for days from 1 January to 24 March. For example, 21 February 1652/3 (alternatively expressed as 1652–1653, 1652–3 or 165$\frac{2}{3}$) refers to 21 February 1653 (NS) or 21 February 1652 (OS). Where no such double indication is given, it is usually safe to assume that an Englishman writing in England reckons from the 25 March as being the first day of the year, although the printed almanacs and some of the early periodicals and newspapers started their year on 1 January. A further discrepancy between the dates appertaining to NS and OS calendar usage arises from the elimination of the accumulated error of ten days in the former (see above). Consequently, careful consideration must be given to the origin of a document and the habits of its author since a difference of dating may amount to 10, 11, 12 or 13 days according as the document was written after 1582, 1700, 1800 or 1900, respectively. Thus, from 1582 English correspondence with countries that had adopted the NS calendar often gave both forms of the date. For example $^{14}/_{24}$ December 1635 indicates 14 December 1635 (OS, then currently in use in England) and 24 December 1635 (NS). When such correspondence was written between 1 January and 24 March, inclusively, a double year-date was also necessary for precision. For example, $^{14}/_{24}$ February 160$^9/_{10}$ refers to 14 February 1609 (OS) and 24 February 1610 (NS).

Clearly, this was a clumsy and unnecessary situation which in England was obviated by Lord Chesterfield's Act in 1751 by which the Gregorian calendar was introduced into England. This provided that the day after 31 December 1751 should be, throughout the Dominions of the British Crown, 1 January 1752. Furthermore, by 1752 the discrepancy of days (see above) between the OS and NS calendars had increased to eleven which was also rectified in the 1751 Act which provided that the eleven days between 2 September and 14 September 1752 should be omitted. However, double dating was still necessary on correspondence between England and countries which still operated on the OS calendar. For example, as late as the early twentieth century we have a letter from the Russian Minister of Foreign Affairs to the British Ambassador dated $^{16}/_{29}$ Août 1907.

APPENDIX 4

Alms Dishes used in the Maundy Service

The Maundy Dish (Plate 13), normally to be seen in the Tower of London where it forms part of the royal regalia, is a plain silver gilt dish with a broad rim and a line around the edge, has a diameter of 25¾in and weighs 202oz. It was made in London in 1660 and given by Charles II, although it is engraved in its centre with the arms and cypher of William and Mary.[67] The maker's mark has been quoted as either an apparent grenade [pomegranate] in a formal shield[68] or an orb and star on a plain shield.[69]

Beginning with the Maundy service in 1971, the use of this dish was transferred from the Second Distribution to the First Distribution and it was replaced in the former by two other alms dishes, known as the Fish Dishes (Plate 21), assorted fish of various sizes being clearly recognized in parts of their designs. These two dishes also date from the time of Charles II and were once part of the Chapel Plate. In 1967 they were added to the collection in the Jewel House at the Tower of London. On their rims are four oval panels, representing on one dish love, death, industry and strength, and on the other dish faith, hope, justice and fortitude.[70]

A third dish was later introduced for use in the Second Distribution. This dish, dating from the reign of Edward VII, is on loan from the Marquis of Exeter, the Hereditary Grand Almoner.[71] Other alms dishes may be used in the ceremony as and when they may be required.[72]

APPENDIX 5

Attendant Persons, excluding the Royal Almonry Officials, at the Royal Maundy Service

The Chapel Royal Choir[73]

The Children and Gentlemen of Her Majesty's Chapel Royal constitute the Chapel Royal Choir. Even when it is held outside of London, the Maundy service still remains a Chapel Royal service and the Chapel Royal Choir is always in attendance. The choir has a notable musical history, originates from a distant date and remains a distinctive part of the royal establishment. The ancient custom of its attendance upon the monarch manifests itself in the command it receives to sing at the Maundy service. It is also in attendance at royal baptisms and weddings. The Children of the Choir wear gold-braided red tunics, red breeches, white lace bands and white gloves, and black stockings and shoes, all of which harmonize with the uniforms of the Yeomen of the Guard, and the Gentlemen of the Choir wear red cassocks with surplices and white ties.

The Children of the Royal Almonry[74]

Prior to 1808, there were entered on the records of the Almonry the names of some elderly men, who were called the Children of the Royal Almonry. Their duties were to attend the Chapel Royal, the then annual venue of the Maundy service, arrayed in linen scarves. For this they received aggregate fees of twenty-one pounds (twenty guineas). This ultimately came to be considered an abuse of the Maundy charity. Consequently, these elderly men were pensioned off and were replaced by real children, two boys and two girls, from parents of a respectable class. Each of them received, whilst they were between the ages of seven and fourteen years, an annual grant of five guineas for the purposes of aiding their education, this sum being paid to their parents. These children did not personally attend the Maundy service but were represented by four children selected from the schools of the parishes of St John the Evangelist and St Margaret, Westminster. These parishes were situated within the bounds of the Broad Sanctuary, thereby fittingly furnishing these representatives, bearing in mind that the annual venue for the service was then in Whitehall. The children were attired in the traditional linen scarves and carried the traditional bouquets during the service and received a fee of five shillings each. Currently, the four children attending the Maundy service as Children of the Royal Almonry are recommended from schools in the locality of the service's venue and each of them receives a set of Maundy money as a fee for their attendance.

The Wandsmen[75]

The original function and, indeed, the origin of the Wandsmen, or wandbearers as they were called in the past, is unknown. Their wands may have been willows or palms and thus connected with Easter or, alternatively, they may have been staves by which the populace in earlier times was held back in order to make way for the Maundy recipients. Nevertheless, whatever their earlier purpose may have been, the present day functions of the wandsmen, which involve rendering assistance to the recipients in every possible way, such as ensuring that they are in their proper places and explaining to them their rôle in the service, began in Victorian times as a result of a request from the Secretary of the Royal Almonry for help in administering to the then large number of recipients.

Until a few years ago there were four wandsmen but this was then increased to six, some of whom are descended from former employees of the Exchequer and Audit Department. Currently numbered amongst the Wandsmen are the son of the late Mr E. E. Ratcliffe, who was the Assistant Secretary of the Royal Almonry, and the younger son of Mr Peter A. Wright, the present Secretary.

The Yeomen of the Guard[76]

The Yeomen of the Guard, the monarch's bodyguard, is the oldest military corps in existence. It was created by Henry VII from his faithful English and Welsh followers who accompanied him into exile in France and subsequently marched with him at the battle of Bosworth Field where he defeated the army of Richard III, thereby claiming the throne. At his subsequent coronation, he proclaimed that the Yeomen were not only for his personal protection but for 'the upholding of the dignity and grandeur of the English crown in perpetuity, his successors, the kings and queens of England for all time'. Since then, they have attended their sovereigns at their coronation, served them during their reign, attended their lying-in-state and escorted them to their grave.

Initially, the Yeomen were virtually the personal servants of the monarch and, in fact, their colloquial name beef-eaters is a corruption of buffetiers, namely personal attendants of the sovereign who, on high festivals and other state occasions, were ranged near the royal sideboard, or buffet. They accompanied their sovereign everywhere, even in battle, but after 1743, the last year in which an English king actually participated personally in battle, their duties have become purely ceremonial. These now include searching the vaults of the Houses of Parliament prior to its official opening by the monarch, lining the Royal Gallery of the Upper House for the State Opening of Parliament, being present at the Epiphany and Maundy services and those of the Orders of the Garter and of the Bath and forming guards of honour and being in attendance at a variety of other royal functions.

In total there are eighty men in the Yeomen of the Guard. These are chosen from all regiments and corps of the Army, the Royal Air Force and the Royal Marines, a roll of candidates being maintained by the Ministry of Defence.

APPENDIX 6
Units of Weight[77]

In the Anglo-Saxon countries, in addition to metric units employed in scientific work, and now in general use, many other groups of mass units have simultaneously been in operation. Amongst these are the avoirdupois weights of commerce and industry, the troy[78] weights for precious metals and coins and the apothecary weights.[79] Common to all these three groups is the troy grain (gr), defined as the 7,000th part of the avoirdupois pound.

In the specification of the size of coin by the number in a weight of one pound, the mint or tower pound was long used. This was equal to 5,400gr and was divided into twelve mint or tower ounces (each of 450gr), this ounce in turn being divided into twenty mint or tower pennyweights (each of 22.5gr). However, this pound was formally abolished by Act of Parliament in 1527 and was replaced by the troy pound of 5,760gr and of twelve troy ounces (each of twenty troy pennyweights or 480gr). The still heavier avoirdupois pound, of 7,000gr, is divided into sixteen avoirdupois ounces (each of sixteen avoirdupois drams or 437.5gr). Fourteen avoirdupois pounds make one stone, two and eight of which make a quarter and a hundredweight (or 1.12 centals or short hundredweights), respectively, twenty hundredweights making one long ton (or 1.12 short tons). Concurrent with the use of troy weights in the weighing of precious metals and precious stones, avoirdupois weights were used by general traders and, in conformity with outside practice, were adopted only for the copper coinage. Also used by moneyers, jewellers, etc. as a unit in the weighing of gold and precious stones is the carat which has a weight equal to four troy grains.

APPENDIX 7

The Trial of the Pyx[80]

This is the procedure by which samples of all the coins produced at the Mint are investigated in order to ensure their fineness. The word 'pyx' is of Roman origin, being derived from the Greek *puxis*, meaning a box, and refers to the box or chest in which the pieces for assay were locked away until such time as the Trial should take place.

In most major countries, mints are subject to a periodic scrutiny, by an external tribunal, of samples of its more important coins. The tribunal is usually composed of representatives of certain other State Departments, commonly contains a judicial element and, also, sometimes nominated distinguished citizens. The United Kingdom is probably unique in resort to a private body, namely the London Livery Company of Goldsmiths, to carry out this examination.

For the Trial at the present time, a jury of Freemen of the Goldsmiths' Company is empanelled by the Queen's Remembrancer at their hall. After taking the oath, the members of the jury count the coins submitted to them by the Deputy Master of the Royal Mint as representative samples of the previous year's work. All the coins are weighed in bulk, and some of them individually, and a certain number are selected for subsequent assay. The Trial is then adjourned *de die in diem* (from day to day). About two months later, the jury is summoned by the Queen's Remembrancer, to whom the Clerk of the Company delivers the jury's verdict in the presence of the Master, the Deputy Master and senior officers of the Royal Mint, the fineness of the gold, silver, nickel-brass and cupro-nickel coins (bronze coins are not submitted) having being determined by comparing them with pure metal trail plates.[81]

The origin of the Trial is obscure. The introduction of the assay of the coinage and the establishment of a standard is variously assigned to the reigns of Henry I, Henry II, Richard I and John. About 1180, the weight and fineness of much of the money received by the Exchequer were regularly examined under the eyes of the Barons of the Exchequer. However, the purpose of this was to establish the value at which each contribution should be accepted rather than to verify the standard of work of the various mints and minters. Moreover, limits of variation of weight and fineness were extremely hazy and no directives by which a trial could operate were in existence. During a demonetization and recoinage nearly seventy years later, a trial of the new and the old coinage was staged in 1248 in the presence of the Barons of the Exchequer and a sworn jury of twelve citizens and of twelve or thirteen goldsmiths of standing. Standard reference bars, one of pure silver and the other of the fineness of the coin, were used in this trial which was, however, less to ascertain how far each mint had complied with standards than to convince the country at large, which was paying heavily for the currency reform, that the fineness of the coin had risen as a consequence of it. Between this date and 1279, a trial before the King's Council of the Pyx of coins set aside by the London Mint must have been established, for in the latter year Edward I issued orders relating to the same and the first known writ for a Trial of the Pyx, which was issued to these Barons in 1282, speaks of it as an established procedure. There is little doubt that the Trial of the Pyx, as now practised, was formally established during this later period.

Until after 1432, the Trial was made before the Barons of the Exchequer, in 1475 it was being made before a jury of four goldsmiths, a jury which by 1534 had grown to sixteen goldsmiths, one gold refiner and twelve members of other London livery companies, although by 1580 these other companies had dropped out and the jury has since been named by the goldsmiths and wholly from their livery.

The Trial of the Pyx was anciently held by royal authority. Indeed, James I usually honoured it with his actual presence, one of the obvious manifestations of his well-known interest in the Mint and its workings, although Charles I did so just once. During the Commonwealth, it was held under special authority of Parliament and later under a warrant from Cromwell, the Lord Protector. Since the Restoration to the present time the authority for the Trial has been the sovereign acting through the Privy Council by special orders under the Great Seal.

From the Restoration until 1870, the Trial took place somewhat irregularly and only at intervals of several years, as the Master's convenience directed. Indeed, by the late eighteenth century it was considered antiquarian and a not very useful survival from the past. Nonetheless, during the following century it became recognized as an important factor in coinage administration and by the Coinage Act 1870 was made statutory and required to be held 'at least once in every year in which coins have been issued from the Mint', and detailed regulations for its conduct were drawn up. At this time also, the preliminaries of the Trial were removed from Westminster, where they had in earlier times been held, to Goldsmiths' Hall, the by then already well-established venue for the task of the examination, and its presidency was transferred from the Lord Chancellor to the Queen's Remembrancer, who was to both charge the jury and receive their verdict.

It is a remarkable testimony to the working of the Mint that in over the 700 years throughout which the Trial had been held up to 1974, there were only five failures. The first of these occurred in 1318 when the jury found that the silver coins were substandard with regard to their purity. Consequently, the Master of the Mint or the moneyer, one Giles de Hertesbergh (or de Herbage) and his assistant, Jerrick de Lose, were both bound to answer to the King (Edward II). In addition, the former was required so to answer for a further £100 of melted silver and when it was found that he was unable financially to meet this order he was committed to prison, apparently for six weeks. In 1349, the Italian master was fined £93 13s 3d, this being the proportionate value over his whole coinage of the deficiency of fineness exhibited by the trial coins. The jury reported on the Trial in 1534 of the first coins of 22 carat gold that the Mint had put more copper and less silver into the alloy for the coins than was in the trial plate. However, in this it would appear that the jury had exceeded its duty, for since the value of silver in the alloy of gold was never taken into account when pricing coins, the Mint rightly retained, or at any rate finally assumed, discretion in the make-up of the alloy. Isaac Newton was the Master of the Mint in 1710 when the third failure from the Trial occurred, the jury finding that the gold coins were below standard. Newton was furious and was able to demonstrate that the fault lay not in the minting but in a defect in the new trial plates that had been supplied that year. In 1926 the jury found that one silver sixpence was underweight by 0.008 grams and a fifth failure arose in 1969 when some of the coinage minted for New Zealand for inclusion in specimen sets was found to be overweight.

On three other occasions some mishap occurred at the Trial but there was no question of an adverse verdict. In 1600 there were defects in the assaying furnaces and the Trial had to be reconvened on the following day. After all the commissioners, judges and mint officials had been assembled on 14 November 1657 for the second Trial during the Commonwealth, it was confessed that the master portions of the trial plates, which had been prepared in 1649, had been lost: after an adjournment for a fortnight it was resumed using those parts of the plates which had been supplied to the Goldsmiths for use in their assay hall. In 1707 the assay furnace was over-stoked and set fire to the Exchequer, the Treasury making the handsome gesture of paying a reward to those who extinguished the flames.

In early times the Trial of the Pyx used to be concluded in a single day and the verdict and close of the proceedings were celebrated by a dinner, at the Mint's expense, for its officers and the jury. Since 1900 the period between submission and verdict has grown and currently stands at some two months. Changes in the dinner have also occurred. Instead of being held at the Dog Tavern in Westminster and at the Mint's expense, as it was at the turn of the seventeenth century, it first of all became the joint financial responsibility of the Mint and the Goldsmiths' Company and has now become a stately banquet at Goldsmiths' Hall with the Company acting as hosts to the Mint and its officers.

APPENDIX 8

Peter Blondeau and the Milled Coinage[82]

Up to, and including, the beginning of the reign of Charles II, with some minor exceptions during the reigns of Elizabeth I and Charles I (see below), the coinage of England was known as hammered coinage by virtue of its method of production. In this, the metal which was to be used to produce the coins was hand hammered into thin plates from which the blanks were either punched, or cut and shaped by hand shearing, and then hand struck using a fixed pile (lower die) and a hand-held trussel (upper die).

However, early ideas and experiments as to the possibility of producing coins by mechanical means, mainly relating to the production of medals, had originated in Italy at the beginning of the sixteenth century. Leonardo da Vinci (1452–1519) devised, toward the end of his life, a mechanical means of producing and striking blanks, probably during his assumed association with the mint at Rome, in about 1512.

Benvenuto Cellini, appointed engraver to the mint at Rome in 1529, was closely involved with the screw-press method of coining and in 1558 a treatise written in Florence dealt with the art of coining by both hammer and screw-press. Though Cellini visited France in 1557, there is no evidence to suggest that this new coining machinery was installed there at that time though the matter was certainly discussed between the artist and Francis I of France.

Francis' son, Henry II of France, appears to have recalled these discussions when faced with reforming the French coinage with a view to protecting against clipping and forgery. Various relevant machines were set up in the grounds of the Palace and in 1552 proof coins were successfully struck. Four years later, the progressive monarch, Henry of Navarre, afterwards Henry IV of France, caused a similar set of coining machinery to be set up at Pau.

It is from this machinery that the milled series of coins takes it name, since the necessary power to drive the machinery was first obtained by the use of a mill. However, the power produced by this mill, whether wind, water or horse driven, was not used in the actual striking of the coins. This was done in manually operated screw-presses until Matthew Boulton and James Watt provided steam engines to drive the actual presses. The mill was used in the earlier period simply to drive the rollers which flattened out the metal into strips of even thickness, nearly that of the finished coin, from which were cut the blanks, of uniform quality, ultimately used in the striking of coin in the screw-press.

This new process of coining reached England during the reign of Elizabeth I, whose administration was, like that earlier in France, faced with a large quantity of base and clipped coins. Eloye Mestrell, who may have been earlier employed at the French mint, came to England and was appointed by the Queen's Council in 1561 to a position at the Tower Mint, at a salary of £25 per annum, together with a house in the new upper mint. Mestrelle's machines which were introduced at the Mint produced coins which are of much finer workmanship than those made by the old method of hand hammering. However, there was considerable opposition toward the introduction of this machinery from the mint workers who feared that it might jeopardize their employment. They found an ally in 1572 in the then newly-appointed Warden of the Mint, Sir Richard Martin who, as part of the extensive exercise with regard to the Mint's cost effectiveness which he undertook, condemned the mechanical process for coining on the grounds that it was ten times slower than the hand method of producing coins. Thus, quality was sacrificed for cheapness, Mestrelle was dismissed – he was, in fact, hanged at Tyburn in 1578 for counterfeiting – and progress was arrested for some ninety years, with the re-establishment of hand hammering as the sole method of producing the nation's coinage until the beginning of the reign of Charles II, with the exception of some coins produced by Nicholas Briot[83] during the reign of Charles I.

Nicholas Briot was Chief Engraver at the Paris mint from 1606 until 1625. During this period he invented a mechanical method for minting which produced a product of a far superior quality and more perfectly round than did the hammer method. However, having been frustrated by the French authorities in his attempts to introduce his machinery into their mint, and being hard-pressed by his creditors, he fled to England in 1625. Here, he began work at the Tower Mint both as a medallist and a designer for the King's portrait on the coinage and attempted to introduce his new coining machines into use. Briot's screw-press could not produce nearly enough coins to satisfy demand and so the bulk of the coinage was still produced by hand-hammering. Even so, the use of his machinery was viewed with considerable hostility by the English mint employees, fearful for their positions.

Subsequent to Briot's departure from the Paris mint, other mechanical methods for the production of coin began to make their appearance there and, after competition between them and the hand method, the use of the coining hammer in French mints was prohibited from 1645 onward. The engineer at the Paris mint at this time was Peter Blondeau and it was he who, in 1649, was invited into the service of the Commonwealth government, at that time desirous of exploring the modernization of English mint practice. Nevertheless, Blondeau, like Briot, received the wrath of the English moneyers but, eventually, he managed to strike a small quantity of coinage in silver, and a trifle in gold, bearing Cromwell's portrait and secured separate premises in Drury House, a safe distance from the Mint, where the Lord Protector promised him £1,400 worth of additional machinery. Unfortunately, the contemporary political scene overtook him, the Protector and the Protectorate passed into history, the coins bearing Cromwell's portrait were never issued and Blondeau took the precaution of returning to France. Three months after the Restoration, the Mint transferred his, and the older machinery of Nicholas Briot, to Edinburgh. As a result, the first coinages of the new monarch, Charles II, were produced using the hammering method from dies produced by Thomas Simon[84] who may, to some extent, have had the co-operation of Thomas Rawlins in some of this work.

However, by 1661, the variability in weight and size of the English coinage and the problems associated with clipping, cutting and counterfeiting had once again become of paramount concern to the Mint. It was thus ordered that, in order to rectify these problems, all coin was to be struck as soon as possible by machinery, with grained or lettered edges. Consequently, Thomas Simon was sent to France on 8 November 1661 to fetch Blondeau back and on 24 January 1661/2 he was ordered to deliver up all the tools, etc. for coinage which were in his possession to the officers of the Mint, although, without doubt, coins produced using his dies were used as Maundy money until 1670. As a result of these moves England had, by 1663, followed France's lead of

1645 and the production of milled coinage had completely superseded that of the hammered type.

The hammered coinage, being produced from blanks which had been shaped by hand, was therefore seldom perfectly circular in shape and was thus always liable to be subject to the fraudulent and prevalent practice of clipping. With the introduction of machine-made blanks and coining presses, the resulting coins were perfectly circular. Nevertheless, the clippers were not finally defeated until the coins were made with graining (milling) or lettering around their edges, such marks being either introduced during the striking process by the use of a suitably marked collar or by using a special edge-marking machine, the castaing machine, which marked the edge of the blanks before they went into the minting press. However, the small silver denominations retained plain edges, a feature which was to remain on all the similar denominations, later to become used exclusively for Maundy purposes, issued up to the present time.

APPENDIX 9

The Groat

The statement that, after 1582, 'the fourpence disappeared altogether, never to return except in the form of Maundy coinage'[85] is clearly without foundation. Indeed, the rôle of the silver fourpence as a denomination in general circulation for long after this date is well established.[86] Even after the early nineteenth century, by which time a small denominational copper coinage was in wide use in general currency, the silver groat, as distinct from the Maundy fourpence, was also so introduced in 1836 (Plate 75). In this year, too, this coin was introduced into British Guiana at a value of a quarter guilder, the old British Guiana bitt, when the rate of 1s 4d per guilder (the mode of reckoning under the previous Dutch administration) was laid down in 1840.[87] This groat, called the Britannia groat because of the seated figure of Britannia on its reverse (Plate 75 and 81), was also known as the Joey in view of the championing of its introduction by Joseph Hume, M.P., as being the London hackney fare for half a mile. However, although they prospered and took root in the colony, these groats were extremely unpopular with the hackney cab drivers who frequently, as a consequence of its introduction, received only a groat where otherwise they would have received a sixpence without any demand for change.[88]

With the exception of 1850, these groats were struck for general circulation in Britain until 1855. Their demise was heralded by the introduction into the general British currency of the silver threepence by a proclamation of 19 May 1845.[89] Confusion resulted from having the two denominations so close together and of the same diameter, although the groat had a grained edge, whereas that of the threepence was plain, and also had the same weight as the Maundy fourpence (0.06060oz) and was thus correspondingly thicker than the threepence which weighed 0.04545oz.[90] Thus, after 1855 the former was discontinued in favour of the latter although the groat would appear to have circulated at least north of the Border for many decades afterwards.[91] Following a request from the colony for further supplies of the groat, it was struck again in 1888 (Plate 88) for use in British Guiana. However, except for a change in the Queen's effigy and the year date, these coins are of the same design as the earlier Victorian issues of the Britannia groat and bear no indication of their locality. Subsequent issues of the fourpence for similar colonial use were not of the Britannia type and specified in their reverse legends their locality: for those issued up to 1916 this was British Guiana and West Indies whereas for those issued from 1917 to 1945 it was British Guiana.[92]

NOTES

1. *DNB*, suppl. 1, pp. 229–230; Dyer and Stocker; Forrer, 1 (1904), p. 204.
2. *DNB*, 6, pp. 51, 52; Forrer, 1 (1904), pp. 258–59, 7 (1923), p. 109.
3. See Appendix 3.
4. *DNB*, 6, pp. 351–52; Helen Farquhar, 'Nicholas Briot and the Civil War', *NC*, 14, fourth series (1914),

pp. 169–235 and Plates XII–XV; Forrer, 1 (1904) pp. 285–94; Mark Jones, (with an appendix by Duncan Hook), *A Catalogue of French Medals in the British Museum*, vol. 2, 1660–1672, (London, 1988), pp. 143–76.
5. Forrer, 1 (1904), pp. 295–96, 7 (1923), p. 124.
6. Forrer, 1 (1904), p. 308, 7 (1923), p. 135.
7. See Appendix 1.
8. *DNB*, 10, pp. 44–47.
9. *DNB*, 13, pp. 121–23; Forrer, 1 (1904), pp. 472–79, 7 (1923), p. 197.
10. See note 7 above.
11. This statute, the Statute of Limitations, was legislation passed during the reign of William III. It debarred a foreigner from holding the custody of the dies for the coinage and thereby effectively barred aliens from positions of responsibility at the Mint since, obviously, no Chief Engraver could work under this condition.
12. Forrer, 1 (1904), pp. 563–64, 7 (1923), p. 217. Linecar (1977), p. 123; Seaby, p. 162.
13. See note 7 above.
14. See note 7 above.
15. *Who was Who*, 6 (1972), p. 429.
16. *DNB* (1941–50), pp. 321–22; Rayner, pp. 22–24.
17. *Who's Who* (1988), p. 1129.
18. Forrer, 8 (1930), pp. 2, 3; *Who was Who*, 3 (1941), p. 865.
19. *Who's Who* (1988), p. 1163.
20. Forrer, 4 (1909), p. 38, 8 (1930), p. 56.
21. See note 11 above.
22. See note 7 above.
23. *DNB*, 41, pp. 353, 416; Dyer; Forrer, 4 (1909), pp. 298–99, 8 (1930), p. 101; Linecar (1977), pp. 80, 81.
24. p. 416.
25. See note 7 above.
26. G. P. Dyer, 'Thomas Humphrey Paget (1893–1974)', *NC*, 140 (20, seventh series) (1980), pp. 165–77 and Plates 21–24.
27. See note 7 above.
28. See note 7 above.
29. See note 7 above.
30. *DNB*, 45, pp. 314–15; Forrer, 4 (1909), pp. 551–61, 8 (1930), pp. 134–36.
31. See note 7 above.
32. See note 7 above.
33. *DNB*, 45, pp. 328–31; Forrer, 4 (1909), pp. 582–620, 8 (1930), pp. 137–38.
34. See note 7 above.
35. See note 11 above.
36. *DNB*, 47, pp. 326–27; Forrer, 5 (1912), pp. 38–52.
37. See note 7 above.
38. See note 3 above.
39. See note 7 above.
40. *DNB*, 49, pp. 98–101; Forrer, 5 (1912), pp. 156–57, 161–74, 183–87; Woolf (1979), p. 110.
41. See Appendix 8.
42. Linecar (1977), p. 70.
43. *DNB*, 52, pp. 265–67; Helen Farquhar, 'Thomas Simon, "one of our Chief Engravers" ', *NC*, 12, fifth series (1932), pp. 274–310; Forrer, 5 (1912), pp. 519–32; Alan J. Nathason, *Thomas Simon, His Life and Work 1618–1665* (London, 1975); H. E. Pagan, Presidential Address 1988 to the British Numismatic Society, *BNJ*, 58 (1988), pp. 177–89.
44. See note 7 above.
45. See note 7 above.
46. See note 7 above.
47. *DNB*, 55, pp. 358–59; Forrer, 6 (1916), pp. 14–17.
48. See note 7 above.
49. See note 3 above.
50. See note 3 above.

51. *DNB*, 63, pp. 268–69; Forrer, 6 (1916), pp. 592–631, 8 (1930), p. 299.
52. See note 7 above.
53. See note 7 above.
54. *DNB*, 63, pp. 269–71; Forrer, 6 (1916), pp. 635–50, 8 (1930), pp. 299–300.
55. *DNB*, 63, pp. 270–71; Forrer, 6 (1916), 650–87, 8 (1930), pp. 300–3.
56. See note 7 above, under Wyon; Thomas junior.
57. See note 7 above, under Wyon; Thomas junior.
58. See note 7 above.
59. See note 7 above.
60. Linecar (1977), p. 99.
61. Dugdale, pp. 18–20, 31, 33–39, 41, 45, 51, 53, 56, 57, 60, 63, 67–72, 75, 76, 90, 91, 99, 107–11, 115, 117, 122, 151, 158, 161, 168; *London Interiors*, pp. 45–46; 'The Banqueting House', in Sheppard, Chapter 3, pp. 35–52 and Plate; 'The Chapel Royal', in Sheppard, Chapter 4, pp. 53–65; 'United Service Institution', in Sheppard, Chapter 10, pp. 100–103.
62. See note 3 above.
63. See note 3 above.
64. See note 3 above.
65. See note 3 above.
66. Cheney, pp. 1–11; *OCEL*, pp. 932–34.
67. Sitwell; Wright (1981), p. 24.
68. Sitwell.
69. Wright (1981), p. 24.
70. See note 69 above.
71. *ORM* (15 April 1976), Hereford Cathedral, pp. 10, 11.
72. Wright.
73. Wright (1981), p. 19.
74. Bidwell, p. 545; Wright (1981), p. 19.
75. Wright; Wright (1981), p. 19.
76. '*London Interiors*', p. 48; Walford, p. 369; Wright (1981) pp. 19, 20.
77. Craig (1953), p. xv; W. S. B. Woolhouse, *The Measures, Weights, and Moneys of All Nations; and an Analysis of the Christian, Hebrew, and Mahometan Calendars*, second edition (London, 1859); Ronald Edward Zupko, *A Dictionary of English Weights and Measures from Anglo-Saxon Times to the Nineteenth Century* (Madison, Milwaukee and London, 1968); Ronald Edward Zupko, *British Weights and Measures. A History from Antiquity to the Seventeenth Century* (Madison and London, 1977).
78. Although the troy pound was probably named from a weight (the marc) used at the fair of Troyes in France, it is certain that the standard for the English troy pound did not come from this source. The Troyes marc had an ounce equal to 472.1 British Imperial grains and thus, although the English troy pound took its name from the Troyes marc, it took its standard from some pound of full weight, probably the Bremen pound whose ounce weighed 480.8 British Imperial grains.
79. In the apothecary weights, 1 pound = 12 ounces, 1 ounce = 8 drams, 1 dram = 3 scruples and 1 scruple = 20 troy grains.
80. Craig (1953), pp. 394–407; Jacob, pp. 24–27; J. H. Watson, *Ancient Trial Plates* (London, 1962), pp. 6–9.
81. In former times, plates of impure metal but of legally prescribed composition were used.
82. Craig (1953), pp. 145, 152, 153, 158–60, 162, 163; *ESC*, pp. 11, 12; Linecar (1977), pp. 39, 40, 45, 46; Morrieson, pp. 117–19; Seaby, pp. xiii, xiv, xvii–xix, 97, 98, 106, 107; See also the second paragraph of note 70 to Chapter 3.
83. See note 7 above.
84. See note 7 above.
85. Sutherland, p. 153.
86. See pages 103, 106, 107 and 113.
87. Pridmore, pp. 9, 33, 34. By authorization of the Treasury on 9 October 1838, approval was also given for the striking of a half-groat, namely a silver twopence, of the same type as the Maundy twopence, for colonial use. Such use of this denomination, was, however, limited to British Guiana, where it circulated as a half-bitt value. Only three such strikings of these twopences, namely of coins dated 1838, 1843 and 1848, took place (Pridmore, pp. 267–68, 274–75).

88. Craig (1953), p. 311; Hawkins, p. 424.
89. Hocking (1906), p. 180. The statement that 'the silver threepence was extended from the Maundy to the public service in August 1839' (Craig (1953), p. 312) would appear to be incorrect, even if it includes such service in selected colonies for which were used, as the equivalent of the Spanish half-reale, threepences dated from 1834 and onward (Pridmore, pp. 267, 273–74). The silver three-halfpence was also issued from 1834 to 1843 (Plates 77 and 83), and then again in 1860 and 1862 and, as patterns or proofs only, in 1870, for selected colonial use as the equivalent of a Spanish quarter-reale (Pridmore, pp. 267, 275–76).
90. See note 6 to Table 12 and the reference quoted therein.
91. *Royal Mint: Ninety-Sixth Annual Report of the Deputy Master and Comptroller for the Year 1965* (London), p.2.
92. Pridmore, pp. 33–35, 46–48.

Bibliography

When, throughout the text, a reference is used on only one occasion, it is quoted in full as an appropriate note. Otherwise, notes quote only the author's name, the page number where appropriate and, where necessary to permit unambiguous referral to this bibliography, the year of publication.

Bidwell, H. J., 'Royal Almsgiving', *Guardian*, no. 2470 (1893), pp. 545–46

BL Addit. MS 7099; Ord's 'Household expenses of Henry VII' (quoted in Farquhar (1927–28), p. 118)

BL Addit. MS 21481, running from 1 May 1509 to 23 March 1518 (quoted in Farquhar (1927–28), pp. 216-17)

BL Harl. MS 829, no. 27, fo. 74: *Relations of the King's washing 33 poor men's feate on Maundy Thursday 1663* (quoted in Farquhar (1929–30), p. 222)

BL Harl. MS 1026 fo. 38; *Justin Pagitt's Memorandum Book* (quoted in Farquhar (1929–30), pp. 221–22)

BL Harl. MS 1644, September 1581 to September 1582, fo. 4, 6 April 1582 (quoted in Farquhar (1925–26), pp. 83, 84, (1927–28), p. 112)

BL Harl. MS 3795, no. 11, fo. 33: *The Service to be done on Maundy Thursday by the Lord Bp Almoner* (quoted in Farquhar (1929–30), pp. 222–23)

Bloch, Marc, *The Royal Touch, Sacred Monarchy and Scrofula in England and France*, translated by J. E. Anderson (Montreal, 1973)

Bond, Francis, *Visitors' Guide to Westminster Abbey* (London, New York, Toronto and Melbourne, 1909)

Brand, John, *Observations on Popular Antiquities Chiefly Illustrating the Origin of our Vulgar Customs, Ceremonies and Superstitions*, vol. 1 (London, 1841)

Brooke, George C., *English Coins*, third edition (London, 1966)

Brown, I. D., 'Maundy Money in General Circulation', *CNJ*, 21 (1976), p. 252

Burns, Edward, *The Coinage of Scotland*, 3 vols (Edinburgh, 1887), ii, p. 535

Calendar of State Papers and Manuscripts, relating to English Affairs, existing in the Archives and Collections of Venice, and in other Libraries of Northern Italy, edited by Rawdon Brown (London, 1877), vi, part I, 1555–56, pp. 428–37

Challis, Dr. C. E., Reader in Modern History, University of Leeds, personal communication

Challis, C. E., 'The Early Story' in *Royal Sovereign 1489–1989*, edited by G. P. Dyer (Llantrisant, 1989), pp. 25–29

Charlton, William, 'Maundy Thursday Observances and the Royal Maundy Money', *Transactions of the Lancashire and Cheshire Antiquarian Society*, 34 (1916), pp. 201–19

Cheney, C. R. (editor), *Handbook of Dates for Students of English History* (reprint with corrections) (London, 1978)

Clay, Rotha Mary, *Samuel Hieronymus Grimm of Burgdorf in Switzerland* (London, 1939)

Coin Year Book 1975 (Brentwood, 1974)

Craig, Sir John, *Newton at the Mint* (Cambridge, 1946)

Craig, Sir John, *The Mint* (Cambridge, 1953)

Crawford, Lord, *Stuart and Tudor Proclamations*, no. 593 and *Calendar of State Papers, Domestic*, 1564, (23 March 1563/4 (see Appendix 3)), p. 236 (quoted in Farquhar (1927–28), p. 111)

Crawfurd, Raymond, *The King's Evil* (Oxford, 1911)

Crawfurd, Raymond, 'The Blessing of Cramp-rings' in *Studies in the History and Method of Science*, edited by Charles Singer, second edition (London, 1955), pp. 165–87

Davies, J. G., *Holy Week: a Short History* (London, 1964)

Davies, Peter J., *British Silver Coins since 1816* (England, n.p. 1982)

Dawks' Newsletter, 8 April 1699, no. 439 (quoted in Farquhar (1929–30), p. 220)

Drake, Francis, *Eboracum: or the History and Antiquities of the City of York, from its Original to the Present Times. Together with the History of the Cathedral Church, and the Lives of the Archbishops of that See, from the first Introduction of Christianity into the Northern Parts of this Island, to the present State of Condition of that Magnificent Fabrick*, 2 books (London, 1736)

Dugdale, George S., *Whitehall through the Centuries* (London 1950)

Dyer, Mr G. P., Librarian and Curator at the Royal Mint, personal communication

Dyer, G. P., *The Proposed Coinage of King Edward VIII* (London, 1973)

Dyer, G. P. and P. P. Gaspar, 'The Striking of Proof and Pattern Coins in the Eighteenth Century', *BNJ*, 50 (1980), pp. 117–27 and Plates V–VIII

Dyer, G. P. and P. P. Gaspar, 'The Dorrien and Magens Shilling of 1798', *BNJ*, 52 (1982), pp. 198–214

Dyer, G. P. and Mark Stocker, 'Edgar Boehm and the Jubilee Coinage', *BNJ*, 54 (1984), pp. 274–88

Farquhar, Helen, 'Portraiture of our Stuart Monarchs on their Coins and Medals. Part V. William III, – continued', *BNJ*, 9 (1912)

Farquhar, Helen, 'Royal Charities. Part I, – Angels as Healing-Pieces for the King's Evil', *BNJ*, 12 (2, second series) (1916), pp. 39–135

Farquhar, Helen, 'Royal Charities. Part II. – Touchpieces for the King's Evil', *BNJ*, 13 (3, second series) (1917), pp. 95–163

Farquhar, Helen, 'Royal Charities. Part III. – Continuation of Touchpieces for the King's Evil. James II to William III', *BNJ*, 14 (4, second series) (1918), pp. 89–120

Farquhar, Helen, 'Royal Charities. Part IV. – Conclusion of Touchpieces for the King's Evil. Anne and the Stuart Princes', *BNJ*, 15 (5, second series) (1919–20), pp. 141–84

Farquhar, Helen, 'Royal Charities. (Second Series). The Maundy', *BNJ*, 16 (6, second series) (1921–22), pp. 195–228

Farquhar, Helen, 'Royal Charities. (Second Series). Part II. Alms at the Gate, Daily Alms and Privy Alms'. *BNJ*, 17 (7, second series) (1923–24), pp. 133–64

Farquhar, Helen, 'Royal Charities. (Second Series). Part III. Largesse and the King's Dole', *BNJ*, 18 (8, second series) (1925–26), pp. 63–91

Farquhar, Helen, 'Royal Charities. (Second Series). Part IV. The Maundy Coins', *BNJ*, 19 (9, second series) (1927–28), pp. 109–29

Farquhar, Helen, 'Royal Charities. (Second Series). Part V. The Maundy Pennies and Small Currencies', *BNJ*, 20 (10, second series) (1929–30), pp. 215–50

Feasey, H. J., *Ancient English Holy Week Ceremonial* (London, 1897)

Forrer, L. (compiler), *Biographical Dictionary of Medallists, Coin-, Gem-, and Seal-Engravers, Mint Masters, etc., Ancient and Modern, with Reference to their Works. B.C. 500 – A.D. 1900*, 8 vols (London, 1904–30)

Freeman-Grenville, G. S. P., *The Queen's Lineage from A.D. 495 to the Silver Jubilee of Her Majesty Queen Elizabeth II* (London, 1977)

Gaspar, Peter P., 'The 1821 BBITANNIAR: Sixpence and the Need for Reexamination of 19th Century Blundered Die Varieties', *NCirc*, 86 (1978), pp. 358–61

Gomme, George Lawrence (editor), *The Gentleman's Magazine Library. Popular Superstitions* (London, 1884)

Graham, T. H. B., 'Charles II's Hammered Silver Coinage', *NC*, 11, fourth series (1911), pp. 57–79 and Plate VI

Grueber, H. A., *Handbook of the Coins of Great Britain and Ireland in the British Museum*, second edition (London, 1970)

Harding, James, *Sales List of Small Silver and Maundy Money*, (December 1979); (June 1980), p. 1; (January 1982)

Hardy, T. D. (transcriber), *Rotuli de Liberate ac de Misis et Præstitis Regnante Johanne* (London, 1844)

Hawkins, Edward, *The Silver Coins of England*, third edition (London, 1887)

Henfrey, H. W., *A Guide to the Study of English Coins, from the Conquest to the Present Time*, revised by C. F. Keary (London, 1885)

Hocking, William John, *Catalogue of the Coins, Tokens, Medals, Dies and Seals in the Museum of the Royal Mint*, vol. 1, *Coins and Tokens* (London, 1906), vol. 2, *Dies, Medals and Seals* (London, 1910)

Hocking, William John, 'Notes on a Collection of Coining Instruments in the National Museum of Antiquities, Edinburgh', *PSAS*, 49 (1914–15), pp. 308–32

Hole, Christina, *English Traditional Customs* (London and Sydney, 1975)

Jacob, J. H., 'Trial of the Pyx', *New Zealand Numismatic Journal*, 14 (1976), pp. 24–27

John Bull (Monday, 8 April 1833) (quoted in *Coin and Medal News* (August 1987))

Johnson, Samuel, *A Dictionary of the English Language: in which the Words are Deduced from their Originals, and Illustrated in their Different Significations by Examples from the Best Writers. To which are Prefixed a History of the Language and an English Grammar. Stereotyped Verbatim from the Last Folio Edition Corrected by the Doctor* (Paris, 1830), p. 739

Kamen, H., 'The Destruction of the Spanish Silver Fleet at Vigo in 1702', *NCirc*, 76 (1968), pp. 186–89

Kelly, E. M., *Spanish Dollars and Silver Tokens. An Account of the Issues of the Bank of England 1797–1816* (London, 1976)

Linecar, H. W. A., *British Coin Designs and Designers* (London, 1977)

Linecar, H. W. A., 'Maundy Money Varieties', *NCirc*, 86 (1978), pp. 184–86

London Interiors with their Customs and Ceremonies (London, 1841)

Manville, Mr Harrington E., personal communication

Mays, James, 'The Lady behind the Northumberland Shilling', *Coins, incorporating Coins and Medals*, 13 (1976), pp. 18, 19

Mays, James O'Donald, 'Northumberland, his Wife and his Shilling', *NCirc*, 96 (1988), pp. 178–81

McAlpine, Ian and Brian Robinson, 'The Royal Coat of Arms on English Coinage'. *NCirc*, 86 (1978), pp. 575–77; 87 (1979), pp. 4–7

McAlpine, Ian and Brian Robinson, 'The Revolution in Coinage Design under Henry VII, *SCMB*, (March 1981), pp. 73–76; (April 1981), pp. 99–102

Mercurius Politicus, 18 April 1661 (quoted in Farquhar (1929–30), p. 223); 23 April 1663; 18 April 1667 (quoted in Farquhar (1925–26), p. 89)

Miles, John, 'The King's Evil', *History of Medicine*, 5, no. 4 (1974), pp. 23, 24

[Montagu, H.], *Catalogue of Sale of Collection of Milled English Coins, from George I to Victoria, including Patterns and Proofs* (London, Spink, 1890)

Morrieson, H. W., 'A Review of the Coinage of Charles II', *BNJ*, 15 (5, second series) (1919–20), pp. 117–39

Nicholls, Cornelius, 'Maundy Celebrations Ancient and Modern' *HCM* (1909), pp. 1–29

Nichols, John, *Progresses, Public Processions, etc. of Queen Elizabeth*, 3 vols (London, 1823)

Nicolas, Nicholas Harris, *Privy Purse Expenses of Elizabeth of York: Wardrobe Accounts of Edward the Fourth. With a Memoir of Elizabeth of York, and Notes* (London, 1830)
Nightingale, Benedict, *Charities* (London, 1973)
Norweb Collection Sale. English Coins – Part 2 (1985). Spink Coin Auction no. 48
Oman, Sir Charles, *The Coinage of England* (Oxford, 1931)
Onions, C. T. (with the assistance of G. W. S. Friedrichsen and R. W. Burchfield), *The Oxford Dictionary of English Etymology* (Oxford, 1966), p. 563
'On the Custom of the Maundy', *Saturday Magazine* (3 April 1841)
Peck, C. Wilson, *English Copper, Tin and Bronze Coins in the British Museum*, second edition (London, 1970)
Perham, Michael, *Liturgy Pastoral and Parochial* (London, 1984)
Pridmore, F. *The Coins of the British Commonwealth of Nations to the End of the Reign of George VI 1952. Part 3. Bermuda, British Guiana, British Honduras and the British West Indies* (London, 1965)
PRO, E101/415/3. Account Book of John Heron, Treasurer of the Chamber, 1 October 1499–31 October 1502
PRO, Accounts of Sir William Cavendish, Knight Treasurer of the King's Chamber, 1st. and 2nd. Ed. VI, bundle 426, vols 5, 6 (quoted in Farquhar (1927–28), p. 118)
PRO, Exchequer accounts various, bundle 415, no. 3, 18 April 1500 (quoted in Farquhar (1927–28), p. 118)
Ratcliffe, E. E., *The Royal Maundy* (London, 1936)
Ratcliffe, E. E., and P. A. Wright, *The Royal Maundy: a Brief Outline of its History and Ceremonial* (London, 1960)
Rayner, P. A., *The Designers and Engravers of the English Milled Coinage 1662–1953* (London, 1954)
Robinson, Brian, previously unpublished observation
Robinson, Brian, *The Royal Maundy* (London, 1977)
Robinson, Brian, 'Die Axis Variations of the Maundy Coinage', *NCirc*, 94 (1986), pp. 46, 47
Ruding, Rogers, *Annals of the Coinage of Britain and its Dependencies*, 4 vols (vol. 4 contains the Plates) (London, 1817); second edition, (6 vols (vol. 6 contains the Plates) (London, 1819); third edition, 3 vols (vol. 3 contains the Plates) (London, 1840)
Sacra Moneta, Galata Coins, Wolverhampton (September 1987), p. 3
Salzman, M. G., *A Handbook of Modern British Coins and their Varieties 1797–1970* (London, 1982)
Seaby, Peter, *The Story of the British Coinage* (London, 1985)
Seaby, Peter and Purvey, P. Frank, *Standard Catalogue of British Coins. vol. 2. Coins of Scotland, Ireland and the Islands (Jersey, Guernsey, Man and Lundy)* (London, 1984), p. 39
Sheppard, Edgar, *The Old Royal Palace of Whitehall* (London, 1902)
Sitwell, H. D. W., 'The Crown Jewels and other Regalia in the Tower of London', (London 1953), p. 95 and plate 29
Skeat, W. W., *An Etymological Dictionary of the English Language* (Oxford, 1882, 1910)
Snelling, Thomas, *A View of the Silver Coinage of England from the Norman Conquest to the Present Time* (London, 1762)
Spink and Son, Ltd, *The Royal Maundy* (London, c. 1902)
Spink Coin Auction, 4 June 1980, No. 9. *The Collection of English Milled Silver Coins 1656–1800 formed by H. E. Manville of Washington DC*, p. 52
Spink Coin Auction, 19 November 1987, no. 62
Squibb, T. F. E., 'Maundy Ceremonies of the Past', *SCMB* (April 1961), pp. 138–40 (a contemporary report quoted from the *Annual Register*, 24 March 1826)
Stewart, Ian H., 'Some Scottish Ceremonial Coins', *PSAS*, 98 (1964–65, 1965–66), pp. 254–75 and Plates XXXV, XXXVI

Stewart, Ian Halley, *The Scottish Coinage*, with supplement (London, 1967), p. 122
Sutherland, C. H. V., *English Coinage 600–1900* (London, 1973)
Symonds, Henry, 'The Pyx Trials of the Commonwealth, Charles II and James II', *NC*, 15, fourth series (1915), pp. 345–50
Symonds, Henry, 'The Mint of Queen Elizabeth and Those Who Worked There', *NC*, 16, fourth series (1916), pp. 61–105
Tanner, Dr Lawrence E., Secretary of the Royal Almonry from 1921 to 1964, personal communication
Tanner, Lawrence E., *The Royal Almonry and the Maundy Service*', presidential address to the British Archæological Society, 1956
Tanner, Lawrence E., 'Lord High Almoners and Sub–Almoners, 1100–1957' *Journal of the British Arahæological Association*, 20, 21 (1957–58), pp. 72–83
Tanner, Lawrence, E., *Recollections of a Westminster Antiquary* (London, 1969), Chapter 10, pp. 120–29
The Diary of Samuel Pepys, M.A., F.R.S., edited with additions by Henry B. Wheatley (London, 1895), vol. 6
'The Royal Cure for the King's Evil', *BMJ* (13 May 1899), pp. 1182–84
Thurston, Herbert, 'Lent and Holy Week' (1904)
Torr, James, *The Antiquities of York City, and the Civil Government thereof: with a List of all the Mayors and Bayliffs, Lord Mayors and Sheriffs, from the Time of King EDWARD the First, to this present Year, 1719. Collected from the Papers of Christopher Hildyard Esq; With Notes and Observations, and the Addition of Ancient Inscriptions, and Coates or Arms, from Gravestones and Church–windows, and since Continued to this present Year 1719, With an APPENDIX of the Dimensions of YORK Minster, the Names of the Founders, Repairers, and Benefactors. A Catalogue of all the Religious Houses, Chapells, and Churches, that have been, and at present are, in the said City. As [sic] also the Gifts and Legacies to the Charity–Schools, with the Names of the first Promotors and Founders thereof* (York, 1719)
Trowbridge, Richard J., *Maundy Coins of Great Britain*, third edition (Glendale, California, 1976)
Urry, William, 'Maundy Rites at Canterbury in the Middle Ages', *Friends of Canterbury Cathedral 25th Annual Report 1965*
Walford, Edward, *Old and New London: a Narrative of its History, its People and its Places*, 6 vols (vols 1 and 2 by Walter Thornbury) (London, Paris and New York, 1873–78). III, *Westminster and the Western Suburbs*, pp. 368–69
Webb, Henry, '*Remarks on the Early Silver Coins of Charles II, with an Attempted Arrangement of the Smaller Pieces not Fully Classified by Hawkins*', *NC*, 19, new series (1879), pp. 92–98 and plate IV
Wingate, James, 'Interesting Discovery in Scotch [sic] Numismatics', *NC*, 9, new series (1868–69), p. 215
Woolf, Noel, 'The Sovereign Remedy: Touch–Pieces and the King's Evil', *BNJ*, 49 (1979), pp. 99–121 and Plates XIX–XXII
Woolf, Noel, 'The Sovereign Remedy: Touch–Pieces and the King's Evil. Part II', *BNJ*, 50 (1980), pp. 91–116 and Plates II–IV
Woolf, Noel, 'The Sovereign Remedy: Touch–Pieces for the King's Evil – supplement', *BNJ*, 55 (1985), p. 195
Woolf, Noel, *The Sovereign Remedy. Touch-Pieces and the King's Evil* (Manchester, 1990)
Wright, Mr Peter A., Secretary of the Royal Almonry, personal communication
Wright, Peter A., *The Pictorial History of the Royal Maundy* (London, 1966, 1971, 1981)

PLATES

The captions to the plates are located on pages xiv-xviii

1   2

3

4

5

De his que facere debet subelemos die cene.

Que qd fer. iiij. post ramos palm̄ subelemos recipe dz a celerar̄ singula sig' videlic' p archiep'o· iij. signa si p'sens sit. Et p priore ij. Et p quolib3 fr̄e p'sente signū j. Et p quolib3 existente in servic' et defūcto eodē anno rec' signū j. Et p hospitib3 religiosis si venerint recipiet pro quolib3 signū unū. Que omnia sig' librabit elemos. de quib3 elemos librabit de consuetud p manū subelemos. suppor' iij. sig'. Tercio por' ij. Quarto priori ij. Celerario iij. subceler' ij. p'centor' ij. succentor' j. tercio antor' j. sacriste ij. magro subsacriste j. camerar' ij. sub camerar' j. magris infirmar' iij. penitenciar' iij. granetar' ij. Refector' ij. socio suo j. hostiler' j. cocinar' j. Et aulẽ infirmo pretinenti baculū j. ceteria v̄o signia in voluntate elemos remanent distribuēda Excepto qd librabit subelemos iiij. Et servienti suo. In refectorio j. Et garcioni panetar' in celar' j.

Die cene post cap'lm subelemos

intrans dz aquam et vocare singulos pauperes et duc' p claustrū ad altare beati Johis uv̄ chorium et celebrare missam de sp̄u sc̄o. q' finita reducere dz pauperes p claustrū in aulam ubi singuli pauperes recipe debent j. panē qui dicitur smalkeys. pisas sal. et iij. allecia. Et potare qn̄tū uoliunt. Residuū potus remanebit ad elemos. Et servientes elemosinar' panē potū pis' sal. Et salsar' allecia recipe dz a celerar'o et thes' prata in aula. antequā redierint de ecc'a post ea lavare debent pauperes pedes suos u' ante si voluerint. Et post missam convectū dn̄i conventū recipit panē et biberes. p visum celerar'ij et gn̄ear' intrabunt pauperes claustrū expectantes mandatū. post p'ndiū p'acto mandato in quentu et totis ec'a cervus p'cata in elemosinar' a: subelemos librabit cuilib3 servienti qui mr̄fuit mandato unā lagenā cervis' de gn̄a.

7

DIE Joṽ Cene aṗd Cnareburḡ, in ma .... Reḡ ad x .... iij. s̃. j. d̃. P robis, illoɤ paupū ... suendis ij. s̃. ij. d̃. P xiij. zonis, ⁊ xiij. cultellis, ⁊ xiij. braccalibʒ ad eosdē paupes ⁊ p xiij. ...... iiij. s̃. iiij. d̃. ob̃ ...... de Binedoñ. Nicoł carpent̃ se iiij[to]. socioɤ eunt̃ ad Hugōem de Nevill, ij. m̃. p Ŗ. Galfr̃ de La Jaił mił ... oti Ivoñ de Lajał, de dono, xx. s̃. p Ŗ.

DIE Veñ Crucis adorande ibid̃, in mił paupibus q°s dñs Rex pavit eadē die iiij. li. xiij. s̃. ix. d̃. It .... upibʒ q°s dñs Rex pavit eo qd̃ Ric̆ de Mari ..... pisces ix. s̃. iiij. d̃. ob̃. Eadē die ib, Odoni caretar̃ de warderoba se alt̃o ad robas e ...... Cointance sūmetar̃ ad robā v. .... Bel sūmet̃ ad robā vij. s̃. vj. d̃. Luc̆ sūmetar̃ ad robā, vij. s̃. vj. d̃. La ... ... obā, vij. s̃. vj. d̃. Rad̃ sūmet̃ ...

Robe carettar̃ ⁊ sūmeł.

Sᵃ viijᵃ. CCC. li. xxxvij. s̃. j. d̃.

D Sab̃ in vigił Pasc̆ aṗ Cnareburḡ, Herneš nūtio Thom̃ de Samford .... eunti c̃ litt̃is ad com̃ Wint̃ .....

D Mart̃ proxᵃ post diē Pasc̆ aṗd Wakefeld̃, Ric̆ nūtio Elie B'nard̃ eunti ...... m̃. P pargameno vij. d̃.

DIE ...... in dignerio dñi Regis ibid̃, p plibʒ carnibʒ xj. s̃. viij. d̃. p Rob̃ de Vet̃i P ......

...... ṗxᵃ aṗ Notingeh̃, Thom̃ de L ...... ⁊ rancino suo aṗ Norhant̃ iij. s̃.

D Sab̃ ib̃, p xj. ulñ de grisenc̃ ad facie ......, qñ ivim⁹ ī exẽrcitū Scoc̆, x. ......

8

D Sab̃ ī septim̃ Pasc̆ aṗ Notingeh̃, Phil de Wigorñ mił, eūti ī nūtiū dñi Reḡ ..., de dono x. m̃. p Ŗ. Ric̆ nūti, ... suū de dono j. m̃. p Regē. Amfredo de Dena militi, eunti ī nūtiū dñi Reḡ ī Hib̃ ..... dono x. m̃. p Ŗ.

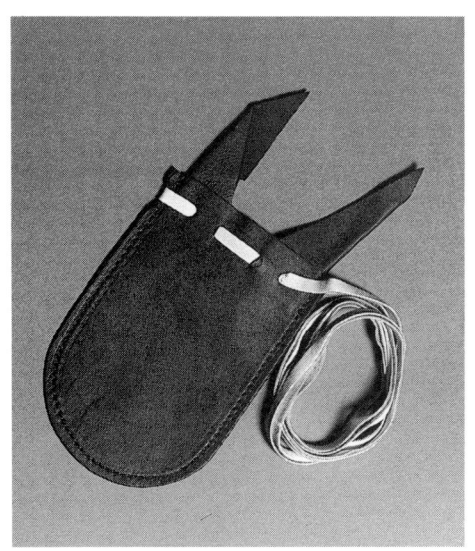

11

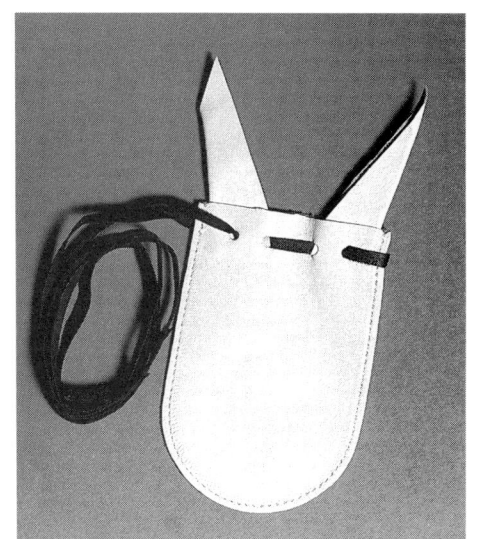

12

13

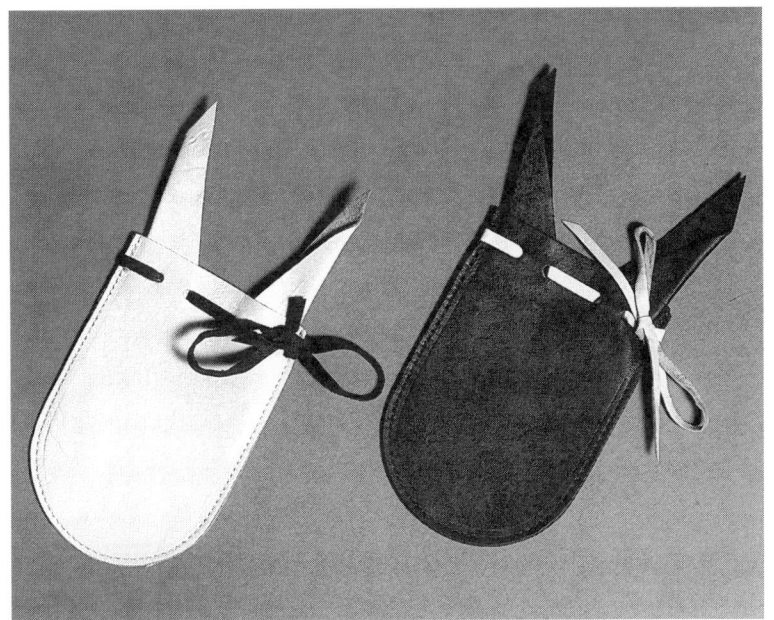

15

16

17

18

19

20

22

23

24

25

26

27

28

29

30

32

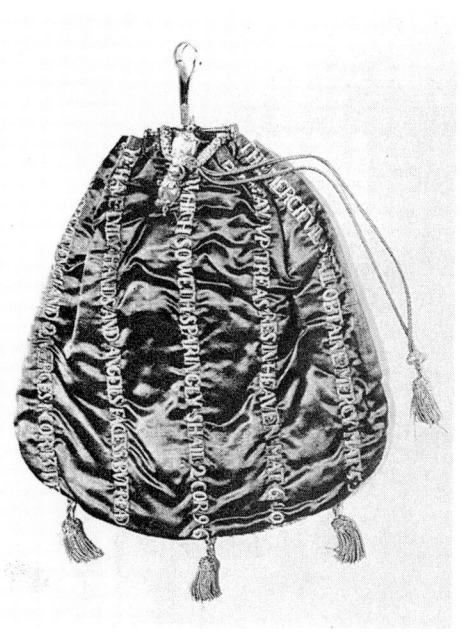 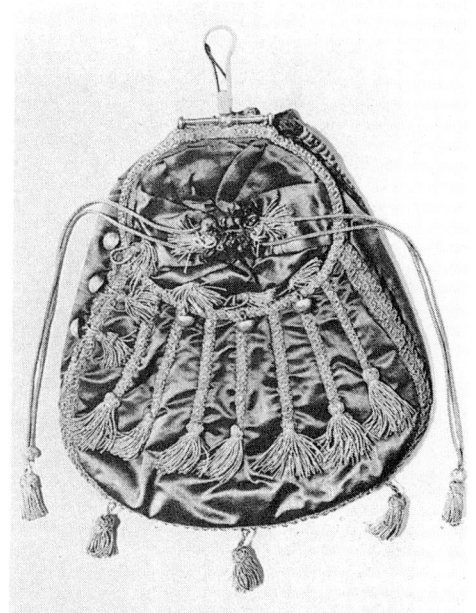

33

34

35

36

37

38   39   40

41

42

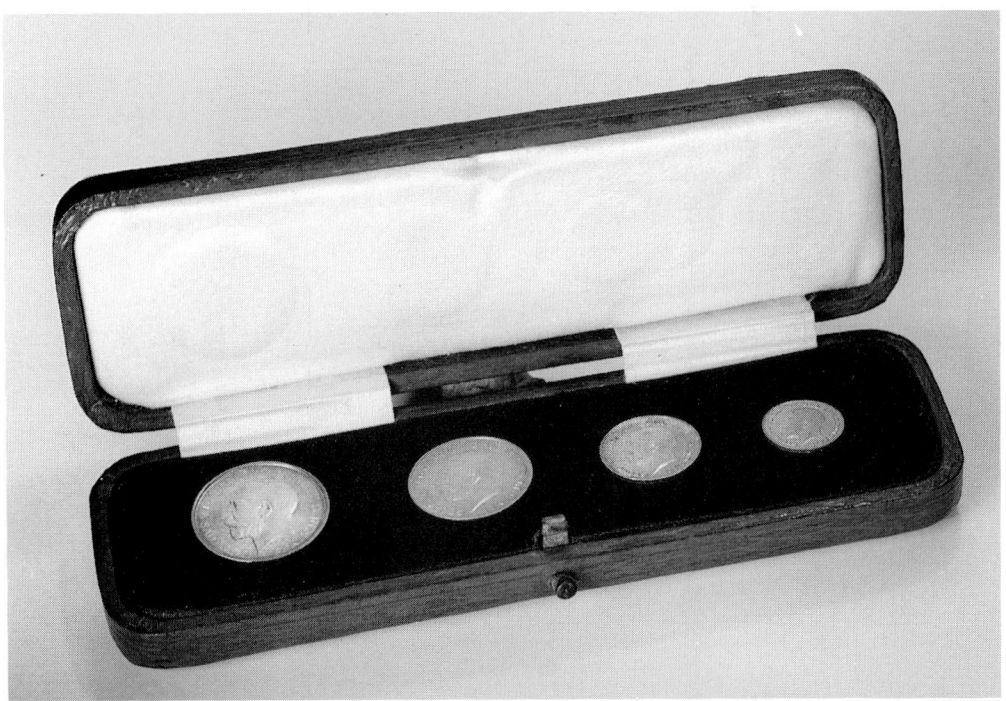

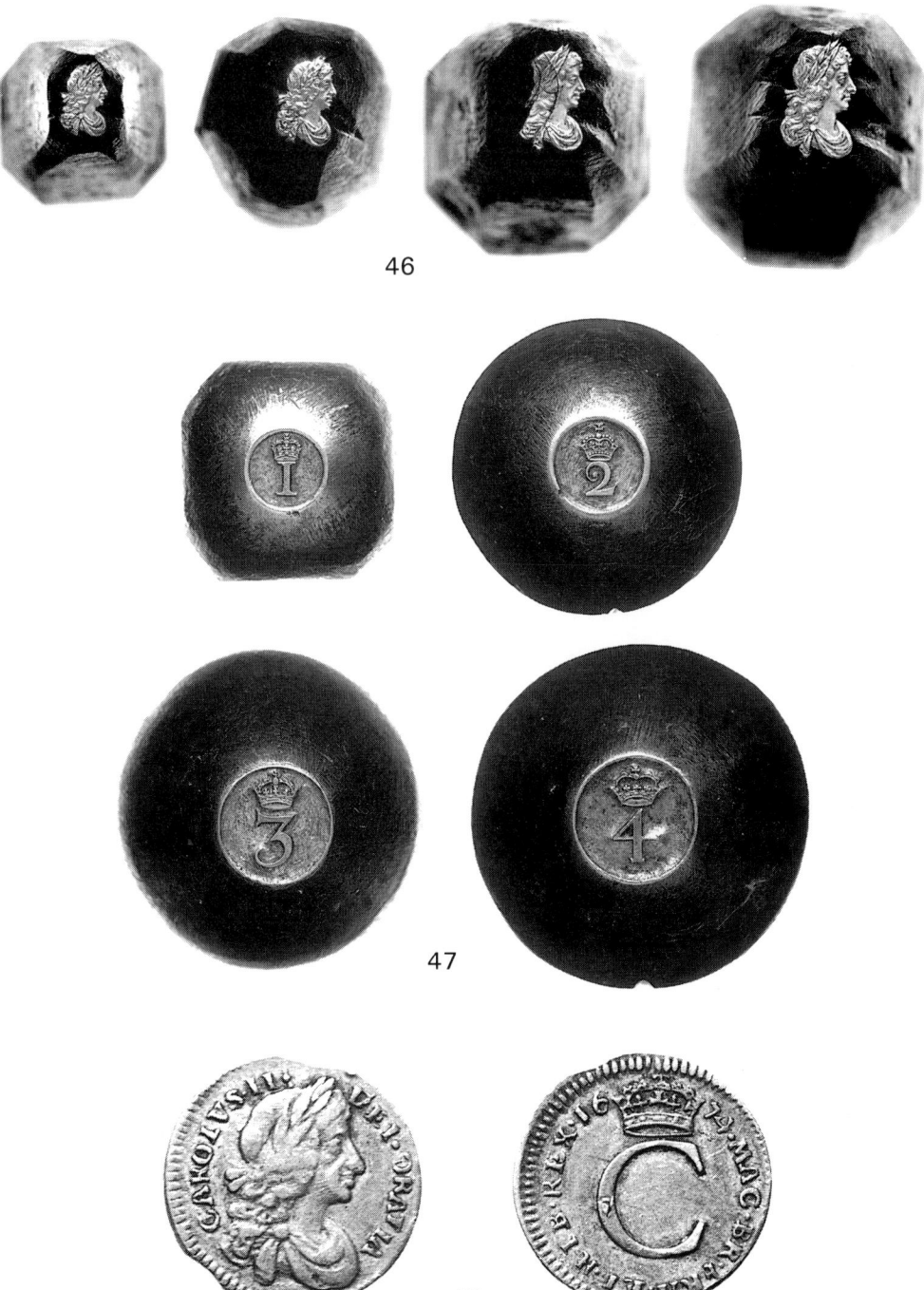

46

47

48

59

60

61

62

63

64

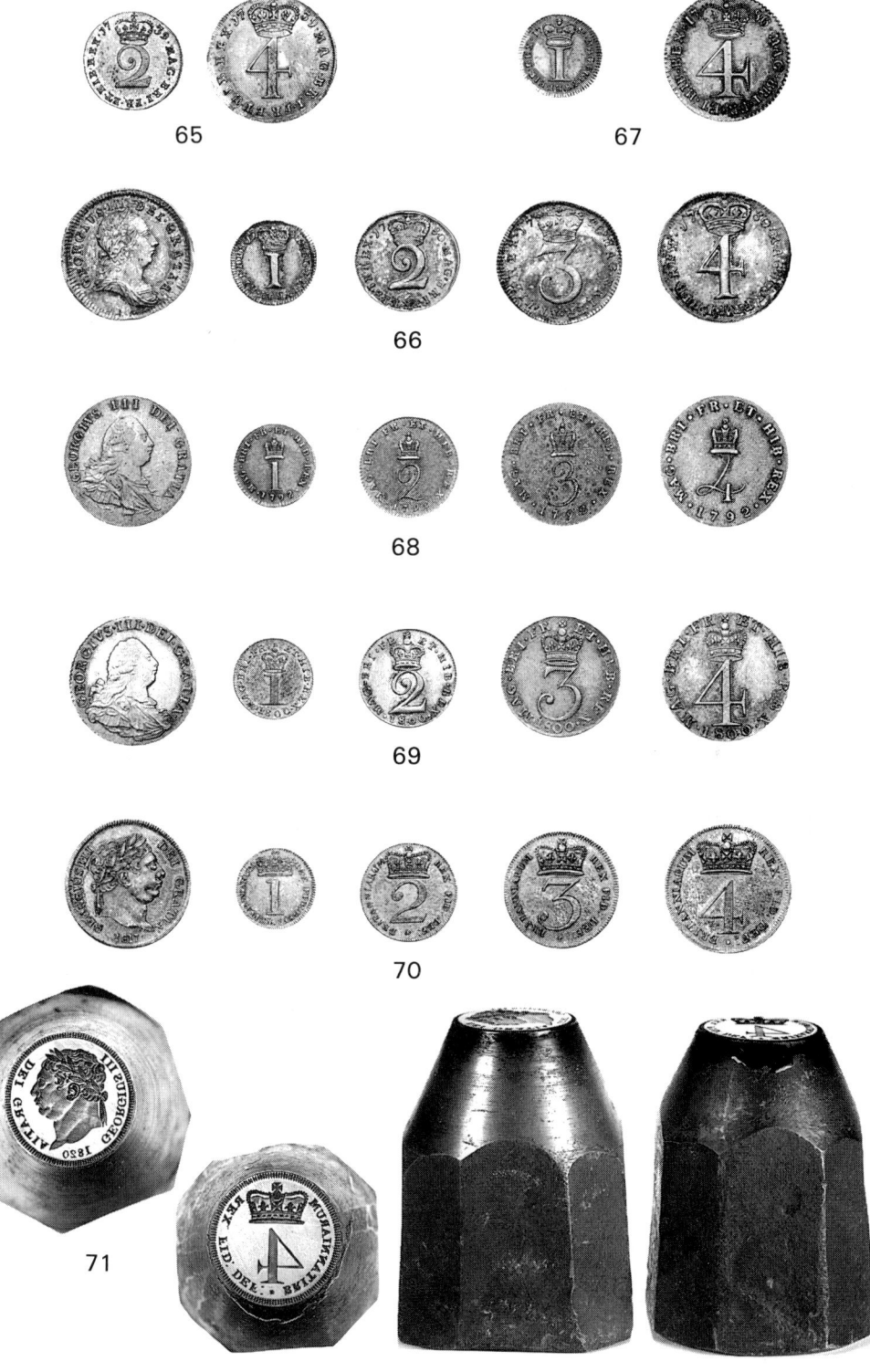

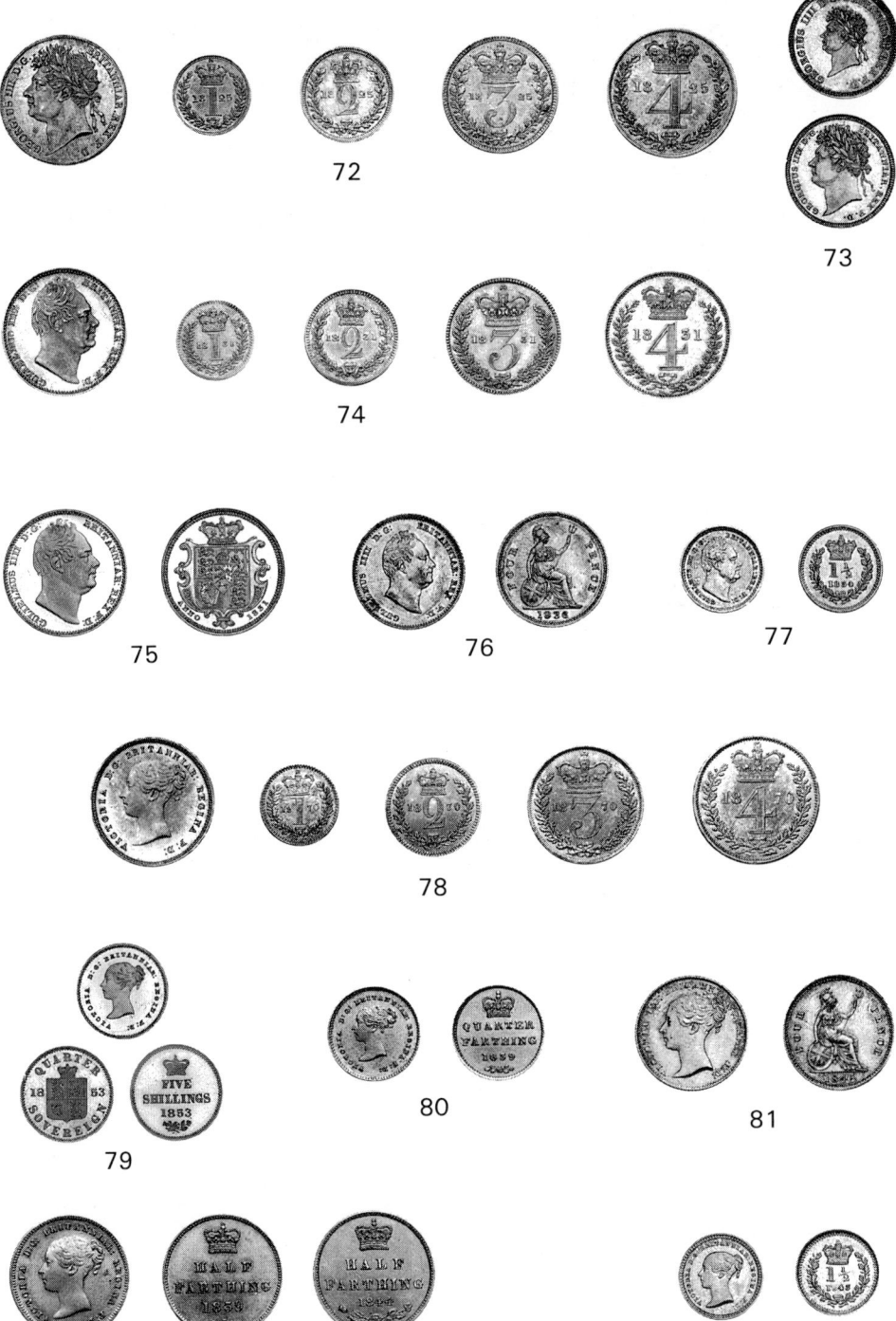

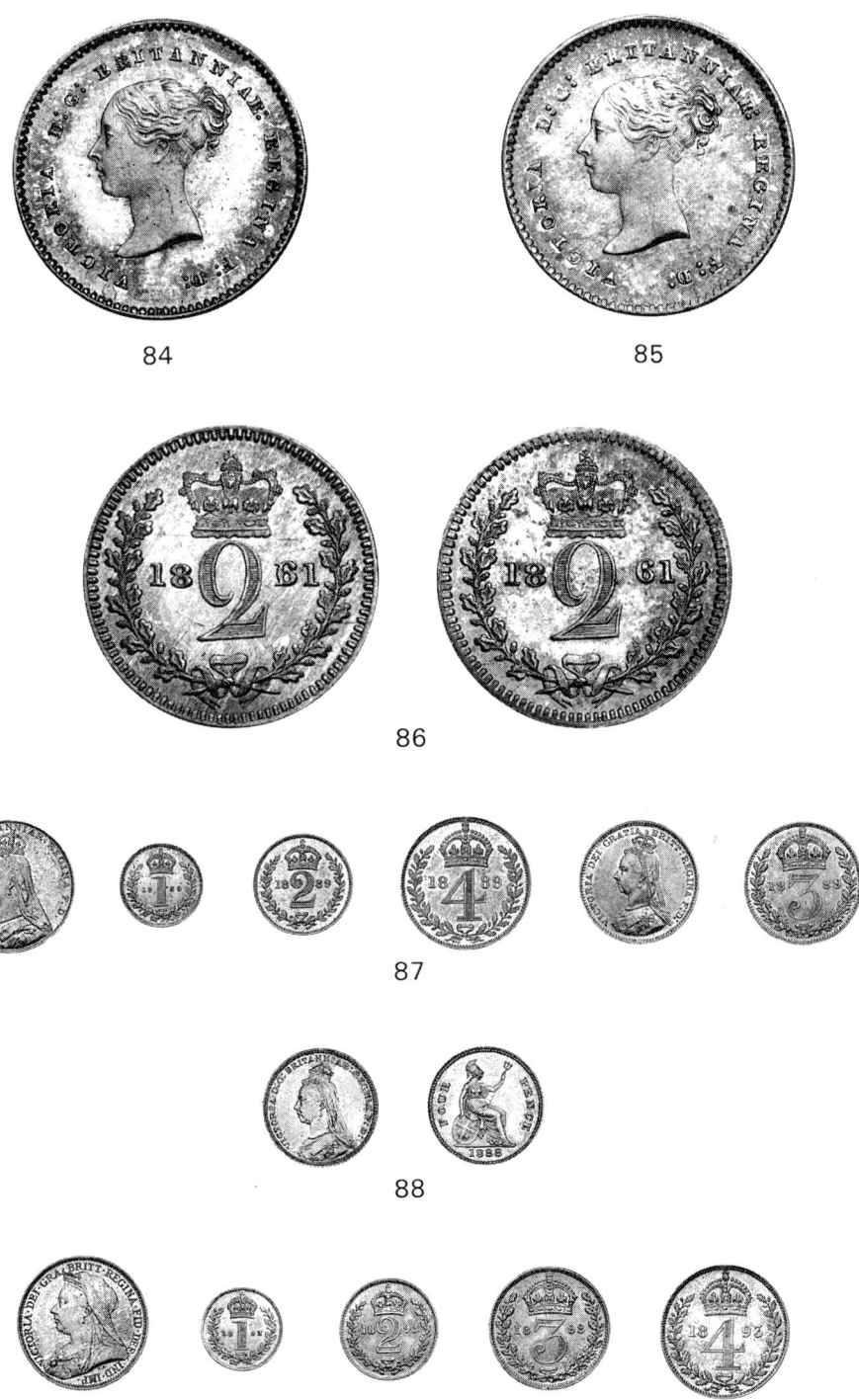

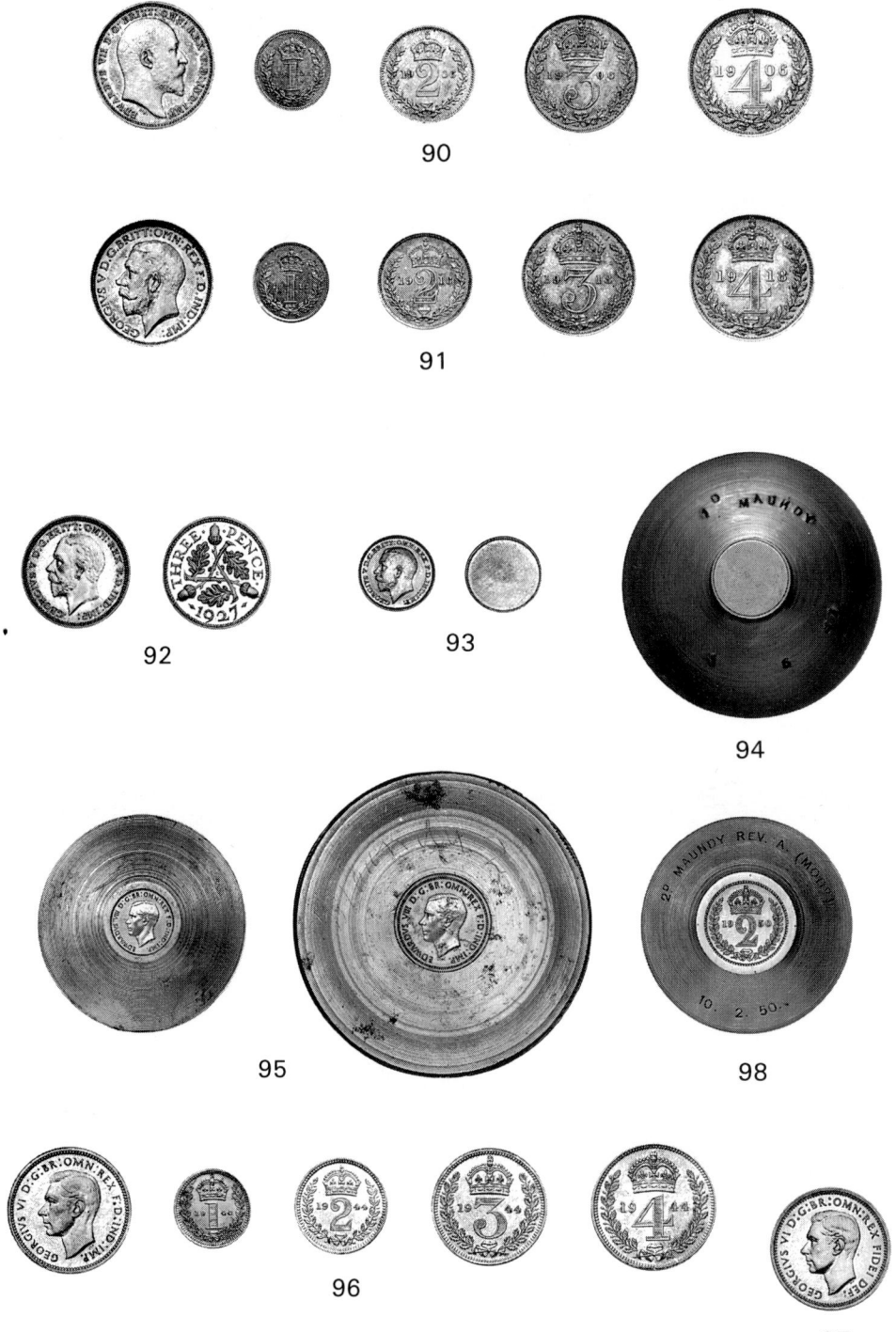

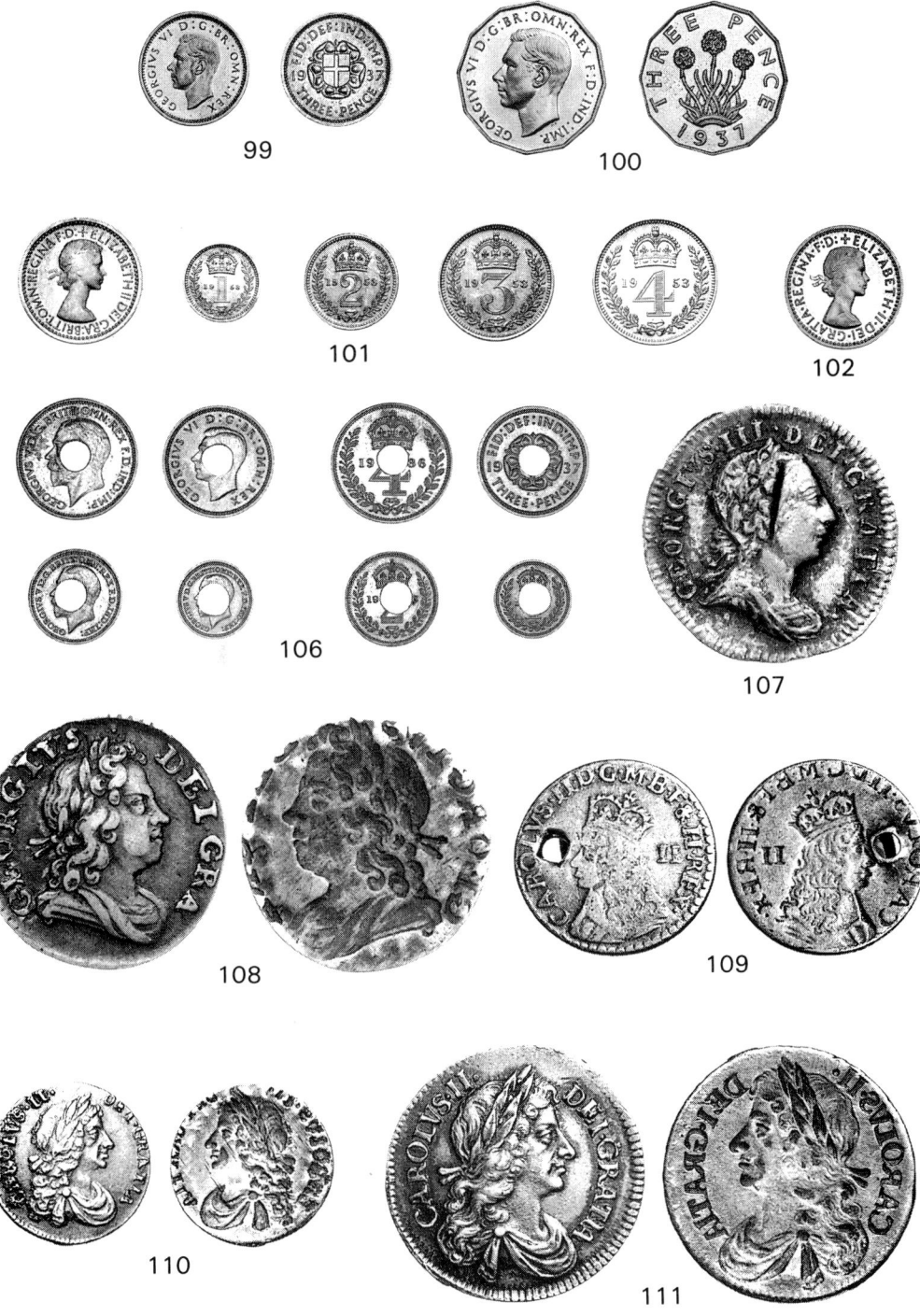

Minute

1831 Mar 23

Mint 9/114

To the Provost and Company of Moneyers
And the ~~Surveyor of Money Presses~~

*
12 Proofs in 1.
12 — in 2.
12 — in 3.
12 — in 4.

You are hereby authorized, in conformity
with the directions of the Master of the Mint, to
allow Mr W. Wyon, the Chief Engraver the use of
the Cutting of Presses for Cutting Blanks ~~striking off~~ a Series of
Proof Impressions in Fine Gold from the Dies
which have been prepared for His Majesty's
New Coinage of Maundy Monies.

Mint Office
23d March 1831.

Signed J.W. Morrison

A similar authority sent to Mr Beaudé
to allow the use of the Die Press.

104

105

Index

Unless otherwise indicated, the pennies, twopences, threepences and fourpences referred to in this index are those which were struck in silver and, likewise, all monarchs referred to are of England.

Abdication of
  Edward VIII, 183
  James II, 10, 149
Act
  Coinage
    1870, 96, 239
    1946, 97, 98
    1971, 96
  Engravers', 89
  Lord Chesterfield's, 233
  of
    Union with Ireland, 164
    Union with Scotland, 92, 111–12, 156
Acts of
  Parliament, 107, 237
  the Council, 100
Adoration of the Cross, 13
Aliens' law of William III, 222, 224, 227, 245
Allowances, *see* Clothing allowance; Food allowance; Robe redemption allowance
Alloy, 96, 97, 103, 111, 178, 183, 185, 187, 196, 223
Almoner, 73
  Grand, 29
  Great, 74
  Hereditary Grand, *see* Hereditary Grand Almoner
  King's, 26, 73, 75, 78
  Lord High, *see* Lord High Almoner; *see also* Great Almoner, High Almoner, King's High Almoner
  sub-, *see* Sub-almoner
  to the Queen (consort), 35
Almonry, *see also* Royal Almonry
  at Windsor, 58
  Office, *see* Royal Almonry
Alms, Daily and Gate; *see also* Royal Gate Alms
  at Easter, 206
  monetary denominations used for, 113, 120
  of
    food, 2
    money, 2
  reason for, 2
  recipients of, 2
  venues for distribution of, 2, 16
Alms dishes, *see* Dishes
America
  United States of, 97
  visitors from, 131
Angel
  (coin)
    as the source of the seal of the Royal Almonry, 80
    attempt to restore as a healing-piece, 9
    change of legend on, 7, 8
    first introduced into coinage, 6
    first regularly used as a healing-piece, 6
    gold, mystic power of, 7
    increases in value of, 7
    legends on, 6–8
    maintenance of fineness, 7
    ship on design of, 6, 80, Plate 1
    specially struck for touching, 8
    striking of ceased, 8
    use as robe redemption allowance, 34
    value of, 6, 7
    weight of, 7
    wyvern on, 6, 16
  (which visited Pope Gregory the Great's table), 25, 61, 95
Anne, 41, 42, 51
  death of, 12
  end of touching by, 12
  gift of purse to William Lloyd, 79, Plate 33
  groove on obverse of some of pennies of, 198, 218; *see also* Groove on the obverse of some post-Restoration silver pennies
  Scotland, popularity in, 112
  small silver coinage of, 104, 111, 154–56, Plate 62
    die-axis of, 192
    slight change in portraiture on, 154
  touching by, 11, 17
  Vigo coinage of, 101, 118
Apostles, 56
  and Jesus, as the prototype for the number (thirteen) of Maundy recipients, 20, 25, 61, 95
  and the angel who came to Pope Gregory the Great's table, as the prototype for the number (thirteen) of Maundy recipients, 25, 61, 95
  as the prototype for the number (twelve) of Maundy recipients, 24, 29, 35, 42, 61, 64, 66
  pence in the Gift of Pennies, 37
  Jesus washed the feet of, 19, 37
Aprons, *see* Maundy aprons
Aragon, Catherine of, 35
Arbuthnot, John, 113
Argyll, Duchess of (Princess Louise), 49
Athlone
  Countess of (Princess Alice), 49
  Earl of, 49
Bank of England, 118–19, 125,

254 Index

130, 210, 214
Banqueting House, Whitehall,
  231; *see also* Chapel Royal,
  Whitehall, 58; Whitehall
  organ lent for Maundy services,
  58
  venue for
    Maundy distributions 42, 43,
    58
    the *pedilavium*, 42
    touching, 8
Barons of the Exchequer, 238–39
Basire, James, 47
Basket, 57, 79
Bath, touching at, 11
Beef-eaters, 236
Beg, 57
Bennett-Levy, Mrs, 44
Bible, New English, 63
Bifurcations, 195
Bimetallism, 206
Birmingham Cathedral, 51–55, 63
Birthdays of monarchs, xii
Bitt (and half-bitt), 244, 246
Blondeau, Peter, 146, 241–42
Board, Goodman, 38
Boehm, Sir Joseph Edgar, 175,
  219
Bonnie Prince Charlie, 12
Bosworth Field, Battle of, 85, 236
Boulton, Matthew, 119, 164, 241
Bounty
  Common, 3
  Discretionary, 3
    recipients, selection of, 3
  Minor, 3
    recipients, selection of, 3
Bower, George, 152, 219, 221–22
Briot, Nicholas, 4, 8, 149, 219,
  220, 228, 242, Plates 56 and 57
Bristol, Bishop of, 77, 78, 81
Britannia Groat, 112, 124, 244
  discontinued, 244
  for colonial use, 244
  general currency in Britain, 244
  known as the Joey, 244
  master-tools for, 168
  of
    Victoria (jubilee head), 175,
      244, Plate 88
    Victoria (young head), 168,
      244, Plate 81
    William IV, 168, 244, Plate
      76
  popularity in Scotland, 244
  shape and size of, 244
  weight of, 244
Britanniar, removed from royal
  titles, 190–1
British Guiana, 124, 244, 246
Brock, Sir Thomas, 175, 220, 222
Brockages, 137, 200–1, Plates 108

to 118
  definition of, 200
  method of production, 200
  obverse, and how to date,
    200–1
  reverse, 200–1
  reasons for production
    (possible), 201
Browne, John, 9, 10
Brystall, Yorkshire, Vicar of, 80
Buffetiers, 236
Bull
  head, 164
  Samuel, 154, 220
Burrs (vertical), 195
  deburring, 194
Bust profile; *see also* Direction of
  profile bust; Effigy
  direction reversed in following
    reign, 212–13
Cæsar, Rev. Anthony Douglass,
  53, 82
Calendar, 232–33
  Gregorian, 232–33
  Julian, 111, 232
  New Style, 111, 232–33
  Old Style, 111, 153, 232–33
Cambridge
  Clare College, Master of, 81
  Colleges, Maundy coins for,
    120, 125, 210
  King's College, Provost of, 76
  King's hall,
    endowment to by Edward
      III, 5
    Warden of, 76
  Lady May, 49
  Pembroke College, Master of,
    81
  royal endowment of a reader
    or professor in Arabic, 5
  Trinity College, Master of, 77
Canterbury
  Archbishop of
    Cranmer, Thomas, 87
      first protestant, 87
    Lanfranc of Bec, 21
    Lord High Almoner, 51, 60,
      61, 78, 90, Plates 28 and 31
    Sub-almoner, 82
  Cathedral, 62, 73
  mediæval Maundy services of
    the monks at, 20–24
Caritatis potum, 50; *see also*
  Drinking the monarch's
  health; Loving cup
Carlisle
  Bishop of, 77, 78
  Cathedral, 62
  Dean of, 48, 81
Cartwheel, 112
Carwood Castle, 37

Cashel, Archbishop of, 78
Castaing machine, 243
Cave, Joseph, 111, 208
Cellini, Benvenuto, 241
Cene, day of, 57
Cena Dni, 24
Cena Domini, 26, 57, 63
Ceylon, 215
Chamberlayne, Wm., 113
Chancellor of the Exchequer, 99,
  205
Chantrey, Sir Francis, 165, 167,
  220–21
Chapel
  Plate
  Royal
    Children of, 48, 52, 60, 235
    choir, 60, 235
    Gentlemen of, 48, 52, 59, 60,
      235
    service, 80
    Whitehall; *see also*
      Banqueting House,
      Whitehall; Whitehall
      Ante-chapel of, 47, 58,
        Plate 23
      ceiling of, 48, 231, Plate 17
      closed for repairs, 58
      conveyance of Maundy
        alms to, 46, Plate 22
      destruction by fire, 231
      Maundy services at, 43,
        45–48, 58, 231, Plates 16,
        17 and 23
      Venue for the Maundy
        service, 235
        ceased as, 60, 89
        reopened as, 48, 60
        temporarily vacated as,
          58, 59
      young gentlemen of, 59
Chapels Royal, Sub-dean of, *see*
  Sub-almoner, 80–82
Char, 56
Charity
  of
    ecclesiastics, 2, 4
    important organisations, 2
    nobles, 4
    organization of, 1
    royal, 111
      details of not publically
        available, 4
      disbanded, 3
      educational endowments
        from, 5
      pensions from, 3, 4
      reasons for, 4, 26
      still payable, 2, 3
Charles I
  angel (coin) of, 7
  coronation medalets of, 4

Index 255

Easter alms of, 206
execution of, 231
hammered coinage of, 241–42
largesse distribution by, 39
Maundy distributions for, 38, 39, 58, 65, 101
milled coinage during reign of, 242
Oxford Declaration Penny, 39, 101, Plate 40
pattern penny and twopences by Briot, 149, Plates 56 and 57
touching by, 8, 39
Trial of the Pyx during reign of, 239
Charles II; *see also* Restoration
coining by the hammer during reign of, 241–42
Commonwealth and foreign coins current during early part of reign of, 141
donation of the Maundy Dish by, 234
endowment of Christ's Hospital by, 5
foundation of the Royal Hospital at Chelsea by, 67
Maundy
distribution by, 40, 65, 101
petitioners of, 66, 67, 93
service
restored by, 40, 65
interest in began to wane, 40
mintmark on coinage of, 212
pattern (?) twopence of, 147–49, 191, 196, 207
robe redemption allowance of, type of coins used, 34
Simon's Maundy money of, 101–2, 106, 142, 145–46, 212
small silver coinage of
hammered (type 1), 101, 141–46, 212, Plates 51 to 54
classification of, 142–43
die-axes of, 193
machine made, 142, 145–46
milled, 146
(type 2), 102–4, 106, 141–42, 146–49, Plate 55
brockages of, 200–1, Plates 109 to 113
die-axes of, 191–92
intradenomination weight variation of, 211
introduced, 242–43
Trial of the Pyx of, 103
state entry into London, 141
surgeon of, 10

touching by, 8, 9
Charwoman, 56
Chelmsford Cathedral, 62
Chelsea, Royal Hospital at, 67
Chester Cathedral, 10
Chesterfield
Act of Lord, 233
fifth Earl of, 209; *see also* Stanhope, Philip
Chichester
Bishop of, 29, 76, 77, 82
Cathedral, 62
Chief Engraver, *see* Engraver, Chief
Chizzolo, Dr Ippolito, 29
Chore, 56
Christie, Mr, 99, 100
Christmas, 2, 3, 118, 120, 220, 232
Eve, 14
for curing, 14
Churchill, Winston Spencer, 99
Cinquefoil, 164
Civil War
Briot during, 220
king in York just prior to, 38, 39, 58
Maundy
distributions during, 39, 58
recipients of Charles II from the injured, 66
Thomas Rawlins' work during, 227
touching during, 8
Cleansing, 56
Clerk, James, 111, 208
Clipping, 242–43
defeated, 243
Clothing allowance, 34; *see also* Maundy gifts of clothing and food
distribution of, 45, 61
by the Lord High Almoner, 45, 50
in
paper packets, 45, 50
purses, 45, 46, 61; *see also* Purses
introduced for
men, 45
women, 45, 89
magnitude of, 45, 61
type of coin used for, 45
Clothing gift, *see* Maundy gifts of clothing and food
Coat of arms, 142, 146, 153–54, 210, 212
last use on the small silver coinage, 211
Cæna Domini, 57
Cænæ Domini, 57
Coinage; *see also* Indentures, for

the coinage
assay of, *see* Trial of the Pyx
dating of, rigid system introduced, 174
hammered, 141, 146, 212, 241–43
machine made, but hammered, 142, 145–46
manufacture of, 136, 241–44
by the screw-press, 241
economic philosophy of, 116, 158, 165
Maundy, *see* Maundy money
milled, 141–42, 146, 212, 241–44
Coining, irons for, 141
Colchester, Archdeacon of, 76
Collar
use of in coining, 101, 145, 164, 195, 243
not used in coining, 164, 195, 211
Collyer, Thomas, 66
Colon in legend
first
appearance in the small silver coinage, 154, 156
standard use in the Maundy coinage, 215
Colsoni, F., 41, 42
Command, 57
Commercialism, 120, 130–32
Committee
advisory, on coin, 225
Privy Council, on Coin, 119, 163
Royal Mint Advisory, 182, 191, 225–26
Commonwealth
coining during, 242
coins current during early part of Charles II's reign, 141
countries, 190
bust on coins of, 216
Maundy distribution in abeyance, 39
"Queen" (bust), 217
Thomas
Rawlins during, 227
Simon during, 228–29
touching during, 8
Trial of the Pyx during, 239–40
Compton, Lord Alwyne, 49, 78, Plate 27
Conway, Right Honourable Sir Edward, 101
Cook, Captain James, 161
Copper
coinage of 1672, 103, 112
Maundy set in, 185, 197–98, Plate 105
die-axis of, 192

raison d'être of, 197–98
pattern groat in, 111–12
penny in (?), 111
Coronation
  crown of 1953, 48
  Hereditary Grand Almoner at, 74
  King's Champion at, 4
  largesse distributed at, 4
  of
    Charles I, 4
    Edward VII, 60
    Edward VIII (proposed), 50
    Elizabeth II, 50, 61
    George V, 60
    George VI, 60
    Henry VII, 236
    Victoria, 74
    William II, 4
Cotton, Billy, 209
Counterfeiting, 117, 119, 242
Counterstamping, *see* Dollars (Mexican and Spanish)
Court Heralds, 4
Craig, Sir John, 97, 98
Cramp rings, *see* Rings, cramp
Cranmer, Archbishop Thomas, 35, 37, 87
  death of, 87
Croker, John, 153–54, 156, 158, 220–22, 229
Cromwell, Oliver, 229, 239, 242; *see also* Commonwealth
Cross
  of Gwyneth, 13
  section, 194
    wedge-shaped, 195
  the, 13, 14
    Adoration of, 13
Crown
  jewels, 175, 234
  mintmark, 212
  of
    1953, 48
    1977, 48
  Petition, 228–29
  wreath, 202
Crowns, multiformity in, 161–62, 175, Figure 1
Curle, Dr, 38; *see also* Curll, Walter
Curll, Walter, 77; *see also* Curle, Dr
Cutting, 242
da Vinci, Leonardo, 241
Damaged letters, 211
Dates, 232–33
de
  Bluntesdon, Henry, 75, 79, 94
    seal of, 79
  Hertesbergh, Giles, 239
  Keynes, Thomas, 25, 75

la Bere, John, 74, 76
Lose, Jerrick, 239
Newbury, John, 25
De Saulles, George William, 175, 177–78, 222–23
Dearmer, Canon Percy, 90, Plate 28
Debasement, 7, 97, 98, 178–79, 184, 186
Decimalization, 125, 191, 216
Defacing, official, 197, Plate 106
Defender of the Faith, 157, 164–65, 167–68, 175, 177–78, 183, 186, 190–91, 213–14; *see also* Fidei Defensor
Delaune, Thomas, 41, 42, 64, 87
Deodands, 74, 94
Deputizing for the monarch, 2, 33, 34, 38–43, 58
  because of plague, 37, 39
  from 1699 until 1932, 42, 50
  since 1932, 51
Derby, Archdeacon of, 75
Derry, Bishop of, 78
Designers, 219, 222; *see also* Chantrey, Sir Francis Legatt; Gillick, Mary; Gray, Kruger; Machin, Arnold; Mackennal, Sir Bertram; Maklouf, Raphael; Metcalfe, Percy; Paget, Thomas Humphrey
Die-axis
  definition of, 191
  on the post-Restoration small silver and Maundy coinage, 146, 149, 191–94, 196
  displacement of, 191
    pattern (?) by, 191, 196
    proofs by, 191–93, 196
  randomization of, 193
  upright on proofs, 191–93, 196, 217–18
  variations in, 191–94
Die
  lower (pile), 200, 218, 241
  mismatching, 149, 193, 196, 199, 200; *see also* Groove on the obverse of some post-Restoration silver pennies; Metal-flow (problems with); Metal theft
  upper (trussel), 200, 218, 241
Dies, 106
  damage to, 141, 156, 198, 218
  errors in, 136–38, 141
  for early Maundy pennies, 101
  for VIGO five-guineas, 101
  hammered and milled not interchangeable, 212
  hand-finishing of, 136, 191
    by probationer, 210
  in the Royal Mint Museum, 138

manufacture of, 136, 138, 141, 191, 211, 218
maximization of use of, 116
multiformity of, 136, 141, 160–3, Figure 1
necks on, for use with a collar, 164
no necks on, 164, Plate 71
produced from 1741 to 1812 in connection with Maundy money manufacture, 138–39, 161
repair of, 141
sinking of, 136, 138
  by smith or smith assistant, 211
sunk for Maundy money production from 1741 to 1812, 138–39
Direction of profile bust, 146, 212–13
Dishes; *see also* Edward VII, alms dish dates from; Fish Dishes; Hereditary Grand Almoner; Maundy Dish
  others as required in the Maundy service, 234
Distinguishing
  Maundy
    from currency threepences, 174, 183, 186–87, 204
    sets of 1937 (those issued in the proof sets from those issued for Maundy purposes), 185, 196
  proofs from non-proofs, 176, 194–96
  threepences of 1920, between the two alloy compositions of, 182, 216
Dissolution of the Monasteries, 26
Distribution
  First, 34, 46, 50, 61, 234
    and Second combined, 46
  Second, 34, 46, 50, 61, 210, 234
Dole, 69
  King's, 2, 3, 206
    coins used in, 113, 120, 206
    distributed on
      Good Friday, 2
      Maundy Thursday, 2
    magnitude of, 2, 3
    monarch deputized for in the distribution of, 2
Dollars (Mexican and Spanish)
  counterstamped, 118–19, 163, 209, Plate 41
  other coins counterstamped, 209
Dorset, Archdeacon of, 75
Drinking the monarch's health,

Index 257

31, 41, 47, 50, 51, 59, 60; *see also* Loving cup
Dublin
  Archbishop of, 75, 80
  arrival of the Duke of Northumberland in, 110, 118
Dunkeld, Bishop of, 75
Durham
  Bishop of, 34, 76, 77
  Cathedral, 62
  mediæval Maundy services of the monks at, 20, 21, 23
  Prebendary of (Kaye, Sir Richard), 81, 89
  rites of, 20
  Stephen Payne, connections with, 94
Dutch War of 1666, 66
Duty mark, 118–19
Early strikes, 190, 194
Easter; *see also* Good Friday, Maundy Thursday
  alms distribution at, 2, 3
Easter Day (Sunday)
  dates of, compilation of, xii
  determination of date of, xii, xiii
Edinburgh
  Duke of, 52–54, 88, 90, 226, Plate 19
  Mint, *see* Scotland, Edinburgh Mint
Educational endowments, 5
Edward I
  almoner to, 79
  stole the Cross of Gwyneth, 13
  Trial of the Pyx, 238
Edward II, 239
  almoner to, 79
  cramp rings introduced by, 13
  pedilavium by, and first monarch yet known to be associated with, 63
  popularity waned, 16
  touching by waned, 16
Edward III
  endowment to King's Hall, Cambridge, 5
  jubilee of, 26
  Maundy distributions of, 25, 26, 63
  pedilavium by, 25
Edward VI
  cramp rings of, 15
  death of, 29
  foundation of Christ's Hospital by, 5
  largesse of, 4
  Maundy distributions of, 29, 33, 64, 65
  restoration of gold fineness by, 7

robe redemption allowance of, 29, 33, 34
  touching not practised by, 7
Edward VII
  alms dish dates from, 234
  born, 127
  coronation of, 60
  Emperor of India, 178
  Maundy coinage of, 178–79, 202–3, Plate 90
    die-axis of, 192
    mintages, 122, 120
  Maundy distribution for, 49, Plate 27
  supernumerary list of, 68
  wife of, 49
Edward VIII
  abdication of, 183, 225
  born, 128
  coinage, patterns for, 183
  coronation (proposed) of, 50
  Maundy
    coinage
      of, 183
      soft reduction obverse punches for, 183, Plate 95
    distribution in 1936 by, 50, 90, 183, 218, Plate 31
    set of 1936 belonging to, sale of, 90, 218
Edward the Confessor
  cramp rings, patronage of under, 14
  ring of, in Westminster Abbey, 14
  touching by, 5, 16
Effigy; *see also* Bust profile; Direction of profile bust
  modified, of George V, 182
  of Elizabeth II (Gillick bust), retention on the Maundy coinage, 191
  not anticipated, 217
  recognizable on coins, 1, 4, 101
Elizabeth I
  angel (coin) of, 7
  death of, 100
  demise of cramp rings during the reign of, 15
  foundation relating to Westminster School, 5
  largesse distribution by, 31, 32
  Maundy
    coins as prizes at Westminster School, sanctioned by, 5, 120, 131, 210
    distribution of in
      1560, 31, 32, 64, Plate 10
      1572/3, 18, 32, 33
      1579, 30, 31
      1582, 33, 64, 65, 95

1595, 34, 64
    distributions, venues for, 58, 60
    money of, 100
    milled coinage during the reign of, 241–42
    orders for coining of, 100
    restoration of the title Fidei Defensor, 213–14
    robe redemption allowance of, 33, 34
  touching by, 7, 17
Elizabeth II
  born, 129
  coronation of, 50, 61
  Maundy
    coinage of, 187–91, 202–3, Plates 101 and 102
    die-axis of, 192
    mintages, 123–24, 132
    retention of the Gillick effigy on, 191
    Trial of the Pyx of, 98–100
    service of in
      1952, 50, 216
      1953, 50, 203–4
      1957, 88, Plate 19
      1974, 65
      1989, 51–55, Plate 20
    Maundy money for, 98
Elizabeth of York, 35
Ellison-Macartney, Sir William Grey, 209
Ely
  Bishop of, 29, 49, 62, 77, 78
  Cathedral, 62
Emblem, national, 146, 149
Emperor of India, 178, 184
  removed from the royal titles, 186
Empire, British, 178
Empress of
  India, 177, 213
  Russia, 49
England
  Bank of, 118–19, 125, 130, 210, 214
  national emblem of, 146, 149
Engraver
  Chief, 156, 158, 210, 220, 224, 226–30
  duty of, 156, 211
  demise of position at the Mint, 222
  Second (Assistant), 67, 156, 158, 163, 210, 220, 224, 228–30
  duty of, 156, 211
Engravers, 219; *see also* Basire, James; Boehm, Sir Joseph Edgar; Bower, George; Briot, Nicholas; Brock, Sir Thomas;

Bull, Samuel; Cave, Joseph; Clerk, James; Croker, John; De Saulles, George William; Harris, Henry; Merlen, Jean Baptiste; Ochs, Johann Rudolph senior; Ochs, John Ralph junior; Pingo, Lewis; Pistrucci, Benedetto; Rawlins, Thomas; Roettiers, James; Roettiers, John; Roettiers, Norbert; Roettiers, Philip; Simon, Thomas; Tanner, John Sigismund; Wade, Edward; Wyon, Leonard Charles; Wyon, Peter; Wyon, Thomas junior; Wyon, Thomas senior; Wyon, William; Yeo, Richard
   in eighteenth and early nineteenth centuries, 211
   recruitment of, 211
   saving working time of, 116
   smith and smith's assistant to, 211
Engravers' Act, 89
Engraving department of the Mint, 211
Epiphany, 236
Errors, in dies and punches, 136–38, 141
Esher, 37
Essex, Archdeacon of, 76
Eton
   College
      foundation of by Henry VI, 5
      Provost of, 76
      Scrofula at, 6
   Maundy distribution at, 37, 58
Evil, King's, see King's Evil; Scrofula
Exchequer, 238, 240
   Barons of the, 238–39
   Chancellor of the, 99, 205
Exeter
   Bishop of, 78, 81
   Cathedral, 62
      Chancellor of, 76
   Dean of, 62, 75, 81
   Marquess of, 74, 234
Failures in the Trial of the Pyx, 239
   of the Maundy money, 98–100
Faitta, Marco Antonio, 29
Feast Thursday, 56, 57
Fidei Defensor, 213–14; see also Defender of the Faith
   first monarch to use in their titles, 156, 213
Fire, destruction by of
   Chapel Royal, 231
   many conventual buildings at Westminster, 79
   part of the Exchequer, 240

   Whitehall Palace, 231
Fish
   Dishes, 46, 54, 234, Plate 21
   -tailing of letters in a legend, 195
Five-guineas, 101
Flan, size of incorrect, 137, 159, 196, Plates 49 and 50
Flaw, see Die mismatching; Groove on the obverse of some post-Restoration silver pennies; Metal-flow (problems with); Metal theft
Folland, Mr W., 49
Food
   allowance, 50; see also Maundy gifts of clothing and food
   in red purse, 34, 48, 50, 61
   introduced, 48
   magnitude of, 48
   type of coin used for, 48, Plates 24 and 25
   gift, see Maundy gifts of clothing and food
Fordham, Rector of, 80
Fourpence (groat); see also Britannia groat; Groat (fourpence); Maundy money; Post-Restoration small silver coinage
as
   general currency, 102–3, 106–7, 111, 113, 116
   Maundy money, 116–17
circulating in Ireland in 1925, 102
Edinburgh Mint, puncheon and patterns for, 111–12, 208
in
   limited general circulation, 102
   Scotland, 111–12, 125, 244
insignificant in ordinary transactions, 111
master tools for, 168
milled, first striking of, 102
numismatic origin of, 98, 100
of
   1697, 106, 153–4, 192
   1702, 153, 192
   1765, 105, 160–1
   1775, 105, 160–1
   James IV of Scotland, 92–3, 112
patterns with Edinburgh mintmark, 111–12
posthumous issue dated 1702, 153, 192
recognizable effigy on, 4
twelvepenny groat in Scotland, 112
use in

Daily Alms, 2, 113
Earl of Northumberland's Maundy, 36
Gate Alms, 113
King's Dole, 2, 113
largesse, 4, 113
some colleges at the Universities of Cambridge and Oxford, 120, 125, 210
weight of, 244; see also Maundy money, weights of
worn specimens of, 102
France
   coining in, 241–42
   engravers from, 211, 241–42
   Francis I of, 241
   Henry II of, 16, 241
   Henry IV of, 16, 241
   King of, title surrendered, 164
   kings of, touching by, 16
   Mal de Roi, 6
   mint in, 241–42
   national emblem of, 146, 149
   Paris mint, 242
   Treaty of Amiens with, 164
   touching in, 5, 16
      by the Stuart Pretenders, 12
Francis I of France, 241
Freeman, Sir Ralph, 141
Fremantle, C.W. (later Hon. Sir Charles Fremantle, K.C.B.), 125, 130
Frozen date, 105, 110, 116, 163, 214
Garter Tower, Windsor, 58
General currency, 103
   all four small silver denominations
      as, 102–3, 106–7, 111–12, 146
      not for use as, 111, 116–17
      unlikely as, 120
   threepence and fourpence remain as when penny and twopence excluded from, 103, 111–13
George I
   appointment of preachers in the Chapel Royal, 231
   declined to touch, 12
   small silver coinage of, 104, 156–58, Plate 63
      brockage of, 200–1, Plate 108
      die-axis of, 192
   titles of, 156–57, 213
George II
   distribution of largesse during reign of, 4
   Maundy
      coinage of, 102, 104, 116, 158–59, Plates 64 and 65
      die-axis of, 192
      mintages, 108

silver struck as, 108
distributions for, 18, 43, 45, 65, 88, 95, 116
silver coined during reign of, 118
George III
born, 126
duty mark of, 118–19
groove on obverse of some pennies of, 140, 198–99
head as counterstamp, 119, 163, 209, Plate 41
Maundy
coinage of, 102, 104, 158, 160–65, 201, Plates 66 to 70
circlet multiformity, 161–62, Figure 1
die-axes of, 192
mintages, 108–9, 121
silver struck as, 108–9, 113, 116
distributions for, 42, 43, 45–48, 51, 64, 65, 95, 115, Plates 16, 22 and 23
George IV
born, 126
Maundy
coinage of, 165–66, Plates 72 and 73
die-axis of, 192
mintages, 121
distribution for, 58, 59
small bust on threepence of 1822, 165–66
George V
born, 128
bronze pennies of, 199
coronation of, 60
death of, 90
Emperor of India, 178
Maundy
coinage of, 178, 180–3, 202–3, Plate 91
die-axis of, 192
mintages, 122–23
distribution by, 50, Plates 29 and 30
distributions for, 65, 96
George VI
born, 128
coronation of, 60
death of, 90
Emperor of India, 184
Maundy
coinage of, 184–87, 202–3, Plates 96 and 97
dated 1937, difference between those in the specimen sets and those used for Maundy purposes, 97, 185, 196

die-axis of, 192
mintages, 123
distribution
by, 51, 96, 210
for, 60, 61
of 1950, 88, Plate 18
proposed modification to design of denominational 2, disapproval of, 186
Gerhard, Dr D.J., 198
Gift, see Allowances; Clothing gift; Food gift; Gift of Pennies (Maundy money); Gift of the Maundy robe
Gift of
clothes, see Clothing gift
food, see Food gift
Pennies (Maundy money), 28, 34, 37, 43, 65, 87, 89, 95, 96, 113, 117, 133, 206; see also Maundy money
denominational compositions of
from 1946 to 1978, 134
in
1914, 96
1915, 96
1948, 96, 134
1953, 134, 203–4
1977, 134, 202
the Maundy robe, 30–33
Gilbert, Rev. Dr John, 43, 81
Gillick, Mary, 190–1, 217, 223, 226
Gladstone, Mr, 79
Gloucester, Bishop of, 78
Gold
Great Recoinage of, 117
Maundy sets in, 167, 169, 187, 190, 193, 197–98, Plate 104
die-axes of not recorded, 193
standard, 96, 206
weighing of, 237
Goldsmiths'
Company, 238, 240
Hall, London, 98, 118, 240
Good Friday, 20, 55, 61
Adoration of the Cross on, 13
blessing of cramp rings on, 14, 30
King's Dole distributed on, 2
production of cramp rings on, 14, 15
Royal Maundy service on, 2, 28, 65, 84, 85
touching on, 39
Goodenough, Rev. Dr Edmund, 59, 81
Googe, Barnaby, 24
Grafton, Duchess of, 103
Graham, Thomas, F.R.S., 174
Graining introduced, 243

Grand
Almoner, 29
Duke Michael, 49
Gray, Kruger, 183, 186, 223, 225
Great
Almoner, 74
Gold Recoinage, 117
Recoinage of
1696 to 1698, 106–7, 111, 154, 206, 220
1816, 165, 214
Wardrobe, keeper of, 30
Greatham Hospital, 94
Greenwich
Maundy service at, 32, 58, 60
Palace of, Great Hall at, 58
Gregory
the Great, Pope, 25, 61, 95
XIII, Pope, 232
Gresford-Jones, Rt Rev. Edward Michael, 51, 78
Grimm, Samuel Hieronymus, 46, 47
Groat, 244; see also Britannia groat; Fourpence (groat)
Groove on the obverse of some post-Restoration silver pennies, 140, 198–200, 218; see also Die mismatching; Metal-flow (problems with); Metal theft
attempt to verify reason for, 200
elimination of, 140, 199
reason for, 199
Gunthorpe, John, 74, 76
Half-
farthing, 168, 215, Plate 82
groat (twopence), see Twopence (half-groat)
sovereign, 34, 168, Plate 75
Hammered coinage, see Coinage, hammered
Hampton Court, 31
Hanby, Mr J., 48, 59, 68
Hanover
Georges of, 42
titles, 156–57
House of, accession, 231
Hardwicke Court, near Gloucester, 79
Harewood, Countess of, 51
Harris, Henry, 210, 220–22
Hatter, Dr, 43
Hawley, Thomas, 27
Healey, Denis, M.P., 99, 205
Healing
divine service of introduced, 6
-pieces, 1, 6; see also Angel (coin)
base-metal coins not as, 8
early use of gold pieces,

other than angels, as, 6
first regular use of the angel as, 6
foreign gold coins as, 9
royal relics as, 8
silver coins as, 8
Henneage, Mr, 33
Henry I
  assay of coinage introduced by (?), 238
  touching by, 5
Henry II, assay of coinage introduced by (?), 238
Henry II of France
  rôle in the reform of the French currency, 241
  touching by, 16
Henry IV, 63, 64
Henry IV of France
  rôle in the reform of the French currency, 241
  touching by, 16
Henry V
  almoner to, seal of, 79
  cramp rings of, 13
Henry VI
  cramp rings of, 14
  foundation of Eton College by, 5
Henry VII
  coronation of, 236
  creation of the Yeomen of the Guard by, 236
  divine service of healing introduced by, 6
  Maundy
    distribution of his wife, 35
    distributions of, 27, 64, 65, 95
  popish ritual of touching of, 10
Henry VIII
  casting out of Cardinal Wolsey by, 37
  cramp rings of, 15
  King's almoner of (Cardinal Wolsey), 76, 79, 94
  Maundy distributions of, 27, 28, 64, 65, 95
  title Defender of the Faith conferred upon, 213
  touching by, 7
Henry, Cardinal Duke of York
  death of, 12
  touching by, 12
Henry Grace de Dieu, 79
Heralds, see Court Heralds
Hereditary Grand Almoner, 74, 234
  loan of alms dish from, 234
Hereford
  Bishop of, 76
  Cathedral, 62

Dean of, 80
High Almoner, see Lord High Almoner
Hill, George F., 182
Hilliard, Nicholas, 31
Hocking, William John, 130
Holy
  Thursday, 29; see also Maundy Thursday
  Week, 55
    Thursday of, names for, 55–57, 91
Hope, Rauf, 30
Hospital
  Christ's
    endowment of by Charles II, 5
    foundation of by Edward VI, 5
  Greatham, 94
  Osprynge, Warden of, 75
  Royal, at Chelsea, foundation of by Charles II, 67
Hume, Joseph, M.P., 244
Hunt and Roskell, 120, 196
Huntingdon, Archdeacon of, 81
Indentures, for the coinage, 96, 100, 103, 106, 111, 212
  objection to, 106–7
India
  Emperor of, 178
    removed from the royal titles, 186
  Empress of, 177, 213
  independence of, 186
Initials on coinage
  of designer or engraver on
    general coinage, 186, 214
    Maundy coinage, 175, 178, 182–84, 214
  of the Master of the Mint, 214
Inns of Court, 2, 73
Ireland; see also Cashel; Derry; Dublin; South Antrim
  Act of Union with, 164
  Bank of, 125, 130, 210
  King of, title surrendered, 164
  Maundy fourpence in general circulation in, 102
  national emblem of, 146, 149
Ironside, Christopher, 226
Jacob, J.H., 98
James I, 60
  accession of, 100, 112
  Chapel Royal ceiling, connection with, 231
  death of, 206
  Maundy coinage of, 100–1, 206, Plates 38 and 39
  touching by, 7, 11
  Trial of the Pyx during reign of,

239
  use of the angel as a touch-piece by, 7, 9
James II
  abdication of, 10, 149
  accession of, 41
  daughters of
    Anne, see Anne
    Mary (wife of William III), 11, see also William and Mary
  Mary of Modena, marriage to, 10
  Maundy distribution by, 41, 43, 50
  pedilavium by, 41, 43
  robe redemption allowance of, type of coins used, 34
  small silver coinage of, 104, 149–50, Plate 58
    brockages of, 200–1, Plates 114 to 117
    die-axis of, 192
  surgeon of, 10
  threepence, weakly struck reverse of, 200
  touching by in
    England, 10
    exile, 11
James III of Scotland, 92
James IV of Scotland, 92, 112
James VI of Scotland, 100, 112
James, Mr, 59
James, Mr John Hasting (later Sir Jack), 125, 132
Jesus (Christ), 19, 20, 25, 50, 61, 95
Joey (Britannia groat), 244
John
  assay of coinage introduced by (?), 238
  Maundy
    distributions of, 24, 25, 61, 63, 95, Plate 9
    money of, 24, 204, Plates 7 and 8
Johnson
  Dr Samuel, 12, 57; see also Touch-piece
  Sir Robert, 225
Jones
  Inigo, 231
  Mr J., 48
Joseph of Arimathea, 14
Journey weight, 130, 209
Jubilee
  Diamond, of Victoria, 131
    official medal for, 220
  Golden, of Victoria, 174–75
  head, 174–76, 193, 201, 216, 219
  Silver, crown of 1977, 48

Judges at assizes, 44
Kaye, Dr (Sir) Richard, 46, 47, 81, Plates 16 and 22
King's
　Almoner, 25, 38, 73, 75, 78
　Champion, 4
　Chapel, 40
　Chaplain, 75
　Clerk, 76
　Dole, see Dole, King's
　Evil, 5–13; see also Scrofula
　High Almoner, 74, 76; see also Lord High Almoner
　Under (or Sub) Almoner, 80; see also Sub-almoner
Knaresborough, 25, 63, Plate 9
Lanfranc of Bec, 21
Lang, Rt Rev. Cosmo Gordon, 51, 78, 90, Plates 28 and 31
Largesse, 4, 31, 32, 39, 110, 112, 118, 149, 207
　denominations used in, 4, 31, 32, 113, 149
　fell into disuse, 4
　medalets for, 4
　use as propaganda, 4
Last Supper, 19, 50, 56, 57
Lavipedium, 19
Law, Aliens, of William III, 222, 224, 227
Legend changes, 154, 156, 177–8, 186, 191, 214
Leicester
　Abbey, 37
　　death of Cardinal Thomas Wolsey at, 37
　Earl of, 209; see also Townsend, George
Lend-Lease agreement, 97
Leukenor, John, 74, 75
Lichfield
　Bishop of, 42, 51, 62, 78, 88, Plate 18
　Cathedral, 20, 62
　Dr Johnson's family home in, 12
Lichfield and Coventry, Bishop of, 78
Lima, 117–18
Lincoln
　Bishop of, 76, 77
　Dean of, 76, 77, 81, 89
Linen
　scarves, 46, 235
　towels, see Maundy towels
Lists, supernumerary, 3, 18, 68
Liverpool, Earl of, 107, 119
Llandaff, Bishop of, 81
Lloyd, William, 42, 78
　purse of, 79, Plate 33
London
　Archdeacon of, 75
　Bishop of, 40, 60, 76–78, 100–1

King's College, Principal of, 82
Lead Company, 113
Livery Company of Goldsmiths, 238, 240
Maundy
　Dish made in, 234
　service confined to, 61–63, 67, 69, 154
　Prebendary of, 75, 76
　Tower of, 234
Lonison, John, 100
Lord Berkeley, Henry, 35
Lord High
　Admiral, 74
　Almoner, see also Grand Almoner; Great Almoner; High Almoner; King's High Almoner and Compton, Lord Alwyne; de Bluntesdon, Henry; de la Bere, John; Gresford-Jones, Rt Rev. Edward Michael; Gunthorpe, John; Lang, Rt Rev. Cosmo Gordon; Leukenor, John; Lloyd, William; Payne, Stephen; Robinson, Dr Joseph Armitage; Taylor, Rt Rev. John Bernard; Woods, Rt Rev. Edward Sydney; Wilberforce, Samuel
　alms distribution by, first known representation of, 79, Plate 34
　appointment of, 42, 73, 74
　apportionment of duties with his monarch in the Maundy service, 39, 40, 42, 50
　badge of office of, 80, Plate 37
　current duty of, 73
　current rôle in the Maundy service, 53
　delivery of Maundy money to, 206
　deputizing for his monarch in the Maundy ceremony, 33, 34, 38, 39, 42, 49, 51, 61
　deputy, 34, 77
　fees for, 74, 79
　former duties of, 74
　former official residence of, 46, 74, 79
　gird with traditional towel during the Maundy service, 44, 53, 91, Plates 18 to 20
　King's High Almoner, 74
　kissed his thumb instead of the Maundy recipients' feet, 38
　Minor and Discretionary Bounty recipients, selection

　by, 3
　nosegay carried by, 44, 53
　office of
　　former personal advantages of, 79
　　nature of, 74
　pre-washing Maundy recipients' feet by, 29, 32, 33
　purse of, 79, Plate 33
　Royal Gate Alms recipients, selection by, 3
Almoners
　artifacts of, 79, Plate 33
　list of, 75–78, 80
　seals of, 76, 79, 80, 94, Plates 34 and 35
　Chancellor, 74, 239
　Constable, 74
　Treasurer, 74
Loving cup, 19, 50; see also *Caritatis potum*; Drinking the monarch's health
Lowndes, Mr, 208
Machin, Arnold, 191, 217, 223, 226
Machine made, but hammered, coinage, 101, 142, 145–46
Mackennal, Sir Bertram, 178, 182, 224
Magens Dorrien Magens, 119
Maklouf, Raphael, 191, 224
Mal de Roi, see Scrofula, 6
Malcolm III of Scotland, 92
Mandate, 19, 53, 57
Mandatum, 19, 57
Manufacture of, see Coinage; Dies; Matrices; Maundy cases; Maundy money, production of; Maundy purses; Punches
March, kalends of, 20
Martin, Mr (later Sir Richard), 100, 205, 242
Mary
　death of, 106, 150
　distribution of the Maundy by, 42
Mary of Modena, 10
Mary, Queen of Scots, 31
Mary Tudor
　accession of, 4
　angel (coin) of, 7, 8
　blessing of cramp rings by, 14, 15, 30
　death of Cranmer, rôle in, 87
　donation of Maundy towels and aprons by, 29, 30, 44
　largesse of, upon her accession, 4
Maundy
　-connected gifts received by, 30

service of, 29, 30, 33, 34, 65
repeal of title Fidei Defensor
  by, 213
robe redemption allowance
  possibly given by, 33, 34
Royal Maundy taken very
  seriously by, 7
touching by, 7, 16, 17, 30
Master tools, 156, 158, 162, 165,
  168, 175; see also Maundy coin
  master tools
Mathewes, Dr, 34; see also
  Matthew, Tobie
Matrices
  fully-inscribed, 138
  in the Royal Mint Museum, 138
  manufacture of, 136
  obverse, carved by the Chief
    Engraver, 158, 210
  produced from 1741 to 1812 in
    connection with Maundy
    money, 140
  reverse, carved by the Second
    Engraver, 156, 158, 163, 210
  use in the manufacture of
    punches, 136, 138
Matt proof Maundy sets, 125,
  179, 184–85, 187, 190, 193,
  195–97; see also Proof
  doubts concerning, 196–97
Matthew, Tobie, 77; see also
  Mathewes, Dr
Maundy
  aprons, 26, 29, 31, 33, Plate 10
    given away, after use, to the
      Maundy recipients, 27, 30,
      33
  cases, 130–1, 197–98, 210,
    Plates 42 to 45
    manufacture of, 130, 197–98
    profits from manufacture of,
      130–1
  ceremony, see Maundy service
  coin master tools, used for
    other coinage, 168
  coinage, see Maundy money;
    Post-Restoration small silver
    coinage
  collective term from royal alms-
    giving, 1, 120, 206
  Dish, 34, 45–48, 50, 53, 59, 60,
    234, Plates 13, 14 and 22
    cypher on, 234
    origin of, 234
  distribution; see also Maundy
    service; Royal Maundy
    adoption by the early
      monarchy, possible reasons
      for, 26
    adverse criticism of, 69, 73
    by
      Cardinal Wolsey, 37, 94

Catherine of Aragon, 35
Earl of Northumberland,
  35, 36
Elizabeth of York, 35
Henry, Lord Berkeley, 35
non-royal personages, 35
Queen consorts, 35
distributors since 1932, 51
earliest by an English
  monarch, 25
early purely ecclesiastic, 20–3
in
  1210, 25, 61, 63, Plate 9
  1213, 24, 61, 63, 95
  1361, 25, 26, 63
  1556, 29, 30, 33, 34, 65
  1560, 31, 32, Plate 10
  1572/3, 18, 32, 33
  1579, 30, 31
  1582, 33, 65, 95
  1595, 34
  1633, 38, 101
  1639, 38, 39, 58, 65, 101
  1643, 39, 58, 101
  1644, 39, 58, 101
  1661, 40, 65, 101
  1663, 40, 65, 101
  1685, 41
  1690, 41, 65
  1698, 42
  1699, 42, 65, 101
  1731, 18, 43, 65, 88, 95,
    116
  1732, 43
  1736, 43
  1737, 43
  1754, 45
  1755, 45
  1765, 45
  1766, 45
  1767, 45
  1772, 45
  1773, 46, 47, Plates 16, 22
    and 23
  1774, 45
  1814, 18, 47, 51, 65, 95,
    115
  1826, 58, 59
  1833, 59, 60
  1838, 18, 48, 60, 68
  1842, 48, 60, Plate 17
  1875, 49, Plate 26
  1900, 65
  1901, 49, Plate 27
  1932, 50, Plates 29 and 30
  1937, 60, 61
  1989, 51–55
    Maundy money for, 98
  other countries, 18
  Scotland, potentially,
    111–12
  Scotland, pre-Union of the

Crowns, 92, 112
sixteenth century, account
  of, 26, 27
distributions of
  Edward VI, 29, 33, 64, 65
  Henry VII, 27, 64, 65, 95
  Henry VIII, 27, 28, 64, 65,
    95
  James IV of Scotland, 92, 93,
    112
gift of clothing commuted to a
  monetary allowance
  for men, 45
  for women, 45, 89
gift of food commuted to a
  monetary allowance, 48, 93
gifts of clothing and food; see
  also Clothing allowance;
  Food allowance
  distribution in the
    Ante-chapel of the Chapel
    Royal, 58, Plate 23
  introduced, 25
  nature of, examples of,
    29–33, 38–43, 45, 47
  reasons for, 26
  supplied pro mandeto regis,
    57
gown; see also Robe
  redemption allowance
  given to one of the Maundy
    recipients, 30, 31
  possibly along with a gift of
    twenty shillings in lieu to
    the others, 33
  replacement of this gift by
    one of twenty shillings
    to every recipient, 33,
    see Robe redemption
    allowance
  reasons for, 29, 33
meal
  example of, 42
  introduction of, and reasons
    for, 24–26
  recent, 63
  replaced by a monetary gift,
    as part of the food
    allowance, 58
money, see also Dies;
  Fourpence (groat); Gift of
  Pennies; Matrices; Maundy
  coinage; Maundy sets;
  Penny; Post-Restoration
  small silver coinage;
  Punches; Threepence;
  Twopence (half-groat)
  collecting of, cautions in,
    203–4, 218
  commercialism associated
    with, 120, 130–2, 201–4
  demand for, increase in, 90,

Index 263

131, 203, 210
denominations
  struck up to 1822, 104–5
  used as the Gift of Pennies
    between 1753 and 1775,
    examples of, 45, 117
  first recorded use of the
    penny to fourpence
    sequence, 43, 116
  John's pennies of the
    Rochester Mint (?), 24,
    204, Plates 7 and 8
  only pennies, 27, 100–1,
    106–7, 111, 113,
    116–17; 206
  only pennies and
    twopences, 100–1, 103,
    111–13
  Oxford Declaration
    Penny (?), 39, 101,
    Plate 40
  penny to fourpence
    sequence used annually
    as Maundy money, 113,
    117
design of
  artistic experiment (?),
    162, 186
  modification of the
    denominational 2, 175
  proposed, 186, Plate 98
  condemned, 182
  crowns, multiformity in,
    161–62, 175, Figure 1
  current design first
    introduced, 165
    slightly modified, 175
  effigy modified, 182
  introduction of
    denominational Arabic
    numerals, 150, 152
  low relief in 1953,
    subsequent re-touching of
    dies, 190
  numerals,
    intradenominational
    changes in, 158, 162,
    175, 186, 199
  proposed, 182, 186,
    Plate 98
  only issue with date on the
    obverse, 215
  re-engraving of reverse
    tools, 158, 161, 182–83
  during the Great Recoinage
    of 1696 to 1698, 106–7, 111,
    154
edges plain, 96, 194, 243
Elizabeth I's, 100
fineness of, 96–98, 178–79
  182, 184–86
  different from the other

    'silver' coinage, 97, 98
first recorded distribution of,
  24, 25, 95, 100
frozen date, 105, 110, 116,
  163, 214
general circulation of, 102,
  116
initials of designer or
  engraver on, *see* Initials on
  coinage
investment potential of, 203
issues of, 136 and onwards
James I's, 100–1, 206, Plates
  38 and 39
legal tender, 98, 102
legend changes of historical
  significance, 156–57, 164,
  177–78, 186, 190–1, 213
magnitude of the Gift of
  Pennies
  related to monarch's
    age, 27–29, 40, 41, 65,
    87–89, 95, 96, 100, 115
  regnal year, 43, 63, 95
    a gift of shillings
      likewise related, 41,
      87
    clearly erroneous, 43
    coincidental, 63, 95
  thirteen pennies and the
    prototypes for, 24, 25, 95
  thirty pence in money, 21
  twelve pence and the
    prototype for, 37
manufacture of, press for,
  164–65, 201; *see also*
  production of
master tools, *see* Master
  tools; Maundy coin master
  tools
mintages, 117
  comparatively very low,
    201
  excess over requirements
    of the Maundy
    recipients, 114–16, 120,
    126–29, 133–35
    adverse criticism of, 133
  from
    1727 to 1816, 108–10
    1816 to 1988, 121–25
    1965 to 1970, 136
    1971 to 1975, 135
  out of control, 130
  reductions in, 130, 132, 204
  related to collector
    demand, 130, 210; *see
    also* 207
  restriction in, 125, 130
missing dates, 116
multiformity in legends, etc.,
  136, 141, 160–2

not referred to in 1762 and
  1817 literature, 102
number four in date,
  variation in, 186
obligation to produce, 113,
  120, 163, 206
oddments, 203–4
of 1800 (frozen date), 105,
  110, 116, 140, 163, 214
pension, regarded as, 132
physical dimensions of, 96,
  97
production of, 115, 198, 218,
  241
  at a loss, 116
  bullion for, 98, 105, 113,
    116, 206
  during silver shortage, 113,
    116–7, 119–20, 206
  frozen date, 105, 110, 116,
    163, 214
  master tools used also for
    other coinage, 168
  Mint's working philosophy
    on, 116, 165, 191
  obligation to produce, 113,
    120, 163, 206
  orders for, 98, 100–1
  press for, 164–65, 201
  tools for, 136–38, 141
  troy pounds of silver
    annually used in from
    1727 to 1816, 108–10
proof issues of, *see* Proof;
  Proofs
remedy allowances of, 96
requirements of the Maundy
  recipients, annually, from
    1727 to 1816, 114–16
    1816 to 1988, 126–29
Scottish
  groats of James IV, 92, 93,
    112
  tools and patterns for,
    111–12, 208
silver, weight of, produced
  annually as, 125, 130
Simon's, 101–2, 106, 142,
  145–46, 212
small silver coinage produced
  solely as, 101–2, 116
Trial of the Pyx of, 98
  failure in, 98–100
types of, 136 and onwards
ultimately must be
  spendable, 101
Undated, 101, 142, 146
use of
  earlier years' coins as, 117
  mixed-date sequences as,
    117
uses of other than as the Gift

of Pennies
for
distribution in other charities, 2, 4, 6, 31, 32, 113, 120
Victoria's private use, 120
pennies as a gift to Queen Charlotte, 120
sets, available for
employees of more than five years standing at the Royal Mint, 132–33
fees, 44, 74, 120, 130–1, 210, 235
presentations, 120, 131, 196
prizes to the pupils at Westminster School, 5, 120, 131, 210
retail trade, 120, 130, 204
souvenir-type gifts, 113
the
Banks of England, Scotland and Ireland, 125, 130, 210
Chief Clerk, 130
Deputy Master of the Mint, 130
general public, 120, 130
Master of the Mint, 210
Queen's household, 120, 210
twopences and fourpences supplied to some colleges at the Universities of Cambridge and Oxford, 120, 125, 210
varieties of, 136 and onwards
weights of, 96, 165, 195, 197, 199, 244
intradenominational variation in, 211; *see also* Maundy money, remedy allowances of
worn specimens of, 102, 146
nosegays, 29, 35, 44, 46, 50, 52, 59, 60, 90, 210, 235, Plates 18, 19, and 22; *see also* Nosegays
petitions, 66, 67, 93
prayer, 53, 91
procession in
1773, 46, Plate 22
1826, 58, 59
1838, 48
1893, 46
1937, 60, 61
1989, 52, 53
purses, Plates 11, 12, 15; *see*

also Red leather purse (with long white strings); White leather purse (with long red strings)
carried on the Maundy Dish, 34, 59, Plates 14, 22 and frontispiece
cost of in the Tudor period, 34, 85
green purse with short white strings, 45, 61, Plate 15
introduced, 45
use of, 45
ceased, 46
manufacture of, materials for, 85
red purse only used, 27, 34
white purse introduced, 27
white purse with short green strings, 45, 61, Plate 15
introduced, 45
use of, 45
ceased, 46
recipients; *see also* Ochs, Frances
absentees from the Maundy service
gifts sent to, 64, 65
possible, 32
admission tickets for, 59
adverse criticism of choice of, 69
ages of, 69–73
all present at a Maundy service, 63
centenarians as, 38, 45, 69, 73
choice of
confined largely to London's residents, 67, 68
residential criteria revised, 69, 132
harassment of by numismatic traders, 131–32
in more than one year as, 66, 67, 93
life-long appointment as, 68, 132
list of for the Maundy distribution in 1969, 70–73
Maundy money requirements of, 114–16, 120, 126–29
number of, *see also* Apostles
fifty desirable in early times, 63
related to
Cardinal Wolsey's age at his Maundy in 1530, 37
Earl of Northumberland's age in his Maundy, 35, 36
monarch's

age, 23, 27, 59, 60, 64, 65, 88, 89, 95, 96, 115
first decreed that, 63, 64
not in the case of Edward VI, 29, 64
resulting usually in excesses at the beginning of a new reign, 18, 68
the practice now and since the Tudor period, 65
regnal year
coincidental, 63, 95
report probably based on misinformation, 43, 64, 95
number of ecclesiastical personnel in a priory, 20, 23
thirteen and the prototypes for, 20, 24, 25, 61, 63, 95
three poor people, 20, 21
twelve and the prototypes for, 21, 24, 29, 35, 42, 61, 64, 66
regarded as a minimum since the Apostles were the prototype, 29
only once as, 69, 132
qualities of, 67–73
reservists, 3, 18, 68
sex of, 64, 65
tickets for admission, 59
why and how chosen, 66–73
criticism of, 69
robe, 30–33; *see also* Robe redemption allowance
service; *see also* Maundy distribution; *Pedilavium*; Royal Maundy
adoption by the early monarchy, possible reasons for, 26
almost in oblivion, 18, 49, 102
artifacts, early locational, of, 20
centred solely in the sovereign, 26
conceived, 19
development by the Tudor period, 26
division into morning and afternoon sessions, 48. 59
held
in
abeyance during the Commonwealth, 39

Index 265

countries overseas, 18, 19, 24
London for over 200 years, 61–63, 67, 69, 154, 235
Scotland
  before the Crowns were united, 92, 112
  not since the Act of Union, 92, 111–12, 156
Wales, 61, 62
on
  Good Friday, 2, 28, 65, 84, 85
  Maundy Thursday, usually, 2
liturgy and order of current, 51–55
in
  1937, 60, 61
  1826, 58, 59
sixteenth century, 26, 27
Stuart, 41, 51
Tudor, 29, 30, 32, 33
mediæval, of monks, 20–24
monarch's rôle in
  active participation returns, 50, 90, 210
  attended as spectator, 42, 43, 47, 48, Plates 16 and 17
  ceased, 42, 45, 50, 51, 112
  outside London after over 200 years, 61–63, 69
  reservists for, 3, 18, 68
  revitalization of in the twentieth century, 49
  revived at the Restoration, 39, 40, 58, 231
  venues of, 48, 58–63, 89, 154, 235
    reasons for, 58, 60–63
sets, *see also* Maundy money, uses of other than as the Gift of Pennies, sets available for; Proof
collecting of, cautions in, 203–4, 218
commercialism associated with, 120, 130–2, 201–4
considered as British proof sets with very low mintages, 201
definition of, 96
investment potential of, 203
mintages of
  comparatively very low, 201
  out of control, 130
  reductions in, 130, 132, 204
  related to collector

demand, 130, 210
restriction in, 125, 130
not referred to in 1762 and 1817 literature, 102
values of
  compared with contemporary coins, 202
  movement in, 203
Thursday
  alternative names for, 55, 56
  dates of, *see* Easter Day (Sunday)
  draws near, 101
  ecclesiastical complexity of, 19
  etymology of, 56, 57
  Holy Thursday, 29
  in Scotland, pre-Union of the Crowns, 92, 112
  King's Dole distributed on, 2
  Latin-derived name for, 57
  pedilavium not confined to, 20
  spelling of, variations in, 91
towels, 26, 29, 32, 33, 38, 40, 41
  given away to the Maundy recipients, 27, 30, 33
  present day, 44
  retained by their wearers, 44
  scarves, linen, 46, 235
  worn symbolically by the Royal Almonry officials, 44, 46, 47, 53, 59–61, 91, Plates 16, 18 to 20, 22, 27 and 28
  Children of the Royal Almonry, 44
  various spellings of, 91
Medalets, 4
Merlen, Jean Baptiste, 165–68, 175, 177, 224, 230
Mestrell, Eloye, 241–42
Metal
  -flow (problems with), 149, 164, 193, 195, 199, 200, 211; *see also* Die mismatching; Groove on the obverse of some post-Restoration silver pennies; Metal theft
  theft, 200; *see also* Die mismatching; Groove on the obverse of some post-Restoration silver pennies; Metal-flow (problems with)
  consequences of, 199, 200
Metcalfe, Percy, 225
Milled coinage, *see* Coinage, milled
Milling introduced in England permanently, 243

temporarily, 241–42
Mint; *see also* Royal Mint
engraving department of, 211
forbidden to strike silver coinage, 119, 163
Maundy money, press for, 164–65, 201
nepotism at, 226
obliged to produce the Maundy money, 113, 120, 163, 206
Solicitor of, 113
Warden of, 100; *see also* Royal Mint, Master of
Mintages, *see* Maundy money, mintages
Mintmark, 142, 145, 212
Monarchs' birthdays, xii
Monarchy; *see also* Maundy service, monarch's rôle in
adoption of the Maundy distribution and the *pedilavium* by, possible reasons for, 26
alleged
  divine right of, 17
  miraculous properties of, 26
  sacred and miraculous properties of, 1, 13
  sacred nature of, 14, 15
  supernatural character of, 7, 14, 15, 39
alms giving by
  noblesse oblige, 1
  public relations' exercise, 1, 7, 13, 26, 39
attendance upon by the Yeomen of the Guard, 236
hereditary healers, monopolization of magical procedures by, 14
Maundy service centred solely in, 26
public relations' exercises by, 1, 7, 13, 26, 39
Stuart, rule by, benefits and glories of, 231
survival instincts of, 7, 8, 11, 26
touching by
  as a manifestation of the sacerdotal and divine power of, 1
  as verification of rightful sovereignty, 4–7, 11, 16
  fragile prestige strengthened by, 13
  miraculous nature of began to be questioned, 7, 11
use of largesse by for propaganda purposes, 4
usurping of spiritual healing power by, 14, 15
Monasteries, 2, 73

dissolution of, 26
Monogram, 146, 149–50
Morbus Regius, 6; *see also* Scrofula
Morrison, James William, 107, 197, Plate 103
Napoleonic Wars, 58
National emblem, 146, 149
New
  English Bible, 63
  Zealand, 61, 161, 239
Newcastle
  Bishop of, 82
  Cathedral, 63
Newton, Isaac, 107, 113, 118, 208, 211, 213, 239
Noblesse oblige, 1, 26, 36, 69
Norgate, Mr T.T., 3, 49
Norman Conquest, 20, 21
Northehill, Rector of, 80
Northumberland
  Duke of, arrival in Dublin, 110, 118
  Earl of, 18
    Maundy distribution by, for himself, 35, 36
    his
      sons, 36
      wife, 36
  Household Book, 36, 86
  shilling, 110, 118, 161
Norton, Collegiate Church of, Vicar of, 75
Norwich
  Archdeacon of, 76
  Bishop of, 77
Nosegays; *see also* Maundy nosegays
  bunch of herbs for the judges at assizes, 44
Nottingham, Archdeacon of, 89
Number four in date, variation in, 186
Ochs
  Frances, 67, 93
  Johann Rudolph senior, 156, 224
  John Ralph junior, 67, 158, 224–26
Office, Almonry, *see* Royal Almonry
Old
  head, 175, 177–78, 216
  Pretender, 12
Omnium
  added to royal titles, 178
  removed from royal titles, 190–1
Orange
  arms of, 153
  House of, 153–54
  Lion of, 154

Order
  of the
    Bath, 236
    Garter, 236
    Treasury, for coining, 118
    Trial of the Pyx 1975, 98
Orders, various, for coining, 100
Oxford
  Bishop of, 78, 80, 81
  Briot retired to, 220
  Charles I in, 39, 58, 101
  Christ's Church
    Canon of, 76
    Dean of, 77
  Colleges, Maundy coins for, 120, 125, 210
  death of Thomas Cranmer at, 87
  Declaration Penny, 39, 101, Plate 40
  Magdalen College, President of, 76
  Maundy distributions at, 39, 58, 101
  Merton College, Warden of, 76
  Oriel College
    Founder and Provost of, 75
    Provost of, 76
  Queen's College, Provost of, 77
  royal endowment of a reader or professor in Arabic, 5
  St Alban Hall, Principal of, 76
Paget, Thomas Humphrey, 183–84, 225–26
Pagn, Maister Richard, 35
Palm Sunday, 22
Papal Legate in England, 29, 37, 87
Paper packets, 45, 50
Parliament
  State opening of, 236
  Trial of the Pyx, 239
Parry, Blanche, 31
Pattern (?), the twopence of 1668, 102, 147–49, 191, 196, 207
Patterns by Briot of silver penny and twopences of Charles I, 149, Plates 56 and 57
Payne, Stephen
  connections with Durham, 94
  Dean of Exeter, 62, 75, 94
  Lord High Almoner, 62, 75, 79
  seal of, 62, 79, Plate 34
Pedilavium; *see also* Maundy service; Royal Maundy
  abandonment (in England)
    altogether, 43, 45, 60
    but not elsewhere, 24
    by the monarch, 41, 42, 60, 66
  regretted, 44
  adoption by the early

monarchy, possible reasons for, 26
as effected by
  bishops and priests, 20–24
  Cardinal Wolsey, 37
  Charles II, 40
  clerics and monarchs in other countries, 18, 19, 24
  Edward II, 25, 63
  Elizabeth I, 31–33
  James II, 41
  Mary Tudor, 29
  monks, 19, 20–24
  William III, 42, 66
death whilst preforming, 20
early venues and sites for, 20, 21
feet
  after washing, by the washer crossed and kissed, 32
  held by the Bishop Almoner who then kissed his own thumb, 378
  kissed, 20, 21, 29, 39–41
  and touched with forehead, 21
  on the instep, 38
  in,
    children's, 21
    merely touched with a wetted finger, 21
    pre-washed by menials and clerics in ascending order of seniority, 29, 32–33, 38, 39
    the
      King's Almoner, 27
      recipients, 20, 23, 33
    scrupulously washed, 21
    sequentially washed by three or four persons before the monarch did so, 26
  washed in
    clear water, 21
    cold water, then in claret wine, 38, 39
    warm water, 21
    and flowers in silver basins, 32
    and then in white wine, 38
  water
    from silver ewers, 29
    in
      silver basins, 27
      which had been boiled bayes and rosemary, 38
    sprinkled from a sprig of hyssop, 41

first monarch associated with, 25
frequency of, 20
not effected by the Earl of Northumberland, 35, 36
origin of, 19
reintroduction into the Maundy service (?), x, 73
remaining symbolism of, 43, 44, 46, 47, 52, 90
resurrection of by the Anglican Church, 44
Pennies, silver, *see* Gift of Pennies; Maundy money
Penny; *see also* Maundy money; Post-Restoration small silver coinage
  cartwheel, 112
  curio, 111, 113
  dies for, 101
  Edinburgh Mint, puncheon for, 111–12, 208
  general circulation
    displacement from begins, 103, 112
    in, 102, 106–7
  general currency
    as, 102–3, 106, 111
    not as, 111, 113, 116
  groove on, *see* Groove on the obverse of some post-Restoration silver pennies
  head as counterstamp, 119, 163, 209, Plate 41
  Maundy money, exclusive use as, 27, 100–1, 106–7, 111, 113, 116–17, 206
  milled, first striking of, 102
  mintages in Elizabeth I's reign (examples of), 100
  numismatic origin of, 97, 98, 100, 205
  of
    coarse alloy, 103
    John's Rochester Mint, 24, 204, Plates 7 and 8
    the year 1765 (?), 105
  Oxford Declaration, 39, 101, Plate 40
  pattern by Briot, 149, Plate 56
  regional variation in demand for, 113
  use
    as gift to Queen Charlotte, 120
    in
      Daily Alms, 2, 113
      Earl of Northumberland's Maundy, 36
      Gate Alms, 113
      King's Dole, 2, 113

    largesse, 4, 113
    touching, as the daily gift, 6
  weights of, *see* Maundy money, weights of
Pepys, Samuel, 40
Percival, Rev. Lancelot Jefferson, 49, 51, 61, 82, 90, Plate 28
Percy
  Henry Algernon, 35, *see also* Northumberland, Earl of
  Lord, 36
  Thomas, Bishop of Dromore, 86
Peterborough
  Bishop of, 81
  Cardinal Wolsey's Maundy at, 37, 62, 94
  Cathedral, 62
Petitions to be put on the Maundy list, 66, 67
Philanthropy, 1, 4, 26, 39
Philip, Thomas, 66
Physicians
  acceptance of touching by, 11, 12
  fee for, an angel, 6
  selection of patients for touching by, 10, 12
Pigeon, N., 31
Pile, 200, 218, 241
Pingo, Lewis, 162, 224, 226
Pistrucci, Benedetto, 164–5, 214, 224, 226–7, 230
Plague
  Maundy service, effect on caused Almoner to deputize for his monarch, 31, 37, 39
    take precautions, 37, 38
    monarch participated in spite of, 40
  touching postponed or cancelled because of, 8, 9
Plate of the Kingdom, 118
Pole
  Cardinal Reginald, 29
    death of Cranmer, rôle in, 87
  William Wellesley, 214, 226, 230
    initials on the coinage, 214
Post-Restoration small silver coinage; *see also* Maundy money
  alloy change for suggested, 111
  brockages of, *see* Brockages
  crowns, multiformity in, 161–62, 175, Figure 1
  demand for, regional variation in, 112–13
  denominations struck from 1668, 104–5

Edinburgh Mint
  die pair for a twopence, 111–12
  patterns of a fourpence, 111–12
  puncheons for, 111–12, 208
fineness of, 96
general currency use of, 102–3, 106–7, 111–12, 146, 154
  not
    for, 111, 116–17
    penny, 154
    and twopence, 103, 111–13
  unlikely, 120
Maundy purposes
  evolution of use for, 102–3, 106–7, 111–13, 116–17
  exclusive use for, 101–2, 113, 116
  first penny to fourpence sequence for, 43, 116
  only
    incidental use for, 106–7, 146
    pennies, 27, 100–1, 106–7, 111, 113, 116–17, 154, 206
Scotland; *see also* Edinburgh Mint, in this entry
  great need for in, 208
  not in demand for, 112
  silver struck as, from 1695 to 1804, 106–7
  standard of, attempted reduction in, 111
  striking of, 110
Trial of the Pyx of, 98, 103
use of in other royal charities, 2, 4, 31, 32, 113, 120, 149, 207
wearing of, rapid, 111
weights of, 96, 103, 110
  intradenominational variations in, 211
worn specimens of, 102, 146
Posthumous
  distribution of the Maundy coinage of
    1936, 50, 183
    1952, 50, 90, 185, 216
  issue of the 1702 fourpence, 153, 192
Press, 164–65, 201
Prince of Wales, children of, 49
Princess
  Alice (Countess of Athlone), 49
  Beatrice, 49
  Christina, 49
  Helena Victoria, 49, 60, 90, Plate 28
    attendance at Maundy services, 49, 60

Louise (Duchess of Argyll), 49
Marie-Louise, 49, 50, 60, 90, Plate 28
  attendance at Maundy services, 49, 60
  Royal, 51
Probationer, duties of, 211
Proclamation, announcing Maundy distribution, 58
Proclamations, for the coinage, 103, 168, 175
Progress, royal, 4, 8, 207
Proof
  -like, 194, 204, 217
  Maundy
    penny dated 1729 (?), 159, 196
    sets
      currently all considered as, 201
      distinguished from non-proofs, 176, 191–96, Figure 2
      in specimen sets, 97, 195
      of
        1763, 160, 192, 195
        1822, 166, 193, 195–96
        1828, 166, 193, 195–96
        1831, 124, 167, 195–96
        1834 (?), 167, 194
        1838, 169, 192, 195
        1839, 124, 169, 192, 195
        1853, 125, 170, 192–93, 195
        1867, 171, 192–3, 195
        1868, 171, 193, 196
        1871, 120, 172, 192, 195
        1878, 172, 192–93, 195
        1881, 173, 192–93, 195
        1888, 176, 195–96
        1902 (matt), 125, 179, 193, 195–96
        1911, 125, 180, 193–96
        1937, 97, 125, 184–85, 193, 195–96
          matt (?), 184–85, 196–97
        1951 (matt) (?), 185, 196–97
        1953 (matt) (?), 187, 196–97
    sets, see Specimen (proof) sets
Proofs
  production of, 194
  upright die-axis on, 191–93, 196, 217–18
  VIP, striking stopped, 210
  weights of, 195–96
Provincial mints, 111, 154
Public demand, 130, 207, 210
Public relations' exercise, 1, 7, 13, 26, 39

Punch for proposed new reverse of the Maundy twopence in 1950, 186, Plate 98
Punches
  damage to, (?) 138, 165, 198, Plate 46
  economic use of, 116
  errors in, 136–38, 141
  fully-lettered, 138
  in the Royal Mint Museum, 138
  manufacture (raising) of, 136, 163
  obverse, carved by the Chief Engraver, 158, 162, 210
  partially dated, 191, 138, 141
  produced from 1741 to 1812 in connection with Maundy money manufacture, 140, 158
  repairs to, 141
  reverse, carved by the Second Engraver, 156, 158, 163, 210
  unlettered, 136, Plates 46 and 47
  use in the sinking of dies, 136, 138, 211
  varieties of, 138
  wearing of, 138, 199
Purse of William Lloyd, 79, Plate 33
Purses, see Maundy purses
Pyx, trial of, see Trial of the Pyx
Quarter-
  farthing, 168, 215, Plate 80
  sovereign, 168, Plate 79
Queen
  Alexandra, 49
  Charlotte, 47, 58, 210
  Charlotte Sound, 161
  Mother, 51, 88, Plate 18
Queen's
  Chaplains, Dean of, 29
  Remembrancer, 98, 238–39
Ratcliffe, Mr E.E., xi, 88, 90, 236, Plates 18 and 28
Rawlins, Thomas, 141, 227, 229, 242
Rawlinson manuscripts, 66
Red leather purse (with long white strings), 45, 47, 50, Plate 11
  cost of in the Tudor period, 27, 28
  only purse used, 27, 34
  use for
    all allowances, 53
    Gift of Pennies, 27, 34
    in 1690 (?), 41, 87
    robe redemption allowance, 27, 28, 33, 34, 40, 46, 48, 50
Reformation, 15, 73
Renaissance in Britain, 1, 4
Research, further, 136, 146, 193–94

Restoration, 8, 9, 39, 40, 141, 220, 227, 229, 231, 242
  revival of
    hammered coinage at, 101, 242
    the Royal Maundy at, 39, 40, 58, 231
    touching for Scrofula at, 8, 40
  Trial of the Pyx from, 239
Returns, Parliamentary, 124
Richard I, assay of coinage introduced by (?), 238
Richard Cœur de Lion, 13
Richmond, 35, 37
  Maundy distribution at, 58
Rings
  healing, 1, 14
  cramp
    cures by, 13
    demise of, 15
    evolution of, 13, 14
    modus operandi of, 15
    production of usurped by the monarchy, 14, 15
Ripon Cathedral, 62
Robe redemption allowance
  abandoned in 1731, 34
  introduction of, 33
  reasons for, 29, 33
  monetary value of, 34, 40, 93
  possibly paid by
    Cardinal Thomas Wolsey, 37
    Mary Tudor, 33
    William III, 41, 87
  purse for, 27, 28, 33, 34, 40, 46, 48, 50
  restored in 1759, 34
  type of coin used in 34, 40, 50, 59, 90
Robert II of the Franks, 5
Robinson, Dr Joseph Armitage, 49, 50, 78
Rochester
  Bishop of, 62, 66, 67, 77, 78, 81, 82
  Cathedral, 62
  Dean of, 81
  Maundy distribution at in 1213, 24, 25
  Mint, pennies of, 24, 204, Plates 7 and 8
Roettiers
  family, genealogy of, 228
  James, 11, 152, 126–29
  John, 9, 146, 149, 191, 207, 210, 226–29
  Norbert, 11, 17, 152, 226–29
  Philip, 17, 226–28
Roman Catholic, 10, 15, 24, 29, 30, 41, 49, 213, 232
Royal

Almonry; *see also* Lord High Almoner(s); Sub-almoner(s)
Assistant Secretary of; *see also* Folland, Mr W.; Ratcliffe, Mr E.E.; Waters, Mr Derek
  Maundy sets as fee for, 120, 130–1, 210
  rôle in the Maundy service, 50, 53
  traditional attire of, in the Maundy service, 44, 53, 80, 91, Plates 18 to 20 and 28
Children of, 31, 53, 60, 88, 90, 235, Plates 18 and 19
  fees for, 235
  Maundy sets as fees for, 130–1, 210, 235
  wearing of symbolic towels by, 44
Gentlemen of, 46, 47, Plate 22
Groom of, *see* James, Mr; Jones, Mr J.
Maundy coin, order for from, 98
office premises of in
  Scotland Yard, 16, 46, 89, 94
    conveyance of Maundy alms from, 46, Plate 22
  Buckingham Palace, 94
procession of, 46, 48, 52, 53, 60, 61, Plate 22
responsible for the Royal Maundy ceremony, 18, 42
seal of, 79, 80, 94, Plate 36
Secretary of; *see also* Hanby, Mr J.; Norgate, Mr T.T.; Tanner, Dr L.E., Wright, Mr P.A.
  brocaded silk bag of, 45
  Maundy sets as fee for, 120, 130–1, 210
  order for Maundy coinage from, 98
  presentation by, of alms to those on the supernumerary list, 68
  Minor Bounty, 3
  presentation of the clothing allowance, rôle in, 45
  rôle in the Maundy service, 50, 53
  traditional attire of in the Maundy service, 44, 53, 80, 91, Plates 18 to 20 and 28

Treasurer of the Chamber, alternative name for, 33, 46, 206, Plate 22
  Wandsmen requested by, 236
Gate Alms; *see also* Alms, Daily and Gate
  recipients for, selection of, 3
Hospital at Chelsea, 67
Maundy; *see also* Maundy ceremony; Maundy distribution; Maundy service; *Pedilavium*
  almost in oblivion, 18, 49, 102
  Commonwealth, in abeyance during, 40
  distributed on
    Good Friday, 2, 28, 65, 84, 85
    Maundy Thursday, usually, 2
  earlier works on, 18, 19
  into perspective, 1
  reservists for, 3, 18, 68
  responsibility for, 18, 42
  Restoration, revival at, 40, 58, 231
  term introduced, 35
Mint; *see also* Mint
  Assistant to the Master, 239
  Chancellor of the Exchequer, Master of, 99, 205
  Deputy Master of, 238; *see also* Christie, Mr; Craig, Sir John; de Lose, Jerrick; Fremantle, C.W.; Gerhard, Dr D.J.; James, John Hasting (later Sir Jack); Johnson, Sir Robert; Morrison, James William
  receives order for Maundy coinage, 98
  engraving department of, 211
  Master of, 238–9; *see also* Churchill, Winston Spencer; de Hertesbergh, Giles; Freeman, Sir Ralph; Healey, Denis, M.P.; Lonison, John (master worker); Martin, Mr (later Sir Richard) (Warden); Newton, Issac (Warden); Pole, William Wellesley; Slingsby, Henry; Stanhope, Philip (Chesterfield, fifth Earl of); Townsend, George (Leicester, Earl of); Yonge, Sir George, bart.
  Master's initials on the

  coinage, 214
  opened, 164
  policy, 207
  Provident Society, 130–1
  regulates physical dimensions of the coinage, 97
  Self Help Society, 130–1
  Work of during the silver shortage, 117
party at the Maundy service in
  1773, 46, 47, Plate 16
  1907, 49
  1909, 49
  1920, 49
  1937, 60
regalia, 234
touching, *see* Touching
United Service Institute, 60
Royalty, *see* Monarchy
Rubens, Peter Paul, 48, 231
Salisbury (Sarum)
  Bishop of, 5, 16, 31, 33, 40, 77, 78, 81
  Canon of, 81
  Cathedral, 62
  Dean of, 76
Sarum, *see* Salisbury
Schir Thursday, 56; *see also* 55
Scotland
  Act of Union with, 92, 111–12, 156
  Bank of, 125, 130, 210
  calendar in, 232
  circulation of groat in, 244
  Dunkeld, Bishop of, 75
  Edinburgh Mint, 111–12
    Blondeau's and Briot's machinery transferred to, 242
    closed, 111
    die pair for a twopence, 111–12
    patterns of a fourpence, 111–12
    puncheons for the small silver coinage, 111–12, 208
  Groat (twelvepenny) of, 112
  James III of, 92
  James IV of, 92, 112
  James VI of, 100
  Malcolm III of, 92
  Master of the Mint in, 93, 112, 220
  Maundy service in
    before the Crowns were united, 92, 112
    not since the Act of Union, 61, 92, 111–12, 156
  national emblem of, 146, 149
  post-Restoration small silver coinage
    great need for in, 208

270 Index

not in demand in, 112
use in, 125, 244
Shetland Islands, 8
threepence remained in favour in, 187
touching in, by the Stuart Pretenders, 12
Yard, 16, 46, 79, 89, 94
Scott, David, 93, 112
Screw-press, 241
Scrofula, 5–13; *see also* King's Evil; Royal touching, Touching
early alleged cures for, apart from touching, 6, 8, 13
nature and diagnosis of, 6, 12
occurrence of, 6
Seal of
Cardinal Thomas Wolsey as the King's Almoner, 76, 79, 80
Henry de Bluntesdon, 79, Plate 34
Stephen Payne, 79, 94, Plate 35
the Royal Almonry, 79, 80, 94, Plate 36
Second Engraver, *see* Engraver, Second (Assistant)
Seez, Bishop of, 75
Selby Abbey
Maundy service at, 62, 73
Maundy recipients at, list of, 70–73
Sheer, 56, 57
Thursday, 56; *see also* 55
Sheppard, Canon Edgar, xi, 49, 82
Sher-Thursday, 56; *see also* 55
Shere Thursday, 26, 56; *see also* 55
shere thursdaye, 20; *see also* 55, 56
Shetland Islands, 8
Shilling
Dorrien and Magens, 119
Northumberland, 110, 118, 161
of
1758, 118
1787, 118
Ship on
the
angel, 6, 80, Plate 1
seal of
Cardinal Wolsey as the King's Almoner, 79, 80
Stephen Payne, 79, Plate 35
the Royal Almonry, 79, 80, Plate 36
touch-piece, 9, 80, Plate 4
wheels, 79
Shire
Thursday, 19; *see also* 55, 56

-Thursday, 35; *see also* 55, 56
Shirethursday, 27; *see also* 55, 56
Shirthursday, 35; *see also* 55, 56
Shrewsbury, St Mary at, Dean of, 80
Silk bag; *see also* Lloyd, William, purse of
used in distribution of clothing allowance, 45
Silver
bullion price of, purchase price greater, 105, 113–14, 116–17, 206
coinage, token, 119, 206, 214
pennies, *see* Gift of Pennies; Maundy money
shortage, 113–14, 116–17, 120, 206
standard, 206
sterling, 96–98, 186
distinguish from other alloys, 216
struck as small coinage, 100, 106–10
Simon, Thomas, 9, 141, 145–46, 227–29, 242
Simon's Maundy money, 101–2, 106, 142, 145–46, 212
die-axes of, 146, 193–94
reverse die, variation in, 146
Undated Maundy money, also known as, 101, 142, 145–46
Sixpence of
1757, 118
1758, 118
1787, 118
Slingsby, Henry, 103
Small
bust on 1822 threepence, 165–66
silver coinage, *see* Post-Restoration small silver coinage
Smith
assistant to the engravers, 211
to the engravers, 211
Solicitor of the Mint, *see* Mint, Solicitor of
South Antrim, 209
Southwark Cathedral, 62
Southwell
Minster, 62
Prebendary of, 89
Sovereign (coin), 34, 50, 90
Sovereignty, verification or strengthening of by touching, 6, 7, 11–13, 16
Specimen (proof) sets, 179, 193–95, 202
containing Maundy sets, 125, 195
not containing Maundy sets,

194–95
of
1887 and 1893, threepences in, 193
1937, Maundy coins in, different from those used for Maundy purposes, 97, 185, 196
Spetisbury, Dorset, Rector of, 81
St
Albans
Bishop of, 51, 62, 78
Cathedral, 61, 62, 69
Asaph, Bishop of, 78
Brendan, 19, 20, 83
Davids
Bishop of, 76
Cathedral, 61, 62
James's
courtyard at, touching in, 11
Park, largesse distribution in, 31, 32
Oswald, Archbishop of York, Bishop of Worcester, 20
Paul's
Cathedral
account of the 1937 Maundy service in, 60, 61
choir of, 60
Dean and Chapter of, 60
Prebendary and Chancellor of, 76
venue for the Maundy service, 60, 61
London
Prebendary and Treasurer of, 76
Prebendary of, 81
Stafford, Archdeacon of, 77
Stanhope, Philip (fifth Earl of Chesterfield), 209
Statute of Limitations, 222, 224, 227, 245
Staves, White, 41
Sterling silver, *see* Silver, sterling
Stowe, Archdeacon of, 75
Strikes
early, 190, 194
weak, 190
Stuart
Charles Edward Louis Philip Casimir, 12
House of
accession to the throne of England, 100
end of, 12
prayers and ceremonies used by, 41, 51
James Francis Edward, 12
monarchical rule, benefits and glories of, 231
Pretenders, 12

Stuarts
  the Roettiers' loyalty to, 228
  touching for Scrofula in exile by, 12
Sub-
  almoner, 49, 53, 73, 74, 101; see also Cæsar, Rev. Anthony Douglass; Gilbert, Rev. Dr John; Goodenough, Rev. Dr Edmund; Kaye, Dr (Sir) Richard; Percival, Rev. Lancelot Jefferson; Sheppard, Canon Edgar
    current rôle in the Maundy service, 53, Plate 20
    delivery of the Maundy money to, 206
    deputized for his monarch, 43, 46, 47, 51, 59, 60, 73
    fee for, 131
    gird with traditional towel during the Maundy service, 44, 53, 91, Plates 18 to 20
    King's Under (or Sub) Almoner, 80
    Minor and Discretionary Bounty recipients, assisted in selection of, 3
    pre-washing of feet by, 29, 32, 33, 38
    Royal Gate Alms recipients, assisted in selection of, 3
    Sub-dean of Chapels Royal, 49, 50, 81, 82
    Under Almoner, 29, 80
  almoners, list of, 80–82
  dean of Chapels Royal, 49, 50, 81, 82
Supernumerary lists, 3, 18, 68
Survival, instinct for
  by the Church, 26
  monarchial, 7, 8, 11, 26
Symbolism
  dangers of, 44
  of the Maundy ceremony censured, 69, 73
  remaining of the *pedilavium*, 43, 44, 46, 47, 52, 90
Tanner, Dr L.E., xi, xii, 18, 49, 50, 88, 90, Plates 18, 19 and 28
Tanner, John Sigismund, 158, 229
Taunton, Archdeacon of, 76
Taylor, Rt Rev. John Bernard, 53, 78, Plate 20
Teerline, Levina, 31
Temple, Master of, 81
Testoon, 4
Tewkesbury Abbey, 62
The
  Royal
    Harry, 79

Sovereign, 9
Sovereign of the Seas, 9
Three-halfpence, 168, Plates 77 and 83
Threepence; see also Maundy money; Post-Restoration small silver coinage
  abhorred, increasingly, in England, 187
  comparison with the Britannia groat, 244
  copper-zinc-nickel dodecagonal type introduced, 187
  Edinburgh Mint, puncheon for, 111–12, 208
  for
    colonial use, 102, 168, 187
    general currency use, 102–3, 106, 111, 113, 116, 124–25, 168, 175–76, 182–83, 204, 216
      different from the Maundy threepence, 183, 186–87, 216, Plates 92, 99 and 100
      distinguishable from the maundy threepence, 174, 183, 186–87, 204
      final striking in silver for, 187
      Maundy threepence of same design as currency threepence, 102, 168, 183, 204
      proclamation for, 168
  in
    Daily Alms, 2
    New Zealand, 161
    proof specimen sets of 1887 and 1893, 193
  insignificant in ordinary transactions by the early eighteenth century, 111
  Jubilee head of
    1887, 193
    1893, 216
  master tools for, 168
  Maundy money, as, 116–17
    general circulation of, 102
    solely, 168, 204
  milled, first striking of, 102
  new designs for, 183, 186–87, Plates 92, 99 and 100
  numismatic origin of, 98, 100
  of
    James II (reverses weak), 200
    1762, 107, 110, 113, 116, 118, 140, 160–1
    1763, 107, 110, 113, 116, 118, 160–1
    1927, 183, 202, Plate 92
    1937, difference between those in the specimen sets

and those used for Maundy purposes, 97, 185, 196
  remained in favour in Scotland and Wales, 187
  replacement of, 187
  Scotland, use in, 187
  small bust in 1822, 165–66
  unpopular in England, 187
  use in royal charities other than the Royal Maundy, 113
  weight of, 244; see also Maundy money, weights of
Token silver coinage, 119, 214
Toledo, Synod of, 20
Torby, Countess of, 49
Touch-pieces
  design of, 9
  Dr Johnson's specimen of, 12, 17
  end of in England, 12
  in
    gold, 1, 9, Plate 4
      charge upon the Exchequer of, 10
      end of in England, 12
      introduced, 9
      number of recipients of, 10
      numbers issued, 10, 11
      numismatic study of, 9, 10
      ship on, 9, 80, Plate 4
      weight reduction in, 9
    silver, 1, 11
      numismatic study of, 12
      ship on, 9, 80, Plate 4
  use of by the Stuart Pretenders, 12
Touching; see also Healing-piece, Scrofula, Touch-piece
  abuse of, 10
  as a verification of rightful sovereignty, 4–7, 11, 16
  beginning of the end of, 8
  by
    Anne, 11, 17
    Charles I, 8, 39
    Charles II, 9, Plate 3
    Edward II, 16
    Elizabeth I, 7, 17
    Henry I, 5
    Henry II of France, 16
    Henry IV of France, 16
    Henry VII, 10
    Henry VIII, 7
    James I, 7, 11
    James II, 10, 11
    Mary Tudor, 7, 16, 17, 30
    Stuart Pretenders in exile, 12
  charge of upon the Exchequer, 10
  control of
    choice of recipients, 10–12

tickets and tokens for admission, 10, 11
declined by George I, 12
dismissed by William and Mary, 11
divine service of healing introduced, 6
during the Commonwealth, 8
end of in
  England, 12
  France, 17
first practised, 5
genuineness of (?), 12, 13
illustrations of, 9, 16
in
  Chester Cathedral, 10
  the Banqueting House, 8, 9, 231
myth of began to wane, 11
not practised
  during hot weather, 9, 10
  by Edward VI, 7
numbers touched, 8–11
postponed or cancelled because of plague, 8, 9
preventing abuse of, 10, 11
revived at the Restoration, 8, 40
seasons and days for, 8–11, 39
using
  angels as healing-pieces, *see* Healing-pieces
  touch-pieces, *see* Touch-pieces
Towels, linen, *see* Maundy towels
Tower Mint, vacated, 164
Townsend, George (Earl of Leicester), 209
Treasurer of the
  Chamber, 33, 46, 206, Plate 22
  Household, 74
Treasury, Secretary to, 208
Treaty of Amiens, 164
Trial of the Pyx, 98, 103, 124, 145, 211, 238–40
  failure of the Maundy money in, 98–100
  failures up to 1974, 239
  mishaps during, 240
Troy weights, 237, 246
Trussel, 200, 218, 241
Tudor period
  end of, 100
  largesse in, 4
  Maundy service, examples of during, 26, 27, 29–33, 35–37
  Royal Maundy, term introduced during, 35
Twopence (half-groat); *see also* Half-groat (twopence); Maundy money; Post-Restoration small silver

coinage
cartwheel, 112
curio, 111, 113
Edinburgh Mint, puncheon and die pair for, 111–12
general circulation
  displacement from begins, 103, 112
  in, 102, 106–7
general currency
  as, 102–3, 106, 111
  not as, 111, 113, 116
master tools for, 168
Maundy money, as, 100–1, 111, 113, 116–17
milled, first striking of, 102
numismatic origin of, 98, 100
of coarse alloy, 103
pattern (?), 102, 147–49, 191, 196, 207
patterns by Briot, 149, Plate 57
proposed reverse design change in 1950, 186, Plate 98
recognizable effigy on, 4
regional variation in demand for, 113
use in
  British Guiana, 102, 124, 246
  Daily Alms, 2, 113
  Earl of Northumberland's Maundy, 36
  Gate Alms, 113
  King's Dole, 2, 113
  largesse, 4, 31, 32, 113, 149
  some colleges at the Universities of Cambridge and Oxford, 120, 125
weights of, *see* Maundy money, weights of
worn specimens of, 102
Undated Maundy money, *see* Simon's Maundy money
Under Almoner, 29, 80, *see* Sub-almoner
Uniface, 181–82, 194
United States of America, 97; *see also* America
Universities, 2, 73; *see also* Cambridge; Oxford
Variation in; *see also* Tables 21 to 33 and 35
  circlets, 161–62, Figure 1
  dies, 136
  legend, Queen Anne small silver coinage, 154, 156
  number four in the date, 186
  punches, 138, 141
  reverse die, 146
Venues for the Maundy service, *see* Maundy service, venues of
Victoria
  born, 126

coronation of, 74
death of, 68
Empress of India, 177, 213
Maundy
  coinage of, 168–78, 201, 203, Plates 78, 87 and 89
  die-axes of, 192
  mintages, 121–22, 130
  proofs, 192–93; *see also* Proof
  service of, in
    1838, 18, 48, 60, 68
    1842, 48, 60, Plate 17
    1875, 49, Plate 26
    1900, 65
  Sculptor in Ordinary to, 219
  supernumerary list of, 18, 68
Vigo, 101, 118
Wade, Edward, 228
Wales
  Llandaff, 81
  Maundy service in, 61, 62
  Prince of, 49
  Royal Mint moved to, 133
St
  Asaph, 78
  Davids, 61, 62, 76
  threepence remained in favour in, 187
Wandsmen, 51, 235–36
Ward, Robert, 66, 67, 93
Warrants, for coining, 9, 100–1, 107, 119, 141, 145, 206, 212
Wassail-bowl, 50
Waters, Mr Derek, 53, Plate 20
Watt, James, 241
Weight
  of Britannia groats, 244
  units of, 130, 209, 237, 246
Weights of Maundy money, *see* Maundy money, weights of
Wells, Dean of, 50, 75, 76, 78, 81
West Hartlepool, 94
Westminster
  Abbey
    annual venue for the Maundy service, 49, 60, 61
    coronations at, 60, 61
    Dean's Steps at, Plates 14, 18 and 28
    Maundy
      bench in the cloisters, 20
      service at, 58, 210
        in 1932, 50
      services at since 1954, 61–63
    mediæval Maundy services of the monks at, 20, 21, 23
    muniments of, 79
    ring of Edward the Confessor in, 14
  Canon of, 82

St Stephen's, 76
  Dean of, 50, 77, 78, Plate 31
  St Stephen's, 75
  destruction by fire of many
    conventual buildings at, 79
  Dog Tavern in, 240
  Head Master of, 81
  National School of St George
    at, children from 48, 59
  parishes of St John the
    Evangelist and St Margaret at,
    235
  Parry, Blanche, monument at,
    31
  Prebendary of, 77, 81
    St Stephen's, 76
  School
    Billy Cotton not at, 209
    Head Master of, 81
    Maundy sets distributed as
      prizes to pupils at, 5, 120,
      131, 210
    new foundation of Elizabeth
      I, 5
  St Margaret's at, 31
Wheels, ship on, 79
White leather purse (with long
  red strings), 45, 47, Plate 12
  introduced, 27, 34
  used for the Gift of Pennies,
    27, 33, 34, 40, 53, 61, 96, 130
Whitehall; see also Banqueting
  House, Whitehall; Chapel
  Royal, Whitehall
  Court at, 66, 67
  Gardens, 58
  Great Hall at, 58
  Palace of, 16, 231
    destruction of by fire, 231
  venue for the Maundy service,
    32, 38, 58, 68
Wilberforce, Samuel, 78, 79
William II, largesse at coronation
  of, 4
William III
  aliens' law of, 222, 224, 227,
    245
  fourpence of 1702
    mintage of, 153
    posthumous issue of, 153,
    192
  groove on the obverse of some
    pennies of, 198
  Lord High Almoner to, 79
  Maundy
    coinage of, 106
    services of, 41, 42, 65, 66,
      101, 106
  pedilavium, last monarch to
    effect, 42, 66
  Scotland, hostility to in, 112
  small silver coinage of, 104,
    153–54, Plate 61
  die-axis of, 192
  surgeon of, 10
William IV
  birth of, 68, 126
  death of, 68
  knighted Francis Legatt
    Chantrey, 221
  Maundy
    coinage of, 167–68, 194,
    Plate 74
    die-axis of, 192
    mintages, 121
    distribution for, 59, 60
William and Mary
  groove on the obverse of some
    pennies of, 198
  Lord High Almoner to, 79
  Maundy
    Dish, arms and cypher of on,
    234
    service of, 41, 64, 65
    offered the Crown, 231
    small silver coinage of, 104,
      106, 150–53, Plate 60
    brockages of, 200–1, Plate
    118
    design of remained
      fundamentally unchanged
      until 1820, 165
    die-axis of, 192
  touching dismissed by, 11
Winchester
  Bishop of, 38, 39, 77, 78, 81, 82
  Canon of, 82
  Cathedral
    Maundy
      bench at, 20
      service at, 62
Windsor
  Almonry at, 58
  Canon of, 75–77, 80
  Dean of, 75–78, 81
  Duchess of, 90, 218
  Duke of, see Edward VIII
  Garter Tower at, 58
  Maundy distribution at, 37, 58,
    62
  St George's Chapel, 62
Wire money, 140, 162, 201
Witness line, 195
Wolsey, Cardinal Thomas
  Archbishop of York, 76
  created a cardinal, 94
  death of, 37
  fall from power of, 37, 94, 231
  King's Almoner, 76, 79, 94
    seal as, 79
  Maundy of, 37, 62, 94
  petitioner for Henry VIII, 213
  wealth of, 86
Wood, Derwent, 225

Woods, Rt Rev. Edward Sydney,
  51, 62, 78, 88, Plate 18
Worcester
  Bishop of, 77
    St Oswald, 20
  Cathedral
    Maundy
      bench table in, 20
      service at, 62
  Dean of, 78
  Prebendary of, 81
  Thomas Brock's birthplace, 220
World War II, 97, 124, 226
Wright, Mr P.A., xi, xii, 18, 53,
  88, 236, Plates 19 and 20
Wyon
  family, genealogy of, 230
  Leonard Charles, 175, 222, 224,
    226, 229
  Peter, 230
  Thomas junior, 164, 224, 226,
    230
  Thomas senior, 230
  William, 120, 164–65, 167–68,
    197, 224, 226–27, 229–30,
    Plate 103
Wyvern, on obverse of the angel,
  6, 16
Year of Grace, 28, 36, 64, 87, 95
Yeo, Richard, 226
Yeomen of the Guard, 34, 46–48,
  50, 52–54, 59, 60, 235–36,
  frontispiece and Plates 14, 18,
  19, 22 and 27
Yonge, Sir George, bart., 209
York; *see also* Wolsey, Cardinal
  Thomas
  Archbishop of, 16, 43, 67,
    76–78, 81, 88, 93
    official London residence of,
    37, 231
    St Oswald, 20
  Archdeaconry of, 73
  Briot in, 220
  Charles I in, 38, 39, 58
  Dean of, 76
  House of, 16
  largesse distribution at, 39
  Maundy services at, 38, 39, 58
  Minster
    Maundy
      service at, 38, 39, 62, 73
      seats in, 20
  Place, 37, 231
  touching for the King's Evil at,
    39
  Wolsey banished to, 37
Young
  head, 168–69, 174
  Matthew, 120, 209
  Pretender, 12
'Zadok, the priest', 50, 54, 61